LEARNING: PRINCIPLES AND APPLICATIONS

LEARNING: PRINCIPLES AND APPLICATIONS

Stephen B. Klein

Fort Hays State University

McGraw-Hill Book Company

New York St. Louis San Francisco Auckland Bogotá
Hamburg Johannesburg London Madrid Mexico Milan Montreal New Delhi
Panama Paris São Paulo Singapore Sydney Tokyo Toronto

IN MEMORY OF MY FATHER,
CLARENCE

AND TO MY MOTHER,
BEVERLY

FOR THEIR LOVE, INSPIRATION,
AND GUIDANCE

This book was set in Times Roman by Bi-Comp, Incorporated.
The editor was James D. Anker; the production supervisor was
Denise Puryear; the cover was designed by Carla Bauer.
Project supervision was done by Chernow Editorial Services, Inc.
R. R. Donnelley & Sons Company was printer and binder.

LEARNING: PRINCIPLES AND APPLICATIONS

1 2 3 4 5 6 7 8 9 0 DOCDOC 8 9 8 7 6

ISBN 0-07-035052-3

Library of Congress Cataloging-in-Publication Data

Klein, Stephen B.
    Learning: Principles and Applications
    Bibliography: p.
    Includes index.
    1. Learning. I. Title.
LB1060.K58 1987   370.15′23   86-676
ISBN 0-07-035052-3

CONTENTS

PREFACE

Psychologists have spent most of this century intensively studying the learning process. They have uncovered many important aspects of how we acquire information about the structure of our environment and how we use this understanding to interact effectively with that environment. This book describes what psychologists have discovered about the nature of the learning process.

Chapter 1 provides a description of learning theory, including what changes have taken place in learning theory during this century and how contemporary views of the learning process have been shaped by the ideas expressed by previous generations of psychologists.

Chapter 2 details Pavlovian conditioning, a process which involves learning when events will or will not occur. This chapter discusses the factors which govern the acquisition or elimination of conditioned responses.

Chapters 3 and 4 describe instrumental conditioning, the process of learning how to behave to obtain the positive aspects (rewards) and avoid the negative aspects (punishers) of our environment. The variables influencing the development or extinction of appetitive or reward-seeking behavior are described in Chapter 3, and Chapter 4 presents the determinants of avoidance behavior.

Chapter 5 discusses the environmental control of behavior and how the stimulus environment can exert a powerful influence on how we act. Cognitions can also have an important influence on our actions, and Chapter 6 describes the cognitive processes which affect how and when we behave.

Chapter 7 details three complex learning processes: how we identify concepts, solve problems, and learn to use language. Chapters 8 and 9 discuss memory, the process which allows us to retain our experiences into the future. The nature of memory storage is described in Chapter 8, and the processes which allow us to retrieve experiences are detailed in Chapter 9. Chapter 9 also discusses the causes of forgetting. Further, the biological basis of memory storage and retrieval is presented in these chapters.

Chapter 10 provides a discussion of the biological processes which influence learning. In some instances, biological systems enhance learning; in other cases, learning is impaired by our biological character. Chapter 10 also describes the biological processes which provide the pleasurable aspects of reward and the negative aspects of punishment.

This book presents the important contributions of both animal and human research, since both are crucial to our understanding of the learning process. In many instances, animal studies and human experimentation have yielded identical results, indicating the generality of the processes governing learning. Although there are many general laws of learning, in some instances species differ in their ability to learn a particular behavior. The use of different animals has shown that biological character affects learning. In some situations, only animal research can be ethically conducted, whereas in other cases only human research can identify the learning process which is unique to people. This book describes the research necessary to illustrate a specific learning process.

Several features have been incorporated into this book to increase the relevance of the abstract concepts which describe the nature of learning. At the beginning of each chapter is a vignette intended to give you a preview of the material to be presented in that chapter as well as to stimulate your interest. Many real-world examples of learning concepts are provided throughout the text, and it is hoped that these examples will allow you to recognize instances where the abstract concepts detailed in the text occur in the real world. Applications of the basic concepts described in the textbook are included to demonstrate that the basic learning principles have been successfully used to alter behavior. My students have appreciated the balanced approach between a description of basic learning processes and a presentation of how these basic principles govern our behavior. I hope that you, too, will like this approach.

The textbook has had input from many people I thank the students in my learning classes who read drafts of the chapters and pointed out which sections they liked, which they disliked, and which were unclear. Not only was their feedback very helpful to me, but I am certain that it contributed to the readability and quality of the text.

The staff at McGraw-Hill played an important role in the creation of this text. The psychology editors, James D. Anker, Pat Nave, and David Serbun, guided the development of the text from its inception to this final product. Barbara Chernow, the editing supervisor, ensured that the text was not only easy to read but also aesthetically appealing.

I also thank my colleagues who reviewed chapters of the text. I am especially grateful to Dr. John D. Batson, Furman University; Dr. Michael R. Best, Southern Methodist University; Dr. E. John Capaldi, Purdue University; Dr. Alexis C. Collier, Ohio State University; Dr. Roy E. Connally, University of Central Florida; Dr. Robert G. Crowder, Yale University; Dr. James J. D'Amato, Rockland Community College; Dr. Hiram E. Fitzgerald, Michigan State University; Dr. Robert Henderson, University of Illinois at Urbana-Champaign; Dr. Charles F. Hinderliter, University of Pittsburgh; Dr. Craig T. Johnson, Towson State University; Dr. John M. Knight, Central State University; Dr. Harry MacKay, Northeastern University; Dr. Robert M. Markley, Fort

Hays State University; Dr. Peter J. Mikulka, Old Dominion University; Dr. Ralph R. Miller, State University of New York, Binghamton; Dr. Robert R. Mowrer, Fort Hays State University; Dr. Robert L. Thompson, Hunter College; Dr. Arno F. Wittig, Ball State University; and Dr. Thomas Zentall, University of Kentucky for their contributions to this book.

Stephen B. Klein

LEARNING: PRINCIPLES AND APPLICATIONS

CHAPTER 1

THEORETICAL APPROACHES TO LEARNING

THE GIFT OF KNOWLEDGE

Robert entered college three years ago to become a lawyer. His interest in the law had been spurred by a United States law course he had taken in high school. However, during the past year, several psychology courses have proved more exciting and challenging than his political science classes, and he now wants to obtain a degree in clinical psychology. Robert's interest in psychology has also been stimulated by his younger sister Sarah's drug problems. Sarah, an excellent student before she began to experiment with drugs several years ago, is now addicted, has quit school, and has left home. Robert wants to understand the factors which lead to addictive behavior, and he hopes to contribute someday to the development of an effective drug-addiction therapy.

Dr. Carson, Robert's advisor, suggested that he enroll in a course on learning to fulfill the psychology department's degree requirements. Spending endless hours watching rats run through mazes and analyzing pages and pages of data did not appeal to Robert. Interested in the human aspect of psychology, Robert wondered how this course would benefit him. However, he worried that not taking the course would adversely affect Dr. Carson's evaluation of him for graduate school; therefore, Robert enrolled in the class.

Robert soon discovered that his preconceived ideas about the learning course were incorrect. The course covered both animal and human research, and Robert found that the various types of experimentation complemented each other in revealing the nature of the learning processes which govern behavior. The experiments, far from boring, made the learning principles described in class seem real. Robert discovered that learning involves the devel-

1

opment of effective methods to obtain reward and to avoid adversity as well as an understanding of when and where these responses are appropriate. Robert was interested to learn how basic research has stimulated the development of techniques for modifying behavior and how understanding the principles of learning benefits even the most ardent student of clinical psychology.

Although psychology has changed dramatically during the past two decades, contemporary learning theory represents a synthesis of the theories proposed by previous generations of psychologists. Although Robert expected to find the study of psychology's past irrelevant, instead he found that these ideas have shaped and determined modern psychology. He found that the learning process is governed by complex, yet lawful, principles. For instance, Robert discovered that although psychologists had attempted to use a single stimulus-response approach to describe the learning process, contemporary psychology now recognizes that several processes are involved in the acquisition or elimination of a behavior.

Robert now thinks that the knowledge gained from the learning class will undoubtedly help him search for an effective treatment of addictive behavior. You will learn from this book what Robert discovered about the learning process in his course. I hope that your experience will be as positive as his.

A DEFINITION OF LEARNING

What is *learning?* Learning is a *relatively permanent change in the ability to exhibit a behavior; this change occurs as the result of successful or unsuccessful experience.* This definition of learning has three important components: First, the change in behavior must be relatively permanent to be considered an example of learning. We often alter our behavior as the result of motivational changes. For example, we eat when we are hungry or study when we are worried about an upcoming exam. However, learning is not necessarily responsible for our behavior. If eating or studying behaviors have already been learned, motivational changes rather than learning trigger the change in behavior. Thus, you have already learned to eat, and your hunger motivates your eating behavior. Likewise, you have learned to study to prevent failure, and your fear motivates studying behavior. These behavioral changes are temporary; when the motivational state changes again, the behavior will also change. Therefore, you will stop eating when you are no longer hungry and quit studying when you no longer fear failing the examination. You should recognize that learning is not always permanent. Our actions often change as the result of new experiences, which occurs when previously learned behaviors are no longer effective. Also, there are times when we forget a previously learned behavior, and therefore, we are no longer able to exhibit that behavior.

Second, learning reflects a change in the potential for a behavior. Learning does not automatically lead to a change in behavior. We must be sufficiently motivated to translate learning into behavior. For example, although you may know the location of the campus cafeteria, you will not be motivated to go there until you are hungry. Also, we might be unable to exhibit a particular behavior even though we have learned it and are sufficiently motivated to exhibit it. For example, you may learn from friends that a good movie is playing but not go because you cannot afford it.

Third, many examples of behavioral change do not reflect the learning process. Lornez (1966) described many situations in which experience alters instinctive behavior. The following examples demonstrate that adaptive modification produced by experience is often programmed into a species's genetic makeup.

Automobiles once had to be driven several hundred miles before they operated at peak efficiency. Likewise, many response systems become more efficient with experience. For example, Wells (1962) discovered that practice improves a young squid's prey-catching ability. Although a young squid's prey-catching form is the same as an adult squid's form, the young squid's response is slower and less certain than the adult's. Also, Hess (1956) observed that the aim of young chickens' food-pecking response improves with experience. To demonstrate that practice rather than success caused the improvement, Hess put goggles on the chicks which caused the food to appear to be several inches from the actual location. Wearing the goggles, the chicks always missed the food; however, the more they pecked, the closer they came to the perceived location of the food. Thus the improvement in pecking behavior was unrelated to the chicken's success in obtaining food.

We have discovered that learning represents a relatively permanent change in the potential for a behavior, a change which develops through successful or unsuccessful experience. Let's now examine the historical origins of this definition and of contemporary learning theory.

HISTORICAL ORIGINS

Early Philosophical Thought

Why are you taking this learning course? Perhaps you found the material on learning in your introductory psychology course interesting and want to know more about the learning process. Or you might believe that a high grade in this course will enhance your chances of being accepted to a good graduate school. Either of these reasons (or another of your own) suggests that you know why you are taking this course and that you freely chose to participate in the class in accordance with your motivation. Your behavior is consistent with the theories by which early philosophers such as Aristotle and Plato portrayed human nature. They believed that people have *free will* and that behavior is governed by intellect and reason. Thus, if we behave in a socially inappropriate manner, we have freely chosen that behavior and are, therefore, accountable for our actions.

In the seventeenth century, René Descartes described his dualistic view of animal and human behavior in which different processes motivate animal and human action. Descartes proposed that animals are similar to small machines in that their behavior is mechanistic and determined by their internal processes—instincts and reflexes. Unlike human beings, they have neither reasoning abilities nor free will. Having no "mind," lower animals cannot be held accountable for their behavior. Human beings, however, can determine their own fate; their minds control their actions, whereas the body determines the behavior of a lower animal. According to the eighteenth-century philosopher Immanual Kant, our knowledge and rationality should control our passions and our body. In 1859, Charles Darwin's *On the Origin of Species* challenged this idealized view of the nature of humans as a unique and essentially cerebral species; his theory admitted the animal nature present in all of us.

Darwin's Influence

The idea that the process which motivates the behavior of humans is distinctively different from that of lower animals came under attack just over a century ago; the controversy concerning the nature of human behavior still rages. Darwin proposed that the differences between humans and lower animals are quantitative rather than qualitative—that the major force motivating all animals, including humans, is survival. Humans may be more adept at survival, but the same general process determines the nature of both humans and lower animals. According to Darwin, survival requires that animals and humans possess specific characteristics—both behavioral and physical—which are *adaptive* to their environment. If an animal, either human or nonhuman, has these characteristics, then it will survive. For example, a deer that can run faster than its predator will survive. In contrast, animals or humans that do not possess the adaptive characteristics will perish; the slow deer becomes the cougar's meal. Darwin's phrase "survival of the fittest" merely reflects his observation that in an environment with limited resources, only the able creatures will live to reproduce. The importance—and one obviously controversial aspect—of Darwin's theory is the assumption that human beings are not unique but are motivated by the same factors that influence the behavior of other animals.

A central aspect of Darwin's theory is his concept of evolution. Darwin asserted that each successful species possesses characteristics enabling it to survive in a particular environment. When an environment changes, the species must either respond to that change or become extinct. If the environmental change is a slow one, some members of the species may adapt through adventitious genetic mutations; others may possess characteristics adaptive to their new environment; they alone will live to reproduce, passing along to their offspring their adaptive characteristics. Thus, the species changes due to the selective loss of some group members. For example, if an environment becomes colder, only those bears with a very thick coat will survive, and future generations of bears will have thicker coats than the average in the preceeding generations. If the environment should continue to change, a different species of animal will evolve—a species that is adapted to the new environment. Unfortunately, too rapid a change in the environment typically results in extinction of the species. *Evolution* represents the changes of the behavioral and physical characteristics that a species undergoes in order to survive in a new environment. Knowledge of the evolutionary process is not limited to biologists. Cattle breeders have known for generations that a fatter or healthier breed of cattle results from selective breeding. During "natural" evolution, the environment itself selectively breeds the members of a species, "choosing" which will survive and reproduce.

Functionalism

Functionalism was an early school of psychology which emphasized the instinctive origins and adaptive function of behavior. To a great extent, functionalism developed to incorporate evolutionary theory into the earlier philosophical view of human nature. The functionalists expressed various ideas concerning the mechanisms controlling human behavior. According to John Dewey (1886), for example, the reflexive survival behaviors of the lower animals have been replaced in the human being by the mind, which has evolved as the primary mechanism for human survival. The brain's function is to enable the individual to adapt to the environment. Thus, although Dewey's functionalism stressed the importance of survival and environmental adaptation—characteristics of Darwin's evolutionary theory—it retained the *dualism* evident in early philosophical thought by asserting that the manner of human survival differed from that of lower animals.

In contrast to Dewey's dualism, William James, a fellow nineteenth-century psychologist, argued that the major difference between humans and lower animals lies in the character of their respective inborn or instinctual motives. According to James, human beings possess a larger number of instincts which guide behavior (for example, rivalry, sympathy, fear, sociability, cleanliness, modesty, and love) than do lower animals. These social instincts directly enhance (or reduce) our successful interaction with our environment and thus our survival. William James (1890) also concluded that all instincts, both human and animal, have a mentalistic quality, possessing both purpose and direction, attributes previously accorded only to people. His is essentially a continuity theory, which, unlike Dewey's dualism, did not demand a distinctive break between humans and lower animals.

Some psychologists (see Troland, 1928), opposed to a mentalistic concept of instinct, argued that internal biochemical forces motivate behavior in all species. This school of thought retained the similarity between humans and lower animals but substituted a mechanistic view for James's mentalism. Energy concepts developed in physics and chemistry during the second half of the nineteenth century provided a framework for the mechanistic approach to motivation. Ernst Brucke stated in 1874 that "the living organism is a dynamic system in which the laws of chemistry and physics apply"—a view which led to great advances in physiology. These functionalists used this physiochemical approach to explain the motivation for human and animal behavior.

Psychologists advocating a mechanistic approach to instinct differed in their views of the nature of this mechanistic process. For instance, Jacques Loeb's (1899) view stressed the influence of external stimulation on behavior. Thinking that animal and human behavior was inflexible and comparable to a plant's trophism to light, he labeled his concept the *tropistic school*. According to Loeb, internal forces, such as emotions, play only a minor role in motivation. In contrast, H. S. Jennings (1904) did not believe that the animal's physiological (internal) state which produced behavior was inflexible; instead, he argued, learning could alter internal systems and thereby influence behavior. A mechanistic view has appealed to many psychologists during this century. We will see attempts to incorporate both Loeb's and Jenning's approaches during the remainder of this chapter.

A number of psychologists strongly criticized the instinct concept proposed by the functionalists on several grounds: (1) Anthropologists pointed to a variety of values, beliefs, and behaviors among different cultures whose existence rendered the idea of universal human instincts inconsistent. (2) Watson and Morgan's (1917) observations of human infants led them to conclude that only three innate emotional responses—fear, rage, and love—existed and that these could be elicited by only a small number of stimuli. (3) The widespread and uncritical use of the instinct concept did not advance our understanding of the nature of human behavior. Let's use Bernard's (1924) analysis of the instinct concept to examine the criticism prominent during the 1920s. Bernard identified several thousand, often conflicting, instincts proposed by the functionalists. One example of Bernard's was the idea that "with a glance of the eye we can estimate *instinctively* the age of a passerby" (page 132). It is not surprising that many psychologists reacted so negatively to the instinctive concept.

In the 1920s American psychology moved away from the instinct explanation of human behavior and replaced it with an emphasis on the learning process. The instinct concept reappeared in American psychology when the writings of the European animal behaviorists, called *ethologists,* who emphasized the importance of inheritance in the determination of behavior, surfaced during the 1950s. The ethological view of instinct was not readily accepted, and American psychology has only recently recognized the importance of instinctive processes in behavior. The influence of instinctive processes on learning will be examined in Chapter 10; we will now look at the theory of behaviorism, which replaced the functionalism theory in American psychology.

Behaviorism

Behaviorism is a theory which emphasizes the role of experience in governing human behavior. According to behaviorists, although we possess instinctual motives, the important determinants of our behavior are learned. Acquired drives typically motivate us, and our behavior in response to these motives is also learned through the process of our interaction with the environment. For example, a behaviorist assumes that your motivation to attend school is a learned one and that your behaviors while you attend school are also learned. One of the behaviorists' main goals is the establishment of the laws governing learning—a concern that has dominated academic psychology for most of this century. A number of ideas contributed to the behavioral view. The Greek philosopher Aristotle's concept of the association of ideas represents one important origin of behaviorism.

Associationism Suppose that a friend approaches you after class and remarks that your party last week was terrific. This remark causes you to recall meeting a very attractive person at your party, which in turn reminds you to ask this person for a date. This whole thought process reflects the concept of association of ideas: two events can become associated with each other; thus, when you think of one event you automatically recall the other. Aristotle proposed that in order for an association to develop the two events must be *contiguous* (temporally paired) and either similar to or opposite from each other.

During the eighteenth century, British empiricists described the association process in greater detail. David Hume (1739) hypothesized that another factor—causal events—might be capable of association. For example, if you overslept and missed your class, your learned association might be that oversleeping causes you not to attend class.

Thorndike The work of Edward Thorndike represented another important influence on the behaviorist view. Thorndike's 1898 publication of his studies established that animal behavior could change as a consequence of experience. His ideas on learning and motivation developed from his research with his famous puzzle box (see Figure 1.1). In these studies, he placed a hungry cat into a locked box and put food outside the box. The cat could escape from the box and then obtain food by exhibiting one of a number of possible behaviors. For example, two such effective behaviors were pulling on a string and pressing a pedal. Not only did the cat escape, but also, with each successive trial, the time needed for escape slowly decreased. It appears that the cat's escape from the box progressed from a chance act to a learned behavior.

Thorndike proposed that the cat formed an association between the stimulus (the box) and the effective response. Learning, according to Thorndike, reflects the development of an S-R (stimulus-response) association. As the result of learning, when the animal reexperiences the specific stimulus, the appropriate response is elicited. Thorndike asserts that the animal is not conscious of this association but is instead exhibiting a mechanistic habit in response to a particular stimulus. The S-R association developed because the cat was *rewarded*: when the cat was hungry, the appropriate response was followed by the presentation of food, which produced a satisfying state and strengthened the S-R bond. Thorndike labeled this strengthening of an association produced by pleasant events *the law of effect*.

FIGURE 1.1
Thorndike's famous puzzle box: The hungry cat can escape
by exhibiting one of several potential responses and thereby
obtain food. From *Theories of learning* by L. C. Swenson ©
1980 by Wadsworth, Inc. Reprinted by permission of the
publisher.

Thorndike did not think that the law of effect represents only animal behavior; he argued that it also reflects the human learning process. Thorndike
(1932) presented his human subjects with a concept to learn. Telling his subjects that they had responded correctly enabled the subjects to learn the appropriate response. Although Thorndike initially proposed that unpleasant events
weakened the S-R bond, his later studies indicated that telling subjects that
they were wrong or not giving feedback about the correctness of their response
did not influence his subjects' behavior. Contemporary researchers have demonstrated that aversive events often can modify both animal and human behavior. We will describe the influence of unpleasant experiences on behavior in
Chapter 4.

Although Thorndike's views concerning the nature of the learning process
are quite specific, his ideas on the motivational process which determines
behavior seem very vague. According to Thorndike, if a particular event is
satisfying, it serves as a reward; however, learning occurs or previously
learned behavior is exhibited only if the animal or human is "ready." Thus in
his *law of readiness* Thorndike assumes that the animal or human must be
motivated to develop an association or to exhibit a previously established habit.
Thorndike did not hypothesize concerning the nature of the motivation mechanism, leaving such endeavors to future psychologists. Indeed, the motivational
basis of behavior became of critical concern to later generations of behaviorists.

Pavlov How did the cat initially choose the correct response in Thorn-dike's puzzle-box studies? Thorndike explained the process as one of trial and error; the cat simply switched behaviors until it discovered the correct one. Reward then functioned to strengthen that correct response. However, the research of Ivan Pavlov (1927) portrayed the learning process as anything but trial and error. According to Pavlov, definite preset rules determine which behavior occurs in the learning situation.

Behaviorists were profoundly influenced by Pavlov's work. His description of the conditioning process first appeared in English when his Huxley lecture, delivered at Charing Cross Hospital, was published in *Science* in 1906. The translation into English of his work *Conditioned Reflexes* in 1927 provided a comprehensive description of his work. Pavlov was a physiologist, not a psy-chologist; his initial plan was to uncover the laws governing digestion. He discovered that animals exhibit numerous reflexive responses when food is placed in their mouths (for example, salivation, gastric secretion). The function of these responses is to aid in the digestion process. Pavlov also developed a unique method for determining the quantity of a dog's gastric secretion in relation to the amount of food placed in its stomach. He cut a slice of the stomach tissue from the body and measured the relative volume of gastric secretion which occurred in response to the food. He discovered that the amount and type of food fed to the dog determined the amount of gastric secretion. Next, Pavlov cut the esophagus and brought it out of the dog's neck; this procedure allowed the dog to chew and swallow food which then fell onto the ground rather than traveling to the stomach. The amount of gastric secre-tion was the same whether the food was in the dog's mouth or in its stomach; Pavlov concluded that food in the mouth produced the gastric secretion in the stomach.

Pavlov then made another important discovery: his dogs began to secrete stomach juices when they saw food or when it was placed in their food dishes. He concluded that the dogs had learned a new behavior, since he had not observed this response during their first exposure to the sight of food. To explain his observation, he suggested that both animals and humans possess instinctual or *unconditioned reflexes*. An unconditioned reflex consists of two components—an *unconditioned stimulus* (UCS—for example, food), which involuntarily elicits the second component, the *unconditioned response* (UCR—for example, saliva or gastric juice). A new or *conditioned reflex* de-velops when environmental events (for example, the sight of food) occur with the unconditioned stimulus. As conditioning progresses, the *conditioned stimu-lus* (CS—for example, the sight of food) becomes able to elicit the learned, or *conditioned response* (CR—in this example, saliva or gastric secretion). The conditioned response is strengthened by increasing the number of pairings of the conditioned stimulus with the unconditioned stimulus. Pavlov assumed a mechanistic view of behavior—stimuli either have an innate capacity or ac-quire the ability to elicit behavior.

The demonstration of a learned reflex in animals stands as an important discovery, illustrating not only an animal's ability to learn but also the mechanism responsible for the learned behavior. According to Pavlov, any neutral stimulus paired with the unconditioned stimulus could, through conditioning, develop the capacity to elicit a CR. In his classic demonstration of the conditioning process, he first implanted a tube, called a fistula, in a dog's salivary glands to collect saliva (see Figure 1.2). He then presented the conditioned stimulus, the sound of a metronome, and shortly thereafter placed the unconditioned stimulus, meat powder, in the dog's mouth. On the first presentation, only the meat powder produced saliva (UCR). However, with repeated pairings of the tone with food, the tone (CS) began to elicit saliva (CR); the strength of the conditioned response increased with increased pairings of the conditioned and unconditioned stimuli. Figure 1.3 presents a diagram of Pavlov's classical conditioning process.

Pavlov conducted an extensive investigation of the conditioning process by identifying many procedures which influence an animal's learned behaviors; many of his ideas are still accepted today. Pavlov showed that if, after conditioning, the conditioned stimulus is presented without the unconditioned stimulus, the strength of the conditioned response diminished. Pavlov named this process of eliminating an established conditioned response *extinction*. Animals also *generalize* their conditioned response to similar stimuli; Pavlov found that his dogs salivated when presented not only with the conditioned stimulus but also with stimuli similar to the conditioned stimulus. For example, Pavlov's

FIGURE 1.2
Pavlov's salivary-conditioning apparatus. The experimenter can measure saliva output when either a conditioned stimulus (for example, a bell) or an unconditioned stimulus (for example, meat powder) is presented to the dog. The dog is placed in a harness to minimize movement, thus ensuring an accurate measure of the salivary response. Adapted from Yerkes, R. M., & Margulis, S. The method of Pavlov in animal psychology. *Psychological Bulletin*, 1909, 6, 257–273. Copyright 1909 by the American Psychological Association. Reprinted by permission.

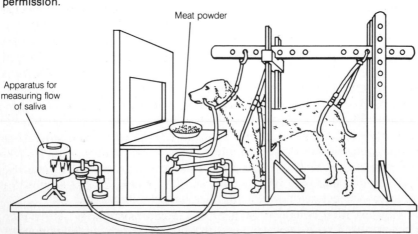

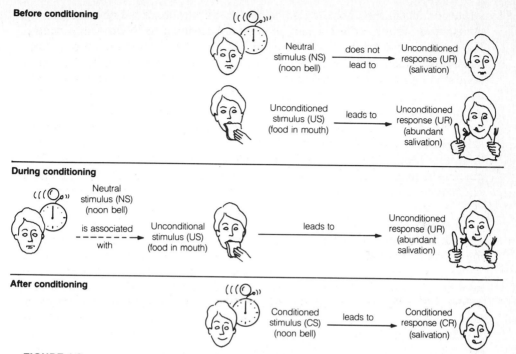

FIGURE 1.3
Schematic illustration of Pavlovian conditioning of salivation to a tone. Before conditioning, the presentation of the tone elicits no response when presented alone. During conditioning, the tone is followed by the unconditioned stimulus, meat powder, which can
produce the physiological response of salivation, the UCR. After conditioning, the presentation of the tone elicits the conditioned salivation response. From Davidoff, L. *Introduction to psychology* (2d ed.). New York: McGraw-Hill, 1980.

dogs salivated to tones which were either louder or softer than the conditioned
stimulus. He also discovered that dogs could learn not only what stimuli to
respond to but also which stimuli not to respond to—a process which Pavlov
labeled *discrimination*. For example, Pavlov discovered that his dogs learned
to salivate to a stimulus paired with food but did not salivate when presented
with a stimulus without food.

Pavlov also found that a stimulus never directly paired with the unconditioned stimulus could produce a response—a process called *higher-order conditioning*. In it, following the direct pairing of a conditioned stimulus (for example, a light) with the UCS (for example, food), the conditioned stimulus is then
paired with another stimulus (for example, a tone) without the presence of the
unconditioned stimulus. After several light and tone pairings, an animal will
salivate to the tone, even though the tone was never paired directly with the
UCS.

Pavlov's observations have profoundly influenced psychology. His conditioning process, often called Pavlovian conditioning, has been demonstrated in

various animals, including humans. Conditioned responses also have been established to many different unconditioned stimuli, and psychologists have shown that most environmental stimuli can become conditioned ones.

Pavlov and Thorndike described two different learning processes—classical conditioning and instrumental conditioning. In the past, especially during the two decades following the publication of Pavlov's work, the classical conditioning process was emphasized. Later, during the 1940s and 1950s, researchers focused on the instrumental or operant conditioning process initially described by Thorndike. A resurgence of interest in Pavlovian conditioning has occurred during the past decade. We will discuss the Pavlovian conditioning process in greater detail in Chapter 2 and the instrumental conditioning process in Chapter 3.

Watson   Neither Thorndike nor Pavlov was a behaviorist. Each merely described the learning process. It was John B. Watson who demonstrated its importance in human behavior. Watson, the chief spokesperson of his day for American behaviorism, rejected mental ideas such as consciousness or awareness and instead emphasized that all behaviors represent either unconditioned or acquired habits. According to Watson (1925), our thoughts are merely feedback from our muscular responses to environmental stimuli.

Watson, arguing that the important adult behaviors are learned, stressed the importance of the learning process. Although Pavlov's research excited Watson, the work of another Russian, Vladimir Bechterev, played a central role in his thinking. Bechterev and Pavlov conducted their research at the same time, and the 1913 American publication of Bechterev's work also contributed greatly to the popularity of behaviorism. Whereas Pavlov used positive or pleasant UCSs, Bechterev employed aversive or unpleasant ones (for example, shock) to study the conditioning process. Bechterev found that a conditioned response (for example, finger withdrawal) could be established by the pairing of a neutral stimuli with the shock. In his duplication of Bechterev's studies, Watson showed that after several pairings, a previously neutral stimulus elicited not only a leg withdrawal response but also emotional arousal (revealed by increased heart rate) as the conditioned response. Although not the first to demonstrate the conditioning, or acquired learning, of emotional responses, this evidence was important to Watson's concepts of human behavior and emotionality.

Watson assumed that abnormal, as well as normal, behavior is learned. He was particularly concerned with demonstrating that human fears are acquired through Pavlovian conditioning. To illustrate this point, Watson and Raynor (1920) showed a white rat to Albert, a healthy infant attending a day-care center. As the child reached for the rat, he heard a loud sound (UCS) produced by Watson's hitting a heavy iron rail with a hammer (see Figure 1.4). After three CS-UCS pairings, Watson and Raynor observed that presentation of the rat (CS) alone produced a fear response in the child. The rat elicited strong emotional arousal, demonstrated by the child's attempts to escape from it, after

FIGURE 1.4
While "little Albert" was playing with a white rat, Watson struck a suspended
steel bar with a hammer. The loud sound disturbed the child, causing him to
develop a conditioned fear of the white rat. Rosalie Raynor, Watson's assistant,
distracted "little Albert" while Watson approached the bar. From *Theories of
learning* by L. C. Swenson © 1980 by Wadsworth, Inc. Reprinted by permission of
the publisher.

six CS-UCS pairings. The authors observed a strong generalization to similar
objects: The child also showed fear of a white rabbit and a white fur coat.

Although Watson had intended to extinguish Albert's fear, Albert's mother
withdrew him from the day-care center before Watson could eliminate the
infant's fear. Mary Cover Jones, a student working with Watson, developed an
effective technique in 1924 for eliminating conditioned fears. A young child
served as the subject. Jones paired a white rabbit with a loud noise often
enough for the rabbit to elicit a fear response on its own. Once the fear was well
established, she brought the rabbit into the same room with the child while the
child was eating, carefully keeping enough distance between the rabbit and
child so that the child was not alarmed. She then moved the rabbit closer and
closer to the eating child, allowing him to grow accustomed to it in gradual
steps. Eventually the child was able to touch and hold the formerly fear-inducing animal. According to Jones, this procedure had eliminated fear by conditioning a positive emotional response, produced by eating, to the rabbit. The
acquisition of such a fear-inhibiting emotional response is called *counterconditioning*. Approximately thirty years later, her study played an important role in

the development of an effective treatment of human phobic behavior. We will discuss this treatment, systematic desensitization, in Chapter 2.

Many different views of human nature developed during the early part of the twentieth century. Some of these views stressed the mentalistic aspect of our behavior; others presented human beings as automatically responding to events in the environment. The role of instincts was central to some theories of behavior; learning as the determinant of human action was the core of others. However, psychology was just in its infancy, and all these views remained essentially untested. Fortunately, our understanding of the learning principles governing our behavior has increased during the past fifty years, as you will discover from the remainder of the text. The theoretical views of learning begin our discussion.

CONTEMPORARY LEARNING THEORY

Two major theoretical approaches have been proposed to explain the nature of the learning process. The S-R theorists advocate a mechanistic view of the learning process in which a stimulus automatically elicits behavior and learning consists of an environmental stimulus developing the ability to elicit a specific response. In contrast, the cognitive theorists advocate a mentalistic view of the learning process. Learning, according to the cognitive approach, involves the recognition of when important events, such as reward and punishment, are likely to occur and an understanding of how to attain reward and avoid adversity. The flexible view of behavior advocated by the cognitive theorists contrasts sharply with the inflexible approach of the S-R theorists. Perhaps you feel that only one of these approaches is correct; however, according to the literature both mechanistic and cognitive processes influence our behavior. We begin by describing the S-R theories and follow with a discussion of the cognitive approach. The importance of both approaches will be evident throughout the text.

S-R Views

The Concept of Drive   In 1918, Robert S. Woodworth introduced the concept of *drive* to psychology. He defines drive as an intense internal force which motivates behavior. Although drive theorists recognized that some drives were innate, they believed that acquired drives motivated most human behavior (see Miller & Dollard, 1941). We will now study Clark Hull's drive approach, the most influential drive theory.

Hull's Drive Theory   Clark Hull's drive theory prevailed for much of this century (see Hull, 1943, 1952). From the 1930s until the mid-1960s, most psychologists assumed that an intense internal arousal, called drive (D), automatically motivates behavior. Hull's view asserts that the combined influence of several factors determines the intensity of instrumental activity. According to Hull, the relationship is represented as behavioral potential ($_sE_R$) = drive (D) ×

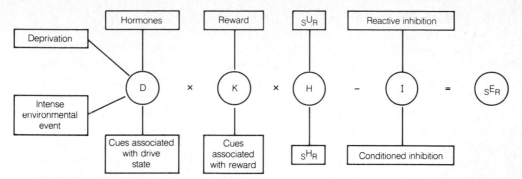

FIGURE 1.5
Diagram of Hull's theory. The terms in the circles show the major variables influencing the likelihood of behavior in Hull's view. The terms in the rectangles represent the processes which influence each major process. From Klein, S. B. *Motivation: Biosocial approaches.* New York: McGraw-Hill, 1982.

incentive (K) × habit strength (H) − inhibition (I). The factors influencing each aspect of Hull's theory are presented in Figure 1.5. In Hull's view, accurate prediction of the behavior of animals or humans is possible only when each factor in the mathematical relationship is known.

Imagine the "butterflies" that you experience before taking a test. The scheduled exam creates this arousal or nervousness; the prior scheduling of the exam is the antecedent condition producing the internal drive state. Your nervousness motivates the behavior which in the past produced drive reduction; it is to be hoped that this behavior includes learning what information will be covered on the exam, learning what kind of exam it will be, and studying. Let's begin our discussion by examining the antecedent conditions inducing drive and motivating behavior.

Unconditioned Sources of Drive Hull (1943) proposed that events which threaten the survival of animals or humans (for example, failure to obtain food) create the internal drive state. For animals or people to survive, their internal biological systems must operate effectively. A deficit in these internal systems threatens survival and represents, according to Hull, the antecedent condition which motivates animals or people to restore these biological systems to normal. In some cases, the animal or human may restore normal functioning through an internal adjustment. For instance, in the absence of food, an individual will use stored energy to maintain normal functioning. However, if the deficiency persists, behavior will be activated to resolve the deficiency. Thus, animals or people using too much stored energy are forced to obtain food and to restore the essential energy reserves necessary for survival.

In 1952, Hull acknowledged that events which do not threaten the animal's or human's survival can also motivate behavior. Several types of studies forced Hull to acknowledge that an internal drive state can appear even in the absence of deprivation. First, animals show a strong preference for saccharin, consuming large quantities even when they are not hungry. Although saccharin has no caloric value, deprived animals eat it rather than a more nutritionally valuable food. In addition, hungry rats can learn an instrumental behavior to secure saccharin (Sheffield & Roby, 1950). Thus, instrumental behavior can obviously occur in the absence of a biologically induced deficiency. Several classes of nondeprivation events can induce drive and thereby motivate behavior.

Hull assumed that intense environmental events motivate behavior by activating the internal drive state. Electrical shock is one external stimulus that can induce internal arousal. The shock may be aversive, but it does not threaten the animal's or person's survival. Yet, the presentation of electrical shock is one antecedent condition motivating defensive behavior.

Internal biological systems unrelated to a deprivation condition can also motivate behavior. For example, the heightened estrogen level during the middle of a female cat's estrus cycle motivates increased sexual responsivity. The female cat without a high estrogen level will not exhibit sexual behavior with a male cat. Thus, sexual behavior seems to be independent of deprivation; rather, it occurs when both the appropriate external (male cat) and internal (estrogen) cues are present for the female cat.

Thus the internal drive state which motivates behavior can be produced by a number of circumstances, including deprivation, intense environmental events, and hormonal changes. The drive produced by these events are instinctive. However, many stimuli in our environment acquire the capacity to induce the internal drive state. Let's next examine the process that allows external cues to develop the capacity to motivate behavior.

Acquired Drives　Hull (1943) suggested that environmental stimuli can acquire the ability to produce internal drive through classical conditioning. From this view, the association of environmental cues with the antecedent conditions which produce an unconditioned-drive state causes the development of a conditioned-drive state. Once this conditioned-drive state has developed, these cues can induce internal arousal and thus can motivate behavior on subsequent occasions, even in the absence of the stimuli that induce the unconditioned drives.

Consider the following example to illustrate Hull's acquired-drive concept: A male factory worker visits a bar every day after work and drinks several glasses of beer before departing. Since he rarely consumes alcohol at other times, the drinking appears to be motivated by a specific environmental circumstance, the end of work. How did this stimulus develop the capacity to motivate this factory worker to walk several blocks to the bar to obtain a few glasses of beer? One possibility is that the internal need state of thirst motivated the initial trip to the bar; this need was created after a very hot day of working indoors without air-conditioning. Thus, thirst motivated the first trip to the bar, and the beer reduced the thirst. Because of this experience, the stimulus of leaving work became associated through classical conditioning with the worker's internal drive state: the end of work was now a stimulus which by itself could produce some internal drive. With each successive trip to the bar on a hot day, the stimulus of work's end developed stronger drive capacities. This person now visits the bar every day after work, even if the weather is not hot and no biologically induced thirst exists. Thus, the ability of the end of work to motivate behavior in the absence of an unconditioned drive state indicates that the end of the day has acquired drive properties.

The Reinforcing Function of Drive Reduction From the Hullian view, drive motivates behavior, but each specific reflexive behavior depends on the environment—that is, environmental events direct behavior. But which behavior does a specific stimulus elicit? Hull thought that when an animal or human is motivated (drive exists), the environmental cue present automatically elicits a response; the response with the strongest innate habit strength ($_sU_R$) to that stimulus will occur. If that stimulus reduces the drive state, the bond between the stimulus and response is strengthened; thus, habit strength is the result of drive reduction. The habit strength increases each time the behavior produces drive reduction. According to Hull, the strength of an S-R association depends on both the innate habit strength ($_sU_R$) and the acquired habit strength ($_sH_R$).

Unsuccessful behavior causes drive to persist in the animal or human. If this happens, all behavior is temporarily inhibited—a process referred to as *reactive inhibition*. If the drive state persists, this habitual behavior will occur again when the reactive inhibition declines. However, the continued failure of the habit to reduce drive leads to a permanent or *conditioned inhibition*. Conditioned inhibition is specific to a particular response and acts to reduce the excitatory strength of the dominant habit. The continued failure of this behavior to reduce drive causes the second strongest response in the *habit hierarchy* to become the dominant habit. If this behavior is successful (produces drive reduction), the response's habit strength increases, and the response is again elicited when the animal is motivated. The conditioned-inhibition process will be repeated if the second habit in the hierarchy is ineffective; thus, the animal will continue down the habit hierarchy until a successful response occurs.

In addition to the inhibition of the dominant habit, the habit hierarchy can be rearranged in a second way. If the strongest habit cannot occur, the next response in the hierarchy will be elicited. According to Hull, the habit strength of this second response will be increased if it produces drive reduction. The continued success of this habit will cause it to become the dominant habit in the hierarchy.

Let's examine how the Hullian view of reinforcement would explain the factory worker's daily trip to the bar. His primary drive initially motivated him to reduce his thirst need. Suppose that the strongest habit in this situation was a trip to the water fountain, but the water in the fountain was lukewarm and his drive persisted. Next, he tried a nearby vending machine, only to find that it was empty. Finally, he walked to the bar several blocks from the factory and ordered a beer to reduce his thirst. Hull would assert that the drive reduction strengthened the bond between the end of work and going to the bar for beer. Each subsequent trip strengthened the bond until the behavior became habitual.

Incentive Motivation   To suggest that the factory worker would continue to visit the bar if it no longer stocked beer is probably inaccurate; his behavior does reflect to some degree his desire to drink beer. Hull's 1943 theory assumed that the value of reward only influenced the strength of the S-R bond; a more valuable reward produced greater drive reduction and, therefore, a stronger habit. Once established, an animal's or human's motivation depended, asserted Hull, on the drive level but not the reward value. However, various studies showed that the value of the reinforcer has an important influence on motivational level. For example, Crespi (1942) found that shifts in reward magnitude produced a rapid change in rats' runway performance for food. When he increased reward magnitude from 1 to 16 pellets on the twentieth trial, performance after just two or three trials equalled that of animals which always received the higher reward. If reward magnitude influenced only learning level, as Hull had suggested, the animals' change in runway speed should have been gradual. The rapid shift in the rats' behavior indicates that reward magnitude influenced their motivation; the use of a larger reward increased the rats' motivational level. A similar rapid change in behavior occurred when the reward was decreased from 256 to 16 pellets. These rats quickly decreased their running speed to a level equal to that of rats receiving the lower reward on each trial. Figure 1.6 presents the results of Crespi's study.

The results of these experiments convinced Hull (1952) that reward magnitude (K) affects the intensity of instrumental behavior. According to Hull, a

FIGURE 1.6
Speed in the runway was a function of the magnitude of reinforcement. The rats received 1, 16, or 256 pellets of food. (The acquisition data for the 1-pellet group are not presented.) Sixteen pellets were given to each rat after trial 20. Adapted from Crespi, L. P. Quantitative variation of incentive and performance in white rats. *American Journal of Psychology*, 1942, *55*, 467–517.

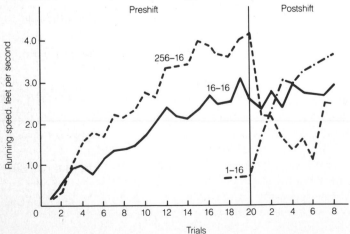

large reward produces a greater arousal level and thereby more motivation to act than does a small reward. Furthermore, he theorized that environmental stimuli associated with reward acquire incentive motivation properties and that the cues present with a large reward will produce a greater conditioned-incentive motivation than those stimuli associated with a small reward. The importance of these acquired-incentive cues is most evident when reward cannot be seen; the cues associated with a large reward elicit a greater approach toward reward than do cues associated with a small reward.

Overview Hull's drive view represented the dominant behavioral theory during the period from the 1930s to the 1960s. Many of Hull's ideas do accurately reflect an important aspect of human behavior: (1) Intense arousal can motivate behavior. (2) Environmental stimuli can develop the ability to produce arousal, thereby motivating behavior. (3) Environmental events do direct one's actions. (4) Habitual reactions are elicited by environmental stimuli. (5) The value of reward influences the intensity of instrumental behavior. Evidence of the validity of these aspects of Hull's theory will be discussed throughout the text. Although Hull's drive theory developed from research with animals, psychologists have adopted it to explain the basis of many behaviors of people.

However, Hull's drive concept has encountered some difficulties. First, cognitive processes, as well as drive, clearly play an important role in a person's behavior. Second, Hull's concept of reinforcement has proved to be inaccurate; that is, reinforcement and drive reduction are not synonymous. Two types of evidence challenge the drive-reduction view of reinforcement. First, numerous experiments—the initial study by Olds and Milner in 1954 is classic—demonstrate that direct stimulation of the brain is reinforcing. Olds and Milner placed a small wire, an *electrode,* into a rat's brain and passed an electrical current through the electrode. They noted that their rats learned to bar press to obtain brain stimulation. Other studies have reported that rats will learn the correct path in a maze for this reinforcement (see Mendelson & Chorover, 1965). The reinforcing property of brain stimulation argues against a drive-reduction interpretation of reinforcement.

Sheffield (1966) argued that drive induction rather than reduction strengthens instrumental behavior. In addition, according to Sheffield, reinforcers produce excitement or arousal, which motivates subsequent behavior. For example, it is the excitement produced by the presentation of food that reinforces the instrumental behavior; the food subsequently motivates eating. This interpretation of reinforcement explains how secondary reinforcers acquire the ability to reinforce behavior through association with primary reinforcers; this characteristic of secondary or learned reinforcers was an enigma to the Hullian view. A secondary reinforcer (for example, money) not only reinforces behavior but also motivates future behavior. Money reinforces our working, and many people are intensely motivated to spend the money as they obtain it. The drive-induction interpretation also appears to explain the observation that sensory-deprived animals are motivated to obtain stimulation. For example, Butler and Harlow (1954) discovered that monkeys learned an instrumental response so that they could view a normal laboratory environment from their isolation chamber.

Hull's drive theory focused on the acquisition of habitual reactions. Although he did indicate that environmental stimuli associated with reward could acquire the ability to motivate behavior through the classical conditioning process, he did not specify the mechanism responsible for the motivational influence of these environmental stimuli. Following Hull's death in 1952, Kenneth Spence described the process responsible for the acquisition of incentive motivation. Other psychologists subsequently used the system detailed by Spence to describe the conditioning of other motives. We will briefly examine their views next; their contribution will be evident throughout the text.

Acquired Motive Approach

Anticipation of Reward   To explain the influence of reward value on behavior, Hull (1952) introduced the concept of incentive motivation (K). Although Hull indicated that an animal or human would be more motivated after receiving a large reward rather than a small one, Kenneth Spence (1956), Hull's student, detailed the transformation of K into behavior. His view explains why an animal or human is more motivated by a large than a small reward. Let's use the behavior of the factory worker to describe Spence's view (refer to Figure 1.7). In our example, the worker starts at the factory (A) and walks 3 blocks until arriving at his goal (the bar, F).

Spence suggested that when a reward (beer) is obtained in a goal environment, this reward elicits a goal response (R_G). For example, when the thirsty

FIGURE 1.7
Route that the factory worker must take from the factory site A to the bar F. From Klein, S. B. *Motivation: Biosocial approaches.* New York: McGraw-Hill, 1982.

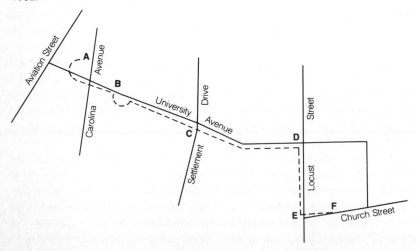

worker smells and tastes the beer, the beer initiates an internal response. This internal response (for example, salivation, gastric secretion) produces an internal stimulus state (S_G) which motivates the worker to drink the beer. The characteristics of S_G resemble those of Hull's drive state (D): they represent an internal arousal which motivates behavior. The internal response is intensified as the worker drinks. Until drinking is inhibited, the beer will continue to elicit the internal goal response. Thus, the intensity of the worker's goal response is determined by the reward value; the greater the reward magnitude, the stronger the goal response.

Spence thought that during the first few experiences, the environmental cues present during reward (for example, the bar) became associated with reward and subsequently produced a conditioned or anticipatory goal response (r_G). This conditioned goal response then causes internal stimulus changes (s_G) which motivate instrumental behavior. After the establishment of the r_G to the bar, the sight of the bar from the intersection of Church and Locust streets (point E) will elicit the r_G-s_G complex, which then motivates the worker to approach the bar more readily than on earlier experiences. As the strength of the r_G-s_G mechanism increases on every reinforced trip to the bar, the factory worker more rapidly approaches the bar. Upon entering the bar, the worker orders a beer and begins drinking. Since he saw the bar from the Church and Locust intersection (point E), the stimulus characteristics of point E also become able to produce the r_G-s_G mechanism through higher-order conditioning. After the establishment of the r_G-s_G complex to point E, the anticipatory goal response will occur when the worker sees point E upon reaching the intersection of University Avenue and Locust Street (point D). The sight of E motivates him to approach point E. Now at the intersection of Church and Locust streets, the worker can see the bar; this causes him to approach it and another reinforcing experience. Because the worker saw the conditioned stimulus (point E) from point D, higher-order conditioning causes the r_G-s_G mechanism to be conditioned to the stimulus characteristics of the corner of University Avenue and Locust Street. Higher-order conditioning will continue until each landmark can produce the r_G-s_G mechanism which will motivate the worker to approach the next landmark. When conditioning is completed, the worker will begin walking from the factory toward the bar. The ability of each landmark (points A, B, C, D, E, and F) to motivate approach behavior increases with each subsequent reinforcing trip to the bar. The effect of this increased incentive motivation makes the worker walk faster on successive reinforced experiences; the walking speed increases until a maximum is reached.

The reward magnitude used during conditioning determined the maximum level of responding. Since a large reward creates a more intense r_G than does a smaller reward, Spence assumed that the environmental cues associated with the large reward produce a stronger r_G than if paired with a small reward. This idea conforms to basic classical conditioning principles: the strength of a CR depends on UCS intensity; the stronger the UCS, the greater the CR. Spence's incentive motivation concept is supported by observations that performance level improves with greater reward (for example, Crespi, 1942). As noted earlier, Crespi found that rats ran down an alley faster for a larger reward than for a smaller one.

Hull recognized the need for the r_G-s_G mechanism as early as 1931. Since the classical conditioning process operated according to a contiguity principle (the greater the delay between CS and UCS, the weaker the CR), a mechanism must exist to enable the worker to associate the end of the workday with walking toward the bar, since the reinforcement in the bar is not likely to be temporally paired with the cues present at the factory. Thus, the higher-order conditioning of the r_G-s_G mechanism to the factory and to intervening points proposed by Spence enables the worker to remain motivated until he reaches the bar and beer.

Spence's anticipatory goal mechanism indicates that the classical conditioning process was responsible for this factory worker's motivation to approach reward. Other psychologists have adopted this acquired motive view to explain an animal's or person's motivation to avoid frustrating or painful circumstances (for example, Amsel, 1958; D'Amato, 1970).

Avoidance of Frustrating Events   According to Hull (1943), the absence of reward, or nonreward, acts to inhibit behavior. Hull proposed two types of inhibition of a specific behavior produced by nonreward: (1) *Reactive inhibition* (I_R) is the temporary inhibition produced when behavior does not produce reward and the animal becomes fatigued. (2) *Conditioned inhibition* ($_sI_R$) represents the process of permanent behavioral inhibition produced when environmental events are associated with the inhibitory nonreward state. These cues subsequently will reduce the likelihood that a particular behavior will occur. Hull thought that drive, incentive motivation, and habit strength facilitate the occurrence of a specific response and that inhibition (both reactive and conditioned) reduces the tendency to respond.

The Hullian view asserts that nonreward inhibits habitual behavior, thereby allowing the strengthening of other behaviors. However, this view does not completely describe the influence which nonreward has on instrumental behavior. Abram Amsel's frustration theory (1958) asserts that frustration both motivates avoidance behavior and suppresses appetitive behavior.

Amsel proposed that the frustration state differs from the appetitive-drive state. Nonreward presented in a situation in which reward previously occurred produces an innate (unconditioned) frustration response (R_F). This frustration response has motivational properties: the stimulus aftereffects (S_F) energize escape behavior. The cues present during the frustration (R_F) become conditioned to produce an anticipatory frustration response (r_F). The anticipatory frustration response also produces internal stimuli (s_F); these stimuli (s_F) motivate an animal or human to avoid a potentially frustrating situation.

The following example illustrates the central characteristics of Amsel's frustration model. Suppose that you have 10 minutes to reach the theater before the movie begins. You get into your old car, but it will not start. The failure of your car to start produces nonreward, which in turn produces frustration (R_F). The stimulus aftereffects of frustration (S_F) motivate escape behavior; that is, you leave the car and return home. If your car continues not to start, you probably will sell it to avoid future frustration. According to Amsel's view, the car becomes associated with nonreward and, therefore, produces an anticipatory frustration response (r_F). The internal stimulus consequences (S_F) of this anticipatory frustration response motivate you to sell your car.

Avoidance of Painful Events   In 1956, O. H. Mowrer proposed a Hull-based view of avoidance learning. According to Mowrer, avoidance behavior is developed in two stages. *In the first stage, a person becomes afraid of a particular object by associating it with an aversive event.* For example, a person bitten by a dog then associates the dog (CS) with the bite (UCS) which elicited pain (UCR). Now the person becomes afraid (CR) when seeing the dog. *During the second phase, fear motivates instrumental behavior, and the instrumental activity which reduces fear becomes habitual.* The person's fear of the dog motivates escape from the dog, perhaps by quickly walking away when seeing it, thus preventing another bite. Mowrer's view assumes that the motive for avoidance behavior is escape from a fearful object and that avoidance behavior is reinforced by fear reduction. Although Mowrer's view received initial support, recent research (Bolles, 1972) has cast doubt on its validity. This research shows that the major problem with Mowrer's theory is that avoidance behavior not only is motivated by fear but also occurs to prevent adversity and is reinforced by the successful prevention of the UCS. Michael D'Amato (1970) has successfully restructured Mowrer's view into an acquired-motive approach. (Chapter 4 describes the avoidance process in greater detail. It should be noted that other psychologists believe that cognitive processes are also involved in avoidance behavior. We will address this view in Chapter 6.)

According to D'Amato, an aversive event (for example, shock) elicits an unconditioned pain response (R_p); the unconditioned stimulus of painful shock (S_p) motivates escape behavior. Through classical conditioning, the environmental cues present during shock acquire the ability to produce an anticipatory pain response (r_p) whose stimulus aftereffects (s_p) also motivate escape behavior. D'Amato's r_p-s_p mechanism motivates an animal or human to escape from the conditioned stimulus, just as Amsel's r_F-s_F system caused an animal to escape from a situation associated with frustration. You may have noticed a similarity between D'Amato's r_p-s_p system and Mowrer's conditioned-fear theory. In both views, the conditioned stimulus associated with an aversive event motivates avoidance behavior. The difference between the two views lies in the reinforcement mechanism responsible for the animal's or person's avoidance behavior.

D'Amato suggested that the termination of an aversive event (UCS; for example, the shock) produces an unconditioned relief response (R_R). The stimulus consequences (S_R) of the relief response are reinforcing. According to D'Amato, the stimuli associated with the termination of the aversive event become capable of producing an anticipatory relief response (r_R); the stimulus consequences (s_R) of this anticipatory response (r_R) are also reinforcing. In addition, the sight of the cues associated with anticipatory relief produces approach behavior in a manner closely resembling Spence's description of the approach response to anticipatory-goal-related cues. This idea suggests a second motivational basis of avoidance responding: the animal or human is not only escaping from an aversive situation but is also approaching a reinforcing one. The avoidance of the aversive event is important, D'Amato claims, because if the animal does not avoid, the r_R-s_R mechanism will not develop. Let's consider how D'Amato's theory would explain the motivational basis of some people's avoidance of dogs.

Being bitten by a dog is an aversive event which produces an unconditioned pain response and causes one to associate the dog with being bitten. Through this conditioning, the dog produces an anticipatory pain response (r_p). The r_p-s_p mechanism motivates a person who has been bitten to get away from a dog when he sees one; this produces an unconditioned relief response. Suppose that such a person runs into a house to escape the dog. The house then becomes associated with relief and is able to produce an anticipatory relief response. Thus, if the dog is seen again, the sight of the house produces the r_R-s_R complex which acts to motivate the person to run into the house. Therefore, the anticipation of both pain and relief motivates this person to avoid the dog.

Nature of Anticipatory Behavior   Rescorla and Solomon (1967) pointed to a serious problem with the r_G-s_G mechanism proposed by Kenneth Spence. Although incentive value does influence an animal's motivation level, there are no peripheral physiological changes (for example, salivation) which are always related to an animal's instrumental behavior. Psychologists who attempted to observe r_G directly and evaluate its influence on behavior have found that salivation might precede or follow instrumental behavior; other times an animal might salivate without responding or respond without salivating (Lewis, 1959; Kintsch & Witte, 1962). Apparently, salivation is not the r_G in Spence's incentive motivational view. Rescorla and Solomon suggested that r_G is a central, rather than peripheral, event. This central process is classically conditioned and has its strength determined by reward magnitude; its effect is to motivate behavior. As we will discover in the next chapter, Rescorla and Solomon also suggested that fear, frustration, and relief are central rather than peripheral events.

Overview   The acquired-motive approach emphasized the important role of classically conditioned emotional responses in motivating instrumental behavior. This approach also described the mechanistic process responsible for an animal's or person's approach toward reward or avoidance of adversity. Empirical research has validated the motivational influence of conditioned responses on instrumental behavior.

A Contiguity View   Hull's drive theory advocated a reinforcement mechanism for the establishment of S-R associations. Although most psychologists during the 1930s and 1940s accepted this S-R approach, Edwin Guthrie (1935,

1942, 1959) rejected the view that reward strengthened the bond between a stimulus and a response. Instead, Guthrie proposed that contiguity was sufficient to establish an S-R association. According to Guthrie, if a response occurs when a particular stimulus is present, the stimulus and response will automatically become associated.

Associative Shifting   Guthrie was not the first psychologist to suggest that an S-R association could be established through contiguous conditioning. Thorndike's (1913) *associative-shifting process* represented an initial contiguity view of conditioning. According to Thorndike, gradually changing the stimulus which elicited a response could result in the association of that response to a totally new stimulus. To illustrate the associative-shifting process, consider Thorndike's example of teaching a cat to stand up on command. At first, a piece of fish is placed in front of a cat; when the cat stands to reach the fish, the trainer says "stand up." After a number of trials, the fish stimulus is omitted, and the verbal stimulus alone can elicit the standing response, even though this S-R association has not been reinforced. Although Thorndike assumed that conditioning could develop through associative shifting, he proposed that the law of effect rather than associative shifting explains most S-R associations. In contrast, Guthrie asserted that contiguity represents the sole process through which associations are formed.

Guthrie's Approach   According to Guthrie, learning is a simple process governed entirely by the contiguity principle: whenever a particular stimulus and response occur simultaneously, an animal or person reencountering that stimulus will exhibit that specific response. Guthrie provided many real-life examples of how a behavior could be changed based on his theory. Consider the following example to illustrate Guthrie's view of learning:

> The mother of a ten year old girl complained to a psychologist that for two years her daughter had annoyed her by a habit of tossing coat and hat on the floor as she entered the house. On a hundred occasions the mother had insisted that the girl pick up the clothing and hang it in its place. These wild ways were changed only after the mother, on advice, began to insist not that the girl pick up the fallen garments from the floor, but that she put them on, return to the street, and re-enter the house, this time removing the coat and hanging it properly. (Guthrie, 1935)

Why was this technique effective? According to Guthrie, the desired response is for the child to hang up her clothes directly when entering the house, that is, to associate hanging up her clothes with entering the house. Having the child hang up the clothes after being in the house will not establish the correct association; learning, in Guthrie's view, will occur only when entering the house and hanging up the coat and hat occur together.

Impact of Reward   Guthrie assumed that reward has an important effect on our response to a specific environmental circumstance; however, he did not believe that reward strengthens S-R associations. According to Guthrie, many responses can become conditioned to a stimulus, and the response exhibited just prior to reward will be associated with the stimulus and will be produced when the animal or person experiences the stimulus again. For example, a child may draw, put together a puzzle, and study at the same desk. If her parents reward the child by allowing her to play outside after she studies but not after she draws or works on the puzzle, the next time the child sits down at the desk she will study rather than draw or play with a puzzle. In Guthrie's view, an animal or person must respond in a particular way—here, to study—in the presence of a specific stimulus—here, the desk—to obtain reward—here, playing outside. Once the animal or person exhibits the appropriate response, the obtained reward acts to change the stimulus context (internal and/or external) which was present prior to reward. For example, the child is no longer sitting at the desk but is outside riding her bike. Any new actions will be conditioned to this new stimulus circumstance—being outside—therefore allowing the appropriate response—studying—to be produced by the stimulus context—desk—when it is experienced again. Thus, reward functions to prevent further conditioning and not to strengthen an S-R association. In the example of the studying child, the reward of going outside prevents her from doing anything else at the desk; the reward does not per se strengthen the child's association between studying and the desk. Also, Guthrie assumed that reward must be presented immediately after the appropriate response if that response is to occur on the next stimulus exposure. If the reward is delayed, the animal's or person's actions occurring between the appropriate response and reward will be exhibited when the stimulus context is encountered again later instead of the response which actually produced reward. For example, if the child did not go outside immediately after studying but instead watched television at the desk and then went outside, the child would watch television at the desk rather than study.

The Function of Punishment How did Guthrie explain the influence of punishment? Punishment decreases the likelihood that the preceding behavior will be repeated; yet, it also acts like reward in that it changes the stimulus context. Thus, in Guthrie's system, punishment, like reward, changes the stimulus context, but its behavioral effect is a decrease rather than an increase in the preceding behavior. To explain this opposite effect, Guthrie assumed that punishment functions like a stimulus rather than a reward, that is, punishment is an unconditioned stimulus capable of eliciting a number of responses, such as crying, pouting, or fleeing. If the escape response terminates the adversity, it will become conditioned to the stimulus context in which punishment occurred. When this stimulus circumstance is encountered again, the conditioned response will be elicited. If this anticipatory response is effective, punishment will not occur. However, if the response which terminates punishment does not prevent punishment, the animal or person will not be able to avoid rather than just escape punishment.

Consider the following example to illustrate Guthrie's view of punishment. The parent of a misbehaving child uses a paddle for spanking. The spanking causes the child to cry, which terminates the spanking. The paddle and the crying will become associated. Whenever the child sees the paddle, he will cry;

if crying prevents the parent from using the paddle for punishment, crying will enable the child to avoid punishment. However, if the escape response of crying does not successfully prevent the aversive event of spanking, the child will not learn to avoid being punished. According to Guthrie, when an effective escape response does not prevent punishment the escape response will continue to be the last response conditioned to the context. Thus the escape response will still be elicited despite its inability to prevent punishment.

Guthrie assumed that punishment may not eliminate the undesired, punished behavior. Punishment will work only if the response elicited by punishment and, therefore, conditioned to the punishment situation is incompatible with the inappropriate response. For example, suppose a child is spanked for hitting a younger sibling. Unfortunately, punishment often acts to elicit aggression. Since the punished response—hitting a younger sibling—is not incompatible with the aggressive response, punishment will not be likely to suppress aggressive behavior in Guthrie's view.

Influence of Motives   In Guthrie's learning approach, motives have two important effects on the learning process. First, *motives determine which response occurs (and the vigor of the response) in a specific environmental context, thereby affecting which response will become associated with that stimulus.* For example, hunger determines whether food will elicit eating, which obviously influences whether a stimulus present with food, such as television, will become associated with eating. Second, *the internal stimuli aroused by a specific motivational state can become conditioned to produce the behavior necessary for a goal to be attained.* Suppose that a rat must run down an alley to receive food. If a hungry rat runs down the alley, the internal stimuli produced by hunger (as well as the stimuli in the alley) will become conditioned to produce running, which enables the rat to obtain the food. Following conditioning, satiation (or lower level of deprivation) will cause the absence of the internal stimuli which produce running; thus, the response necessary to obtain reward—running down the alley—will not be exhibited if the rat is no longer hungry. Guthrie referred to these internal stimuli, which are produced by motivation and result in the behaviors which are reinforced, as *maintaining stimuli.*

Importance of Practice   According to Guthrie, learning occurs in a single trial; that is, the strength of an S-R association reaches its maximum value following a single pairing of the stimulus and a response. You might wonder why Guthrie believed that learning could occur on a single trial when it is obvious that the efficiency and strength of behavior (or both) improve with successful experience. Guthrie did not deny that behavior improves with successful experience; however, he did reject the Hullian view that the strength of the S-R bond slowly increases with successful experience. According to Guthrie, performance gradually improves for three reasons. First, *although many potential stimuli are present during the initial conditioning, only a portion of these stimuli will be active (or attended to).* The exact stimuli present when an animal or person responds vary from trial to trial. For a stimulus active on a particular trial to produce a response, this stimulus must have also been active during a previous response. For example, suppose that in a classical conditioning situation, a tone had been present while a dog salivated, but the dog was not attending to the tone on this trial. Therefore, the dog will not salivate to the tone, even though the tone and salivation had been paired previously. Although the dog's behavior may change from trial to trial, this change reflects an attentional process rather than a learning process. Second, *many different stimuli can become conditioned to produce a particular response*. As more stimuli become able to elicit a response, the strength of the response will increase. However, this increased intensity of a response is not caused by an increased S-R association but rather by the increased number of stimuli able to produce the response. Third, *a complex behavior actually consists of many separate responses*. For the behavior to be efficient, each response element must be conditioned to the stimulus. As each element is conditioned to the stimulus, the efficiency of behavior will improve. According to Guthrie, the more varied the stimuli and/or the responses which must be associated to produce effective performance, the more practice is needed to make behavior efficient.

Overview The S-R contiguity view proposed by Guthrie during the 1930s and 1940s was not accepted by many psychologists. During his career as a professor at the University of Washington, he conducted few studies to validate his approach. The lack of empirical evaluation meant that Guthrie's theory remained unrevised from its original proposal in 1935 until his final writings in 1959. Recent experiments to test Guthrie's theory have found some ideas inaccurate and others accurate.

Some parts of Guthrie's theory do accurately describe certain aspects of the learning process. First, punishment can intensify an inappropriate behavior when the response elicited by punishment is compatible with the punished response; however, the impact of this facilitatory influence of punishment is limited. Chapter 4 will more closely examine the consequences of punishment. Second, contiguity between a response and reward is critical to prevent the acquisition of competing associations. (The child must go outside immediately after studying; if she watches television first, she will associate her desk with watching television rather than with studying.) Third, a particular internal stimulus can produce a specific behavioral response as the result of prior association of the internal stimulus and the response. (A hungry rat will run down the same alley in which it previously found food.) Fourth, only a portion of the environmental stimuli are active at a particular moment; therefore only a segment of potential stimuli can become associated with the response. Later chapters will examine evidence supporting these aspects of Guthrie's view.

Some aspects of Guthrie's theory, however, do not accurately describe the learning process. First, although Guthrie rejected the law of effect, suggesting instead that reward functions to change the stimulus situation, numerous experiments (see Bower & Hilgard, 1981) have disproved his reward concept. An experimenter can arrange for many changes (for example, jiggling the box or having the floor drop out from under the box) to occur after a response, but these actions do not act like a reward and the response will not be conditioned, even though substantial stimulus change followed the response. Second, Guthrie assumed that for an animal or person to avoid adversity, the avoidance response must be like the escape response. Although often difficult to learn, responses do occur in which the escape and the avoidance response differ. For example, we may install an alarm in our home to prevent being burned in a fire (avoidance response); but we run out of our house if it is burning (escape response). In an experimental test, O. H. Mowrer (1947) discovered that rats learned to press a bar to terminate shock; this response differed from the one (rearing on hind legs) they learned to avoid shock. Third, Guthrie believed that recency and frequency determined which response a particular stimulus would produce. However, Noble's (1966) extensive research indicated that reinforcement predicted a subject's response significantly better than did either frequency or recency. Fourth, Guthrie assumed that learning occurs on a single trial; that is, a single, simultaneous pairing of a stimulus and response results in the development of the maximum S-R associative strength. Many studies have evaluated Guthrie's view that learning occurs after a single S-R pairing. To test this view, the conditioning situation must be simple, and the trial-to-trial behavior of each subject must be assessed. In an eye-blink conditioning study using humans, Voeks (1954) conducted a well-controlled evaluation of Guthrie's view. Voeks observed that most subjects showed all-or-none learning; they showed no CR on one trial and an intense CR on the next trial. However, other studies have not reported single-trial learning for individual subjects: instead, they have found a gradual conditioning of a response in learning curves of individual subjects (see Bower & Hilgard, 1981). Spence (1956), accepting that jump-type conditioning does occur in some circumstances, indicated how an incremental learning approach could explain these results. (An incremental view assumes that the strength of learned behavior increases slowly over trials.) According to Spence, although S-R habit strength increases slowly over trials, the response will not be elicited until its strength exceeds the threshold of response evocation. According to Spence, if the threshold is near maximum strength, the learning process will appear to be of the all-or-none type. Spence's analysis allowed an incremental theory to explain the apparent single-trial learning curve, but recent theorizing suggests that some aspects of learning could develop on a single trial and others develop slowly. We will discuss this idea in greater detail in Chapter 5.

The S-R theories assume that a mechanistic process governs our behavior. In contrast, the cognitive approach suggests that one's actions are guided by purpose rather than by internal and external forces. Furthermore, the cognitive approach asserts that one's behavior is a flexible reaction rather than a habitual response. Although we will briefly examine the cognitive view of learning, Chapter 6 discusses this approach to learning in greater detail.

Cognitive Approaches

Tolman's Purposive Behaviorism Edward Tolman proposed a cognitive view of learning during the 1930s and 1940s that was not accepted by most psychologists. Instead, Hull's mechanistic drive theory represented the accepted view of learning during that period. During the 1950s the cognitive view gained some acceptance and other psychologists expanded Tolman's original approach. In the past decade, the cognitive approach has become a major theory of learning. Our discussion begins with Tolman's work. His research stands as a remarkable achievement; while Hull and his students were diligently working to disprove Tolman's view, he alone developed his theory of behavior. Later in the chapter, we'll study contemporary cognitive theories.

Flexibility of Behavior Edward Tolman's view (1932, 1959) conflicted with Hull's drive theory described earlier in this chapter. Tolman did not believe that behavior was an automatic response to an environmental event. Instead, he proposed that our behavior has both direction and purpose. Tolman assumed that behavior is goal-oriented; that is, we are motivated either to achieve a desired condition or to avoid an aversive situation. According to Tolman, there are both paths leading to our goals as well as tools which we can employ to obtain these goals. In Tolman's view, we can understand the structure of our environment, thus, through experience, we learn how to use these paths and tools to reach our goals. It is important to recognize that although Tolman believed that behavior is purposeful and that we develop expectancies, he did not mean that we are aware of either the purpose or the direction of our behavior. Tolman assumed only that we act *as if* we expect a particular behavior to lead to a specific goal.

Not only is our behavior goal-oriented, but also we expect specific outcomes to follow specific behaviors. For example, you may expect to receive an A for working hard in this class. If you do not receive an A, you will continue to work hard for the reward and will not be satisfied with a less-valued goal object. Thus, if you received a B on your first test in this class, you would not be satisfied with the B and would work even harder for an A on the next test. Tolman also believed that certain events in the environment convey information about where our goals are located. We can reach our goals only after we have learned the signs leading to reward or punishment in our environment. For example, you must learn the signs leading to the cafeteria to obtain food.

Tolman proposed that learning can occur without reinforcement. We learn about the structure of the environment merely as the result of experience. However, our expectations will not be translated into behavior unless we are motivated. And the presence of reward is one process which motivates our behavior. Thus, from Tolman's perspective, we may have acquired sufficient knowledge, but, unless we are motivated, our learning will not be evident in our behavior. According to Tolman, motivation has two functions. First, motivation produces a state of internal tension which creates a demand for the goal object. Second, it determines the environmental features to which we will attend. For example, if we are not hungry, we are less likely to learn where food is located than if we are starving. However, tension does not possess the mechanistic quality which it did in Hull's theory. According to Tolman, our expectations control the direction of our drives. For example, if we are motivated by hunger, our behavior will be directed toward the expected location of food, sometimes the cupboard, sometimes the refrigerator, and sometimes the grocery store. However, when we are motivated, we do not respond in a fixed, automatic, or stereotyped way to reduce our drive, but rather our behavior will remain flexible enough to enable us to reach our goal. Thus, Tolman assumed that the means (or behavior) necessary to reach a goal can vary and only the end product (or goal) is fixed.

Consider the following example to illustrate Tolman's approach. Your goal is to clean your room. Although you usually manage to complete this task, the disarray in your room differs every day, and you do not use the same motor movements with each cleaning. Your behavior varies each time, but your knowledge of the means necessary to obtain your goal will enable your drive to be converted into successful behavior.

Motivational Processes   According to Tolman, there are two types of motivations. Deprivation is one source of motivation. In Tolman's view deprivation conditions produce an internal drive state which increases demand for the goal object. Tolman also suggested that the value of reward affects the intensity of our motivations; we are more motivated to obtain a large reward than a small one. Tolman referred to the influence of reward on motivating behavior as *incentive motivation*. Environmental events can also acquire motivational properties through association with either a primary drive or a reinforcer (1959). The following example illustrates Tolman's view. A thirsty child sees a soda. According to Tolman, the ability of thirst to motivate behavior transfers to the soda. Tolman called this transference process *cathexis,* a term he borrowed from psychoanalytic theory. As a result of cathexis, the soda is now a preferred goal object, and this child, even when not thirsty, will be motivated to obtain a soda in the future. The preference for the soda is a positive cathexis. In contrast, our avoiding a certain place could reflect a negative cathexis. In Tolman's opinion, if we associate that place with an unpleasant experience, we will think of the place as an aversive object. You might remember that Hull suggested that drives could be conditioned. Tolman's cathexis concept is very similar to Hull's view of acquired drive. And Tolman's equivalence belief principle is comparable to Hull's acquired incentive concept. Animals or people react to a secondary reinforcer (or subgoal) as they do to an original goal object; for instance, our motivation to obtain money reflects our identification of money with a desired goal object such as food.

Is Reinforcement Necessary for Learning?   We learned earlier in this chapter that Thorndike assumed that S-R associations are established when the response leads to a satisfying state of affairs. Hull (1943) adopted Thorndike's law of effect concept and suggested that habit strength increases when a particular response decreases the drive state. In contrast to these views, Tolman

(1932) felt that reinforcement is not necessary for learning to occur and that the simultaneous experiencing of two events is sufficient for learning. Thus, according to Tolman, an understanding of when events will occur can develop without reinforcement. What is the influence of reward in Tolman's view? Tolman proposed that reward affects performance but not learning. The presence of a reward will motivate an animal or person to exhibit a previously learned behavior. For example, a child may have learned how to mow the yard but needs to be rewarded to do the job.

Not Every Reward Will Do   After playing outside, my oldest son is thirsty. However, unless juice or soda is available, he will not drink anything. Although water will satisfy his thirst, he is motivated to obtain a specific reward and does not find a less desirable reward satisfactory.

My son's behavior is one example of Tolman's assertion that we are motivated to obtain specific reinforcers. If we do not receive one of these rewards, we will not accept a less-valued reinforcer, and we will continue to act until we obtain the desired reward.

Overview   Edward Tolman proposed that the expectation of future reward or punishment motivates instrumental activities. Furthermore, the knowledge of the paths and/or the tools which enable us to obtain reward or avoid punishment guides our behavior. Although the research designed by Tolman and his students did not provide conclusive evidence for his cognitive approach, his work caused Hull to make major changes in his theory to accomodate Tolman's observation. For example, the idea that a conditioned anticipation of reward (r_G) motivates us to approach reward is clearly similar to Tolman's view that the expectation of reward motivates behavior intended for obtaining reward. Furthermore, Hull's drive view that frustration can motivate both the avoidance of a less-preferred reward and the continued search of the desired reward represents the drive explanation of the observation that not any reward will be acceptable. It should be noted that once Tolman's observations were incorporated in drive theory, most psychologists ignored Tolman's cognitive view, and the drive view of learning continued to be generally accepted. However, as problems developed within the drive approach during the 1960s and 1970s, the cognitive view gained wider approval. Psychologists began to use a cognitive approach to explain how behavior is learned. The next two sections of this chapter will look at a contemporary cognitive approach.

Expectancy-Value Theory   Tolman's cognitive approach is the foundation of Julian Rotter's (1954) social-learning theory. Rotter expanded Tolman's view by describing the types of expectancies we develop. In addition, his interest in clinical psychology led Rotter to describe how certain expectancies can lead to behavior pathology.

Basic Tenets   There are three main ideas expressed in Rotter's expectancy theory. First, Rotter suggested that *our preference for a particular event is determined by its reinforcement value*. According to Rotter, the value of a particular event is relative; its value reflects a comparison with other events. Thus, some of us may find an event highly reinforcing because we have not experienced many reinforcing events; others who have experienced many reinforcing events may not find this event as reinforcing. Rotter also suggested that a reinforcer can change its value when new reinforcers are introduced. A restaurant you have valued may lose its appeal when compared to a new restaurant.

The second component of Rotter's expectancy-value theory is that *each person has a subjective expectation concerning the likelihood of obtaining a particular reinforcer*. We believe that there is a specific probability of reaching a desired goal; these beliefs may or may not reflect reality. For example, you may feel that someone whom you like will not accept your dinner invitation, even though he or she will, in fact, come if you extend an invitation. The actual probability that an event will occur does not influence your behavior; you simply will not ask because your expected probability is low. Thus, in Rotter's view, even if you are motivated, you will not behave if you do not expect reward. Attractive women not being asked for dates because men expect to be rejected is yet another example of the influence of belief on instrumental behavior.

The third aspect of Rotter's expectancy-value theory says that *our expectation of obtaining reinforcement is determined by the situation*. We may expect to receive reward in one setting but not in another. Our past experiences determine this situational dependence; we acquire the expectation that a particular goal is more likely to occur under some circumstances than others. For example, suppose that you have a strong preference for Italian food. You would then be more likely to expect reward in an Italian restaurant than in a French café. Your relative expectations act to guide your behavior: if you have to choose between these two restaurants, you are more likely to choose the Italian restaurant than the French one.

Yet, sometimes we encounter new experiences. How do we respond to these new events? According to Rotter, *our generalized expectations from past experiences guide our actions*. Our behavioral potential represents our expectation of obtaining reward in a particular situation as well as the value of that reward. In Rotter's view, we can predict our behavior if we multiply our expectation of reward by our value of the reward. This mathematical formula has proved useful in describing and predicting behavior. See Atkinson's (1964) research on achievement motivation as one example of its use.

Rotter believed that unrealistic expectations often cause psychological disturbance. For example, if a person expects that no member of the opposite sex will accept an invitation for a date, the individual will avoid asking members of the opposite sex out and become depressed. According to Rotter, a clinical psychologist must modify a disturbed person's cognitions before treatment can permanently modify the psychopathology. In terms of our example, the therapist showing the depressed individual similar people who have dated is one method of altering the depressed person's inaccurate expectation.

Types of Expectations Bolles (1972, 1978) proposed that through our interaction with the environment, we develop two types of expectations which guide our instrumental activity. Bolles called the first type an *S-S* expectancy*.

According to Bolles, many environmental events (S), such as dinner bells or tones, are present when a biologically important event (S*), such as food or shock, occurs. The association of an environmental event (S) with a biologically significant event (S*) typically means that we will expect S* the next time we encounter S. However, this is not always true; Bolles suggested that S must reliably predict the occurrence of S* in order for the S-S* expectancy to develop. Thus, according to Bolles, contiguity is not sufficient for learning: Events must *consistently* occur together before we can acquire an S-S* expectancy. In addition, when two or more stimuli are present with the S*, only the more reliable predictor of the S* will become associated with the S*.

In our environment, there are many contingencies between behavior (R) and outcomes (S*), such as the relationship between studying and good grades. According to Bolles, we can learn to recognize the relationship between behavior and outcomes. Bolles called an understanding of the contingency between a behavior and an outcome an *R-S* expectancy*. Although many of our R-S* expectancies are acquired through experience, Bolles suggested that innate R-S* expectations also influence behavior. Note that our R-S* expectations do not necessarily reflect the contingencies in the environment; only the belief that a specific response leads to reinforcement or prevents punishment is important. In some situations we are rewarded or punished independent of our behavior, but in most circumstances reinforcement or aversive events depend on our exhibiting a specific behavior. Therefore, under these conditions, our S-S* expectancies predict the likelihood of a biologically important event occurring, and our R-S* expectancies lead us to the predicted result—either the presence of an appetitive event (for example, food) or the prevention of an aversive event (for example, shock).

Consider the following example to illustrate Bolles's view of an S-S* and an R-S* expectancy. Having refused to go to bed, a child receives a spanking from her father. This father uses a belt to administer the punishment. Does the child expect to be spanked when her father removes the belt? If the child usually sees her father remove his belt only before a spanking, the child probably will expect a spanking (S*) when she sees her father remove the belt (S). The child's expectation of punishment activates the S-S* expectancy that the child believes will prevent the spanking: the child starts to cry when father removes the belt. Although not always effective, this child's crying has frequently prevented past spankings; these experiences cause her to expect that crying (R) will prevent her from being punished (S*).

Walter Mischel (1973) suggested that three types of expectancies influence our actions. The first two expectancies, *stimulus outcome* and *behavior outcome,* are identical to the S-S* and R-S* expectancies described in Bolles's writings. In Mischel's view, stimulus-outcome expectations represent the belief in the consequences of the environmental stimuli which we experience, whereas behavior-outcome expectations represent our understanding of the consequences of our actions. According to Mischel, we do not believe that a particular behavior will be successful in all circumstances; instead a particular behavior-outcome expectation is activated only under specific environmental conditions.

Note that although we may expect to receive reward in a particular setting, we may still not exhibit a specific behavior. We will execute a certain response only when we feel competent or possess *self-efficacy*. According to Albert Bandura (1977), an efficacy expectancy refers to the belief that we are capable or are not capable of exhibiting a particular response. For example, suppose that you want to surf fish. The presence of a nice day predicts good fishing, and you expect to make your catches by casting your rod into the surf. However, unless you feel able to place a worm on your hook, you will be unable to obtain reward. Many people feel capable of placing a worm on their hooks and, therefore, are able to obtain their expected reward. However, some people want to fish but cannot place worms on hooks. Unless these people can alter their lack of perceived competence or self-efficacy, they will not experience the rewarding aspect of fishing.

Covariation   What is an expectancy? According to Alloy and Tabachnik (1984), an expectancy is a mental representation of the degree of covariation between events. (*Covariation* refers to the level of the relation between stimuli, behavior, and outcomes; the greater the relation, the higher the covariation.) In Alloy and Tabachnik's view, the level of relation between events differs. Some relations are perfect: one event always follows the other. Some relations are weak: one event sometimes follows the other. In many conditions, no relation exists among stimuli, behavior, and outcomes. According to Alloy and Tabachnik, it is important to know about the degree of covariation. This information provides people and animals with "a means of explaining the past, controlling the present, and predicting the future." Thus, covariation data allow a person to maximize the likelihood of obtaining desired outcomes and minimize the likelihood of experiencing aversive results.

It is important to recognize that the differences in covariation among stimuli, behavior, and outcomes per se are not the central aspect of Alloy and Tabachnik's theory. Instead, the main point of their view is that animals and people *know* the level of covariation among stimuli, behavior, and outcomes. This knowledge is contained in a mental representation of the degree of covariation; this mental representation or expectation is gained through experience and acts to guide instrumental activity.

Suppose you turn on a radio and then hear music. How did you learn that there is a high covariation between turning on the radio and hearing music? Alloy and Tabachnik suggest that two types of information determine the perceived level of covariance. First, an animal or person has a prior expectation or belief about the degree of covariation among stimuli, behavior, and outcomes. Through experience you have developed a preconceived idea about the relation between turning on the radio and hearing music. Second, information about the contingency among stimuli, behavior, and outcomes is contained in the situation itself. Thus, if you do not hear music after turning on the radio, you may conclude that the radio is broken. According to Alloy and Tabachnik, the combined influence of both prior expectations and situational information determines the level of perceived covariation. In the ideal, the animal or person weighs both prior expectations and current circumstance to develop an idea of covariation of stimuli, behavior, and outcomes. However, previous expectancies often have a much more profound influence on the perceived level of covariation than does situational information. Animals and people often ignore information contained in the environment and respond solely on their preconceived beliefs about the contingency or the covariation between stimuli, behavior, and outcomes. Alloy and Tabachnik present evidence indicating that people can detect the contingency among stimuli, behavior, and outcomes. Chapter 6 looks at evidence showing that the perceived relation between events influences instrumental activity.

Overview   Psychologists have suggested that expectancies play an important role in determining many human behaviors. For example, Bandura's research (Bandura, Ross, & Ross, 1963) argued that the expectation of reward and punishment influenced the likelihood of aggression, and Seligman (1975) has related the expectation of an inability to control events to depression. In addition, expectancy theory has been used to explain avoidance behavior, achievement motivation, and social behavior. Furthermore, effective clinical treatment for various behavior disorders has been developed by applying the expectancy-value approach. The ability of these treatments to alter behavior pathology lies in their modification of the individual's expectations responsible for the behavioral disturbance.

Skinner's Behaviorist Methodology

The work of B. F. Skinner, a noted American behaviorist, spans more than half a century and has contributed greatly to our understanding of the learning process. Skinner's behaviorism, often referred to as *behaviorist methodology,* is quite different from theories advocated by the other behaviorists we have discussed in this chapter. In his 1938 text *The Behavior of Organisms,* Skinner asserted that the goal of behaviorism should be to identify and isolate the environmental factors which govern behavior. Further, Skinner stated that we will understand a particular behavior only after we have learned how to predict and control the behavior. Also, Skinner suggests that the ability to predict and control a behavior depends on understanding the circumstances governing the occurrence of the behavior. Skinner's first step toward his goal was to examine the variables responsible for a rat's behavior—pressing a lever for food—in an operant chamber. His experimental analysis of the rat's behavior explained the environmental factors influencing the rat's lever pressing as well as produced a methodology with which to predict and control the rat's responding. Skinner then expanded his analysis of behavior to include other animals, humans, and situations and behaviors which differed greatly from operant chambers and bar pressing. For example, in his 1957 text, *Verbal Behavior,* Skinner argued that people do not have an instinctive capacity for "expressing our ideas." Instead, he believed that verbal behavior, like any other instrumental behavior, is controlled by differential reinforcement and punishment administered by significant others, such as parents and friends. Skinner's methodology led to the development of behavior modification, an effective approach to treating behavior pathology. We will see much evidence of Skinner's contribution in Chapter 3.

How does Skinner's view differ from those of the other behaviorists described in this chapter? Skinner (1938) asserted that the use of theory and "theoretical constructs" does not contribute to our understanding of behavior; in fact, he argued that theory can actually hamper the accumulation of knowledge. In Skinner's view, the search for evidence to validate a particular theory of behavior interferes with the functional analysis of the variables controlling the behavior, and, thereby, precludes the discovery of the environmental variables which control responding. Consider the following example to illustrate Skinner's approach. Many psychologists have speculated that stimulus-response associations are strengthened as the result of reinforcement, and years of research have been devoted to validating this view. According to Skinner, understanding the "theoretical construct" underlying the strengthening effect of reward on stimulus-response associations is useful only in that it points out that reinforcement is one environmental variable which can control how frequently a specific behavior occurs in a particular context.

Many psychologists do not agree with Skinner's view. Theory guides research, which in turn identifies the variables controlling behavior as well as explains similar results of various experiments. As Kendler stated in 1959:

> This "option-play" (or "playing-by-ear") type of research generates a mass of data that is most difficult to analyze systematically. Each experimental article contains many more variables than subjects. The knowledge obtained, as well as the interpretation offered, is that some variables in conjunction with other variables, result in changes in behavior.
>
> Where does the Skinnerian formulation go from here? At present the Skinnerians have been able to generate an enthusiasm and conviction among themselves resembling a quaint mixture of that found in a revolutionary party, a revival meeting, and a homecoming football gathering. Can this enthusiasm and conviction maintain itself on such a skimpy diet of theoretical notions? This writer thinks not. . . .

The work of psychologists who do use theory to guide their research has contributed greatly to our understanding of behavior and has increased our ability to predict and control behavior. For example, Hull's drive theory, discussed earlier, greatly influenced the development of systematic desensitization, a behavior therapy which effectively modifies phobic behavior (we will describe systematic desensitization in Chapter 2). The contribution of Hull and other theorists will be evident throughout the text.

SUMMARY

We have defined learning as a relatively permanent change in the ability to exhibit a behavior that occurs as the result of successful or unsuccessful experience. Many psychologists have speculated about the nature of the learning process, and two opposing viewpoints have characterized the debate over what mechanism underlies the development or the elimination of behavior. For most of this century, the majority of psychologists advocated a mechanistic process, that is, that an environmental event automatically produces a response. In contrast, a few psychologists suggested that learning reflects a mental process in which behavior is flexible and goal-oriented. Contemporary learning theory assumes that a complex interaction of mechanistic processes and mentalism underlies learning.

This century began with the functionalists emphasizing the instinctive character of human behavior. However, this approach was found to be inaccurate and was replaced with behaviorism, the belief that most human behavior is learned. The accomplishments of three men were primarily responsible for the acceptance of the behavioral approach: (1) Thorndike's observation that hungry animals learned a behavior to obtain reward, (2) Pavlov's demonstration that the pairing of a novel stimulus (the conditioned stimulus) with a biologically important event (the unconditioned stimulus) results in the ability of the conditioned stimulus to elicit the conditioned response, and (3) Watson's experiments showing that an emotional fear response could be conditioned in both animals and humans.

Two mechanistic S-R views were presented during the 1930s: Hull's approach emphasized the importance of reward in the learning process; Guthrie's approach proposed that contiguity was sufficient for learning. The Hullian drive view was the dominant behavioral approach from the 1930s to the middle 1960s, and only recently have some of Guthrie's views been recognized as playing an important role in learning.

Hull theorized that a nonspecific intense internal arousal—drive—motivates behavior. Several classes of stimuli (deprivation, intense environmental events, and hormonal changes) appear inherently capable of initiating drive, and any stimuli associated with these innate-drive stimuli develop the capacity to produce drive through the classical conditioning process. Also, reward, and stimuli associated with reward, are able to produce arousal and motivate behavior. According to Hull, once drive has motivated action, behavior is then directed by the specific prevailing stimulus conditions. A specific stimulus is capable of eliciting several behaviors, and the behavior with the strongest bond (or habit strength) will be repeated; the bond strengthens if the behavior produces drive reduction. In contrast to the excitatory influence of drive and habit strength on behavior, the continued presence of drive is an aversive situation which results in permanent inhibition, called conditioned inhibition; this continued presence of drive antagonizes the excitatory effect of drive and habit strength.

Although Hull's theory focused on the unlearned sources of drive and the development of habit strength, contemporary drive theories emphasize the importance of acquired motives. Spence developed his incentive-motivation system to explain animal and human approach responses to reward. According to Spence, the presentation of reward elicits an unconditioned emotional response (R_G); the stimulus consequences (S_G) of the R_G motivate consummatory behavior. The association of environmental events with reward causes the development of a conditioned anticipatory goal response (r_G). The stimuli (S_G) produced by this conditioned response motivate the approach to reward. As environmental events distant from reward become capable of eliciting the r_G-s_G mechanism through higher-order conditioning, approach behavior is activated by these cues.

Amsel described another acquired motivational system to explain the influence of nonreward on behavior. According to Amsel, the presentation of nonreward in a situation previously associated with reward produces an unconditioned frustration response (R_F). The stimulus consequences of frustration (S_F) motivate escape from the frustrating situation. Just as the conditioning of the r_G-s_G mechanism motivates approach behavior toward potential reward, the anticipatory-frustration-response mechanism (r_F-s_F) motivates avoidance of a potentially frustrating situation.

D'Amato proposed additional learned motivational systems—anticipatory pain and relief—to describe the mechanism responsible for the avoidance of painful events. D'Amato asserts that the classical conditioning of the anticipatory-pain-response mechanism (r_p-s_p) to the environmental cues associated with an aversive painful event provides motivation to escape from this environment. Furthermore, the termination of pain produces an unconditioned relief response (R_R). The stimulus consequences (S_R) of relief motivate further appetitive behavior. The establishment of the anticipatory-relief-response mechanism (r_R-s_R) provides motivation to approach the cues associated with unconditioned relief; this approach behavior is established in a manner similar to the conditioning of approach to a potential reward.

Guthrie advocated a contiguity approach to S-R learning. According to Guthrie, when a stimulus and response occur together, they automatically become associated, and when encountered again, that stimulus will produce the response. Guthrie rejected the view that reward strengthens S-R associations; instead, he assumed that reward alters the stimulus environment, thereby precluding the acquisition of any new S-R associations that would inhibit the occurrence of a previously established response to the stimulus. Furthermore, Guthrie asserted that punishment suppresses an inappropriate behavior only if the response produced by punishment is incompatible with the punished response; in contrast, punishment can actually increase responding if the response elicited by punishment is compatible with the punished response. In Guthrie's view, motivation determines which response will occur in the presence of a particular stimulus and thus determines which responses will become associated with that stimulus. Furthermore, the internal stimuli aroused by a specific motivational state can become conditioned to produce a response if the response has previously been followed by reward.

Practice increases the likelihood, intensity, and efficiency of a response. According to Guthrie, practice increases the number of stimuli associated with a response and thereby the intensity of that response. Also, the likelihood of the response occurring increases as more elements of the stimulus complex become associated with the response. In addition, for a complex response to become efficient, each response element must be conditioned to the stimulus.

During the past two decades, many psychologists have recognized that cognitive processes play an important role in learning. In contrast to the mechanistic view that we automatically respond to environmental events, the cognitive approach assumes that we are actively involved in determining our responses to environmental circumstance.

Cognitive psychology began in the 1930s and 1940s with Tolman's ideas. Although Tolman's cognitive approach did not initially receive much acceptance, his views represent the foundation of current cognitive theories. Tolman proposed that our behavior is goal-oriented: we are motivated to reach specific goals and continue to search until we obtain them. Rather than believing that behavior represents an inflexible habit, Tolman assumed that our behavior remains flexible enough to allow us to reach our goals. Our expectations determine the specific behavior we use to obtain reward or avoid punishment. Our expectations are derived from our understanding of the means necessary to reach our goals; this understanding is inferred from the environment.

Tolman theorized that although we may know how and where to obtain our goals, we will not behave unless we are motivated. He proposed two classes of motives: (1) deprivation conditions and (2) incentive motivation. According to Tolman, deprivation increases our demand for goal objects, and greater reward value increases our motivation to obtain goals.

Three types of expectancies appear to influence behavior: stimulus-outcome, response-outcome, and efficacy expectations. Stimulus-outcome expectancies involve our understanding of the predictive relationships in our environment—we expect a particular stimulus to predict a biologically important event. Response-outcome expectancies represent our belief in the consequences of our action—we expect a specific outcome when we behave in a particular way. Our efficacy expectation reflects our perceived ability to execute a particular action—we feel competent when efficacy expectations are high and inadequate when they are low. Stimulus-outcome and efficacy expectancies control whether we will act; response-outcome expectancies determine which behavior we will exhibit to obtain desired goals.

What exactly is an expectation? According to Alloy and Tabachnik, an expectation is a mental representation of the degree of covariation among stimuli, behavior, and outcomes. Not only can we detect the level of covariation between events, but also this perceived covariation influences our instrumental activities.

B. F. Skinner argued that theory interferes with the discovery of the causes of behavior. Instead of wasting time attempting to validate a particular "theoretical concept," Skinner believed that psychologists should seek to identify and isolate the environmental factors governing behavior. Once these variables have been discovered, Skinner assumed that we would be able to predict and control behavior. Skinner's analysis of behavior increased the understanding of the circumstances which influence responding and contributed to a methodology which allows reliable prediction and effective control of behavior. However, the theoretical emphasis criticized by Skinner has motivated important research—research that has contributed to our understanding of the common elements of various situations and behaviors and produced effective procedures for controlling behaviors. Throughout the text, we will see the importance of both theoretical and experimental analyses of behavior.

CHAPTER 2

PAVLOVIAN CONDITIONING

A LINGERING FEAR

Diane is a secretary for a prominent local lawyer. Although her coworkers often ask her to socialize after work, Diane always rejects their requests; instead, driving directly home, she proceeds hurriedly from her car to her apartment. Once inside, Diane locks the door and refuses to leave until the next morning.

On weekends, Diane will shop with her sister who lives with their parents several blocks away. However, once darkness approaches, Diane compulsively returns to her apartment. Although her sister, her parents, and close friends sometimes visit during the evening, Diane refuses any of their invitations to go out after dark.

Several men—all seemingly pleasant, sociable, and handsome—have asked Diane for dates during the past year. Although desperate to socialize with them, Diane has been unable to accept any of their invitations.

Diane's fear of going out at night and her inability to accept dates began thirteen months ago. She had dined with her parents at their home and had left about 9:30 p.m. Because it was a very pleasant fall evening, she decided to walk the several blocks to her apartment. Within a block of her apartment, a man grabbed her, dragging her to a nearby alley. He gagged her with a handkerchief, preventing her from screaming, and raped her. Because she did not see her assailant, the police doubted that they could apprehend him. The few friends and relatives Diane had told about the attack tried to support her, but she found no solace from their efforts.

During the few occasions after the attack that Diane did go out after dark, she felt very uncomfortable: she was repulsed by the sight of any man. This intense reaction forced her to return home. She did accept one date after her rape, but she became so frightened that she had to end the evening by claiming that she had become ill. Diane wants to overcome her fears but does not know how.

Diane's fears reflect two separate classically conditioned emotional reactions acquired from being raped: she is now afraid of darkness and men. These fears motivate Diane to avoid going out at night and dating men. In this chapter, we will describe the classical conditioning process responsible for Diane's intense internal reactions to men and darkness. (The learning mechanism which causes Diane to avoid men and darkness will be detailed in Chapter 4.) We'll also detail an effective behavior therapy, systematic desensitization, which uses the classical conditioning process to eliminate conditioned fear reactions like Diane's.

THE ENVIRONMENTAL CONNECTION

Our environment contains an enormous amount of information. Knowledge of relevant environmental information is essential to our effective interaction with our environment. Some of this information predicts when important environmental events (pleasant or unpleasant) will or might occur. Other information concerns the location of rewarding or punishing events. The environment also contains information indicating how we can behave to obtain reinforcement or avoid punishment. Thus, if we do not detect important environmental information, we will not know (1) *whether reinforcement or punishment will or might occur,* (2) *where rewards and aversive events are located,* and (3) *how to behave to receive reinforcement or prevent adversity. Classical conditioning* provides information about what events are pleasant or unpleasant, when these important events will or might occur, and where they are located. *Instrumental conditioning* allows us to know how to behave to obtain reward or avoid punishment.

Consider the following two examples to illustrate the information provided by classical conditioning and instrumental conditioning. Arriving home after class, you notice that your stomach is growling. You go to the kitchen, put your books on the table, and proceed to the refrigerator. Upon opening the refrigerator, an apple pie strikes your fancy; you take it as well as the milk container out of the refrigerator. After eating a large piece of the pie and drinking a glass of milk, you no longer feel hungry. In this situation, you know that a piece of apple pie and a glass of milk are reinforcers; the environment indicated that the refrigerator contained reinforcement. In addition, the knowledge that going to the refrigerator and removing the apple pie and milk would relieve your hunger enabled you to obtain the desired rewards.

For the second example, suppose that your instructor reminded you today that you will have an examination on three chapters next week. Since you have not read the assigned material for the test, you decide that tonight you will read it. The instructor's message indicated when an aversive event (an examination) will occur and when an even more aversive event (failure of the examination) might take place. You have chosen to study for the test to prevent failure. This chapter will detail how the classical conditioning process determines what events are important, when they will or might occur, and where they are located. (Chapter 3 describes instrumental conditioning.)

We know that the information necessary for our behavior to be effective, that is, for us to consistently obtain reward and avoid punishment, is in our environment. However, we do not always use the knowledge contained in our environment. For example, sometimes we know that adversity is imminent but do not act to prevent it; sometimes we know that reward is available, but do not behave in ways that will obtain it. We must be motivated to translate our knowledge into action. Under some conditions, innate factors provide the motivational basis for our behavior. For example, if you had not eaten for hours when you arrived home after class, deprivation probably motivated your trip to the refrigerator. However, in other situations, the environment may produce an internal reaction which motivates our behavior. If, for example, we arrive home shortly after having eaten our lunch and go to the refrigerator, the arrival home reflects an environmental condition which produces hunger and motivates us to seek food. Or, for example, the announced examination induces fear, thereby causing us to read the assigned material. Later in the chapter we will discuss why certain environmental events can produce internal changes, such as hunger and fear, as the result of a classical conditioning experience. These internal reactions to environmental events represent the motivating force behind much of the behavior of animals and humans.

ACQUISITION OF A CONDITIONED RESPONSE

The Conditioning Paradigm

Four basic components make up the conditioning paradigm: (1) the *unconditioned stimulus* (UCS), (2) the *unconditioned response* (UCR), (3) the *conditioned stimulus* (CS), and (4) the *conditioned response* (CR). Prior to conditioning, the UCS elicits the UCR, but the CS cannot elicit the CR. During conditioning, the CS is paired with the UCS. Following conditioning, the CS can elicit the CR. The strength (or intensity) of the CR increases steadily during acquisition until a maximum or *asymptotic level* is reached (see Figure 2.1). The UCR is an innate reflexive response to the UCS. The UCS-UCR complex is referred to as the *unconditioned reflex;* the CS-CR complex is called the *conditioned reflex.*

Note that although the pairing of the CS and UCS is essential to the development of the CR, other factors determine whether conditioning occurs and what the final asymptotic level of the CR is. We will detail the conditions which influence the ability of the CS to elicit the CR later in the chapter. Let's now return to the eating and studying examples to illustrate the basic elements of conditioning.

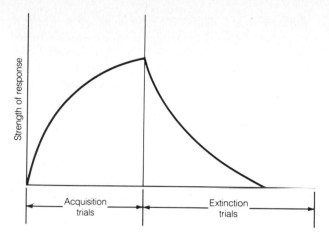

FIGURE 2.1
Acquisition and extinction
of a conditioned response.

Conditioning of Hunger   Some of us become hungry when arriving home after class; the home environment at this time of day is the CS eliciting the hunger reaction (CR). This conditioned hunger is assumed to reflect the conditioning of arriving home with deprivation-induced hunger: deprivation is the UCS; hunger, the UCR (see Hull, 1943). One probable cause of this conditioning is that very often you arrive at home late in the day, have not eaten for awhile, and are hungry.

Your hunger undoubtedly intensifies when you go into the kitchen and see the refrigerator. Opening the refrigerator, you notice the milk and pie. Why does the sight of the refrigerator and the food increase your hunger and motivation to obtain food? The answer lies in the association of the kitchen, the refrigerator, and the sight of the food (CSs) with the taste and the smell of the food (UCSs). When animals or people are exposed to food, they exhibit a set of unconditioned responses which prepare them to digest, metabolize, and store ingested food. These internal preparatory responses are called *cephalic reflexes* (see Powley, 1977). (A reflex is *cephalic* when input to the brain originates in the head region, output to the periphery goes to the autonomic nervous system and endocrine system, and the central nervous system mediates the input and output.) Elicited by the taste and smell of food, these cephalic responses include the secretion of saliva, gastric juices, pancreatic enzymes, and insulin. One important action of insulin is to lower blood glucose, which in turn stimulates hunger and motivates eating (see Mayer, 1953). Thus, we become hungry when we taste or smell food. The intensity of these cephalic responses is directly related to the palatability of food. The more desirable the food, the greater the cephalic responses and the larger the meal.

Cephalic responses can be conditioned (see Powley, 1977). The conditioning of the cephalic responses to environmental cues plays an important role in your motivation to eat when you arrive home. Since the cues such as the kitchen and the refrigerator have been associated with food, they can elicit the cephalic responses and, therefore, produce hunger. Thus, when you go to the kitchen and see the refrigerator, your body reflexively releases insulin, which lowers your blood glucose level and thus makes you hungry. As we will discover shortly, the strength of the conditioned reflex depends on the intensity of the unconditioned stimulus. If you have associated the environment of the kitchen with highly palatable foods capable of eliciting an intense cephalic reaction, the stimuli in the kitchen will elicit an intense conditioned cephalic response, and your hunger will be great.

Our discussion indicates that the environmental cues present when you arrive home from school can elicit a conditioned hunger reaction; this conditioned hunger motivates you to eat, even when you are not deprived. These environmental cues have developed the ability to arouse hunger through association with deprivation, food, or both. A different type of conditioned emotional reaction motivates your study behavior. Let's now examine the conditioning of fear and its ability to motivate studying.

Conditioning of Fear   For most people, an examination is an aversive event. When you take a test (UCS), the examination elicits an unconditioned pain reaction (UCR; see Chapter 1). The psychological distress which you experience when an instructor hands you a test is one aspect of your pain reaction; the increased psychological arousal is another part of your response to receiving an examination. Although the adversity does lessen while you are taking a test, you will not experience relief until you complete it.

Examinations differ considerably in their degree of aversiveness. You respond intensely to some tests; others elicit only a mild pain reaction. Many factors determine the aversiveness of an examination. The *severity* of the test is one factor influencing how intensely you will respond; a difficult test eliciting a stronger pain reaction than an easy exam is one example of how the severity of the test (UCS) influences the intensity of the pain reaction (UCR). Another factor often affecting the aversiveness of a test is the number of examinations you *experience*. You probably experience more distress while taking the first test in a course than during subsequent examinations. Your experience with prior tests may cause the development of tolerance (see Solomon, 1980) and, thereby, a reduced pain reaction to a later test.

Through past experiences, the cues which predict an examination can elicit an anticipatory pain reaction (the CR, see Chapter 1). We typically call this anticipatory pain reaction fear. One stimulus associated with an examination is the announcement of an impending test. Thus, you become frightened (CR) when an instructor announces (CS) that an examination will be given during the next class period. As the time of the test approaches, you become more aroused. This arousal motivates you to study to prevent failure. Psychologists have consistently observed that *fear is conditioned when a novel stimulus (the CS) is associated with an aversive event*. The Russian physiologist Bechterev's 1913 observation that a conditioned response (for example, withdrawal of the finger) can be established by pairing a neutral stimulus with shock was the first experimental demonstration of fear conditioning. In 1916, John Watson showed that emotional arousal was conditioned during the pairing of a novel stimulus with shock. Other researchers have consistently reported the development of fear through classical conditioning in animals (see Miller, 1948) and humans (see Staats & Staats, 1957). Also, it has been found that *fear motivates an instrumental behavior which both terminates the conditioned fear response and prevents the unconditioned aversive event*. Neal Miller's classic 1948 study demonstrates the motivational properties of fear. Miller first conditioned fear in rats by presenting electric shock in the white compartment of a shuttle-box apparatus (see Figure 2.2). Once the shock was administered, Miller allowed the rats to escape into the black compartment. After the initial pairings of the white compartment with shock, he confined the animals in the white compartment without any additional shock. However, each rat could escape the white chamber by turning a wheel to open the door to the black compartment. Miller found that about half of the rats learned to turn the wheel to escape the aversive white chamber; the other half "froze" and did not learn the required response. The results show that the association of an environment (the white chamber) with an unconditioned aversive event (shock) can cause the environment to acquire some of the properties of the UCS; that is, the CS can elicit a response (fear) which is similar to the response (pain) elicited by the UCS.

FIGURE 2.2
Apparatus similar to that employed by Miller (1948) to investigate acquisition of a fear response. The rat's emotional response to the white chamber, previously paired with shock, motivates the rat to learn to turn the wheel which raises the gate and allows escape. From *Theories of learning* by L. C. Swenson © 1980 by Wadsworth, Inc. Reprinted by permission of the publisher.

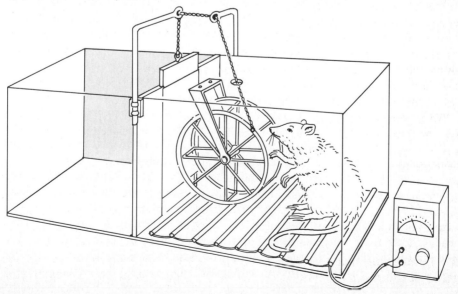

We learned earlier that the degree of hunger induced by environmental events depends on the UCS intensity—the stronger the UCS, the more intense our conditioned hunger reaction. Our conditioned fear reaction is also influenced by the strength of the aversive unconditioned event. We fear a difficult test more than an easy one. Similarly, more fear will be elicited by an important test than by an unimportant test.

Not all students become frightened by an impending examination, and some do not learn that studying represents an effective way of reducing fear and preventing failure. This chapter describes the conditions which influence the development of a conditioned fear response. Chapter 4 will detail the factors which govern avoidance acquisition.

Examples of Various Conditioned Responses   Many different responses can be conditioned as a result of CS-UCS pairings. In addition, numerous unconditioned stimuli other than food or shock can be employed in the conditioning process. Table 2.1 presents a list of unconditioned stimuli which can be used in conditioning and of the responses elicited by these stimuli.

Most experiments on classical conditioning have investigated the conditioning of a single conditioned response. Actually, several responses are conditioned during CS-UCS pairings. The conditioning of several responses has an obvious adaptive value. For example, when a CS is experienced with food, several different digestive responses are conditioned. The conditioned salivary reflex aids in swallowing, the conditioned gastric-secretion response facilitates digestion, and the conditioned insulin release enhances storage. Similarly, when a cue is paired with adversity, autonomic and cortical arousal is conditioned. It is this conditioned arousal which provides the motivational basis of escape and avoidance responding. Further, conditioned defensive reactions allow the animal to avoid potential adversity.

The Character of the Conditioned Response   Pavlov (1927) suggested that as a result of conditioning the conditioned stimulus becomes able to elicit the same response as the unconditioned stimulus. This stimulus-substitution view holds that the conditioned and unconditioned responses are the same response elicited by different stimuli. Although the conditioned and unconditioned responses are often similar (e.g., the conditioned stimulus paired with a food unconditioned stimulus elicits similar digestive responses as both the CR and UCR), in some circumstances conditioned and unconditioned responses are dissimilar (see Hollis, 1982, for a review of this literature).

The research of Shepard Siegel and his colleagues represents an impressive accumulation of evidence that the conditioned and unconditioned responses can be different (Siegel, 1975, 1976, 1978, 1979; Siegel, Hinson, & Krank, 1978; Siegel, Hinson, Krank, & McCully, 1982; Siegel, Sherman, & Mitchell, 1980). In several of their studies, Siegel and his associates used morphine as the unconditioned stimulus (Siegel, 1976, 1978; Siegel, Hinson, & Krank, 1978). *Analgesia,* or reduced sensitivity to pain, is one unconditioned response to

TABLE 2.1
A SAMPLE OF UNCONDITIONED STIMULI AND RESPONSES

Responses	Stimuli
Salivation	Dry food, acid
Clocking of EEG alpha rhythm	Light
Change in skin resistance (GSR)	Electric shock
Pupillary reflex	Change in illumination, shock
Gastrointestinal secretions	Food
Vasomotor reactions	Shock, thermal stimuli
Nausea, vomiting, etc.	Morphine
Immunity reactions	Injection of toxin and antigen
Diuresis	Increased water intake
Flexion reflex	Electric shock
Knee jerk	Patellar blow
Eye-blink reflex	Shock, sound, air puff
Eye movements	Rotation
Change in respiration	Electric shock
Change in pitch of voice	Electric shock
Withdrawal movements	Electric shock
Mouth opening, swallowing	Food
Locomotion	Shock
Instructed responses	Various
Previously conditioned (higher-order responses)	Various
Novel-food aversion	X-irradiation, lithium chloride ingestion, apomorphine injection, others
Change in blood sugar	Insulin injection

Source: Flaherty, C. F., Hamilton, L. W., Gandelman, R. J., & Spear, N. E. *Learning and memory.* Chicago: Rand McNally, 1977.

morphine. Siegel reported that the conditioned response to stimuli such as lights or tones paired with morphine was *hypoanalgesia,* or increased sensitivity to a painful event. How did Siegel know that a conditioned stimulus associated with morphine makes an event more unpleasant? To illustrate both the analgesic effect of morphine and the hypoanalgesic effect of a stimulus paired with morphine, Siegel placed a rat's paw on a hot plate and measured how long it took the rat to remove its paw. He observed that rats injected with morphine (the UCS) took longer to remove the paw from the heated plate than did animals not receiving the morphine injection. In contrast to the analgesia produced by the morphine, presentation of the CS (light or tone) resulted in the rat removing its paw more quickly than animals which had been presented a stimulus not paired with the UCS. Similar results have been observed by others (see Tiffany & Baker, 1981, for another example). Siegel (1975) as well as several other researchers (e.g., Flaherty et al., 1980) also found that while the UCR to insulin is hypoglycemia, the CR to a stimulus paired with insulin is hyperglycemia. Additional studies reported that the UCR to alcohol is hypothemia and that the CR to a stimulus associated with alcohol is hyperthermia (refer to Crowell, Hinson, & Siegel, 1981; Le, Poulos, & Cappell, 1979).

Siegel's research shows not only that the CR can be opposite of the UCR but also that conditioning is responsible at least in part for the phenomenon of drug tolerance. Tolerance to a drug develops because, with repeated use of a drug, the effectiveness of the drug declines, and thus larger doses are necessary to achieve the same pharmacological effect. According to Siegel, conditioning of a response, opposite of the unconditioned drug effects, to the environmental cues present during drug administration antagonizes the drug's action and results in a lower pharmacological reaction to the drug. Two lines of evidence support a role of conditioning in drug tolerance. First, Siegel, Sherman, and Mitchell (1980) found that exposure to the CS (environment) with the UCS (drug), once the association has been conditioned, results in the extinction of the CR; the elimination of the response to the CS produces a stronger reaction to the drug itself. Comparable results were obtained by Mansfield and Cunningham (1980). Second, Siegel, Hinson, and Krank (1978) reported an increased response to the drug can be induced by changing the stimulus context in which the drug is administered. The novel environment does not elicit a CR opposite to the drug's unconditioned effect; the absence of the opposing CR results in a stronger unconditioned drug effect. Other researchers (see Tiffany & Baker, 1981) have also discovered that a change in context leads to reduced drug tolerance. A heightened drug response in a new environment is not limited to animals. Siegel, Hinson, Krank, and McCully (1982) observed that drug overdose typically occurs when addicts take their usual drug dose in an unfamiliar environment. Without the protective opposing response, the effect of the drug is increased, resulting in the overdose.

Why is the CR sometimes similar to the UCR and sometimes dissimilar to the UCR? Although there is no definite answer to this question, the most reasonable explanation lies in the way that a conditioned response enables animals or people to adapt to their environment. The CR is an anticipatory response; that is, it occurs prior to the UCS. It is adaptive for a person to salivate prior to ingesting food. Similarly, becoming frightened before an aversive event motivates us to prevent the undesirable event. Since drugs alter normal physiological function, the conditioning of an opposite CR reduces the impact of the drug (UCS) and, thereby, aids in the maintenance of homeostasis. It may be that the CR is dissimilar to the UCR when an opposite response is the most adaptive way to respond to the UCS.

Conditioning Procedures

Five procedures have been employed in conditioning studies (see Figure 2.3). These procedures, representing the different ways in which a CS can be paired with the UCS, are not equally effective (see Keith-Lucas & Guttman, 1975; Sherman, 1978). The delayed-conditioning procedure is the most effective;

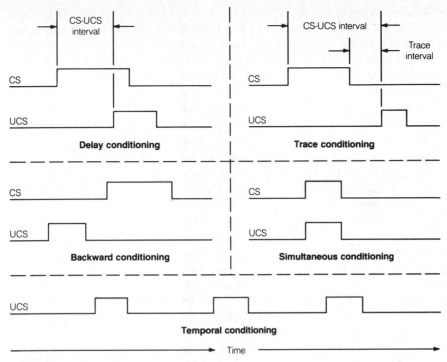

FIGURE 2.3
Schematic drawing of the five major classical conditioning procedures. The temporal relationship between the CS and the UCS in delay, trace, backward, and simultaneous conditioning is depicted. Note that there is no explicit CS in temporal conditioning.

backward conditioning is the least effective. The other three procedures have intermediate levels of effectiveness.

Delayed Conditioning In delayed conditioning, CS onset precedes UCS onset. The termination of the CS occurs either with the UCS onset or during UCS presentation. If, for instance, a father removes his belt before spanking his child, he is employing the delayed-conditioning procedure. The removal of the belt is the CS; its occurrence precedes the spanking (UCS) and remains present until the spanking occurs. Having experienced this type of conditioning, this child probably will be quite frightened whenever the father removes his belt.

Trace Conditioning During a trace-conditioning procedure, the CS is presented and terminated prior to UCS onset. Parents who threaten their children prior to punishment are using a trace-conditioning procedure. As we will discover in the next section, fear developed with this procedure will be quite weak unless the interval between CS termination and UCS onset is very short.

Simultaneous Conditioning   The CS and UCS are presented together when the simultaneous-conditioning procedure is employed. A parent whose threat and spanking occur simultaneously is using this procedure. The child's fear of the threat is weaker with the simultaneous-conditioning procedure than with the delayed-conditioning procedure.

Backward Conditioning   In the backward-conditioning procedure, the UCS is presented and terminated prior to the CS. Parents threatening their children after punishing them are practicing a backward-conditioning procedure. With the use of this procedure, fear of the threat probably will not develop. In fact, contemporary research indicates that using the backward-conditioning procedure results in the development of another type of CR (see Rescorla & Lo-Lordo, 1965). According to Rescorla and LoLordo, the backward-conditioning procedure is actually a conditioned-inhibition procedure; that is, the CS is paired with the absence of shock, producing relief; a child would experience a conditioned relief rather than fear when the threat is presented. Obviously, the CS must occur prior to the UCS if fear rather than relief is to be conditioned to the threat.

Temporal Conditioning   There is no distinctive CS in temporal conditioning. Instead, the UCS is presented at regular intervals. To show that conditioning has occurred, the UCS is omitted and the strength of the CR assessed. Animals and humans learn to exhibit the CR just prior to the onset of the UCS in temporal conditioning. What mechanism allows for temporal conditioning? In temporal conditioning, biological state provides the CS. Biological state changes during each day; this twenty-four-hour cycle is called the *circadian rhythm*. When the same internal state precedes each UCS exposure, that state will be conditioned to elicit the CR.

Consider the following example to illustrate the temporal-conditioning procedure. You set your alarm to awaken you at 7 a.m. for an 8 a.m. class. After several months, you awaken just prior to the alarm's sounding. The reason for your actions lies in the temporal-conditioning process. The alarm (UCS) produces an arousal reaction (UCR) which awakens you. Since a twenty-four-hour cycle of biological changes occurs each day, your internal state present every day just before the alarm rings (the CS) becomes conditioned to produce arousal; this arousal (CR) awakens you prior to the alarm's sounding.

How Readily Is a Conditioned Response Learned?

In the last section we discovered that a conditioned response develops when a novel stimulus is paired with an unconditioned stimulus. However, the pairing of a CS and a UCS does not automatically ensure that a conditioned response will be acquired. A number of factors determine whether a CR will develop following CS-UCS pairings. First, *the CS and UCS must be contiguous; that is, the conditioned stimulus must precede the unconditioned stimulus by only a brief time.* As we will learn shortly, the longer the delay between the CS and the UCS, the weaker the CR. Second, *the CS must consistently precede the occurrence of the UCS.* Even though the CS and UCS may be frequently paired, no CR will develop if the UCS occurs without the CS as often as with it. Also, little or no conditioning of the CR will develop if the CS occurs frequently in the absence of the UCS. Thus, the greater the predictive value of the CS, the stronger the CR elicited by the CS. Third, *the CS must provide more reliable information concerning the occurrence of the UCS than do other cues in the environment.* The presence of another predictive cue will prevent, or *block,* the development of the CR to a second cue which is also being paired with the UCS (see Kamin, 1968). Although the second cue predicts the occurrence of the UCS, it does not provide new information; thus no CR develops. Fourth, *the salience of the CS affects the strength of the CR acquired following CS-UCS pairing.* Although Pavlov (1927) suggested that any neutral stimulus paired with the unconditioned stimulus could, through conditioning, develop the capacity to elicit a CR, contemporary research shows that some stimuli are readily associated with a specific unconditioned stimulus (see Seligman, 1970). Seligman introduced the concept of *preparedness* to indicate that animals have an evolutionary predisposition (preparedness) to associate a particular stimulus with a specific unconditioned stimulus. Further, other CS-UCS associations cannot be learned. Seligman's *contrapreparedness* concept suggests that some stimuli, despite repeated CS-UCS pairings, cannot become associated with a particular UCS. Finally, *the strength of the CR is affected by the intensity of the CS, the UCS, or both.* Although increases in the UCS intensity typically lead to faster conditioning and a higher level of the conditioned response, a stronger CS does not always produce a stronger CR. Under some conditions, a higher CS intensity leads to a greater CR; under others, there is little difference in CR strength as a function of CS intensity. Grice (1968, 1972) suggests that context determines the influence of CS intensity on the strength of the CR. According to Grice, comparing a weak CS to a strong CS causes a person or an animal to respond more intensely to the strong one. Without a comparison, there is little difference between the response to a weak CS and a strong CS. Evidence for Grice's view will be presented later in this section. We have learned that many factors affect the classical conditioning process. Let us now look at the evidence indicating that these factors play an important role in classical conditioning.

Contiguity   Consider the following example to illustrate the importance of contiguity on the development of a conditioned response. An 8-year-old boy hits his 6-year-old brother. The mother informs her aggressive son that his father will spank him when he gets home from work. Even though his father frequently punishes his older son for aggression toward his younger brother, the mother's threat instills no fear. The failure of her threat to elicit fear renders the mother unable to curb her son's inappropriate behavior.

Why doesn't the boy fear his mother's threat, since it has been consistently paired with his father's punishment? The answer to this question is in the significance of the close temporal pairing, or *contiguity,* in classical conditioning. A threat (the CS) provides information concerning future punishment and elicits the emotional state which motivates avoidance behavior. Although the mother's threat does predict future punishment, the child becoming frightened when the threat is given is not adaptive since the punishment will not occur for several hours. Instead of being frightened from the time that the threat is made until the father's arrival, the older boy becomes afraid only when his father arrives. This boy's fear now motivates him to avoid punishment, perhaps by crying and promising not to hit his little brother again. However, this effort typically is ineffective, and his father spanks him. If the youngster had behaved following his mother's threat, he probably would not have been punished. However, the delay between the threat and the punishment was too long, and therefore the threat did not develop the ability to elicit fear and prevent parental punishment.

The Optimal Interval Many studies document the importance of contiguity in the acquisition of a conditioned response. Experiments designed to evaluate the influence of contiguity on classical conditioning have varied the interval between the CS and UCS and then evaluated the strength of the CR. The results of these studies show that the optimal CS-UCS interval, or interstimulus interval (ISI), is very short (see Figure 2.4). Intervals even shorter than the optimal ISI produce weaker conditioning, and the strength of the CR increases as the ISI becomes longer until the optimal CS-UCS interval is reached. Furthermore, an ISI longer than the optimal CS-UCS interval leads to less conditioning, and the intensity of the CR decreases as the ISI increases beyond the optimal ISI.

The optimal CS-UCS interval is different for different responses. For example, the optimal conditioning interval is 450 milliseconds for eyelid conditioning. This 450-millisecond ISI for the conditioning of the eyelid-closure reflex has been observed in both animals (see Frey & Ross, 1968; Smith, Coleman, & Gormezano, 1969) and humans (see Kimble & Reynolds, 1967). Figure 2.4 presents the CS-UCS interval gradient for eyelid conditioning in rabbits and people. Some other optimal ISIs include 2 seconds for skeletal movements (Noble & Harding, 1963), 4 seconds for salivary reflexes (Gormezano, 1972), and 20 seconds for heart-rate responses (Church & Black, 1958).

Why does the optimal CS-UCS interval vary between responses? The optimal ISI is thought to reflect the latency to respond in a particular reflex system (Hilgard & Marquis, 1940). Hilgard and Marquis suggested that the different optimal CS-UCS intervals occur because the response latency of the autonomic nervous system is longer than that of the eyelid-closure reflex. However, the optimal CS-UCS interval may change during the course of an experiment (see Flaherty, Hamilton, Gandelman, & Spear, 1977). For example, Kimmel (1965) found that the optimal CS-UCS interval increased as the CR was being acquired, whereas Suboski (1967) observed that increased conditioning trials

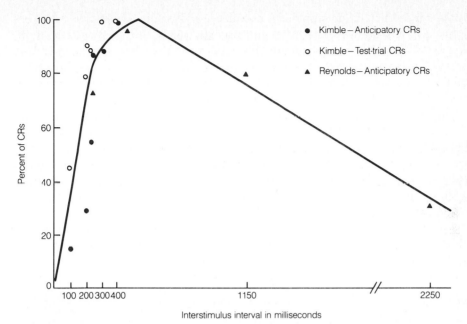

FIGURE 2.4
An idealized interstimulus interval (ISI) gradient obtained from eye-blink conditioning data in humans. From Kimble, G. A., & Reynolds, B. Eyelid conditioning as a function of the interval between conditioned and unconditioned stimuli. In G. A. Kimble (Ed.), *Foundations of conditioning and learning.* New York: Irvington, 1967.

caused the optimal CS-UCS latency to decline. Although optimal conditioning obviously occurs with a short latency, what process determines the exact interval that is best for a particular form of conditioning is unclear.

A Bridge between CS and UCS We have learned that the acquisition of the CR is impaired when the CS-UCS interval is longer than a few seconds. Several recent studies (see Bolles, Collier, Bouton, & Marlin, 1978; Kaplan, 1984; Kaplan & Hearst, 1982; Kehoe, Gibbs, Garcia, & Gormezano, 1979; Pearce, Nicholas, & Dickinson, 1981; Rescorla, 1982) have reported that the attenuation of conditioning produced by a temporal gap between the CS and UCS can be reduced if a second stimulus is presented between the CS and UCS.

Consider the Rescorla (1982) study to illustrate this phenomenon. Rescorla's subjects, pigeons, were shown a colored light followed by food 10 seconds later. When one color, for example, red, was presented, a second stimulus, either a white light or a tone, was presented during the 10 seconds between the colored light and the food. The white light or tone was not presented on trials in which a different color light, say green, was used. Rescorla found that the level of conditioning was significantly greater to the color paired with the white light or tone (in this case, the red light) than to the color which was not followed by an intermediate stimulus (the green light).

Why does the "filler stimulus" produce conditioning despite a delay between the CS and UCS? According to Rescorla (1982), the intermediate stimulus acts as a catalyst, enhancing the association of the CS and the UCS. This observation suggests that with appropriate procedures, a high level of conditioning can develop even though there is a significant delay between the CS and the UCS.

Long-Delay Learning   There is one noteworthy exception to the contiguity principle. Animals and humans can associate a taste stimulus (CS) with an illness experience (UCS) that occurs several hours after the taste cue exposure. The association of taste with illness, called *flavor-* or *taste-aversion learning,* contrasts sharply with the other forms of classical conditioning, in which no conditioning occurs if the CS-UCS interval is longer than several minutes. Although taste-aversion learning can occur with long delays, there is a CS-UCS interval gradient, and the strongest conditioning occurs when the taste and illness are separated only by 30 minutes (see Garcia, Clark, & Hankins, 1973). We will take a more detailed look at flavor aversion learning in Chapter 10, which discusses the biological influences on learning.

Cue Predictiveness   Robert Bolles (1972, 1979) proposed that contiguity alone is not sufficient for the development of a conditioned response. In Bolles's view, events must consistently occur together before we can acquire a conditioned response. A neutral stimulus may be simultaneously paired with a UCS, but unless the neutral stimulus reliably predicts the occurrence of the UCS, the CR will not be elicited by the neutral stimulus. In addition, when two or more stimuli are presented with the UCS, only the most reliable predictor of the UCS will become associated with the UCS.

The following example illustrates the important influence of predictiveness on the development of a conditioned response. Many parents threaten their children prior to punishment; yet, their threats instill no fear, despite repeated threat-punishment (CS-UCS) pairings. Why is parental threat ineffective? One likely reason is that these parents may often punish their children without threatening them. Or, the parents may frequently threaten their children without punishing them. Under these circumstances, the threat is not a reliable predictor of punishment, and its presentation will elicit little or no fear, even though the threat and punishment have been frequently experienced together. We will first examine evidence showing that the acquisition of the CR is impaired if the UCS is often presented without the CS, and follow this with a description of research which shows that presentations of the CS alone decrease the development of the CR.

UCS-Alone Presentations   Robert Rescorla's (1968) research demonstrates the influence of cue predictiveness in classical conditioning. After his rats learned to bar press for food, Rescorla divided the two-hour training sessions into 2-minute segments. One of the three events occurred in each segment: (1) a distinctive cue (CS; tone) was paired with a shock (UCS), (2) shock was presented without the distinctive cue, or (3) neither tone nor shock occurred during the interval. Rescorla varied the likelihood that the shock would occur with (or without) the tone in each 2-minute segment. He found that the tone suppressed bar-press responding for food when the tone reliably predicted shock. However, the influence of the tone on the rats' behavior diminished as the frequency of shock occurring without the tone increased. The tone had no effect on behavior when the shock occurred as frequently in the absence of the tone as it did when the tone was present. Figure 2.5 presents the results of the subjects who received a .4 CS-UCS probability (or CS paired with the UCS on 40 percent of the 2-minute segments).

One important aspect of Rescorla's data is that even with only a few pairings, the presentation of the tone produced intense fear and suppressed bar pressing if the shock was applied only with the tone. However, when the shock occurred without the tone as frequently as it did with it, no conditioning was found, even with a large number of tone-shock pairings. Apparently, the pre-

FIGURE 2.5
Suppression of bar-pressing behavior during six test sessions (a low value indicates that the CS elicits fear and thereby suppresses bar pressing for food). The probability of the UCS occurring with the CS is .4 for all groups, and the values shown in the figure represent the probability that the UCS will occur alone in a 2-minute segment. Note that when the two probabilities are equal, the CS does not elicit fear and, therefore, does not suppress responding. Only when the UCS occurs more frequently with than without the CS will the CS elicit fear and suppress bar pressing. Adapted from Rescorla, R. A. Probability of shock in the presence and absence of CS in fear conditioning. *Journal of Comparative and Physiological Psychology*, 1968, *68*, 1–5. Copyright 1968 by the American Psychological Association. Reprinted by permission.

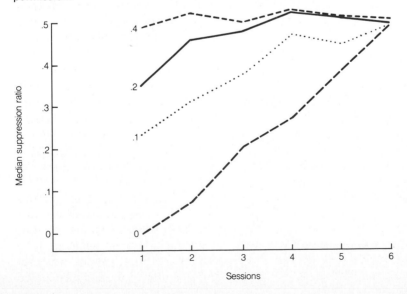

dictability of a stimulus, not the number of CS-UCS pairings, determines an environmental event's ability to elicit a CR. Other investigators have documented the significant influence of cue predictiveness on our behavior; refer to a study by Bolles et al. (1975) for another example.

CS-Alone Presentations   The acquisition of a CR is also impaired or prevented when the CS is presented alone during conditioning. Many studies have documented the attenuation of conditioning when the CS is presented alone as well as with the UCS (see Hall, 1976).

The level of conditioning also depends on the percentage of trials pairing the CS with the UCS; the greater the percentage, the greater the conditioning. Hartman and Grant's (1960) study provides one example of the influence of the percentage of paired CS-UCS presentations on the CR strength. All Hartman and Grant's human subjects received 40 light–air puff (CS-UCS) pairings. For subjects in the 25 percent group, the UCS occurred following 40 of the 160 CS presentations; for subjects in the 50 percent group, the air puff followed the tone on 40 of 80 CS presentations; for subjects in the 75 percent group, the UCS followed the CS on 40 of 54 trials; for subjects in the 100 percent group, the air puff was presented after the light on 40 of 40 trials. Hartman and Grant's results showed that the strength of conditioning was an increasing function of the percentage of trials which paired the CS with the UCS (see Figure 2.6). Similar findings were reported by Grant and Schipper (1952) and Moore and Gormezano (1963).

Cue Blocking   Recall the example of the failure of parental threat to instill fear. In addition to a lack of predictiveness, another possible explanation for this lack of fear is that the children are already afraid when the threat is

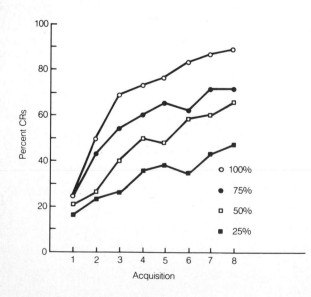

FIGURE 2.6
Percentages of conditioned responses during each block of acquisition trials as a function of the percentage of trials in which the UCS follows the CS. Adapted from Hartman, T. F., & Grant, D. A. Effect of intermittent reinforcement on acquisition, extinction, and spontaneous recovery of the conditioned eyelid response. *Journal of Experimental Psychology*, 1960, *60*, 89–96. Copyright 1960 by the American Psychological Association. Reprinted by permission.

presented. Perhaps they are afraid of their parents; if so, parental presence (the CS) will interfere with the acquisition of fear to the threat, despite repeated threat-punishment pairings.

The Blocking Paradigm   For a cue to elicit a CR, and thereby influence behavior, Bolles (1978) suggested that the cue not only must predict the occurrence of the UCS but also must provide information not signalled by the other cues present in the environment. The classic research of Leon Kamin (1968) demonstrates that the presence of a predictive cue (CS_1) will prevent, or *block,* the development of an association between a second cue (CS_2) also paired with the UCS. To demonstrate the importance of relative cue predictability, Kamin presented all his subjects with a distinctive cue (S_1, a light) paired with a shock (UCS) eight times during the first phase of the study. In the second phase of the study, the experimental group subjects received eight pairings of the light (CS_1), a new cue (CS_2, a tone), and shock (UCS) (see Figure 2.7). Kamin observed that although presentation of the light (CS_1) suppressed bar-press responding, the tone cue (CS_2) alone had no influence on instrumental behavior. He gave control-group animals only tone-shock pairings during the second phase of study and noticed strong suppression caused by the tone (CS_2).

After Kamin's original studies, many other researchers observed the blocking phenomenon. Numerous experiments (for example, Dickinson, Hall, & Mackintosh, 1976; Gray & Appignanesi, 1973; Kremer, Specht, & Allen, 1980; Mackintosh, Bygrave, & Picton, 1977; Rescorla & Wagner, 1972; Wagner, Rudy, & Whitlow, 1973) have shown that the association of one cue (CS_1) with shock caused the blocking of fear to a second cue (CS_2) when both CS_1 and CS_2 were presented with shock.

FIGURE 2.7
The design of Kamin's blocking study. In phase 1, the CS_1 (light) is paired with the UCS (shock); in the second phase, both the CS_1 and CS_2 (tone) are paired with the UCS (shock). The ability of the CS_2 (tone) to elicit fear is assessed during phase 3.

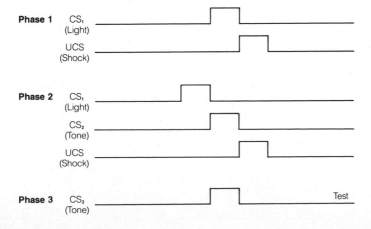

The Nature of Blocking   Why did the tone suppress instrumental behavior in the control animals but not in the experimental subjects in Kamin's blocking study? Kamin (1969) offered two explanations for the blocking phenomenon. One states that the presence of the predictive light cue (CS$_1$) caused the experimental group animals to ignore the tone (CS$_2$). In the absence of the light, the control-group rats paid attention to the tone and associated its presence with shock. A study by Wagner (1969) shows that animals in the blocking condition were aware of the presence of the tone but did not use this information. Wagner reported that when the light and tone cues together predicted no shock, the tone cue developed the ability to inhibit avoidance behavior.

Kamin's second explanation assumes that when animals first experience shock they are surprised by this unanticipated event. The surprise causes the rats to associate a light cue with shock; learning, according to Kamin, only takes place when surprising events occur. Following conditioning, encountering the light cue causes no surprise. Since the light produced an anticipation of shock in Kamin's experimental animals, the tone was not experienced when the rats were surprised, and therefore the tone did not develop the ability to produce fear.

Mackintosh and his associates (Dickinson, Hall, & Mackintosh, 1976; Mackintosh, Bygrave, & Picton, 1977) demonstrated that a surprising event can prevent the CS$_1$ from blocking the CS$_2$-CR association. In the first phase of their studies, animals received CS$_1$-UCS-UCS pairings until CS$_1$ suppressed bar pressing. Following the acquisition of fear to CS$_1$, some subjects were given CS$_1$-CS$_2$-UCS pairings; other rats received CS$_1$-CS$_2$-UCS-UCS pairings. Mackintosh and his associates observed that when they omitted the second UCS, creating a surprising event, no blocking occurred and fear was conditioned to the CS$_2$. In contrast, the development of fear was blocked in those subjects who received the anticipated second UCS. These results indicate that the omission of the UCS can diminish the blocking effect. Other studies have also shown that unexpected or surprising events can reduce blocking and thereby result in the ability of the CS$_2$ to elicit the CR; refer to Kremer, Specht, and Allen (1980) for another example.

Why is surprise necessary for conditioning? Why can surprise eliminate the blocking phenomenon? Two theories (Mackintosh, 1975; Rescorla & Wagner, 1972) have proposed answers to why surprise is essential for the development of a CR. According to Rescorla and Wagner (1972), only surprising or unpredicted UCSs are reinforcing; that is, surprise enables the UCS to be effective. In contrast, Mackintosh (1975) asserted that surprising UCSs serve to maintain the associability of the CS; that is, a CS is only relevant when the occurrence of the UCS is surprising. Although a large number of studies (for example, Dickinson, Colwill, & Pearce, 1980; Dickinson, Hall, & Mackintosh, 1976; Kremer, Specht, & Allen, 1980; Mackintosh, Dickson, & Cotton, 1980; Maleske & Frey, 1979; Neely & Wagner, 1974; Randich & LoLordo, 1979) have attempted to discover the underlying mechanism responsible for the influence of surprise in conditioning, the reason why a surprising UCS is necessary for the acquisition of a conditioned response is unclear (refer to Dickinson, 1980, for a discussion of the issue).

Salience   As we learned earlier, Seligman (1970) suggested that animals or humans are prepared to acquire certain associations but are contraprepared to develop other conditioned responses. The likelihood that a particular neutral stimulus will become able to elicit a conditioned response after pairing with a specific unconditioned stimulus is called the *salience* of the neutral stimulus. Salient stimuli rapidly become associated with a particular unconditioned stimulus, whereas nonsalient stimuli do not, despite repeated CS-UCS pairings. It should be noted that many, perhaps most, stimuli arc ncithcr salicnt nor nonsalient; these stimuli will gradually develop the ability to elicit a conditioned response as the result of conditioning experiences. Also important is that salience is *species-dependent;* that is, a stimulus may be salient to one species but not to another. Chapter 10 discusses the biological significance of stimulus salience in classical conditioning and the influence of species-specific stimulus salience on the acquisition of a conditioned response.

On many occasions, two or more cues are presented together with the UCS; this procedure is called *compound conditioning*. Which cue will become associated with the UCS? Most of the time, a greater CR will develop to the more salient (or intense) CS than to the less salient (or intense) CS. Also, the larger the difference in salience (or intensity), the greater the difference in CR strength elicited by the cues. Thus, the presence of a more salient (or intense) cue interferes with, or overshadows, the association of the less salient (or intense) cue with the UCS. This phenomenon, called *overshadowing,* was originally observed by Pavlov (1927). Pavlov found that a more intense tone overshadowed the association of a less intense tone with the UCS. Overshadowing is readily observed in flavor-aversion experiments. For example, Lindsey and Best (1973) presented two novel fluids (saccharin and casein hydrosylate) prior to illness, finding that a strong aversion developed to the salient saccharin flavor but only a weak aversion was established to the less salient casein hydrosylate solution. Similar overshadowing by a salient taste cue of the development of an aversion to a less salient cue was observed by Green and Churchill (1970), Kalat and Rozin (1970), Klein, Davis, Cohen, and Weston (1984), and Smith and Roll (1967).

The Influence of Intensity

CS Intensity   Suppose that you were bitten by a dog. Would you be more afraid of the dog if it were large or small? If we assume that the pain induced by bites (the UCS) from each is equivalent, research on the intensity of the CS and the strength of conditioning indicates your fear of each would be equivalent only if one dog bites you. However, if you were bitten by both sizes of dogs (not necessarily at the same time), you would be more afraid of the more intense CS, the large dog. Let's now look at research examining the influence of CS intensity on CR strength.

Initial research (see Hall, 1976) indicated that the intensity of the CS does not affect CR strength. For example, Grant and Schneider (1948, 1949) reported that CS intensity did not influence the classical conditioning of the eyeblink response in humans. Carter (1941) and Wilcott (1953) showed similar results. However, more recent research clearly points out that CS intensity can affect the strength of the conditioned response. The production of a stronger CR through a more intense CS has been shown in dogs (Barnes, 1956), rabbits (Frey, 1969), rats (Kamin & Schaub, 1963), fish (Woodard, 1971), pigeons (Cohen, 1974), and humans (Beck, 1963; Grice & Hunter, 1964; Mattson & Moore, 1964).

An intense CS does not always elicit a CR stronger than that elicited by a weak CS. When an animal or person experiences only a single stimulus (either weak or intense), an intense CS does not produce an appreciably greater CR than a weak CS. However, if an animal or person encounters both the intense and the weak CS, the intense CS will produce a significantly greater CR than the weak CS will.

A study by Grice and Hunter (1964) shows the important influence of the type of training procedure on the magnitude of CS-intensity effect. In Grice and Hunter's study, one group of human subjects received 100 eye-blink conditioning trials of a loud (100 dB) tone (CS) and a 1-lb/in² air puff (UCS). A second group of subjects had a soft-tone (50 dB) CS paired with the air puff for 100 trials. The third group of subjects was given 50 trials with the loud tone and 50 trials with the soft tone. Grice and Hunter's results, presented in Figure 2.8, show that the effect of CS intensity (loudness of tone) on conditioning was much greater when a subject experienced both stimuli than when a subject was exposed to only the soft or the loud tone. Beck (1963) also found that the influence of CS intensity was greater when subjects experienced both stimuli than when they were exposed to only one. In addition, using rabbits, Frey (1969) observed that the CS intensity had greater impact on the CR (eye-blink response) when the rabbit experienced both stimuli during a single session than when the stimuli were experienced in separate sessions. Frey's results demonstrate that the ability to compare the weak CS with the strong CS also influences the magnitude of the effect of the CS intensity and that the strongest effect occurs when both stimuli are experienced close together.

Our discussion indicates that the CS intensity does influence CR strength, although the type of conditioning experience affects the magnitude of this CS intensity effect. Further, research has shown that UCS intensity also has a strong effect on classical conditioning.

UCS Intensity Consider the following example to illustrate the influence of the UCS intensity on the strength of a CR. You have the misfortune of being in an automobile accident. How much fear will be elicited the next time you get into a car? Research on UCS intensity and CR strength indicates that your level

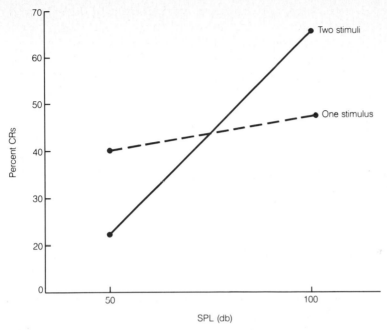

FIGURE 2.8
Percentage of conditioned responses during last sixty trials to soft (50 dB) or loud (100 dB) tones under one or two stimulus conditions. From Grice, G. R., & Hunter, J. J. Stimulus intensity effects depend upon the type of experimental design. *Psychological Review,* 1964, *71,* 247–256. Copyright 1964 by the American Psychological Association. Reprinted by permission.

of fear will depend on the intensity of the accident; the more severe the accident, the greater your fear of automobiles. Thus, if the accident was minor, causing only slight discomfort, your subsequent fear will be minimal. However, a severe accident that inflicts severe damage on you will cause an intense fear.

The literature (see Hall, 1976) provides conclusive documentation that the strength of the CR increases with higher UCS intensity. To show the influence of UCS intensity on eye-blink conditioning, Prokasy, Grant, and Myers (1958) gave their human subjects 50-, 120-, 190-, or 260-mm air-puff UCS paired with a light CS. They found that the strength of the CR was directly related to the UCS intensity; that is, the more intense the air puff, the stronger the eye-blink CR (see Figure 2.9). Spence (1956) reported a similar effect of UCS intensity on eye-blink conditioning.

Other studies have evaluated the influence of shock intensity on fear conditioning. For example, Wickens and Harding (1965) presented human subjects with one CS (tone or light) paired with an intense UCS (2.5-mA shock) and another CS (light or tone) paired with a weak UCS (1.5-mA shock). Wickens and Harding reported that their subjects showed a greater galvanic skin re-

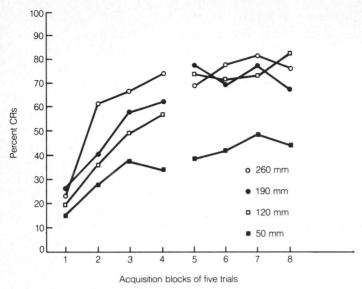

FIGURE 2.9
Percentage of conditioned responses during acquisition as a
function of the UCS intensity. Adapted from Prokasy, W. P., Jr.,
Grant, D. A., & Myers, N. A. Eyelid conditioning as a function of
unconditioned stimulus intensity and intertrial interval. *Journal of
Experimental Psychology,* 1958, *55,* 242–246. Copyright 1958 by
the American Psychological Association. Reprinted by permission.

sponse (GSR) to the stimulus paired with the intense shock than to the cue
paired with the weaker shock. These results point out that the more intense
UCS produced a stronger CR than did the weak UCS.

Annau and Kamin (1961) evaluated the influence of UCS intensity on the
strength of a conditioned emotional response in rats. A tone was paired with a
0.28-, 0.49-, 1.55-, or 2.91-ma shock. Annau and Kamin reported that the
strength of the CR increased as the UCS intensity increased.

The Nature of the Acquisition Process

We have learned that the predictiveness of the conditioned stimulus influences
how readily a conditioned response is acquired. We also discovered that the
predictive value of other stimuli also affects the rate at which a CR is learned.
How does an animal or person judge the relative predictiveness of a stimulus?
Two theories have been developed to explain the mechanism by which predictiveness affects classical conditioning. The Rescorla-Wagner theory suggests
that an associative process enables predictiveness to influence the strength of a
CR, whereas Mackintosh argues that attentional processes account for the
impact of predictiveness on conditioning. Note that these are complex theories;

we will only briefly examine the main points of both views. The interested reader should refer to Rescorla and Wagner (1972) for a detailed discussion of their theory and to Mackintosh (1975) for an in-depth description of his theory.

Rescorla-Wagner Associative Model   Robert Rescorla and Allan Wagner (1972) suggested an associative model of classical conditioning of four main components. First, *there is a maximum associative strength which can develop between a CS and UCS as the result of conditioning.* The limit of associative strength, or asymptote of conditioning, is determined by the UCS; different UCSs support different maximum levels of conditioning, and, therefore have different asymptotic values. Second, *although the associative strength increases with each training trial, the amount of associative strength gained on a particular training trial is affected by the level of prior training.* Since the typical learning curve in Pavlovian conditioning is negatively accelerated (refer to Figure 2.10), more associative strength will accrue during early training than during later training. In fact, as can be seen in Figure 2.10, the increment on each conditioning trial declines with each CS-UCS pairing. Third, *the rate of conditioning varies depending on the CS and the UCS used.* Associative strength accrues quickly to some stimuli and slowly to others. Figure 2.10 shows the learning curve of two stimuli: one stimulus readily gains associative strength while conditioning to the other stimulus occurs slowly. Fourth, *the*

FIGURE 2.10
The change in associative strength during conditioning for two different stimuli. One stimulus rapidly develops associative stimulus; the other acquires associative strength more slowly.

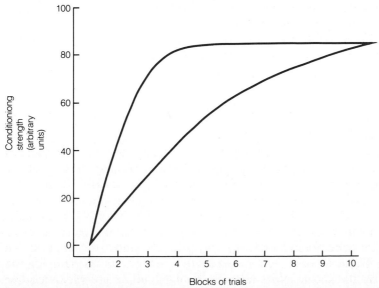

level of conditioning on a particular trial is influenced not only by the amount of prior conditioning to the stimulus but also by the level of previous conditioning to other stimuli associated with the UCS. According to Rescorla and Wagner, a particular UCS can only support a certain amount of conditioning, even when more than one stimulus is paired with the UCS. When two (or more) stimuli are presented prior to the UCS, these stimuli must share the associative strength that can be supported by that UCS. Thus, associative strength that accrues to one stimulus is not available to be conditioned to the other stimuli. Consider this example to illustrate Rescorla and Wagner's view: Suppose two stimuli are paired with a UCS and the maximum associative strength which can be supported by that UCS is ten. If seven units are conditioned to one cue paired with the UCS, only three units can develop to the other cue.

Rescorla and Wagner (1972) developed a mathematical equation based on the four ideas outlined. Their mathematical model of Pavlovian conditioning is $\Delta V_A = K(\lambda - V_{AX})$. In this formula, V is associative strength between the conditioned stimulus A and the UCS, and ΔV is the change in associative strength which develops on a specific trial when the CS_A and UCS are paired. K refers to the rate of conditioning which is determined by the character of the CS_A and the UCS, and λ defines the maximum level of conditioning supported by the UCS. V_{AX} indicates the level of conditioning which has already accrued to the conditioned stimulus A as well as to other stimuli (X) which are also present during conditioning. Thus, $V_{AX} = V_A + V_X$.

To see how this mathematical model works, suppose that a light stimulus is paired with shock on five trials. The value of K is 0.50, λ is 90, and $V = 0$. When we apply these values to the Rescorla-Wagner model, we get:

Trial 1: $\Delta V_A = 0.50 (90 - 0) = 45$
Trial 2: $\Delta V_A = 0.50 (90 - 45) = 22.5$
Trial 3: $\Delta V_A = 0.50 (90 - 67.5) \doteq 11.25$
Trial 4: $\Delta V_A = 0.50 (90 - 78.8) = 5.6$
Trial 5: $\Delta V_A = 0.50 (90 - 84.4) = 2.8$
Total associative strengths after five trials = 87.2

The data provided by the above equation show that conditioning to CS_A occurs rapidly; associative strength grows 45 units on Trial 1, 22.5 units on Trial 2, 11.25 units on Trial 3, 5.6 units on Trial 4, and 2.8 units on Trial 5. Thus, 87.2 units of associative strength accrued to the CS_A after just five trials of conditioning. Evidently, associative strength develops rapidly to CS_A; thus, CS_A is either an intense or a salient stimulus, or both, and/or the UCS strong.

The Rescorla-Wagner model has been used to explain a number of conditioning phenomena. Let's see how it explains blocking. Suppose that we initially pair a light with shock for five trials. The K value for the light is 0.5 and the maximum level of conditioning, or λ, is 90 units of associative strength. As we learned earlier, 87.2 units of associative strength would accrue to the light after five pairings with the shock. Next we pair the light, tone, and shock for five more trials. The K value for the tone is 0.5, and we would expect that five pairings of the tone and shock would yield strong conditioning. However, only 2.8 units of associative strength are still available to be conditioned according to the Rescorla-Wagner model. And the tone must share this associative strength with the light cue. Because strong conditioning has already occurred to the light, little conditioning to the tone will take place. The Rescorla-Wagner equation predicts weak conditioning to the tone.

Trial 1: $\Delta V_{light} = 0.5\ (90 - 87.2) = 1.4$ $\Delta V_{tone} = 0.5\ (90 - 87.2) = 1.4$
Trial 2: $\Delta V_{light} = 0.5\ (90 - 90) = 0$ $\Delta V_{tone} = 0.5\ (90 - 90) = 0$
Trial 3: $\Delta V_{light} = 0.5\ (90 - 90) = 0$ $\Delta V_{tone} = 0.5\ (90 - 90) = 0$
Trial 4: $\Delta V_{light} = 0.5\ (90 - 90) = 0$ $\Delta V_{tone} = 0.5\ (90 - 90) = 0$
Trial 5: $\Delta V_{light} = 0.5\ (90 - 90) = 0$ $\Delta V_{tone} = 0.5\ (90 - 90) = 0$
Total associative strength:
light = 88.6   tone = 1.4

We learned earlier that blocking occurs when a stimulus previously paired with a UCS is presented with a new stimulus and the UCS. The Rescorla-Wagner model suggests that blocking occurs because the initial CS has already accrued most or all of the associative strength, and little is left to condition to the other stimulus. As shown in the above equations, little conditioning occurred to the tone because most of the associative strength had developed to the light prior to the compound pairing of the light, tone, and shock. Based on this explanation, the equation generated by the Rescorla-Wagner model can also predict cue blocking.

The Rescorla-Wagner model can also predict the results of other Pavlovian conditioning phenomena. Earlier we learned that the presence of a more salient cue will overshadow the development of a CR to a less salient cue when both are paired in compound with the UCS. According to the Rescorla-Wagner model, overshadowing occurs because a salient cue has a higher K value and therefore acquires associative strength more readily than a less salient cue. Since there is a limited amount of associative strength which a UCS can support, the rapid development of associative strength to the salient cue will leave little associative strength available for conditioning after the first few trials. Therefore, since the less salient cue acquires associative strength slowly, little conditioning to it will occur after the initial training trials.

Many studies have evaluated the validity of the Rescorla-Wagner model of Pavlovian conditioning. Most of these studies have supported the model, but some observations have not been consistent with the Rescorla-Wagner model. We will now discuss one area of research—the UCS preexposure effect— which has provided data that support the Rescorla-Wagner model. Then we will discuss three areas of research—potentiation, CS preexposure, and cue predictiveness—which provide findings that are not predicted by the Rescorla-Wagner model. Finally, an alternative view of Pavlovian conditioning—Mackintosh's attentional approach—will be discussed.

Support for the Rescorla-Wagner Model: The UCS Preexposure Effect
Suppose that several months after recovering from the flu, you become sick
after eating a distinctive food. Would you develop an aversion to this food?
Probably not; your previous experiences with the flu independent of the particular food would prevent the conditioning of an association between eating this
food and being sick.

The previous example illustrates the effect of preexposure to the UCS (illness) without the CS (food) on the acquisition of a CR (aversion) when the CS
is later presented with the UCS. Psychologists (see Baker & Mackintosh, 1979,
or Randich & Ross, 1985) refer to this phenomenon as the *UCS preexposure
effect*. Many studies have consistently observed that preexposure to the UCS
impairs subsequent conditioning; for example, several researchers have demonstrated that the presentation of a drug which induces illness (UCS) prior to
conditioning impairs the subsequent association of a distinctive food (CS) with
illness (Best & Domjan, 1979; Cain & Baenninger, 1977; Cannon, Berman,
Baker, & Atkinson, 1975; Domjan & Gemberling, 1980; Mikulka, Leard, &
Klein, 1977). Similar preexposure interference has been reported with other
UCSs (e.g., shock: Baker & Mackintosh, 1979; Baker, Mercier, Gabel, &
Baker, 1981; Mis & Moore, 1973; Rescorla, 1974; Randich & LoLordo, 1979;
and food: Balsam & Schwartz, 1981; Engberg, Hanson, Welker, & Thomas,
1972; Tomie, Murphy, & Fath, 1980).

Why does preexposure to the UCS impair subsequent conditioning? The
Rescorla-Wagner model provides an explanation: the presentation of the UCS
without the CS occurs in a specific environment or context; this results in the
development of associative strength to the context. Since the UCS can only
support a limited amount of associative strength, conditioning of associative
strength to stimulus context reduces the maximum level of possible conditioning to the CS. Thus, the presence of the stimulus context will block the acquisition of a CR to the CS when the CS is presented with the UCS in the stimulus
context.

Many experiments have presented evidence supporting a context-blocking
explanation of the UCS preexposure effect (see Baker, Mercer, Gabel, &
Baker, 1981; Balsam & Schwartz, 1981; Randich & Ross, 1985; Rescorla,
Durlach, & Grau, 1985; Tomie, Murphy, & Fath, 1980). These studies show
that the UCS preexposure effect is attenuated when the preexposure context is
different from the conditioning context. Because of the change in context, no
stimuli present during conditioning can compete with the association of the CS
and the UCS. Therefore, the CR is readily conditioned to the CS when paired
with the UCS in the new context. We will briefly discuss the Randich and Ross
study to illustrate the effect of context change on the impact of the UCS
preexposure effect.

Randich and Ross (1985) placed three groups of rats in context A during the
first phase of the study. Context A was characterized by noise from a fan and
did not have a light, painted walls, or the odor of Pine-Sol. Two of these

groups—the experimental groups—received a 10-second unsignaled shock (UCS) in context A; the other group—the control group—did not receive the shock in context A. After ten trials in context A, one experimental group was placed again in context A and received pairings of a 3-minute noise CS and shock. The control-group animals also were given noise-shock (CS-UCS) pairings in context A. Randich and Ross observed that the rats which had been preexposed to the shock in context A and were then conditioned in context A showed much less fear of the noise CS than did the control-group animals who had not been preexposed to shock. The second experimental group of animals received noise CS and shock pairings in context B. Context B was quite different from context A; it had a light, black-and-white striped walls, and Pine-Sol odor, but no fan. Strong fear of the noise CS was exhibited by animals given UCS preexposure in context A but conditioned in context B. These results provide persuasive evidence that context associations formed during UCS preexposure are responsible for the decrease in the conditioning to the CS when paired with the UCS.

Our discussion provides strong support for the context-blocking explanation of the UCS preexposure effect. Although this explanation is consistent with and predicted by the Rescorla-Wagner model, several aspects of Pavlovian conditioning are not consistent with the Rescorla-Wagner model.

Problems with the Rescorla-Wagner Model   Several observations are not predicted by the Rescorla-Wagner model, and one problem area is the *potentiation effect*.

Potentiation of a Conditioned Response   As stated earlier, the Rescorla-Wagner model predicts that when a salient and a nonsalient cue are presented together with the UCS, the salient cue will accrue more associative strength than will the nonsalient cue. However, overshadowing does not always occur when two cues of different salience are paired with a UCS; in fact, in some circumstances the presence of a salient cue leads to a stronger CR than would have occurred had the nonsalient cue been presented alone with the UCS. The increased conditioned response to a nonsalient stimulus as the result of also presenting a salient cue during conditioning was first described by John Garcia and his associates (see Garcia & Rusiniak, 1980; Palmerino, Rusiniak, & Garcia, 1980; Rusiniak, Palmerino, & Garcia, 1982). They observed that the presence of a salient flavor *potentiated* rather than overshadowed the establishment of an aversion to a nonsalient odor cue paired with illness.

The Rusiniak, Palmerino, and Garcia (1982) study illustrates the potentiation of an odor aversion by a salient taste stimulus. The experimenters presented to one group of rats an odor cue (either almond or vanilla) and a salient saccharin taste cue prior to illness; other subjects received only the odor cue before experiencing lithium chloride–induced illness. Tests showed that a strong aversion to almond or vanilla developed rapidly when the odor cue was presented with the saccharin taste cue, but only a weak odor aversion was established when the odor alone occurred prior to illness. Other researchers (see Klein, Freda, & Mikulka, 1985; Rescorla & Holland, 1982) have also reported that a taste stimulus potentiated the formation of a place as well as an odor aversion.

Why does the presence of a salient taste cue potentiate rather than over-shadow the acquisition of an odor aversion? According to Garcia and Rusiniak (1980), the taste stimulus "indexes" the odor stimulus as a food cue and thereby mediates the establishment of a strong odor aversion. This indexing process has considerable adaptive significance. The potentiation of the odor aversion by the taste cue enables an animal to recognize a potentially poisonous food early in the ingestive sequence. Thus, a strong odor aversion causes animals to avoid dangerous foods even without tasting them.

Rescorla (1982) presents a different view of the potentiation effect, a view consistent with the Rescorla-Wagner model. According to Rescorla, potentiation occurs because the animal perceives the compound stimuli (taste and odor) as a single unitary event and then mistakes the individual elements for the compound. If Rescorla's view is accurate, the potentiation effect should depend on the strength of the taste-illness association: Potentiation should occur with a strong taste aversion, and weakening the taste-illness association should result in an elimination of the potentiation effect. Rescorla (1981) presented evidence to support his view, that is, he found that extinction of the taste aversion also attenuated the animal's aversion to an odor cue. This result indicates that the strength of the odor aversion depends on a strong taste aversion. It should be noted that Lett (1982) observed that taste-alone exposures eliminated the taste aversion but not the potentiated odor aversion. Thus, the cause of potentiation remains unclear, and the potentiation effect continues to present a problem for the Rescorla-Wagner model of conditioning.

CS Preexposure   Many times we eat a certain food and become ill but do not develop an aversion to that food. The CS preexposure effect provides an explanation. Many studies have reported that preexposure to a specific stimulus (food) subsequently retarded the development of a CR (aversion) to that stimulus when paired with a UCS (illness). The CS preexposure effect has been reported in a variety of Pavlovian conditioning situations, including conditioned licking of water in rats (e.g., Baker & Mackintosh, 1979), conditioned fear in rats (e.g., Dickinson, 1976; Rescorla, 1971), eye-blink conditioning in rabbits (Siegel, 1969), leg-flexion conditioning in sheep and goats (Lubow & Moore, 1959), and flavor aversion learning in rats (e.g., Best & Gemberling, 1977; Elkins, 1973; Fenwick, Mikulka, & Klein, 1975; Revusky & Bedarf, 1967).

Why is the CS preexposure effect a problem for the Rescorla-Wagner model? According to Rescorla and Wagner (1972), exposure to the CS prior to conditioning should have no effect on its subsequent association with the UCS. This prediction assumes that readiness of a stimulus to be associated with a UCS depends only on the intensity and salience of the CS; these values are represented by the parameter K in the Rescorla-Wagner model. Although neither the intensity nor the salience of the CS is changed as the result of CS preexposure, the subsequent interference with conditioning indicates that the associability of the CS changes when the CS occurs without the UCS prior to conditioning.

How can the influence of CS preexposure on subsequent conditioning be explained? One explanation involves modifying the Rescorla-Wagner model to allow for a change in the value of K as the result of experience. Yet, the effect of CS preexposure on the acquisition of a CR to the preexposed stimulus appears to involve more than just a reduction in the value of K. Instead, Mackintosh (1983) argues that animals learn that a particular stimulus is irrelevant because it predicts no significant event; the recognition of stimulus irrelevance causes the animal to ignore that stimulus in the future. This failure to attend to the CS and the events that follow the CS is responsible for the interference with conditioning produced by CS preexposure. We will look more closely at this attentional view of CS preexposure when we describe Mackintosh's view of conditioning. However, let's first return to the Rescorla-Wagner Model and examine a study by Lubow, Rifkin, and Alek (1976) which shows that the CS preexposure effect involves more than a reduction in the value of K.

Lubow, Rifkin, and Alek (1976) preexposed one group of rats to either a light alone or a light followed by a tone. Other rats received no preexposure stimulus. Following preexposure, all animals experienced the light paired with shock. Lubow, Ritkin, and Alek discovered that less interference with conditioning to the light occurred when the light had been followed by the tone during preexposure than when only the light was presented. Evidently, presenting the CS (light) without the UCS (shock) is not sufficient to produce the CS preexposure effect; only when the CS occurs alone is subsequent conditioning impaired by preexposure. These results argue against the view that CS preexposure results in less associability; if the associability theory were correct, equivalent interference should have been caused by both preexposure treatments, since the tone is not a UCS. Yet, because the animal learned that the light predicted the tone during preexposure, it continued to attend to the light and, thereby, associated the light and the shock. We will further address the effects of learning that a stimulus is irrelevant later in the chapter.

A Better Predictor of the Future   We discovered earlier that conditioning is impaired when a CS is not predictive of the UCS, that is, when a UCS occurs both with and without the CS during conditioning. According to the Rescorla-Wagner model, context blocking is responsible for the reduced conditioning caused when the UCS occurs more without the UCS as with it. While the UCS occurs without the CS, the UCS is always presented in a specific environment or context. The pairing of the stimulus context with the UCS will result in the development of associative strength to the context. Since the UCS can only support a limited amount of associative strength, the conditioning of associative strength to the stimulus context will reduce the amount available to the CS. In contrast, when the CS is always paired with the UCS, more associative strength will develop to the CS because it is more salient than the background context. However, as the UCS is repeatedly presented without the CS, the context can accrue associative strength without being overshadowed by the CS. And, as the context develops associative strength, it will block the conditioning to the CS. Therefore, the Rescorla-Wagner model assumes that associative blocking is responsible for the influence of cue predictiveness on the development of a CR.

Whereas the Rescorla-Wagner model indicates that context blocking accounts for the decreased conditioning when the CS is not predictive of the UCS, a study by Klein, Davis, Cohen, and Weston (1984) suggests that predictiveness involves more than context blocking. Their research indicates that an animal plays an active role in determining whether a cue is predictive, in contrast with the passive role assumed by the Rescorla-Wagner associative model of conditioning. In the Klein, Davis, Cohen, and Weston study, one group of animals received four trials of a nonsalient strawberry flavor prior to illness. On each trial, a different but more salient flavor was also paired with illness. Thus, the strawberry flavor was more predictive of illness than any of the other flavors. Although no aversion was established to the nonsalient strawberry flavor after a single pairing with illness, a strong aversion to the strawberry flavor was present after the fourth flavor-illness pairing. It was assumed that the predictive value of the nonsalient strawberry flavor was responsible for the development of the aversion. Note that although this predictiveness treatment resulted in a strong aversion to strawberry, only a weak aversion developed to the salient lemon flavor which was presented with the strawberry cue on the fourth trial. Why did the predictiveness treatment result in an aversion to the strawberry but not the lemon flavor? Associative blocking is a possible cause of the results seen in the predictiveness treatment. To assess the influence of blocking in cue predictiveness, a second group of animals received only strawberry paired with illness on the first three trials and strawberry, lemon, and illness on the fourth trial. If blocking is responsible for the strong aversion to strawberry and weak aversion to lemon, similar results should be seen in the blocking treatment. However, although a modest aversion to strawberry was conditioned in the blocking treatment, it did not block the development of an aversion to the lemon flavor. These results indicate that associative blocking is not entirely responsible for the influence of cue predictiveness on the development of a conditioned response and thus that the impact of predictiveness on conditioning cannot be explained by the associative blocking theory of the Rescorla-Wagner model.

Mackintosh's Attentional View   Nicholas Mackintosh (1975) suggested that animals seek information which predicts the occurrence of biologically significant events (UCSs). Once an animal has identified a cue which reliably predicts a specific biologically significant event, the animal ignores other stimuli which also provide information about the event. Attention is an important part of Mackintosh's approach; animals attend to stimuli that are predictive and ignore those that are not essential.

You might wonder what the key difference is between Mackintosh's view and the Rescorla-Wagner model. Both theories assume that associations are developed when a CS and UCS are paired, but the two approaches advocate different views of the subject's role in conditioning. The Rescorla-Wagner model suggests that the subject plays a passive role in the development of a CR; the level of conditioning is determined by the K value of the CS and the UCS, the λ value of the UCS, the amount of prior conditioning to the CS, and the effect of other stimuli present during conditioning. In contrast, Mackintosh's view assumes that the subject plays an active role in the conditioning process; the amount of conditioning depends not only on the physical characteristics of stimuli but also on the subject's recognition of the correlation (or lack of correlation) between events (CS and UCS). Mackintosh's theory is also relevant to other learning processes. We will briefly describe its application to Pavlovian conditioning next; its importance in explaining other types of learning will be discussed in later chapters.

Mackintosh's view of Pavlovian conditioning explains two phenomena—CS preexposure and predictiveness—which present problems for the Rescorla-Wagner model. We discovered earlier in the chapter that CS preexposure impairs the acquisition of the CR when the CS and UCS are later paired. According to Mackintosh, an animal learns that the CS is irrelevant as the result of preexposure to the CS; in other words, that the CS is uncorrelated with any significant event. In Mackintosh's view, once the animal discovers that a stimulus is irrelevant, it will stop attending to that stimulus, and, therefore, will have difficulty learning that the CS is correlated with the UCS. Support for a learned irrelevance view of CS preexposure is provided by studies in which uncorrelated presentations of the CS and UCS prior to conditioning led to substantial interference with the acquisition of the CR. In fact, significantly greater interference is produced by uncorrelated presentations of the CS and the UCS than by only CS or UCS preexposure. This greater impairment of subsequent conditioning when the CS and UCS are paired has been demonstrated by studies conditioning fear in rats (Baker, 1976; Kremer, 1971), lick training in rats (Baker & Mackintosh, 1977), and the nictating response in rabbits (Siegel & Domjan, 1971).

These observations coincide with Mackintosh's theory of learned irrelevance; a CS is easier to identify as irrelevant when it is presented, but not correlated, with the UCS. Thus animals are able to learn uncorrelated as well as correlated relationships; unpaired presentation of the CS and UCS allows the subject to identify the CS as irrelevant, and thus subsequent conditioning is impaired.

Mackintosh's (1975) view asserts that the predictive value of the CS plays a significant role in the development of a conditioned response. Mackintosh argues that once the subject has learned that a stimulus reliably predicts the UCS, the animal will have difficulty recognizing the predictive value of other stimuli. Mackintosh's view of blocking illustrates his approach. According to Mackintosh, during the initial stage of a blocking study when cue A and the UCS are paired, the animal learns that cue A predicts the UCS. Having learned the predictiveness of cue A, when cues A and B are subsequently paired with the UCS, the animal recognizes that cue B is redundant; that is, cue B provides no additional relevant information. Thus, associative blocking in Mackintosh's view reflects an animal learning to ignore irrelevant or redundant stimuli.

A series of studies provides support for Mackintosh's predictiveness view of the blocking phenomenon (Mackintosh, 1978; Mackintosh, Bygrave, & Picton, 1977; Mackintosh, Dickinson, & Cotton, 1980). This research indicates that some learning about the second stimulus (cue B) does take place on the first blocking trial when the two stimuli are paired together with the UCS. This finding is inconsistent with the Rescorla-Wagner model of blocking, which argues that no conditioning to the second stimulus occurs on the first blocking trial when all the associative capacity of the UCS has already been conditioned to the first stimulus (cue A). This lack of available associative strength should result in no conditioning to the second stimulus; yet, conditioning to the second stimulus does occur on the first blocking trial. Mackintosh (1983) offers an explanation for this conditioning. According to Mackintosh, conditioning takes place on the first trial in which the new stimulus is added because the animal attends to this new CS and, therefore, associates it with the UCS. However, since in the blocking paradigm the UCS is not surprising, the subject will not attend to the new CS on subsequent trials. Thus, the recognition that the second CS is redundant causes the animal to ignore it and thus not to associate it with the UCS.

Mackintosh (1978) presents evidence to support the argument that the animal stops attending to the second stimulus after the first blocking trial. Recall that presenting a surprising event (i.e., one shock instead of two) after the first conditioned stimulus and the second added stimulus disrupts blocking; that is, the CR was conditioned to the second added CS when an unexpected UCS was presented. Mackintosh (1978) reported that although conditioning to the second stimulus occurred when a surprising UCS was also presented on the first blocking trial, no conditioning took place if an unexpected UCS occurred on the second trial of compound conditioning. According to Mackintosh, the animal had already learned that the second CS was irrelevant when an expected UCS was presented on the first trial. Because it recognized the stimulus irrelevance, the animal did not attend to that stimulus on the second trial, and, therefore, no conditioning to the second stimulus occurred, despite the presentation of the unexpected UCS. Apparently, once an animal discovers that a stimulus is irrelevant, it has a hard time learning that the stimulus provides information about an unexpected event.

Overview   Perhaps you believe that Mackintosh's attentional view is valid and that the Rescorla-Wagner associative approach does not accurately describe the Pavlovian conditioning process. It is important that you recognize that the weaknesses in the Rescorla-Wagner model do not indicate that it has no value. A great deal of research has supported the predictions of their model, and it does accurately describe many significant aspects of the conditioning process. However, there is more to Pavlovian conditioning than just the pairing of a CS and a UCS; the animal's biological character and attentional processes affect what associations it will learn. A number of psychologists have recognized the significance of both associative and attentional processes in Pavlovian conditioning. The interested reader should refer to Pearce and Hall (1980) for a discussion of a theory which incorporates both of these processes— associative and attentional—into a theory of Pavlovian conditioning.

EXTINCTION OF THE CONDITIONED RESPONSE

Earlier in the chapter, the example of conditioned hunger demonstrated that environmental stimuli, through their association with deprivation, reward, or both, can acquire the ability to elicit hunger. Similarly, we learned that students can become afraid of examinations by associating them with their aversive consequences. Our conditioned responses typically have an adaptive function; the development of a conditioned hunger and fear reaction enables us to eat at regularly scheduled times and study for scheduled examinations. However, the conditioning of hunger and fear can also be harmful. Clinical research (Rimm & Masters, 1979) has revealed that overweight people eat in many situations (for example, while watching television, driving, or at the movies). To lose weight, these people must restrict their food intake to the dining room (or the room where they usually eat), a process called *stimulus narrowing*. How can those who are overweight control their intake in varied environmental circumstances? One answer lies in *extinction,* a method of eliminating a conditioned response. As the obese person's hunger response to varied environmental circumstances has developed through the classical conditioning process, the extinction of the conditioned hunger reaction represents one approach to losing weight.

Extinction can also be effective therapy for the many people who are extremely fearful of examinations. Test anxiety motivates these people to avoid tests rather than to study for them. Since an intense fear of examinations is acquired through the classical conditioning process, again, extinction represents a potentially effective method of eliminating an intense fear reaction.

Extinction Paradigm

The extinction of a conditioned response will occur when the conditioned stimulus is presented without the unconditioned stimulus. The strength of the CR decreases as the number of CS-alone experiences increases, until eventually no CR is elicited by the CS (refer to Figure 2.1).

Pavlov reported in his classic 1927 book that a classically conditioned salivation response in dogs could be rapidly extinguished by presenting the CS (tone) without the UCS (meat powder). Since Pavlov's initial observations, many psychologists have documented the extinction of a CR by using CS-alone presentations; the extinction process is definitely one of the most reliable conditioning phenomena.

How can a person's intense hunger reaction to environmental stimuli such as watching television be eliminated? Extinction is one method which can be used to suppress the elicitation of a CR; in this case, the hunger response can be eliminated by repeatedly watching television without eating food (the UCS). Note that people experiencing hunger-inducing circumstances are not always able to refrain from eating. Other behavioral techniques (for example, aversive counterconditioning, reinforcement therapy) are often necessary to ensure the inhibition of eating and, thereby, the extinction of the conditioned hunger response. The use of reward is examined in the next chapter; the use of adversity is looked at in Chapter 4.

An extreme fear of examinations can also be eliminated by extinction. If a person takes an examination and does not fail, this person's fear will be diminished. However, fear is not only an extremely aversive emotion but also an intense motivator of avoidance behavior. Thus, persons having test anxiety may not be able to withstand the fear to inhibit avoidance behavior. Other techniques (for example, desensitization and participant modeling) are available to further the inhibition of avoidance behavior and, thereby, the extinction of fear. Desensitization is discussed later in this chapter; participant modeling is examined in Chapter 6.

How Rapidly Does a Conditioned Response Extinguish?

Three factors influence the extinction of a conditioned response. First, *the strength of the CR* can affect the extinction of the conditioned response. The stronger the CR at the end of acquisition, the longer it will take to extinguish the CR, unless the extinction process radically changes the stimulus context from that experienced during acquisition. Second, *the percentage of trials in which the UCS follows the CS* can influence the extinction of a conditioned response. The literature shows that presenting the UCS without (as well as with) the CS during acquisition will result in a slower CR extinction than will presenting the UCS always after the CS; this relationship is observed if there are not substantial differences in CR strength due to the greater conditioning caused by presentation of a predictive rather than a nonpredictive conditioned stimulus. Third, *the length of exposure to the CS during extinction* affects the level of extinction. Empirical investigation reveals that the longer the CS-alone exposure, the greater the reduction in CR strength.

The Strength of the CR   Hull (1943) envisioned the extinction process as a mirror image of acquisition; that is, the stronger the CS-CR bond, the more difficult it is to extinguish the association. Thus, Hull assumed that the stronger the CR, the slower the extinction of that response. Although many studies have found that acquisition levels do influence resistance to extinction, other research has not observed a perfect relationship between the strength of the CR revealed in acquisition and the rate of the extinction of that response. As Hall (1976) stated, one reason for this discrepancy is that the omission of the UCS during extinction changes the subject's motivation level from that which existed during acquisition. This altered motivation level makes extinction differ from acquisition and thereby decreases the correlation between the CR acquisition level and the resistance to extinction.

The Influence of Predictiveness In 1939, Humphreys examined how the percentage of trials in which the UCS followed the CS during acquisition influenced the resistance to extinction. To study this effect, an eye-blink response was conditioned in humans. During acquisition, subjects in the first group received ninety-six CS-UCS pairings and no CS-alone presentations; subjects in the second group received forty-eight CS-UCS pairings and forty-eight CS-alone presentations; subjects in the third group were given forty-eight CS-UCS pairings and no CS-alone presentations. Humphreys discovered that the subjects who received CS-UCS pairings 50 percent of the trials (group 2) extinguished the conditioned eye-blink response significantly more slowly than did those subjects given CS-UCS pairings on 100 percent of the trials (groups 1 and 3). Humphrey's results are presented in Figure 2.11.

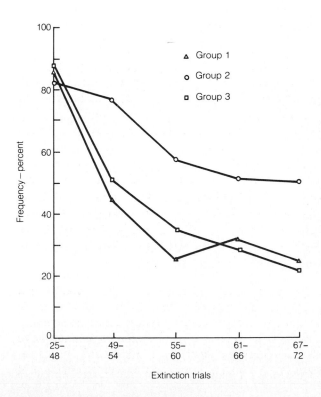

FIGURE 2.11
The extinction of the conditioned response as a function of the percentage of trials where UCS followed the CS during acquisition. Subjects in groups 1 and 3 received CS-UCS pairings on 100 percent of the acquisition trials; those in group 2, on 50 percent. Adapted from Humphreys, L. G. The effect of random alternation of reinforcement on the acquisition and extinction of conditioned eyelid reactions. *Journal of Experimental Psychology*, 1939, *25*, 141–158. Copyright 1939 by the American Psychological Association. Reprinted by permission.

Although studies with people have shown that extinction is slower when the CS is not always followed by the UCS, the results with animals have been inconsistent (Hall, 1976). Some research has shown that there is more resistance to extinction when the CS is less predictive during conditioning; other studies have found that the resistance to extinction is greater when the CS is more predictive during acquisition; still other studies have found no differences in rate of extinction as a function of percentage of trials that the UCS follows the CS. In some studies in which the terminal level of responding was not controlled, the strength of the CR probably was higher as well as being more predictive during acquisition; this difference could explain the greater resistance to extinction observed in some studies using a more predictive CS.

In those studies where the final acquisition level is equivalent for all subjects, slower extinction with less predictive CS is thought to be due to a greater inability to detect extinction. When the UCS does not always follow the CS during acquisition, discriminating the change from acquisition to extinction is more difficult. Subjects whose only experience with a CS alone is during extinction find this discrimination easier.

Longnecker, Krauskopf, and Bitterman's (1952) study provides a test of the discrimination view of the influence of CS predictiveness during acquisition on the rate of extinction. Half the subjects in this study received Galvanic Skin Response (GSR) conditioning on random presentations of CS-UCS and CS-alone trials; the other subjects were given CS-UCS pairings on odd-numbered trials and CS-alone presentations on even-numbered trials. This alternate training procedure made the presentation of the UCS predictable, thereby increasing the discriminability of extinction. Longnecker, Krauskopf, and Bitterman observed significantly faster extinction with the alternate-treatment procedure than with the random-treatment presentation. These results indicate that the ability of people or animals to detect the difference between acquisition and extinction influences the rate of the extinction of the CR. Thus, the occurrence of the CS without the UCS during acquisition increases resistance to extinction by reducing the distinction between acquisition and extinction.

Thus the combined influence of discriminability and response strength governs the effect of exposure to the CS alone during acquisition or extinction. CS-alone exposures during acquisition (1) decrease discriminability, thereby increasing resistance to extinction and (2) reduce response strength, thereby decreasing resistance to extinction. The relative contribution of both factors determines whether CS-alone presentation in acquisition will increase, decrease, or have no effect on resistance to extinction.

Duration of CS Exposure We have discovered that the strength of the conditioned response declines as the CS-alone experience increases. You might have the impression that the number of CS-alone presentations determines the level of extinction, that is, that as the number of extinction trials increases, the strength of the CR declines. However, research clearly shows that the total duration of CS-alone exposure, not the number of extinction trials, determines the amount of extinction (Berman & Katzev, 1972; Monti & Smith, 1976; Shipley, 1974; Shipley, Mock, & Levis, 1971). These studies demonstrate that the strength of the CR weakens as the duration of CS exposure increases. Three articles included in this research (Berman & Katzev, 1972; Monti & Smith, 1976; Shipley, Mock, & Levis, 1971) assessed the extinction of fear in terms of the decline in avoidance responding when the duration of CS exposure was increased; the fourth article (Shipley, 1974) examined the extinction of fear relative to the reduced water consumption produced by the CS when the duration of CS exposure was increased. We will briefly focus on Shipley's study to see the influence of CS-alone duration on the extinction of a CR.

Shipley (1974) initially trained water-deprived rats to lick a water tube to obtain liquid reinforcement. Following lick training, the animals received twenty exposures to a tone paired with electric shock. Extinction occurred following fear conditioning. Half the animals were given 25-second CS exposures during extinction; the other half received a 100-second CS-alone experience during extinction. One-third of the animals in both the 25-second and the 100-second CS-duration groups were given sufficient extinction experience so that they received a total of 200 seconds of CS exposure, another third received 400 seconds, and the last third received 800 seconds of exposure. For example, to have 200 total seconds of CS exposure, the animals given 25 seconds on each trial received eight trials compared to two trials for subjects receiving 100 seconds on each trial. Shipley reported that the suppression of licking produced by the CS was not affected by either the number of CS-alone exposures or the duration of each exposure. Only the total duration of CS exposure during extinction determined the rate of extinction of the CR; the greater the length of the total CS exposure during extinction, the less suppression produced by the tone (see Figure 2.12). Thus, the total duration of the CS exposure seems to be the most important influence on the rate of the extinction of a CR. We have examined the variables which affect extinction rate; let's look at the process responsible for the extinction of a CR.

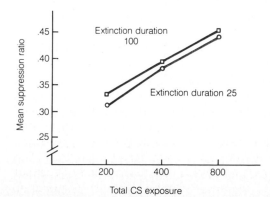

FIGURE 2.12
Suppression of bar-press response to the conditioned stimulus as a function of the duration of exposure to the CS on each extinction trial and total duration of CS exposure during extinction. Adapted from Shipley, R. H. Extinction of conditioned fear in rats as a function of several parameters of CS exposure. *Journal of Comparative and Physiological Psychology*, 1974, 87, 699–707. Copyright 1974 by the American Psychological Association. Reprinted by permission.

The Nature of the Extinction

Pavlov (1927) proposed that the extinction of a CR is caused by the *inhibition* of the CR. This inhibition develops as the result of the activation of a central inhibitory state, which occurs when the CS is presented without the UCS. This inhibitory state is strengthened by the continued presentation of the CS without the UCS and acts to prevent the occurrence of the CR.

The initial inhibition of the CR which occurs as the result of extinction is only temporary. According to Pavlov, the arousal of the inhibitory state declines following the initial extinction. As the strength of the inhibitory state diminishes, the ability of the CS to elicit the CR increases. (The inhibition of a CR can become permanent as a result of conditioned inhibition; we will discuss the conditioned inhibition process shortly.)

Guthrie (1935) suggested a different explanation for the extinction of a conditioned response. According to Guthrie, the presentation of the CS without the UCS causes the conditioning of another response to the CS; this new response will interfere with the ability of the CS to elicit the CR. As the strength of the interfering response increases, the CR will decrease in strength. A number of types of studies have evaluated Pavlov's inhibitory view and Guthrie's response-competition view of extinction. This research supports Pavlov's approach; we will now examine some of this evidence. (See Hall, 1976, for a more detailed review of this literature.)

Evidence supporting Pavlov's view of extinction can be seen in the data comparing massed versus spaced extinction. According to Pavlov, during spaced extinction trials the level of inhibition declines in the interval between trials, thereby slowing the strengthening of the inhibitory state to a level sufficient to suppress the CR. In contrast, the level of inhibition does not decline during the interval between trials during massed extinction, and therefore the strengthening of the inhibitory state occurs quickly. Massed extinction, producing a more rapid intensification of the inhibitory state than spaced extinction, should thus lead to faster extinction than does spaced extinction. Guthrie's approach makes the opposite prediction. Since spaced practice produces faster acquisition of the CR than does massed practice, spaced practice should also produce faster extinction. This conclusion is based on Guthrie's theory that extinction represents the conditioning of a competing response. The research, however, clearly demonstrates that extinction is faster with massed extinction than with spaced extinction (see Hilgard & Marquis, 1940; Pavlov, 1927).

Further evidence that Pavlov's theory is correct is provided by a number of studies which show that acquisition and extinction are also affected by various drugs (see Hilgard & Marquis, 1940). For example, both caffeine and benzedrine (two stimulants) increase the rate of acquisition but interfere with extinction. In contrast, sodium bromide (a depressant) retards the rate of acquisition but enhances the extinction of a CR. Since Pavlov assumed that acquisition and extinction involve different processes and Guthrie suggested that acquisition and extinction reflect the same process, the observation that stimulant and depressant drugs have opposite effects on the acquisition and extinction of a CR supports Pavlov's view.

Rescorla (1969) presents evidence suggesting that extinction may not reflect inhibition. Two types of inquiry support his view. The first support comes from studies using the *summation test*. The summation test involves presentation of the extinguished CS with another CS. If the extinguished CS has inhibitory properties, it should act to suppress responding to the other CS. Rescorla found that an extinguished CS failed the summation test; that is, the extinguished CS did not suppress responding to the other CS. The second type of research involves the *retardation test*. In the retardation test, the CS is again paired with the UCS. If the extinguished CS has inhibitory properties, reacquisition of the CR should be impaired. However, Rescorla found that an extinguished CS also failed the retardation test; that is, reacquisition of a CR was not slower after extinction than had been the original acquisition.

While these results suggest that extinction is not due to inhibition, Mackintosh (1983) argued against this conclusion. According to Mackintosh, extinction involves not only inhibition but other processes as well; the omission of the UCS may change the stimulus context from that during acquisition as well as lead to a decline in motivational state. Several studies have tried to determine if extinction involves processes other than inhibition (Frey & Butler, 1973; Rescorla & Skucy, 1969). In these studies, an extinction procedure in which the UCS is omitted is compared to a procedure in which both the CS and UCS are presented but not paired. This second procedure produces a decline in responding, but that decline is not as rapid as that caused by the traditional extinction procedure. Since the rate of extinction differed depending on the type of extinction process used, extinction probably involves more than just one process. Further, the influence of these other processes probably prevents the inhibitory aspects of extinction from being detected on the summation and retardation tests, although the fact that stimulants impair extinction while depressants facilitate extinction provides support for the view that at least one process involved in extinction is inhibition.

Other Inhibitory Processes

A temporary internal inhibition is one process involved in the extinction of a conditioned response. The inhibition of the CR can become permanent, a process which Pavlov called conditioned inhibition. There are also several other types of inhibitions: external inhibition, latent inhibition, and inhibition of delay. Inhibition can also be eliminated through a process called disinhibition.

Conditioned Inhibition   The initial inhibition of a CR can become permanent. If a new stimulus (CS−) similar to the conditioned stimulus (CS+) is presented in the absence of the unconditioned stimulus, the CS− will act to inhibit a CR to the CS+. The process of developing a permanent inhibitor is called *conditioned inhibition*. Conditioned inhibition is assumed to reflect the acquisition of the ability of the CS− to activate the inhibitory state, which can suppress the CR.

Consider the following example to illustrate conditioned inhibition. Recall our discussion of conditioned hunger; because of past experiences, you became hungry when arriving home after your classes. Suppose that when you open the refrigerator, you find no food. In all likelihood, the empty refrigerator would act to inhibit your hunger. This inhibitory property of the empty refrigerator developed due to past pairings of the empty refrigerator with an absence of food. Many studies have shown that associating new stimuli with the absence of the UCS causes these stimuli to develop permanent inhibitory properties; let's examine two of these studies.

Rescorla and LoLordo (1965) initially trained their dogs to avoid electric shock using a Sidman avoidance schedule. With this procedure, the dogs received a shock every 10 seconds unless they jumped over a hurdle dividing the two compartments of a shuttle box (see Chapter 1). If a dog avoided a shock, the next shock was postponed for 30 seconds. The advantage of this technique is twofold: no external CS is employed during Sidman avoidance conditioning, and the influence of fear-inducing cues (CS+) and fear-inhibiting cues (CS−) can be assessed. After three days of avoidance conditioning, the dogs were locked in one compartment of the shuttle box and exposed on some trials to a 1200-Hz tone (CS+) and shock (UCS) and on other trials to a 400-Hz tone (CS−) without shock. Following conditioned-inhibition training, the CS+ and the CS− were presented. Rescorla and LoLordo found that the CS+ aroused fear and, thereby, increased avoidance responding. In contrast, the CS− inhibited fear, causing the dogs to stop responding. These results indicate that the CS+ elicits fear and the CS− inhibits fear and that conditioned stimuli have an important motivational influence on instrumental behavior; we will examine that influence later in the chapter.

Mellgren and Ost (1969) demonstrated the inhibitory properties of a CS− in an appetitive conditioning situation. First, Mellgren and Ost trained their rats to press a lever to obtain water reward. Then they gave the animals a series of Pavlovian conditioning trials in which a tone (CS+) was followed by water, and a light (CS−) was paired with no water. Mellgren and Ost then presented the CS+ or the CS− while the rats were bar pressing. They reported that the CS+ increased bar pressing and the CS− decreased responding.

External Inhibition   Pavlov (1927) suggested that inhibition could affect behavior in situations other than extinction. To support his theory, he observed that the presentation of a novel stimulus during conditioning reduces the strength of the conditioned response. Pavlov labeled this process reflecting a temporary activation of the inhibitory state *external inhibition*. During external inhibition, the inhibition of the CR will not occur on a subsequent trial unless the novel stimulus is presented again; if the novel stimulus is not presented during the next trial, the strength of the conditioned response will return to its previous level.

Latent Inhibition   Recall that preexposure to the CS impairs subsequent conditioning, when the CS and UCS are then presented together. Lubow and Moore (1959) suggested that the effect of CS preexposure resulted from "latent inhibition"; that is, exposure to the CS prior to conditioning caused the CS to acquire inhibitory properties which subsequently interfered with excitatory conditioning when the CS and the UCS were paired. We discovered earlier that Mackintosh believed that CS preexposure leads to learned irrelevance—the subject learns that a stimulus does not predict any significant event and, therefore, has difficulty recognizing the correlation between the stimulus and the UCS.

A number of studies have determined the effect of CS exposure on the acquisition of conditioned inhibition (see Baker & Mackintosh, 1977; Halgren, 1974; Rescorla, 1971). If the impact of CS preexposure resulted from latent inhibition, then the CS preexposure should enhance conditioned-inhibition training. However, these studies showed that preexposure to a stimulus not only retards excitatory conditioning but also interferes with inhibitory conditioning. Thus, it appears that CS preexposure does not lead to the development of latent inhibition.

Inhibition of Delay   On many occasions a short delay separates a CS and a UCS. For example, several minutes elapse from the time that we enter a restaurant until we receive our food. Under these conditions, we inhibit our responding until just prior to receiving the food. (If we did begin to salivate as soon as we entered the restaurant, our mouths would be dry when we received our food and our digestion process would be impaired.) Note that the ability to inhibit responding until the end of the CS-UCS interval improves with experience. At first, we respond immediately when a CS is presented; our ability to withhold the CR improves with increased CS-UCS pairings.

Pavlov's classic research (1927) with dogs demonstrated the development of the ability to suppress the CR until the end of the CS-UCS interval, a phenomenon he labeled *inhibition of delay*. Other experimenters have also shown that animals and humans can inhibit the CR until just before the UCS presentation (see Ellison, 1964; Kimmel, 1965; Sheffield, 1965). For example, Kimmel (1965) gave human subjects fifty trials of red light (CS) and shock pairings (UCS). The red light was presented 7.5 seconds prior to shock, and both were terminated simultaneously. Kimmel reported that the latency of the GSR response increased with increased training trials (see Figure 2.13).

Disinhibition   The presentation of a novel stimulus during conditioning causes the CS to inhibit the elicitation of the CR. Presenting a novel stimulus during extinction also causes disruption; however, the novel stimulus causes an increase in the strength of the conditioned response. The extinction process

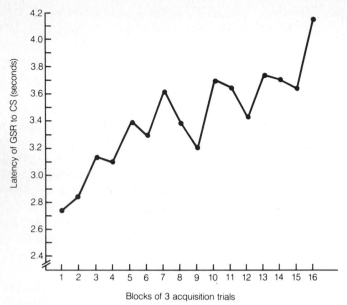

FIGURE 2.13
The average latency of GSR response to a conditioned stimulus
which preceded the unconditioned stimulus by 7.5 seconds.
From Kimmel, H. D. Instrumental inhibitory factors in classical
conditioning. In W. F. Prokasy (Ed.), *Classical conditioning: A
symposium.* New York: Irvington, 1965.

will proceed normally on the next trial if the novel stimulus is not presented.
Pavlov labeled the process of increased CR strength *disinhibition*.

Kimmel's (1965) study shows the disinhibition phenomenon in an inhibition-
of-delay paradigm. Kimmel observed that a novel tone presented during the CS
disrupted the ability of the subjects to withhold the CR during the 7.5-second
CS-UCS interval. Whereas the CR was exhibited approximately 4 seconds
after the CS was presented following fifty acquisition trials, the CR latency
dropped to 2.3 seconds when the novel stimulus was presented with the CS.
These results indicate that a novel stimulus can disrupt the inhibition of a CR
and also that inhibition is responsible for the suppression of the CR observed in
the inhibition-of-delay phenomenon.

GUILT BY ASSOCIATION

Although many conditioned responses are acquired through direct experiences,
many stimuli develop the ability to elicit a conditioned response indirectly; that
is, a stimulus which is never directly paired with the UCS nevertheless elicits a
CR. For example, although many people with test anxiety have developed their
fear because of the direct pairing of a test and failure, many people who fear
tests have never failed an exam.

A stimulus can acquire the ability to elicit a CR indirectly in four ways. First, *a stimulus never paired with the UCS can elicit the CR through the stimulus-generalization process.* A person with test anxiety may have failed similar events (for example, homework).

Second, *a stimulus never directly paired with the UCS could produce the CR through the process of higher-order conditioning.* In higher-order conditioning, following the direct pairing of a CS (for example, a tone) with the UCS (for example, food), the conditioned stimulus is then paired with another stimulus (for example, a light). After several tone-light pairings, an animal or person will salivate when presented the light, even though the light was never paired directly with the UCS. Let's see how test anxiety could be acquired through higher-order conditioning. Perhaps leaving home to go to school was very distressing to you as a youngster. The association of this distress with school caused you to fear the school itself. Since schools give exams, tests (CS_2) become associated with school (CS_1); thus, as the result of higher-order conditioning, examinations elicit fear.

Third, *sensory preconditioning can cause the development of a CR to a stimulus never paired directly with the UCS.* Sensory preconditioning is similar to higher-order conditioning except that during sensory preconditioning, the CS_1 and CS_2 are paired prior to conditioning instead of presented after CS-UCS pairing (as in higher-order conditioning). Let's use the text-anxiety example to illustrate the sensory-preconditioning process. Exams are a typical school activity, and, as the result of attending school, students will associate school (CS_1) with exams (CS_2). Aversive experiences sometimes occur at school; for example, a child may be teased by other children during recess. This abuse causes the child to dislike school. Because the child associates school with tests, this child now fears tests even though examinations never have been directly paired with adversity.

Fourth, *the ability of a stimulus to elicit a CR can be acquired vicariously.* Observing the pairing of a CS with a UCS in other people can cause us to respond to the CS as if we had experienced the CS-UCS presentation. Suppose that someone observed another person fail an examination. As the result of this experience, the observer associates an examination with failure and is now afraid of tests.

Thus, a stimulus can develop the ability to elicit a CR indirectly through generalization, higher-order conditioning, sensory preconditioning, and/or vicarious conditioning. Note that several sources may contribute to the intensity of the conditioned response. For example, the combined influence of vicarious conditioning and sensory preconditioning may cause an intense conditioned reaction to the CS. Chapter 1 briefly discussed the generalization process; Chapter 5 will examine it in greater detail.

Higher-Order Conditioning

Conditioning Paradigm   Pavlov (1927) observed that following CS-UCS pairings, presenting the CS with another neutral stimulus (CS_2) enabled the CS_2

to elicit the CR. In one of Pavlov's studies using dogs, a tone (the beat of a metronome) was paired with meat powder. After this first-order conditioning, the tone was presented with a black square, but the meat powder was omitted. Following the pairings of tone and black square, the black square (CS_2) alone was able to elicit salivation. Pavlov called this conditioning process *higher-order conditioning*. (In this particular study, the conditioning was second order.) Figure 2.14 presents a diagram of the higher-order conditioning process. Note that the strength of a CR acquired through higher-order conditioning is weaker than that caused by first-order conditioning. Pavlov discovered a second-order CR to be approximately 50 percent as strong as a first-order CR and a third-order CR to be very weak. He found it impossible to develop a fourth-order CR.

Psychologists since the time of Pavlov's original studies have not always succeeded at producing a CR through higher-order conditioning. Why was not apparent until Rescorla's elegant analysis of higher-order conditioning (see Holland & Rescorla, 1975; Rescorla, 1973, 1978; Rizley & Rescorla, 1972). According to Rescorla, the problem with higher-order conditioning is that the pairing of CS_2-CS_1 without the UCS during the second phase of conditioning also represents a conditioned-inhibition paradigm. Thus, not only is the excitation of the CR being conditioned to the CS_2 during CS_2-CS_1 pairings, but also the inhibition of the CR is being conditioned as the result of the pairing of the compound stimulus (CS_2 and CS_1) in the absence of the UCS. Rescorla and his associates discovered that conditioned excitation develops more rapidly than the acquisition of conditioned inhibition. Thus, CS_2 will elicit the CR with only a few pairings. However, as conditioned inhibition develops, CR strength in response to the CS_2 declines until the CS_2 can no longer elicit the CR. At this

FIGURE 2.14
The higher-order conditioning process. In phase 1, the CS_1 (light) was paired with the UCS; in phase 2, the CS_1 (light) and the CS_2 (buzzer) were presented together. The ability of the CS_2 to elicit the CR was evaluated in phase 3.

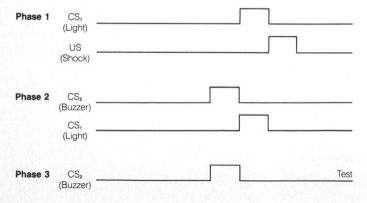

time, the conditioned inhibition equals the conditioned excitation produced by the CS_2.

Rizley and Rescorla's (1972) study illustrates the influence of the number of CS_2-CS_1 pairings on the strength of a higher-order conditioned fear. Rizley and Rescorla gave rats eight presentations of a 10-second flashing light (CS_1) paired with a 1-mA 0.5-second electric shock (UCS). Following first-order conditioning, the light (CS_1) was paired with an 1800-Hz tone. Rizley and Rescorla discovered that the strength of fear of the CS_2 increased with each CS_2-CS_1 pairing, reaching a maximum strength after four pairings (see Figure 2.15). However, the intensity of fear elicited by the CS_2 declined with each additional pairing until the CS_2 produced no fear after fifteen CS_2-CS_1 presentations. Holland and Rescorla (1975) observed a similar influence of the amount of higher-order conditioning on the development of a conditioned appetitive response. In summary, the work of Rescorla and his colleagues demonstrates that higher-order conditioning will be evident after a few but not after many CS_2-CS_1 presentations.

The observation that the strength of a second-order CR diminishes after the presentation of more than a few CS_2-CS_1 pairings does not indicate that higher-order conditioning has no role in real-world settings. For example, once a CR such as fear is conditioned to a CS_2 such as high places, the fear produced by the CS_2 will motivate avoidance behavior. An animal or person will quickly avoid; this results in only a brief exposure to the CS_2. As we learned earlier, the amount of CS_1 exposure without the UCS influences the rate of extinction; the longer the exposure, the greater the extinction. Therefore, a rapid avoidance response will produce a short exposure to the CS_2 and will result in slow development of conditioned inhibition. The slow acquisition of conditioned inhibition to the CS_2 can allow a CS_2 to elicit fear for a very long, possibly indefinite, period of time. The discussion of avoidance learning in Chapter 4 demonstrates that eliminating all avoidance behavior is very difficult because of the intense motivational properties of fear.

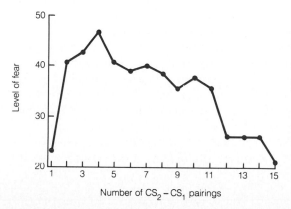

FIGURE 2.15
Changes in fear response to CS_2 after various numbers of CS_1 and CS_2 pairings. Adapted from Rizley, R. C., & Rescorla, R. A. Associations in second-order conditioning and sensory preconditioning. *Journal of Comparative and Physiological Psychology*, 1972, *81*, 1–11. Copyright 1972 by the American Psychological Association. Reprinted by permission.

The Nature of Higher-Order Conditioning What mechanism is responsible for the CS_2 eliciting the CR? Rescorla (1973, 1978) suggested three possibilities: (1) The CS_2 causes an animal or a person to recall the CS_1, which, in turn, elicits the CR. (2) During CS_2 and CS_1 pairings, the presence of CS_1 elicits the memory of the UCS, which then elicits the CR. The animal or person will then associate the CS_2 with the memory of the UCS. (3) The CS_2 directly elicits the CR. Rescorla and his associates' research (Holland & Rescorla, 1975; Rizley & Rescorla, 1972) indicates that the CS_2 directly elicits the CR. Let's see how they arrived at this conclusion.

To test the first alternative, Rizley and Rescorla (1972) presented the CS_1 alone after second-order conditioning of fear to the CS_2. If the ability of the CS_2 to elicit fear reflects the aversiveness of the CS_1, then extinguishing the CR to the CS_1 should also eliminate the fear-eliciting ability of the CS_2. Rizley and Rescorla discovered that the CS_2 continued to produce fear, even after the CS_1 no longer did. Apparently, the ability of the CS_2 to elicit fear does not depend on the aversiveness of the CS_1. Holland and Rescorla (1975) observed similar results with an appetitive conditioned response.

Rizley and Rescorla (1972) evaluated the second alternative by eliminating the aversiveness of the UCS after higher-order conditioning. To accomplish this objective, they used a 2-second 112-dB noise as the UCS. (Unlike a shock UCS, continued presentation of a loud noise results in reduced aversiveness until the noise is no longer aversive.) In the first phase of the study, a light (CS_1) was paired with the loud noise, followed by tone-light (CS_2-CS_1) pairings in the second phase. Following higher-order conditioning, the animals received thirty-six UCS exposures; this procedure eliminated the aversiveness of the loud noise. Rizley and Rescorla reported that the CS_2 continued to elicit fear even though the UCS was no longer aversive. Thus, it appears that the ability of the CS_2 to elicit fear does not depend on the aversiveness of either the CS_1 or the UCS. In contrast, Rizley and Rescorla found that the CS_1 no longer could elicit the CR when the UCS lost its aversiveness.

Rizley and Rescorla's observations may enhance our understanding of the etiology of people's phobias, the origins of which are often quite difficult to uncover. If phobias develop through higher-order conditioning, the original source of the phobia may no longer be aversive, but the phobic object will still elicit fear because it has become independent of the CS_1 and the UCS. Recall our example of test anxiety used to explain higher-order conditioning. The aversiveness of leaving home to attend school typically declines with repeated experiences. Whereas the loss of the UCS aversiveness causes the child to lose fear of school (CS_1), tests (CS_2) continue to elicit fear. Rizley and Rescorla's findings also suggest that there is no need to search for the origins of a phobia; the only way to eliminate a higher-order CR is to present the CS_2 alone. The applicability of the animal research conducted by Rescorla and his associates to the higher-order-conditioned responses of humans awaits future investigation.

Sensory Preconditioning

Consider the following example to illustrate the sensory preconditioning process: Your neighbor owns a large German shepherd; you associate this neighbor with his dog. As you are walking down the street, the dog bites you, causing you to become afraid of the dog. You will also develop a disliking for your neighbor as the result of your previous association of the neighbor with the dog.

Conditioning Paradigm   In sensory preconditioning, two neutral stimuli, CS_1 and CS_2, are paired (see Figure 2.16). Following the association of CS_1 and CS_2 (neighbor and dog), CS_1 is presented with an unconditioned stimulus (bite). The CS_1-UCS pairings result in the ability of the CS_2, as well as the CS_1, to elicit the CR (fear). Thus, as a result of the initial CS_2-CS_1 association, the CS_2 can produce the CR even though it is not paired directly with the UCS.

Empirical Support   Brogden's (1939) classic research represents an early successful study of sensory preconditioning. In the first phase of Brogden's experiment, dogs in the experimental condition received 200 simultaneous pairings of a light and buzzer. Control animals did not receive light-buzzer pairings. Following this initial conditioning, one of the cues (either the light or the buzzer) was presented with an electric shock to the dog's foot. Brogden reported that presentation of the other cue not paired with shock elicited the CR (leg flexion) in experimental but not in control animals. Although Brogden's results showed that a cue can develop the ability to elicit a CR through the sensory preconditioning process, the leg flexion CR to the CS_2 was weak. Other

FIGURE 2.16
The sensory preconditioning process. In phase 1, the CS_1 (light) and CS_2 (buzzer) were paired; the CS_1 (light) was presented with the UCS in phase 2. The ability of the CS_2 to elicit the CR was evaluated in phase 3.

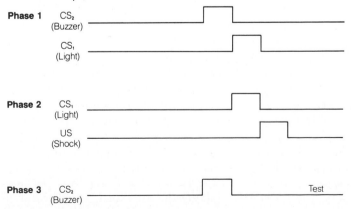

researchers during the 1940s and 1950s also discovered that the magnitude of the sensory preconditioning effect was small (see Kimble, 1961).

Recent studies (Prewitt, 1967; Rizley & Rescorla, 1972; Tait, Marquis, Williams, Weinstein, & Suboski, 1969) indicate that the early studies did not employ the best procedures to produce a strong, reliable sensory preconditioning effect. These studies show that the CS_2 will elicit a strong CR if during the initial conditioning (1) the CS_2 precedes the CS_1 by several seconds and (2) only a few CS_2-CS_1 pairings are used to prevent the development of learned irrelevance. Recall that when the CS is presented without the UCS prior to conditioning, there is a diminished conditioning of a CR when the CS and UCS are paired during training.

The Nature of Sensory Preconditioning   Mediation appears to be responsible for the sensory preconditioning effect. According to this view, the presentation of the CS_2 causes an animal or person to recall CS_1, which results in the elicitation of the CR. Thus, the memory of CS_1 mediates the ability of the CS_2 to elicit the CR. Rizley and Rescorla's (1972) study provides support for a mediation approach.

Rizley and Rescorla (1972) presented their standard sensory preconditioning treatment to two groups of rats. After CS_2-CS_1 pairings and CS_1-UCS (shock) pairings, one group of rats was given repeated CS_1-alone presentations until the CS_1 no longer elicited the CR. The other group of animals did not receive CS_1-CR extinction trials. Both groups of rats were then exposed to the CS_2. Rizley and Rescorla found that animals given CS_1-alone experience (extinction) did not respond to the CS_2, whereas the CS_2 did suppress behavior in those animals that had not received CS_1-alone presentations. These observations indicate that the ability of the CS_2 to elicit the CR depends on the continued ability of the CS_1 to elicit the CR. Therefore, unlike in higher-order conditioning, an animal's response to CS_2 acquired through sensory preconditioning is not independent of its reaction to CS_1.

Vicarious Conditioning

A person can develop an emotional response to a specific stimulus through direct experience; an individual can also learn to respond to a particular stimulus as a result of observing the experiences of others. For example, a person can become afraid of dogs after being bitten; this person can also learn to fear dogs after seeing another person being bitten. The development of a CS's ability to elicit a CR following such an observation is called *vicarious conditioning*.

Although many emotional responses clearly are developed through direct conditioning, the research also demonstrates that CS-UCS associations can be acquired through vicarious conditioning experiences (see Bandura, 1977); we will now discuss several studies which examine the vicarious conditioning of a CR.

Empirical Support   Berger's study (1962) demonstrates the vicarious conditioning of a conditioned fear reaction to a neutral stimulus. Berger's subjects listened to a neutral tone and then saw another person receiving an electric shock and exhibiting pain reactions (this other person, a confederate, pretended to be shocked and hurt). Berger found that subjects who repeatedly witnessed the scene, which was preceded by the tone, developed an emotional response to the tone. Bandura and Rosenthal (1966) also observed that vicarious conditioning of fear occurred when a subject observed another person being shocked.

An emotional reaction can develop by observing people fail a task as well as watching individuals receiving electric shock (see Bandura, Blanchard, & Ritter, 1969; Craig & Weinstein, 1965). In the Craig and Weinstein study, subjects watched another person succeed or fail at a motor task. The subjects who witnessed the other person fail showed a stronger conditioned GSR reaction to the task than did those subjects who saw the other person succeed at the task. Furthermore, subjects who were told that shock was contingent on the person's failure did not show a stronger conditioned affective reaction than did subjects who only witnessed failure. Apparently, we can learn to fear a task merely by watching others fail it.

Vicarious conditioning is not unique to humans. Crooks (1967) reported that monkeys can develop a fear of certain objects after viewing the experience of another monkey with these objects. In Crooks's study, the subjects heard a tape-recorded distress when a model monkey touched some particular objects; they did not hear the emotional reaction when the model touched other objects. Crooks discovered that subjects subsequently played with those objects not associated with distress but would not touch the objects which appeared to have hurt the other monkey.

The Importance of Arousal   We do not always develop a CR after watching the experiences of others. For vicarious conditioning to occur, we must respond emotionally to the scene we witness. Bandura and Rosenthal (1966) evaluated the level of vicarious CR conditioning as a function of the subjects' arousal level during conditioning. They found that observers moderately aroused by the sight of a confederate being shocked would subsequently show strong autonomic reaction to the tone which had been paired with shock experienced by the confederate; subjects either minimally distressed or intensely upset from viewing the confederate being shocked displayed only a weak vicarious conditioning. The highly aroused subjects stopped attending to the person receiving the shock; Bandura and Rosenthal suggested that the altered attention of these subjects reduced the association of the tone with shock. Apparently, we must be aroused—but not too aroused—if we are to develop conditioned responses from observing the experiences of others.

Conditioned stimuli not only elicit or inhibit the occurrence of conditioned responses but also influence instrumental activity. The next section will discuss how conditioned stimuli can also arouse or suppress instrumental behavior.

CONDITIONED STIMULI AND INSTRUMENTAL BEHAVIOR

Central Motivational States

Consider the following two situations: (1) You are in a movie theater when a fire alarm sounds inside, causing you to stop watching the movie and rush from the theater. (2) You are studying for an exam to be taken tomorrow when you realize it's time for your favorite television show. You stop studying to watch the show. Both examples contain a particular element (the fire alarm and the scheduled time) which suppressed one behavior and evoked another. The fire alarm motivated you to terminate watching the movie and escape from the theater. In contrast, the scheduled time acted to inhibit your studying and motivate you to watch television.

Rescorla and Solomon's (1967) theory offers an explanation for the behavior exhibited in the two examples. According to Rescorla and Solomon, two central motivational states govern behavior. Arousal of an appetitive state motivates approach behavior; activation of an aversive state arouses avoidance behavior. Two types of conditioned stimuli stimulate the appetitive state and inhibit the aversive state. Since you associate the scheduled time of your favorite television show with past reward, that specific time can excite the central appetitive state and suppress the aversive state as a conditioned response. Spence (1956) called this response the *anticipatory goal response* (r_G—see Chapter 1); Mowrer (1960) called it *hope*. The other conditioned stimulus that activates the central appetitive state and inhibits the aversive state is associated with the absence of an aversive event. For example, if you bolted from the theater when the fire alarm sounded, you would probably reenter when the alarm stopped (if, of course, you have been reassured of safety) and resume watching the movie. Rescorla and Solomon would assert that through conditioning, the termination of a stimulus (the fire alarm) associated with the absence of an aversive event (fire) stimulated the central appetitive state and suppressed the aversive state. D'Amato (1970) labeled this response an *anticipatory relief response* (r_R—see Chapter 1); Tarpy (1975) labeled it *relief*. Thus, hope and relief motivate appetitive behavior and suppress avoidance behavior by influencing the functioning of the central motivational states.

Two types of conditioned stimuli also stimulate the central aversive state and inhibit the appetitive state. Because the fire alarm had been associated with fire, the alarm inhibited the appetitive state and therefore suppressed the watching of the movie. In addition, the alarm activated the aversive state, which in turn motivated escape behavior. Mowrer (1960) referred to this response as *fear;* D'Amato called it an *anticipatory pain response* (r_P—see Chapter 1). When a stimulus is associated with the absence of reward, the conditioned response produced by this stimulus is also an excitation of the central aversive state and an inhibition of the appetitive state. Amsel (1958) labeled this an *anticipatory frustration response* (r_F—see Chapter 1); Tarpy referred to it as *disappointment*. Thus, both *fear* and *frustration* stimulate avoidance behavior and suppress appetitive behavior by influencing the function of the central motivational states.

Why does a conditioned stimulus excite one state yet inhibit the other state? Suppose that the scheduled television show in our example aroused only the appetitive state and did not inhibit the aversive state. If this were the case, we would be unable to respond because our approach and avoidance tendencies would have equal motive strength. Judson Brown's classic research (1948) on approach-avoidance conflict shows that equivalent approach and avoidance motive strengths produce vascillation; that is, the animal or person can neither approach reward nor avoid adversity. Therefore, the scheduled television show must inhibit the aversive state as well as excite the appetitive state to induce you to stop studying and turn on your favorite show.

Interaction Studies

Many studies support the theory that conditioned stimuli influence instrumental behavior through their effect on the two central motivational states. To validate this theory, a study must classically condition a response to a specific stimulus, establish an instrumental behavior, and then evaluate how the conditioned stimulus affects the instrumental activity. Figure 2.17 presents a diagram

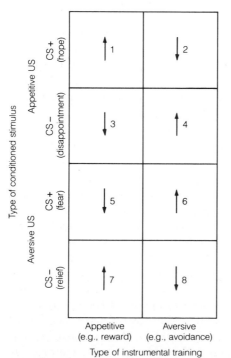

FIGURE 2.17
Matrix illustrating the interaction between conditioned stimuli and instrumental behavior. Arrows indicate whether the conditioned stimulus facilitates (↑) or suppresses (↓) behavior. The terms in parentheses show the conditioned emotional response elicited by a particular conditioned stimulus. Adapted from Rescorla, R. A., & Solomon, R. L. Two-process theory: Relationships between Pavlovian conditioning and instrumental learning. *Psychological Review*, 1967, *74*, 151–182. Copyright 1967 by the American Psychological Association. Reprinted by permission.

of the behavioral predictions of the Rescorla-Solomon theory. The figure indicates the predicted direction of behavioral change produced by each type of conditioned stimulus. For example, hope and relief should increase appetitive behavior (cells 1 and 7) and decrease aversive behavior (cells 2 and 8). Trapold and Winokur's (1967) study shows the influence of a conditioned stimulus paired with food on instrumental appetitive bar-pressing behavior. The authors found, as predicted in cell 1, that the CS previously paired with food increased bar-pressing behavior. In contrast, Trapold and Winokur observed that another stimulus paired with the absence of food decreased the instrumental appetitive bar-press response. These results agree with the cell-3 prediction. Bolles, Grossen, Hargrave, and Duncan (1970) made a similar observation: hope increased rats' appetitive instrumental alley running while disappointment decreased it.

A study by Grossen, Kostensek, and Bolles (1969) illustrates how hope (cell 2) and disappointment (cell 4) influence aversive behavior. In the first phase of the study, rats were trained to postpone shock by running from one compartment of a shuttle box to a second chamber and then back to the original compartment. Following the establishment of the avoidance response, one group of rats was exposed to tone-food pairings and another group to tones with no food. Results indicated that the tone suppressed avoidance behavior for the rats that received tone-food pairings but increased response for the rats given tones with no food. Apparently, the emotional response of hope inhibits an aversive instrumental behavior; disappointment, in comparison, increases avoidance behavior.

The emotional responses (fear and relief) acquired in aversive situations also influence instrumental behavior. A study by Annau and Kamin (1961) demonstrated how fear affects an appetitive bar-press response. The authors observed that a stimulus previously paired with shock suppressed their rats' bar-press behavior for food. These results support the prediction of cell 5: the aversive state, when activated by the feared stimulus, suppresses instrumental appetitive behavior. In addition to suppressing appetitive behavior, fear also enhances avoidance behavior (cell 6). The influence of fear on avoidance behavior is exemplified in a study by Martin and Riess (1969). Following the pairing of a light with shock, the conditioned fear stimulus increased the level of a previously learned instrumental bar-press avoidance response. Rescorla and Lo-Lordo (1965) demonstrated that a stimulus associated with the absence of shock suppressed an instrumental avoidance response. These results support the prediction of cell 8: stimuli associated with relief suppress avoidance behavior by activating the central appetitive state. Finally, Hammond (1966) showed that a stimulus paired with the absence of shock enhanced appetitive responding for food (see cell 7).

Our discussion indicates that emotional responses acquired through classical conditioning influence instrumental behavior. It should not be surprising that an appetitive emotional response (hope or disappointment) affects appetitive behavior or that an aversive emotional response (fear or relief) influences aversive behavior. What is surprising is the influence of appetitive conditioned responses on aversive behavior and aversive conditioned responses on appetitive behavior. Why should your relief which occurred when the fire alarm terminated stimulate your return to the theater and the movie? Or why should your anticipation of a pleasant television show reduce your aversive studying behavior? In asserting the existence of two central motivational states, Rescorla and Solomon's theory provides an answer to these questions. The aversive state is activated by stimuli associated with pain and frustration; the appetitive state stimulated by cues associated with reward and relief. An aversive conditioned response motivates avoidance behavior and suppresses approach behavior. However, an appetitive conditioned response initiates approach behavior and inhibits avoidance behavior. Considerable evidence indicates that there are two neural systems involved in the functions of the two central motivational states; that is, one system motivates us to approach reward, and the other system motivates us to avoid adversity. Furthermore, the appetitive system is activated by reward or stimuli associated with reward; the aversive system is aroused by adversity or stimuli associated with adversity. Chapter 10 describes where these two motivational states are located in the central nervous system as well as evidence that these two particular neural systems represent the two central motivational states in Rescorla and Solomon's theory.

APPLICATION: SYSTEMATIC DESENSITIZATION

Our discussion has focused on the principles governing the acquisition and extinction of a conditioned response. These principles have been applied in studies involving development or elimination of conditioned responses in real-world settings. One important application of classical conditioning has been the systematic desensitization therapy developed by Wolpe to inhibit phobic behavior (a *phobia* is an unrealistic fear of the phobic object). Let's now examine this technique's use of Pavlovian conditioning to alter pathological behavior; refer to Rimm and Masters (1979) for a more detailed discussion of these and other clinical applications.

Original Animal Studies

Wolpe's therapy evolved from his animal research. In an initial study (Wolpe, 1958), he shocked one group of cats in their home cages after they heard a buzzer. For the other cats, he paired the buzzer with eating in the home cages and then shocked them. Both groups of cats later showed extreme fear of the buzzer. One indication of their fear was their refusal to eat when hearing the buzzer. These results indicated to Wolpe that conflict—as proposed by Masserman in 1943—was not essential to produce neurotic reactions; Wolpe felt that human neurosis represented a classically conditioned fear response to a specific stimulus.

Since fear inhibited eating, Wolpe reasoned that eating could—if sufficiently intense—suppress fear. Also, Wolpe proposed that the repeated pairing of the reinforcing aspects of eating with the feared stimulus would cause the fear stimuli to become a permanent inhibitor rather than an elicitor of fear. The process of establishing a response which competes with a previously acquired response is called *counterconditioning* (see Chapter 1). Wolpe suggested that counterconditioning represented a potentially effective way of treating human phobic behavior. He based this idea on three lines of evidence: (1) Sherrington's statement (1906) that an animal can only experience one emotional state at a time—a process Wolpe termed *reciprocal inhibition,* (2) Jones's report (1924) that she had successfully eliminated a young boy's conditioned fear of rabbits by presenting the feared stimulus (a rabbit) while the boy was eating (see Chapter 1), and (3) Wolpe's research using a graduated counterconditioning process to eliminate his cats' phobia of their home cages.

Wolpe initially placed his phobic cats in a cage with food; this cage was quite dissimilar to their home cage. He used the dissimilar cage (which produced only a low fear level due to generalization) because use of the home cage would produce too intense a fear and therefore would inhibit eating. Wolpe observed that his cats ate in a dissimilar cage and did not appear afraid after eating. Wolpe concluded that in the dissimilar environment, the eating response had replaced the fear response. Once the fear to the dissimilar cage was extinguished, the cats were less fearful in another cage more closely resembling the feared home cage. The fear was reduced because the inhibition of fear conditioned to the dissimilar cage generalized to the second cage. The counterconditioning was now employed with this second cage, and Wolpe found that presentation of food in this cage quickly reversed the cats' fear. Wolpe continued the gradual counterconditioning treatment by slowly changing the characteristics of the test cage until the cats could eat in their home cage without any evidence of fear. Wolpe also found that a gradual exposure to the buzzer paired with food modified the cats' anxiety toward the buzzer.

Clinical Treatment

Wolpe (1958) asserted that human phobias could be eliminated in a manner similar to that employed with his cats. Wolpe chose not to use eating to inhibit human fears but instead used three classes of inhibitors: relaxation, assertion, and sexual responses. This chapter will discuss the use of relaxation.

Wolpe's therapy using relaxation to counter human phobic behavior is called *systematic desensitization*. Desensitization requires a patient to relax and to imagine anxiety-inducing scenes. To induce relaxation, Wolpe used a series of muscle exercises developed by Jacobson in 1938. These exercises involve tensing a particular muscle and then eliminating this tension. It is assumed that tension is related to anxiety and that tension reduction is relaxing (or reinforcing). The patient tenses and relaxes each major muscle group in a specific sequence. Rimm and Masters (1979) indicated that relaxation is effective when the tension phase lasts approximately ten seconds and is followed by 10–15 seconds of relaxation for each muscle group. The typical procedure requires about 30–40 minutes to complete; however, less time is needed later in therapy as patients become more adept. Once relaxed, patients are required to think of a specific word (for example, calm). This procedure, called *cue-controlled relaxation* by Russell and Sipich in 1973, causes the development of a conditioned relaxation response which enables relaxation to be elicited promptly by a specific stimulus; the patient is then quickly able to inhibit any anxiety occurring during therapy.

Once the patient has learned to relax, therapy can begin. The desensitization treatment consists of three phases: (1) the construction of the anxiety hierarchy, (2) actual counterconditioning—the pairing of relaxation with the feared stimuli, and (3) an assessment of whether the patient can successfully interact with the phobic project. In the first stage, patients are instructed to construct a graded series of anxiety-inducing scenes related to their phobia. The level of induced-anxiety must differ for the scenes; a 10- to 15-item list of low-, moderate-, and high-anxiety scenes is typically employed. Using index cards, a patient writes descriptions of the scenes and then ranks them in a hierarchy. To evaluate the level of anxiety elicited, the therapist then reads the descriptions of the scenes while the patient imagines them.

Paul (1969) identified two major types of hierarchies: thematic and spatial-temporal. In *thematic hierarchies,* the scenes relate to a basic theme. Table 2.2 presents a hierarchy detailing the anxiety experienced by an insurance sales-

TABLE 2.2
THEMATIC HIERARCHY OF ANXIETY

Level	Scene
1	You are in your office with an agent, R. C., discussing a prospective interview. The client in question is stalling on his payment, and you must tell R. C. what to do.
2	It is Monday morning and you are at your office. In a few minutes you will attend the regularly scheduled sales meeting. You are prepared for the meeting.
3	Conducting an exploratory interview with a prospective client.
4	Sitting at home. The telephone rings.
5	Anticipating returning a call from the district director.
6	Anticipating returning a call from a stranger.
7	Entering the Monday sales meeting unprepared.
8	Anticipating a visit from the regional director.
9	A fellow agent requests a joint visit with a client.
10	On a joint visit with a fellow agent.
11	Attempting to close a sale.
12	Thinking about attending an agents' and managers' meeting.
13	Thinking of contacting a client who should have been contacted earlier.
14	Thinking about calling a prospective client.
15	Thinking about the regional directors' request for names of prospective agents.
16	Alone, driving to prospective client's home.
17	Calling a prospective client.

Note: In the anxiety hierarchy, a higher level represents greater anxiety.
Source: Rimm, D. C. & Masters, J. C. *Behavior therapy: Techniques and empirical findings* (2d ed.). New York: Academic Press, 1979.

man when anticipating interactions with coworkers or clients. It is a thematic hierarchy; each scene in the hierarchy is somewhat different, but all relate to the salesman's fear of possible failure in professional situations. In contrast, a *spatial-temporal* hierarchy is based on a phobic behavior which has intensity determined by distance (either physical or temporal) to the feared object. The test-anxiety hierarchy shown in Table 2.3 indicates that the level of anxiety is related to the proximity to exam time.

One important aspect of the hierarchy presented in Table 2.3 needs mention. Perhaps contrary to your intuition, the patient experienced more anxiety enroute to the exam than when actually at the test area. Others have a different hierarchy such that they experience the most fear when taking the exam. Each phobic response is highly idiosyncratic and depends on one person's unique learning experience. Therefore, a hierarchy must be specially constructed for each patient. Some phobias combine thematic and spatial-temporal hierarchies. For example, a height phobic can experience varying levels of anxiety—at different places and at different distances from the edges of these places.

After the hierarchy is constructed, the counterconditioning phase of treatment begins. The patient is instructed to relax and imagine as clearly as possible the lowest scene on the hierarchy which the therapist is describing. Since even this scene elicits some anxiety, Rimm and Masters (1979) suggested that the first exposure be quite brief (5 seconds). The duration of the imagined scene can then be slowly increased as counterconditioning progresses. It is important that the patient not become anxious while picturing the scene; otherwise, additional anxiety rather than relaxation will be conditioned. The therapist instructs the patient to signal when anxious by raising a finger, and the therapist terminates the scene. After a scene has ended, the patient is instructed to relax. The scene can again be visualized when relaxation is reinstated. If the individual can imagine the first scene without any discomfort, the next highest scene in

TABLE 2.3
SPATIAL-TEMPORAL HIERARCHY OF ANXIETY

Level	Scene
1	Four days before an examination.
2	Three days before an examination.
3	Two days before an examination.
4	One day before an examination.
5	The night before an examination.
6	The examination paper lies face down before the student.
7	Awaiting the distribution of examination papers.
8	Before the unopened doors of the examination room.
9	In the process of answering an examination paper.
10	On the way to the university on the day of an examination.

Note: In the anxiety hierarchy, a higher level represents greater anxiety.
Source: Wolpe, J. *The practice of behavior therapy* (3rd Edition) Oxford: Pergamon, 1982.

the hierarchy is imagined. The process of slowly counterconditioning each level of the hierarchy is continued until the patient can imagine the most aversive scene without becoming anxious.

Clinical Effectiveness

The last phase of desensitization evaluates the therapy's success. To demonstrate the effectiveness of desensitization, the individual is required to encounter the phobic object. The success of desensitization as a treatment of phobic behavior is quite impressive. Wolpe (1958) reported that 90 percent of 210 patients showed significant improvement with desensitization compared to the 60 percent success rate when psychoanalysis was used. The comparison is more striking because desensitization produced a rapid extinction of phobic behavior (according to Wolpe, 1976, a range of twelve to twenty-nine sessions was effective) compared to the slower length of treatment (three to five years) necessary for psychoanalysis to cure phobic behavior. Although Lazarus (1971) reported that some patients showed a relapse in one to three years after therapy, their renewed anxiety could be readily reversed with additional desensitization. The list of phobias successfully treated or extinguished by desensitization is striking: fears of height, driving, snakes, dogs, insects, tests, water, flying, rejection by others, crowds, enclosed places, and injections are a few in a long list. In addition, desensitization apparently can be used with any behavior disorder initiated by anxiety. For instance, desensitization should be used to treat an alcoholic whose drinking occurs in response to anxiety.

Besides evaluating the effectiveness of desensitization, clinical research has determined the necessity of including relaxation or graded exposure into the desensitization treatment. Some studies (for example, Davison, 1968) found no improvement when relaxation was not part of the desensitization process, but other experiments (for example, Miller & Nowas, 1970) indicated that relaxation was not essential. Schubot (1966) reported that only extremely phobic individuals needed relaxation. Rimm and Masters (1979) suggested that only severely phobic people seek treatment; thus relaxation should be included in the desensitization therapy. In addition, Krapft (1967) discovered that presenting the scenes in a descending order was approximately as effective as the typically employed ascending order. The reduction in phobic behavior with use of the descending order is not surprising; the flooding technique (or forced exposure to the CS, see Chapter 4) shows that exposure to the feared stimulus is sufficient to eliminate phobic behavior. However, Rimm and Masters (1979) pointed out that intense fear is experienced if the items at the top of the hierarchy are presented first. In contrast, the generalization of relaxation occurring during the standard desensitization procedure reduces the anxiety level produced when the patient reaches the items at the top of the hierarchy. Thus, the graded ascending exposure is needed because it reduces the aversiveness of the therapy. Perhaps the most positive aspect of desensitization treatment is that it represents a relatively painless method of suppressing phobic behavior.

SUMMARY

Many environmental stimuli can produce internal reactions; these emotional responses often act to motivate our overt behavior. The hunger you experience while watching a commercial about food on television or the fear you experience when told of an impending exam are two examples of our emotional reaction to environmental stimuli. Furthermore, the hunger reaction may be sufficiently intense to motivate you to get a sandwich from the refrigerator, or the fear response may be sufficiently intense to motivate you to open your book and study for the test.

The ability of these environmental events to produce internal emotional reactions that motivate instrumental behavior develops through the classical conditioning process. Conditioning involves the pairing of a neutral environment cue with a biologically important event. Prior to conditioning, only the biologically important stimulus, called an unconditioned stimulus, can elicit a response. This response, called the unconditioned response, consists of both an overt muscular reaction and an internal emotional response. As the result of conditioning, the neutral environmental stimulus, now a conditioned stimulus, can also elicit a response, called the conditioned response. Although the conditioned response is often similar to the unconditioned response, it can be quite different. Research has demonstrated that the conditioned response is opposite to the unconditioned response when drugs are used as the unconditioned stimuli. The conditioning of responses opposite to the unconditioned responses appears to contribute to the development of tolerance and may occur as a conditioned homeostatic response which has adaptive value to an animal or person.

Although the pairing of the conditioned and the unconditioned stimulus is essential for the development of a conditioned response, it is not sufficient to ensure the acquisition of a conditioned response. Five additional factors determine whether a stimulus develops the ability to elicit a response. First, temporal contiguity must exist between the conditioned and the unconditioned stimuli. Second, the CS and the UCS must be sufficiently intense to ensure the development of the CR. Third, the conditioned stimulus must be a salient cue. Fourth, the conditioned stimulus must be a reliable predictor of the unconditioned stimulus. Fifth, the stimulus must not provide redundant information.

A number of theories regarding the nature of the process responsible for the acquisition of a conditioned response have been proposed. The Rescorla-Wagner model proposed that there is a maximum level of associative strength which can develop between a CS and a UCS as the result of conditioning. Furthermore, the amount of conditioning on a particular training trial depends not only on the strength of the CS and UCS but also on the level of prior training to the CS and on other stimuli present during conditioning. Although the Rescorla-Wagner model of conditioning has received considerable empirical support, three phenomena—potentiation, CS preexposure, and predictiveness—do not seem to be explainable within the context of the Rescorla-Wagner theory. According to Garcia and Rusiniak, potentiation may reflect a biological preparedness to associate odor cues with gastrointestinal distress when a taste cue is also present during conditioning. Mackintosh's attentional view suggests that the influence of CS preexposure on subsequent conditioning is due to subjects learning that the cue is irrelevant and consequently failing to attend to that cue when it is later paired with the UCS. Mackintosh also proposed that predictiveness influences the development of a conditioned response such that the identification of a cue which reliably precedes a biologically significant event causes a subject to ignore stimuli which provide redundant information.

Sometimes stimuli produce undesired conditioned emotional reactions. Extinction represents an effective method of eliminating the ability of the conditioned stimulus to elicit the conditioned response; the presentation of the CS without the UCS will cause a reduction in CR strength. With continued CS-alone presentations, eventually the conditioned stimulus will not elicit any response. Extinction of a conditioned response is thought to reflect an inhibitory process as well as changes either in an animal's motivational state or from the stimulus context present during conditioning. Other inhibitory processes which suppress conditioned responses include conditioned inhibition, external inhibition, and inhibition of delay. These inhibitory processes can be disrupted by presentation of a novel stimulus, causing a dishibition effect and resulting in an increased CR strength.

Conditioned stimuli not only elicit emotional reactions but also motivate instrumental activity. Stimuli paired with reward or with the absence of adversity motivate appetitive behavior and suppress avoidance responding. That these stimuli can influence behavior is due to their activation of a central appetitive motivational state or inhibition of a central aversive motivational state as a conditioned response. Other stimuli which are present with adversity or with the absence of reward motivate avoidance behavior and suppress appetitive behavior. These stimuli's ability to affect behavior is caused by their arousal of the central aversive motivational state and their inhibition of the central appetitive motivational state.

A conditioned stimulus can develop the ability to elicit the conditioned response indirectly; that is, without being directly associated with the UCS. Generalization represents one way that a CR can be acquired indirectly. Other methods include higher-order conditioning, sensory preconditioning, and vicarious conditioning.

The classical conditioning process has been applied in many natural settings. In one example, the association of a phobic object with relaxation suppresses phobic behavior. Classical conditioning plays an extremely important role in our lives; this chapter illustrates that significant contribution.

CHAPTER 3

INSTRUMENTAL APPETITIVE CONDITIONING

A LACK OF CONTROL

Professor Simpkins, Julia's teacher for her introductory psychology course, has just finished lecturing to the class about instrumental conditioning. Impressed by the powerful influence of reinforcement on behavior, Julia asks if instrumental conditioning can be used to teach her 6-year-old son to make his bed and clean his room. All other attempts to instill a sense of responsibility have been futile. Professor Simpkins tells Julia that reinforcement could, indeed, alter her son's behavior and gives a brief outline to be followed to obtain the desired results.

First, Julia must decide exactly what she wants her son to do to receive reward. Julia decides that her son should return his toys to the toy box before going to bed, put his clothes in the hamper, and make his bed. Second, a reinforcer must be chosen. Since movies are one of her son's favorite pastimes, Julie chooses going to the movies on Saturday afternoon as a reinforcer. Also, since the child must be aware of the specific behavior to be exhibited to receive reward, Dr. Simpkins suggests writing a contract specifying exactly what the boy must do to obtain his reward.

Dr. Simpkins also tells Julia that initially people sometimes have difficulty performing the required behavior and maintaining consistency. To ensure that Julia's son learns to behave effectively and consistently, Dr. Simpkins suggests using shaping—selecting a level of behavior that can be easily performed and then slowly changing the response requirement until only the final desired behavior will produce reinforcement. Julia decides that her son initially has to make his bed and clean his room only on weekends to obtain reward. Over a period of several weeks, Julia's son will be required to perform the tasks every other day. Furthermore, during the early phases of shaping, the boy needs only to provide a path to his bed and to place his clothes in the hamper. Also, he only has to spread the cover over his bed until required to clean his room everyday; then, the efficiency of bedmaking must improve until the bed is made neatly. To ensure accurate recording of the boy's behavior, Dr. Simpkins suggests keeping a chart on his door and checking it for appropriate behavior. He also emphasizes that this shaping procedure works only if record keeping is accurate and if reward is provided for appropriate behavior.

In this chapter, we will discuss how a reinforcement procedure similar to that outlined by Professor Simpkins has successfully altered behavior. We will also discuss the variables which influence the acquisition and the extinction of instrumental appetitive behavior. Let's begin by examining B. F. Skinner's contribution to our understanding of instrumental conditioning.

SKINNER'S BEHAVIORISM

Types of Learning

In 1938, Skinner identified two types of learning: respondent and operant conditioning. *Respondent conditioning* refers to the learning situation investigated by Pavlov: the conditioned and unconditioned stimuli are paired, and the conditioned stimulus subsequently elicits the conditioned response. In this type of learning, the animal or human passively responds to an environmental stimulus. Respondent behaviors are primarily internal responses in the form of emotional and glandular reactions to stimuli. However, Skinner was most interested in operant conditioning, the type of learning situation investigated by Thorndike (see Chapter 1). Skinner asserted that in *operant conditioning,* an animal or human actively interacts with the environment to obtain reward. Operant behavior is not elicited by a stimulus; rather, in anticipation of the consequences of the behavior, an animal or person voluntarily emits specific behavior when that behavior produces reinforcement. Skinner called this relationship between behavior and reinforcement a *contingency*. The environment determines contingencies, and the animal or human must emit the appropriate behavior to obtain a reinforcer.

Consider the following two examples to illustrate the instrumental conditioning process. Recall from Chapter 2 that you become hungry when arriving home from school. Your hunger motivates you to go to the refrigerator and to remove pie and milk. The action of going to the refrigerator is an instrumental response which occurs because you have learned the contingency between going to the refrigerator and obtaining food. Chapter 2 also detailed the development of fear; fear is induced when an examination is scheduled, motivating you to study. Studying for an examination is also an instrumental behavior. There is a contingency between studying and avoiding adversity; our understanding of this contingency motivates us to study when the scheduled examination is announced. Since much of our behavior is instrumental, the acquisition of instrumental appetitive behavior is detailed in this chapter. The process responsible for the development of instrumental aversive behavior will be described in the next chapter.

Skinner, wanting to use terminology that pointed out the critical difference between the two forms of learning, replaced the terms *Pavlovian* and *instrumental conditioning* with *respondent* and *operant conditioning*. However, although two forms of learning do clearly exist, Skinner's terminology does not accurately describe their characteristics. Conditioned responses are not a passive reaction to an environmental event; instead, the perceived predictiveness of the conditioned stimulus determines whether an animal or person exhibits the conditioned response. Also, although instrumental behavior is not elicited by conditioned stimuli, central-nervous-system structures aroused by conditioned stimuli and unconditioned stimuli motivate instrumental behavior. Skinner's terminology has not replaced the Pavlovian and instrumental conditioning terms, and the terms *Pavlovian* and *instrumental conditioning* are used frequently in this book.

Methodology

Skinner was extremely imaginative. Since he needed only a simply structured environment to study instrumental behavior, he invented his own. This apparatus, called an *operant chamber* by Skinner, creates an enclosed environment with a small bar on the inside wall. There is a dispenser for presenting either food or liquid reinforcement when a rat presses the bar. (A more elaborate version of an operant chamber presents tones or lights to study generalization and discrimination.) The operant chamber has been modified to accommodate many different animal species. Figure 3.1 presents a basic operant chamber, for use with pigeons, in which a pecking key replaces the bar press used for rats and some other species.

In addition to his well-known box and many other ingenious inventions, Skinner developed his own methodology to study behavior. More interested in observing the rate of a behavior than the intensity of a specific response, he developed the cumulative recorder (refer to Figure 3.1). The pen attached to the recorder moves at a specific rate across the page; at the same time, each bar-press response produces an upward movement on the pen, thus enabling the experimenter to determine the rate of behavior.

Other apparatuses have been used to investigate the instrumental conditioning process. For example, psychologists have designed runways and T-mazes to evaluate the factors which affect the acquisition of an instrumental response (see Figure 3.2). Research using each apparatus has enhanced our knowledge of the instrumental conditioning process; similar results from research using many different apparatuses point to the generality of the principles governing instrumental conditioning.

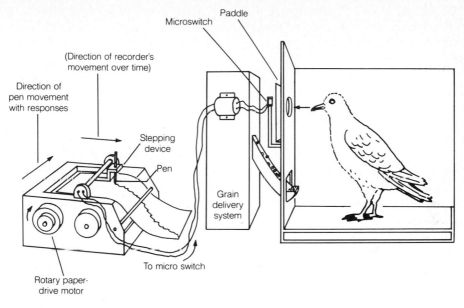

Cumulative recorder   Operant chamber

FIGURE 3.1
Operant chamber designed for pigeons. When the pigeon pecks the key, reinforcement (a pellet) is delivered. Each peck produces an upward deflection on the cumulative recorder, providing a permanent record of the pigeon's behavior. From *Theories of learning* by L. C. Swenson © 1980 by Wadsworth, Inc. Reprinted by permission of the publisher.

ACQUISITION OF INSTRUMENTAL APPETITIVE BEHAVIOR

Most people not only recognize that reinforcement has an important impact on behavior but also suggest that reward can be used to motivate people to act in a certain manner. Furthermore, when asked to define a reinforcer, these individuals most often say that reward is something a person likes. The following section points out that this intuitive understanding of reinforcement, although not very scientific, is fairly accurate.

The Reinforcement Process

Unlike the learning theories described in Chapter 1, Skinner's theories (1938) did not specify the underlying mechanism of reinforcement; instead, Skinner considered showing the effect of reinforcement on behavior to be sufficient. According to Skinner, a *reinforcer* is an event which increases the frequency of the behavior preceding it. One cannot predict whether an event will be a reinforcer: the influence of the event on behavior determines if it is a reinforce-

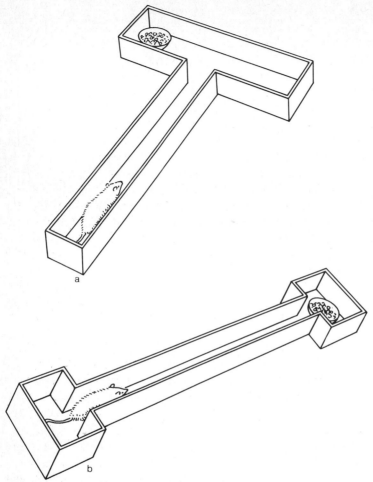

FIGURE 3.2
(a) A simple T maze. In this maze, the rat must learn whether to turn
left or right to obtain reinforcement. (b) A runway. In this apparatus,
the rat receives reward when it reaches the goal box; latency to run
down the alley is the index of performance. Adapted from Fantino, E.,
& Logan, C. A. *The experimental analysis of behavior: A biological
perspective.* San Francisco: Freeman, 1979.

ment. For example, a piece of candy may be an effective reinforcer for some
children but not for others. Only observing what influence candy has on a
particular child's behavior can determine its reinforcing value.

Activities as Reinforcers   We usually assume that reinforcers are things like
food or water. However, activities can also be reinforcement for behavior. For
example, allowing children to watch television or to go to the movies can be

reinforcement for studying. Although food and going to the movies appear to be very different types of reinforcers, Premack's (1959, 1965) analysis of reinforcement indicates that all reinforcers share a common attribute. According to Premack, a reinforcer is any activity whose probability of occurring is greater than the reinforced behavior. Therefore, a movie can be a reinforcer for studying if the likelihood of going to the movie is greater than the probability of studying. In Premack's view, it is the eating response to food, not food per se, which is the reinforcer. Since eating is a more probable behavior than bar pressing, eating can reinforce bar pressing.

Premack's study (1965) using rats illustrates the reinforcing character of high-probability activities. In this study, two behaviors were possible: running on a wheel or drinking from a tube. The probability of these two activities could be controlled: the running response, by engaging or releasing a brake; the drinking response, by moving the tube into or out of an opening on the cage. Premack maintains that restriction should increase the probability of a behavior; that is, a restricted response is more probable than a freely available response. For some rats, drinking was restricted while running was possible; thus, drinking was the more probable response. Premack reported that the running rate for these subjects was higher when running produced the drinking tube than when it had no influence on the likelihood of drinking. For other rats, running was the more probable response because running was restricted while the lick tube was available. Lick rate for these subjects was higher when licking released the brake on the wheel than when the lick response had no effect on running. Other experiments with rats have also found that a higher-probability response reinforces a lower-probability response; see Premack, Schaeffer, and Hundt (1964) for another study.

Premack (1959) has also evaluated his view of reinforcement with children. He placed a pinball machine next to a candy dispenser. In the first phase of the study, Premack observed the children's relative rate of responding to each activity. Some children played pinball more frequently than they ate candy and were labeled "manipulators"; other children ate candy more often than they played pinball and were labeled "eaters." During the second phase of the study, manipulators had to eat to play the pinball machine, and eaters were required to play the pinball machine to get candy. Premack reported that eating increased the number of times the eaters played the pinball machine; playing the pinball machine increased the number of pieces of candy eaten by manipulators.

Homme, deBaca, Devine, Steinhorst, and Rickert (1963) evaluated the ability of activity to control the behavior of nursery-school children. In their study, low-probability behaviors like sitting quietly and looking at the blackboard were reinforced with the opportunity to engage in high-probability behaviors such as running around the room and pushing chairs. During the early stage of the study, the high-probability activities followed the low-frequency behaviors; later in the study, the children could earn tokens for low-probability behaviors that allowed them to purchase high-probability preferred activities. Homme, deBaca, Devine, Steinhorst, and Rickert reported that after a few days this reinforcement procedure resulted in the children being quiet and attentive. These results suggest that any response can act as a reinforcer when the probability of that activity occurring is greater than that of the reinforced behavior.

Why are certain activities reinforcing? Timberlake and Allison's (1974) theory provides one likely explanation. According to Timberlake and Allison, animals are programmed to exhibit a specific level of responding to objects important to their survival. For example, a rat given free access to food will consume approximately the same amount of food each day; the rat responds to food at the same level each day because it is adaptive and enhances the rat's chances of survival. When an animal's access to an object is restricted and, therefore, its level of responding is lowered, the animal will be motivated to return to its previous level of responding. As the result of food deprivation, the rat's biological structure will cause it to engage in behavior which will gain access to food and, thereby, restore responding to the predeprivation level. Further, Timberlake and Allison assert that a certain activity is a reinforcer when the establishment of a behavior-reward contingency restricts the opportunity to participate in that activity; in turn, the animal increases the level of instrumental behavior to return the performance of the restricted activity to its baseline precontingency level.

Timberlake and Allison conducted a number of studies which support their theory that an animal increases the level of instrumental behavior to reestablish the baseline level of the restricted activity. In one study, animals were deprived access to a running wheel, and a contingency was established so that the rat had to drink to gain access to the wheel. Even though the rat's baseline level of responding was higher for drinking than running, Timberlake and Allison found that the contingency between drinking and running led to an increase in the rat's level of drinking. Apparently, restricting access to an activity causes that activity to act as a reinforcer. These results indicate that the relative level of responding does not determine whether an activity acts as a reinforcer. Instead, restriction can cause any activity to increase the response level of another activity that will provide access to the restricted one.

Termination of Adversity The occurrence of a desired event (or a high-probability activity) is not the only type of reinforcer. Termination of an aversive event (for example, shock) can also be reinforcing. When the reinforcer is the termination of an aversive event, the reinforcer is referred to as a *negative reinforcer*. In contrast, a *positive reinforcer* is an activity such as eating food or going to the movies. Skinner (1938) observed that an animal can learn to bar press not only to produce food but also to turn off shock. The acquisition of a behavior which terminates an aversive event is called *escape conditioning*. This chapter describes the development of responses using positive reinforcers; the acquisition of an escape response as the result of negative reinforcement will be detailed in Chapter 4.

Types of Reinforcers   Skinner identified two types of reinforcers, primary and secondary. *Primary reinforcers* have innate reinforcing properties; *secondary reinforcers* develop their reinforcing properties through their association with primary reinforcers. For example, food is a primary reinforcer; money is a secondary one.

A number of variables affect the strength of a secondary reinforcer. First, *the amount of primary reinforcement paired with a secondary reinforcing stimulus influences the reinforcing power of a secondary reinforcer.* D'Amato (1955) placed five pellets in one arm of a T-maze and one pellet in the other arm. When he later tested animals without reward present, he found that rats made significantly more responses to the cue associated with the large reward. Thus a stimulus paired with a large reward acquires more reinforcing properties than does a cue associated with a small reward. Other experiments have also reported that the value of the primary reward influences the strength of a secondary reinforcer (see Lawson, 1957, for a similar study).

Second, *the number of pairings of the secondary reinforcing stimulus and primary reinforcer affects the strength of the secondary reinforcer.* Many experiments showed that the more often a secondary reinforcing stimulus is paired with a primary reinforcer, the stronger the reinforcing power of the secondary reinforcer (see Bersh, 1951; Hall, 1951a; Miles, 1956). For example, Bersh (1951) presented a 3-second light cue prior to 10, 20, 40, 80, or 120 reinforcements (food) for bar pressing. After training, primary reinforcement was discontinued and the bar-press response extinguished; this procedure reduced the bar-press response strength for all subjects. The testing phase consisted of the presentation of the light following a bar-press response. As seen in Figure 3.3, the number of responses to the light cue during testing increased as a function of light-food pairings; thus the reinforcing power of a secondary reinforcer increases with more pairings of the secondary reinforcing stimulus and the primary reinforcer.

Third, *the time elapsing between the presentation of a secondary reinforcing stimulus and the primary reinforcer affects the strength of the secondary reinforcer.* Bersh (1951) varied the interval between light and food reinforcement in an operant chamber; the food followed the light stimulus by 0.5, 1, 2, 4, or 10 seconds. Bersh observed that the number of responses emitted to obtain the light cue decreased as the interval between the secondary and the primary reinforcer increased. Bersh's results indicate that the power of a secondary reinforcer decreases as the interval between the secondary reinforcer stimulus and the primary reinforcer increases. Jenkins (1950) also observed that the strength of a secondary reinforcer was influenced by the temporal delay between the onset of the secondary and primary reinforcers.

We have discovered that the value of the primary reinforcer, the number of pairings, and the temporal delay affect the reinforcing strength of a secondary reinforcer. The influence of these variables is not surprising: secondary reinforcers acquire their reinforcing ability through the Pavlovian conditioning pro-

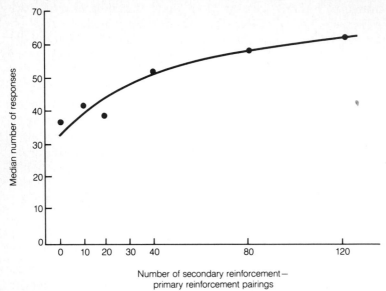

FIGURE 3.3
The strength of a secondary reinforcer as a function of the number of secondary and primary reinforcer pairings during acquisition. The measure of the power of the secondary reinforcer is the number of responses emitted during the first 10 minutes of testing. Adapted from Bersh, P. J. The influence of two variables upon the establishment of a secondary reinforcer for operant responses. *Journal of Experimental Psychology*, 1951, *41*, 62–73. Copyright 1951 by the American Psychological Association. Reprinted by permission.

cess. As we learned in Chapter 2, these variables influence the association of a conditioned stimulus and an unconditioned stimulus.

Conditioned and unconditioned stimuli possess motivational properties (see Chapter 2). Primary and secondary reinforcers also motivate behavior; for example, food motivates you to eat, and money motivates you to spend. Secondary reinforcers acquire motivational character through the Pavlovian conditioning process; that is, primary and secondary reinforcers can motivate behavior because the secondary reinforcer (for example, money) is a conditioned stimulus and the primary reinforcer (for example, food) is an unconditioned stimulus. Recall from Chapter 2 that both conditioned stimuli (secondary reinforcers) and unconditioned stimuli (primary reinforcers) arouse the appetitive motivational state, which results in the activation of instrumental appetitive behavior. Chapter 10 will discuss how both primary and secondary reinforcers activate the central nervous system's reward system. Activity in this reward system reinforces behavior and produces the arousal that motivates further appetitive responding.

Shaping

The environment specifies the behavior necessary to obtain reinforcement. However, many operant behaviors occur infrequently or not at all, making it unlikely that the animal or person will experience the behavior-reinforcement contingency. Such conditions result in either no change or only a slow change in the frequency of the behavior's occurrence. Skinner (1938) developed a procedure called *shaping,* also known as the *successive approximation procedure,* to ensure that the instrumental behavior would be learned quickly. During shaping, a behavior whose baseline rate of responding is higher than that of the desired behavior is selected and reinforced. When this behavior increases in frequency, the contingency is then changed, and behavior which is a closer approximation to the desired final behavior is reinforced. The contingency is slowly changed until the only way the animal or person can obtain reward is to emit the appropriate behavior.

Training a Rat to Bar-Press   Many scientists have demonstrated that the successive-approximation technique effectively and quickly modifies behavior. Let us consider two examples of shaping behavior. How can an experimenter train a rat to bar-press to obtain reinforcement? A rat's operant rate of bar pressing is not zero, since an animal exploring a small operant chamber may hit the bar. Therefore, the rat could possibly learn on its own. However, this self-training procedure is often slow, and the speed of learning varies considerably between animals. Shaping of bar pressing ensures a rapid acquisition of desired behavior. The first stage of the shaping procedure involves reinforcing the high operant feeding response which occurs at the beginning of training when hungry rats exhibit a high rate of eating food from the dispenser. When this feeding behavior occurs consistently (which will be only a short time after training begins), the contingency must be changed to a closer approximation of the final bar-press response.

The second stage of shaping reinforces the rat when it is moving away from the food dispenser (refer to Figure 3.4). The change in contingency causes the rat to move away from the empty dispenser. This response triggers the dispensation of food. The clicking sound made by the pellet dispenser, a cue the rat associated with food in the first stage of training, motivates the animal to return to the dispenser. This procedure reinforces moving away from the dispenser, a behavior closer to the bar-press response than to eating from the food dispenser. The moving-away response continues to be reinforced until the behavior occurs consistently; then the contingency is changed again.

In the third phase of shaping, the rat is reinforced only for moving away from the dispenser in the direction of the bar. The change in contingency causes the rat to move in a number of directions. The experimenter must wait, reinforcing only movement toward the bar. Once this response occurs consistently, the contingency is again changed; the rat must move closer to the bar. The shaping

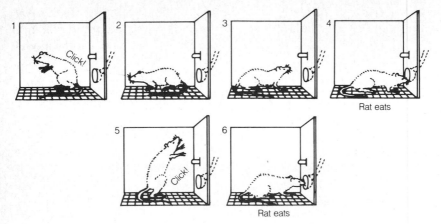

FIGURE 3.4
Shaping a bar-press response in rats. In the initial phase, the rat is reinforced for eating out of the pellet dispenser (not pictured). During the second phase of shaping (scenes 1, 2, 3, and 4), the rat must move away from the dispenser to receive reward. The click sound motivates the rat to return to the food. Later in the shaping process (scenes 5 and 6), the rat must move toward the bar for food. From *Psychology,* by Camille Wortman and Elizabeth F. Loftus. Copyright 1981 by Alfred A. Knopf, Inc. Reprinted by permission of the publisher.

procedure reinforces closer and closer approximations until the rat presses the bar. At this point, shaping is complete, and the final behavior is reinforced automatically. The use of shaping to develop a bar-press response is a reliable technique; most rats learn to bar-press in approximately an hour. Let's consider a real-world application of the shaping technique.

Learning to Use a Knife   Many parents struggle to teach their children how to use knives. Although most children in our culture eventually learn to use a knife, the rate at which this skill is acquired varies greatly from one child to the next. Some learn slowly; others require an enormous amount of time to discover this simple action. Many parents undoubtedly use reinforcement (probably praise) as well as punishment (probably scolding) for attempting proper usage, but parents typically reinforce only the final response. Since children need considerable practice to learn to use a knife effectively, they may experience much frustration before acquiring the proper technique.

Parents can employ the shaping technique to help their children to learn rapidly to eat with a knife. Parents should begin by reinforcing a behavior their children can readily perform (for example, simply holding the knife) and should then change the contingency once the child has learned this first step. Now the child must attempt to cut food with a knife to be reinforced. By successively reinforcing behavior which more closely resembles the final desired behavior, parents can quickly have their children eating properly with knives.

We have learned that the contingency between behavior and reinforcement influences how we act. Our discussion has focused on situations in which a single behavior produces reinforcement. However, reinforcement typically is not programmed to occur like this: usually, we must learn not only how to act but also how often and/or when. Skinner's research (Ferster & Skinner, 1957; Skinner, 1938) called the aspect of the contingency that specifies how often or when we must act to receive reinforcement the *schedule of reinforcement*.

Schedules of Reinforcement

Reinforcement can be provided on the basis of the number of responses emitted. A situation in which the contingency specifies that a certain number of responses are necessary to produce reinforcement was labeled a *ratio schedule of reinforcement* by Skinner (1938).

Reinforcement can also be scheduled on a time basis; Skinner called the programming of reinforcement on the basis of time an *interval schedule of reinforcement*. In an interval schedule, reinforcement becomes available at a certain period of time after the last reinforcement. Any behavior occurring during the interval receives no reinforcement, and the first response occurring at the end of the interval is reinforced. Note that in an interval schedule reward must be obtained before another interval begins. For example, if a rat is scheduled to be reinforced for bar pressing on a 1-minute interval schedule of reinforcement but waits 2 minutes to respond, it is reinforced then and the next reward becomes available 1 minute later. Since the rat could have earned two rewards, the delay in its behavior cost it the reward that would have been obtained if the animal had responded at the end of the 1-minute interval.

Furthermore, both ratio and interval schedules can be further classified into fixed and variable reinforcement schedules. In a fixed-ratio (FR) schedule, a constant number of responses are necessary to produce reinforcement. For example, in an FR-10 schedule, a rat must bar-press ten times to receive reward. The person who gets a dollar for every ten telephone books delivered is being rewarded on a fixed-ratio schedule. In contrast, in a variable-ratio (VR) schedule, an average number of responses produces reinforcement; the exact number of responses required for reinforcement varies from reward to reward. For example, a rat must bar-press on the average of ten times to receive reward on a VR-10 schedule; in this schedule, sometimes two bar presses produce reward, whereas other times fifty bar presses are needed. A real-world example of a VR schedule would be a door-to-door salesperson who makes two consecutive sales on one occasion and at other times knocks on fifty doors between sales.

In a fixed-interval (FI) schedule of reinforcement, the same interval always intervenes between available rewards. For example, in an FI 1-minute schedule, the rat must wait 1 minute following reinforcement for the opportunity to receive another reinforcement. A real-world example of an FI schedule would be making gelatin. After cooking, the gelatin is placed in the refrigerator to harden. After a while the gelatin is ready, but the individual can wait a few hours or even a few days before going to the refrigerator and obtaining the gelatin reward. Also, reinforcement can become available after a varying interval of time. With a variable-interval (VI) schedule, there is an average interval between available reinforcements, but the exact interval between each reinforcement differs. A rat reinforced on a VI 1-minute schedule must wait on the average 1 minute between rewards; however, the exact time between rewards changes after each reinforcement. Consider the following example to illustrate a variable-interval schedule. Suppose that a child regularly mows a neighbor's yard; the child is instructed to mow the yard when the grass is approximately two inches high. Although this contingency means that the child will mow approximately every week, mowing may be required more often than weekly if it rains heavily; no rain may mean that the child can wait 10 days or 2 weeks to mow.

We have discussed four types of reinforcement schedules, FR, VR, FI, and VI, in which reinforcement is programmed on the basis of either time between available reinforcement, called interval schedules, or number of responses necessary to obtain reinforcement, called ratio schedules. Furthermore, reward can occur after a fixed or a variable number of responses or after a fixed or a variable amount of time. These schedules of reinforcement have an important influence on our behavior. Pattern and intensity of behavior are very different depending on the type of reinforcement schedule. Let's now briefly examine the behavioral characteristics of these reinforcement schedules. [See Ferster and Skinner (1957) for a detailed discussion of schedules of reinforcement.]

Fixed-Ratio Schedules   On a fixed-ratio schedule, a specific number of responses are necessary to produce reinforcement. The animal or person receives reinforcement after a single response in an FR-1 (or continuous reinforcement schedule, CRF) schedule. Likewise, ten responses must occur to receive reinforcement on an FR-10 schedule.

Fixed-ratio schedules produce a consistent response rate, that is, an animal or person responds at a steady rate during the entire time that reinforcement is possible or until satiation occurs (refer to Figure 3.5). Furthermore, the intensity of responding increases with higher FR schedules. For example, Collier, Hirsch, and Hamlin (1972) notes that rats bar-press at a higher rate on an FR-20 than FR-10 schedule and higher still on an FR-60 than FR-40 one (see Figure 3.6). Similar results were obtained with pigeons (Felton & Lyon, 1966), cats (Kanarek, 1974), prairie dogs (Todd & Cogan, 1978), and children (Stephens, Pear, Wray, & Jackson, 1975).

Fixed-ratio schedules have a distinctive characteristic. Following reinforcement, responding will stop. The pause after reinforcement is called a *postreinforcement pause*. After the pause, responding resumes at the rate present before reinforcement. Therefore, the animal or person on a fixed-ratio schedule either responds at the intensity characteristic of that ratio or does not respond at all. A postreinforcement pause is not observed with all fixed-ratio schedules.

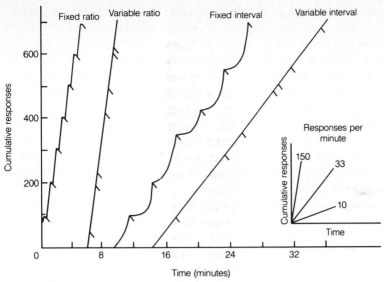

FIGURE 3.5
Samples of cumulative records of bar-press responding under the simple
schedules of reinforcement. The slash marks on the response records
indicate the presentations of reward.

FIGURE 3.6
Cumulative response records on various fixed-ratio schedules. Note that the rate of
responding increases with higher FR ratios, and the postreinforcement behavior occurs
only at highest FR schedules. From Collier, G., Hirsch, E., & Hamlin, P. H. The ecological
determinants of reinforcement in the rat. *Physiology and Behavior*, 1972, *9*, 705–716.
Copyright 1972, Pergamon Press, Ltd.

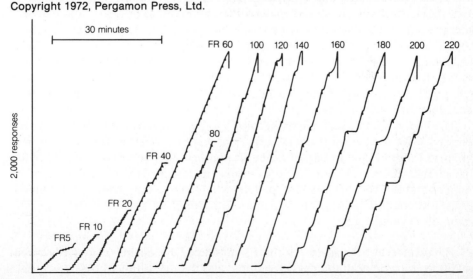

The higher the number of responses needed to obtain reinforcement, the more likely it is that a pause will follow reinforcement. As seen in Figure 3.6, there is no pause after reinforcement on an FR-100 schedule, but pause behavior follows reward on an FR-200 schedule. The length of the pause also varies; the higher the ratio schedule, the longer the pause (see Felton & Lyon, 1966; Todd & Cogan, 1978). Felton and Lyon observed that pigeons pause for about 1.5 seconds on an FR-25 schedule compared to a pause of almost a minute on an FR-150 schedule; Todd & Cogan found that prairie dogs paused longer on an FR-90 than an FR-60 schedule of reinforcement. Other researchers (for example, Collier, Hirsch, & Hamlin, 1972) have noted that the greater the effort necessary to obtain reward, the longer the pause after receiving reinforcement. The length of the pause also depends on satiation (Sidman & Stebbins, 1954). Sidman and Stebbins found that the greater the satiation, the longer the pause following reinforcement.

Postreinforcement pause behavior can be seen in humans. The persistent writing behavior of an author while writing a textbook followed by a vacation after the book is completed is one example of a pause in behavior after reinforcement on a fixed-ratio schedule.

Variable-Ratio Schedules   On a variable-ratio schedule, an average number of responses produces reinforcement, but the actual number of responses changes from reinforcement to reinforcement. Like the fixed-ratio schedules, VR schedules produce a consistent response rate (refer to Figure 3.5). Furthermore, the greater the average responses necessary to produce reinforcement, the higher the response rate. For example, Felton and Lyon (1966) found that rats bar-press at a higher rate on a VR-200 than a VR-50. Similarly, Ferster and Skinner (1957) observed that pigeons' rate of key pecking was higher on a VR-100 than a VR-50 and still higher on a VR-200 schedule of reinforcement.

In contrast to the pause after receiving reinforcement on a fixed-ratio schedule, postreinforcement pauses occur only occasionally on variable-ratio schedules (see Felton & Lyon, 1966, or Ferster & Skinner, 1957). The relative absence of pause behavior after reinforcement on VR schedules results in a higher response rate on a VR than on a comparable FR schedule. Thus, rats bar-press more times during an hour session with a VR-50 than an FR-50 schedule (see Figure 3.5).

The high response rate occurring with VR schedules can explain the persistent and vigorous behavior characteristic of gambling. For example, a slot machine is programmed to pay off after an average number of operations. However, the exact number of operations necessary to obtain reward is unpredictable. The behavior of people who play a slot machine for hours, constantly putting money into it, occurs because of the variable-ratio programming of slot machines.

Fixed-Interval Schedules   In the FI schedule, the occurrence of reinforcement depends on both the passage of time and the exhibition of the appropriate behavior. Reinforcement is not available until after a specified period of time, and the first response emitted after the interval is reinforced. Therefore, a rat on an FI 1-minute schedule is reinforced for the first bar press after the minute interval has elapsed; in contrast, a rat on an FI 2-minute schedule must wait 2 minutes before its response is reinforced.

Fixed-interval schedules also produce a characteristic response pattern (refer to Figure 3.5). An animal or person stops responding after receiving reinforcement on an FI schedule and then slowly increases responding as the time for reinforcement to become available approaches. The pause after reinforcement and the slow increase in response rate observed on the cumulative record was referred to as the *scallop effect* by Ferster and Skinner (1957). The scallop effect has been observed in a number of species, including pigeons (Catania & Reynolds, 1968; Dews, 1962), rats (Innis, 1979; Madigan, 1978), and humans (Shimoff, Catania, & Matthews, 1981).

Two variables affect the length of the postreinforcement pause seen on FI schedules. First, the ability to withhold responding until close to the end of the interval increases with experience (Cruser & Klein, 1984; Schneider, 1969). Second, the pause is longer with longer FI schedules (Gentry, Weiss, & Laties, 1983; Schneider, 1969).

Although a considerable amount of research has investigated fixed-interval schedules, few real-world situations reward behavior on a fixed-interval schedule. Consider the example of a person being paid once a week, a situation often used to illustrate behavior rewarded on a fixed-interval schedule. In reality, being paid weekly is not an example of a fixed-interval schedule; instead, a weekly paycheck reflects the operation of response-cost or negative punishment (refer to Chapter 4). In a response-cost situation, a person receives reward (money) noncontingently or without having to perform a specific behavior but can lose the money by failing to perform the appropriate behavior (and thus getting fired). Interestingly, people often act as if they are being paid on a fixed-interval schedule, indicating that individuals do not always recognize the actual environmental contingencies and behave according to the perceived contingency between behavior and reinforcement.

Variable-Interval Schedules   On a VI schedule, the interval of time between available reinforcements is an average; however, the interval of time varies from one reinforcement to the next. For example, the average interval is 2 minutes on a VI 2-minute schedule, but the rat may wait 1 minute between reinforcements one time and 5 minutes the next time.

Variable-interval schedules are characterized by a steady rate of responding (see Figure 3.5). Furthermore, the rate of responding is affected by VI length— the longer the average interval between reinforcements, the lower the response rate. For example, Catania and Reynolds (1968) discovered that pigeons responded 60 to 100 times per minute on a VI 2-minute schedule, but only 20 to 70 times per minute on a VI 7.1-minute schedule. Similar results were obtained by Nevin (1973) in rats and by Todd and Cogan (1978) in prairie dogs.

The scallop effect characteristic of FI schedules does not occur on VI schedules: no pause follows reinforcement on a VI schedule. However, Catania and Reynolds (1968) reported that the maximum rate of responding on VI schedules occurred just prior to reward.

Differential-Rate Schedules   In many situations, a specific number of behaviors must occur or not occur within a specified amount of time for reinforcement to be obtained. When reinforcement depends on both time and the number of responses, the schedule uses a *differential rate of reinforcement*. For example, students required to complete an assignment during a semester are being reinforced on a differential-rate schedule. Why is this not an example of a fixed-interval schedule? A fixed-interval schedule uses no time limit for the occurrence of the appropriate behavior; in a differential rate schedule, if the behavior does not occur within the time limit, no reinforcement is provided. We will now discuss three important types of differential-rate schedules.

DRH Schedules   Reinforcement can be scheduled contingent on a high rate of responding; this schedule is called a *differential rate of high responding (DRH) schedule*. Consider the following example of a DRH schedule. Your instructor assigns a paper due in two weeks. It must be at least 10 typed pages. In this situation, a substantial amount of effort must be exerted in a short time to complete the assignment. Although aversive, you will work hard to complete the assignment if your behavior is controlled by the DRH schedule of reinforcement.

DRH schedules are extremely effective. Animals exhibit a consistently high rate of responding when reinforcement is provided on a DRH schedule (Catania, 1979). For example, a pigeon on this schedule can learn to peck a key more than ten times per second. However, DRH schedules contain an inherent danger. If the high level of responding needed to produce reward cannot be maintained, the animal will receive less reward. This lowered reinforcement further decreases the response rate. In a vicious cycle, the response rate and the obtained reward decline until no responses are emitted. Therefore, the response rate of the DRH schedule must not be too high, ensuring that consistent responding occurs.

Interestingly, people often respond to a DRH schedule as if it is an FI schedule. For example, a scheduled exam is a DRH schedule; that is, a high rate of responding is necessary to obtain a good grade. However, most students treat exams as they would an FI schedule: they stop responding after an exam and slowly increase their response rate until they are "cramming" for the next test. By limiting studying to just prior to examinations, students are not likely to respond enough to do well. Thus, students do not always respond appropriately. Obviously, the most effective strategy is to respond throughout the interval, which is the response pattern characteristic of DRH schedules. Several ways exist to ensure that students respond appropriately. For example, the interval between tests could be shortened to reduce pause behavior, or papers due shortly after their assignment could replace exams.

DRL Schedules   Reinforcement can be scheduled contingent upon a low
rate of responding; this schedule is a *differential rate of low responding (DRL)
schedule*. On this schedule, a certain interval of time must elapse without a
response, and the first response at the end of the interval is reinforced. If an
animal or person responds during the interval, the interval is reset and the
response withheld for the length of time specified in the contingency. The
following example illustrates the DRL schedule: Attempting to start your car,
you flood the engine. If you try to start it before waiting several minutes, it will
flood again, and you will have to wait a few more minutes before it will start.
Thus, to start your engine after flooding it, you must withhold your starting
behavior for several minutes.

DRH schedules produce high rates of responding. In contrast, DRL schedules limit the response rate. DRL schedules, like DRH schedules, provide for
effective control of behavior; that is, animals or persons respond according to
the schedule of reinforcement. However, DRL schedules, unlike DRH schedules, require time to become effective (Reynolds, 1968). The effect of reinforcement is an increase in the frequency of a reinforced behavior, but with DRL
schedules an increase in the response rate acts to prevent reinforcement. The
absence of reinforcement lowers the response rate. Eventually, the influence of
the schedule appears, and the animal or person is able to withhold responding
until the end of the interval (see Figure 3.7).

DRO Schedules   Providing reinforcement only if there is an *absence* of a
particular response in a specified period of time is called *differential reinforcement of other behaviors* (DRO). The DRO schedule is unique in that it reinforces the failure to exhibit a specific behavior in a particular time period.
Suppose that a parent informs his or her child that hitting a younger sibling

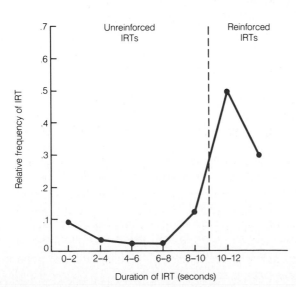

FIGURE 3.7
Relative frequency distribution of
interresponse times in rats
receiving reward on a 10-second
DRL schedule. Adapted from *A
primer of operant conditioning* by
G. S. Reynolds. Copyright 1968 by
Scott, Foresman, and Company.
Reprinted by permission.

again before dinner will result in no television viewing that evening. In this situation, the parent is using a DRO schedule; that is, in order for the child to watch television (reinforcement), no aggressive responses can occur prior to dinner.

Compound Schedules The contingency between behavior and reward sometimes involves more than one schedule. In compound schedules, two or more schedules are combined. As one example of a compound schedule, consider the child who must make the bed everyday (FR-7) and mow the yard on Saturday (FR-1) to receive reward. The child must complete both schedules to receive reward. Compound schedules of reinforcement will not be discussed here, but interested readers should consult D'Amato (1970) for a discussion of the varied compound schedules of reinforcement.

We have learned that to obtain reinforcement, animals or people must discover the contingency which exists between behavior and reinforcement. A number of variables affect the acquisition of instrumental behavior. Let's now turn our attention to the factors which influence whether we respond according to the contingency and thus obtain reinforcement.

How Readily Is an Instrumental Response Learned?

Although many variables affect the development of instrumental behavior, three factors play significant roles in determining the strength of conditioning. First, the *delay of reinforcement* affects the level of conditioning. Contiguity has a dramatic impact on instrumental behavior; the closer in time the response and the reinforcement, the greater the conditioning of the instrumental response. However, contiguity alone does not determine the level of conditioning; other factors affect the instrumental conditioning process, even when reinforcement directly follows the instrumental behavior.

Second, the strength of conditioning is affected by the *magnitude of reward*. The literature shows that in many situations the greater the magnitude of the reinforcer, the faster and stronger the conditioning of the instrumental response. However, the impact of the magnitude of reward is affected by prior experience with reinforcement and the magnitude of this previous reward. Prior experience with reinforcers of large magnitude acts to decrease the effectiveness of a reward of lower magnitude. In contrast, past exposure to a reward of small magnitude causes an increase in the effectiveness of a reward of higher magnitude.

Third, the *motivation level* influences the acquisition of an instrumental response. Motivation has a positive influence on instrumental conditioning; the higher the motivation level, the more rapid the acquisition of an instrumental response. In addition, a higher asymptotic level of performance is produced with a greater motivation level. The next three sections briefly examine evidence indicating how these three factors—contiguity, reinforcer magnitude, and motivation level—affect the strength of instrumental conditioning.

Contiguity You help a friend change a tire on his or her car; you are thanked for your assistance. The effect of the social reward is to increase your likelihood of future helping behavior. However, if your friend waits several minutes before thanking you, the impact of the reinforcement is reduced. This observation points to the importance of contiguity on instrumental conditioning: reward can lead to the acquisition of an instrumental response if it immediately follows the instrumental behavior, whereas instrumental learning is impaired if reward is delayed after the instrumental response. Furthermore, the longer the delay between the response and reinforcement, the less conditioning that occurs. Many studies have documented the importance of delay on the acquisition of an instrumental behavior; several of them are discussed next.

Delay In a classic study, Grice (1948) investigated the role of reinforcement delay on the rat's learning to go into a black chamber instead of a white one. Grice varied the delay between the correct response and reinforcement. In his study, the delay interval was either 0, 0.5, 1.2, 2, 5, or 10 seconds. As seen in Figure 3.8, there is a very steep delay gradient: little conditioning occurred

FIGURE 3.8
Amount of learning as a function of the delay of reinforcement. The measure of level of learning is the reciprocal × 1000 of the number of trials to reach 75 percent correct choices; thus, the higher the value, the greater the level of learning. From Grice, G. R. The relation of secondary reinforcement to delayed reward in visual discrimination learning. *Journal of Experimental Psychology*, 1948, *38*, 1–16. Copyright 1948 by the American Psychological Association. Reprinted by permission.

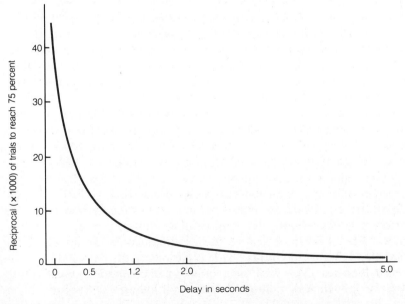

with delay intervals as short as 1.2 seconds. Other experiments have obtained results similar to Grice's; see Smith (1951) for another study.

However, not all experiments have reported a delay gradient comparable to Grice's data (Logan, 1952; Perin, 1943; Skinner, 1938). For example, Perin (1943) found moderate levels of conditioning of bar-press responses even with a 10-second delay, and with a delay of 30 seconds or more rats were unable to learn to bar press to obtain reinforcement.

Why do the delay gradients differ between Grice's and Perin's experiments? The presence or absence of secondary reinforcement cues appears to be an important factor in the delay gradient. The presence of a secondary reinforcer during the interval provides some strengthening of the instrumental behavior, despite the delay of primary reinforcement, and therefore lessens the influence of delay. In contrast, when no cues are associated with reinforcement during the delay, even a very short delay produces little conditioning. In support of this approach, animals in Grice's study spent the delay interval in an environment not associated with reinforcement. In contrast, during the delay interval the rats in Perin's experiment remained in the conditioning environment (the operant chamber) associated with reinforcement.

Perin's (1943) results provide direct support for the influence of secondary reinforcement on the delay gradient. Perin, using a 45-second delay between the correct response and reinforcement, placed some animals in their training chamber for the delay interval and other rats in one of two different chambers (one, for correct responding; the other, for incorrect responding). The subjects spending the delay interval in a chamber associated with reinforcement after a correct response showed significantly more conditioning than did rats that had spent the interval in the training chamber.

Delay of Reinforcement and Conditioning in Humans The importance of reinforcement delay has also been demonstrated using children. These studies consistently show that the longer the delay between the instrumental behavior and reinforcement, the poorer the conditioning of the instrumental response (Hall, 1976). Table 3.1 presents a sample of these delay-of-reinforcement studies; let's examine one of them closely.

Terrell and Ware (1961) gave kindergarten and first-grade children two easy problems to solve. The children received immediate reward for responding correctly to one of the problems; a 7-second delay of reward followed the correct solution of the other problem. Terrell and Ware reported that to learn the problems, the children required approximately seven trials with immediate reward compared with an average of seventeen trials when reward was delayed. These observations indicate that a delay between the correct response and reinforcement interferes with the acquisition of that response.

Interference Why is delay critical to the development of an instrumental behavior? Chapter 1 discussed Guthrie's idea that contiguity between a stimulus and response is critical to prevent the acquisition of competing associations. This view of the influence of contiguity on conditioning has recently been addressed by Samuel Revusky (1971, 1977). Revusky's concurrent-interference theory was initially developed to explain why animals and humans can associate a taste cue with illness, even though the illness occurs several hours after the taste experience. According to Revusky, the absence of interference causes long-delay learning; that is, there are no other tastes between the taste cue and illness which can interfere with the long-delay acquisition of the taste aversion. Revusky's extensive investigation of taste-aversion learning demonstrates that if either a novel taste cue or a taste previously paired with illness occurs in the interval between taste and illness, long-delay aversion will not occur. It should be noted that interference does not always occur; if the intervening taste has previously been associated with the absence of illness and, therefore, is not easily associated with illness, interference with long-delay learning is not observed. Revusky calls the interference produced by the intervening taste *concurrent interference;* Chapter 10 discusses Revusky's flavor-aversion research in greater detail.

Revusky's concurrent interference hypothesis can also explain why contiguity is important in the acquisition of an instrumental behavior. According to this view, contiguity will not be critical if interfering associations are eliminated. To evaluate this approach, Lett (1973, 1975) showed in an extensive series of studies that animals could learn to go to the correct arm of a T-maze, even with a 2-minute interval between the correct response and reinforcement, if interference was minimized. To accomplish this goal, Lett removed some subjects from the T-maze after they had responded, placing them in their home cage during the interval; other rats were left in the correct arm of the T-maze. At the end of the interval, all the rats were returned to the start box and rewarded if they had responded correctly 2 minutes earlier. Lett predicted that interference should be minimal for the animals that spent the interval in their home cages, since the events there have little relevance to the events occurring in the T-maze. Interference should be great for animals left in the T-maze, where other responses could be associated with reward. In support of the interference theory, animals spending the interval in the T-maze showed no change in their behavior as the result of reward; yet, learning was as efficient for animals spending the interval in their home cages as for animals that experienced no delay between the correct behavior and reward. Apparently, the importance of delay can be reduced when interfering associations are not acquired during the delay interval. Results comparable to those of Lett have been obtained by other researchers; see D'Amato, Safarjan, and Salmon (1981) for a series of studies with monkeys.

Reward Magnitude

Acquisition of an Instrumental Response   Suppose that parents decide to reward their children for learning vocabulary words. The rate of acquisition of the vocabulary words will depend on the magnitude of the reward provided; the larger the reward magnitude, the faster the acquisition of vocabulary words.

Many studies show that the magnitude of reward affects the rate of acquisi-

TABLE 3.1
SOME STUDIES INVESTIGATING DELAY OF REWARD WITH NORMAL AND RETARDED CHILDREN

Subjects	Task	Delay intervals	Response measure	Results	Investigators
Preschool children	2-stimulus, 1-choice apparatus, with reward delivered immediately to one stimulus and after 7 seconds to the other	0 and 7 seconds	Response speed and preference for one of the two stimuli	Subjects preferred to respond to immediate rewarded stimulus; no difference in response speed.	Lipsitt and Castaneda (1958)
Fourth-grade children	Simultaneous and successive discrimination tasks	0, 3, or 6 seconds	Number correct	No delay-of-reinforcement gradient obtained, although 6-second group performed most poorly.	Erickson and Lipsitt (1960)
Fourth-grade children	2-stimulus (easy) and 3-stimulus (difficult) successive discrimination problems	0, 10, or 30 seconds	Number correct	Increasing delay had progressively deleterious effect on difficult discrimination; no difference among groups with easy task.	Hockman and Lipsitt (1961)
Kindergarten and first-grade children	(1) Discrimination learning with Ss required to learn a size and form problem concurrently (2) Three-stimulus size and form problem learned concurrently	In both (1) and (2), one problem learned with 0-second delay, other problem with 7-second delay.	Number correct	Both (1) and (2) revealed delay resulted in poorer learning.	Terrell and Ware (1961)

Moderately and severely retarded children; also normal first graders	2-choice discrimination problem	0, 1.5, 6, or 12 seconds	Errors and trials to criterion	Twelve-second delay significantly increased errors and trials to criterion for all groups. No difference among other delay intervals.	Hetherington, Ross, and Pick (1964)
Mental retardates	Discrimination of geometric forms, e.g., square, Ss required to solve 10 problems (1 problem per day)	0 or 5 seconds	Errors	Delay increased difficulty of problem. Effect appeared to be limited to initial trials on each problem.	Schoelkopf and Orlando (1965)
Mental retardates	2-choice discrimination problem; chosen stimulus was visible or not visible during delay	0, 12, or 18 seconds	Errors and trials to criterion	Zero-second delay significantly superior to 12- or 18-second groups for both conditions.	Ross, Hetherington, and Wray (1965)
Normal and moderately retarded children	Simple discrimination	0 or 12 seconds	Errors and trials to criterion	Twelve-second delay increased errors for retardates; no difference between 0- and 12-second delay for normals.	Hetherington and Ross (1967)
Mental retardates	2-choice discrimination problem	0 or 15 seconds	Number of correct responses	Zero-second delay significantly superior to 15 seconds.	Keeley and Sprague (1969)

Source: Hall, J. F. *Classical conditioning and instrumental learning: A contemporary approach.* Philadelphia: Lippincott, 1976.

tion of an instrumental response; let's look at several. Crespi's 1942 study demonstrates the significance of reward magnitude on the acquisition of an instrumental running response in an alley. Upon reaching the goal box, Crespi's rats received either 1, 4, 16, 64, or 256 units of food (a unit equals 0.02 g). Crespi observed that the greater the reward magnitude was, the faster the animals ran down the alley. Other investigators have also observed that reward magnitude affects the acquisition of an instrumental running response; see Armus (1959), Mellgren (1972), Osborne (1978), or Reynolds and Pavlik (1960) for other examples.

Researchers have also shown that reward magnitude affects the acquisition of a bar-press response in an operant chamber. For example, Guttman (1953) varied the amount of reward rats received for bar pressing; animals were given a 4, 8, 16, or 32 percent sucrose solution following the instrumental response. Guttman discovered that the greater the reward magnitude was, the faster the animals learned to bar-press to obtain reinforcement (refer to Figure 3.9). Other studies have also demonstrated that the magnitude of reward affects the rate of acquisition of an instrumental bar-press response (Butter & Thomas, 1958; Conrad & Sidman, 1956).

Reward magnitude influences the acquisition of other instrumental responses. For example, several studies (Clayton, 1964; Cowles & Nissen, 1937;

FIGURE 3.9
Number of bar-press responses per minute as a function of the concentration of sucrose in water. Note that rate of responding increases with greater reward magnitudes used in training. Adapted from Guttman, N. Equal reinforcing values for sucrose and glucose solutions compared with sweetness values. *Journal of Comparative and Physiological Psychology*, 1954, *47*, 358–361. Copyright 1954 by the American Psychological Association. Reprinted by permission.

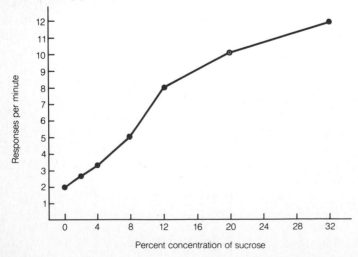

Denny & King, 1955; Greene, 1953; Leary, 1958; Powell & Perkins, 1957; Schrier & Harlow, 1956) have found that the development of the correct response in a discrimination task depends on the magnitude of reward; the greater the magnitude, the faster the appropriate response acquired in a discrimination situation.

Performance of an Instrumental Response   Several weeks ago, my youngest son informed me that 2 dollars was no longer enough money for mowing the yard; he wanted 3 dollars to do the job. His response indicates the critical influence that the magnitude of reward has on the performance of an instrumental behavior. The likelihood and intensity of an instrumental response depends on the magnitude of reward provided following the occurrence of a particular response. In many instances, the magnitude of reward must be sufficient for the behavior to occur; thus, my son's mowing response would occur only if the payment was sufficiently high. At other times, the instrumental behavior may occur but the intensity of the response depends on the reward magnitude; under these circumstances, the greater the reward magnitude, the higher the level of performance of the instrumental response. The literature (Pubols, 1960) consistently shows that reward magnitude affects instrumental-task performance.

Capaldi's 1948 study detailed earlier also evaluated the asymptotic level of instrumental performance as a function of reward magnitude. Capaldi discovered that the greater the magnitude was, the faster the rats ran down the alley to obtain reinforcement, indicating that the magnitude of reward influences the asymptotic level of instrumental behavior. Other studies show that reward magnitude determines the final level of instrumental performance in the runway situation (Armus, 1959; Hill & Wallace, 1967; Mellgren, 1972; Reynolds & Pavlik, 1960), in the operant chamber (Butter & Thomas, 1958; Conrad & Sidman, 1956; Gutman, Sutterer, & Brush, 1975), and in discrimination situations (Clayton, 1964; Denny & King, 1955; Greene, 1953; Powell & Perkins, 1957; Schrier & Harlow, 1956).

You may have the impression that the magnitude of reward influences the final level of conditioning. Evidence indicates, however, that the differences in asymptotic performance reflect motivational rather than learning differences. According to this view, the greater the reward magnitude, the greater the motivation to obtain the reinforcer. How can this approach be validated? To assess the relative contribution of learning and motivation, the reward value must be shifted to a higher (or lower) level. If the reward-magnitude shift causes a slow alteration in behavior, the change in responding is thought to reflect a learning influence, since learning changes occur slowly; if the alteration in behavior following the shift is rapid, motivational processes are assumed to cause the behavior change.

Many studies (Crespi, 1942; Zeaman, 1949) report a rapid change in behavior when reward magnitude is shifted, indicating that motivational differences cause the asymptotic performance differences occurring as a function of differences in reward magnitude. For example, Crespi (1942) shifted some animals from a high-reward magnitude (256 units) to a moderate reward level (16 units) on trial twenty; other animals were shifted from a low- (1 pellet) to a moderate reward magnitude (refer to Figure 1.6). The animals showed a rapid change in behavior on the trial following the shift in reward magnitude: the high-to-moderate shift's animals exhibited a significantly lowered response time on trial twenty-one, whereas the low-to-moderate shift's subjects ran significantly faster on trial twenty-one than on the preceding trial. Other experiments have documented this rapid change in behavior after a shift in the magnitude of reward; see Zeaman (1949) for another example of this effect.

Experience   Suppose that your boss's marginal profits cause your salary to be decreased. Under these conditions, your behavior will be less efficient as the result of the lowered magnitude of reward. How much will your output decline? Research (Crespi, 1942) indicates that you will exhibit less output now than if your salary had always been low (see Figure 3.10). The process in which a shift from a high to a low reward magnitude produces a level of instrumental behavior below that which would be exhibited if the level of reward had always been low is called the *depression effect.*

Perhaps your boss's profits increase and you receive a raise. Under these conditions, your behavior will become more efficient as a result of the higher magnitude of reward. In contrast to the depression effect, a shift from low to high reward magnitude produces a level of instrumental behavior greater than that which would occur if the higher level had always been used. The height-

FIGURE 3.10
Higher level of performance with large rather than small reward magnitude during preshift phase, and the positive and negative contrast which occur in the postshift phase.

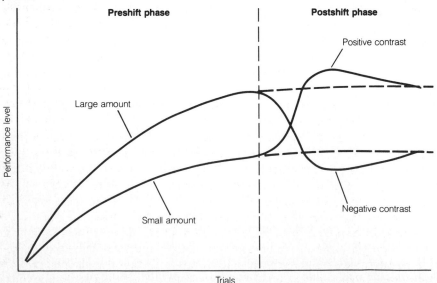

ened performance produced by a shift from low to high reward and occurring above that exhibited with a constant high level of reward is called an *elation effect*.

Zeaman (1949) suggested replacing the terms *elation* and *depression* with those of *positive* and *negative contrast* effects: literature on perception had already used the phrase *contrast effects* to indicate that the specific context in which a stimulus is experienced can produce exaggerated or reduced effects of this stimulus. Thus, experience with low reward heightens the influence of a high reward (positive contrast effect); that is, a large reward is more effective than it normally would be because of previous experience with a small reward. In contrast, experience exaggerates the impact of a low-reward magnitude (negative contrast effect); that is, a small reward is less effective than it would normally be because of experience with a large reward.

Experimental investigations (Flaherty, Hamilton, Gandelman, & Spear, 1977) since Crespi's original study have consistently produced a negative contrast effect; yet, research conducted during the 1960s seemed to indicate that the positive contrast effect could not be induced (see Black, 1968). However, Bower (1981) suggested that a ceiling effect was responsible for the inability to produce a positive contrast effect, that is, high reward magnitude alone was causing maximum responding, and therefore the shift from low to high could not raise performance above that of the level exhibited by animals always experiencing the high reward magnitude. A number of studies conducted in the late 1960s and early 1970s demonstrated that a positive contrast effect can be produced if animals are initially responding at a level below the upper limit. To demonstrate this theory, Mellgren (1972) and Shanab, Sanders, and Premack (1969) trained rats with a delayed reward, a procedure which results in performance in a high reward magnitude condition below maximum responding. These investigators found that a shift from low to high reward magnitude caused animals to respond greater than the level exhibited by animals always receiving the high reward magnitude. Thus, a positive contrast effect can be produced when initial responding is below the maximum level.

We should note that the contrast effects last for only short periods of time. Thus, animals shifted from high to low (or low to high) reward respond at a lower (or higher) level than animals always experiencing the low (or high) reward magnitude for only a few trials.

Why do the contrast effects occur? The emotion of frustration seems to play an important role in the negative contrast effect. According to Flaherty (1985), an animal establishes an expected level of reward during initial acquisition training. The presentation of a lower than expected level of reward in the second phase causes frustration, which interferes with instrumental activity and thereby produces a response level lower than would have been found had the low reward magnitude been the expected reward. Support for this view is provided by the observation that drugs which reduce anxiety in humans eliminate the negative contrast effect; this result has been found with the tranquilizer Librium (Becker & Flaherty, 1983), with alcohol (Becker & Flaherty,

1982), and with barbiturates (Flaherty & Driscoll, 1980; Ridgers & Gray, 1973). Flaherty suggests that the emotional response of elation produced by receiving a reward greater than the expected magnitude may explain the positive contrast effect; however, evidence validating this view is not available.

· *Reward Magnitude and Humans* Chapter 1 discussed the assumption by many psychologists that reward magnitude (or incentive value) influences the acquisition and performance of an instrumental behavior. Although most of the research on reward magnitude has used animals as subjects, some research with people has indicated that reward value affects the acquisition and performance of an instrumental response. However, differences in reward magnitude are not always reflected in behavioral differences. Research with young children (Hall, 1976) has shown that the magnitude of reward does affect the development of an instrumental response. For example, Siegel and Andrews (1962) found that 4- and 5-year-old children responded correctly more often on a discrimination task when provided a large reward (for example, a small prize) rather than a small reward (a button).

Experimentation also shows that reward magnitude influences instrumental behavior in adults. For example, Atkinson's research (1958) found that the amount of money paid for successful performance influences the level of achievement behavior. In one study, Atkinson told some of his subjects that they were to receive $1.25 for successfully performing each of two 20-minute achievement tasks; other subjects were told they would receive $2.50 for the same tasks. Atkinson discovered that the higher-paid subjects performed at a significantly higher level than did the subjects given the lower monetary incentive.

The magnitude of reward can also influence the level of cooperative behavior. For example, to determine whether reward magnitude affects cooperative behavior, McClintock and McNeel (1966) conducted an investigation in which subjects could earn either a small (up to 66¢) or a large (up to $13.20) reward for cooperative behavior. McClintock and McNeel reported that high reward magnitude increased the level of cooperative behavior. It should be noted that reward magnitude influences cooperative behavior only when an opponent's performance is unknown. Half of McClintock and McNeel's subjects received the results of both their own and an opponent's progress. Reward magnitude did not influence these subjects' cooperative behavior. McClintock and McNeel concluded that many people have a strong motivation to compete and obtain great satisfaction, or reward, from winning. Therefore, for these people, an extrinsic reward will motivate cooperative behavior only if the intrinsic reward of winning does not inhibit the influence of extrinsic reinforcers.

Motivation How much will you study to earn a high grade on your next exam? Recall from the last section that the higher the value of attaining a high grade, the more intense your study. The next section points out that the greater your motivation to do well on the exam is, the harder you will study.

The level of motivation clearly affects the acquisition of an instrumental behavior; the greater the level of motivation, the faster the acquisition of the instrumental response (Hall, 1976). Barry's 1958 study illustrates the influence of motivation level on instrumental conditioning. The rats in Barry's study were trained to run down a 4-foot alley to obtain food after being deprived of food for either 2.5 or 26.5 hours. The study's results (see Figure 3.11) show that the rats under the high drive (26.5 hours of food deprivation) increased their speed more rapidly to reach the goal than did the rats exposed to low drive (2.5 hours of food deprivation).

An animal's level of motivation also affects the final level of instrumental behavior: the higher the motivation level, the more intense the instrumental response. Consider the results of Barry's experiment shown in Figure 3.11. The asymptotic runway speed was greater with high than with low drive, which indicates that the rats' final speed to obtain food reward is greater after 26.5 hours of food deprivation than after 2.5 hours.

The positive influence of the level of motivation on the acquisition and performance of an instrumental response has been demonstrated in animals

FIGURE 3.11
Rats' speed to reach reward in the runway during training as a function of motivation level. Adapted from Barry, H., III. Effects of strength of drive on learning and on extinction. *Journal of Experimental Psychology*, 1958, *55*, 473–481. Copyright 1958 by the American Psychological Association. Reprinted by permission.

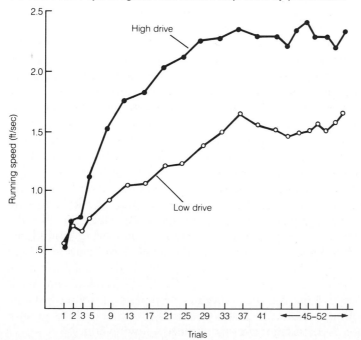

using a number of different conditioning apparatuses. For example, increased food deprivation produces a more rapid acquisition and higher final performance in the runway (Barry, 1958; Campbell & Kraeling, 1953; Lewis & Cotton, 1960; Reynolds & Pavlik, 1960), the T-maze (Jensen, 1960; MacDuff, 1946), an operant chamber (Batten & Shoemaker, 1961; Carlton, 1961), and the Y-maze (Lachman, 1961).

The level of motivation also affects the instrumental behavior of people. For example, Lowell (1952) reported that people with a high need to achieve completed either an arithmetic or a verbal task more readily than did persons with a low level of achievement motivation. Testing whether a person's motivation determines the likelihood of cooperative behavior, Tyszka and Grzelak (1976) discovered that people with competitive or individualistic motives show a lower level of cooperative behavior than did individuals with cooperative motives, even in a situation where reward can be attained only through cooperation. The research of other social psychologists (Guyer & Rapoport, 1972; MacCrimmon & Messick, 1976) also shows that the cooperative-behavior level is greater with cooperative than with either competitive or individualistic motives. The influence of the level of motivation on instrumental behavior has also been demonstrated with food-seeking behavior (Schachter, 1971a, 1971b) and sexual behavior (Catell, Kawash, & De Young, 1972; Mann, Berkowitz, Sidman, Starr, & West, 1974).

Animals and people respond more intensely when the level of motivation is high rather than low. Is this behavior difference due to differences in performance, or have animals and people learned more with high than with low motivation levels? The research of several psychologists (Capaldi, 1971; Capaldi & Hovancik, 1973; Eisenberger, Myers, & Kaplan, 1973) indicates that the higher level of instrumental behavior occurring with high levels of motivation reflects a difference in both learning and performance. To illustrate this point, let's examine Capaldi and Hovancik's 1963 study. Rats under either high or low drive levels received thirty-four trials in a straight alley to obtain food reward and were then shifted to a low level of drive for thirty-four more trials. Capaldi and Hovancik observed that a shift of drive level from high to low caused a decline in running speed; however, the level of performance did not drop to that exhibited by animals trained under low drive (see Figure 3.12). The fact that the level of performance in the study's second phase was greater for shifted groups than for nonshifted groups points out that the animals had learned more under high than low drive and that the greater learning with the high reward remained when both groups experienced low-drive conditions. Yet, the level of performance did drop when the level of motivation shifted from a high to a low level, which shows that some of the behavioral differences in the first phase of the study were caused by the greater motivational impact of the high level of drive. Thus, the more intense responding produced by the high-level-of-drive group results from the greater learning as well as greater motivation occurring under a high level than under a low level of drive.

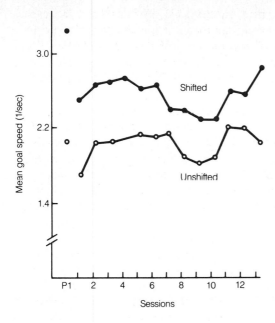

FIGURE 3.12
The response latency to reach the goal box for shifted and unshifted groups on the last day of phase 1 (preshift) and the sessions of phase 2 (postshift). From Capaldi, E. D., & Hovancik, J. R. Effect of previous body weight level on rats' straight-alley performance. *Journal of Experimental Psychology,* 1973, 97, 93–97. Copyright 1973 by the American Psychological Association. Reprinted by permission.

We have learned that reinforcement causes the acquisition of the instrumental response which produces that reinforcer. Typically, the exhibition of an instrumental behavior is appropriate; that is, society approves of animals or people responding in a particular fashion. However, sometimes it is inappropriate for animals or people to exhibit a specific response that had been producing reinforcement. Several methods can be employed to inhibit an inappropriate response. One effective method is *extinction,* the discontinuance of reinforcement when the inappropriate behavior occurs. Other techniques involving aversive control are detailed in Chapter 4.

THE EXTINCTION OF AN INSTRUMENTAL APPETITIVE RESPONSE

Extinction Paradigm

An instrumental appetitive response, acquired when reinforcement follows the occurrence of the behavior, can also be extinguished when the reward no longer occurs after the response. Continued failure of the instrumental behavior to produce reinforcement causes the strength of the instrumental response to diminish until eventually the animal or person no longer emits the instrumental action.

Consider the following examples to illustrate the extinction of an instrumental response. (1) A hungry rat has been given food reinforcement for bar pressing; the presentation of food contingent on bar pressing causes the rat to bar-press frequently. During extinction, food reinforcement is no longer presented, and the rate of bar pressing declines until the rat stops pressing the bar. (2) A child shopping with his or her mother sees a favorite candy bar and discovers that a temper tantrum causes the mother to buy the candy. The contingency between the temper tantrum and candy causes the child to have a tantrum every time he or she shops with mother and wants a candy bar. The child's mother, tired of being manipulated, decides to submit no longer to her child's unruly behavior. Although the mother is annoyed by the child's tantrums, she no longer reinforces them with candy, and the incidence of tantrums declines slowly until the child can enter a store and behave when candy is refused. (3) A man eats in a specific restaurant nightly; an attractive waitress rather than the quality of the food draws him. Arriving at the restaurant one night, he finds that the waitress has quit. For a while the man continued to eat at the restaurant infrequently, but he eventually stopped. Many studies have shown that when reinforcement is no longer provided, the instrumental behavior ceases to be emitted; let's now examine several experiments demonstrating the extinction of an instrumental response when reinforcement is discontinued.

In 1938, Skinner observed that the failure to reinforce a previously acquired bar-press response in rats caused the extinction of that response. At the beginning of extinction, the rate of responding is high (see Figure 3.13). Continued failure of the response to produce reinforcement causes the rate of responding to decline until the rat stops bar pressing. Note that responding is erratic during extinction; some periods have high response rates, and sometimes no responding occurs prior to the complete elimination of responding. Other psychologists

FIGURE 3.13
Cumulative response record during the extinction of a bar-press response.

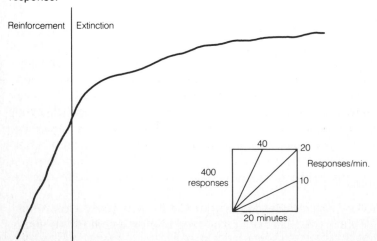

Reinforcement | Extinction

40
20
Responses/min.
400
responses
10

20 minutes

(Perin, 1942; Williams, 1938) have reported that animals cease bar pressing when reinforcement is no longer provided following an instrumental bar-press response. Furthermore, researchers have found that extinction of a previously reinforced instrumental response occurs when reward is no longer presented in a runway apparatus (Bacon, 1962; Hill & Spear, 1963; Weinstock, 1958).

Extinction of a previously reinforced instrumental behavior has also been documented in humans. For example, Lewis and Duncan (1956, 1957, 1958) reinforced college students for pulling the lever of a slot machine. When reinforcement (a disk exchangeable for 5 cents) was discontinued, the students eventually stopped pulling the lever. Lewis (1952) noted a similar extinction pattern in 6- and 7-year-old children who were no longer reinforced with toys for pressing a button.

Development of Inhibition

Chapter 1 discussed Hull's suggestion that nonreward during extinction inhibits a previously reinforced instrumental habit. Initially, a temporary reactive inhibition (I_R) suppresses all responding due to fatigue occurring when behavior does not produce reinforcement; later, a permanent conditioned inhibition ($_sI_R$) develops specifically to the nonreinforced behavior if the behavior continues to be unrewarded. According to Hull, the conditioned inhibition of a response occurs because the environmental events present during the nonreinforced behavior become associated with the inhibitory nonreward state. When these cues are experienced again, the inhibitory state is aroused and the instrumental behavior suppressed.

The following example will illustrate Hull's view of extinction: A rat bar-presses but no reward occurs; nonreward elicits inhibition, which, in turn, becomes associated with the operant chamber through the classical conditioning process. When the rat is again placed in the operant chamber, inhibition is elicited as a conditioned response, and the rat's bar-pressing response is suppressed.

We know that stimuli associated with nonreward can inhibit appetitive instrumental behavior; this suppression of the appetitive instrumental response is thought to result from the inhibition of the central appetitive motivational state by cues associated with nonreward. Thus, Hull's view of conditioned inhibition does appear to reflect accurately the development of a conditioned response which can inhibit an instrumental appetitive response. Nonreward and the cues associated with nonreward can motivate avoidance behavior; the ability of frustration to elicit avoidance behavior is described next.

Aversive Quality of Nonreward

According to Amsel's view, nonreward in a situation previously associated with reward is aversive and escape from this aversive situation is reinforcing. Adelman and Maatsch (1956) provided evidence of the aversiveness of frustration and the reinforcing quality of escaping from a frustrating situation. They found that animals jumped out of a box previously associated with reward and up onto a ledge within 5 seconds if they were not rewarded. In contrast, animals which had been rewarded with food for jumping across the ledge took 20 seconds to jump. In addition, although the rewarded animals stopped jumping after about 60 extinction trials, the frustrated animals did not quit responding even after 100 trials, even though their only reward was escape from a frustrating situation.

Ludvigson and his associates (Collerain & Ludvigson, 1977; Ludvigson, McNeese, & Collerain, 1979) provided additional evidence of the aversiveness of nonreward. They reported that animals experiencing nonreward after previously receiving reinforcement leave odor trails that other rats find aversive and that motivate escape behavior. Collerain (1978) found that odors are produced by nonreward after as few as four rewarded trials.

Other researchers (Brooks, 1980; Daly, 1974) have shown that the cues associated with nonreward develop aversive qualities. Let's briefly examine Daly's study to demonstrate the aversive quality of cues associated with nonreward. Daly presented a cue (either a distinctive box or a light) during nonreinforced trials in the first phase of her study; during the second part of the experiment, the rats learned a new response—jumping a hurdle—which enabled them to turn off the light or to escape from the box. Apparently, the cues (distinctive box or light) had acquired aversive qualities during nonrewarded trials; the presence of these cues subsequently motivated the new response. Termination of these cues reinforced the acquisition of the hurdle-jump response.

Activation of Instrumental Behavior

One additional point about the influence of nonreward on instrumental behavior deserves our attention. Nonreward sometimes increases rather than decreases the intensity of instrumental behavior. Amsel and Roussell's (1952) study shows that frustration can motivate appetitive behavior. They used a double runway apparatus (see Figure 3.14) in which rats in the first stage of the study ran from the start box (SB) to the first goal box (GB_1), where they received reward (food). After consuming their food, the rats were allowed to go to the second goal box (GB_2) for a second reward. In the second phase of the study,

FIGURE 3.14
Double runway similar to one used in Amsel and Roussell's study (1952). When placed in the start box (SB), rats ran to the first goal box (GB_1). After a short confinement in GB_1, the rats were allowed to go to the second goal box (GB_2).

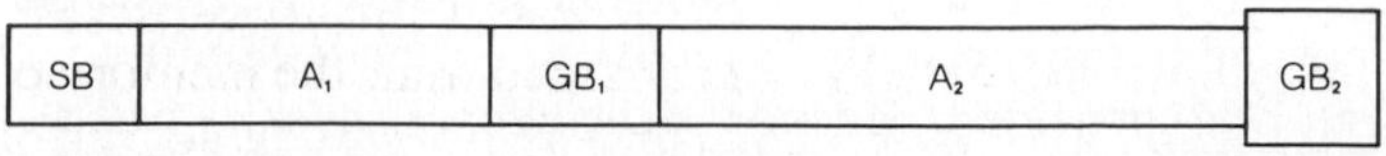

the experimental group of rats received food only 50 percent of the time in GB_1, and a control group continued to receive a reward in GB_1 on every trial. Reward continued to be presented on every trial to all the animals in the second goal box. The authors found that the experimental group rats ran to the second goal box more quickly if they had not been rewarded in GB_1 than if they had. Also, the experimental group animals ran faster than did control animals which received reward in GB_1. The faster response of the experimental group was not due to lack of motivation in the control group; Wagner (1963) discovered that control animals that never received reward in the first goal box also ran slower than experimental animals. Apparently, frustration produced by the absence of anticipated reward in the first goal box intensified the rats' motivation to reach the second goal box.

Why did nonreward increase the intensity of instrumental responding? Frustration will increase appetitive instrumental behavior if the animal's or person's escape response is either similar to or compatible with the attainment of reward. The results of Amsel and Rousell's study support this approach: the rats' approach to GB_2 was also an escape response to GB_1. Furthermore, a frustrated animal or person could become conditioned to exhibit appetitive behavior if this behavior has reduced frustration in the past. Chapter 1 noted a similar matching of approach and avoidance processes in response to painful events.

Nonreward can also motivate instrumental appetitive responding if the frustration cues have been conditioned to elicit appetitive instead of avoidance behavior. E. J. Capaldi's sequential theory (Capaldi, 1966, 1967, 1971) explains this conditioning process. According to Capaldi, an animal remembers at the beginning of a trial whether reward or nonreward occurred on the last trial; Capaldi labels the memory of reward as S^R and the memory of nonreward, S^N. When an instrumental response produces reinforcement following a nonreinforced trial, the memory of the nonreward (S^N) becomes associated with the instrumental response. Although the memory of nonreward (S^N) should motivate avoidance behavior, the external cues present during conditioning have been associated with reward; therefore, an approach rather than an avoidance response is elicited.

An animal's behavior on a single alternation task illustrates that nonreward can become conditioned to motivate an appetitive instrumental response (Burns, 1976; Capaldi, 1971; Flaherty & Davenport, 1972). In the single alternation situation, reward and nonreward trials are alternated. Studies using the single alternation task report that the intensity of instrumental responding increases following a nonrewarded trial but declines after a rewarded trial. According to Capaldi, since reward always follows a nonrewarded trial, the memory of nonreward (S^N) is associated with reward, resulting in the conditioning of the appetitive instrumental response to S^N. Therefore, the memory of nonreward elicits the instrumental appetitive behavior; the increased intensity of the instrumental appetitive response after nonrewarded trials supports this view. Furthermore, since nonreward always follows a rewarded trial, the memory of reward (S^R) is associated with nonreward, which results in the conditioning of an avoidance response to S^R. Thus, the memory of reward elicits instrumental avoidance behavior; the decreased intensity of the instrumental appetitive response after rewarded trials provides support for Capaldi's approach.

We should note that continued nonreward will eventually lead to extinction, even in animals that have associated S^N with reward. However, the ability of S^N to elicit the instrumental appetitive response slows the extinction process. The impact of the association of S^N and the appetitive behavior on the resistance to extinction is detailed later in the chapter when we discuss the partial reinforcement effect.

Resistance to Extinction

Three factors appear to contribute significantly to the persistence of behavior during extinction. First, the *reward magnitude* experienced during acquisition influences the resistance to extinction of an instrumental response. The effect of the reward magnitude on the extinction of an instrumental behavior depends on the level of acquisition training: when the level of training is minimal, the higher the reward magnitude employed in acquisition, the greater the resistance to extinction. In contrast, extended acquisition training results in an inverse relationship between the reward magnitude employed in acquisition and the resistance to extinction; that is, the higher the reward magnitude used in acquisition, the less persistence exhibited during extinction. Second, resistance to extinction is affected by the *delay of reinforcement* used in acquisition training. Research on the influence of the delay of reinforcement indicates that if reward is sometimes delayed in acquisition, resistance to extinction is enhanced. However, the persistence of extinction is not affected if reward is always delayed. Third, the *consistency of reinforcement* in acquisition influences the persistence of an instrumental response during extinction. During extinction, an animal or person will continue to emit an instrumental behavior that has not been reinforced every time it occurred longer than a response that has always been reinforced. The greater resistance to extinction which occurs with intermittent rather than continuous reinforcement is referred to as the *partial reinforcement effect* (PRE).

Reward Magnitude   D'Amato (1970) suggested that the influence of the reward magnitude experienced in acquisition on the resistance to extinction depends on the amount of acquisition training. As seen in Figure 3.15, when the level of acquisition training is low, a large reward produces a greater resistance to extinction than does a small reinforcer. However, the opposite effect is observed with extended acquisition: a small reward magnitude in acquisition produces more persistence of the instrumental behavior during extinction than does the use of a large reward magnitude in acquisition.

The literature provides support for D'Amato's interpretation of the effects of reward magnitude on the extinction of an instrumental behavior. Hill and Spear (1963), giving their subjects only a few acquisition trials in the runway and

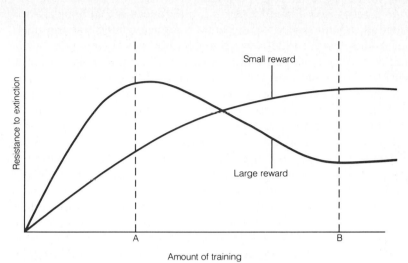

FIGURE 3.15
Hypothesized resistance to extinction of an instrumental response as a
function of level of acquisition training and magnitude of reinforcement.
From D'Amato, M. R. *Experimental psychology: Methodology,
psychophysics, and learning.* New York: McGraw-Hill, 1970.

providing either a small or large reward in the goal box, found that the rats
given the large reward during acquisition showed more resistance to extinction
than did those rats that received a small reward during acquisition. In contrast,
Armus (1959) and Hulse (1958) provided a large number of acquisition trials in
the runway and presented either a small or large reward magnitude in the goal
box. Both Armus and Hulse observed that during extinction rapid running
persisted much longer for the animals given the smaller reward during acquisition. These results indicate that with extended acquisition training, a small
reward magnitude produces more resistance to extinction than does a large
reward magnitude. Furthermore, several studies (Ison & Cook, 1964;
Senkowski, 1978; Traupman, 1972) varied both the acquisition reward magnitude and the number of acquisition trials; the results of the studies support the
relation depicted in Figure 3.15.

Why does the influence of reward magnitude on the resistance to extinction
depend on the level of acquisition training? According to D'Amato (1970),
when a small reward magnitude is used in acquisition, the r_G-s_G mechanism
develops very slowly (see Chapter 1 for discussion of this acquired motive
concept). During extinction, substantial differences between reward magnitude
conditions in the r_G-s_G mechanism will not exist and, therefore, the differences
in frustration produced during extinction will be small. (This assertion assumes
that frustration is not produced until an animal or person is anticipating reward
and that the amount of frustration produced depends on the strength of the

anticipatory goal response.) Since frustration differences are minimal, resistance to extinction should depend on the amount of acquisition training only. The results of studies using a small reward magnitude support this prediction; the greater the level of acquisition training with a small reward magnitude, the more resistant the instrumental behavior to extinction.

In contrast, the anticipatory goal mechanism (r_G-s_G) is conditioned rapidly when a large reward is used in acquisition. During the initial phases of training, the r_G-s_G mechanism is being established. Frustration will not be elicited if extinction occurs following low levels of training; however, resistance to extinction will decrease as r_G-s_G is conditioned. Once the r_G-s_G association is strong enough to produce frustration, increases in r_G-s_G should lead to higher levels of frustration during extinction. These increases in frustration, produced as a result of extended training with a large reward, lead to a more rapid extinction of the instrumental response. Researchers employing a large reward magnitude have observed that increased acquisition training leads first to an increase in resistance to extinction and then to a decline in the difficulty of eliminating an instrumental response.

Delay of Reward   The effect of the delay of reinforcement on the resistance to extinction depends on the consistency of the reward delay. When a constant delay is used in acquisition, resistance to extinction is not affected by acquisition delay. (Note that terminal acquisition differences are produced with different delay intervals and that these terminal differences must be equated; Anderson in 1963 suggested guidelines for controlling for asymptotic differences in performance.)

Consider Tombaugh's 1966 study to illustrate the influence of consistent delay of reward in acquisition on the resistance to extinction. Tombaugh's rats were given seventy acquisition trials in a runway apparatus; reward in the goal box was delayed for periods of 0, 5, 10, or 20 seconds. During the sixty extinction trials, the rats were confined in the goal box for a period of delay equivalent to that experienced during acquisition. Upon equating terminal acquisition performance levels, Tombaugh found no differences in the resistance of extinction as a function of the delay of reward used in acquisition. Other studies (Habley, Gipson, & Hause, 1972; Renner, 1965; Sgro, Dyal, & Anastasio, 1967) have also found that resistance to extinction is not affected when a constant delay of reinforcement is employed during acquisition training.

Comparison of varied and constant delay of reward in acquisition shows clearly that the delay of reinforcement does influence resistance to extinction. A number of researchers (Logan, 1960; Schoonard & Lawrence, 1962; Shanab & Birnbaum, 1974), using either an immediate reward throughout acquisition or a delayed reward on some of the acquisition trials, reported a greater increased resistance to extinction when the reward presented during training was sometimes delayed rather than always consistent. Note that in order for varied delay to increase persistence effectively in extinction, the delay must be substantial (20 to 30 seconds).

Consistency of Reinforcement   Earlier in the chapter we described an example of a mother extinguishing her child's temper tantrums in a grocery store. Suppose that after several nonreinforced trips to the store and a reduction in the duration and intensity of the temper tantrums, on the next trip to the store, the mother has a headache when the child starts to cry. The headache seems to intensify the unpleasantness of the tantrum, and she decides to buy her child candy to stop the crying. If the mother had headaches infrequently but reinforces a tantrum whenever she does have a headache, this mother is now intermittently rather than continuously reinforcing her child's temper tantrums. As we learned earlier, this intermittent reinforcement causes the intensity of the temper tantrum to return to its original strength. The intensity of the child's behavior will soon exceed that level produced when the response was continuously reinforced. Despite how she feels, in all likelihood, the mother will eventually become so annoyed that she will decide to tolerate her child's intense temper tantrums no longer; unfortunately, extinguishing this behavior will be extremely difficult because she has intermittently reinforced the child's temper tantrums.

Partial Reinforcement   The previous example illustrates the influence of the consistency of reinforcement on the extinction of an instrumental behavior: extinction is slower following partial rather than continuous reinforcement. Humphreys (1939) and Skinner (1938) were the first to describe this greater resistance to extinction with partial rather than with continuous reinforcement. Many studies since these early observations have demonstrated a partial-reinforcement effect (PRE); this effect is one of the most reliable phenomena in psychology.

Jenkins, McFann, and Clayton (1950) trained rats to bar-press for food reinforcement. Half the rats were reinforced on a VI schedule; the others, on a continuous schedule. As can be seen from Figure 3.16, rats receiving intermittent reinforcement emitted five times as many responses during extinction as did rats given continuous reinforcement. Other researchers have found that partial reinforcement in the operant chamber produces greater resistance to extinction than does continuous reinforcement; see Mowrer and Jones (1945) for another example.

Most research on the partial-reinforcement effect has used the runway apparatus; these results have consistently shown the PRE effect. Consider Weinstock's 1958 study to illustrate this effect in the runway. Weinstock's rats received 108 acquisition trials with reinforcement occurring on 16.7, 33.5, 50, 66.7, 83.3, or 100 percent of the trials; each rat was then given 60 extinction trials. Weinstock found an inverse relationship between resistance to extinction and the percentage of reinforced trials. These results indicate that as the likelihood of an instrumental response producing reinforcement in acquisition decreases, the persistence of the behavior during extinction increases. Many other experiments have demonstrated that intermittent reinforcement during acquisition increases resistance to extinction in the runway; see Robbins (1971) for a review of this literature.

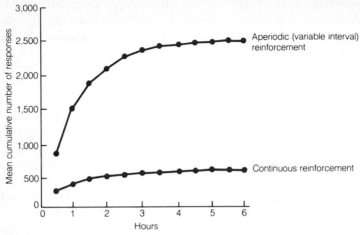

FIGURE 3.16
Mean cumulative bar-press response during extinction in rats
receiving intermittent or continuous reinforcement. From Jenkins,
W. O., McFann, H., & Clayton, F. L. A methodological study of
extinction following aperiodic and continuous reinforcement.
Journal of Comparative and Physiological Psychology, 1950, *43,*
155–167. Copyright 1950 by the American Psychological Association.
Reprinted by permission.

The PRE has also been demonstrated with humans (Lewis, 1952; Lewis &
Duncan, 1956, 1957, 1958). College students in Lewis and Duncan's (1958)
study were given reinforcement (a disk exchangeable for 5 cents) for pulling the
arm of a slot machine. The percentage of reinforced lever-pulling responses
varied: subjects received reinforcement after 33, 67, or 100 percent of the
responses. Lewis and Duncan allowed subjects to play the slot machine as long
as they liked during extinction, reporting that the lower the percentage of
responses reinforced during acquisition, the greater the persistence of subjects
during extinction. To determine whether the PRE effect also occurs in children,
Lewis's (1952) study used 6- and 7-year-old children who participated in a task
involving pressing buttons; they were reinforced with toys after each correct
response or after several correct behaviors. Lewis found that resistance to
extinction was greater with partial reinforcement (reinforcement given after
several correct responses) during acquisition than if the correct response was
rewarded each time it occurred.

Note that the percentage of reinforced trials cannot be too low (see Lewis,
1960) or learning will be minimal and extinction will be rapid. Studies using a
very small or very large percentage of reinforced trials generally produce a U-
shaped relation between the percentage of reinforced responses and resistance
to extinction; that is, low and high percentages of reinforcement produce more
rapid extinction than do situations in which an instrumental response is reinforced on some but not all occurrences.

Many explanations of the PRE have been proposed since Humphreys's and Skinner's initial observations: E. J. Capaldi's sequential theory (see Capaldi, 1966, 1967, 1971) appears to best describe the process responsible for the increased resistance to extinction following intermittent compared with continuous reinforcement. Capaldi provides a complex explanation of the effect. Although a brief summary is provided here, the interested reader should see Capaldi (1971) for a more detailed description of his theory.

Recall that if reward follows a nonrewarded trial, the animal will then associate the memory of the nonreinforced experience (S^N) with the appetitive instrumental response. According to Capaldi, the conditioning of the S^N-R (memory of nonreward–instrumental behavior) association accounts for the increased resistance to extinction with partial reinforcement. This S^N-R association develops due to the transition from a nonrewarded to rewarded trial; this is an NR transition in Capaldi's theory.

During extinction, the only memory present after the first nonreinforced experience is S^N. Animals receiving continuous reinforcement do not experience S^N during acquisition; therefore, S^N is not associated with the instrumental response. The presence of S^N in continuously reinforced animals during extinction produces a stimulus context which is different from the context present during acquisition. The change in the stimulus context during extinction produces a reduction in response strength due to *generalization decrement,* a reduced intensity of a response occurring when the stimulus present is dissimilar to that conditioned to the response (see Chapter 5 for a discussion of generalization). The loss of response strength due to generalization decrement, combined with the inhibition developed during extinction, produces a rapid extinction of the instrumental response in animals receiving continuous reinforcement in acquisition. However, another type of situation occurs in animals receiving partial reinforcement in acquisition: S^N is associated with the appetitive instrumental response during acquisition, and therefore no generalization decrement occurs during extinction in animals experiencing partial rather than continuous reinforcement in acquisition. The absence of the generalization decrement with partial reinforcement causes the strength of the instrumental response at the beginning of extinction to remain at the level conditioned during acquisition. Thus, the inhibition developed during extinction only slowly suppresses the instrumental response; as a result, extinction is slower with partial than with continuous reinforcement.

Capaldi and his associates (Capaldi, Hart, & Stanley, 1963; Capaldi & Spivey, 1964) conducted several studies to point out the importance of S^N experienced during a reinforced trial on the resistance to extinction. In these studies, during the interval between the nonrewarded and rewarded trials, reward was given in an environment other than the runway. The effect of this intertrial reinforcement procedure is the replacement of the memory of nonreward (S^N) with a memory of reward (S^R) and thus a reduced resistance to extinction. Compared with control animals receiving only partial reinforcement, rats given intertrial reward showed a faster extinction of the instrumental response.

According to Capaldi, partial reinforcement causes the memory of nonreward (S^N) to elicit the instrumental response. The strength of the association between the S^N and the instrumental response affects the resistance to extinction of that instrumental behavior. Capaldi suggests that three sequential factors influence the level of resistance to extinction produced by partial reinforcement. First, *the greater the number of N-R transitions during acquisition, the slower the resistance to extinction.* In Capaldi's view, NR transitions act to condition the memory of S^N to the instrumental response; therefore, the greater the number of conditioning trials (NR transitions), the stronger the association of S^N to instrumental response. To support his theory, Capaldi (1964) gave his rats 3, 10, or 20 NR transitions during the acquisition of a running response (experiment 3). He found that the persistence of responding during extinction increased as the number of NR transitions experienced in acquisition increased. Other studies have demonstrated that the number of NR transitions during acquisition affects the resistance to extinction of an instrumental response; see Seybert, Mellgren, and Jobe (1973) or Spivey (1967) for other examples.

Second, *the greater the number of consecutive nonrewarded trials prior to reward, the slower the extinction of the instrumental response.* According to Capaldi, the memory of nonreward (S^N) intensifies with consecutive nonreinforced trials. The presentation of reinforcement causes a stronger S^N to be associated with the instrumental response when more than one nonreward trial precedes reward than when only a single nonrewarded experience occurs prior to reward. Furthermore, the larger the number of nonrewarded trials, or *N-length,* the stronger the S^N conditioned to the instrumental response. Two processes contribute to the increased resistance to extinction which occurs with greater N-length: (1) the stronger the stimuli present during reinforcement (such as S^N), the greater the strength of the association of that stimulus with the instrumental response. Thus, the stronger memory of nonreward (S^N) produced by a longer N-length results in a greater S^N–instrumental-response association. (2) The level of generalization decrement is affected by the degree of similarity of the two stimuli; the more similar the training and test stimuli, the less generalization decrement that occurs. Many nonrewarded trials occur during extinction; thus, a larger number of nonrewarded trials experienced during acquisition prior to reward create more similar acquisition and extinction experiences and thereby result in less generalization decrement of the instrumental response present during extinction.

The literature shows that the longer the N-length, the greater the resistance to extinction. Consider Capaldi's (1964) experiment to illustrate the influence of N-length. Two groups of rats in Capaldi's study (experiment 1) received an identical sequence of rewarded and nonrewarded trials (RNNRRNNR) during each acquisition session. The groups also received two intertrial reinforcements during acquisition. The intertrial reward for one group occurred between nonreward trials (RN$_r$NRRN$_r$NR); this procedure reduced the N-length from 2 to 1. The subjects in the other group received the intertrial reinforcements after a reward trial (R_rNNRR$_r$NNR); this technique enabled the N-length to remain at 2. Although the two groups did not differ in the acquisition of the running response, the subjects in the group with an N-length of 2 were more resistant to extinction than were animals in the N-length one group (see Figure 3.17). These results indicate that the greater the N-length experienced in acquisition, the slower the extinction of the instrumental response. Seybert, Baer, Harvey, Ludwig, and Gerard (1979) noted a similar increased resistance to extinction with a greater number of nonreinforced trials.

Third, *the greater the number of different N-lengths experienced during acquisition, the slower the extinction of the instrumental response.* According to Capaldi, there is a maximum level of conditioning that can develop to a particular N-length. Once this asymptotic level of conditioning has occurred, further experience with the N-length will have no additional effect. Resistance to extinction can only be increased in this situation if other N-lengths are also experienced. The increased resistance to extinction which occurs with varied N-lengths was documented in Capaldi's (1964) study (experiment 3). During acquisition, Capaldi gave his rats either a single N-length of 3 or varied N-lengths (1, 2, and 3). An equal number of rats from the constant and varied treatment conditions received 24, 60, or 120 acquisition trials. If the animals

FIGURE 3.17
Mean log response latency to reach the goal box during acquisition and extinction in rats having one or two nonrewarded trials prior to reward during acquisition. From Capaldi, E. J. Effect of N-length, number of different N-lengths, and number of reinforcements on resistance to extinction. *Journal of Experimental Psychology*, 1968, *68*, 230–239. Copyright 1964 by the American Psychological Association. Reprinted by permission.

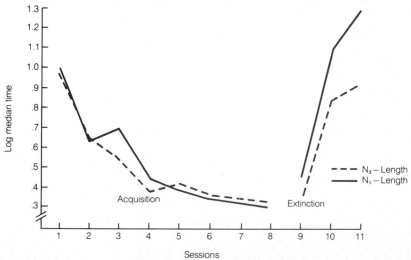

received only 24 acquisition trials, greater resistance to extinction occurred in the subjects experiencing only the N-length of 3 than in those receiving varied N-lengths (see Figure 3.18). Capaldi asserts that the strength of conditioning to N-length of 3 for subjects in group N_3 had reached the maximum level; in contrast, only weak conditioning to each N-length had developed in animals in group N_{123} after 24 acquisition trials. Thus, the stronger conditioning to the single N-length observed in Group N_3 animals was responsible for the greater resistance to extinction observed after 24 trials. In contrast, the animals receiving the varied N-lengths of 1, 2, and 3 showed more resistance to extinction after 120 acquisition trials when compared with the animals given only a single N-length of 3. According to Capaldi, maximum conditioning of all three N-lengths had occurred for animals in group N_{123}, and therefore the cumulative conditioning of the three N-lengths in group$_{123}$ exceeded the single N-length conditioning in group N_3 rats. Other researchers (Campbell, Knouse, & Wroten, 1970) have also found that extinction is slower as the number of different N-lengths experienced during acquisition increases.

The discussion of the PRE effect mentioned that the percentage of rewarded trials affects resistance to extinction. According to Capaldi, the percentage of reward affects extinction only because a lower reward percentage, compared with a higher reward percentage, produces more NR transitions and longer,

FIGURE 3.18
The mean log response latency to reach the goal box during extinction in animals receiving 24, 60, or 120 acquisition trials and a single N-length of 3 or varied N-lengths of 1, 2, and 3 during acquisition. From Capaldi, E. J. Effect of N-length, number of different N-lengths, and number of reinforcements on resistance to extinction. *Journal of Experimental Psychology,* 1964, *68,* 230–239. Copyright 1964 by the American Psychological Association. Reprinted by permission.

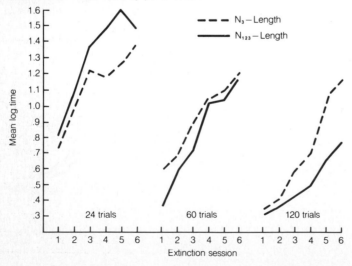

more varied N-lengths. To illustrate this explanation, Capaldi and Stanley (1965) exposed rats in a high percentage of reward group to an N-length during acquisition that was longer than the N-length to which the rats in a low percentage of reward condition were exposed. The animals in the higher percentage of reward condition were more resistant to extinction than were those in the lower percentage of reward group.

Our discussion indicates that sequential variables govern the resistance to extinction observed in the PRE effect. The importance of the sequence of reward and nonreward on resistance to extinction has also been shown in humans; the Grosslight, Hall, and Murnin (1953) study illustrates this effect. They asked college students to predict whether or not a second light would follow the presentation of a first light. The correctness of their prediction was considered to be a reward, and its presentation was governed by the experimenter. Subjects received a series of training trials using either an RN, NR, or RR sequence for each session, followed by ten extinction trials. Grosslight, Hall, and Murnin discovered that the subjects given the NR sequence showed significantly more resistance to extinction than did the subjects who received either the RN or RR sequence.

What is the significance of the partial-reinforcement effect? According to Flaherty (1985), observations of animals in their natural environments indicate that an animal's attempts to attain a desired goal are sometimes successful, and at other times the animals fail to reach the goal. Flaherty asserts that the PRE effect is adaptive because it allows animals not to give up too soon and thereby lose an opportunity to be successful. Yet, animals receiving partial reinforcement do not keep responding indefinitely without reward, an observation indicating that animals do not persist forever and, therefore, experience continued frustration.

In this chapter we have learned that the way we act is affected by the presentation of reward and nonreward. The importance of reinforcement and nonreinforcement on instrumental behavior has impressed many psychologists, who have designed instrumental conditioning procedures to control human behavior. These psychologists have used reinforcement to institute more effective patterns of behavior and nonreward to eliminate inappropriate behavior patterns.

CONTINGENCY MANAGEMENT

In 1953, B. F. Skinner suggested that poorly arranged reinforcer contingencies are sometimes responsible for people's behavior problems. In many instances, effective instrumental responding does not occur because reinforcement is unavailable. At other times, reinforcing people's behavior problems sustains their occurrence. Skinner believed that rearranging reinforcement contingencies could eliminate behavior pathology and increase the occurrence of more effective ways of responding. Many psychologists (Ullman & Krasner, 1965) accepted Skinner's view, and the restructuring of reinforcement contingencies emerged as an effective way of altering human behavior. The use of reward and nonreward to control people's behavior was initially labeled *behavior modification*. However, behavior modification refers to all types of behavioral treatments, and thus behavior therapists (refer to Rimm & Masters, 1979) now use the term *contingency management* to indicate that contingent reinforcement and nonreinforcement are being used to increase the frequency of appropriate behaviors and to eliminate or reduce inappropriate responses. We begin by examining the procedures necessary for effective use of reward and nonreward to alter instrumental behavior. Evidence of the effectiveness of contingency management is described later in this section.

There are three main stages in the effective implementation of a contingency-management program (see Rimm & Masters, 1979, for a more detailed discussion of these procedures). The initial stage of therapy assesses the frequency of appropriate and inappropriate behaviors and determines the situations in which these instrumental behaviors occur. In addition, the reinforcement maintaining the inappropriate responding, as well as potential reinforcers for the appropriate behavior, are determined in the assessment phase. The second phase of therapy, the contingency-contracting stage of treatment, specifies the relationship between responding and reinforcement. Also, the method of administering the reinforcement contingent on appropriate behaviors is determined. During the final stage of contingency management, the treatment is implemented. The changes in responding during and following treatment are evaluated in the last phase of contingency management: this procedure ensures that (1) behavioral changes are produced by the therapy program and (2) these changes continue after the termination of formal treatment. As we will discover shortly, contingency management is an effective way to alter behavior; the failure of the treatment to change responding means that the program was developed and/or implemented incorrectly, and changes in the treatment are necessary to ensure behavioral change.

Assessment Phase

The therapist must define the behavior problem and determine the situations in which it does or does not occur. Discussions with the patient, others who are familiar with the patient, or both, are the initial source of information concerning the behavior problem. However, the therapist cannot rely solely on this subjective reporting, which merely provides the therapists with an impression of the problem. For example, the incidence of the appropriate or inappropriate behavior may be higher or lower than that revealed from informal impressions. Therefore, direct observations are needed to establish the precise baseline level of responding of the target behaviors prior to the specification of the new contingency. The observations may be made by the staff of an institution, other people significant to the patient, or the patient. Regardless of who observes the target behavior, accurate observations are essential, and training is needed to ensure reliable data recording. Consider the following example to illustrate the observational training process. Parents complain to a behavior therapist that their child frequently has temper tantrums, which they have tried but failed to eliminate. The therapist instructs the parents to fill in a chart (see Table 3.2) indicating the number and duration of tantrums occurring each day for a week plus their response to each tantrum. The parents' observations provide an accurate recording of the frequency and intensity of the problem behavior.

The parents' observations also indicate the reinforcement of the problem behavior. As can be seen from Table 3.2, parental response to the tantrum increased the frequency of the response; parents ignoring the behavior decreased the frequency of temper tantrums. Therefore, it is essential in the assessment phase to record the events following the target behavior; this information signifies the reinforcer of the problem behavior.

The assessment must also indicate when and where the target behavior occurs. For example, the child may be having tantrums at home every day after school but not at school. This information about the target behavior shows the extent of the behavior problem as well as the stimulus conditions which precipitate the response.

During the second, or contingency-contracting phase, the contingency between appropriate responding and reinforcement is specified; however, this contracting cannot be accomplished without an effective reinforcement. In the assessment phase of treatment, the reinforcer to be used during therapy is determined. In some cases, the behavioral recording indicates what can be used as a reinforcer for appropriate behavior; in other instances, the therapist must

TABLE 3.2
INSTANCES OF TANTRUM BEHAVIOR AND PARENTAL REACTION TO TANTRUMS
DURING 7-DAY BASELINE ASSESSMENT PERIOD

Day	Tantrums	Duration (minutes)	Response
1	1	4	Comforted child when he slipped and banged head during crying
2	1	5	Told child to be quiet but finally gave cookie to quiet him down
	1	6	Ignored until couldn't stand it; gave cookie
3	1	5	Ignored
	2	6	Ignored
	3	8	Ignored until child took cookie himself; spanked child
4	1	4	Ignored; child stopped spontaneously
5	1	4	Company present; gave child cookie to quiet him
	2	5	Ignored; finally gave in
6	1	8	Ignored; went into bathroom, had cigarette, read magazine until child quieted himself
	2	4	Ignored; just as I was about to give in, child stopped
7	1	3	Ignored; child stopped, began to play

Source: Rimm, D. C. and Masters, J. C. *Behavior therapy: Techniques and empirical findings* (2d ed.). New York: Academic Press, 1979.

discover what can be employed. Behavior therapists (see Rimm & Masters, 1979) have developed a number of reinforcer assessment techniques. For example, the Mediation-Reinforcer Incomplete Blank (MRB), a modified incomplete-sentence test developed by Tharp and Wetzel (1969), reveals the patients' view of a reinforcer. A patient's response to the question "I will do almost anything to get _____" shows what the patient considers to be a material reinforcer.

The assessment stage of therapy provides information regarding the frequency and intensity of target behaviors, the situations in which these behaviors occur, and effective reinforcers. In the contracting phase, a plan for developing appropriate and suppressing inappropriate instrumental responses is developed.

Contingency Contracting

In contingency contracting, the desired instrumental response is specified, and the precise relation between that response and reinforcement is indicated. This indication involves deciding the schedule of reinforcement necessary to establish the desired response. In addition, if a shaping procedure is needed, the contract will detail the changes in the contingency to occur at various stages of treatment. Furthermore, an inappropriate instrumental response often has elicited reinforcement in the past; the contingency will indicate that this inappropriate response will no longer be rewarded.

Who will administer the reinforcer? In the traditional application of contingency management, people other than the patient (for example, a nurse in a mental hospital, a teacher in a school setting, or a parent in the home) have provided reinforcement contingent on the occurrence of the appropriate instrumental behavior. During the contracting stage, the individuals administering reinforcement are trained to identify and reinforce appropriate behavior.

Assigning people significant to the patient to provide reinforcement is ideal for many situations. However, in some circumstances this technique is not feasible. This is especially true of adults seeking to change their behavior by using outpatient therapy; self-reinforcement often has proved effective in these situations. Although psychologists (Skinner, 1953) were initially skeptical of the efficacy of self-reinforcement in behavioral management, Bandura and Perloff (1967) demonstrated the self-reinforcement technique to be as effective in changing behavior as the typical reinforcement procedure. In their study, 7- to 10-year-old children received reinforcement for exerting effort on a wheel-turning task. Some children given supply tokens at the beginning of the experiment provided their own reward (the tokens could be exchanged for prizes) for attaining a high level of performance; other children attaining a high level of performance received tokens from the experimenter. Bandura and Perloff reported that the self-imposed-reward groups and the externally imposed reward groups showed equal levels of performance, responding at a higher level than children given reward prior to the task or no reward at all. Self-reinforcement procedures have effectively modified a number of undesired behaviors: impulsive overspending (Paulsen, Rimm, Woodburn, & Rimm, 1977), depression (Fuchs & Rehm, 1977; Rehm, 1977), inadequate study habits (Beneke & Harris, 1972; Greiner & Karoly, 1976), and overeating (Harris, 1969; Stuart, 1971). Let's discuss the control of eating behavior as an example of the self-reinforcement procedure.

The self-reward procedure has three separate stages: self-monitoring, contingency contracting, and self-reinforcement. During the self-monitoring stage, the patients record the frequency of eating behavior, including the quantity and caloric content of all food eaten. Surprisingly, overweight individuals typically are unaware of the amount they consume. The self-monitoring procedure serves to enlighten the patients concerning the extent of their overeating. Often patients show a weight reduction in the self-monitoring phase (Green, 1978), probably because they simply recognize the extent of their food intake. Patients are also required to record the stimulus conditions that precede eating and the consequences of eating. The self-monitoring stage establishes the baseline level of eating performance and provides a means of evaluating the behavior change produced by the self-reinforcement treatment.

In the contracting stage, the behavior-reward contingency is established. Reinforcement (for example, money or some enjoyable activity) is provided when the individual meets the food-reduction requirement. The patient is given realistic goals, recognizing that behavior change cannot occur quickly. A shaping procedure is usually employed by slowly reducing caloric intake. The self-monitoring phase reveals that the obese person eats in many situations (for example, while watching television, driving, or at the movies), and therefore eating in these situations must be eliminated. Thus, the patient is allowed to eat only in the dining room. The individual is also rewarded for avoiding situations leading to eating. Competing responses must be identified and reinforced. For instance, the patient should provide some form of reinforcement for reading a book rather than eating. Finally, the self-control procedure reinforces the behavior itself rather than the effect of the behavior. For example, the patient would earn the reward (going to a movie) by limiting his or her daily intake to 1000 calories rather than by losing a pound. The objective of the therapy is to develop new, permanent, and effective modes of eating which will continue after treatment ends and after the weight goal has been met.

The self-reinforcement treatment is implemented during the last phase of the procedure. In general, self-reinforcement produces modest weight losses over the typical ten-week therapy period. Some experiments have yielded more impressive effects. For example, Musante (1976), working with 229 overweight patients at Duke University, reported an average weight loss per week of 3.5 lb in males and 2.3 lb in females, and Stuart (1967) observed an average weight loss of 38 lb during a twenty-week session. However, most studies indicate an average loss of 1 lb per week. Follow-up studies show that many patients regain weight, and some lose even more weight after the study ends. Social support (Mahoney, 1974) and periodic maintenance sessions (Stuart, 1967) are two important factors in enhancing and maintaining weight loss: failure to incorporate these factors will lead to smaller behavioral change during treatment and less consistent maintenance of the new behavior after therapy.

Implementation of the Contingency-Management Program

Skinner's idea that reinforcement could be systematically employed to modify behavior was empirically tested in the early 1960s by Ayllon and Azrin at Anna State Hospital in Illinois (Ayllon & Azrin, 1965, 1968, 1969). Ayllon and Azrin established a contingency-management program for institutionalized adult female psychotic patients. These patients received tokens, which could later be exchanged for desired primary reinforcers, when they engaged in instrumental responses that they had not exhibited while hospitalized and that they would need for effective adjustment to the "real world." Two classes of instrumental behaviors were reinforced: (1) self-care activities such as grooming and bathing and (2) job activities such as washing dishes and serving food. Ayllon and Azrin reported that the frequency of appropriate instrumental responding significantly increased as the result of their contingency-management program. (Their approach is often called a token economy program due to the use of tokens as secondary reinforcers.) Ayllon and Azrin's treatment shows that psychiatric patients can develop behaviors necessary for successful adjustment through the reinforcement of those behaviors. In fact, many studies (Fairweather, Sanders, Maynard, & Cressler, 1969; Paul & Lentz, 1977; Schaefer & Martin, 1969) have found that psychotic patients receiving contingency-management treatment adjust significantly better to daily living than do patients given standard hospital treatment programs. The efficacy of instrumental conditioning to alter the behavior of hospitalized psychotic patients appears to be a well-established finding.

Contingency-management programs have been used to alter behavior in a variety of settings. Some of these programs are shown in Table 3.3. Contingency management appears to be an effective treatment for a number of behavior pathologies in addition to the lack of real-world living skills. Depression is one behavior problem which has been modified by contingent reinforcement (see Burgess, 1968; Lieberman & Raskin, 1971). Contingency management has also been used in the treatment of anxiety (Barlow, Agras, Leitenberg, & Wincze, 1970; Marshall, Boutilier, & Minnes, 1974; Reisinger, 1972; Rimm & Mahoney, 1969; Vasta, 1975) and pain (see Cautela, 1977; Kallman, Hersen, & O'Toole, 1975; Sand & Biglan, 1974). In these studies, reinforcement occurred when the patients showed decreases in anxiety, depression, or pain and increases in responses incompatible with the behavior problem.

Token economy systems have been established at a number of residential treatment centers for delinquent and predelinquent children and adolescents. The aim of these contingency-management programs is to establish appropriate social and lawful behavior as well as academic competencies. These programs have shown that contingent reinforcement can decrease inappropriate social behavior and increase desired social and academic responses (Bailey, Wolf, & Phillips, 1970; Emshoff, Redd, & Davidson, 1976; Hobbs & Holt, 1976; Maloney, Harper, Braukmann, Fiven, Phillips, & Wolf, 1976; Phillips, 1968; Phillips, Phillips, Fixen, & Wolf, 1971).

A contingency-management program can also increase effective responding in retarded children and adults. For example, contingent reinforcement has been used with retarded children to teach toilet training (Azrin, Sneed, & Foxx, 1973; Giles & Wolf, 1966; Siegel, 1977), personal grooming (Horner & Keilitz, 1975), and mealtime behavior (Plummer, Baer, & LeBlanc, 1977). Furthermore, contingency management can suppress several behaviors characteristic of some retarded children; for example, the incidence of self-injurious behavior (Griffin, Locke, & Landers, 1975; Solnick, Rincover, & Peterson, 1977), aggression and disruptive behavior (Plummer, Baer, & LeBlanc, 1977), and self-stimulation (Wells, Forehand, Hickey, & Green, 1977) will decrease when reinforcement is contingent on the suppression of these behaviors.

Childhood hyperactivity is another behavior which appears to respond to contingency-management treatment (Ayllon, Layman, & Kandel, 1975; Christensen & Sprague, 1973; Kaufman & Hallahan, 1973; Shafto & Sulzbacher, 1977; Wulbert & Dries, 1977). These programs, which provide reinforcement for proper classroom behavior and academic competency, consistently show that the contingency-management program produces a decline in activity and an improvement in academic performance in hyperactive children. Furthermore, whereas drug treatment using the stimulant Ritalin (methylphenidate) appears to reduce activity, studies demonstrate that it has no influence on academic competency; therefore, contingency management should be incorporated in any treatment of hyperactive children.

Contingent reinforcement has been used to improve the academic performance of normal children and adults also. For example, Lovitt, Guppy, and Blattner (1969) found that contingent free time and listening to the radio increased the accuracy of spelling in fourth-grade children. Other studies have also found that academic competency in children can be increased with a contingency-management procedure; refer to Chadwick and Day (1971), Harris and Sherman (1973), McLaughlin and Malaby (1972), Rapport and Bostow (1976) for other examples. Also, contingent reinforcement has been shown to increase the studying behavior of college students; however, this procedure appears to be effective only with students of below-average ability (Bristol & Sloane, 1974) or students with low or medium grade averages (DuNann & Weber, 1976). The other students are probably already exhibiting effective studying behavior, and therefore reinforcement is not likely to increase their responding. Thus, contingent reinforcement will increase academic performance for only those students not already responding effectively.

Contingency management is also effective with large groups of people. For example, Hayes and Cone (1977) found that direct payments to efficient energy users produced large reductions in energy consumption, and Seaver and Patterson (1976) discovered that informational feedback and a contingent decal for

TABLE 3.3
SAMPLE OF BEHAVIORS INFLUENCED BY A CONTINGENCY-MANAGEMENT PROGRAM

Target	Behavior/competency	Population	Outcome	Source of report
Social	Social and emotional behaviors	Handicapped children	Increased	Cooke & Apolloni (1976)
	Prosocial verbal behavior	Delinquent adolescent	Increased	Emshoff, Redd, & Davidson, (1976)
	Social interaction	Chronic psychotic adults	Increased	Fichter, Wallace, Liberman, & Davis (1976)
	Social interaction	Retarded adolescents	Increased	L. Williams, Martin, McDonald, Hardy, & Lambert (1975)
	Reluctant speech	Preadolescents	Decreased	Williamson, Sewell, Sanders, Haney, & White (1977)
	Sharing, praising	Children	Increased	Rogers-Warren & Baer (1976)
	Social speech	Retarded children	Increased	Mithaug & Wolfe (1976)
	Social greeting	Retarded children	Increased	Stokes, Baer, & Jackson (1974)
	Positive reinforcement of children	Adult teacher	Increased	Breyer & Allen (1975)
	Social skills	Predelinquent adolescents	Increased	D. M. Maloney, Harper, Braukmann, Fixsen, Phillips, & Wolf (1976)
	Peer interaction, obedience	Delinquent adolescents	Increased	Hobbs & Holt (1976)
	Extreme withdrawal	Children	Improved	Allen, Hart, Buell, Harris, & Wolf (1964); Brawley, Harris, Allen, Fleming, & Peterson (1969)
	Extreme passivity	Children	Improved	Johnston, Kelley, Harris, & Wolf (1966)
	Sharing	Children	Increased	Warren, Rogers-Warren, & Baer (1976)
	Social disruption	Children	Decreased	MacPherson, Candee, & Hohman (1974)
Self-control	Hyperactivity/attention span	Retarded children	Decreased/increased	Alabiso (1975)
	Hyperactivity	Children	Decreased	Wulbert & Dries (1977)
	Hyperactivity	Children	Decreased	Ayllon, Layman, & Kandel (1975)
	Hyperactivity and aggression	Children	Decreased	Allen, Henke, Harris, Baer, & Reynolds (1967); Hall, Lund, & Jackson (1968)

	Target	Population	Outcome	Reference
	Obesity	Children	Decreased	Epstein, Parker, McCoy, & McGee (1975)
	Classroom disruption	Children	Decreased	Todd, Scott, Bostow, & Alexander (1976)
	Family interaction	Mother and adolescent	Improved responsibility	Blechman, Olson, Schornagle, Halsdorf, & Turner (1976)
	Enuresis	Adolescent	Eliminated	Popler (1976)
	Rumination	Infant	Eliminated	Linscheid & Cunningham (1977)
	Hirschsprung's disease	Child	Controlled	Epstein & McCoy (1977)
	Classroom disruption	Children	Decreased	Robertson, DeReus, & Drabman (1976)
	Classroom disruption	Children	Decreased	Ayllon, Garber, & Pisor (1975)
	Classroom task attention	Children	Increased	Hay, Hay, & Nelson (1977b)
	Classroom task attention	Children	Increased	Marholin & Steinman (1977)
	Academic task completion	Children	Increased	Rapport & Bostow (1976)
	Homework	Children	Improved	Harris & Sherman (1974)
	School attendance	Predelinquent	Improved	Alexander, Corbett, & Smigel (1976)
	Curfew obedience	Adolescents	Improved	Alexander, Corbett, & Smigel (1976)
	Self-control	Normal adult	Improved	Whitman & Dussault (1976)
	Writer's block	Adult	Eliminated	Passman (1976)
	Stuttering	Adults	Eliminated	Ingham & Andrews (1973)
Cognitive-emotional	Complex language	Autistic child	Acquired	Stevens-Long & Rasmussen (1974)
	Creativity	Children	Increased	Henson (1975)
	Intelligence score	Handicapped children	Increased	Smeets & Striefel (1975)
	Intelligence/vocabulary	Normal children	Increased	Clingman & Fowler (1976)
	Creativity	Normal children	Increased	Glover & Gary (1976)
	School performance	Adolescent	Improved	Schumaker, Hovell, & Sherman (1977)
	Reading/comprehension	Autistic child	Improved	Rosenbaum & Breiling (1976)
	Arithmetic competence	Children	Improved	Hundert (1976)
	Autisticlike behavior	Child	Eliminated	Moore & Bailey (1973)
	Anxiety and depression	Adult	Eliminated	Vasta (1975)
	Anxiety and depression	Adult	Eliminated	Reisinger (1972)
	Phobia	Adults	Eliminated	Marshall, Boutilier, & Minnes (1974)
	Conversion reaction	Adult	Eliminated	Kallman, Hersen, & O'Toole (1975)

TABLE 3.3 (continued)

Target	Behavior/competency	Population	Outcome	Source of report
	Anxiety and hyper-dependency	Children	Improved	Wahler & Pollio (1968)
	Autism	Children	Improved	Lovaas (1968); Wetzel, Baker, Rooney, & Martin (1966)
	Mutism	Adults	Improved	Sherman (1965); Straughan (1968)
	School phobia	Children	Eliminated	G. R. Patterson (1965)
	Psychogenic seizures			Gardner (1967)
	Psychogenic blindness	Adult	Improved	Brady & Lind (1961)
	Maladaptive or reduced responsiveness of various sorts in schizophrenics	Adult	Improved	Ayllon & Azrin (1968a); King, Armitage, & Tilton (1960); Peters & Jenkins (1954); Schaefer & Martin (1966); Thompson & Grabowski (1972, 1977)
	Inappropriate gender identity	Child	Made appropriate	Rekers, Yates, Willis, Rosen, & Taubman (1976)
	Pain	Adult	Eliminated	Cautela (1971c)
	Stuttering	Adults	Reduced	Ingham & Andrews (1973)

Source: Rimm, D. C. and Masters, J. C. *Behavior therapy: Techniques and empirical findings* (2d ed.). New York: Academic Press, 1979.

efficient energy use resulted in a significant decrease in home fuel consumption. Also, McCalden and Davis (1972) discovered that reserving a special lane of the Oakland-San Francisco Bay Bridge for cars with several passengers increased car pooling and improved traffic flow. Finally, Reiss, Piotrowski, and Bailey (1976) reported that dental care for children of rural areas improved when their parents received incentives for taking their children to a dentist.

Thus contingency management is an effective technique for increasing appropriate responding and for decreasing inappropriate behavior. Although the use of contingency-management techniques has increased over the past decade, it could be employed in many more circumstances to produce more effective responding. It is to be hoped that contingency-management programs will become more prevalent in the future.

SUMMARY

Reinforcement has a powerful influence on instrumental behavior. When reinforcement is contingent on the occurrence of a particular instrumental response, the incidence of that response increases. Although reinforcers typically are thought of as objects, such as food or water, Premack's analysis indicates that activities such as watching television or going to a dance can also be reinforcers. An object or activity will serve as a reinforcer if a response contingency limits access to that object or event; such a contingency causes an increase in the instrumental activity to restore access to the object or event to the prerestriction level of responding. Research indicates that the termination of adversity can also be reinforcing.

Primary reinforcers possess innate reinforcing ability, and secondary reinforcers develop the capacity to reinforce instrumental behavior. The reinforcing properties of many objects or activities, although seemingly obvious, may not occur in certain individuals or under some circumstances. Therefore, a specific object or activity is reinforcing when its influence on behavior is ascertained through observation. If the object or activity increases the frequency of a contingent instrumental behavior, it is a reinforcer.

The environment specifies the relation between the instrumental response and reinforcement; however, when the operant rate is zero, the instrumental response will not increase in frequency, despite the contingency between reinforcement and the instrumental response. Furthermore, learning is slow if the operant rate of the instrumental behavior is low. The shaping procedure can be used to ensure rapid conditioning. Shaping involves reinforcing a high-operant-rate response and then changing the contingency so that closer and closer approximations to the final behavior are necessary to produce reinforcement.

The contingency specifies not only the response which will lead to reinforcement but also the manner in which the behavior must occur. In fixed-ratio schedules, reward requires a fixed number of responses; a variable-ratio schedule uses an average number of responses for reward, but the number of responses varies from reinforcement to reinforcement. In contrast, on an interval schedule of reinforcement the first response after a specified interval of time produces reward; the interval remains constant throughout a fixed-interval schedule and varies from reward to reward on a variable-interval schedule. More complex schedules include differential-rate schedules and compound schedules. With differential rate schedules, a specified number of behaviors must occur within a specific period in order for reward to be presented. Compound schedules combine two (or more) schedules of reinforcement. Each schedule produces a characteristic response rate and pattern, and an animal or person will exhibit behavior characteristic of that schedule.

Three variables influence the acquisition of an instrumental response. An instrumental response will be acquired rapidly and performance will be at a high level if (1) reward immediately follows the instrumental response, (2) the reward received for the instrumental response is valued, and (3) motivation is high.

The strength of the instrumental response increases during acquisition; the frequency and intensity of the instrumental behavior declines during extinction. Extinction of an instrumental response occurs when that behavior no longer produces reinforcement. Nonreward of the instrumental response inhibits that response and elicits avoidance behavior. The avoidance behavior initially is a response to escape from the frustration induced by nonreward. Association of environmental cues with nonreward causes an animal or person to avoid receiving nonreward and, therefore, to decrease the strength of the instrumental response. However, nonreward sometimes increases rather than decreases the intensity of an instrumental response. It is argued that this intensification occurs when the avoidance response elicited by frustration is compatible with the appetitive response to obtain reward or when memory of nonreward has been conditioned to elicit the appetitive response.

A number of variables affect the extinction of an instrumental response. Extinction is governed by the reward magnitude experienced in acquisition, the delay between the instrumental response and reward during acquisition, and the consistency of reward for acquisition of the instrumental response. A large reward magnitude produces greater resistance to extinction than does a small reward magnitude when the amount of acquisition training is low, but the opposite is true with extended acquisition training. Also, resistance to extinction is higher when reward delay is varied rather than constant. Furthermore, partial rather than continuous reinforcement leads to slower extinction of the instrumental behavior. Capaldi's research indicates that the conditioning of the memory of nonreward and instrumental activity in the partial-reinforcement condition, but not in the continuous-reward condition, accounts for the greater resistance to extinction with partial rather than with continuous reinforcement.

Contingent reinforcement has been used in many real-world situations to increase appropriate instrumental behaviors and decrease inappropriate instrumental responses. The application of the instrumental conditioning process to alter human behavior is called contingency management. The three phases of contingency management are assessment, contracting, and implementation.

The assessment phase determines the level of appropriate and inappropriate instrumental behavior as well as the situations where these behaviors occur and the potential reinforcers of the appropriate instrumental response. The precise relation between the instrumental response and reinforcement is decided during the contracting phase, and the reinforcement is provided contingent on the appropriate instrumental response, suppression of the inappropriate instrumental behavior, or both in the implementation phase. Contingency management has successfully modified many different behaviors, including inadequate living skills, phobias, depression, poor study habits, antisocial responses, and energy consumption. The expanded use of this procedure offers hope for an improved society.

CHAPTER 4

INSTRUMENTAL AVERSIVE CONDITIONING

THE PAIN OF LONELINESS

Susan dreads her husband Bill's upcoming two-year deployment. After Bill's last sea duty, Susan had pleaded with him to leave the Navy. Sixteen months of his two-year tour had been served at sea, while she alone cared for their two young children. However, Bill will not consider resigning; he will reach retirement after only six more years of service.

Remembering the loneliness she felt last time Bill was at sea, Susan wonders if she can survive the next two years. The family's transfer from Virginia to California just before Bill's last deployment had intensified Susan's problems. When they lived in Virginia, her parents and a few close friends had lived nearby, but in California, although the wives of the men in Bill's squadron were friendly, Susan felt awkward and attended only a few social functions. Susan missed her family and friends in Virginia.

Susan enjoys caring for her two young children, a task which consumes most of her time and energy. Yet, the absence of Bill and her family and friends created a void. During Bill's last deployment, Susan found that a glass or two of wine with dinner dulled her senses, eased the pain of her loneliness, and enabled her to sleep soundly. Soon Susan was consuming a bottle or two nightly. Her children began to notice her moodiness; Susan's care of them had, in fact, diminished to the point of negligence.

Susan's drinking declined when Bill was at home or a relative was visiting. However, as his departure approached each time, Susan would begin to drink heavily again, continuing until he came home or someone visited. After this two years of sea duty, Bill spent two years at home. His presence produced a remarkable change in Susan: she drank less, her moodiness disappeared, and her care of her children improved. Unfortunately, as the time for another sea duty approaches, Susan feels panic-stricken. She realizes that she needs help but does not know where to turn.

Susan's loneliness during Bill's sea duty represents a reaction to the loss of social support and security (see Chapter 3 for a discussion of the negative emotional state of frustration elicited by the loss of reward). Susan responded to her husband's absence by drinking. Alcohol dulled her feelings of separation, and her increased drinking had become a habitual way to cope with her loneliness. Other people who lose, even temporarily, valued interpersonal relationships may also drink to reduce their loneliness. In contrast, some people feel that they are helpless and, therefore, become clinically depressed; still others react by forming new relationships. Chapter 4 describes how people respond when attempting to terminate unpleasant events like the loss of an interpersonal relationship. Chapter 6 details the circumstances that lead people to become depressed rather than to cope with adversity.

THE ADVERSITY AROUND US

We all encounter many unpleasant events; no one is immune to adversity. Unless we learn how to cope with adversity, our lives will become quite miserable.

Some aversive events can be escaped but not avoided. We cannot anticipate these circumstances but must be prepared to respond to terminate them. For example, walking to the store, you are attacked by a thief who wants your money. You can end the attack by surrendering your money or by counterattacking. You will escape if your aggressive response is effective; however, if it is not, your counterattack probably will lead to even greater adversity.

Other aversive events can be avoided. To prevent adversity, you must learn when the aversive event will occur and also how you can act to prevent it. For example, many elderly people know that they may be mugged if they go out at night; therefore, their refusal to leave their homes after dark represents an avoidance behavior which allows them to avoid being mugged. This chapter describes the learning processes governing whether we are able to escape or avoid an aversive event.

A parent spanks his or her child after receiving a teacher's note indicating poor behavior. The spanking is intended to inhibit future misbehavior in the classroom; this parent's behavior toward the child is called *punishment*. If punishment is effective, the child will no longer misbehave in school. What factors determine whether punishment suppresses inappropriate behavior will be detailed later in the chapter.

You might think that a parent spanking a child for misbehaving does not relate to an elderly person's remaining inside at night to avoid being mugged, but punishment and avoidance conditioning typically detail two aspects of the same process: the child can avoid being punished (spanked) by not misbehaving in school, and the elderly person can avoid being mugged by not going out at night. Thus, to be effective, punishment must motivate the inhibition of the inappropriate response. However, in some circumstances a person or an animal learns to prevent punishment, but this response differs from inhibition of inappropriate behavior. For example, a child may be able to avoid a spanking by crying rather than by not misbehaving. Although we will describe punishment and avoidance behavior separately in this chapter, remember that if punishment is to be successful, inhibition of the inappropriate response must be the only response that can prevent punishment.

Some aversive events cannot be escaped or avoided. For example, a child who is abused by a parent cannot escape or prevent the abuse. Chapter 6 discusses how an animal or person becomes helpless upon learning that adversity can be neither escaped nor avoided.

ESCAPE CONDITIONING

Many people close their eyes during a scary scene in a horror movie, reopening them when they believe the unpleasant scene has ended. This behavior is one example of an *escape response*—an instrumental behavior motivated by an aversive event (for example, the scary scene, S^{R-}) and reinforced by the termination of the adversity.

Many studies (Brush, 1970; Campbell & Church, 1969) show that people and animals will try to escape from aversive events; let's examine two. Miller's classic 1948 study (see Chapter 1) showed that rats could learn to escape painful electric shock. Miller placed rats in the white compartment of a shuttle box and exposed them to electric shock. The rats could escape the shock by turning a wheel and then running into the black compartment; Miller reported that the rats rapidly learned to use this escape route. In a similar study using human subjects, Hiroto (1974) exposed college students to an unpleasant noise that they could terminate by moving their finger from one side of a shuttle box to the other. Hiroto found that his subjects quickly learned how to escape the noise.

Not all people close their eyes during a horror movie; some people may not find the scenes scary (or may even consider them reinforcing) or have not learned the escape response of closing their eyes. Thus aversive events are not always escaped.

Escape from Adversity

Three factors play an important role in determining whether a person or animal learns to escape from adversity and how efficient the escape response is. First, *the intensity of the aversive event affects escape conditioning*. Research evaluating the effect of the severity of adversity indicates that the greater the intensity of the aversive event, the faster the conditioning of the escape response and the higher the asymptotic level of responding. However, the intensity of adversity is affected by experience: exposure to a low-level aversive event increases the aversiveness of exposure to a higher intensity of the same event. In contrast, previous experience with a high level of an aversive event decreases the aversiveness of a lower level of this adversity. Second, *the amount of reinforcement influences the acquisition of an escape response*. Experimentation investigating the effect of reward magnitude shows that the greater the decrease in the severity of adversity produced by the escape response, the faster the acquisition of an escape as well as the higher the final level of escape responding. Third, *delay of reward affects the development of an escape response*. Research evaluating the effect of reward delay indicates that the longer the delay in the termination of the aversive event, the slower the acquisition of the escape response and the lower the asymptotic response level.

Intensity of the Aversive Event   Walking to class, you see a student stumble and fall. Will you stop to help? A number of variables affect helping behavior. One critical factor is the aversiveness of the emergency. According to Jane Piliavin and her associates (Piliavin, Dovidio, Gaertner, & Clark, 1981), the more unpleasant the situation, the higher the cost of helping and, therefore, the greater the motive to escape from the emergency. Thus, the more serious the injury is, the less likely you are to help.

Many studies have supported this cost analysis of helping. For example, Piliavin, Piliavin, and Roden (1975) created a simulated emergency on subway cars in New York City. A confederate acting as a victim would moan and then faint. The experimenters increased the discomfort of some bystanders by having the victim expose an ugly birthmark just before fainting. The victim did not expose the unpleasant birthmark to other bystanders. Piliavin, Piliavin, and Roden's results indicate that the bystanders who saw the ugly birthmark helped the victim less often than those who did not. As the cost of helping increases—in this case, the cost included enduring the sight of an ugly birthmark—the likelihood of helping behavior decreases.

People's escape response in other unpleasant situations also is influenced by the degree of the aversiveness of the situation. The escape response when anticipating failure on an achievement task provides another illustration of the influence of the intensity of the aversive event. The more unpleasant the task, in this case the greater the expectation of failure, the higher the motivation to escape and, therefore, the less persistence exhibited by subjects (Atkinson, 1964; Feather, 1967).

Research with animals has documented the effect of the intensity of adversity on escape behavior. Most studies have used electric shock as the aversive event. For example, Trapold and Fowler (1960) trained rats to escape electric shock in the start box of an alley by running to an uncharged goal box. The rats received 120, 160, 240, 300, or 400 V of electric shock in the start box. Trapold and Fowler reported that the greater the shock intensity, the shorter the latency to escape from the start box (see Figure 4.1). Other studies (refer to Amsel, 1950; Campbell & Kraeling, 1953) discovered that the bigger the increase in the

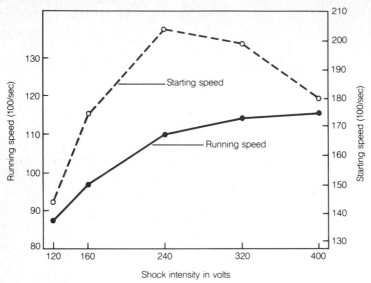

FIGURE 4.1
Mean escape performance as a function of shock intensity over last
eight trials of training. Adapted from Trapold, M. A., & Fowler, H.
Instrumental escape performance as a function of the intensity of
noxious stimulation. *Journal of Experimental Psychology*, 1960, *60*,
323–326. Copyright 1960 by the American Psychological Association.
Reprinted by permission.

electric shock, the faster the escape response. Additional research showed that
escape latency is influenced by the intensity of loud noise (Bolles & Seelbach,
1964; Masterson, 1969) and light (see Kaplan, Jackson, & Sparer, 1965).

   Is It Really That Bad?   Chapter 3 pointed out that the value of a reinforcer is
influenced by experience with other rewards. Similarly, the aversiveness of an
event is affected by previous exposure to other aversive situations. When
contrasted with a less aversive circumstance, an unpleasant experience seems
more aversive; however, this adversity contrasted with more aversive situations appears less unpleasant. For example, you may have thought that a
certain "horror" movie was extremely scary until you saw a film which frightened you even more.
   Nation, Wrather, and Mellgren's (1974) study demonstrates how prior experience with high or low levels of electric shock influences aversiveness of
moderate shock intensity. Nation, Wrather, and Mellgren initially trained their
rats to escape from either a 0.2-, 0.4-, or 0.8-mA electric shock. After twenty
escape-conditioning trials, the shock level shifted to the 0.4-mA level for all
subjects for twenty additional trials. Nation, Wrather, and Mellgren found that
the rats shifting from 0.2-mA to 0.4-mA escaped most rapidly and that the rats
shifted from 0.8-mA to 0.4-mA shock escaped more slowly than even the

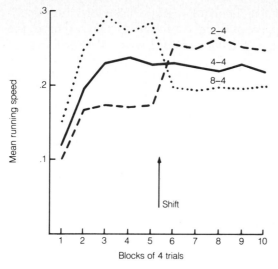

FIGURE 4.2
Mean running speed in the alley during escape training. Animals received either 0.2, 0.4, or 0.8 mA electric shock in the start box and were shifted to 0.4 mA following trial block 5. From Nation, J. R., Wrather, D. M., & Mellgren, R. L. Contrast effects in escape conditioning of rats. *Journal of Comparative and Physiological Psychology*, 1974, *86,* 69–73. Copyright 1974 by the American Psychological Association. Reprinted by permission.

subjects that always received the 0.4-mA shock (see Figure 4.2). These results show that the 0.4-mA shock was more aversive when contrasted with a lower level shock than when no comparison could be made; it was less aversive when compared with a higher shock level. Apparently, the intensity of an animal's escape reaction to an aversive event depends on both the intensity of that situation and the intensity of similar unpleasant events already experienced.

No Place to Run   Why do many people remain in unsatisfying social relationships? One likely reason is that past escape reactions from unpleasant social relationships did not lead to positive relationships, and therefore these individuals have not learned to use an escape response to get out of aversive situations. Many studies show that amount of reward (degree of decrease in adversity) affects the intensity of escape behavior. In these experiments, the greater the reward, the higher the asymptotic level of escape performance.

Campbell and Kraeling (1953) exposed rats to a 400-V electric shock in the start box of an alley. Upon reaching the goal box, the shock was reduced to 0, 100, 200, or 300 V. Campbell and Kraeling reported that the greater the reduction in shock intensity, the faster the rats escaped from the 400-V electric shock. Other experiments (Bower, Fowler, & Trapold, 1959) have discovered that the level of escape behavior relates directly to the level of shock reduction produced by the escape response. Reward magnitude has been found to have a positive influence on the asymptotic level of escape performance with cold water as the aversive stimulus (Woods, Davidson, & Peters, 1964; Woods & Holland, 1966).

How Long Does the Pain Last?   In the last section we discovered that the magnitude of reward affects the intensity of escape responding. Research has indicated that the delay of reward also influences escape behavior. This experimentation shows that the longer the reward delay after an escape response, the slower the acquisition of the escape behavior and the lower the final level of escape performance.

Fowler and Trapold's (1962) study illustrates the impact of reward delay on escape conditioning. In their study, the termination of electric shock was delayed 0, 1, 2, 4, 8, or 16 seconds after the rats entered the goal box of the alley apparatus. Fowler and Trapold reported that how long the rats took to reach the goal box was a direct function of reward delay; the longer the delay, the slower the acquisition of a rapid escape response (see Figure 4.3). Furthermore, reward delay also determined the maximum escape speed; the longer the delay, the lower the final level of escape performance. Other studies using animals (Milby, 1971; Tarpy, 1969; Tarpy & Koster, 1970) and humans (Penney, 1967) have found that reward delay plays an important role in escape conditioning.

However, some experiments reported that a delay of even 3 seconds results in no escape conditioning. According to Tarpy and Sawabini (1974), differences in delay gradients reflect the presence or absence of cues associated with reward (termination of aversive event). The experiments showing very short delay gradients have used the operant chamber apparatus, with bar pressing as the escape response to terminate shock. Since no cues are typically associated with shock termination in the bar-press situation, no secondary reinforcement cues can enhance performance when reward is delayed. If cues are presented

FIGURE 4.3
Mean running speed during escape training as a function of the delay in shock termination. Adapted from Fowler, H., & Trapold, M. A. Escape performance as a function of delay of reinforcement. *Journal of Experimental Psychology*, 1962, *63*, 464–467. Copyright 1962 by the American Psychological Association. Reprinted by permission.

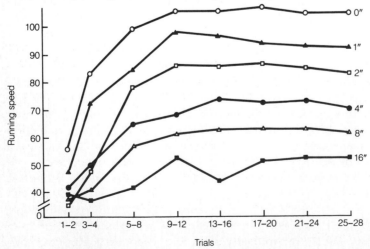

following a bar-press response, these stimuli will be associated with shock termination, and some escape conditioning will occur despite a short delay of reward. Recall from Chapter 3 that a similar influence of cues associated with rewards occurs when positive reinforcement is delayed. Apparently, one significant influence of secondary reinforcers is overcoming the effect of primary reward delay and, therefore, the conditioning of an instrumental response.

Extinction of an Escape Response

A rat shocked in the start box of an alley learns to escape by running into the goal box. Using extinction, a psychologist can stop the rat from escaping the start box. Extinction of an escape response can be accomplished by no longer presenting the aversive event (S^{R-}) or no longer terminating the S^{R-} following the escape response.

Removal of Reward   An escape response is eliminated when S^{R-} continues despite the performance of the escape response. However, an animal or person will continue to respond for some time; the adversity continues to motivate the escape response until an animal or person learns that the escape response no longer terminates the aversive event.

The number of training trials affects the resistance to extinction of an escape response: the greater the acquisition training, the slower the extinction of the escape behavior. To illustrate the influence of the acquisition level on resistance to extinction, Fazzaro and D'Amato (1969) trained rats to bar-press to terminate electric shock. Rats received 200, 400, 800, or 1600 training trials prior to extinction. Fazzaro and D'Amato found that the number of bar-press responses emitted during extinction increased with greater numbers of acquisition trials (see Figure 4.4). Other studies have found that the greater the training, the slower the extinction of an escape response; the Campbell (1959) study provides one example.

Absence of Adversity   Extinction of an escape response also occurs when the aversive event is no longer experienced, but an animal or person exhibits a number of escape responses during extinction even though the S^{R-} no longer occurs. When the aversive event is not experienced, the motive for escape is not present; this observation leads to the expectation that during extinction no escape responses will occur. Why, then, do escape responses occur when the aversive event is not present?

D'Amato (1970) suggests an explanation for why escape responses occur even after the presentation of the aversive event has been discontinued. According to D'Amato, the cues that were present when the aversive event occurred during escape conditioning elicit the r_p-s_p (anticipatory pain response mechanism; see Chapter 1). During extinction, these stimuli produce the r_p-s_p and therefore motivate the escape response even though the aversive event

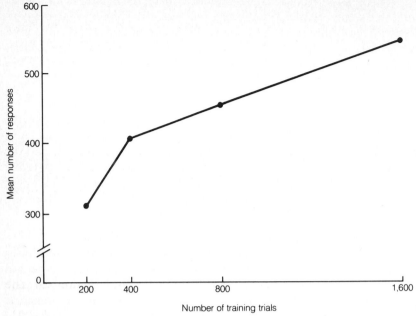

FIGURE 4.4
Mean number of escape responses duration during extinction as a function of
the number of acquisition trials. (From Fazzaro, J., & D'Amato, M. R. Resistance
to extinction after varying amounts of nondiscriminative or cue-correlated
escape training. *Journal of Comparative and Physiological Psychology,* 1969,
68, 373–376. Copyright 1969 by the American Psychological Association.
Reprinted by permission.

(S^{R-}) is no longer presented. The animal will continue to respond until the
anticipatory pain response is extinguished.

Our discussion indicates that we can learn how to escape from aversive
situations. However, avoiding adversity is more desirable than escaping adversity. In the next section we will examine the development of instrumental
responses, responses that allow us to prevent aversive events.

THE AVOIDANCE OF ADVERSITY

A teenager is invited to a party by a boy she does not like. Not wanting to hurt
his feelings, she says that she would like to go but cannot because she must
study for a test. This teenager is exhibiting an avoidance response: her "little
white lie" enabled her to prevent an unpleasant evening without harming anyone. Animals and people exhibit many different avoidance responses to prevent adversity.

Types of Avoidance Behavior

There are two classes of avoidance behavior: active and passive avoidance responses. Under some circumstances, an overt response is necessary to prevent an unpleasant event, that is, an *active avoidance response* is necessary to avoid the aversive event. The teenager exhibited an active avoidance response: she formulated an excuse to prevent adversity. In other circumstances, an animal or person can avoid an aversive event by not responding, that is, a *passive avoidance response* will prevent adversity. Suppose you receive a note from your dentist indicating that it is time for your six-month checkup. Since you do not like going to the dentist, you ignore the note. This is passive avoidance behavior: you avoid the dentist by not responding to the note. Many studies have demonstrated that animals and people can learn to avoid adversity both actively and passively.

Active Avoidance Learning O. H. Mowrer's classic research (Mowrer, 1938, 1939) showed that rats could learn to exhibit an overt response to avoid electric shock. In these studies, a cue (for example, a buzzer) was paired with painful electric shock in one chamber of a shuttle box (see Figure 4.5). The rats could avoid shock by jumping across a barrier between the two compartments when the cue (CS) was presented but before the shock onset (UCS). The animals in Mowrer's studies learned to exhibit the active avoidance hurdle-jump response when exposed to the CS and, therefore, avoided the electric shock. Many other psychologists since Mowrer have discovered that rats can learn to cross a barrier to avoid electric shock in the shuttle box apparatus (Black, 1963; Bower, Starr, & Lazarovitz, 1965; Kamin, 1956; Moyer & Korn, 1966; Theios, Lynch, & Lowe, 1966). The shuttle box apparatus has also been employed to train other animal species to avoid adversity. This research indicates that to avoid shock, dogs (Moscovitch & LoLordo, 1967; Rescorla & LoLordo, 1965; Solomon & Wynne, 1953), cats (Lockhart & Steinbrecher, 1965; Steinbrecher & Lockhart, 1966), mice (Winston, Lindzey, & Connor, 1967), and rabbits (Flakus & Steinbrecher, 1964) can learn to jump over the hurdle in a shuttle box.

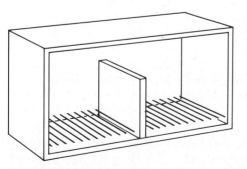

FIGURE 4.5
Illustration shows shuttle box used to study avoidance learning. Each compartment has an electrified grid floor. When the conditioned stimulus is presented, animal must jump to other compartment to avoid electric shock.

The hurdle-jumping response in the shuttle box is one of many behaviors which animals can learn to avoid aversive events. Miller (1941, 1948) discovered that rats could learn to turn a wheel to avoid electric shock. Other psychologists have reported that rats can learn to press a bar in an operant chamber (Biederman, D'Amato, & Keller, 1964; D'Amato, Keller, & DiCara, 1964; Hurwitz, 1964) or even rear up on their hind legs (Bolles & Tuttle, 1967) to prevent shock.

People learn many different responses to avoid adversity. A person opening an umbrella to stay dry, a child doing homework to avoid failing, and an adult paying the mortgage to avoid foreclosure are three examples of humans responding to avoid unpleasant events.

Many, perhaps most, of our avoidance responses are acquired during childhood. Research with children shows that they are very adept in learning how to avoid adversity. Unlike most experiments with animals which use electric shock as the aversive event, research using children typically employs loud tones as the unpleasant event. In these experiments (Penney & Croskery, 1962; Penney & Kirwin, 1965; Robinson & Robinson, 1961) preschool-aged children could press a lever to prevent hearing a loud noise. The children readily learned the avoidance response in these studies.

Passive Avoidance Learning   Psychologists have also shown that animals can learn to avoid adversity passively. In one setting, an animal placed on top of a ledge above a grid floor receives an electric shock upon stepping down. Researchers (Chorover & Schiller, 1965; Geller & Jarvik, 1968; Hines & Paolino, 1970; Lewis & Maher, 1965; McGaugh & Landfield, 1970) report that rats refuse to leave the platform after a single training trial. Other studies demonstrate that animals readily learn to avoid shock by not entering an environment where they had been shocked the previous day (Baron, 1965; Kamin, 1959) or by refusing to bar-press after having been shocked for bar pressing (Camp, Raymond, & Church, 1967; Seligman & Campbell, 1965; Storms, Boroczi, & Broen, 1962).

The Nature of Avoidance Learning

We have discovered that animals and people can readily learn to avoid unpleasant events. What process enables animals or people to prevent adversity? The avoidance-learning research of the 1930s presented the Hullian drive theory (see Chapter 1) with a major dilemma. The observation that animals can act to avoid unpleasant events suggests a cognitive process, that is, they are behaving *in order to prevent* adversity. Yet, the Hullian drive theory argued that mechanistic rather than cognitive processes govern behavior. O. H. Mowrer (1939, 1947, 1956) developed a drive-based view of avoidance behavior, an approach regarded as an accurate explanation of avoidance behavior until its problems became apparent during the 1960s. Recent drive theorists (D'Amato, 1970) have restructured Mowrer's view into a contemporary drive theory of avoidance behavior. Others (Bandura, 1977; Bolles, 1978) have argued that cognitive processes are involved in avoidance learning. Let's first examine Mowrer's two-factor theory of avoidance learning.

Mowrer's Two-Factor Theory   Mowrer proposed a drive view of avoidance behavior which did not assume that avoidance behavior is motivated to prevent future adversity, a cognitive process. According to Mowrer, although animals or people appear to be avoiding painful events, they are actually escaping a feared stimulus. Thus, their behavior is an escape response from a feared object, not an avoidance response to future adversity. Consider Miller's classic study (1948) to illustrate Mowrer's view of avoidance behavior.

In Miller's study, rats were shocked in a white chamber and learned to avoid shock by running from the white chamber through a doorway into a non-shocked black chamber. According to Mowrer, the rats were simply escaping the feared white compartment and were not behaving to avoid being shocked. In Mowrer's view, the fear reduction as the result of termination of the feared stimulus (white compartment) reinforced the rats' behavior. Fortunately for the rat, the environment was structured so that nonoccurrence of an aversive event is a by-product of escaping the feared environment. However, Mowrer believed that the motivation is to escape fear, not to avoid an aversive event, and that the instrumental response is reinforced by fear reduction, not by the avoidance of adversity.

Thus Mowrer's view assumes that avoidance behavior is learned in two stages. In the first stage, fear is developed through the classical conditioning process. In the second stage, this fear motivates escape behavior, and an instrumental response is learned which terminates the feared stimulus. The reduction of fear reinforces the instrumental avoidance behavior. Recall Susan's avoidance response of drinking alcohol described in this chapter's vignette; how would Mowrer's two-factor theory explain her behavior? Susan associated her husband's sea duty with loneliness and therefore developed a fear of sea duty. Her fear motivated her escape behavior. Since drinking reduced her fear, she began to drink whenever she anticipated her husband going to sea. Thus, Susan does not drink to prevent her husband from going to sea but rather because it successfully terminates her fear of his departure.

Initial research evaluating Mowrer's theory was positive. Several studies (for example, Miller, 1948; Brown & Jacobs, 1949) observed that once fear of a distinctive cue was established, an animal learned a new response to escape from the fear stimulus. Perhaps the strongest support—and the evidence which Mowrer used to develop his view—came from his and Lamoreaux's experiment. Mowrer and Lamoreaux (1942) used three groups of rats in their study. The CS (fear stimulus) was terminated in the experimental group immediately after performance of the avoidance response. In the first control condition, using a trace conditioning procedure, the CS was removed before the rats' response, but in the second control condition the conditioned stimulus remained even after the rats' avoidance behavior. Mowrer and Lamoreaux reported that the rats in the experimental group learned the avoidance response more quickly than did subjects in either of the two control groups. The authors contended that the superior avoidance learning of the experimental group demonstrated that fear reduction reinforced the avoidance response, because only in the experimental group did the rats' behavior immediately terminate the fear stimulus.

Drive theorists (Miller, 1951) believed that they had discovered how avoidance behavior is learned. However, some problems with Mowrer's view surfaced during the 1950s and 1960s. First, although exposure to the conditioned stimulus without the UCS should eliminate avoidance behavior, avoidance behavior is often extremely resistant to extinction. For example, Solomon and Wynne (1954) reported that their dogs, even after receiving over 200 extinction trials, continued to perform a previously established avoidance response. The apparent failure of extinction represents a problem for the two-factor theory: if fear is acquired through classical conditioning and is responsible for motivating the avoidance behavior, then the presentation of the CS during extinction should cause a reduction in fear and a cessation of avoidance behavior. Levis (1976) offered an answer to this problem: it is not the number of extinction trials but rather the duration of exposure to the CS that determines the reduction of fear and thus the elimination of an avoidance response. Levis found that the likelihood that avoidance behavior will occur depends on the duration of exposure to the fear stimulus: the longer the exposure, the weaker the avoidance response. Thus, Solomon and Wynne's extinction results do not necessarily contradict Mowrer's two-factor theory.

A second problem for the two-factor theory concerns the apparent absence of fear in a well-established avoidance response. For example, Kamin, Brimer, and Black (1963) observed that a CS for a well-learned avoidance behavior did not suppress an instrumental response for food. The failure of the conditioned stimulus to reduce responding is thought to reflect an absence of fear, since one indication of fear is the suppression of appetitive behavior. However, absence of suppression may indicate not that an animal shows no fear in response to the CS but rather that an animal's motivation for food is stronger than the fear induced by the CS. In addition, strong fear is not necessary to motivate a habitual avoidance response—an observation consistent with Hull's idea that the tendency to respond is a joint function of drive and habit strength. However, the next two problems cannot be explained with Mowrer's drive view of avoidance behavior.

The frequent observation that some animals, even under optimal conditions (see Turner & Solomon, 1962), fail to learn to avoid an aversive event creates yet another problem for the traditional drive view. These studies showed that a CS associated with shock (or with another aversive event) terminates with the avoidance response—but the animal does not learn. For example, D'Amato and Schiff (1964) found that over half of their subjects, even after having participated in more than 7000 trials over a four-month period, failed to learn an avoidance response. These animals escaped but did not learn to avoid the shock—a result not predictable from Mowrer's two-factor theory.

Kamin's classic experiment (1956) demonstrating the importance of the avoidance of the aversive event during conditioning is perhaps the most damaging to Mowrer's theory. Kamin compared avoidance learning in four groups of rats: (1) rats whose response both terminated the CS and prevented the UCS (normal condition), (2) rats shocked at a predetermined time but whose behavior terminated the CS (terminate-CS group), (3) rats who avoided the UCS while the CS remained for a short time after the response (avoid-UCS group), and (4) rats in a classical conditioning control group given CS and UCS but not allowed to escape or avoid the shock. Although the two-factor theory would predict that the avoid-UCS group would not learn because their fear remained after their response, these subjects showed greater avoidance responding than did control animals. Also, the avoid-UCS subjects responded as often as the rats whose behavior terminated but did not prevent shock. Figure 4.6 presents the results of Kamin's study; the results indicate that two factors—the fear

FIGURE 4.6
Percentage of avoidance responses as a function of the rats' ability to terminate the CS, avoid the UCS, or both. From Kamin, L. J. The effects of termination of the CS and avoidance of the UCS on avoidance learning. *Journal of Comparative and Physiological Psychology*, 1956, *49*, 420–424. Copyright 1956 by the American Psychological Association. Reprinted by permission.

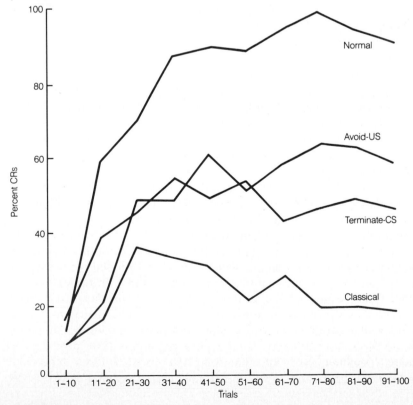

reduction and the avoidance of the aversive event—play an important role in avoidance learning. Recall that Susan's drinking terminated her fear but did not prevent her husband's departure. Kamin's results show why most people do not drink as a means of coping with adversity.

D'Amato's Theory of Avoidance Learning   Michael D'Amato (1970) developed a drive view to explain why the ability to prevent the aversive event is important for avoidance behavior (see Chapter 1). According to D'Amato, an aversive event such as a shock elicits an unconditioned pain response (R_P), and the stimulus consequences of the painful event (S_P) motivate escape behavior. As the result of conditioning, the environmental cues present during shock can eventually produce an anticipatory pain response (r_p) with its stimulus aftereffects (s_p) also motivating escape behavior.

D'Amato's r_p-s_p mechanism motivates an animal or human to escape from the conditioned stimulus, just as Amsel's r_F-s_F system causes an animal or person to escape from a situation associated with frustration. You may have noticed a similarity between D'Amato's r_p-s_p system and Mowrer's conditioned-fear theory. In both views, the conditioned stimulus associated with an aversive event motivates avoidance behavior. The difference between the two views lies in the reinforcement mechanism which causes the acquisition of the avoidance response.

In D'Amato's view, the termination of an aversive event (the UCS; for example, shock) produces an unconditioned relief response (R_R). The stimulus consequences (S_R) of the relief response are reinforcing. According to D'Amato, the stimuli associated with the termination of the aversive event develop the ability to elicit an anticipatory relief response (r_R), and the stimulus aftereffects (s_R) of this anticipatory response are also reinforcing. Furthermore, the sight of the cues associated with anticipatory relief motivates approach behavior in a manner comparable to Spence's description of the approach response to anticipatory-goal-related cues (see Chapter 1). This idea suggests a second motivational basis of avoidance behavior. The animal or human not only is escaping from an aversive situation but also is approaching a reinforcing one. According to D'Amato, the avoidance of the aversive event is important because if the animal does not avoid, the r_R-s_R mechanism will not develop and, therefore, the avoidance response will not be reinforced.

How would D'Amato's view explain how some children learn to avoid going to school when they have an exam by pretending to be sick? For many children, an exam is an aversive event which produces an unconditioned pain response (R_p). The announcement of an exam becomes associated with the exam. The result of this conditioning is that attending school on the day of an exam produces an anticipatory pain response (r_p). The r_p-s_p mechanism motivates some of these children to fake sickness to avoid school. In addition, since the time to leave for school is aversive, the passage of this time produces an unconditioned relief response (R_R). The relief that these children experience when able to avoid school acts to strengthen the habit of pretending to be sick.

D'Amato suggested that the anticipation of relief, as well as pain, motivated avoidance behavior. In our example, the passing of the time for departure to school becomes associated with relief and produces an anticipatory relief response (r_R). Thus, when an exam is scheduled again, the thought of being at home produces the r_R-s_R complex which acts to motivate the child to pretend to be ill. Therefore, the anticipation of both pain and relief motivates many children to pretend sickness.

Two lines of evidence support D'Amato's contemporary drive view of avoidance behavior. First, D'Amato, Fazzaro, and Etkin (1968) maintained that the reason an animal does not learn to avoid when using a trace-conditioning procedure (in this technique, the CS terminates prior to the UCS presentation) is that no distinctive cue is associated with the absence of the UCS. If a cue were present when adversity ended, an avoidance response would be learned. To demonstrate this idea, D'Amato, Fazzaro, and Etkin presented a second cue (in addition to the CS) when their subjects exhibited an avoidance response. Although learning was slow—only reaching the level observed with the traditional delayed procedure (the CS and UCS terminated at the same time) after 500 trials—these subjects performed at a higher level than did rats which did not receive the second cue (see Figure 4.7). According to D'Amato's

FIGURE 4.7
Percentages of avoidance responses during 700 trials for standard delayed-conditioning group (group C), trace-conditioning group (group T), and group receiving a cue for 5 seconds after each avoidance response (group TS). The break in curves indicates that a twenty-four hour interval elapsed between the fifth and sixth blocks of trials. From D'Amato, M. R., Fazzaro, J., & Etkin, M. Anticipatory responding and avoidance discrimination as factors in avoidance conditioning. *Journal of Experimental Psychology*, 1968, *77*, 41–47. Copyright 1968 by the American Psychological Association. Reprinted by permission.

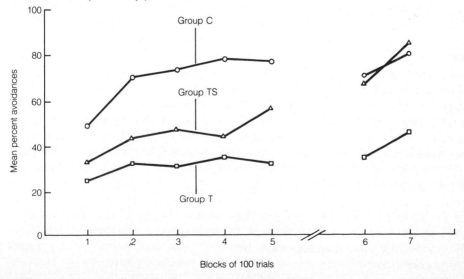

view, once the rat associated the second cue with the termination of shock, the r_R-s_R mechanism was acquired which then acted to reinforce avoidance behavior.

D'Amato's view asserts that we are motivated to approach situations associated with relief and to escape those events paired with adversity. Furthermore, the relief experienced following avoidance behavior reinforces that response. M. Ray Denny's research (1971) demonstrates the motivational and reinforcing character of relief. Let's examine Denny's evidence validating each aspect of D'Amato's view.

Denny and Weisman (1964) demonstrated that animals anticipating pain approach those events associated with the greatest amount of relief. They trained rats to escape or to avoid shock in a striped shock compartment of a T-maze by turning either right into a black compartment or left into a white chamber. One of the chambers was associated with a 100-second intertrial interval, but the rat spent only 20 seconds between trials in the other compartment. The authors found that their rats learned to go to the color associated with the longer interval before the next trial. Apparently, when the rats anticipated adversity, they did not go to any place but rather were motivated toward an environment which was associated with the longest relief.

Denny asserts that the amount of relief depends on the length of time between aversive events: the longer the nonshock interval (or intertrial interval, ITI), the greater the conditioned relief. In Denny's view, the greater the relief, the faster the acquisition of an avoidance habit. To test this idea, Denny and Weisman varied the time between trials from 10 to 225 seconds and observed that acquisition of an avoidance response was directly related to ITI: animals allowed a longer interval between trials learned the avoidance response more readily than did those given a shorter time between trials. These results show that the longer the period of relief after an aversive event is, the more readily rats learn to avoid adversity.

Denny believes that extinction of an avoidance response occurs when an animal begins to relax in the shock (fear) compartment. This happens if the shock and nonshock environment share common characteristics, causing an animal to begin to relax in the aversive environment. In support of this view, Denny, Koons, and Mason (1959) observed that extinction of an avoidance response was faster if the shock compartment and nonshock compartment were similar rather than dissimilar. In addition, extinction eventually takes place, even in a dissimilar environment, owing to the higher-order conditioning of relaxation to the aversive (shock) compartment; it happens once the relaxation produced in the shock chamber can successfully compete with the anticipatory pain (or fear) response.

A Cognitive View   Several psychologists (Bandura, 1977; Bolles, 1970, 1978) theorized that expectancies play an important role in avoidance behavior. According to a cognitive approach, three types of expectancies affect avoidance behavior (see Chapter 1 for a review of expectancy-value theory). Stimulus outcome (S-S*) expectancies indicate when and where aversive events will occur. Also, S-S* expectancies tell us which events are associated with the absence of adversity. The stimulus outcome expectancies indicate when we need to act; the response outcome (R-S*) expectancies inform us when responding will prevent adversity. Consider Susan's avoidance behavior detailed in the vignette to illustrate the influence of outcome expectancies. Susan expects her husband's sea duty to be an aversive event (S-S* expectancy) and has learned that drinking alcohol will decrease her loneliness (R-S* expectancy).

Efficacy expectancies indicate whether we feel capable of exhibiting a particular response. An efficacy expectancy is critical with phobic behavior. *Phobic behavior* represents a circumstance during which an individual exhibits an unrealistic avoidance response; that is, there is no aversive event but the avoidance response occurs anyway. According to Bandura (1977), phobic persons lack self-efficacy: they feel compelled to exhibit phobic avoidance. For example, a person who is *acrophobic* may recognize that no aversive event will occur at the top of a tall building but will still be unable to go there. The role of cognitions in avoidance behavior will be addressed in greater detail in Chapter 6.

Bolles (1975) pointed to one weakness in the cognitive approach: What process transforms an expectation into overt behavior? A number of psychologists have suggested that cognitive processes determine how we interpret our emotions but that once we are aroused, drive processes automatically motivate behavior. The combined influence of cognitive and drive processes has been suggested for a number of behaviors, including achievement behavior (Atkinson, 1958, 1964), aggression (Berkowitz, 1980), interpersonal attraction (Berscheid & Walster, 1978), and sexual behavior (Klein, 1982).

How Readily Is Avoidance Behavior Learned?

Three variables appear to have important influence on avoidance learning. First, *the severity of the aversive event* influences avoidance behavior. The severity of an aversive event depends on the intensity and duration of the adversity, and the influence of severity depends on the type of avoidance task: In simple tasks, the more severe the aversive event, the faster the acquisition and the higher the asymptotic level of avoidance behavior. In contrast, the effect of severity is the opposite with difficult avoidance tasks: the greater the severity of the aversive event, the slower the acquisition and the lower the final level of performance of an avoidance response. Second, *the intensity of the feared object (CS)* affects avoidance responding. Research indicates that the greater the feared object's intensity is, the more readily the avoidance response will be learned. Finally, *the length of the interval between presentation of the feared object and adversity* influences avoidance behavior. As the CS-UCS interval increases, so does the time needed for the acquisition of avoidance response.

Severity of Adversity   You might suspect that the greater the adversity of an event, the more likely an animal or person is to avoid that situation. This relation holds true in most avoidance situations; that is, the greater the adversity of an event, the more readily the avoidance response will be learned and the higher the final level of avoidance performance will be. However, the opposite relationship is valid in a two-way active-avoidance task: the greater the severity of adversity, the longer the time required for acquisition of the avoidance response and the lower the final level of avoidance performance. We will first examine evidence indicating the influence of the severity of the aversive event on avoidance learning, including a discussion of why severity influences two-way avoidance behavior differently than it does other avoidance responses. Note that most studies have varied the intensity of the aversive event; however, adversity can also depend on duration: the longer the aversive event, the more aversive the situation.

Passive-Avoidance Behavior Investigators (Camp, Raymond, & Church, 1967; Church, Raymond, & Beauchamp, 1967; Seligman & Campell, 1965; Storms, Boroczi, & Broen, 1962) have evaluated the effect of shock severity on the acquisition of a passive-avoidance response. In these studies, rats were initially trained to bar-press for food. After learning to bar-press, the animals were given electric shock following a bar-press response; each rat could avoid being shocked by inhibiting its bar-press response. The severity of shock varied in these studies: subjects received low-, moderate-, or high-severity electric shock. The results showed that the higher the shock severity, the faster the acquisition of the passive-avoidance response and the higher the final performance level of the passive-avoidance behavior.

One-Way Active-Avoidance Behavior Shock severity also has an important influence on the acquisition and performance of a one-way active-avoidance response. To illustrate this situation, the animal is shocked in one chamber of a shuttle box and can avoid shock by running to the other chamber. The shocked chamber is painted one color (for example, white), and the goal box is another color (for example, black). Many studies (Kurtz & Pearl, 1960; McAllister, McAllister, & Douglass, 1971; Moyer & Korn, 1966, Theios, Lynch, & Lowe, 1966) have discovered that increases in the severity of the aversive event lead to faster acquisition of the one-way active-avoidance response as well as a higher level of asymptotic avoidance performance. Let's examine the Moyer and Korn (1966) study to document the role of shock intensity on a one-way active-avoidance response.

Moyer and Korn placed their rats on one side of a shuttle box, giving them an electric shock unless they had run to the other compartment within 5 seconds. Each rat remained in the safe chamber for 15 seconds and was then placed in the dangerous chamber to begin another trial. Animals received 0.5, 1.5, 2.5, or 3.5 mA of electric shock during acquisition training. Each subject was given fifty acquisition trials on a single day. Moyer and Korn reported that the more severe the electric shock was, the faster the animals learned to avoid the electric shock (see Figure 4.8). Furthermore, the higher the intensity of shock, the more rapidly the animals ran from the dangerous to the safe compartment of the shuttle box.

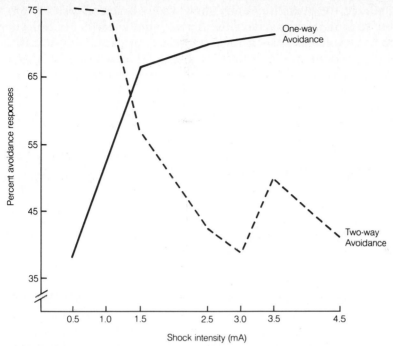

FIGURE 4.8
Influence of shock intensity on the acquisition of a two-way and a one-way
active avoidance response. From Flaherty, C. F., Hamilton, L. W.,
Gandelman, R. J., & Spear, N. E. *Learning and memory.* Chicago; Illinois:
Rand McNally, 1977.

Two-Way Active-Avoidance Behavior   In a two-way active-avoidance situation, the animal is placed in one chamber (side A) of the shuttle box and exposed to a specific stimulus (for example, a light) prior to the presentation of electric shock. To avoid the electric shock, the animal must run to the other chamber (side B) before the electric shock is presented. After this trial, the animal remains in side B for a short time (for example, 60 seconds). At the end of this ITI, the stimulus is again presented, and the animal must run from side B to side A to avoid a shock; thus, the animal in this situation avoids the aversive event only by returning to the place where it had been shocked. Learning a two-way active-avoidance response requires an animal to ignore situational cues (the place where shock was presented) and to attend to a specific cue (for example, the light) which will indicate when electric shock will occur again. The two-way active-avoidance training continues until the animal responds consistently to the specific cue (CS) and, therefore, avoids the aversive electric shock.

We learned earlier that increases in the adversity of an event facilitate the acquisition of a passive-avoidance response and a one-way active-avoidance behavior. In contrast, the literature clearly shows that a severe aversive event impairs rather than enhances the acquisition and asymptotic performance level of a two-way active-avoidance response; furthermore, the greater the severity, the slower the acquisition and the lower the final performance level of the avoidance behavior (Bauer, 1972; Cicala & Kremer, 1969; Johnson & Church, 1965; Levine, 1966; McAllister, McAllister, & Douglass, 1971; Moyer & Korn, 1964; Theios, Lynch, & Lowe, 1966). Let's examine one study to illustrate the important influence of the severity of an aversive event on two-way active-avoidance learning.

Moyer and Korn (1964) gave their rats two-way active-avoidance response training in periods of thirty trials per day for four days. In their study, the rats had 5 seconds after the CS, a tone, was presented in one chamber to run to the other chamber to avoid being shocked. Rats failing to respond within the 5-second interval received a 0.5, 1, 1.5, or 2.5 mA electric shock. Moyer and Korn found that as shock intensity increased, the percentage of avoidance responses made during acquisition declined (refer to Figure 4.8). These results show that high levels of electric shock impair an animal's ability to avoid being shocked in a two-way active-avoidance task.

Why do increases in shock severity impair two-way active-avoidance learning but facilitate other forms of avoidance learning? Theois, Lynch, and Lowe (1966) suggested that in a two-way active-avoidance task the animal experiences conflict between running away from the feared stimulus and running into an environment where adversity occurred on the previous trial. According to Theios, Lynch, and Lowe, the higher the severity of the aversive event, the greater the animal's reluctance to enter the environment associated with prior adversity and, therefore, the poorer the acquisition of an avoidance response. In contrast, this form of conflict (avoidance-avoidance conflict) is not present in other avoidance tasks; thus, the greater the severity of shock, the quicker the animal learns to avoid adversity. Many studies (see Tarpy & Mayer, 1978) support Theios, Lynch, and Lowe's view.

Freedman, Hennessy, and Groner (1974) compared the efficiency of avoidance behavior that occurred when animals ran from a compartment associated with a high level of aversiveness into a compartment associated with less aversiveness with avoidance performance that occurred when both compartments were paired with equal shock adversity. Freedman, Hennessy, and Groner assumed that the reluctance to avoid shock actively would decrease if animals had to run to a less aversive place rather than associating each compartment with equal shock intensities. In support of this view, they found that avoidance performance was better if an animal had run into a place associated with a lower shock intensity.

Intensity of the CS   Suppose that you were bitten by a large dog and by a small one. Chapter 2 showed that you would be more afraid of the more intense CS (large dog) than of the weaker CS (small dog). You would also learn to avoid the large dog more readily than the small one.

The literature consistently shows that the acquisition of an avoidance response is directly related to CS intensity; the greater the intensity of the CS, the more rapidly an avoidance response will be acquired. For example, Bauer (1972) found with rats that the more intense the CS, the higher the level of avoidance performance. Also, James, Ossenkop, and Mostoway (1973) increased or decreased the intensity of a white noise CS during the acquisition of a two-way active-avoidance response. They found a significant increase in avoidance behavior when CS intensity increased; however, decreasing CS intensity did not affect avoidance performance. The most reasonable explanation for this result is that once an avoidance response is acquired, the intensity of the CS loses its impact on avoidance behavior.

Delay Interval between CS and UCS   Remember from Chapter 2 that the level of fear conditioning depends on the CS-UCS interval; the longer the interval, the weaker the conditioning of the fear response. The interval between the CS and the UCS also affects the acquisition of an avoidance response. The literature (Hall, 1979) shows that the longer the CS-UCS interval, the slower the acquisition of the avoidance behavior. It seems reasonable to assume that the influence of the CS-UCS interval on fear conditioning is also responsible for its effect on avoidance learning; as the level of fear is reduced with longer CS-UCS intervals, an animal's motivation to escape the feared stimulus weakens and, therefore, the opportunity to learn to avoid decreases.

Kamin (1954) trained dogs to avoid electric shock by jumping over a barrier in a two-way active-avoidance situation. The CS, a 2-second duration buzzer, preceded the shock UCS. The interval between the CS and UCS varied: subjects received a 5-, 10-, 20-, or 40-second CS-UCS interval. Kamin reported that the shorter the interval between the CS and UCS, the quicker the acquisition of the avoidance response; also, the shorter the CS-UCS interval, the more resistance to extinction. Davitz, Mason, Mowrer, and Vick (1957) noted a similar effect of the CS-UCS interval on the acquisition of an avoidance response in rats.

Note that the reduced avoidance conditioning with longer CS-UCS intervals only occurs with a trace-conditioning procedure (see Chapter 2). In the trace-conditioning paradigm, the CS ends prior to the onset of the UCS. When a delayed conditioning paradigm is employed, the CS-UCS interval has no effect on avoidance learning (Church, Brush, & Solomon, 1956). Recall that in the delayed-conditioning procedure the CS does not terminate until after the UCS begins. Apparently, when the CS is experienced during the UCS, avoidance learning is not affected by how long the CS began before the UCS.

PUNISHMENT

A parent spanks a child for hitting a younger sibling. A teacher sends a disruptive student to the principal to be punished. A soldier absent without leave is ordered to the stockade by the military police. An employee who is late for work is reprimanded by the boss. Each of these situations is an example of punishment. *Punishment* is defined as the use of an aversive event contingent on the occurrence of an inappropriate behavior. The intent of punishment is to suppress an undesired behavior; if punishment is effective, the frequency and/or intensity of the punished behavior will decline. Thus, the parent who spanks a child for hitting a younger sibling is using punishment to decrease the occurrence of the child's aggressive behavior. The spanking is an effective punishment if the youngster hits the sibling less frequently after being punished. Similarly, the teacher who sent the disruptive child to the principal is attempting to stop the child's disruptive behavior; this technique is an effective punishment only if the child's disruptive behavior in the classroom decreases. The soldier placed in the stockade is being punished for going AWOL (absent without leave); this punishment is effective only if the soldier displays this behavior less frequently. Finally, the reprimand for the tardy employee is an effective punishment only if the worker's promptness improves.

Types of Punishers

We have defined punishment as a response-contingent presentation of an aversive event. There are two types of punishment: positive punishment and negative punishment. *Positive punishment* refers to the use of a physically or psychologically painful event as the punishment. A spanking is one example of a positive punisher; verbal criticism is another. In *negative punishment,* reward is lost or unavailable as the consequence of the occurrence of an inappropriate behavior.

There are two categories of negative punishment. One is called *response cost,* a technique in which an undesired response results in either the withdrawal of or failure to obtain reinforcement. In laboratory settings, a response-cost contingency means that an undesired response will cause an animal or person to lose or not to obtain either a primary reinforcer (e.g., candy or food) or a secondary reinforcer (e.g., chips, tokens, or points). Real-world examples of response-cost punishment include the withdrawal or failure to obtain material rewards (e.g., money) or social rewards (e.g., approval).

The other kind of negative punishment is called *time-out* (or time-out from reinforcement). Time-out from reinforcement is a period during which reinforcement is unavailable; a time-out is presented contingent on the occurrence of an undesired behavior. Sending a child to his or her room after misbehaving is one example of time-out.

Is punishment effective? The extensive use of it in our society suggests that we believe punishment to represent an effective technique to suppress inappropriate behavior. However, psychology's view of the effectiveness of punishment has changed dramatically during the past 100 years.

The Effectiveness of Punishment

Chapter 1 discussed Thorndike's (1898) proposal that stimulus-response associations are strengthened when followed by a satisfying state of affairs (or reward). Thorndike initially felt that unpleasant events weakened the S-R bond; however, he later suggested that annoying events or punishment do not weaken S-R associations (1932). Thorndike's studies caused him to repudiate his law of punishment. In a typical experiment, his human subjects were read a long list of words and told that a number from 1 to 10 was associated with each word. The subjects were instructed to guess the number for each word. Some of the subjects' responses were reinforced with the feedback "Yes, that's right"; other responses were punished with the response "No, that's wrong." Most items were followed by no feedback. Whereas reward increased the rate of correct responses, the repetition rate of responses followed by punishment did not decline. On the basis of this research, Thorndike concluded that S-R bonds could be strengthened by reward but not weakened by punishment.

Estes (1944) and Skinner (1953) assumed that punishment could only *temporarily* suppress behavior. The classic Skinner study (1938) supports their view. In his experiment, two rats were trained to bar-press for food reinforcement. The rats' bar-press responding was then extinguished by discontinuing reinforcement. One rat was also punished for bar-pressing by having his paw slapped when it touched the bar during the first few responses of extinction. The other rat did not receive punishment. Skinner observed that punishment initially produced a lower response rate from the punished rat than from the unpunished rat (see Figure 4.9). However, the suppressive effect of punishment was short-lived; bar pressing was resumed at an equivalent rate in the punished and the nonpunished rats within 30 minutes after punishment.

FIGURE 4.9
Effect of punishment on the extinction of bar-press response. Adapted from Skinner, B. F. *The behavior of organisms: An experimental analysis.* New York: Appleton-Century-Crofts, 1938.

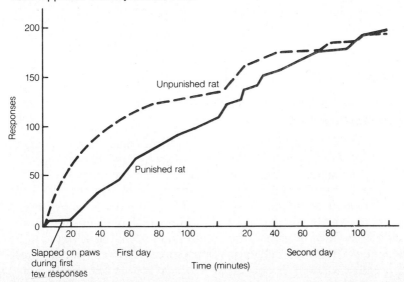

Skinner also noted that the punished rat continued to respond at a high rate even after the nonpunished rat had slowed down. Note that when both rats had stopped responding, both had made the same number of responses. Skinner's observations clearly show that punishment may temporarily suppress responding but does not eliminate it. Estes (1944) conducted a more extensive investigation of the effects of punishment. Instead of a slap of the paw, Estes used electric shock as the punisher. Estes also observed that the suppressive effects of punishment were only temporary. These results and similar observations led Estes (1944) and Skinner (1953) to conclude that punishment is an ineffective technique for eliminating an undesired behavior. They suggested that extinction instead of punishment should be used to suppress an inappropriate response permanently. Their conclusions certainly conflict with our society's belief that punishment is an effective method of suppressing inappropriate behavior.

Research evaluating the influence of punishment on behavior during the 1950s and 1960s shows that under some conditions punishment does permanently suppress inappropriate behavior (see Campbell & Church, 1969, for a review of the punishment literature). However, in other circumstances, punishment either has no effect on behavior or only temporarily suppresses behavior. It is important to recognize that even when the effects of punishment are only temporary, the temporary suppression of an undesired behavior provides an excellent opportunity to reward desired responses. Unfortunately, these opportunities are often lost. For example, a parent punishes a child for misbehaving and the child reads a book for a while. Most parents will feel fortunate for quiet time and ignore the child. However, the parent should reward reading so that the child reads rather than misbehaves to obtain reward in the future.

A number of variables determine whether punishment will suppress behavior and how long the punished behavior will be inhibited. The next section discusses the conditions necessary for effective punishment and the circumstances in which punishment does not suppress inappropriate behavior. Since some negative effects may result from the use of punishment (punishment can under certain circumstances lead to aggression or depression), we will also describe situations in which punishment may cause these negative effects in addition to suppression of punished behavior.

When Is Punishment Effective?

Four factors have an important influence on the effectiveness of punishment. First, *the severity of the punishment* affects the degree of behavioral suppression produced by punishment. The literature shows that the more severe the punishment, the more suppression of the punished behavior. Second, the level of suppression is influenced by the *consistency of punishment administration*. Research documents that the more consistency with which punishment follows an inappropriate behavior, the greater the suppression of that behavior. Third, *delay of punishment* affects the influence of punishment on behavior. Experimentation shows that the level of behavioral suppression decreases as the interval between the behavior and punishment increases. Finally, the *motivational level* of an animal or person influences the effectiveness of punishment. The psychological literature demonstrates that the greater the motivation level, the lower the suppression of the punished behavior. In the next sections, we will look at evidence documenting the influence of these variables on the effectiveness of punishment.

Severity of Punishment   Most people in our society recognize the dangers of driving while under the influence of alcohol. Local newspapers routinely report traffic fatalities caused by drunk drivers. Over 26,000 individuals were killed in 1981 in traffic accidents related to drunk drivers (*Newsweek,* Sept. 13, 1982). Yet, people continue to drive while intoxicated. It is estimated that one in ten drivers on Friday and Saturday nights is driving intoxicated. At other times, the estimate is one in fifty. Thousands of drunk drivers are ticketed each year. These drivers, though punished when apprehended, are very likely to drink and drive again. Over 20 percent of people charged with drunk driving are repeaters. Why are the punishments given to drunk drivers ineffective? One likely reason is that the punishment is too mild to suppress drunk driving effectively. In most cases, the first offense is punished with a small fine. For example, 1800 people were arrested in Idaho for drunk driving in 1981. Only one-third were convicted, and only two people spent time in jail. Unfortunately, these figures are representative of the rest of the country. Research investigating the influence of the severity of the aversive event on the effectiveness of punishment has consistently shown that mild punishment produces little if any suppression of the punished response. If any suppression does occur, it will be short-lived. Furthermore, this research also has found that as the severity of the punishment is increased, the amount of suppression is heightened. Thus, a moderately severe punishment produces more suppression of an inappropriate behavior than a mild punishment, and a strong punishment is likely to produce a complete suppression of the punished behavior. Also, the duration of suppression is related to the punishment's severity: the more severe the punishment is, the longer the punished behavior is inhibited. In fact, a severe punishment will lead to a permanent suppression of the punished response. Many states have recently passed laws providing a mandatory jail sentence for a drunk-driving conviction. It seems reasonable to expect that this more severe punishment will be more effective in suppressing drunk driving than the less severe warning system has been.

Note the two key dimensions to the severity of punishment: intensity and duration. An increase in either a punisher's intensity or duration will make the punishment more effective. In fact, the most effective punishment is intense and lasts a long time.

Animal Studies   Numerous studies using animal subjects (see Church, 1969) have reported that the greater the intensity of punishment, the more the suppression of the punished behavior. Camp, Raymond, and Church's 1967 study provides an excellent example of the influence of punishment's intensity on the degree of suppression of an instrumental behavior. In their study, forty-eight rats initially were given eight sessions of training to bar-press for food reward on a VI 1-minute schedule of reinforcement. Following initial training, the rats were divided into six groups and given 0, 0.1, 0.2, 0.3, 0.5, or 2 mA of electric shock punishment lasting for 2 seconds. An animal was punished if its response rate had not changed within the minute since it had last received punishment. As can be seen in Figure 4.10, the higher the intensity of shock, the greater the suppression of the instrumental response. Apparently, the more severe the punisher, the more effective the electric shock in suppressing the punished response. The importance of shock intensity on the suppression of an instrumental response has been shown in a number of animal species, including monkeys (Appel, 1963; Hake, Azrin, & Oxford, 1967), pigeons (Azrin, 1960; Azrin & Holz, 1966), and rats (Karsh, 1962; Storms, Boroczi, & Broen, 1962).

FIGURE 4.10
Mean suppression ratio as a function of the intensity of electric shock during punishment training. To obtain a suppression ratio, the number of responses to the CS and the number of responses to an equal amount of time without the CS is recorded. The suppression ratio is the number of responses to the CS divided by the total number of responses; the lower the suppression ratio, the greater the conditioning of fear to the CS. Adapted from Camp, D. S., Raymond, G. A., & Church, R. M. Temporal relationship between response and punishment. *Journal of Experimental Psychology,* 1962, *74,* 114–123. Copyright 1967 by the American Psychological Association. Reprinted by permission.

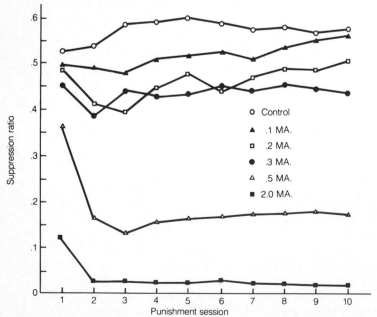

Research (Church, 1969) also demonstrates that the longer the punishment, the greater the inhibition of the punished behavior. For example, Church, Raymond, and Beauchamp (1967) reported that the longer the duration of electric-shock punishment, the greater the suppression of an instrumental bar-press response. After teaching rats to bar-press to obtain reward, Church, Raymond, and Beauchamp gave their rats electric shock punishment for durations of 0, 0.15, 0.30, 0.50, 1.00, or 3.0 seconds. The intensity of shock, 0.16 mA for all subjects, was presented on a 2-minute variable-interval schedule. As can be seen in Figure 4.11, Church, Raymond, and Beauchamp found that the longer the shock duration, the greater the suppression of the punished bar-press response. Seligman and Campbell (1965) and Storms, Borozzi, and Broen (1963) found similar results.

Recall our example of the drunk driver. Remembering that punishment can differ in intensity (for example, a $100 versus a $500 fine) or duration (for example, one day versus sixty days in jail), the larger fine or the longer jail time probably would produce a greater inhibition of this person's future driving while intoxicated than would either a small fine or short jail sentence. Church, Raymond, and Beauchamp's 1967 study provides evidence that the greatest punishment of drunk driving is a large fine (high intensity) and a long-term jail sentence (long duration). In their study, rats were initially trained to bar-press for food reward and then punished on a 2-minute variable-interval schedule. The electric shock punishment varied in intensity from 0.05 (low) to 0.25 (high) mA and in duration from .25 (short) to 2 (long) seconds. Church, Raymond, and Beauchamp found that the amount of suppression of the punished bar-press

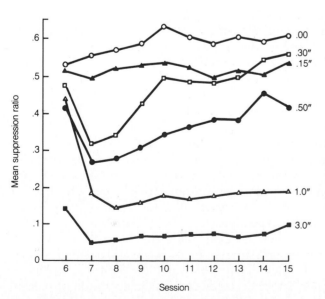

FIGURE 4.11
Mean suppression ratio as a function of the duration of electric shock (in seconds) during punishment training. Adapted from Church, R. M., Raymond, G. A., & Beauchamp, R. D. Response suppression as a function of intensity and duration of punishment. *Journal of Comparative and Physiological Psychology,* 1967, *63,* 39–44. Copyright 1967 by the American Psychological Association. Reprinted by permission.

response was a linear function of the logarithm of the intensity and duration of the electric shock.

Human Studies Research using animal subjects has shown that increases in the severity of punishment produce greater suppression of the punished response. Experimentation with human subjects has also demonstrated that severity affects the effectiveness of punishment. A number of studies (Aronfreed & Leff, 1963; Cheyne, Goyeche, & Walters, 1969; Parke & Walters, 1967) have evaluated the effect of the intensity of punishment on the suppression of playing with a forbidden toy. In these studies, children were punished with a loud noise for selecting one of a pair of toys. The noise ranged from 52 to 96 dB (60 dB is the loudness of normal conversation). After punishment, each child was isolated with toys which were identical or similar to the toys presented at the beginning of the experiment. The studies recorded the latency of each child before touching the "wrong" toy and also the number of times and the length of time the child played with this toy. The results of these experiments show that the higher the intensity of punishment, the greater the suppression of the child's playing with the toy for which he or she had received punishment.

The severity of punishment also affects the level of response suppression in adult humans. Powell and Azrin (1968) punished their subjects for smoking cigarettes by using a specially designed cigarette case which delivers an electric shock when opened. Powell and Azrin reported that the smoking rate decreased as the intensity of shock increased. Similarly, Davidson (1972) found that as the punishment intensity increased, the rate of an alcoholic patient's pressing a lever to obtain alcohol declined.

The Consistency of Punishment A severe punishment may not always be an effective method for suppressing behavior. The literature shows that punishment must be consistently administered if it is to be a reliable technique for eliminating inappropriate behavior. Thus, punishment should be given every time a person drives while intoxicated. Unfortunately, the odds that a drunk driver will be caught are 1 in 2000 (*Newsweek,* Sept. 13, 1982). Rigorous observation of drivers is essential to detect drunk drivers, and this high level of recording is not always feasible; drunk driving probably will continue despite the institution of more severe penalties. Let's now examine evidence indicating that consistency is vital for punishment to suppress a response.

Animal Studies Azrin, Holz, and Hake (1963) trained rats to bar-press for food reward on a 3-minute variable-interval schedule. A 240-V punishment was delivered following responding on varying fixed-ratio punishment schedules for FR-1 to FR-1000. As can be seen in Figure 4.12, the level of suppression decreases as the punishment schedule increases. These results indicate that the less consistent the punishment administered following bar pressing, the less effective the punishment in suppressing bar-press responding. Other studies (e.g., Camp, Raymond, & Church, 1966; Ferraro, 1967; Kelleher & Morse, 1968) have also reported that the consistency of the administration of punishment is a significant variable in the level of suppression of a punished response.

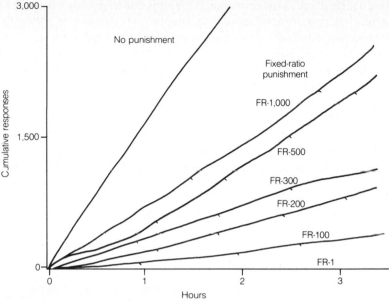

FIGURE 4.12
Figure shows rate of bar-press responding for food reinforcement delivered on a 3-minute variable-interval schedule as a function of fixed-ratio schedule of punishment. Short oblique lines indicate when punishment was delivered. From Azrin, N. H., Holz, W. C., & Hake, D. F. Fixed-ratio punishment. *Journal for the Experimental Analysis of Behavior,* 1963, *6,* 141–148. Copyright 1963 by the Society for the Experimental Analysis of Behavior, Inc. Reprinted by permission.

Human Studies   Research (Walters & Grusec, 1977) points out that consistency is important in determining the effectiveness of punishment on humans. For example, Parke and Deur (1972) rewarded 6- to 9-year-old boys with marbles for hitting a life-size Bobo doll. Then without warning the boys, Parke and Deur began punishing half of them with a loud buzzer every time they hit the doll; the other half was punished only 50 percent of the time they hit the doll and was rewarded the other half of the time. Parke and Deur found that the boys who received continuous punishment stopped hitting the doll sooner than did those boys who were punished only intermittently. In another experiment, Leff (1969) demonstrated that continuous punishment, compared with intermittent punishment, more effectively caused children to stop choosing an attractive toy and to select an unattractive toy instead. Continuous punishment also more effectively suppresses physiological responses than intermittent punishment does (Crider, Schwartz, & Shapiro, 1970).

Correlational studies have evaluated the relation between delinquency and the consistency of parental punishment. This research (Glueck & Glueck, 1950; McCord, McCord, & Zola, 1959) reported that delinquent boys were more likely to have received inconsistent parental discipline than were nondelinquent boys. Apparently, parents who want to suppress their children's socially inappropriate behavior must be consistent in punishing that behavior.

Delay of Punishment   We know that to suppress drunk driving effectively, the punishment must be severe and consistently administered. In this section, we will discover that punishment must also be immediate. The literature shows that the longer the delay between the inappropriate response and punishment, the less effective the punishment will be in suppressing the punished behavior. In our society, there is usually a long delay between the time that a person is apprehended for drunk driving (the response) and the time that this person receives a fine or jail sentence (the punishment). Since research on delay of punishment shows this method to be ineffective, obviously a shorter interval between offense and sentencing must be implemented to maximize the effect of punishing drunk driving. In fact, if punishment is to be most effective, it must be immediate in all instances in which it is used: it is as important for a parent to punish an undesired response (i.e., disruptive behavior) immediately as it is for society to punish drunk driving without delay.

Animal Studies   The literature using animal subjects (Church, 1969) consistently demonstrates that immediate punishment is more effective than delayed punishment. The Camp, Raymond, and Church (1967) study provides an excellent example of this observation. After being trained to bar-press for food reward, rats in the Camp, Raymond, and Church experiment received a 0.25-mA 1-second electric shock either immediately after a bar-press response or 30 seconds after responding. Camp, Raymond, and Church reported significantly greater suppression of the bar-press response when shock occurred immediately after responding than when shock occurred after 30 seconds (see Figure 4.13).

Further evidence is provided by Baron (1965). In a runway task, Baron initially provided food reward when his rats reached the goal box of the runway. Following initial reward training, the rats were punished immediately or 5, 10, 20, or 30 seconds after reaching the goal box. Baron reported that the greater the delay, the faster the rats ran down the alley and, thus, the less effective the punishment in suppressing the rats from running to obtain food. Other studies using animal subjects (Kamin, 1959; Myer & Riccio, 1968; Renner, 1966) have also shown that the greater the delay between the response and punishment, the less that punishment inhibits the response.

Human Studies   Banks and Vogel-Sprott (1965) investigated the influence of delay of punishment (electric shock) on the level of suppression of their human subjects' reaction to a tone in a digit-symbol task. These authors reported that although an immediate punishment inhibited responding, delayed punishment (for 30, 60, or 120 seconds) did not affect responding. Delayed punishment was found similarly ineffective in college students by Trenholme and Baron (1975) and in children by Walters (1964).

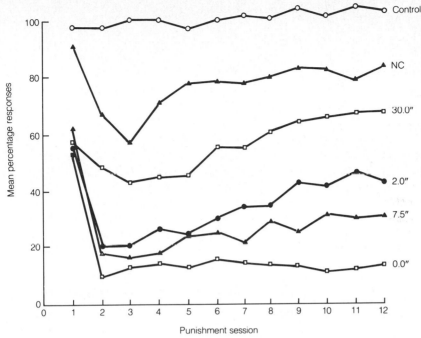

FIGURE 4.13
Mean percentage of response as a function of delay of punishment (in seconds).
Control group did not receive electric shock, and NC group was given
noncontingent shock. Adapted from Camp, D. S., Raymond, G. A., & Church,
R. M. Temporal relationship between response and punishment. *Journal of
Experimental Psychology*, 1967, *74*, 114–123. Copyright 1967 by the American
Psychological Association. Reprinted by permission.

Level of Motivation   People differ in their motivation to consume alcohol:
some are highly motivated to drink; others have only a modest interest in
alcohol. A study by Azrin, Holz, and Hake (1963) suggests that punishment
more effectively suppresses drinking when motivation is low rather than high.
Azrin, Holz, and Hake initially trained pigeons to peck at a key for food reward
on a VI 3-minute schedule of reinforcement. During training, the pigeon's body
weight was decreased to 85 percent of initial body weight (this decreased
weight is typically employed in operant conditioning studies), and an electric
shock was administered after every hundredth response. Azrin, Holz, and
Hake noted that the pigeons almost completely stopped responding when punishment was applied (see Figure 4.14). The authors then increased the pigeons'
motivation for food by decreasing their body weight to 70 percent, then to 65
percent, and finally to 60 percent of the free-feeding body weight. As can be
seen in Figure 4.14, as the pigeons' motivation increased, the suppressive
effects of punishment decreased. In fact, at very high motivation levels, the

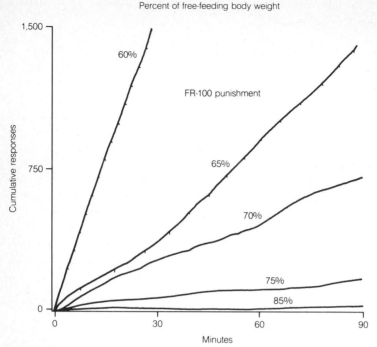

FIGURE 4.14
Rate of bar pressing for food reinforcement delivered on a 3-minute variable-interval schedule with punishment provided after every hundredth response as a function of level of food deprivation. Short oblique lines indicate point of punishment. From Azrin, N. H., Holz, W. C., & Hake, D. F. Fixed-ratio punishment. *Journal of Experimental Psychology,* 1963, *6,* 141–148. Copyright 1963 by the American Psychological Association. Reprinted by permission.

pigeons exhibited an extremely high rate of response, despite repeated punishment. It should be noted that when responding is completely suppressed by punishment at low motivation levels, an increase in the intensity of motivation does not restore response (Boroczi, Storms, & Broen, 1964; Storms, Boroczi, & Broen, 1962). Apparently, once responding no longer occurs, intensifying motivation does not cause an animal to resume exhibiting a punished response.

The Nature of Punishment

Thorndike's Negative Law of Effect   As we learned earlier in the chapter, Thorndike (1913) suggested that punishment weakened the strength of an S-R bond. The recovery of responding shortly after exposure to a mild punishment clearly rejects this view of punishment (Estes, 1944; Estes & Skinner, 1941; Skinner, 1938). If punishment acted to weaken S-R strength, the effect would be permanent, not temporary. Clearly, the effect of punishment on behavior must be caused by a process other than weakening S-R strength.

Guthrie's Competing Response View   Edwin Guthrie (1934) (see Chapter 1) suggested that an aversive event can elicit a number of unconditioned responses (e.g., flinching, jumping, or freezing). These unconditioned responses will then be conditioned to the environment present during the aversive event. According to Guthrie, the punished behavior will be suppressed if the response elicited by the aversive event and conditioned to cues surrounding the adversity are incompatible with the punished response. Therefore, punishment suppresses bar pressing in Guthrie's theory because a response preventing the rat from bar pressing has been conditioned to the operant chamber.

Fowler and Miller's classic study (1963) supports Guthrie's theory. In their study, rats were initially trained to run down an alley for food reward. In one group, the rats were then shocked when their forepaws touched the metal rods in front of the goal box. Electric shock applied to the forepaw elicits a flinching reaction, a response which is incompatible with foreward running; shock therefore should result in rapid suppression of the running response, according to Guthrie. A second group of rats were shocked on the hindpaws; this elicits a lurching response, a behavior which is compatible with the running response; lurching, again according to Guthrie, should therefore increase the speed of rats' response toward reward. A third group of rats was not shocked. Fowler and Miller reported that running was suppressed by forepaw shock but was facilitated by hindpaw shock. Apparently, the response elicited by punishment does influence the effectiveness of punishment.

Other studies also support Guthrie's view of punishment. Morse, Mead, and Kelleher (1967) punished monkeys for struggling on a leash by shocking them. However, punishment increased rather than suppressed struggling, presumably because the shock elicited struggling rather than a behavior which would have competed with struggling. Also, when Walters and Glazer (1971) punished gerbils for standing in an upright posture, they discovered that punishment increased rather than decreased the occurrence of the punished response.

Our discussion suggests that to be effective punishment must elicit a behavior incompatible with the punished response. However, other research indicates that response competition alone is insufficient to make punishment effective. Quite a few studies (Azrin, 1956; Boe & Church, 1967; Camp, Raymond & Church, 1967; Schuster & Rachlin, 1968) show that the suppression of a response is significantly greater when an aversive event is contingent on the occurrence of the response than when adversity occurs independently of behavior. Guthrie's view suggests that contingent and noncontingent adversity have an equal effect on behavior: conditioning of a competing response should occur regardless of whether the presentation of the aversive event depends on the occurrence of a response. The observation that contingency does influence the level of response suppression indicates that response competition alone is insufficient to suppress a response. Mowrer's two-factor theory suggests why response contingency affects the influence of punishment on response suppression.

Mowrer's Two-Factor Theory   Mowrer's view of the process responsible for the effect of punishment on behavior is similar to his theory of avoidance learning described earlier. According to Mowrer, the suppressive influence of punishment occurs in two stages. In the first stage, fear is classically conditioned to the environmental events present during punishment. Fear is elicited when an animal or person experiences the environmental events preceding punishment; this fear acts to motivate the animal or person to escape from the feared stimulus. Any behavior, either overt response or failure to respond, which terminates the feared stimulus will be acquired through instrumental conditioning in the second stage. The reinforcement of the escape response causes the animal or person to exhibit the escape response rather than the punished response in the punishment situation. Thus, the suppressive effect of punishment results from elicitation of a behavior other than the punished behavior.

You may have noticed the similarity between Mowrer's view of avoidance learning and his theory of punishment. In fact, Mowrer is describing two aspects of the same process: fear motivates an avoidance behavior, which enables an animal or person to prevent punishment. Also, the occurrence of the avoidance behavior causes an animal or person not to exhibit the punished response, which is thus responsible for the suppressive effect of punishment.

There is evidence supporting Mowrer's idea that fear is involved in the suppression of punished behavior. Chapter 2 detailed a number of studies in which a stimulus that had been classically conditioned to elicit fear in one situation suppressed an appetitive instrumental behavior when experienced in an entirely different situation. Further, a feared stimulus also increased the level of avoidance responding.

However, learning theorists (Estes, 1969) have pointed to a weakness in Mowrer's view of punishment: It is often difficult to identify the overt behavior motivated by fear which prevents an animal from exhibiting the punished response. Estes's motivational view of punishment indicates why an overt response is not essential.

Estes's Motivational View of Punishment.   According to Estes, when a behavior is reinforced, the motivational system present prior to reward and the response become associated. When this motivational system is activated again, the response is elicited. For example, if a hungry rat is reinforced for bar pressing, the bar-pressing response and hunger become associated. The presence of hunger in the future will act to elicit bar pressing in this rat. Similarly, when a child seeking approval of peers is disruptive in school and obtains approval for these actions, the disruptive responding and the approval of peers become associated. When the child wants approval again, she or he will be disruptive. In Estes's view, the primary mechanism underlying the influence of punishment on behavior is the competition of motives. If a stimulus precedes punishment, it develops the ability to inhibit the motive associated with the punished behavior. Thus, Estes asserts that the main reason punishment works is because an animal or person is no longer motivated and therefore the response is no longer elicited. Let's see how Estes's view of punishment explains the suppression of rats' bar pressing and children's disruptive classroom behavior. According to Estes's approach, punishment does not directly suppress rats' bar pressing or children's disruptive behavior; instead, punishment inhibits the rat's hunger or the child's need for approval. Therefore, since the punished rat or child is no longer motivated, the punished responses of bar pressing or disruptive behavior will no longer be elicited.

There is evidence (Walters & Grusec, 1977) supporting Estes's view. Wall, Walters, and England (1972) trained water-deprived rats to lever-press for water and to "dry-lick" for air; these behaviors were displayed on alternate days. The rate of both responses increased to a stable level after sixty-two days of training. Although each behavior was then punished, the rats showed greater suppression of the dry-licking response than of the lever-pressing response. According to Walters and Grusec, the internal stimuli associated with dry licking are more closely tied in with the thirst motivational system than are the internal stimuli associated with lever pressing. Therefore, if punishment acts to decrease the thirsty rats' motivation for water, it should have more influence on dry licking than on lever pressing. Wall, Walters, and England's results support this view: punishing thirsty rats suppresses dry licking more effectively than lever pressing. However, punishing hungry rats does not suppress dry licking more than lever pressing for food. According to Walters and Grusec, dry licking is not more closely associated with the hunger system than is lever pressing, and thus reducing animals' motivation for food will not suppress dry licking any more than it suppresses lever pressing.

Thus punishment suppresses behavior by inhibiting the motivational system responsible for eliciting the punished response. Note that external stimuli present during punishment can become conditioned to produce fear, and this emotional response of fear represents a general motivational response capable of suppressing any reward-seeking behavior or arousing any avoidance response (see Chapter 2). However, the desired effect of punishment is to suppress a specific behavior, and the evidence indicates that punishment works best by only inhibiting the specific motivational state which has been associated with the punished response.

The Negative Consequences of Punishment

Pain-Induced Aggression   When animals or people are punished, they experience pain. This pain response may elicit anger, which, in turn, arouses aggressive behavior. A number of psychologists have investigated pain-induced aggressive behavior in rats (Moyer, 1976; Ulrich, 1966). In a typical study, two rats placed in a small chamber are given a series of periodic electric shocks to the feet. These rats adopt the boxing posture: They face one another and rear up on their hind legs. The rats do this only when they are being shocked. After the shock has terminated, the rats avoid any social interaction. Although psychologists have used laboratory rats in research to explain the causes of human behavior, it is clear that laboratory rats and humans respond quite differently to painful events. Laboratory rats react by adopting the defensive threat posture. They do not physically attack each other except when they are trying to avoid contact with the shock grids by climbing on top of each other. In contrast, other animals and humans respond with an intense overt attack.

Azrin, Hutchinson, and Sallery (1964) observed that when primates are shocked, they attack other monkeys, rats, or mice. In addition, monkeys which are being shocked will attack a toy tiger (Plotnick, Mir, & Delgado, 1971), a stuffed doll, or a ball (Azrin, 1964). Shock-induced aggressive attack has also been reported in cats (Ulrich, Wolff, & Azrin, 1964), wild rats (Galef, 1970a, 1970b; Karli, 1956), and gerbils (Dunstone, Cannon, Chickson, & Burns, 1972).

During the past twenty years, Leon Berkowitz and his associates (Berkowitz, 1962, 1969, 1971, 1978) have conducted research supporting the theory that anger induced by exposure to painful events can lead to aggression in humans. In one of these studies (Berkowitz & LePage, 1967), subjects were asked to list, within a period of 5 minutes, ideas which could be used by a publicity agent to increase sales of a product. A confederate then rated some subjects' performance as poor by giving these subjects seven electric shocks; this confederate shocked other subjects only once, to indicate a positive evaluation. According to Berkowitz and LePage, the seven-shock evaluation angered subjects, but the one-shock evaluation did not. Next, all the subjects evaluated the confederate's performance by giving the confederate from one to seven shocks. Subjects who had received seven shocks retaliated by giving the confederate significantly more shocks than the other subjects gave. These results clearly indicate that painful events can motivate aggressive behavior.

We have seen that anger can result in aggressive behavior. However, this aggressive reaction is not motivated by the expectation of avoiding punishment; rather, it reflects an impulsive act energized by the emotional arousal which is characteristic of anger. Furthermore, the expression of aggressive behavior in angry animals or people appears to be highly reinforcing. Many studies show that annoyed animals will learn a behavior which allows them the opportunity to be aggressive. For example, Azrin, Hutchinson, and McLaughlin (1965) discovered that squirrel monkeys loosely restrained in a chair bit inanimate objects (for example, a ball) after being shocked. However, if no object was present, they learned to pull a chain which provided them with a ball to bite. Similarly, Dryer and Church (1970) reported that shocked rats chose the appropriate arm in a T-maze which provided another rat to fight.

Bramel, Taub, and Blum (1968) reported that irritated people report "feeling good" after being aggressive. During the early 1960s, Hokanson and his colleagues (Hokanson & Burgess, 1962a, 1962b; Hokanson, Burgess, & Cohen, 1963; Hokanson & Shetler, 1961) found that angry people who were either verbally or physically aggressive toward the instigator of their anger showed a rapid decrease in systolic blood pressure until it reached the initial resting level. In contrast, the decline in systolic blood pressure was much slower in angry subjects who were not given the opportunity to be aggressive. Evidently, aggressive behavior reduces arousal.

Note that punishment does not always elicit aggressive behavior. Hokanson (1970) reported that people's experiences influence their reaction to painful events. If individuals have been rewarded for nonaggressive reactions to adversity, punished for aggressive responses to painful events, or both, the likelihood that punishment will elicit aggression is diminished. Furthermore, the level of anger produced by pain differs among individuals (Klein, 1982). Some people react intensely to a level of adversity that elicits only mild anger in others. Since the probability that painful events will motivate aggression depends on the level of anger induced by the aversive circumstance, individuals who respond strongly to adversity are much more likely to become aggressive than people who are not very angered by aversive events.

Modeling of Aggression   We know that a child who has been spanked for misbehaving may learn to suppress the inappropriate behavior and/or to elicit aggressive behavior caused by the pain of the spanking. The child may also discover aggression to be an effective method of controlling the behavior of others; this knowledge, in turn, may cause this child to imitate the parent's aggressive behavior in an attempt to control other people's actions. The behavior that we learn without receiving explicit reinforcement but by observing another person's actions is called *modeling* (Bandura, 1971). Research has shown that children can learn to be aggressive through modeling; let's now examine this evidence.

The classic experiment by Bandura, Ross, and Ross (1963) illustrates the influence of a model on aggressive behavior. In this study, children saw a preschool model act aggressively toward a life-sized plastic doll called a Bobo doll. The model sat on this doll, punched it, hit it with a mallet, kicked it, and tossed it up and down. Other children in the study did not watch a model behave in this manner. After the initial phase of the study, all children first were allowed to play with attractive toys and then were frustrated by being required to leave these attractive toys for less attractive ones, including a Bobo doll. Bandura, Ross, and Ross recorded the level of imitative aggression (attacking the Bobo doll) and nonimitative aggression (behavior not performed by the model). They found that while all the children exhibited nonimitative forms of aggression when they were frustrated, only the children who had watched the model showed the imitative patterns of aggression. One striking aspect of this study is that a live model did not precipitate any more imitative aggression in these children than a filmed model did. We can apparently learn how to perform a particular behavior merely by watching others exhibit it.

Other studies have also reported that children will imitate a model's aggressive behavior (Grusec, 1972; Hanratty, Liebert, Morris, & Fernandez, 1969;

Steuer, Applefield, & Smith, 1971). For example, Steuer, Applefield, and Smith (1971) discovered that children who had viewed cartoons depicting aggressive behavior became more aggressive toward other children than did children who did not see the cartoons. The imitated aggression included hitting, pushing, kicking, squeezing, choking, or throwing objects at the other children. Furthermore, Hanratty, Liebert, Morris, and Fernandez (1969) reported that as the result of a modeling experience, children will even act aggressively toward an adult. In their study, young boys, after watching an aggressive model, attacked an adult dressed as a clown.

Do children who are physically punished, in turn, model this aggressive behavior? Two types of evidence support the view that they do. First, experimental research shows that *children punished during a study use the same method of punishment when attempting to control the actions of other children*. In one study, Mischel and Grusec (1966) verbally punished preschool-age children for their certain actions during a game; the children, in turn, employed verbal abuse toward other children playing the game. Similarly, Gelfand, Hartmann, Lamb, Smith, Mahan, and Paul (1974) found that children who had been penalized for incorrect responses during a game used this form of punishment when teaching another child to play. Second, correlational studies report *a strong relationship between the use of punishment by parents and the level of aggressive behavior in their children*. The classic Bandura and Walters research (1959) reported that highly aggressive boys had parents who severely punished them for inappropriate behavior in the home. Furthermore, many studies (Spinetta & Rigler, 1972) have found that parents who abuse their children were, in fact, abused as children by their parents. This observation suggests that children abused by their parents attempting to control their actions may imitate this extreme form of punishment by abusing their children as a method of parental control.

The Aversive Quality of a Punisher   Chapter 2 demonstrated that environmental events present during adversity will become classically conditioned to elicit fear. In addition, we saw earlier in this chapter that fear motivates escape behavior. On the basis of these two observations, we should expect that since punishment is a painful event, the person providing the punishment, the punisher, will become a conditioned stimulus capable of eliciting fear. This in turn should motivate the individual to escape from the punisher.

Consider the following example to illustrate this effect of punishment. A child punished by a parent becomes afraid of the parent; this fear motivates the child to escape when encountering the parent. However, note that parental reinforcement does condition positive emotions which then act to counteract the effects of parental punishment, thereby eliminating this child's motive to escape from the parents. Thus, parents need to reward as well as punish children to prevent their offspring from being motivated to avoid them.

Azrin, Hake, Holz, and Hutchinson's study (1965) provides evidence that escape behavior occurs as the result of the use of punishment. These psychologists first trained pigeons to key-peck for food reward on a fixed-ratio schedule and then punished each key-peck response with electric shock. A distinctive stimulus was present during the punishment period, and the pigeons could peck at another key to terminate the cue-signaling punishment. The escape response also produced another stimulus indicating that the original reinforcement-punishment key could be pecked safely. After the pigeons pecked this original key and received reward, the safe cue was terminated and the dangerous stimulus reintroduced. Azrin, Hake, Holz, and Hutchinson reported that although the pigeons emitted few escape responses if the punishment was mild, the frequency of the escape response increased as the intensity of punishment increased until the pigeons spent the entire punishment period escaping from punishment. Moreover, the intensity of electric shock which motivated high levels of escape behavior caused little or no suppression of responding in a standard punishment procedure having no possible escape. Other studies (Buchanan, 1958; Hearst & Sidman, 1961) have also found that punishment motivates rats to escape from the cues associated with punishment.

The aversive quality of a punisher on humans is illustrated in a study by Redd, Morris, and Martin (1975). In their study, 5-year-old children performed a task in the presence of an adult who made either positive comments (for example, "You're doing well") or negative comments (for example, "Stop throwing the tokens around" or "Don't play with the chair"). Redd, Morris, and Martin reported that although the punitive person more effectively kept the children working on their task, the children preferred working with the complimentary person.

We should note that little evidence of patients' escaping a punitive behavior therapist has been reported (Walters & Grusec, 1977). For example, Risley (1968) discovered that punishing autistic children's undesirable behavior with electric shock did not alter the children's eye contact with the therapist, who also reinforced the children's desirable responses. Other studies (Lovaas & Simmons, 1969) have also documented additional support for patients' absence of fear of and escape behavior from a therapist who had punished them. Walters and Grusec (1977) suggested that the use of reward as well as punishment by the therapist prevented the therapist and the therapy situation from becoming aversive and, thereby, from motivating escape behavior. The absence of escape behavior allowed the therapist to suppress undesirable actions successfully and to motivate desirable behavior in the patients. These observations indicate why it is essential that parents reward desired actions as well as punish undesired behaviors; the failure to use reward as well as punishment will cause a child to be afraid of the parent and motivate escape behavior.

There are two additional negative effects of punishment. First, *the suppressive effects of punishment may generalize to similar behaviors*. The inhibition of these responses may be undesirable. For example, if a parent punishes a child for fighting with other children in the neighborhood, the punishment of fighting may generalize, causing the child to stop playing with these children. The generalization of the suppressive effects of punishment from fighting to playing may lead to more harm than allowing the fighting to continue. The effects of punishment do not always generalize to similar behavior. Chapter 5 discusses the circumstances under which punishment does and does not generalize to other responses. Second, *the contingency between punishment and the undesired behavior may not be recognized; the aversive events may be perceived as independent of behavior.* Chapter 6 will discuss how noncontingent aversive events lead to helplessness and depression. Punishment is most likely to be perceived as noncontingent when a delay occurs between the undesirable behavior and punishment. The interval between a response and punishment makes it difficult for an animal or person to recognize that the behavior is responsible for the adversity. Chapter 6 discusses why it is imperative for people to know how their actions relate to punishment to prevent the helplessness which results from noncontingent aversive events. This chapter will detail the ways in which the influence of noncontingent events can be prevented or reversed.

APPLICATION: THE USE OF PUNISHMENT

The use of punishment to control human behavior is widespread in our society. The literature shows that most parents use punishment to govern the actions of their children. For example, Sears, Maccoby, and Levin (1957) discovered that 99 percent of the parents of 379 kindergarten children used spanking as a form of punishment. Furthermore, Lefkowitz, Walder, and Eron (1963) reported that 57 percent of the parents of third-grade children in their study used physical punishment to control their children's actions. Teachers also employ negative events to modify students' disruptive actions. Illustrating the use of punishment in classroom situations, White's analysis (1975) of teacher-pupil interactions reported that although teachers showed approval of good academic performance, appropriate social behavior was expected. Any disruptive behavior by a student produced strong disapproval from teachers in White's study. Interestingly, Madsen, Madsen, Saudargas, Hammond, and Edgar (1970) found that 77 percent of elementary school teachers' interactions with their students were negative. This observation indicates that teachers frequently use aversive events to control their students' actions.

Other individuals in our culture also employ punishment to control behavior. Police officers ticket traffic violators, the IRS jails tax evaders, the army courtmartials AWOL soldiers, and employers fire employees who are often late for work. These examples merely illustrate the extensive use of adversity in controlling human behavior. Psychologists also employ aversive events to modify behavior. The difference between the use of punishment by laypeople and by psychologists lies in psychology's search for effective techniques for applying aversive events to control behavior and for empirically evaluating the level of success of these aversive techniques.

Positive Punishment

Remember that positive punishment is the presentation of a painful event contingent on the occurrence of an undesired behavior. Punishment will be effective when it is severe, occurs immediately after the undesired response, is consistently presented, and the motivation level is not too high. Can positive punishment be used to alter behavior problems in humans? The literature (Rimm & Masters, 1979) clearly points out that punishment can suppress undesired human behavior. Let's now examine evidence showing that punishment can be effectively applied to modify human activity.

Lang and Melamed (1969) describe the use of punishment to suppress the persistent vomiting of a 12-lb 9-month-old child. The child vomited most of his food within 10 minutes after eating, despite the use of various treatments (e.g., dietary changes, use of antinauseants, small feedings at a time). Lang and Melamed detected the beginning of vomiting with an electromygram (EMG), which measures muscle activity. When the EMG indicated that vomiting had begun, the child received an electric shock to the leg; the shock stopped when the child ceased vomiting. After the child had received six punishment sessions (one per day), he no longer vomited after eating. Six months following treatment, the child no longer vomited and was of normal weight. Cunningham and Linscheid (1976), Sajwaj, Libet, and Agras (1974), and Toister, Condron, Worley, and Arthur (1975) have also used punishment effectively to suppress life-threatening vomiting in very young children. Galbraith, Byrick, and Rutledge (1970) successfully used punishment to curtail the vomiting of a 13-year-old retarded boy, and Kohlenberg (1970) reported that punishment suppressed the vomiting of a 21-year-old retarded adult.

Clinical research (Lovibond & Caddy, 1970; Vogler, Lunde, Johnson, & Martin, 1970; Vogler, Lunde, & Martin, 1971; Wilson & Tracey, 1976) indicates that contingent adversity will inhibit drinking in alcoholics. In the Wilson and Tracey study (1976), one group of alcoholics self-administered electric shock contingent on alcohol consumption; other alcoholics received either a covert sensitization treatment (during which the client simultaneously imagines drinking and being shocked) or a counterconditioning procedure (during which the alcoholics imagined drinking while actually being shocked). Wilson and Tracey reported that only the contingent punishment treatment successfully suppressed drinking in the alcoholics. Punishment suppressing drinking in alcoholics was also noted by Lovibond and Caddy (1970), Volger, Lunde, Johnson, and Martin (1970), and Vogler, Lunde, and Martin (1971).

Many other behaviors have been successfully modified through the use of response-contingent punishment. Behaviors suppressed by punishment include obsessive ideation (Kenny, Solyom, & Solyom, 1973; Kushner & Sandler, 1966; McGuire & Vallance, 1964; Wolpe, 1958), hallucinations (Alford & Turner, 1976; Bucher & Fabricatore, 1970; McGuigan, 1966), self-mutilating behavior and tantrum activity of autistic and retarded children (Lovaas, Koegel, Simmons, & Long, 1973; Prochaska, Smith, Marzilli, Colby, & Donovan, 1974; Schreibman & Koegel, 1975; Tanner & Zeiler, 1975), transvestism (Blakemore, Thorpe, Barker, Conway, & Lavin, 1963), chronic cough (Creer, Chai, Hoffman, 1977), chronic sneezing (Kushner, 1968), compulsive behavior (Scholander, 1972), and homosexual behavior (Feldman & MacCulloch, 1971).

Although positive punishment has been effectively used to suppress a wide variety of undesired behaviors, one problem sometimes encountered with punishment therapy involves patient difficulty with generalizing suppression from the therapy situation to the real world. The generalization of the effect of punishment can be accomplished; the Risley (1968) study provides evidence of the generalization of the suppression of a punished behavior. (A detailed discussion of the generalization process is presented in Chapter 5.) Risley (1968) used electric-shock punishment to treat the continual climbing behavior of a 6-year-old hyperactive girl. Although Risley's treatment suppressed the climbing during the therapy situation, there was no change in the frequency of this behavior at the girl's home. Risley then visited the home and showed the mother how to use the device. When the mother punished her daughter's climbing, the frequency of this behavior declined from twenty-nine to two instances a day within four days and disappeared completely within a few weeks. This procedure might seem barbaric. However, the mother had attempted to control the climbing by spanking the child and believed the spanking to be more unpleasant and "brutalizing" for both herself and her daughter than the shock, not to mention less effective. As Rimm and Masters (1979) point out, "many therapists feel that a minimum number of mild shocks is more humane than the continual but ineffective, spanking or shaming of a child."

Response Cost

A colleague recently told me of a problem with his teenage daughter who was having trouble seeing the blackboard at school. When he suggested that she move to the front row of her classes, she informed him that she was already sitting there. Upon taking her to the optometrist, he discovered that her eyesight was extremely poor; she needed to wear glasses all the time. Despite choosing a pair of glasses which she liked, she indicated an extreme dislike for wearing them. After waiting a reasonable adjustment period and discovering that encouragement and praise were ineffective in persuading her to wear the glasses, he informed her that she would lose 50 cents of her weekly allowance every time he saw her without them. Although she was not pleased with this arrangement, she did not lose any of her allowance and no longer expresses unhappiness about wearing her glasses. My colleague was able to modify his daughter's behavior by using a response-cost procedure. Response cost refers to a penalty or fine which is contingent on the occurrence of an undesired behavior. Thus, my colleague's daughter was to be fined 50 cents when she did not wear her glasses. The response-cost procedure motivated her to wear her glasses. Psychologists (Kalish, 1981) have consistently observed that response cost represents an effective technique for suppressing inappropriate behavior.

Peterson and Peterson's study (1968) illustrates the effectiveness of response cost in suppressing self-injurious behavior. These experimenters rewarded a 6-year-old boy who had been severely mutilating himself by giving him small amounts of food when no self-injurious behavior occurred during a 3-

to 5-second period. However, if the boy did exhibit self-injurious behavior, the reward did not occur. Peterson and Peterson reported that they completely eliminated the boy's self-injurious behavior with their response-cost procedure. LeBoeuf (1974) found the loss of reward contingent on self-destructive behavior to be effective in suppressing the head-banging behavior of a normal adult.

A wide range of other undesired behaviors have also been successfully eliminated by using a response-cost procedure. In an extensive investigation of the application of response cost, Kazdin (1972) discovered that response cost inhibited smoking, overeating, stuttering, psychotic speech, aggressiveness, and tardiness. In addition, response cost eliminated perseverative speech (Reichle, Brubakken, & Tetreault, 1976), anxious and depressive behavior (Reisinger, 1972), and hyperactive behavior (Wolf, Hanley, King, Lachowicz, & Giles, 1970).

The response-cost punishment technique has also been used to suppress undesired responding in several or more individuals. For example, Burchard incorporated response cost into a token economy program (see Chapter 3). In Burchard's study, twelve mildly disturbed retarded boys with a long history of antisocial behavior placed in an intensive training unit could receive tokens for school work, cooperating with peers, and proper care of clothing. These tokens could be exchanged for candy, recreational activities, or trips to town. However, the boys lost tokens for antisocial behavior (i.e., fighting, lying, and cheating). Burchard reported that the response-cost procedure effectively suppressed the undesired antisocial behavior. Phillips (1968) and Phillips, Phillips, Fixen, and Wolf (1971) also discovered that response cost represents a successful method of suppressing fighting, stealing, carelessness, and tardiness in predelinquent boys in a home-style rehabilitation center, and Kaufman and O'Leary (1972) found that response cost suppressed disruptive behavior in adolescents institutionalized in a psychiatric hospital.

The classroom also appears to be an appropriate setting for the application of a response-cost punishment system. For example, McLaughlin and Malaby (1972) reported eliminating inappropriate verbalizations in young children. Iwata and Bailey (1974) found a similar effectiveness of response-cost technique in suppressing undesired disruptive classroom behavior.

Time-Out from Reinforcement

Time-out from reinforcement refers to a program in which the occurrence of an inappropriate behavior results in loss of access to reinforcement for a specified period of time. The time-out represents the removal of the individual from a reinforcing environment or the removal of the reinforcement itself. For example, a child who hits a sibling while watching television is sent to his or her room for half an hour and an overweight person is forbidden to dine out for a week for doing poorly on a test are both examples of the use of time-out. Note that if a time-out area is employed, it must not be reinforcing. Thus, sending disruptive children to their room as a time-out may not stop the disruptive behavior if the room contains attractive toys and the child finds being there pleasurable. In fact, the frequency of disruptive behavior may actually increase if the time-out area is reinforcing. Solnick, Rincover, and Peterson's 1977 study illustrates the importance of ensuring that time-out is not reinforcing. The study included a time-out contingent on tantrum behavior in the treatment of a 6-year-old autistic child. Exposure to a sterile time-out environment was contingent on the occurrence of self-stimulating behavior, and presentation of this environment increased rather than decreased the occurrence of tantrum behavior. When the investigators made physical restraint contingent on tantrum behavior, the frequency of tantrums rapidly declined to zero.

A wide variety of behaviors have been suppressed using time-out from reinforcement. For example, Drabman and Spitalnik (1973) reported that time-out suppressed disruptive behavior of male adolescents in a psychiatric hospital. Initial recordings showed that the adolescents exhibited very high rates of several disruptive behaviors: physical aggression, verbal abuse, and disregard of rules. Drabman and Spitalnik instituted a time-out procedure during which the boys were placed in a small room for 10 minutes if they had been physically aggressive or had left their seat without permission (the verbal abuse was not a target of intervention and, therefore, its occurrence did not result in time-out). Drabman and Spitalnik found that the level of physical aggression and the occurrence of patients' leaving their seats decreased significantly after the time-out procedure had been established. In contrast, the unpunished verbal abuse did not decline since its occurrence did not result in time-out. These observations demonstrate that time-out from reinforcement produces a specific reduction of behaviors contingent on its presentation and does not affect unpunished activity. Similarly, Barton, Guess, Garcia, and Baer (1970) discovered that the disruptive meal-time behavior of retarded children could be suppressed by the use of a time-out from reinforcement procedure. MacPherson, Candee, and Hohman (1974) found that time-out could inhibit disruptive lunchroom activity in elementary-school children. Other behaviors which have been suppressed by time-out include thumb-sucking (Baer, 1962), tantrum behavior in autistic children (Wolf, Risley, & Meis, 1964) and normal children (Wahler, Winkel, Peterson, & Morrison, 1965; Williams, 1959), self-stimulation in autistic children (Koegel, Firestone, Kramme, & Dunlap, 1974), and perserverative speech (Reichle, Brubakken, & Tetreault, 1976).

The time-out does not have to be administered in a separate room. Porterfield, Herbert-Jackson, and Risley (1976) instructed 1- and 2-year-old children in a day-care center to "sit and watch" the other children for 1 minute when they exhibited undesired behavior, such as aggression or destruction of toys. Porterfield, Herbert-Jackson, and Risley found that time-out effectively suppressed the young children's disruptive activity. Murry and Hobbs (1977) used a 15-minute time-out from social reinforcement (e.g., talking, playing cards) to suppress drinking in alcoholics. In their study, time-out was contingent on the consumption of more than four drinks a day and/or consumption of any drink in a period of less than 30 minutes. Murry and Hobbs found that consumption of alcohol dropped significantly after the institution of the time-out from reinforcement procedure.

Ethical Use of Punishment

Should punishment be used to suppress undesired behavior? We have learned that inappropriate activity can be eliminated by the use. of punishment. However, for punishment to be effective it must be severe, it must be consistently employed, and it must immediately follow the undesired response. We also discovered that there are negative consequences of the use of punishment; it can induce anger and lead to aggressive behavior, it can be modeled as a method of behavior control, and it can result in the punisher becoming a feared stimulus. There is one additional issue—the rights of the individual being punished—that we will address in our discussion of punishment.

When is the use of punishment permissible? The Eighth Amendment of the Constitution of the United States states: "Excessive bail shall not be required, nor excessive fines imposed, nor cruel and unusual punishments inflicted." What constitutes cruel and unusual punishment? When can a teacher use punishment to discipline a disruptive student or a psychologist use punishment in therapy? The federal courts have indicated that some use of aversive remedial treatment is permissible. However, the treatment may be considered to violate the Eighth Amendment if it "violates minimal standards of decency, is wholly dispropriate to the alleged offense, or goes beyond what is necessary" (Schwitzgebel & Schwitzgebel, 1980).

There have been many unjustified uses of punishment in our society. For example, the courts ruled in *Wright* v. *McMann* (1972) that forcing an inmate in a "psychiatric observation cell" for disciplinary purposes to sleep nude on a concrete floor in cold temperatures without soap, towels, or toilet paper constitutes cruel and unusual punishment. Similarly, the courts found that it is cruel and unusual punishment to administer apormorphine (to induce vomiting) to nonconsenting mental patients (*Knecht* v. *Gillman,* 1973) or to forcefully administer an intramuscular injection of a tranquilizer to a juvenile inmate for a rules infraction (*Nelson* v. *Heyne,* 1974).

Do these abuses mean that aversive punishment procedures may never be employed? Punishment can be used to eliminate undesired behavior; however, the rights of the individual must be safeguarded. Recognition of the importance of protecting the individual was clearly evident in the American Psychological Association's *Ethical Principles of Psychologists* (1971). The preamble of this document states that "psychologists respect the dignity and worth of the individual and strive for the presentation and protection of fundamental human rights. They are committed to increasing knowledge of human behavior and of people's understanding of themselves and others and to the utilization of such knowledge for the promotion of human welfare. While pursuing these objectives, they make every effort to protect the welfare of those who seek their skills."

The welfare of the individual has been safeguarded in a number of ways (Schwitzgebel & Schwitzgebel, 1980). For example, the doctrine of "the least restrictive alternative" requires that less severe methods of punishment be tried before severe treatments are used. For example, Ohio law (1977) requires that "aversive stimuli" be used for seriously disruptive behavior only after other forms of therapy have been attempted. Further, an institutional review board or human rights committee should evaluate whether the use of punishment is justified. According to Stapleton (1975), justification should be based on "the guiding principle (in the use of aversive procedures) is that the procedure should entail a relatively small amount of pain and discomfort relative to a large amount of pain and discomfort if left untreated."

Consider the precautions outlined by the Program and Health Services Division of the State of Minnesota (1977) to safeguard the rights of patients receiving electric shock in their behavior-therapy program: an aversive conditioning program must (1) have specific goals and guidelines for treatment which are written in advance and approved by a review panel, (2) use electric shock only to treat self-destructive behavior when less aversive treatments have been used and found ineffective, (3) obtain written consent from proper authorities before they have experienced the shock, (4) obtain written outside consultation, (5) have the therapist administer the shock to himself or herself, (6) use graduated shock intensities, beginning with sight of the shock device and increasing to intense shock, (7) discontinue procedure if no substantial improvement occurs within first hour or after ten shocks, (8) maintain a record of each treatment and of staff review sessions, and (9) include a treatment procedure to establish positive behaviors at the same time that aversive treatment is given so that aversive shocks can be discontinued.

Concern for the individual should not be limited to institutional use of punishment. The ethical concerns outlined by the American Psychological Association should apply in all instances in which punishment is used. Certainly abuse by parents, family, and peers is as great or greater than that produced by psychologists in the treatment of behavior disorders. A child has as much right to be protected from cruel and unusual punishment by a parent as does a patient from a therapist. Adherence to ethical standards of administering punishment can provide an effective yet humane method of altering inappropriate behavior.

SUMMARY

There are many unpleasant events in our environment. In some instances, an aversive event can be escaped but not prevented; sometimes the adversity can be avoided as well as escaped. Sometimes unpleasant events occur following a specific behavior; these occasions are called punishment; if effective, the punishment will suppress the behavior. At other times, adversity occurs independently of behavior. If this noncontingent exposure to aversive events cannot be escaped or avoided, helplessness will ensue.

Animals and people can learn to escape from an aversive event. Three variables affect the rate of acquisition of a behavior which terminates adversity: (1) the intensity of the aversive event—the greater the aversive event's intensity, the faster the acquisition of an escape response; (2) the amount of reward—the greater the decrease in adversity following the escape behavior, the more rapid the learning of the escape response; (3) the delay of reward—the greater the delay of reward following the escape behavior, the slower the acquisition of the escape response. An escape response can also be extinguished. An animal or person may stop responding if the aversive event is no longer presented; however, fear conditioned during escape learning may prevent extinction of the escape response. Extinction will occur if the escape response is punished. The amount of acquisition training affects resistance to extinction: the greater the level of acquisition training, the slower the extinction of the escape response.

Some unpleasant circumstances can be prevented, and in some cases an animal or person must exhibit a specific overt behavior to avoid adversity; in other instances, the suppression of responding will prevent the aversive event. Psychologists have speculated about the nature of avoidance learning. Mowrer suggested that fear is conditioned during the first phase of learning. In the second stage fear motivates an animal or person to respond. Any behavior which successfully terminates the fear will be reinforced and elicited upon future presentations of the feared stimulus. According to Mowrer, an animal or person will successfully prevent adversity only if the escape response to the feared stimulus will also result in the avoidance of adversity. Although Mowrer's two-factor theory of avoidance learning had a number of problems, the most significant problem was Kamin's demonstration that the prevention of the aversive event is as important in the acquisition of an avoidance response as the termination of the feared stimulus. D'Amato proposed that avoidance behavior reflects a behavior motivated not only by the anticipation of pain but also by the anticipation of relief. D'Amato also theorized that the anticipatory relief response cannot be acquired if the avoidance response does not prevent the aversive event. In contrast, Bolles suggested a cognitive view of avoidance behavior: expectations that (1) an aversive event will occur in the absence of avoidance behavior and that (2) the avoidance response will prevent adversity are acquired during avoidance learning. A contemporary view of avoidance learning suggests that both drives and cognitions play an important role in avoidance behavior.

Three variables affect the rate of acquisition of an avoidance response. First, the severity of the aversive event influences the acquisition of the avoidance response. In some tasks (passive-avoidance learning and one-way active-avoidance learning), increases in adversity lead to faster avoidance learning; in other tasks (two-way active-avoidance learning), an increase in the intensity of the aversive event produces slower acquisition. Second, the intensity of the CS affects avoidance learning: the greater the CS intensity, the faster the acquisition of the avoidance response. Finally, the rate of avoidance acquisition is influenced by the CS-UCS interval: the longer the interval between the CS and UCS, the slower the acquisition of the avoidance response.

Punishment represents the presentation of an aversive event contingent on the occurrence of an undesired response. There are two classes of punishment: positive punishment represents the presentation of a painful event after the occurrence of an undesired response, and negative punishment is the loss of reward (response cost) or inability to obtain reward for a specified period of time (time-out) contingent on the occurrence of an inappropriate behavior. Although Estes and Skinner assumed that punishment only temporarily suppresses the punished response, in some circumstances behavior can be permanently suppressed by punishment. Four variables influence the degree of the effectiveness of punishment: (1) severity of punishment—the more severe the aversive event, the greater the behavioral suppression, (2) consistency of the presentation of punishment—the more consistent the punishment, the more suppression of the behavior, (3) delay of punishment—the longer the delay between punishment and occurrence of the undesired behavior, the less suppression of the punished response, and (4) motivational level—the higher the motivation, the weaker the suppression of the behavior.

Several processes appear to contribute to the effect of punishment on behavior. Guthrie proposed that punishment elicits behavior; if the response elicited by punishment is antagonistic to the punished behavior, punishment will suppress the undesired behavior, but punishment may increase the response if it elicits a compatible response. Mowrer assumed that fear is conditioned by the use of punishment and that it is this fear that motivates escape behavior. As the result of the escape behavior, the punished response does not occur. Although response antagonism and fear do influence the effectiveness of punishment, punishment can suppress behavior normally elicited by punishment, and the punished behavior can be suppressed in the absence of fear. Estes's motivational view suggests that as the result of punishment, an association develops between the specific motivation present and the punishment. This association reduces the motivation level; the absence of motivation suppresses the undesired response, according to Estes.

Punishment has a number of potential negative effects. First, punishment can elicit aggressive behavior. Second, the punished individual may model the use of punishment as a means of behavioral control. Third, the environment in which punishment takes place may become aversive, thereby motivating escape behavior. Fourth, the effects of punishment may generalize to other nonpunished behaviors. Finally, the animal or person may not recognize the contingency between behavior and punishment, and the failure to detect this contingency may result in feelings of helplessness.

Aversive events have been successfully employed to alter undesired human behavior. Punishment—a painful event, loss of reward (response cost), or inability to obtain reward for specified period of time (time-out)—has been successfully employed to suppress undesired responding in humans. Although punishment does represent an effective method of behavior control, safeguards must be employed to protect individuals from cruel and unusual punishment. Adherence to ethical standards of conduct will enable society to use punishment as a method of discipline while ensuring that those punished will experience less discomfort than if the treatment had not been employed.

CHAPTER 5

STIMULUS CONTROL
OF BEHAVIOR

A CASE OF MISTAKEN IDENTITY

Walking to the grocery store, James was approached by a tall thin man who suddenly jumped directly in front of him and within a split second drew a large knife. The stranger grabbed James's arm and demanded his money. Frightened, James surrendered the $25 with which he had planned to buy food. After grabbing the money, the thief bolted down the street, disappearing into an alley. James began yelling, "I've been robbed! I've been robbed!" But the criminal had fled, and the several people who had witnessed the robbery had dispersed.

A merchant hearing James's screams did call the police, who arrived within 5 minutes. The police first questioned James, asking him to describe the robber. The merchant, upon questioning, denied witnessing the crime, and attested only to hearing James's screams.

Several weeks passed before the police contacted James, informing him that they had a suspect meeting James's description of the assailant and having a record of attacks similar to the one on James. The police asked James to come to the police station to try to identify his assailant from a lineup. The lineup was a cinch; James immediately recognized his attacker. On the basis of his criminal record and James' identification, the suspect was charged with assault and robbery.

Unfortunately, the person identified by James was not his assailant. Two weeks after the lineup, another man was apprehended while attempting to rob a woman on her way home from work. During his interrogation, the man confessed not only to this crime but also to robbing James. Since James had had a close view of his assailant, why had he identified the wrong man? To answer, we must examine the five individuals in the lineup. Although five men were in the lineup, only two were as tall as James's assailant. Of these two men, one was thin; the other, fat. The choice seemed obvious to James, and he picked the man he believed had robbed him. James's behavior reflects the operation of discrimination learning: he had learned several important attributes of his assailant, and he used this knowledge to discriminate his assailant from the other men in the lineup. However, his discrimination was not perfect; although James's assailant and the man he identified in the lineup shared two attributes—they were very thin and tall, their facial characteristics differed significantly. James's identification of the wrong man reflects the operation of generalization. He responded only to the similar characteristics of the two men, and he ignored their facial differences.

Chapter 5 discusses the generalization and discrimination processes. *Generalization* is a process in which an animal or person responds in the same way to similar stimuli. In the opening vignette of the chapter, James responded in the same manner to both the assailant and the man in the lineup. Frequently occurring in the real world, generalization in many instances is adaptive. Generalization enables us to know the significance of stimuli we have encountered and how to respond to them. For example, as students you have learned to be on time with assignments to receive a good grade. The generalization of this behavior to work situations will motivate you to complete work assignments on time, thereby gaining advancement. However, generalization is not always constructive. For example, someone fails a test in school and not only becomes afraid of tests in this course but also generalizes the fear to all tests. In this instance, generalization is undesirable; this student now is afraid of all tests. Furthermore, this test anxiety may motivate withdrawal from school.

Discrimination is the process in which an animal or person learns to respond in different ways to different stimuli. In the chapter-opening vignette, James discriminated between the assailant and four of the five men in the police lineup. Discrimination also occurs frequently in the real world—it keeps us from blindly generalizing our response to all stimuli. In many cases, an animal or person responds effectively only when discriminating. Consider the following example to illustrate the discrimination process. A store open from 9 a.m. until 9 p.m. is closed from 9 p.m. until 9 a.m. If you discriminate, you will go to the store when it is open, not when it is closed. However, if you do not discriminate (that is, if you do not know the store's schedule), you will waste time and experience frustration. However, sometimes discrimination is maladaptive: Suppose that an alcoholic in therapy receives electric shock while drinking. If the alcoholic discriminates between therapy and the real world, therapy will be ineffective. Since alcoholics are not shocked for drinking in the real world, this likely discrimination represents a real problem for treating alcoholics. The discrimination between what occurs in therapy and what occurs in the real world also reflects a most significant problem for all types of therapy.

THE GENERALIZATION PROCESS

During World War II, the United States placed thousands of Japanese-American citizens in detention camps, where they were forced to remain until the end of the war. Why did the U.S. government intern thousands of its citizens for almost three years? Generalization was responsible. The Japanese attack on Pearl Harbor caused white Americans to develop a strong negative-conditioned emotional response toward Japan. Unfortunately, white Americans generalized this dislike of Japan to Japanese Americans.

Generalization frequently occurs in the real world. Sometimes, generalization is undesirable, as in the case of the treatment of Japanese Americans during World War II. Racial, ethnic, and religious prejudice are examples of undesirable generalization that occurs when someone who has had an unpleasant experience with one member of a racial, ethnic, or religious group generalizes this dislike to other members of that group.

However, generalization is often adaptive. For example, parents read a book to their children, the children enjoy it, and a positive emotional experience is conditioned to the book. These children then generalize their positive emotional response to other books, and thus they read more and learn more about their environment. The children's generalization also enables them to like books that they have never read. To use another example, preschool children may enjoy playing with the other neighborhood children; this enjoyment reflects a conditioned response acquired through past experience. When these children attend school, they generalize their conditioned social responses to new children and are motivated to play with them. This generalization enables children to socialize with new children; otherwise children would have to learn to like new acquaintances before they would want to play with them. Thus, generalization allows people to respond positively to strangers. Imagine how difficult life would be if you had to have a positive experience with someone before you would talk to him or her. Clearly, generalization makes our lives much easier.

Thus we respond to stimuli similar to the stimulus present during training. However, different amounts of generalization occur. In some instances, we respond the same to all stimuli resembling the stimulus associated with conditioning. For example, people who become ill after eating in a specific restaurant may generalize their negative emotional experiences and avoid eating out again. In other situations, less generalization is observed as the similarity to the conditioned stimulus lessens. Suppose a person has been bitten by a large dog. This individual may not show intense fear of all dogs (complete generalization). Instead, the person is very afraid of large dogs, moderately frightened of medium-sized dogs, and only slightly fearful of small dogs. In this case, the bigger the difference in size of the two dogs, the less generalization of fear that occurs. Or the person might be afraid only of large dogs; if so, only stimuli very similar to the conditioning stimulus (the large dog) will elicit fear. To study level of generalization, psychologists have constructed generalization gradients. A *gen-*

eralization gradient is a visual representation of the strength of the response produced by stimuli of varying degrees of similarity to the stimulus associated with training; these gradients show the level of generalization which occurs to stimuli similar to the one present during conditioning. A steep generalization gradient indicates that people or animals respond very little to stimuli that are not very similar to the training stimulus, while a flat generalization gradient shows that responding occurs even to stimuli quite unlike the conditioning stimulus. Let's next look at the research on generalization gradients.

Generalization Gradients

Much of the research on generalization gradients has been conducted using pigeons as subjects. Pigeons have excellent color vision, and their generalization to stimuli similar to the color used in training can be easily established. Most generalization studies have investigated generalization of excitatory conditioning. Recall from Chapter 2 that in excitatory conditioning, a specific colored stimulus is presented prior to either reward or punishment. Following acquisition, the colored stimulus (S+) paired with reward or punishment and several test stimuli varying in color from very similar to very dissimilar to the S+ are presented. The amount of responding to the test stimulus in comparison to the amount of responding to the training stimulus indicates the level of generalization of excitatory conditioning. A graph of the response to each stimulus provides a visual display of the level of excitatory generalization. Note that the use of stimuli of different colors is a matter of convenience; the principles discussed apply to other stimulus dimensions.

Some research has studied the generalization of inhibitory conditioning. Remember that inhibitory conditioning presents one colored stimulus with either reward or punishment and another with the absence of the event (see Chapter 2). Conditioning of inhibition to the second colored stimulus (S−) will cause it to suppress responding to the excitatory stimulus (S+). After training, the second colored stimulus (S−) and several test stimuli varying in color from very similar to very dissimilar to the inhibitory colored stimulus are presented before the colored stimulus, which was paired with either reward or punishment (S+). The amount of suppression of responding produced by the inhibitory stimulus compared with that produced by the test stimuli indicates the amount of generalization of inhibition. A graph of the level of suppression produced by each stimulus can provide a visual display of the level of inhibitory generalization.

Excitatory-Conditioning Generalization Gradients Guttman and Kalish's (1956) classic experiment, investigating generalization of excitatory conditioning, trained hungry pigeons to peck a small illuminated disk to obtain food reinforcement. Four groups of pigeons were shown one of four colors (530, 550, 580, and 600 nm) ranging from yellowish green to red as training stimuli. During training, the key was illuminated for 60-second periods, and these periods alternated with 10-second periods of no illumination. The pigeons were re-warded on a VI 1-minute schedule of reinforcement when the key was illumi-nated; reward was unavailable when the key was not illuminated. After acquisi-tion training, Guttman and Kalish tested for generalization of responding to similar-colored stimuli. The generalization test consisted of presenting the color illuminated during training and ten other stimuli (five were higher on the wavelength color spectrum and five were lower). Each stimulus was presented randomly twelve times for a period of 30 seconds. Guttman and Kalish's results showed that the pigeons made the maximum number of responses to the train-ing stimuli (see Figure 5.1). Guttman and Kalish noted that the level of respond-ing declined as the difference between training and test stimuli increased. Note that Guttman and Kalish reported symmetrical generalization gradients; this symmetry is an important characteristic of generalization gradients. Further-more, the general shape of each gradient was similar for all four subject groups, regardless of the training stimulus. Other experiments with pigeons have re-ported generalization gradients similar to that observed by Guttman and Kal-ish; see Hearst and Koresko (1968) for another study and Blough and Blough (1977) for a review of the generalization gradient literature.

FIGURE 5.1
Generalization gradients obtained using four different wave lengths in separate groups of pigeons trained to key-peck for food reward.
Adapted from Guttman, N., & Kalish, H. I. Discriminability and stimulus generalization. *Journal of Experimental Psychology*, 1956, *51*, 79–88.
Copyright 1956 by the American Psychological Association. Reprinted by permission.

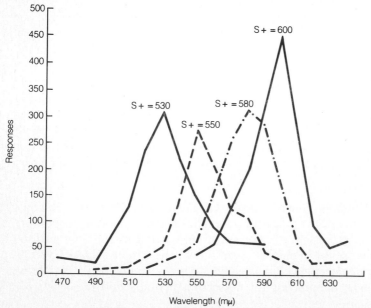

Researchers using species other than pigeons have reported generalization gradients similar to those found by Guttman and Kalish in pigeons. Moore (1972) provides an illustration of this generalization gradient form in rabbits. Moore initially conditioned an eye-blink response to a 1200-Hz tone in rabbits. Following conditioning, the S+ and other stimuli varying from 400 Hz to 2000 Hz were presented to the rabbits. Moore reported that the highest percentage of responding was to the 1200-Hz tone (S+) and that the rabbits' responding declined as the similarity of the test and training stimulus decreased. Razran (1949) describes the results of fifty-four different experiments in Pavlov's laboratory examining the generalization of salivary conditioning in dogs. The results of these experiments show a convex upward generalization gradient.

Generalization gradients like those reported by Guttman and Kalish have been observed using a wide variety of stimuli and responses in humans (refer to Bass & Hull, 1934; Hoveland, 1937; and Razran, 1949). For example, Hoveland (1937), pairing a tone (S+) with electric shock and then investigating the generalization of the galvanic skin response to other stimuli, reported that less generalization occurred as the test and conditioning tone became more dissimilar (refer to Figure 5.2). Bass and Hull (1934), using a tactile stimulus (stimulation of the shoulder) as the S+ and electric shock as the UCS, presented the S+ and other tactile stimuli after conditioning of the electrodermal response. The form of the generalization gradient for tactile stimuli observed by Bass and Hull was similar to that found by Hoveland for auditory stimuli. Razran (1949) examined

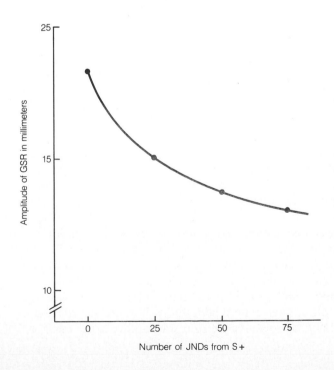

FIGURE 5.2
Amplitude of galvanic response in millimeters during generalization testing as a function of the number of just noticeable differences from the S+. From Hoveland, C. I. The generalization of conditioned responses. II, The sensory generalization of conditioned responses with varying frequencies of tones. *Journal of General Psychology*, 1937, *17*, 125–148. Published by Heldref Publications, 4000 Albemarle St., N. W., Washington, D.C. 20016.

generalization of a salivary response conditioned to words such as *style* and *urn* after pairing the training words with stimuli such as *pretzels* and *candy*. Razran noted that synonyms and homophones of the training stimuli also elicited a salivary response, and the amount of generalization increased with greater semantic similarity.

Perhaps you think that the level of generalization shown in Figure 5.1 is characteristic of all situations. In many circumstances an animal or person will respond to stimuli similar to the conditioning stimulus, but in other situations animals or people may generalize to stimuli only remotely similar to the conditioning stimulus. Consider the following example: Some people who do not interact easily with others find that being around people elicits anxiety, and, although they may be lonely, they avoid contact. These socially anxious people probably experienced some unpleasantness with another person (or persons)—perhaps the other person rebuked an attempted social invitation or said something offensive. As a result of a painful social experience, a conditioned disliking to the other person occurred. Although everyone has had an unpleasant social experience, most people limit their disliking to the person associated with the pain or perhaps to similar individuals. Socially anxious individuals generalize their dislike to all people, and this generalization makes all interacting difficult.

Many studies have reported flat generalization gradients; that is, an animal or person responds to stimuli which are quite dissimilar to the conditioning stimulus. The Jenkins and Harrison (1962) study is one example: Jenkins and Harrison trained two groups of pigeons to key-peck for food reward. A 1000-Hz tone was present for the control group during the entire conditioning phase. In contrast, animals in the experimental group received some training periods during which reward was contingent on key pressing; reward was unavailable despite key pecking during other training periods. The 1000-Hz tone was present during the training period when reward was available; no tone was present when the reward was not available. Generalization testing followed conditioning for both groups of pigeons. Seven tones (300, 450, 670, 1000, 1500, 2250, and 3500 Hz) were presented during generalization testing. Jenkins and Harrison's results, presented in Figure 5.3, show that experimental animals exhibited a generalization gradient similar to that reported by Guttman and Kalish, and control animals responded to the stimulus present during conditioning and the other seven tones equally.

Inhibitory-Conditioning Generalization Gradients   In all likelihood, you are apprehensive when you start dating a person. If this is your initial date with this person, you did not acquire your fear directly; your fear could be caused by one of several factors (i.e., excitatory generalizations from a negative experience with another person). Suppose that your fears are unfounded and you have an enjoyable time. As the result of your experience, you will associate your date with the absence of adversity, the occurrence of a reinforcing experience, or

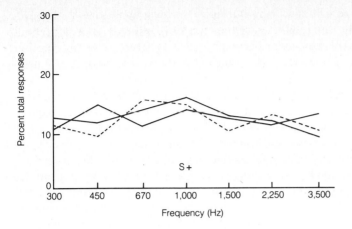

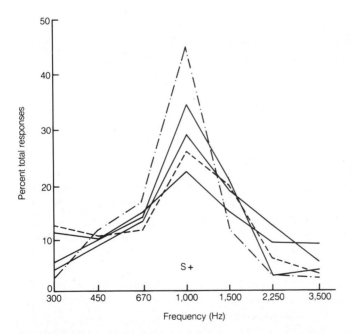

FIGURE 5.3
Percentage of total responses to S+ (1000-Hz tone) and other
stimuli (ranging in loudness from 300 to 3500 Hz) during
generalization testing for control-group subjects receiving
only the S+ in training (top panel) and for experimental group
animals given both S+ and S− in acquisition (bottom panel).
From Jenkins, H. M., & Harrison, R. H. Effect of discrimination
training on auditory generalization. *Journal of Experimental
Psychology*, 1960, *59*, 246–253. Copyright 1960 by the
American Psychological Association. Reprinted by permission.

both. This conditioning will diminish your apprehension about dating this person again. Fortunately, the inhibition of fear not only reduces your apprehensiveness about dating this particular person but also generalizes to dating other new people. Thus, the generalization of inhibition allows you to be less fearful of dating others.

Weisman and Palmer's study (1969) illustrates the generalization of inhibition. In their study, pigeons learned to peck at a green disk (S+) to receive reinforcement on a VI 1-minute schedule. When a white vertical line (S−) was presented, the pigeons were not rewarded for bar pressing. Recall from Chapter 2 that conditioned inhibition is established when one stimulus (S+) is associated with the UCS and another stimulus (S−) is paired with the absence of the UCS; thus, the white vertical line is a conditioned inhibitor because its presence is associated with the absence of food. After conditioning, the pigeons received a conditioned-inhibition generalization test. In this phase of the study, the white vertical line (S−) plus six other lines which departed from the vertical line by −90, −60, −30, +30, +60, and +90 degrees were presented to the subjects. As can be seen in Figure 5.4, the presentation of the vertical line (S−) inhibits pecking. Furthermore, the amount of inhibition that generalized to other lines differed depending on the degree of similarity to the S−; the more dissimilar the line to the S−, the less inhibition of responding. Other psycholo-

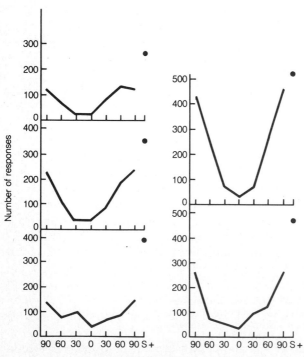

FIGURE 5.4
Figure shows inhibitory generalization gradient for five subjects receiving vertical line as S−. The number of responses to the test stimuli and S+ are shown in the figure. From Weisman, R. G., & Palmer, J. A. Factors influencing inhibitory stimulus control: Discrimination training and prior nondifferential reinforcement. *Journal of Experimental Analysis of Behavior,* 1969, *12,* 229–237. Copyright 1969 by the Society for the Experimental Analysis of Behavior, Inc. Reprinted by permission.

Line orientation (degrees from vertical)

gists have reported similar inhibitory generalization gradients; see Hearst, Besley, and Farthing (1970) and Jenkins and Harrison (1962) for other studies.

Note that the inhibitory generalization gradient shown in Figure 5.4 is similar in form to the excitatory generalization gradient observed by Guttman and Kalish (refer to Figure 5.1). In both examples of generalization, maximal excitation was conditioned to the S+ or maximal inhibition was conditioned to the S−, and the degree of generalization gradually declined with decreasing similarity to the S+ or S−. As is true of excitatory generalization gradients, in certain circumstances inhibition generalizes to stimuli quite dissimilar to the training stimulus. Even dissimilar stimuli can sometimes produce responding equivalent to that elicited by the conditioning stimulus.

Generalization of inhibition to stimuli quite dissimilar to the training stimulus can be seen in a study by Hoffman (1969). In his study, pigeons first learned to key-peck for food reward. Following this initial training phase, the birds were exposed to twenty-four conditioning sessions. During each session, a 2-minute 88-dB noise preceding electric shock was presented three times, and a 2-minute 88-dB 1000-Hz tone not followed by electric shock was presented three times. Hoffman's procedure established the 88-dB noise (S+) as a feared stimulus, and the presentation of the 88-dB noise suppressed key pecking. In contrast, little suppression was noted when the tone (S−) was presented. Furthermore, the presence of the tone inhibited fear to the noise. Generalization of inhibition testing consisted of presenting the noise (S+) and several test tones. The tones varied in pitch from 300 to 3400 Hz. Hoffman reported that each tone equally inhibited the suppressive ability of the noise. Almost complete generalization of inhibition was noted, that is, tones with very dissimilar pitches produced about as much inhibition as did the S− (1000-Hz tone).

Measuring Generalization Gradients   Unless an animal or person responds equally to the training and test stimuli or responds only to the conditioning stimulus, the slope of the generalization gradient (or, the degree of generalization) may be misleading. A considerable amount of research indicates that the method of measurement used has an important influence on the slope of the generalization gradient (see Mackintosh, 1974). One significant methodological issue is whether the gradient shows the absolute number of responses to the training and test stimuli or presents the proportion of responses made to the conditioning and test stimuli. As can be seen in Figure 5.5, the generalization gradient differs when the absolute number of responses rather than the percentage of responses is used to construct the generalization gradient. Figure 5.5 also shows that the steepness of the gradient does not depend on how the generalization gradient is determined. Thomas and Switalski (1966) reported that the steepness of the generalization gradient was greater with an absolute than with a relative generalization gradient, but Hearst and Koresko (1968) found the opposite.

The shape of the generalization gradient is also affected by whether a within-subjects or between-subjects methodology is employed to measure the level of

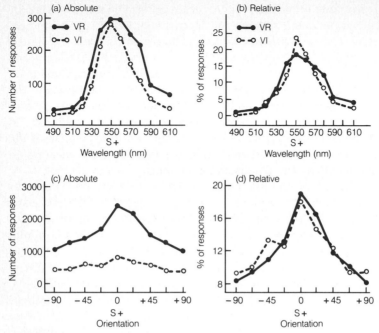

FIGURE 5.5
Absolute and relative generalization gradient for two different studies.
The top two panels present the absolute and relative generalization
gradients in a study by Thomas and Seritalski (1966) in which two
groups of pigeons were reinforced on either a VR (closed circles, solid
line) or VI (open circle, dashed line) schedule. The bottom two panels
show the absolute and relative generalization gradients in an
experiment by Hearst and Koresko (1968) in which two groups of
pigeons received either 2 (open circle, dashed line) or 14 (closed
circles, solid line) days of VI training. From Mackintosh, N. J. *The
psychology of animal learning.* New York: Academic Press, 1974.

generalization. In a within-subjects design, all subjects are tested at all points
on the test stimulus dimension; in a between-subjects design, different subjects
are tested at each point on the test stimulus dimension. The within-subjects
design (each subject receives a number of test stimuli) produces a steeper
generalization gradient than does the between-subject design (each subject
is given only one test stimulus). The important point here is that the shape of
the generalization gradient is influenced by the testing procedure (see Macin-
tosh, 1974). These results indicate that the shapes of generalization gradients
differ.

The observations that the shape of the generalization is affected by both the
testing and scaling procedures has led psychologists to recognize that there is
no uniform shape of a generalization gradient. This research has also caused

psychologists to examine other aspects of the generalization process, and one important question concerns the nature of the generalization process.

The Nature of the Generalization Process

Why do we generalize our response to stimuli similar to the stimulus associated with conditioning at certain times but show no generalization to similar stimuli at other times? Many theories have been proposed to explain stimulus generalization (refer to Prokasy & Hall, 1963, for a review of these theories). The Lashley-Wade view of stimulus generalization is presented here as it seems to best explain why generalization occurs on some occasions but not others.

Lashley and Wade (1946) suggested that animals and people respond to stimuli which differ from the training stimulus because they are unable to distinguish between the generalization test stimulus and the conditioned stimulus. Thus, they conclude that the failure to discriminate between the training and test stimuli is responsible for stimulus generalization. Furthermore, Lashley and Wade proposed that if animals or people could differentiate between the CS and other stimuli, they would show no generalized response to the other stimuli. Therefore, according to Lashley and Wade, generalization represents the failure to discriminate; discrimination precludes generalization, and a failure to discriminate leads to generalization.

Several lines of evidence support the Lashley-Wade view of stimulus generalization. First, *generalization to stimuli even dissimilar to the training stimulus is found when nondifferential reinforcement training is used.* In this task, the conditioned stimulus is present during the entire training session when the nondifferential reinforcement is employed. Thus, the only stimulus the subject experiences during nondifferential reinforcement training is the S+. The Lashley-Wade view assumes that without experience with stimuli other than the S+, the subject will generalize to all similar stimuli. The Jenkins and Harrison study (1962) provides an excellent example of the flat stimulus generalization gradient observed with nondifferential training; this result is consistent with the Lashley-Wade theory of stimulus generalization. In the Jenkins and Harrison study, a 1000-Hz tone was present during the entire conditioning session in which pigeons learned to peck at a key to receive reward. Following training, each subject was exposed to 7 tones ranging from 300 to 3500 Hz and to a nontone presentation. As can be seen in the top panel of Figure 5.3, the pigeons responded equally to all stimuli. Other experiments also show flat generalization gradients with nondifferential training; see Heinemann and Rudolph (1963) for another example.

The second line of evidence is that *discrimination training results in generalization only to stimuli very similar to the conditioning stimulus.* As discussed earlier, during discrimination training, the S+ is present when reward is available, the S− when reward is unavailable. According to the Lashley-Wade view, an animal or person learns to differentiate between the S+ and other stimuli as the result of discrimination training. This knowledge indicates that responses are almost always limited to the S+, and few or no responses are made to other stimuli; that is, little or no stimulus generalization occurs when an animal or person recognizes the specific stimulus associated with reinforcement. A number of studies show that discrimination training leads to steep generalization gradients. We described a few of these experiments earlier in the chapter. The Jenkins and Harrison (1962) study evaluated the influence of discrimination training on stimulus generalization gradients. A brief review of this experiment will document the effect of discrimination training on the level of stimulus generalization. Jenkins and Harrison gave pigeons discrimination training in which pecking at a key with the S+ (a 1000-Hz tone) present resulted in reward; key pecking with the S− (no tone presented) did not lead to reward. After training, stimulus generalization testing consisted of seven tones ranging from 300 to 3500 Hz. The bottom panel of Figure 5.3 illustrates that this discrimination training produced a steep generalization gradient.

The third line of evidence, according to Lashley and Wade, is that *generalization occurs when an animal cannot differentiate between the training stimulus and generalization test stimuli.* An extension of this view suggests that little generalization should occur and that a discrimination should readily be formed when an animal can easily differentiate between S+ and S−. The literature (see Kalish, 1969, or Mostofsky, 1965, for a review) indicates that the more able an animal is to differentiate between the S+ and S−, the easier it learns a discrimination. Furthermore, a steeper generalization gradient is observed when an animal can easily distinguish between the S+ and S− than when this discrimination is difficult.

Haber and Kalish's 1963 study illustrates the influence of discriminability on the ease of establishing a discrimination. Haber and Kalish initially showed that pigeons have more difficulty differentiating between a 550- and a 540-nm light than between a 540- and a 530-nm light. This observation was established by pairing either a 550-nm light or a 540-nm light with reward; greater generalization developed to the 540-nm light with the 550-nm light as the S+ than to the 530-nm light with the 540-nm light as the S+. Two other groups of pigeons learned to discriminate between these two pairs of stimuli; some pigeons had the 550-nm light as the S+ and the 540-nm light as the S−; the other pigeons were trained with the 540-nm light as the S+ and the 530-nm light as the S−. Haber and Kalish reported that animals more easily learned to discriminate between the 540-nm light and the 530-nm light than between the 550-nm light and the 540-nm light.

The final evidence supporting the Lashley-Wade theory is that *perceptual experience influences the amount of stimulus generalization.* The Lashley-Wade view assumes that animals learn to distinguish similarities and differences in environmental events. This perceptual learning is essential for animals to discriminate between different stimuli yet generalize to similar stimuli. Without this perceptual experience, different environmental events would appear similar, thereby making discrimination very difficult. For example, a person with little or no experience with varied colors would find distinguishing between green and red difficult; this difficulty could result in failing to learn to observe traffic lights. Several studies have evaluated the influence of various levels of perceptual experience on the level of stimulus generalization (see Houston, 1981). These results, consistent with the Lashley-Wade view, show that as the perceptual experience of an animal or person increases, the generalization gradient becomes steeper. This demonstrates that perceptual experiences allow animals or people to differentiate between similar stimuli and not to generalize their response from the S+ to other stimuli.

Peterson's classic study (1962) illustrates the effect of perceptual experience on the amount of stimulus generalization. Peterson raised two groups of ducks under different conditions. The experimental group ducks raised in cages illuminated by a 589-nm light experienced only a single color. In contrast, control-group animals were raised in normal light and therefore were exposed to a wide range of colors. During the initial phase of this study, Peterson trained the ducks to peck at a key illuminated by the 589-nm light. After training, both groups received generalization testing using stimuli varying from a 490-nm to a 650-nm light. The top panel of Figure 5.6 illustrates that ducklings raised in a monochromatic environment showed a flat generalization gradient. These results indicate that ducks without perceptual experience with various colors generalized their response to all colors. In contrast, the ducks raised in normal light displayed the greatest response to the S+ (the 589-nm light) (see bottom panel of Figure 5.6). As the result of perceptual experience with various colors, animals apparently learn to differentiate between colors and therefore are less likely to generalize to similar colors. A similar influence of restricted perceptual experience on stimulus generalization was also observed in rats by Walk and Walters (1973), in ducks by Tracy (1970), in monkeys by Ganz and Riesen (1962), and in congenitally blind humans by Ganz (1968).

The Lashley-Wade view of stimulus generalization assumes that failure to differentiate the conditioning stimulus from other stimuli accounts for an animal or person generalizing. With perceptual experience or explicit discrimination training, animals or people become able to distinguish between stimuli, and they then generalize less.

Under some circumstances, generalization is undesired. In these situations, reward is available only when a specific stimulus is present, and generalized responses are ineffective in producing reward. Reward available only under certain conditions creates a situation in which an animal or person must learn to discriminate between when responding is effective and when it is not.

DISCRIMINATION LEARNING

We know that during some occasions reward is available and will occur contingent on an appropriate response and that during other occasions reward is unavailable and will not occur despite continued responding. To respond when reward is available and not when reward is unavailable, we must learn to

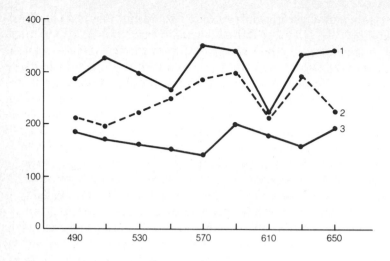

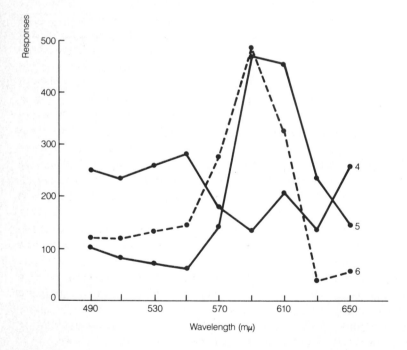

FIGURE 5.6
Generalization gradients obtained with ducklings reared in
monochromatic light (top panel) and in white light (bottom panel).
From Peterson, N. Effect of monochromatic rearing on the control of
responding by wavelength. *Science*, 1962, *136*, 774–775. Copyright 1962
by the American Association for the Advancement of Science.
Reprinted by permission.

discriminate; that is, we must not only discover the conditions indicating re-ward availability and respond when those conditions exist; we must also recognize the circumstances indicating the unavailability of reward and not respond during these times. We are faced with thousands of discrimination learning tasks during our lives. For example, suppose that you want to see a particular movie at your local theater. In many movie theaters you cannot just walk in; you must first get in the right line. If the line for the movie that you want to see is indicated by a blue line or specified number ($S^D{}_s$), then reward (the movie) is available only if you get into the right line. However, you will not be able to see the movie if you get into the wrong line (S^Δ).

We must learn to discriminate the conditions which indicate reward availability (S^D) from the conditions which do not (S^Δ) to interact effectively with our environment. The failure to discriminate will cause us not to respond when reward is available, to respond when reward is unavailable, or both. Thus, you will miss the movie that you wanted to see if you get into the wrong line at the movie theater. In most cases, the failure to discriminate will cause you to be inconvenienced. For example, you lose time and effort going to the library if it's closed. Embarrassment may occur during some circumstances if you do not discriminate. If you go to the movies with friends, you will feel foolish if you have them get into the wrong line. In some cases, behavior pathology can result from discriminative failure. To illustrate this process, consider a lonely person desiring to be with others. This individual's loneliness may stem from a failure to recognize when people will be friendly and when they will not. As a result of the failure to discriminate when to approach others, this lonely person just avoids all social contact. Disruptive behavior in school may also reflect a discriminative failure. The behaviors (e.g., talking) leading to social reward outside school do not lead to reward in school. The child failing to discriminate will talk in school, and this behavior may be considered a problem. The conditions leading to discrimination as well as circumstances causing a failure to discriminate will be described later in the chapter.

Discrimination learning involves discovering not only when reward is available or unavailable but also when aversive events may or may not occur. For example, some conditions forecast rain, and some predict no rain. Since you get wet if you go out in the rain (typically an aversive event), you need to carry an umbrella when it rains to avoid becoming wet. If you fail to learn the conditions indicating impending rain, you will often become wet. Similarly, you need not carry an umbrella on a clear, sunny day. Nothing appears quite as foolish as someone carrying an umbrella when the sun is shining. However, it is difficult to learn when to carry an umbrella and when not to, because no stimuli always signal rain (the aversive event) or always indicate no rain (the absence of the aversive event). We will discuss the influence of predictiveness on discrimination learning later. However, in many circumstances the occurrence or nonoccurrence of aversive events is easily predicted. A course outline for this class indicates that an exam is impending, but the absence of an announcement means that you will have no exam. If you recognize the significance of the schedule, you will study before the next class, but you will not study if no exam is scheduled. The failure to discriminate may cause you to study even though you have no exam or to fail to prepare for a scheduled exam. Another example of discrimination in aversive situations is seen in children who misbehave for a substitute teacher but behave appropriately with their regular teacher. Their behavior is based on the recognition that their regular teacher sometimes punishes them but that a substitute is not likely to do so.

You might have noticed that the abbreviations changed from S+ and S− in the generalization discussion to S^D and S^Δ in the discussion of discrimination learning. This change reflects the conventional terms used in each area of research; it indicates not that we are talking about different stimuli but instead that we are referring to different properties of the same stimulus. Consider the following example to illustrate that a stimulus can function as both a discriminative stimulus and a conditioned stimulus. On a hot summer day going to the beach can be quite reinforcing. The hot summer day is a discriminative stimulus which indicates that reward is available; it is also a conditioned stimulus producing an anticipatory goal response and motivating the instrumental activity of going to the beach.

Discrimination Paradigms

Two-Choice Discrimination Tasks   In a two-choice discrimination learning situation, the S^D (the stimulus signalling reward or punishment availability) and the S^Δ (the stimulus signalling reward or punishment unavailability) are on the same stimulus dimension (for example, the S^D is a red light and the S^Δ a green light). Responding to the S^D produces reward or punishment, and choosing the S^Δ leads to neither reward nor punishment. Consider the following example. Suppose that one of a child's parents is generous and the other parent is conservative. Asking one parent for money to go to the video arcade will be successful; a request to the other will result in failure. The first parent is an S^D since his or her presence indicates that reward is available. Because reward is unavailable when the other parent is asked, the presence of this parent is an S^Δ.

Research evaluating two-choice discrimination learning shows that animals or people begin by responding equally to the S^D and S^Δ. With continued training, response to the S^D increases and the response rate to S^Δ declines. At the end of training, an animal or person is responding at a high rate to the S^D and responding little or not at all to the S^Δ.

Reynolds (1961a) initially trained his pigeons to peck for food reward on a multiple VI 3-minute, VI 3-minute schedule. (A multiple schedule is a compound schedule that consists of two or more independent schedules presented successively; each schedule is associated with a distinctive stimulus.) In Reynolds's study, a red light and a green light were associated with the separate components of the multiple schedule. As can be seen in Figure 5.7, Reynolds's pigeons exhibited equal response to the red and green lights during the prediscrimination phase of his study. In the discrimination stage, the schedule was

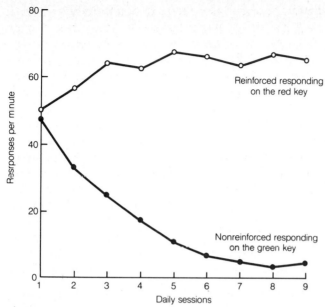

FIGURE 5.7
Mean number of responses per minute during discrimination
learning. From *A primer of operant conditioning* by G. S.
Reynolds. Copyright 1968 by Scott, Foresman and Company.
Reprinted by permission.

changed to a multiple VI 3 extinction schedule. In this schedule, the red light
continued to be correlated with reward, and the green light was associated with
the extinction (or nonreward) component of the multiple schedule. During the
discrimination phase of the study, Reynolds noted that the response rate to the
red light (S^D) increased, and response to the green light (S^Δ) declined (refer to
Figure 5.7). To show that the change in response during the discrimination
phase was due to differential reinforcement, Reynolds shifted the schedule
back to a multiple VI 3, VI 3 schedule in the third phase of his study. Reynolds
found that response to the red light declined and response to the green light
increased during the third (nondiscrimination) phase until an equivalent response rate was made to both stimuli. This finding indicates that responding
during the discrimination phase was controlled by the differential reinforcement procedure. Note two important observations about Reynolds's results.
First, the animals stopped responding to the green light (S^Δ) associated with the
absence of reward. Second, the pigeons increased their response rate to the red
light (S^D) during the discrimination phase. Reynolds called the increased responding to the S^D during the discrimination phase of the study *behavioral
contrast*. Behavioral contrast has been consistently observed by Reynolds
(1961a, 1961b, 1961c) and other psychologists (Bloomfield, 1967; Lombardi &
Flaherty, 1978; Nevin & Shettleworth, 1966; Rovee-Collier & Capatides, 1979;

Terrace, 1966b; Woodruff, 1979). We will discuss behavioral contrast when we examine the nature of discrimination learning.

The behavioral contrast phenomenon points to one problem with discrimination learning: it can have negative consequences. To recognize this problem, consider the following situation. The teacher of a disruptive child decides to extinguish the disruptive behavior by no longer rewarding (perhaps by discontinuing attention) the child's disruptive activities. But the child's parents may continue to attend to the disruptive behavior. In this case, the child will be disruptive at home (S^D) but not at school (S^Δ). In fact, the parents will probably experience an increase in disruptive behavior at home due to behavioral contrast; that is, as the rate of disruptive behavior during school declines, the child will become more disruptive at home. Parents can deal with this situation only by discontinuing reward (e.g., attention) of the disruptive behavior in the home. This observation points out that one consequence of extinguishing an undesired behavior in one setting is an increase in that behavior in other situations. Thus, the desired method is to extinguish an undesired behavior in all situations.

Studies (Hall, 1982) using human subjects indicate that people are sensitive to two-choice discrimination tasks. Illustrating the acquisition of a two-choice discrimination in people, Terrell and Ware (1961) trained kindergarten and first-grade children to discriminate between three-dimensional geometric forms. In one discrimination, the children needed to distinguish between large and small cubed boxes; in the other discrimination, between a sphere and pyramid. A light indicated a correct response. Terrell and Ware reported that the children quickly learned to discriminate between the geometric forms. Other psychologists have also reported two-choice discrimination learning in humans; see Hockman and Lipsitt (1961) and Lipsitt and Castaneda (1958) for other examples.

Conditional Discrimination Tasks   According to D'Amato (1970), in a conditional discrimination task, the reinforcement contingency associated with a particular stimulus depends on the status of a second stimulus. In other words, a specific stimulus does not always signal either the availability or nonavailability of reward in a conditional discrimination task. Instead, in some circumstances a particular cue indicates that reward will be presented contingent on the occurrence of an appropriate response, whereas under other conditions, the cue does not signal reward availability. Consider the following example to illustrate a conditional discrimination. Suppose that a child wants a dollar to spend at the store. The child may ask his or her parents but knows that under most conditions the request will be denied. Suppose that when a relative is with the parents, the child's request is granted. This child will eventually learn to ask for money only when a relative is nearby. In this example, the parents' and relative's presence is an S^D signalling the availability of reward. Thus, the child's request to the parents for money will be effective when a relative is present but ineffective when no relative is visiting (S^Δ). There are many instances of conditional discrimination situations in the real world. For example, a store is open at certain hours and closed at others, or a spouse is friendly sometimes but hostile at other times. It is more difficult to learn that a particular cue signals reward availability sometimes but not at other times than to learn that a specific stimulus always is associated with either reward availability or nonavailability. However, we must discover when a cue signals reward availability and when it does not if we are to interact effectively with our environment. Psychologists have observed that both lower animals and people can learn a conditional discrimination. See D'Amato (1970) for a review of this literature.

Nissen (1951) discovered that chimpanzees can learn a conditional discrimination. In Nissen's study, large and small squares were the discriminative stimuli; the brightness of the cues was the conditional stimulus. When the squares were white, the large square was the S^D and the small square was the S^Δ; when the squares were black, the small square was the S^D and the large square was the S^Δ. Nissen reported that his chimpanzees learned to respond effectively; that is, they responded to the large square when it was white but not black and to the small square when it was black but not white. In fact, Nissen discovered that the chimpanzees could learn an even more complex conditional discrimination. In this second task, the chimpanzees needed to recognize not only the color of the form but also the shape (square or triangle), the presence or absence of a margin, and the presence or absence of a wooden peg to know which stimulus was the S^D. Although it was difficult to learn, the chimpanzees did master this complex conditional discrimination.

People can also learn a conditional discrimination. Gollin's (1966) study provides an example of one of these studies. Gollin trained 37- and 60-month-old children to discriminate between pictures of people and pictures of objects, rewarding them with a marble if they identified the correct stimulus. The status of the people and objects depended on background (stripes versus no stripes): the people were the S^D in one background, and the objects were the S^D in the other background. Gollin reported that all the children except the youngest (37 to 40 months old) learned the conditional discrimination.

An Insoluble Discrimination Problem

Pavlov (1928) initially trained one group of dogs to discriminate between a circle and an ellipse by associating one stimulus—the circle—with food, while the other stimulus—the ellipse—was not followed by food. After discrimination training, the ellipse was made progressively more like the circle. Pavlov observed that as the two stimuli became very similar, the dogs were no longer able to discriminate and responded to both stimuli. However, salivating to both stimuli was not the only change that Pavlov noted in his dogs' behavior. He observed that the dogs showed extreme agitation; they whined, howled, and tried to escape from the restraining harness. Further, Pavlov noted that these behaviors also occurred outside of the experimental situation. According to Pavlov, the dogs experienced strong conflict, attempting to continue to respond to one stimulus but not to the other. This conflict caused the dogs to develop a behavioral disturbance which Pavlov called an *experimental neurosis*. This disorder explains the deterioration of the dogs' behavior—the inability to respond appropriately to the circle and ellipse—when they were returned to the original discrimination task.

Experimental neurosis has been consistently observed when animals are placed in an insoluble discrimination task (see Gantt, 1971, for a review of this literature). For example, Brown (1942) trained rats to discriminate between two lights of different brightness. Brown reinforced approach to the bright light and avoidance of the dim light. If the rats did not respond correctly, they received an electric shock. After the rats learned to discriminate, Brown changed the brightness of the two stimuli so that they were more similar. As the discrimination became more difficult, Brown noted that the rats became extremely agitated. The rats trembled, defecated, and urinated, and some even experienced convulsions.

In the previous examples, neurosis was produced when the two stimuli were made very similar and thus impossible to discriminate. Extreme behavioral disturbances (Maier, 1949; Maier, Glazer, & Klee, 1940; Maier & Klee, 1945) may also occur when an animal can perceive the differences between two stimuli but reward is randomly associated with the two stimuli. Maier and his associates studied the insoluble discrimination problem using a Lashley jumping stand, which forces the rat to jump (by shocking them for not jumping) across a space and through one of two doors. One door is usually black, the other white. In the soluble discrimination situation, one door is the S^D and the other is the S^Δ. If the rat responds to the S^D door it can safely pass through; if the rat responds to the other door it runs into a closed door and falls into a net. To prevent the rat from learning to respond to one particular door, the safe and the dangerous doors are switched after each trial. The rat quickly learns to respond to the S^D in the soluble problem, but there is no correct response to the insoluble problem. Maier observed that although there was no solution to the problem, the rats responded in a specific manner. Some rats always jumped right, others left, still others to the black door, and the rest to the white door. In addition to developing a "fixated" way of responding, the rats lost muscle tone and became unresponsive. Also, they continued to exhibit the "fixated" response even when the problem was made soluble.

Predictiveness plays an important role in discrimination learning. Apparently, animals have a strong need for predictiveness, and severe behavioral disturbances result when animals experience insoluble discrimination problems. These animals can still receive reinforcement half of the time, but the conflict produced by uncertain circumstances is disruptive even though no physical pain such as shock is experienced. Do these studies of experimental neurosis have relevance to humans? While no comparable experiments have been conducted in humans—it would be obviously unethical to do so—certain analogous real-world situations involve insoluble discrimination problems. For example, parents who do not provide consistent reward and punishment create a home environment in which the child cannot discriminate when reward or punishment will occur. Considerable evidence indicates that inconsistent parental discipline leads to behavior problems in children; this information suggests that experiencing insoluble discrimination problems leads to self-doubt, conflict, uncertainty, and behavior pathology (see Baumrind, 1975, for a review of the literature on how parents' child-rearing styles affect their children's emotional development). Every attempt should be made to provide children (and adults) with an environmental structure in which they can predict when reward or punishment will and will not occur.

The Development of a Discrimination

We have seen that animals and people can learn when to respond to receive reinforcement or avoid punishment and when responding will be ineffective. The acquisition of a discrimination occurs in three stages: First, *animals or people must be able to differentiate (or distinguish) between the S^D and the S^Δ.* Second, *they must attend to the relevant dimension.* Third, *the discriminative stimuli must gain control over their behavior.* Two important points concerning the development of a discrimination need to be mentioned before we examine each stage. If an animal or person does not exhibit the behavior characteristic of each stage, the discrimination will not be learned. Thus, an animal or person may be able to differentiate between the discriminative stimuli while attending to the relevant dimension and still not learn to discriminate because the discriminative stimuli did not gain control over the animal's or person's responding. Remember that these stages refer to the sequence of events involved in the development of a discrimination; since discrimination learning is a continuous process, when one stage ends and the next begins is impossible to discern.

Stimulus Differentiation Recall from the vignette of this chapter that a man wrongly accused a particular tall thin man of attacking him. One likely cause of the victim's failure to discriminate was his inability to differentiate between tall thin men. It is also possible that the victim was not attending to differential facial characteristics and thereby did not discriminate. Selective attention and discrimination learning are discussed in the next section of this chapter.

There are obvious instances during which discrimination based on differences between stimuli in a particular dimension is impossible due to an inability to differentiate between discriminative stimuli. For example, some color-blind people cannot discriminate between red and green, and therefore cannot learn when to go and stop for red and green traffic lights. Because these color-blind people can also use traffic light location cues, they can discriminate between the red and the green lights.

Does differentiation failure stem entirely from inherited deficiencies in an animal's or person's perceptual system? Perceptual-system failure can be inherited; color-blindness is merely one example of an inherited trait which can lead to discrimination failure. However, the ability to distinguish between discriminative stimuli also depends on perceptual experience, and the failure to discriminate can result from the absence of essential perceptual experience.

Eleanor Gibson's perceptual learning theory (1969) explains why perceptual experience is essential for discrimination learning. According to Gibson, animals and people have an inherent motivation to discover salient characteristics of their environment. These salient characteristics include the stimuli which remain the same despite changes in the surrounding environment. Perceptual constancies represent the outcome of this discovery. For example, we can recognize that a person's size remains constant despite changes in retinal image size caused by increased distance. While the retinal image of a 6-foot person becomes smaller as the person moves away from us, we can still recognize the size of this person standing 3 or 30 feet away from us. The recognition that size remains constant despite increased distance is one example of what Gibson calls *perceptual learning,* or an increase in an animal's or person's sensitivity to the environment. According to Gibson, perceptual learning occurs as the result of experience but does not involve reward; instead, it is motivated by an inherent need to discover important characteristics of the environment, which will enable survival. Perceptual learning involves not only learning existing constancies but also recognizing differences in the environment; and it is the discovery of differences between stimuli which enables an animal or person to discriminate between stimuli.

Many articles have evaluated the influence of perceptual experience on discrimination training (see Hall, 1982, for a review of this literature). In these studies, rats were raised in environments containing the stimuli which would serve as the S^D and S^Δ when the animals became adults. In the classic study by Gibson, Walk, and Tighe (1959), rats were raised in cages containing metal cutouts of circles and triangles. Remaining in these cages until 90 days of age, the rats were then trained to discriminate between a black triangle and black circle. The authors reported that rats given early perceptual experience learned to discriminate more readily than did those without this early experience. Apparently, the animals receiving early perceptual experience had already learned to differentiate between stimuli of a particular dimension and were able to use this knowledge to discriminate between stimuli of that dimension. Other studies by Gibson and her associates (Gibson, Walk, & Tighe, 1959; Walk, Gibson, Pick, & Tighe, 1959) have reported a similar facilitation of discrimination learning as the result of prior perceptual exposure.

Several recent studies (Channell & Hall, 1981; Hall, 1979) indicate that the facilitative influence of prior perceptual experience occurs only when the initial perceptual experience and later discrimination training take place in different environments. If the perceptual preexposure and subsequent discrimination training occur in the same environment, initial perceptual experience actually impairs subsequent discrimination learning. According to Mackintosh (1983), learned irrelevance is responsible for the impairment of discrimination learning when initial perceptual experience and subsequent discrimination occur in the same environment. As we learned in Chapter 2, learned irrelevance represents the knowledge that a particular stimulus has no significance. When different environments are used for perceptual preexposure and discrimination training, learned irrelevance is attenuated, and the animal's knowledge about the stimuli can act to enhance subsequent discrimination training.

Selective Attention Recall the opening vignette of the chapter. The victim may have been able to recognize his assailant's physical characteristics that differentiated him from other people, but he did not attend to them. Instead, the victim attended only to the size of his assailant and was therefore unable to discriminate his assailant from other people.

The phenomenon of attending to one aspect of a situation while ignoring other dimensions is called *selective attention* (see Howard, 1983, or Posner, 1982, for a review of the literature). Selective attention has adaptive significance. If we attend to too much environmental information, we will be unable to detect important events effectively; thus, limiting the amount of information processed allows us to process information efficiently. For example, suppose that you are reading a textbook. If you attend to all the stimuli in the environment, you would be unable to study; the distraction of other events would prevent you from concentrating sufficiently to interpret the information presented in the text. Thus, you attend only to the text—not to other events in the environment.

While selective attention enables you to study effectively, it can prevent discrimination learning. If you do not attend to the relevant dimension, you cannot learn the discriminative stimuli and therefore will not interact effectively with the environment; that is, sometimes you will fail to respond to the S^D, responding to the S^Δ instead.

Consider the following example. Suppose that you sell automobiles. Some customers will buy a car; others are just looking. Which customers do you approach? If you can learn whom to approach and whom not to approach, you will earn more money. Perhaps age is the relevant dimension. If so, attending to dress and not to age will cause you to approach some people who will not buy and fail to approach others who will. Obviously, to maximize your success, you must attend to the *dimension* associated with reward.

The Filter Theory of Selective Attention Why are people sensitive to some environmental information but unaware of other events? Broadbent (1958) has proposed a *selective filter* explanation of selective attention. Broadbent suggested that animals and people have a limited information-processing capacity. To process information effectively, some information reaching an animal's or person's sensory receptors is not processed: it is rejected because a selective filter allows some information to be processed and rejects other information. The selective filter works by permitting information on only one "channel" to be transmitted beyond the sensory receptors and processed by the central nervous system while preventing other information from being transmitted by the sensory receptors.

Broadbent proposed that the selective filter blocks information on unattended channels from being processed. However, evidence (Treisman, 1960) indicates that the selective filter attenuates the intensity of unattended messages rather than blocks the processing of information on unattended channels. The attenuation rather than blocking has considerable adaptive significance. Because the intensity of unattended information is reduced, most of this information is not processed. However, important information coming over the unattended channel could not be detected if it was blocked. People can detect important information by increasing their sensitivity to it.

Consider the following example. You are reading; visual information from your book is the attended information. You are not attending to auditory information. Your selective filter attenuates the noise around you, and you are unaware of the noise. We have all undoubtedly experienced not hearing someone talking to us while we're reading. However, what if the fire alarm sounds or a baby cries? If our selective filter did not allow any auditory information to pass, we would hear neither sound. Although the intensity of the message is reduced, our sensitivity to important auditory stimuli allows us to hear the fire alarm or the baby's cry.

Selective-Listening Experiments Selective-listening studies have documented the selectivity of perception. In these studies, a subject is exposed to two messages simultaneously. The message can be presented in one of two ways: (1) In *dichotic listening,* one message is presented to the left ear and another to the right ear. (2) In *binaural listening,* both messages are presented to each ear. The task for the subject is to attend to only one message, an objective accomplished by having the subject repeat the words presented in one of the messages (see Figure 5.8). This technique is called *shadowing,* and subjects who practice can effectively shadow the desired message, although binaural listening is more difficult and thus requires more practice. To illustrate the difference between dichotic and binaural listening, imagine that you are trying to listen to one of two people talking to you; during dichotic listening, the two people are seated on either side of you. During binaural listening, they are both standing in front of you. Research on selective listening has shown that usually a subject is unaware of information presented in the nonshadowed message. Let's look briefly at evidence of the selectivity of a person's attention.

Moray's (1959) study shows that subjects can be unaware of information presented on a nonshadowed channel. In a dichotic-listening study, Moray presented a list of words thirty-five times over the nonshadowed channel. Subjects were then presented a larger list of words and were asked to identify words from it which they had heard over the nonshadowed channel. Moray reported that subjects had no recognition of the words presented over the nonshadowed channel. To evaluate the possibility that subjects had heard the words but could not remember them, Treisman and Geffen (1967) asked subjects to tap when certain target words were presented. Although the subjects identified the target words presented over the shadowed channel 86.5 percent

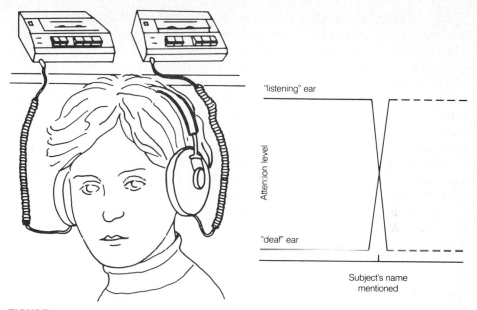

FIGURE 5.8
Dichotic listening studies. Each subject is presented two different messages, one message over each earphone. The subject is instructed "to listen" to one message by repeating the words presented to one ear. This procedure called "shadowing" typically causes subjects to be unaware of words presented to unattended or deaf ear. Note that when an important item (e.g., subject's name) is presented to "deaf" ear, the subject hears it. From *Psychology* (2d ed.). by G. R. Lefrancois © 1983 by Wadsworth, Inc. Reprinted by permission of the publisher.

of the time, the target words presented over the nonshadowed channel were detected only 8.1 percent of the time. These results indicate that failure to report information presented over the nonshadowed channel is a perceptual process, not a memory process. Cherry's investigation (1953) provides dramatic evidence that subjects can be unaware of information coming over the nonshadowed channel. Cherry presented two different messages in a dichotic-listening study; halfway through the study, the message over the nonshadowed channel switched from English to German, and the subjects did not notice the change.

You might think that the selective listening studies indicate that subjects are always unaware of information presented over a nonshadowed channel. However, under some conditions subjects do report information presented on a nonshadowed channel. For example, Moray (1959) reported that subjects can often detect their own name presented over a nonshadowed channel. This research shows that the sensory systems do not block all information of an unattended message but instead process important material. Thus, a person can detect important information (i.e., a name) in a nonshadowed message.

Recall Cherry's subjects who did not detect a shift from English to German. Interestingly, Cherry (1953) reported that starting with a male's voice in both messages followed by switching the nonshadowed message to that of a female's voice causes subjects to notice a change. Subjects also detected a change in the nonshadowed message when it was changed from a recorded human voice to that of a 400-Hz pure tone. Also, Lawson (1966) reported that subjects could detect target tones, but not words, of the nonshadowed message as well as those presented over the shadowed channel. This research demonstrates that some information is processed prior to the selective-attention stage; however, this processing is based on the physical characteristics of an event but not on the content of a message. Thus, over a nonshadowed message, subjects can differentiate a male's voice from a female's voice because both have different physical characteristics, but they cannot recognize a switch from English to German because the differences are in terms of content. If important physical changes are not detected in a nonshadowed message, the selective filter reduces the intensity of the nonshadowed message so that only important content information is detected.

Controlled versus Automatic Processing of Information Recent research (Howard, 1983) argues against a filter explanation of selective attention because people can process more than one piece of information at a time. For example, many people who drive an automobile can converse with a passenger without having an accident.

How can two different pieces of information be processed simultaneously? Shiffrin and Schneider (1977) suggest that there are two types of information processing: controlled processing and automatic processing. *Controlled processing* requires attention, and usually only one piece of information can be attended to at a time. In our example, to understand the conversation, the driver must attend to it; thus, understanding a conversation requires controlled processing. In contrast, *automatic processing* requires little or no attention and occurs when a person is participating in a highly practiced activity, such as driving.

Let's look at one study by Schneider and Shiffrin (1977) to illustrate the difference between automatic and controlled processing. In this study, subjects were visually presented a target letter or number to identify. For some subjects, the target was a letter mixed with other letters in a visual array, a treatment referred to as the same-category condition. For other subjects, the target was a number, and the other items in the visual array were letters (different-category condition). The experimenters also varied the number of other items (letters) in the visual array from zero to three. The total number of items in the visual array, called the *frame size,* ranged from one to four. On some trials the target item was present; on others, it was not. The subject's task was to indicate whether the target item was present. Figure 5.9 presents a diagram of the two treatment conditions in Schneider and Shiffrin's study.

Schneider and Shiffrin observed that with or without the target present, subjects required more time to accurately identify the target in the same-cate-

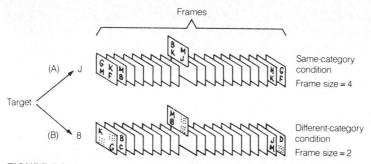

FIGURE 5.9
Trials from each of the two treatment conditions in the Schneider and
Shiffrin experiment: (a) The same category condition, in which the
target and distractors are letters and (b) the different-category
condition, in which the target is a number and letters, the distractors.
Adopted from Schneider, W., & Shiffrin, R. M. Controlled and
automatic human information processing: I. Detection, search, and
attention. *Psychological Review*, 1977, *84*, 1–66. Copyright 1977 by
the American Psychological Association. Reprinted by permission.

gory condition than did subjects in the different-category condition. According
to Schneider and Shiffrin, subjects began the study with a great deal of practice
detecting numbers among letters, and therefore could readily detect the presence of the target number in the different-category condition. In contrast,
subjects trying to identify a target letter from other letters in the same-category
condition needed to inspect each item to determine the target's presence or
absence accurately. These observations indicate that automatic processing was
sufficient for effective performance in the different-category condition but that
controlled processing was necessary in the same-category condition.

The influence of frame size on performance further supports the view that
there are two types of processing of information. Frame size did not affect
performance level in the different-category condition, but it did detrimentally
affect performance in the same-category condition. In the different-category
condition, subjects simply looked for a number; this process could be done
automatically and, therefore, increasing the number of letters did not affect
performance. However, since subjects had to check each item deliberately in
the same-condition category, increasing the frame size added more letters to be
evaluated, thereby making it more difficult for subjects to accurately identify
whether the target was present or absent.

Our discussion indicates that to learn a discrimination we must differentiate
between the S^D and S^Δ and then process the information in the relevant dimension. However, even if we can differentiate between the discriminative stimuli
and are processing data in the relevant dimension, we still might respond to the
S^Δ. To learn a discrimination, the S^D must also gain control over our behavior;
that is, an animal or person must respond to the S^D but not to other stimuli.

Stimulus Selection   The literature (D'Amato, 1970) points out that stimuli in some modalities gain control over responding, whereas stimuli in other modalities are not used because an animal or person does not know when to respond and when not to respond. An animal or person may not respond to stimuli in a particular modality even though (1) these stimuli are correlated with reward, (2) the stimuli can be differentiated, and (3) the animal or person is attending to the stimuli.

D'Amato and Fazzaro's study (1966) demonstrates the stimulus selection process. They trained two capuchin monkeys to discriminate using a compound S^D (a vertical white line superimposed on a red background) and a compound S^Δ (a horizontal white line superimposed on a green background). These compound stimuli were simultaneously presented on twenty of the forty trials that the monkeys received each day. The color components were presented in only ten trials; the horizontal-vertical bar components were presented in the remaining ten trials. On the twenty trials providing one component, the monkeys could respond on the basis of the single compound, or they could press a white illuminated key and see the compound stimuli. Thus, by pressing the white key, called a *cue-producing response,* the monkeys were indicating that they needed the other dimension stimuli to respond effectively. D'Amato and Fazzaro reported that although the monkeys exhibited few cue-producing responses when the color component was given, they almost always emitted the cue-producing response when the bar component was presented. These results indicate that the color dimension controlled the monkeys' behavior and that the bar component had little control over behavior. You might think that primates cannot learn a horizontal-vertical discrimination. However, monkeys can learn to discriminate between horizontal and vertical lines if no other cues are associated with reinforcement. But when color is also associated with reward, the horizontal-vertical cues just do not influence the responding of primates.

Other psychologists have also reported that when more than one stimulus dimension is associated with reward, one cue will gain control while the other cue (or cues) will not influence an animal's responding. For example, Reynolds (1961b) trained pigeons to discriminate between a triangle on a red background (S^D) and a circle on a green background (S^Δ). He reported that the pigeons responded to one of the cues but not to the other cue. The stimulus dimension which gained control differed: for some pigeons, the color dimension gained control; for others, the form controlled behavior (see Figure 5.10).

Stimulus selection has also been demonstrated in studies with human subjects. Trabasso and Bower (1968) trained college students in a concept-identification task (see Chapter 9). In their experiment, two dimensions (shape and location of a dot) were the relevant cues, and three other dimensions were irrelevant. Following the students' training, Trabasso and Bower tested for the learning which occurred to the shape and dot-location dimension. They found that most subjects solved the concept based entirely on one dimension; that is, they could identify the correct stimulus when one dimension was present but

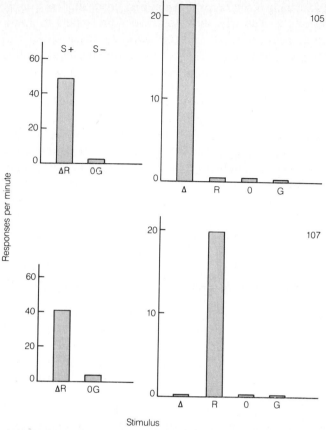

FIGURE 5.10
Number of responses per minute for two pigeons when both
components of the compound were presented (left panels)
and when each component of the compound was presented
separately (right panels). From Reynolds, G. S. Attention in the
pigeon. *Journal of the Experimental Analysis of Behavior,*
1961, *4*, 203–208. Copyright 1961 by the Society for the
Experimental Analysis of Behavior. Reprinted by permission.

responded only at a chance level in the presence of the other dimension. These
observations indicate that in the concept identification task, one dimension
gained control of behavior and the other dimension did not.

Other studies have documented the selective control of responding in humans. For example, Underwood, Ham, and Ekstrand (1962) trained college
students on a paired-associate task. Each subject's task was to associate a list
of seven different 3-consonant nonsense syllables (e.g., GWS) placed on different colored backgrounds (e.g., red) with the single-digit response that was
paired with each colored trigram. After training, each subject was given ten

transfer trials to determine which stimulus dimension had controlled responding during the acquisition phase. The trigrams alone were presented to some subjects during the transfer trials, and the other subjects received either the background colors or both the trigrams and colors as the transfer trial stimuli. As can be seen in Figure 5.11, complete transfer occurred when the color cue was present, but the subjects exhibited little transfer with only the trigrams present. These results demonstrate that subjects during the acquisition phase had responded to the color but not to the trigram dimension.

One treatment can reduce stimulus selection, enabling other stimulus elements to gain control over responding. Research (D'Amato, 1970) indicates that overtraining can increase the number of stimulus elements controlling behavior. D'Amato (1970) trained capuchin monkeys on a compound discrimination task. In the training phase of the study, a vertical line and a circle served as the S^D; a horizontal line and a plus, as the S^Δ. Control subjects were trained to a criterion of 90 percent correct responses; experimental subjects received 800 trials beyond the 90 percent criterion. After training, the monkeys were tested on each stimulus element. D'Amato reported that the experimental subjects responded appropriately to both cues, although only one stimulus element affected the control subjects' behavior. This observation points out that overtraining can increase the number of stimuli which control responding. Other studies have also reported that overtraining decreases stimulus selection in animals; see Sutherland and Holgate (1966) for another example.

James and Greeno (1967) trained college students on a paired-associate learning task using a compound consisting of a three-letter word of high asso-

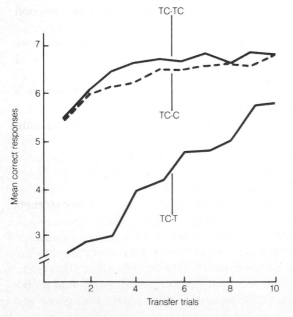

FIGURE 5.11
Mean correct responses on transfer task which began 45 seconds after subjects reached criterion with compound stimuli (trigrams and color cues). From Underwood, B. J., Ham, M., & Ekstrand, B. Cue selection in paired associate learning. *Journal of Experimental Psychology,* 1962, *64,* 405–409. Copyright 1962 by the American Psychological Association. Reprinted by permission.

ciative value and a nonsense syllable of low associative value as the stimulus element and digits from 1 to 8 as the responses. Control subjects who did not receive overtraining responded to the word but not to the nonsense syllable, whereas 20 trials of overtraining in experimental subjects resulted in the non-sense syllables also gaining control of responding.

We should note that overtraining does not always reduce stimulus selection. For example, Houston (1967) used trigrams and colors as the stimulus com-pound in a paired-associate learning task and did not find that overtraining increased the amount of responding controlled by the trigrams. Discussing Houston's study, D'Amato (1970) suggested that color may be such a dominant or salient cue that the nonsalient trigram can gain little or no control of be-havior.

Recall that in order for animals or people to learn to discriminate between the S^D and S^Δ, (1) they must be able to differentiate between the S^D and S^Δ, (2) they must be attending to the relevant dimension, and (3) the relevant dimen-sion must gain control over responding. But what process enables us to learn a discrimination?

The Nature of Discrimination Learning

Hull-Spence Theory   Clark Hull (1943) and Kenneth Spence (1936) pro-vided an explanation of discrimination learning. Although not a completely accurate view of the nature of discrimination learning, their theory does de-scribe some essential aspects of the discrimination-learning process.

Development of Conditioned Excitation and Inhibition   According to the Hull-Spence view, discrimination learning develops in three stages. First, con-ditioned excitation develops to the S^D as the result of reinforcement. Second, nonreward in the presence of the S^Δ results in the development of conditioned inhibition to the S^Δ. As we learned earlier in the chapter, conditioned inhibition suppresses responding to the S^D. Finally, the excitation and inhibition general-ize to other stimuli (see Figure 5.12); the combined influence of excitation and inhibition determines the level of responding to each stimuli. As can be seen in Figure 5.12, the Hull-Spence model predicts that a steeper generalization gradi-ent is found with discrimination training than with nondiscrimination training. Also, their model assumes that maximum responding is not to the S^D but rather to a stimulus other than the S^D and in the stimulus direction opposite to that of the S^Δ. The reason for this prediction is that although the S^D (256 in the figure) has the greatest excitatory strength, it also has accrued inhibitory strength. Although another stimulus (409 in the figure) may have less excitatory strength than the S^D, it also has accrued little inhibitory strength. Thus, the resultant "effective" strength of the S^D will be less than that of the other stimulus.

The Peak Shift Phenomenon   Hanson (1959) tested the assumptions of the Hull-Spence model of discrimination learning. In Hanson's study, pigeons re-ceived either discrimination training using a 550-nm light as the S^D and a 560-nm as the S^Δ or nondiscrimination training with a 550-nm light present during

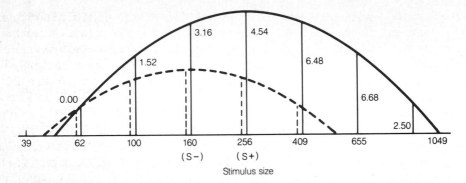

FIGURE 5.12
Figure presents Spence's theoretical view of the interaction of excitatory and inhibitory generalization gradients on discriminated behavior. During acquisition, reward is available when 256 stimulus size is present but not when 160 stimulus size is present. Excitatory potential (solid lines) generalizes to similar stimuli as well as does inhibitory potential (broken lines). The resultant reaction tendency, indicated by the value above each stimulus size, is obtained by substracting the inhibitory from the excitatory potential. From Spence, K. W. The differential response in animals to stimuli varying within a single dimension. *Psychological Review*, 1937, *44*, 430–444. Copyright 1937 by the American Psychological Association. Reprinted by permission.

the entire training session. Following training, both groups of pigeons were given a generalization test using stimuli ranging from 480 to 620 nm. Hanson reported three important differences between discrimination and nondiscrimination generalization gradients (see Figure 5.13). First, a steeper generalization gradient was found with discrimination than with nondiscrimination training, a prediction in accord with the Hull-Spence model. Second, the greatest responding for discrimination-training subjects was not to the S^D but to the 540-nm stimulus. In contrast, pigeons receiving nondiscrimination training responded maximally to the 550-nm stimulus. This observation, referred to as the *peak shift*, also agrees with the Hull-Spence view of discrimination training. Third, the level of responding was higher with discrimination training than nondiscrimination training, an observation not predicted by the Hull-Spence model.

The Aversive Character of S^Δ Terrace (1964) suggested that behavioral contrast is responsible for the heightened responding with discrimination training. Terrace assumes that exposure to the S^Δ is an aversive event and that the "emotional effects of nonreinforced responding" or frustration produced during S^Δ periods increases the intensity of responding to other stimuli. Recall from Chapter 3 that nonreward or stimuli associated with nonreward are aversive, and exposure to either of these stimuli can increase the intensity of responding for reward. Terrace's view that behavioral contrast is responsible for the heightened responding with discrimination training is consistent with the literature presented in Chapter 3.

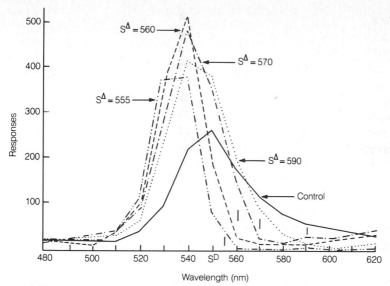

FIGURE 5.13
Mean number of responses on a generalization test (using wavelengths varying from 480 to 620 nm) for four experimental groups receiving prior discrimination training with 550 nm as the S[D] and either 550, 560, 570, or 590 nm as the S[Δ]; the control group did not receive discrimination training. From Hanson, H. M. Effects of discrimination training on stimulus generalization. *Journal of Experimental Psychology*, 1959, *58*, 321–324. Copyright 1959 by the American Psychological Association. Reprinted by permission.

Several other types of research support Terrace's approach. A number of drugs (e.g., chlorpromazine, imipramine) appear to reduce the aversive effects of nonrewarding events. Evidence of this effect is the elimination of frustration-induced behavior (e.g., aggressive behavior) with their use. Another influence of these drugs is the disruption of performance on a discrimination task (Bloomfield, 1972; Terrace, 1963c). Animals receiving chlorpromazine or imipramine exhibit a high level of response to the S[Δ]. It is thought that the reduced aversiveness of the S[Δ] caused by the drugs is responsible for the lack of inhibition of response to the S[Δ]. These drugs not only caused increased responding to the S[Δ] but also eliminated both behavioral contrast and the peak shift. Thus, the heightened response to the S[D] and the maximum responding to a stimulus other than the S[D], both of which are characteristic of discrimination learning, are not seen when either chlorpromazine or imipramine is administered. These observations suggest that (1) S[Δ] must be an aversive event to inhibit responding and (2) the aversiveness of S[Δ] causes both behavioral contrast and the peak shift.

The Hull-Spence model of discrimination learning suggests that conditioned excitation and inhibition develop during training. The generalization of excitation and inhibition leads to a steep excitatory generalization gradient and the peak shift. Hanson's (1959) research supports the Hull-Spence model. However, his study and Terrace's research indicate that nonreward leads not only to the development of conditioned inhibition but also to the establishment of aversive properties to the S^Δ. This aversive character of the S^Δ causes the heightened responding to the S^D (behavioral contrast) and maximum responding to a stimulus other than the S^D (peak shift).

You should not conclude that discrimination learning merely reflects the development of excitatory tendencies to the S^D and inhibitory (and aversive) tendencies to the S^Δ. Although excitation and inhibition do play an important role in discrimination learning, other processes (e.g., attention) also affect the establishment of a discrimination.

Transposition Effect   Although the peak-shift phenomenon appears to support the Hull-Spence view, the noted Gestalt psychologist Wolfgang Kohler (1939) provides an alternative view of discrimination learning which can also explain the peak shift. According to Kohler, stimuli are not evaluated in absolute terms but instead in relation to other stimuli. For example, a 75-dB tone may seem loud in a quiet room but soft in a noisy room. Thus, when we say that a noise is loud or soft, the perceived loudness depends on the context in which the noise is heard.

Kohler's view is important when applied to discrimination learning. For example, suppose that a rat learns to discriminate between an 80-dB S^D and a 60-dB S^Δ. Has the rat learned to respond to the 80-dB tone and not to the 60-dB tone? In Kohler's view, the animal has merely learned to respond to the louder of the two tones. How would the rat react to a 90-dB tone? From what we learned in our discussion of the peak shift, the rat would react more intensely to the 90-dB tone than to the 80-dB tone, even though the 80-dB tone was the S^D. Recall also that the Hull-Spence theory suggests that the greater combined excitatory and inhibitory strength is responsible for the higher level of response to the 90-dB than to the 80-dB tone. Kohler explains peak shift in a different way: since the rat learned to respond to the louder tone, it is logical to expect it to react more intensely to the 90-dB than the 80-dB tone. Kohler evaluated his view by training chickens and chimpanzees to respond to the brighter of the two stimuli (the S^D). When he tested his subjects with the S^D and a brighter light stimulus, the animals chose the brighter of the two lights. Kohler called the phenomenon *transposition,* drawn from the analogy that the relation among notes comprising musical compositions does not change when the melodies are *transposed* to a different key.

Which view of discrimination learning is accurate: the Hull-Spence absolute view or the Kohler relational view? According to Schwartz (1984), there is evidence supporting both views. Studies which give animals choice between two stimuli support the relational or transposition view; that is, the animals respond to the relative rather than absolute qualities of the stimuli. One study providing support for the relational view was conducted by Lawrence and DeRivera (1954). Lawrence and DeRivera initially exposed rats to cards which were divided in half. During training, the bottom half of the card was always an intermediate shade of gray, and the top half was one of the lighter or one of the three darker shades of gray. A lighter top half meant that the rats needed to turn left to obtain reward; a darker top half signaled a right turn for reward. Figure 5.14 presents a diagram of this procedure. During testing, the intermediate shade of gray was no longer presented; instead, two of the six shades of gray presented on top during training were shown (one on the top, the other on the bottom). Although a number of combinations of these six shades were used, only one combination is provided to illustrate how this study supports a relational view. On some test trials, two of the darker shades were used, with the lighter of the two on top (refer to Figure 5.14). If the animals had learned based

FIGURE 5.14
Diagram showing the procedure used by Lawrence and DeRivera (1954) in their analysis of the absolute versus relational view of discrimination learning. The numbers indicate darkness of gray used in their study. Reproduced from *The psychology of learning and behavior,* Second Edition, by Barry Schwartz, by permission of W. W. Norton & Company, Inc. Copyright 1984, 1978 by W. W. Norton & Company, Inc.

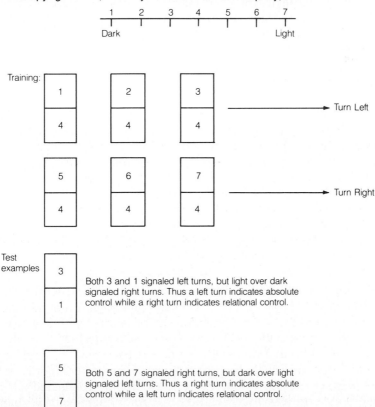

on absolute values, they would turn right, since the darker shade had always been on the top in training. However, if the animals had learned based on the relation between stimuli, they would turn left during testing, since the darker stimulus was still on the bottom. Lawrence and DeRivera reported that on the overwhelming majority of such test trials, the animals' responses were based on the relation between stimuli rather than on the absolute value of the stimuli. Thus, in explaining our example, most of the animals turned left because the darker shade of gray was on the bottom half of the card.

Although some studies support a relational view of discrimination, other experiments support the Hull-Spence absolute stimulus view. Hanson's study (1959) provides support for the Hull-Spence theory. Hanson trained pigeons to peck at a 550-nm (S^D) lighted key to receive reward; pecking at a 590-nm (S^Δ) light yielded no reward. On generalization tests, the pigeons were presented a range of lighted keys varying from 480 to 620 nm. According to the Hull-Spence view, at a point on the stimulus continuum below the S^D the inhibitory generalization gradient does not affect excitatory responding. At this point on the gradient, responding to the S^D should be greater than the responding occurring at the lower wavelength test stimuli. In contrast, the relational view suggests that a lower wavelength of light will always produce responding greater than the S^D does. Hanson's results showed that while greater responding did occur to the 540-nm test light than to the 550-nm S^D, less responding occurred to the 530-nm light than to the S^D (refer to Figure 5.13). Thus, on generalization tests, greater responding only occurs to stimuli close to the S^D.

You might wonder why some results support the Hull-Spence absolute-value view and others suggest that Kohler's relational approach is true. As Schwartz (1984) points out, the relational view is supported on choice tests; that is, subjects must choose to respond to one or two stimuli. In contrast, on generalization tests where a subject just responds to one stimulus, results support the Hull-Spence approach. In Schwartz's view, it is not unreasonable for both approaches to be valid; animals could learn about both the relation between stimuli as well as the absolute characteristics of the stimuli. In choice situations, the relation between stimuli is important, and the animal responds to the relational aspects of what it has learned. In contrast, when only a single stimulus is presented, the absolute character of a stimulus will determine its level of behavioral control.

Errorless Discrimination Training Can an animal or person acquire a discrimination without responding to the S^Δ? Although you might think no, psychologists have discovered that a discrimination can be learned with few or no errors. Several studies during the 1930s and 1940s (Schlosberg & Solomon, 1943; Skinner, 1938) showed that with sufficient care a discrimination could be learned with few errors. However, the significance of these studies was not recognized until Terrace (1963a, 1963b, 1963c, 1964, 1966a) conducted a detailed examination of "errorless discrimination." Terrace examined the characteristics of an errorless discrimination and developed a technique for establishing a discrimination without errors. His research also points out that specific procedures must be used for an animal to learn a discrimination without errors.

Errorless Discrimination Training   Terrace (1963a) trained pigeons on a red-green (S^D-S^Δ) discrimination. Each pigeon was trained to peck at a red illuminated key (S^D) to receive food reward on a VI 1-minute schedule. The pigeons were divided into four groups, and each group received a different combination of procedures to introduce the S^Δ. Two groups of pigeons received a progressive S^Δ introduction. During the first phase of this procedure, the presentation of the S^Δ, a dark key, lasted 5 seconds and then increased by 5 seconds with each trial until reaching 30 seconds. In the second phase of S^Δ introduction, the duration of the S^Δ was kept at 30 seconds, and the intensity of the S^Δ was increased until it became a green light. During the final phase of the study, the duration of the S^Δ was slowly increased from 30 seconds to 3 minutes. (Note that the duration of the S^D was 3 minutes during all three phases.) In contrast, for pigeons receiving constant training, the S^Δ was initially presented at full intensity and full duration. One progressive training group and one constant training group were given an early introduction of S^Δ—the S^Δ was presented during the first session that a pigeon was placed in the training chamber. The other two groups (one progressive, one constant) received late S^Δ introduction—the S^Δ was introduced following fourteen sessions of key-peck training with the S^D present.

Figure 5.15 presents the results of Terrace's study. Terrace reported that pigeons receiving early progressive training did not emit many errors (a range of two to eight during the entire experiment). In contrast, the animals in the other three groups emitted many responses during S^Δ periods. Furthermore, the errors made by early progressive subjects occurred at either the beginning or the end of the S^Δ period, whereas errors for the other three groups of pigeons occurred any time during S^Δ exposure and often in bursts of responses. These results show that a discrimination can be learned with few errors only when the S^Δ has been gradually introduced early in training. In later articles Terrace reported completely errorless discrimination training with the use of slight variations in the early progressive procedure.

As discussed earlier in this chapter, some discriminations are more difficult to acquire than others. For example, pigeons learn a color (red-green) discrimination more readily than a line-tilt (horizontal-vertical) discrimination. Furthermore, not only are pigeons slow to acquire a horizontal-vertical discrimination but also they make many errors to the S^Δ. Terrace (1963b) found that this difficult line-tilt discrimination could be learned without errors. To accomplish this goal, Terrace first trained pigeons on a red-green color discrimination using the early progressive errorless training technique. After training, the vertical and horizontal lines were superimposed on the colors to form compound stimuli (the red vertical line was the S^D; the green horizontal line, the S^Δ). During this segment of training, the intensity of the colors was reduced until they were no longer visible. Terrace found that this "fading" procedure helped the pi-

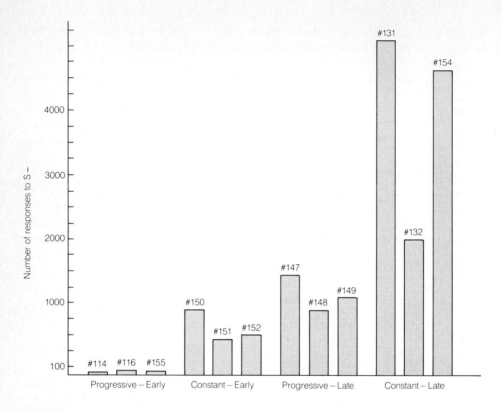

FIGURE 5.15
Number of responses emitted by each bird during twenty-eight trials of training as a function of discrimination-training procedure. Adapted from Terrace, H. S. Discrimination training with and without "errors." *Journal of the Experimental Analysis of Behavior,* 1963, *6,* 1–27. Copyright 1963 by the Society for the Experimental Analysis of Behavior. Reprinted by permission.

geons to learn quickly the horizontal-vertical discrimination without making any errors. In contrast, if the colors were quickly removed or never were presented superimposed on the horizontal-vertical lines, the pigeons made many errors before learning the line-tilt discrimination. Terrace's observations show that the fading technique is an effective way to teach a difficult discrimination. This fading technique was also used by Schusterman (1966) to train a sea lion under water on a series of three-form discriminations without error.

Application of Errorless Discrimination Training Errorless discrimination training has been used to teach humans a discrimination problem. Gollin and Savoy (1968) taught preschool children a shape discrimination using the fading technique. This procedure was also used by Moore and Goldiamond (1964) to teach matching a pattern to its sample and by Corey and Shamow (1972) to teach oral reading. In each of these studies, the preschool children given the faded series of S^Δ stimuli made few errors; other subjects receiving standard discrimination training emitted many incorrect responses to the S^Δ.

The fading technique has been especially helpful in teaching discriminations to retarded individuals. For example, Sidman and Stoddard (1967) compared the effectiveness of both errorless and standard discrimination training in 9- to 14-year-old retarded children trying to learn a circle-ellipse discrimination. These experimenters found that although the retarded children could not learn using the standard training procedure, many did learn the discrimination with the errorless procedure. Furthermore, Sidman and Stoddard argued that the instructional procedure was responsible for the failure of some of the retarded children to learn the discrimination using the errorless technique. Due to the design of the training procedure, a child who persevered in choosing an answer correctly on the first trial continued to be rewarded only 50 percent of the time; this was apparently sufficient to prevent the child from learning the discrimination even with the errorless procedure. Touchette (1968) taught 9- to 16-year-old retarded children a simple discrimination using either a trial-and-error or a fading procedure. He reported that the retarded children did not learn the discrimination using the standard discrimination, but all but one of them acquired the discrimination with the fading procedure.

The significance of Terrace's fading procedure can best be seen in the research of Dorry and Zeaman (1973, 1975). Using the fading procedure they trained retarded children to identify vocabulary words. In their studies, the retarded children were initially taught picture discriminations. After picture discrimination training, words were presented with the pictures; the pictures were then slowly faded out. Dorry and Zeaman compared the effectiveness of the fading procedure with that of normal discrimination training and reported that the retarded children learned more words using the fading procedure than did those children given standard discrimination training. Thus we can conclude that animals and people learn complex discriminations more readily using errorless discrimination training than standard discrimination training. There are other important differences between the behavior of animals receiving errorless discrimination and the behavior of those receiving standard discrimination training.

Nonaversive S^Δ   Remember from earlier in the chapter that there are three important behavioral characteristics seen in excitatory-generalization gradients obtained after standard discrimination training. The maximum responding is to a stimulus other than the S^D. Also, a steeper excitatory-generalization gradient and a higher level of responding are obtained with standard discrimination training than are obtained with nondiscrimination training. Furthermore, presentation of the S^Δ and no other stimuli inhibits responding, but administration of drugs which reduce frustration (e.g., chlorpromazine or imipramine) disrupts effective discrimination performance by increasing responding to S^Δ. These results demonstrate that S^Δ is an aversive agent and that this aversiveness is responsible for the inhibitory ability of the S^Δ. These observations are consistent with the Hull-Spence approach to discrimination learning.

However, the behavioral characteristics found with standard discrimination training are not observed with errorless discrimination training (Terrace, 1964). The peak shift (or maximum responding to a stimulus other than the S^D) is not found using errorless discrimination training. Errorless discrimination training produces the same steepness of the generalization gradient and level of responding to S^D as are found with nondiscrimination training. Furthermore, the presentation of the S^Δ as well as stimuli other than S^D inhibits responding in subjects receiving errorless discrimination training. Finally, the administration of chlorpromazine or imipramine does not disrupt discrimination performance; that is, the animal continues to respond to the S^D but not the S^Δ.

Terrace's observations have important implications for understanding the nature of discrimination learning. These data indicate that with errorless discrimination training, the S^Δ is not aversive. Also, Terrace argues that with errorless discrimination training the S^Δ does not have inhibitory control; instead, animals learn to respond only to the S^D. These results suggest that excitatory and inhibitory control are not the only responses acquired during discrimination training. In fact, inhibitory control does not seem to be essential for effective discrimination performance. Sutherland and Mackintosh's (1971) attention view of discrimination learning suggests that attentional processes play an important role in discrimination learning, and we will discuss this theory next. First, however, it is important to recognize that the motivational aspects of discrimination learning often govern discriminative performance, but animals or people can respond to the S^D but not the S^Δ even when the motivational attributes characteristic of the Hull-Spence model are not present.

Sutherland and Mackintosh's Attentional View   Sutherland and Mackintosh (1971) suggested that discrimination learning occurs in two stages. During the first stage, an animal's or person's attention to the relevant dimension is strengthened. The second phase involves the association of a particular response to the relevant stimulus.

Recall that an animal or person viewing a compound stimulus attends to one dimension. According to Sutherland and Mackintosh, each stimulus dimension can activate an *analyzer*. The arousal of a particular analyzer causes an animal or person to attend to that dimension. Thus, the presentation of a compound stimulus arouses the analyzer of the relevant dimension but not the analyzers of the other stimulus dimensions. Consider the following example to illustrate Sutherland and Mackintosh's view. A person viewing a 5-in red horizontal bar projected onto a gray background could attend to several dimensions—for example, the color, brightness, length, or orientation of the bar. However, this person notices only the color of the bar. In Sutherland and Mackintosh's view, the reason for this phenomenon is that the analyzer for the color dimension is aroused but the analyzers for the other dimensions are not.

What determines which analyzer will be aroused? Initially, the level of arousal of a particular analyzer is related to the intensity of the stimulus dimension; the greater the strength of a particular stimulus dimension, the more likely that dimension will activate the analyzer sufficiently to arouse attention. With certain types of experiences, the ability of analyzers to attract attention changes. According to Sutherland and Mackintosh, the predictive value of a particular stimulus dimension influences the amount of attention produced by the analyzer of a particular stimulus dimension. The analyzer will arouse more attention if the stimulus dimension predicts important events. However, an analyzer will arouse less attention if the stimulus dimension for that analyzer does not predict future events.

In the second phase of discrimination learning, the output from the analyzer is attached to a particular response. The connection between the analyzer output and the response is strengthened as the result of reward. Thus, in Sutherland and Mackintosh's view, reinforcement increases both the attention to a particular dimension and the ability of a particular stimulus to elicit the response.

Predictive Value of Discriminative Stimuli Research indicates that predictiveness has an important influence on discrimination learning. Recall from Chapter 2 that the predictive value of the CS determines whether it becomes able to elicit a CR. Similarly, the ability of the S^D to predict reinforcement is important; the predictiveness of the S^D determines whether it will gain control over responding. If the S^D reliably predicts reward, an animal or person will respond when the S^D is present. However, the S^D will not control responding if it does not reliably predict the occurrence of reward.

Consider the following example. A store posts its business hours. The store and the business hours are the compound S^D. If the store maintains reliable hours (that is, the S^D predicts reward), you will go to that store when it is scheduled to be opened. However, if the store is sometimes closed when it is scheduled to be open, the store's business hours do not reliably predict reward, and you are not likely to shop there; that is, the store's business hours (the S^D) will not control responding.

Wagner, Logan, Haberlandt, and Price (1968) investigated the influence of predictiveness of the S^D on its control of instrumental responding. Two groups of rats were trained to lever-press for reinforcement. Subjects in the first group were reinforced on 50 percent of the trials in which the light–tone-1 compound stimulus was presented, and they were reinforced on 50 percent of the trials in which the light–tone-2 compound stimulus was presented (see Figure 5.16). The rats in the second group received the light–tone-1 stimulus paired with reinforcement 100 percent of the time; the light–tone-2 stimulus was presented with reward 0 percent of the time. Wagner, Logan, Haberlandt, and Price were interested in the degree of control gained by the light cue. For subjects in the first group, the light cue was as predictive of reward as were tones 1 and 2, since each cue was present when reward was available on 50 percent of the trials. In contrast, tone 1 was much more predictive of reward than the light cue for subjects in the second group: for these subjects, tone 1 was present on 100 percent of the trials on which reward was available, but the light was paired with reward on only 50 percent of the trials. Note that although the light was

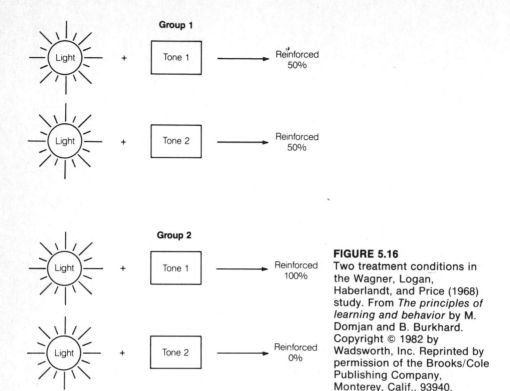

FIGURE 5.16
Two treatment conditions in the Wagner, Logan, Haberlandt, and Price (1968) study. From *The principles of learning and behavior* by M. Domjan and B. Burkhard. Copyright © 1982 by Wadsworth, Inc. Reprinted by permission of the Brooks/Cole Publishing Company, Monterey, Calif., 93940.

paired with reward availability on 50 percent of the trials in both groups, the light was a better predictor in the first group than in the second: no cue in the first group predicted reward more reliably than did the light, whereas tone 1 predicted reward better than the light in the second group. Wagner, Logan, Haberlandt, and Price reported that the light better controlled responding for subjects in the first group than in the second group. These results indicate that it is the relative predictiveness of an S^D—not the percentage of trials in which the S^D is associated with reward—which determines its ability to control responding.

Attention and Discrimination Learning The selective-attention literature described earlier provides evidence of the role of attention in discrimination learning. A study by Lawrence (1952) provides additional support for an attentional view. Lawrence trained rats to jump from a start box into one of two goal boxes. The brightness of both of these goal boxes, visible from the start box, varied from very light to very dark. To receive reward, the rats had to choose the box with the correct brightness. The control group of rats received eighty trials of a difficult discrimination using two intermediate grays. As seen in Figure 5.17, the control animals erred frequently, learning the difficult discrimination slowly. Subjects in a gradual discrimination condition received ten trials

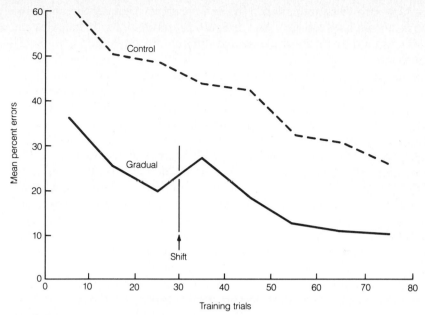

FIGURE 5.17
Mean number of errors during discrimination training for experimental subjects receiving gradual training from easy to difficult discrimination training, or control subjects only receiving difficult discrimination training. The arrow indicates when shift to difficult discrimination was made for experimental subjects. From Lawrence, D. H. The transfer of a discrimination along a continuum. *Journal of Comparative and Physiological Psychology,* 1952, *45,* 511–516. Copyright 1952 by the American Psychological Association. Reprinted by permission.

with an easy problem using boxes of contrasting brightness, ten trials with a somewhat more difficult problem, ten more trials with an even more difficult problem, and finally fifty trials with the most difficult problem. Lawrence reported that rats in the gradual condition learned the most difficult discrimination to a greater level than did the control-condition subjects (refer to Figure 5.17).

Why does the shift from an easy discrimination to a more difficult discrimination facilitate the acquisition of the difficult discrimination? According to the Sutherland-Mackintosh attention view, animals trained on the easy problem learned to attend to the relevant stimulus dimension. This enabled them to learn the difficult discrimination readily, because they were already attending to the relevant stimulus dimension. In contrast, the analyzer output from the relevant stimulus dimension did not arouse the attention of the subjects receiving only the difficult discrimination. Thus, they had difficulty correlating analyzer output with reward and erred frequently.

Additional support for this attentional view can be found in Marsh's study (1969). Marsh reported facilitation of the acquisition of a difficult discrimination as the result of prior discrimination training for subjects having the same dimension relevant on both the easy and difficult discriminations. If the relevant stimulus dimension differed for the easy and difficult discriminations, no facilitation was found.

The results of other experiments are consistent with an attention view. Sutherland and Holgate (1966) reported that if the relevant stimulus dimension on one discrimination is irrelevant on a second discrimination task, the acquisition of the second discrimination is impaired relative to a group of rats receiving only the second discrimination. Similar results were reported in rats (Mackintosh, 1965), cats (Hirayoshi & Warren, 1967; Warren & McGonigle, 1969), and pigeons (Johnson & Cumming, 1968). Also, Waller (1973) observed more impaired discrimination learning for subjects given partial reinforcement than for subjects given continuous reward. According to the Sutherland and Mackintosh view, partial reinforcement leads to poor discrimination learning because the limited ability to predict reward interferes with the strengthening of the analyzer output. The failure to readily strengthen analyzer output results in a slow increase of attention to the relevant dimension and therefore in a slow increase in discrimination learning. Apparently, a stimulus must consistently predict reward before an animal or person attends to it.

Continuity versus Discontinuity   The Hull-Spence view asserts that excitation and inhibition gradually increase during the acquisition of a discrimination. This position is referred to as a *continuity theory* of discrimination learning because it assumes that the development of a discrimination is a continuous and gradual acquisition of excitation to the S^D and inhibition to the S^Δ. Krechevsky (1932) and Lashley (1929) presented a view of discrimination learning which was quite different from the Hull-Spence approach. According to Krechevsky and Lashley, the learning of a discrimination is not a gradual, continuous process. Instead, they believe that an animal or person acquires a discrimination by establishing a "hypothesis" about which stimulus is associated with reward. While testing this hypothesis, the animal attends to the stimulus relevant to its hypothesis and learns nothing about other stimuli. The view exposed by Krechevsky and Lashley is referred to as a *noncontinuity theory* of discrimination learning because it assumes that once an animal focuses its attention on the relevant stimuli, the discrimination is rapidly acquired.

A considerable amount of research has been conducted in attempts to evaluate the continuity versus the noncontinuity views of discrimination learning. Some of this research has been supportive of the Hull-Spence continuity view, and other research has agreed with the noncontinuity approach of Krechevsky and Lashley. It is not surprising that there is research to validate both points of view, since discrimination learning reflects the acquisition of excitatory and inhibitory strength and the development of attention to predictive events in the environment. It seems reasonable that continuity theory explains how the motivational components of a discrimination are learned and that noncontinuity theory describes the attentional aspects of discrimination learning. The interested reader should see Flaherty, Hamilton, Gandelman, and Spear (1977) for a more extensive treatment of the continuity-noncontinuity issue.

SUMMARY

This chapter describes both generalization and discrimination. Generalization is a process in which animals or people respond in the same way to similar stimuli; discrimination is a process in which animals or people learn to respond in different ways to different stimuli. In some cases, generalization and discrimination are adaptive. Generalization enables us to respond to unfamiliar stimuli without having to discover directly their significance, and discrimination allows us to know when to respond and when not to respond. However, animals or people must know when to generalize and when to discriminate to interact effectively with the environment: generalization or discrimination at inappropriate times leads to failure to obtain reward, or the experience of adversity.

There are two major types of generalization: excitatory and inhibitory. In excitatory generalization, a cue is associated with reward or punishment, and stimuli similar to the S+ will elicit the response. In contrast, in inhibitory generalization, a cue is associated with the absence of reward or punishment and stimuli similar to the S− will inhibit responding. The level of generalization differs between situations. A steep generalization gradient is obtained when an animal or person only responds to stimuli very similar to the S+ or S−. A flat generalization gradient occurs when the animal or person exhibits the same amount of excitation or inhibition to any stimuli resembling the S+ or S−.

The Lashley-Wade view of generalization emphasizes the role of discriminability of the S+ and S− in the level of generalization. According to the Lashley-Wade view, animals and people generalize to stimuli quite dissimilar to the conditioning stimulus when they fail to distinguish between the S+ and other stimuli. In contrast, learning to differentiate between the S+ and other stimuli results in little or no generalization.

Reward is available in some circumstances and unavailable in others. In discrimination learning, an animal or person discovers the stimuli (S^D) signalling reward availability and the events (S^Δ) indicating that reward is unavailable. Learning the discrimination results in responding when the S^D, not the S^Δ, is present. Animals and people must also learn to discriminate between when punishment will occur and when it will not.

Animals and people have an inherent need to know when reward or punishment is available. Experimental neurosis occurs when animals are exposed to insoluble discrimination problems; these insoluble problems involve either changing the S^D and the S^Δ so that they are no longer discriminable or presenting reward or punishment inconsistently so that they are not predictable. The behavioral disturbances produced by insoluble discrimination involve extreme agitation or unresponsiveness.

Discrimination learning occurs in three stages. In the first stage, animals or people must be able to differentiate between the S^D and the S^Δ. In the second phase, they must attend to the relevant dimension. In the last phase, the discriminative stimuli must gain control over responding. The discrimination is not learned (1) if an animal or person cannot differentiate between the discriminative stimuli, (2) if the animal or person is not attending to the relevant dimension, or (3) if the discriminative stimulus does not gain control over responding.

Several processes contribute to learning to discriminate. According to the Hull-Spence view, conditioned excitation develops to the S^D as the result of reinforcement; this conditioned excitation allows the S^D to produce the instrumental response. After conditioned excitation is established, nonreward in the presence of the S^Δ results in the development of conditioned inhibition to the S^Δ; this decreases responding to the S^Δ. Kohler's relational or transposition view assumes that animals or people learn the relative relationship between the S^D and the S^Δ. Rather than just responding to a particular stimulus, they learn, for example, to choose the larger or smaller stimulus, or the louder or softer stimulus. According to Schwartz, animals and people learn about both the absolute and relative character of discriminative stimuli, and how they respond depends on the circumstance.

The inhibition conditioned to the S^Δ causes suppression of instrumental responding. Terrace suggested that the association of the S^Δ with nonreward results not only in the development of conditioned inhibition but also in the establishment of aversive properties to the S^Δ. Although S^Δ usually has both inhibitory and aversive qualities, the literature on errorless discrimination learning indicates that a discrimination can be learned when S^Δ has neither inhibitory nor aversive properties. For a discrimination to be learned without errors, the S^Δ must be introduced using an early progressive treatment. According to Terrace, this procedure allows an animal or person to learn to respond only to the S^D.

Attentional processes also play an important role in discrimination learning. Sutherland and Mackintosh suggest that during discrimination learning, an animal's or person's attention to relevant dimensions is strengthened. The ability of a stimulus analyzer to attract attention enables the animal or person to respond appropriately to the discriminative stimuli. After an animal or person is attending to the relevant dimension, the association between the instrumental response and the relevant stimulus is strengthened.

The continuity view of discrimination learning assumes that excitation and inhibition gradually increase during the acquisition of a discrimination; this approach appears to describe the development of the motivational components of discrimination learning. In contrast, the noncontinuity approach asserts that there is an abrupt recognition of the salient features of a discrimination; this approach seems to describe the attentional aspects of discrimination learning.

CHAPTER 6

COGNITIVE CONTROL OF BEHAVIOR

THE INSURMOUNTABLE BARRIER

Math has always been an obstacle for Marie. Her distaste for arithmetic was evident even in elementary school. She dreaded working with numbers, and her lowest grade was always in math. Marie's high marks in her other classes came without much effort, but she always had to struggle to earn an acceptable grade in her math courses. In college, she avoided the high-level math courses and chose only the ones which other students had said were easy. She did well in these courses because they resembled her high school math classes.

During her junior year in college, Marie decided to major in political science. Two Bs in college math were the only marks to mar her superior grade record. To earn her political science degree, Marie should have completed a statistics course during the fall semester of her junior year, but she did not. The hour was not right that fall, and she did not like the professor last spring. Determined, Marie enrolled in the statistics course this past fall—only to drop out three weeks later. She could not comprehend the material and had failed the first exam.

Marie knows that she cannot finish in political science without the statistics class, and only one semester remains until she is scheduled to graduate. However, she does not believe that she can pass the course. She has even begun to wonder if she is capable of exerting the effort to attend this class and to study the material. She had discussed her problem with her parents and friends, and they, in turn, regularly offered encouragement. Unfortunately, their good wishes could not make her problem go away.

Yesterday, Marie learned from a friend that he had a similar problem with chemistry and that a psychologist at the University Counselling Center helped him overcome his "chemistry phobia." This friend suggested to Marie that the center might help her, too. Marie had never considered her math aversion a psychological problem and was reluctant to accept any need for clinical treatment. She knew that she must decide before next week's registration whether to seek help at the center. If Marie does go for help, she may learn several things: Her fear of the course was caused by her attribution of past math failures to a lack of ability in math. On the basis of this attribution, Marie expects to fail in the future. Also, Marie expects to be unable even to attend the class regularly; her lack of a sense of self-efficacy developed further because of her recent inability to remain in the course. Later in the chapter we will discuss a cognitive treatment which has successfully modified the expectations that maintain the phobic behavior of people like Marie.

The term *cognition* refers to an animal's or person's knowledge of the environment. Psychologists investigating cognitive processes have focused on two distinctively different areas of inquiry. Many psychologists have evaluated an animal's or person's understanding of the structure of the psychological environment (i.e., when events occur and what has to be done to obtain reward or avoid punishment) and how this understanding, which is referred to as an *expectancy,* acts to motivate instrumental behavior. The role of cognitions in instrumental activity will be discussed in this chapter. Other psychologists have evaluated the processes which enable an animal or person to have knowledge of the environment. This research has investigated complex learning processes, such as concept formation, problem solving, language acquisition, and the memory process. These processes provide the mental structure or organization for thinking and will be discussed in later chapters.

Recall the discussion of cognitive approaches to learning, which were described in Chapter 1. Although Edward Tolman proposed a cognitive view of learning during the 1930s and 1940s, this approach was unacceptable to most psychologists. Hull's mechanistic approach was the accepted view of learning during that period. The cognitive view gained some acceptance during the 1950s as other psychologists expanded Tolman's original cognitive approach, but only in the past decade have psychologists recognized the important contribution of cognitions in the learning process. Our discussion begins with Tolman's work—his research stands as a remarkable achievement. While Hull and his students were diligently working to disprove Tolman's view, Tolman alone developed what was to become modern cognitive psychology. Later in the chapter, we'll look at the ideas and research of these contemporary cognitive psychologists.

TOLMAN'S PURPOSIVE BEHAVIORISM
Learning Principles

Edward Tolman's (1932, 1959) view of learning contrasts with the mechanistic view described in Chapter 1. Tolman did not envision that behavior reflects an automatic response to an environmental event; rather he thought that our behavior has both direction and purpose. According to Tolman, our behavior is goal-oriented because we are motivated either to approach a particular reward or to avoid a specific aversive event. In addition, we are capable of understanding the structure of our environment. There are (1) paths leading to our goals and (2) tools which we can employ to obtain these goals. Through experience, we gain an expectation of how to use these paths and tools to reach goals. Although Tolman used the terms *purpose* and *expectation* to describe the process which motivates our behavior, he did not mean that we are aware of either the purpose or the direction of our behavior. He theorized that we act *as if* we expect a particular action to lead to a specific goal.

According to Tolman, not only is our behavior goal-oriented, but also we expect specific outcomes to follow specific behaviors. For example, we expect that going to a favorite restaurant will result in a great meal. If we do not obtain our goal, we will continue to search for the reward and will not be satisfied with a less-valued goal object. If our favorite restaurant is closed, we will not accept any restaurant and instead choose a suitable alternative. Also, certain events in the environment convey information about where our goals are located. According to Tolman, we are able to reach our goals only after we have learned the signs leading to reward or punishment in our environment. Thus, we know where our favorite restaurant is located and use this information to guide us to that restaurant.

Tolman suggests that we do not have to be reinforced to learn. However, our expectations will not be translated into behavior unless we are motivated. Tolman proposed that motivation has two functions: (1) It produces a state of internal tension which creates a demand for the goal object and (2) it determines the environmental features to which we will attend. For example, if we are not hungry, we are less likely to learn where food is located than if we are starving. However, tension does not possess the mechanistic quality that it did in Hull's theory. According to Tolman, our expectations control the directions of our drives. Therefore, when we are motivated, we do not respond in a fixed, automatic, or stereotyped way to reduce our drive; rather, our behavior will remain flexible enough to enable us to reach our goal.

Motivational Processes

Tolman proposed two classes of motivators. The first, *deprivation conditions,* produces an internal drive state which increases our demand for the goal object. The value of the goal also influences the intensity of our motivations; we are more motivated to obtain a large reward than a small one. Tolman referred to the motivational qualities of a reward as *incentive motivation.* In addition, Tolman (1959) suggested that environmental events can acquire motivational properties through association with either a primary drive or a reinforcer. Suppose that a hungry child sees a cheeseburger (primary drive). According to Tolman, the ability of hunger to motivate behavior transfers to the cheeseburger. Tolman called this transference process *cathexis,* a concept he borrowed from psychoanalytic theory. As a result of cathexis, the cheeseburger is now a preferred goal object, and this child, even when not hungry, will be motivated to obtain a cheeseburger in the future. The preference for the cheeseburger is a positive cathexis. In contrast, our avoiding a certain person could reflect a negative cathexis. In Tolman's opinion, our association of that person with an unpleasant experience leads us to think of this person as an aversive object. Recall Chapter 1's discussion of conditioned drives—Tolman's cathexis concept is very similar to Hull's view of acquired drive. Tolman's equivalence-belief principle is also like Hull's acquired-incentive concept. Animals or people react to a secondary reinforcer (or subgoal) as they do to an original goal object. For instance, our motivation to obtain money reflects our belief that money is equivalent to a desired goal object such as food.

Much research has been conducted to evaluate the validity of Hull's mechanistic approach. In comparison, the research effort to validate Tolman's cognitive view has been meager, although Tolman and his students conducted several key studies providing support for his approach. The next sections will examine these studies and describe what they tell us about learning. Even though Tolman's studies seriously challenged some of the postulates derived from Hull's drive approach, the cognitive view was forgotten by all but a few psychologists during the 1950s and early 1960s when the drive approach dominated American psychology. The psychologists who continued to use Tolman's cognitive approach provided more evidence for a cognitive view by describing additional cognitive processes involved in motivating behavior. The impact of this contemporary cognitive psychology became evident in the late 1960s.

Place-Learning Studies

Tolman asserted that people expect reinforcement in a certain place and that they follow the paths leading to that place. In contrast, Hull proposed that environmental cues elicit specific motor responses which have led to reinforcement in the past. How do we know which view is valid? Under normal conditions, we cannot determine whether our expectations or habits will lead us to reward. Tolman designed his place-learning studies to provide us with an answer. The following story illustrates the rationale behind Tolman's experiments: Every day you walk the same route from your dorm to class. You can awaken 10 minutes before class and still be prompt because you take the shortest route. However, before your first class today, you have another course assignment which must be turned in to a professor's office across campus. You then will not have enough time before your first class to return to your dorm. Although you have been to this part of the campus before, you have never gone from there to your first morning class. Necessity now causes you to use this new route. Will you arrive on time for your class? Tolman would believe that you would be prompt without much difficulty; your prior experience with the campus has provided you with a cognitive map. Using important landmarks as a guide, you would walk in the direction in which you expect your classroom. In contrast, Hull's view predicts that you would probably be late for class, because the responses you must use in the new route differ from those of your usual route. Although Tolman's initial place-learning studies predict a prompt arrival, later experiments by other psychologists have indicated that there are some conditions in which habit, not expectation, governs behavior. Let's briefly examine these studies.

   T-Maze Experiments Tolman, Ritchie, and Kalish (1946) designed a study to distinguish behavior based on movement habits from behavior based on spatial expectations. Figure 6.1 depicts the apparatus in which they placed the rats for half of the trials in place S_1; on the other trials, the rats began in place S_2. For the place-learning condition, reward was always in the same location, but the turning response necessary to produce reward differed for each trial. In contrast, although the response-learning-condition rats received reward in both places, only one response—either right or left—produced reinforcement. Tolman, Ritchie, and Kalish found that all the place-condition animals learned within eight trials and continued to behave without errors for the next ten trials. None of the rats in the response condition learned this rapidly; even after responding correctly, they continued to make errors. The results of Tolman, Ritchie, and Kalish's study illustrate that superior learning occurs when we can obtain reward in a certain place rather than by using a habit.
   A second study by Tolman, Ritchie, and Kalish (1946) demonstrates that a rat will go to a place associated with reward even though an entirely new motor response is required to reach the place containing the reward. During the first phase of their study, they always put their rats in location S_1 and placed reward

FIGURE 6.1
Schematic diagram of typical apparatus for a place-learning study. Rat can start at either S_1 or S_2 and receive reward in either F_1 or F_2. From Tolman, E. C., Ritchie, B. F., & Kalish, D. Studies of spatial learning: II. Place learning versus response learning. *Journal of Experimental Psychology*, 1946, *36*, 221–229. Copyright 1946 by the American Psychological Association. Reprinted by permission.

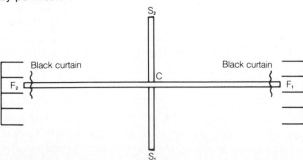

in F_1. For these rats, both a habit (right turn) and an expectation of where food is located (F_1) produced reinforcement. During the second phase of their study, they placed the rats at location S_2. In this stage, the rats reached the goal only by turning left toward F_1; the habitual right response led to an empty goal box. Tolman, Ritchie, and Kalish reported that their subjects turned left and went to F_1, the place associated with reward. These results indicate that expectancies, not habits, controlled behavior in this study.

Numerous studies have compared place versus response learning. Many of these studies demonstrate that spatial relationships govern behavior, whereas other studies indicate that response learning is superior to place learning. Fortunately, there are several likely explanations for these different results. One cause of the conflicting results is the presence of cues to guide behavior (Blodgett & McCutchan, 1947, 1948). For example, place learning is superior to response learning when extra maze cues are present to allow spatial orientation to guide the rats to the correct location. Without extra maze cues, the animals are forced to rely on motor responses to produce reward.

The degree of experience with the task is another reason for the different results. I have sometimes experienced the following situation while driving home. Instead of turning from my typical path to run a planned errand, I continue past the turn and arrive home. Why did I follow the signs home rather than those leading to my errand? One likely answer is that I have driven home so often that the response has become habitual; an automatic response process controls my driving-home behavior unless I exert considerable effort to inhibit this habit so that I take a less habitual route. Kendler and Gasser's (1948) study indicates that well-learned behavior is typically governed by mechanistic processes rather than by cognitive ones. They found that with fewer than twenty trials, animals responded to place cues, whereas with greater training, the rats exhibited the appropriate motor response.

Alternate-Path Studies Examine the map in Figure 6.2. Pretend that these paths represent routes to school. Which path would you choose? In all likelihood, you would use path A, the shortest path. However, what would you do if path A were blocked at point Y? If you were behaving according to your spatial knowledge, you would choose path C. Even though path C is longer than B, your cognitive map would produce the expectation that B is also blocked and thus would motivate the choice of C. In contrast, a drive interpretation predicts that you would choose B since it represents the second dominant habit. Path C is your choice if you behave like the rats did in Tolman and Honzik's 1930s study. In their study, animals were familiar with the entire maze but usually chose Path A to reach the goal. However, most rats chose path C when path A was blocked at point Y. These results point out that knowledge of our environment, rather than "blind habit," often influences our behavior. Although other psychologists have replicated Tolman and Honzik's study (e.g., Caldwell & Jones, 1954), animals have not always chosen path C. For example, Keller and Hull (1936) discovered that changing the width of the alleys caused their rats to

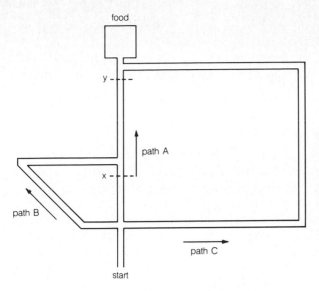

FIGURE 6.2
Apparatus used in Tolman
and Honzik's alternate-path
experiment. Obstacle Y
blocks not only the shortest
path A but also the
middle-length path B. With
paths A and B blocked, the
only available route to the
goal is the longest route,
path C. From Tolman, E. C.,
& Honzik, C. H. *University of
California Publications in
Psychology*, 1930, *4*,
215–232.

respond according to habit and choose the blocked path. Unfortunately, there
has been no definitive evaluation of why the blocked path is sometimes chosen.
We can conclude from our prior discussion that the salience of cues leading to
the goal and the degree of experience with the paths probably determine the
processes controlling behavior. Thus, if we attend to paths leading to reward
and the paths have not been employed frequently, our expectations rather than
habits will determine our action.

Response-Alteration Studies   Suppose that your car stalled 3 miles from
school. Could you walk to school, even though you had always driven? The
drive and cognitive approaches predict different outcomes. Changes in both the
environmental stimuli and the motor responses which occur when you switch
from driving to walking should, according to a drive view, lead to a difficult
trip. However, since the paths leading to reward are not altered, a cognitive
view suggests that you will have no problem with your walk. The results of
several studies support Tolman's cognitive approach. Let's look at several of
these experiments.

MacFarlane (1930), one of Tolman's students, filled a maze with several
inches of water and then trained his rats to swim through the maze to obtain
food reward. After the rats had learned to go through without errors, Mac-
Farlane drained the maze. This change altered the stimulus characteristics of
the maze (for example, the floor was now solid) and the motor response
(walking instead of swimming) necessary to obtain reward, even though Mac-
Farlane had not changed the spatial design of the maze; the same paths led to
reward in both mazes. MacFarlane reported that his rats encountered no difficulty with the altered maze. Apparently, the cognitive map acquired in the

water maze was still valid in the land maze. In an interesting variation of these altered-response studies, McNamara, Long, and Wike (1956) initially gave their rats a ride on a small cart which went through a maze. Later, they found that their rats experienced no difficulty running through the maze to obtain reward.

Is Reinforcement Necessary for Learning?

Recall our discussion of the law of effect in Chapter 1. According to Thorndike, S-R associations are established when the response leads to a satisfying state of affairs. Hull (1943) expanded Thorndike's early view and asserted that habit strength increases when a particular response decreases the drive state. Tolman (1932) thought that reinforcement is not necessary for learning to occur and that the simultaneous experiencing of two events is sufficient. Chapter 1 discussed the development of the incentive motivation process initially detailed by Hull in 1952 and then later described by Spence in 1956. The research of Tolman and his students strongly influenced the nature of the incentive motivation concept.

Latent-Learning Studies   Tolman felt that knowledge of the spatial characteristics of a specific environment can be acquired merely by exploring the environment. Reinforcement is not necessary for the development of a cognitive map; reward influences behavior only when we must use that information to obtain reward. Tolman distinguished between learning and performance by asserting that reward motivates behavior but does not affect learning.

Tolman and Honzik's (1930a) classic study directly assessed the importance of reinforcement on learning and performance. Tolman and Honzik assigned their subjects to one of three conditions: (1) Hungry animals in the R group always received reinforcement (food) in the goal box of a 22-unit maze. (2) The rats in the NR group were hungry but never received reward in the goal box. (3) Hungry rats in the NR-R group were not given reward on the first ten days of conditioning; they received reward for the last ten days. Tolman and Honzik found that animals which received reward on each trial (R group) showed a steady decrease in the number of errors during training, whereas animals not given reward (NR group) showed little improvement in their performance (see Figure 6.3). Does this failure of the unrewarded rats to perform indicate a failure to learn? Or have the nonrewarded rats developed a cognitive map which they are not motivated to use? The behavior of those animals which did not receive reward until the eleventh trial answers this question. Since the development of a habit was envisioned by Hull (1943) as a slow process, animals in the NR-R group should have shown a slow decline in errors when reward began. However, if learning has already occurred by the eleventh trial but all that these rats needed was to be motivated, they should have performed well on the twelfth trial. The results indicate that on the twelfth day and all the subsequent days, animals in the R group (which were always rewarded) per-

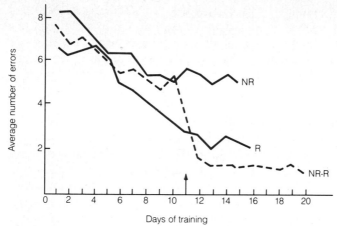

FIGURE 6.3
Results of Tolman and Honzik's latent-learning study. Animals
in the NR group received no reward during the experiment;
those in the R group received reward throughout the study;
those in the NR-R group received reward from only day 11
through day 20. From Tolman, E. C., & Honzik, C. H. Degrees of
hunger; reward and nonreward; and maze learning in rats.
University of California Publications in Psychology, 1930, *4,*
241–256.

formed no differently than did those in the NR-R group (which were only
rewarded beginning trial eleven). Apparently, NR-R animals were learning
during the initial trials even though they did not receive any apparent reinforcement.

The latent-learning studies present the Hullian drive view with a dilemma,
and many mechanistic-oriented psychologists attempted to show that latent
learning was not a real phenomenon. When it became clear that latent learning
can be reliably produced under some conditions, the drive view was modified to
explain the latent-learning studies.

MacCorquodale and Meehl (1954) reported that thirty of forty-eight studies
were able to replicate the latent-learning effect. Although latent learning appears to be a real phenomenon, under some conditions it is likely and in other
circumstances it is not. MacCorquodale and Meehl observed that in studies
where reward was present for nondeprived animals during the initial trials and
motivation was introduced during later experience with the same reward, latent
learning was typically found. However, in other studies latent learning was not
typically found where rewards present during the initial trials were irrelevant to
the motivation existing at that time and reward only became relevant during
later trials. These results suggest that a motivated animal will ignore the presence of a potent but irrelevant reward; thus, the results agree with Tolman's
belief that motivation narrows an animal's attention to those cues which are
salient to its motivational state.

Johnson's (1952) study provides direct support for this interpretation. Johnson varied the level of deprivation during initial exploration in a T maze and found that as deprivation increased, the likelihood of observing latent learning decreased. Apparently, we learn about the general aspects of our environment unless our motivation restricts our attention to some specific part of the environment.

The Drive Response The most consistent observation of latent learning occurs in animals not deprived when initially exposed to reward. The r_G-s_G mechanism described in Chapter 1 was developed to explain the results of these latent-learning studies. The anticipatory goal response (r_G-s_G) is established during initial exposure with reward but is not apparent until the motivating influence of deprivation is added. However, some latent-learning studies—the original Tolman and Honzik study is one example—employ no obvious reward. Yet, the nonrewarded animals in those studies such as Tolman and Honzik's do show a slight improvement in their performance, and this indicates, according to drive-view advocates (see Kimble, 1961), that reward was present in these animals. These advocates suggested that handling or removing the animals from the strange maze to the familiar home cage represented sufficient reward to sometimes establish the r_G-s_G mechanism during initial nonreward. Although the strength of the r_G-s_G was not intense enough to motivate behavior, additional arousal produced by the introduction of reward resulted in rapid improvement in performance.

Any Reward Will Not Do

Suppose that you go into a bar and order a specific beer. You are informed that your favorite beer is no longer available, but a lower grade of beer is now stocked. Will you stay in the bar? It is highly probable that you will seek another bar which has your brand of beer.

This example illustrates Tolman's view that we are motivated to obtain a specific reinforcer. We will not accept a less valued reward when expecting to receive a desired one, and we will continue to act until we obtain the desired reward. Many animal studies demonstrating the incentive motivational process have been reported since Tinklepaugh's 1928 study (see Bolles, 1975, for a review). In Tinklepaugh's study, primates learned to obtain a banana by choosing the container which had a banana under it. The subsequent placement of a piece of lettuce, rather than a banana, under the correct container produced a typical response: The primates refused to eat the lettuce, a less desirable food than bananas, and continued to search the room for the expected banana and shrieked at those people with them to indicate their displeasure.

Recall the discussion of frustration in Chapter 1. We saw that the absence of an anticipated reward produces the aversive emotional state of frustration. Frustration can motivate avoidance of a less desirable reward and continued search for the desired reinforcer. Therefore, as with latent learning, the motivation for a specific reward can be incorporated into drive theory.

THE COVARIATION OF EVENTS

Edward Tolman believed that the expectation of future reward or punishment motivates our behavior. He also believed that this behavior is guided by our knowledge of the paths and/or tools which lead us to obtain reward or to avoid punishment. Research designed by Tolman and his students did not provide conclusive evidence for his cognitive approach, but it did force major changes in Hull's drive view. The idea that a conditioned anticipation of reward motivates us to approach a goal is clearly similar to Tolman's view that the expectation of reward motivates the behavior which we believe will obtain reward. However, once these changes were made, most psychologists ignored Tolman's cognitive view, and the drive approach continued to be generally accepted.

A few psychologists continued the cognitive tradition in the 1950s, and, as problems developed with the drive view during the 1960s and 1970s, the cognitive view gained wider appeal. The next section describes the cognitive approach advocated by a number of contemporary psychologists. Note that although many psychologists today assume that animals and people develop mental representations of contingencies (i.e., when events occur and how we must act to obtain reward and avoid punishment), other psychologists do not believe that subjective representations or expectancies are formed as the result of experience. Instead of a cognitive view, these psychologists advocate a mechanistic or associationistic view. We will explore the continued objections to a cognitive view in this chapter.

Expectation of Reward and Punishment

The cognitive learning theorist Robert Bolles (1972, 1978) suggested that during our interaction with our environment, two types of expectations develop which guide us to obtain reinforcement or to avoid punishment. Bolles called the first type of expectancy an *S-S* expectancy*. According to Bolles, many environmental events (S) are present when a biologically important event (S*), such as food or shock, occurs. However, a particular event (S₁) happening simultaneously with the S* does not mean that we will expect S* when we encounter S₁. Bolles felt that S₁ must reliably predict the occurrence of S* for the S₁-S* expectancy to develop. Contiguity, in Bolles's view, is not sufficient for learning: Events must consistently occur together before we can acquire an S-S* expectancy. In addition, when two or more stimuli are present with S*, only the most reliable predictor of the S* will become associated with it.

Bolles referred to the second type of expectancy as an *R-S* expectancy*. An R-S* expectancy reflects our understanding of the response or responses necessary to produce reward or avoid punishment. Although R-S* expectancies can be acquired through experience, Bolles stressed the importance of innate expectations which govern behavior. Our R-S* expectations do not necessarily reflect the contingencies in the environment; we must believe only that a specific response leads to reinforcement or prevents punishment. Although under some conditions the attainment of reward or the presentation of an aversive event takes place independently of our behavior, in most circumstances the occurrence of reward or adversity depends on our exhibiting a specific response. Under these conditions, our S-S* expectancies predict the potential occurrence of a biologically important event, and our R-S* expectancies lead us to the predicted goal—either the presence of an appetitive event (for example, an appropriate sexual partner) or the prevention of an aversive event (for example, failing an examination).

Walter Mischel, a noted personality theorist, proposed in 1973 three types of expectancies which determine how we act. The first two expectancies, *stimulus outcome* and *behavior outcome,* are identical to the S-S* and R-S* expectancies described by Bolles. According to Mischel, stimulus-outcome expectations reflect our belief in the consequences of the environmental stimuli which we experience. For example, Mischel described one of his female patients as capable of experiencing sexual pleasure in the dark but not under other environmental conditions. According to Mischel, this patient's behavior resulted from her belief that only darkness predicted a safe sexual encounter. Behavior-outcome expectations represent our belief in the consequences of our actions. However, we do not expect a particular behavior to have the same consequences each time we perform it; a particular behavior-outcome expectation is activated only under specific environmental conditions. Thus, Mischel's patient expected sexual intercourse to produce pleasure—but only in the dark. In a lighted environment, this woman expected sexual intercourse to be aversive. This expectation caused her to avoid sex unless she was in a dark room.

Although we may expect to receive reward in a particular setting, we may still not behave. We will not exhibit a specific behavior unless we feel competent. *Competency* refers to a belief in our ability to behave in a certain fashion. (This competency concept is identical to Bandura's self-efficacy idea described in Chapter 1.) For example, suppose that you want to ski. Other people have told you that skiing is enjoyable, and you expect to have a good time. However, unless you feel able to ride on the ski lift, you will be unable to obtain reward. Many people feel capable of getting on the lift and, therefore, are able to obtain their expected reward. However, some people want to ski but think that they cannot ride the lift—these people will be unable to experience the rewarding aspect of skiing unless they can change their feelings of incompetency.

Generalized Expectancy

We are often faced with new situations. How do we know how to act? According to the social-learning theorist Julian Rotter (1966), our generalized expectancies from past experiences guide our actions. Recall your initial feeling when you were a first-year college student. You had never attended college and, therefore, had no direct experience on which to base your expectancies. Under these circumstances, your past expectations governed your behavior. Since you probably did well in high school, an expectation of success motivated you to attend college. Hopefully, your generalized expectations are valid.

Rotter suggested that there are two kinds of generalized expectations: internal expectancy and external expectancy. An *internal expectancy* represents your belief that obtaining your goal depends on your own actions. Thus, your expectation that hard work brings success will motivate you to spend long hours studying for an exam. However, you will not exert much effort studying if you believe that luck will determine whether you receive a high grade on the exam. Rotter refers to this type of cognition as an *external expectation*. When making an external expectation, you believe that events are beyond your control. For example, you exhibit an external expectation if you assume that luck, chance, or the power of others is responsible for your attaining a desired reward. Since you believe little connection to exist between your behavior and reward when you make an external expectation, you will make no effort to obtain reinforcement.

There are environmental situations in which each expectation is appropriate. In skill tasks, you can obtain reward by exhibiting the appropriate ability. Chance tasks, in contrast, do not rely on any specific behavior for reward. Many of us are aware of the distinction between external and internal expectations and exhibit different expectations in each type of setting. We assume in skill situations that our behavior enables us to obtain reward. When we are successful in skill tasks, we increase our expectation of future success, whereas failure often causes us to decrease our expectation of future reward. Our response during chance situations is quite different from how we respond in skill tasks: Since we assume that reward occurs independently of our actions in chance tasks, we are unlikely to change our expectations of future reward following either success or failure.

A study by Phares (1957) illustrates the influence of success and failure on our expectations in skill and chance situations. Phares placed his subjects in an ambiguous setting and provided them information which indicated that they were participating in either a skill or a chance situation. In fact, however, all subjects were in a chance task. During the course of study, the subjects received random experiences of success and failure. The subjects were asked prior to each trial to indicate how many chips they wanted to bet on their next trial's performance. Phares assumed that the subjects' bets reflected their expectations of future successes or failures. He reported that in the skill situations, the subjects increased their bets after success and decreased them after failure. In contrast, the subjects were unlikely to change their bets after either succeeding or failing in a chance setting. Phares's study is important for two reasons. First, he obtained the predicted expectancy differences between skill and chance situations. Second, these differences occurred even though none of the subjects really had control over the attainment of reward. A belief in our ability to control events—not the actual contingencies which exist in our environment—determines our behavior. Therefore, if our inappropriate actions are to be altered, our expectations must also be changed.

It is most appropriate for us to perceive each situation separately. We should attempt to obtain reward in skill settings but either avoid or cope with those situations in which success or failure occurs independently of our actions. However, many people show a generalized expectation by treating all situations as being either skill or chance. In Rotter's view, internally oriented persons believe that success and/or failure is caused by their own skills. Externally oriented individuals, however, assume that they have no control over their fate. Rotter coined the term *locus of control* to refer to our generalized expectation that either internal or external factors control our behavior.

A Mental Representation of Events

What is an *expectancy*? Several psychologists have suggested that an expectancy is a mental representation of event contingencies (see Hulse, Fowler, & Honig, 1978, or Roitblat, Bever, & Terrace, 1979, for a detailed description of this idea). According to this view, an internal or mental representation of an experience is established when an animal or person experiences an event. This representation contains information about the relations among previously experienced events and about relations between behavior and the consequences of this behavior. Instead of environmental stimuli's evoking behavior, these internal representations or expectancies guide instrumental activity.

Some learning theorists (Levis, 1976; Rescorla & Wagner, 1972) reject the idea that subjective representations of event contingencies are formed. Instead, they argue that stimulus-response associations rather than expectancies are formed as the result of experience and that concrete environmental events rather than subjective representations motivate behavior.

Recall our discussion of the Rescorla-Wagner model of conditioning in Chapter 2. This model was developed to explain several Pavlovian conditioning phenomena (i.e., blocking, cue predictiveness, overshadowing) which are not predicted by a simple contiguity model of Pavlovian conditioning. Although the Rescorla-Wagner model can explain Pavlovian conditioning processes like blocking, overshadowing, and UCS preexposure, the model cannot explain other observations. For example, the Rescorla-Wagner model cannot readily account for the CS preexposure phenomenon described in Chapter 2. In a recent article, Alloy and Tabachnik (1984) argued that a cognitive view not only best explains all the Pavlovian conditioning research with animals but also represents the most accurate view of the learning process in both animals and humans.

The Importance of Covariation

According to Alloy and Tabachnik (1984), in our environment there are relations among, or contingencies between, stimuli, behavior, and outcomes. For example, the contingency between working and being paid is a relationship between a specific behavior and a particular outcome. Similarly, the relationship between thunder and rain is a contingency between two stimuli. Alloy and Tabachnik assert that the level of covariance differs; that is, some relations are perfect: One event always follows the other. Other relationships are weak: One event sometimes follows the other one. However, no relations exist among stimuli, behaviors, and outcomes in some environments. Alloy and Tabachnik assert that animals or people need information about the level of covariation between stimuli, behavior, and outcomes. (*Covariation* is the level of relation between stimuli, behaviors, and outcomes; the greater the relationship, the higher the covariation.) This information provides people and animals with "a means of explaining the past, controlling the present, and predicting the future." Thus, covariation data allow a person to maximize the likelihood of obtaining desired outcomes and minimize the likelihood of experiencing aversive results.

The central aspect of Alloy and Tabachnik's view is not that differences in covariation exist between stimuli, behavior, and outcomes. Rather, the main point of their theory is that animals and people know the level of covariation among stimuli, behavior, and outcomes. There is a mental representation of the degree of covariation; this knowledge is gained through experience and acts to guide instrumental activity.

Suppose you hear a loud noise and then see a person fall down. Do you think that there is a covariation between the sound and the person falling down? According to Alloy and Tabachnik, two types of information determine the assessed level of covariance. First, an animal or person has a prior expectation or belief about the degree of covariation between stimuli, behavior, and outcomes. You might have a preconceived belief about how a loud noise and a person's falling relate. Second, the situation contains information about the contingency between stimuli, behavior, and outcomes: you did see someone fall down after the loud noise. Alloy and Tabachnik assert that the combined influence of both prior expectations and situational information determines the level of perceived covariation. In the ideal, the animal or person weighs both prior expectations and current circumstance to develop an idea of covariation of stimuli, behavior, and outcomes. However, as we will discover shortly, previous expectancies often have a much more profound influence on the perceived level of covariance than does situational information. Alloy and Tabachnik present an eloquent discussion and detailed description of research which supports their view that animals and people acquire a mental representation of the contingency or covariation between stimuli, behavior, and outcomes as the result of experience. Furthermore, they present evidence indicating that a covariation cognition influences instrumental activity. (Interested readers should refer to Alloy and Tabachnik's 1984 article for a more detailed discussion.)

There are four main aspects of Alloy and Tabachnik's view. First, *animals and people can detect the contingency between stimuli, behavior, and outcomes*. Second, *animals and people enter into situations with a belief about the degree of covariation between stimuli, behavior, and outcomes*. This preconceived belief represents either an instinctive knowledge of environmental contingencies or a knowledge based on experiences with similar events. Recognize that not only do these covariance estimates exist but they also influence the level of instrumental behavior. Third, *the situation conveys information about the covariation between stimuli, behavior, and outcomes*. This information can be used by an animal or person to know which events are likely to occur or how to act to obtain reward or avoid punishment. Fourth, *although both prior estimates of covariance and information conveyed by the environment about the level of covariance can affect how they act, animals and people often ignore the current situation and respond based solely on preconceived beliefs concerning the covariation between stimuli, behavior, and outcomes*. In these circumstances, the animal's or person's prior beliefs bias the response to the environment. The next four subsections briefly examine evidence to support the four main ideas of Alloy and Tabachnik's view. Most of the research documenting the view that covariance affects instrumental activity has come from research with human subjects, although some research with animals supports this cognitive view of the processes controlling instrumental behavior. We will discuss studies using both animals and humans.

Aspect 1: The Detection of Covariation   Can we detect the level of covariation between events? The evidence indicates that animals and people are able to detect environmental contingencies (see Alloy & Tabachnik, 1984, for a review of this literature). Let's next look at two studies (one using human subjects; the other, animals) which indicate that covariation can be detected.

Alloy and Abramson (1979) asked college students to make one of two possible responses: to press or not to press a button. After each response, one of two outcomes occurred: either a green light or no light was presented. After forty trials, each subject was asked to indicate the relationship between pressing the button and the green light coming on. Each subject did not receive the same contingency; Alloy and Abramson varied the degree of contingency from 0 (no relationship) to 75 percent (on 75 percent of the trials, pressing a button would result in the turning on the green light). Alloy and Abramson reported that their subjects accurately detected the level of covariance between pressing the button and the occurrence of the green light.

Evidence that animals can detect the contingency between events can be seen in the research on predictiveness (see Chapter 2 for a discussion of this research). Recall that Rescorla (1968) varied the contingency between a stimulus (tone) and an outcome (shock). He reported that the greater the contingency, the higher the level of fear exhibited by the rats to the presentation of the stimulus (tone). These observations strongly suggest that animals can detect the level of covariation between events.

Aspect 2: The Influence of Covariation Judgments on Behavior   Do our judgments of covariation affect our behavior? The research indicates that the knowledge of covariation can influence how we act. The attribution literature provides evidence that people make covariation judgments and that these covariation judgments affect instrumental activity. Attribution theory was first outlined by Frits Heider in 1958. Heider suggested that we examine our successes and failures to determine why we believe that these events occurred. We might attribute our experience to personal, or *internal,* causes. Or we might perceive that environmental, or *external,* factors caused our successes and failures; these expectations then determine our subsequent instrumental behavior. Note that internal and external attributions differ from internal and external expectations. For example, a person might attribute failure to lack of ability (an internal causal attribution) which leads to an expectation of being unable to succeed in the future (an external expectation).

Causal Attributions   According to Heider, we can attribute our experiences to two types of internal causal attributions: We can attribute our success to *power* or to *motivation,* and we might believe that lack of power or motivation produced our failure. Power refers to our perceived level of such factors as ability, strength, and attractiveness. Motivation represents the level of exertion or effort which we feel we have exhibited to reach our goals.

We can also attribute success or failure to environmental factors. Heider proposed that environmental forces either impede us from reaching our goal or cause success. In Heider's view, environmental barriers frequently reduce the likelihood of our reaching goals, although some environmental forces aid in obtaining a desired goal. The success or failure of others can provide us with information enabling us to judge the presence of these environmental forces. If most people have successfully completed a certain task, environmental events probably will enable us to be successful at this same task. In contrast, the failure of most people to reach their goals may be attributed to the presence of environmental factors which would also block our successes, although environmental forces can also influence each of us differently. For example, the effect of the environmental event luck fluctuates among people. We assume that good luck enables us to be successful and that bad luck prevents—or at least impairs—us from reaching our goals.

We are also concerned whether the factors to which we attributed our success or failure will or will not continue to influence our ability to reach our future goals. Heider (1958) assumed that some factors are *stable* and others are *unstable*. When we attribute our success or failure on a certain task to a stable factor, we assume that this factor will continue to determine our future successes or failures on this specific task. In contrast, since the influence of unstable factors can change as time progresses, we are uncertain whether these factors will continue to influence our being able to reach a desired goal.

This dimension—stability—influences both internal and external attributions. Power is typically assumed to be a stable factor; motivation, an unstable element. For example, most of us do not believe that our ability will change in the course of time. In contrast, we *are* likely to feel that our level of motivation will fluctuate. Environmental forces can also be stable or unstable. We might believe that some environmental forces which either promote or prevent success will remain effective, whereas other external factors may cease to influence us. For example, we assume that the difficulty of a task will not change. However, luck can change; good luck can become bad luck or vice versa.

Expectations of the Future   Heider assumed that our causal attributions determine our expectations of future success or failure. Rosenbaum's (1972) study documents this influence. Rosenbaum told some of his subjects about the success of one individual working on a project, whereas other subjects were informed that this person's project had failed. All the subjects were provided information that enabled them to make a causal attribution for the project's success or failure. Half the subjects in both the success and failure conditions were given a story which indicated that a stable factor—high or low ability— was responsible for the project's outcome. The other subjects were told that an unstable factor—high or low effort—produced the project's results. Thus, the subjects were able to make a causal attribution for success or failure during the first phase of Rosenbaum's study. In the second phase, Rosenbaum asked his subjects to indicate their expectation of this person's success on the next project. Although the expectation of future success is always greater after we have succeeded than after we have failed, the stability attribution was extremely important in this study (see Figure 6.4). Attributing success to an unstable factor produced a lower expectation of future success than did attributing success to a stable factor. On the other hand, the attribution of failure to an unstable factor produced a higher expectation of future success than did attribution of failure to a stable factor. As Heider predicted, our expectations of future success depend on whether we attribute our successes and failures to stable or unstable factors.

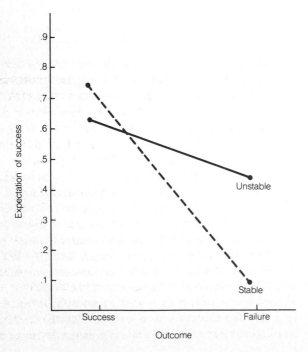

FIGURE 6.4
Subjects' expectation of success as a function of previous success or failure and the attribution of the outcome to a stable or unstable factor. Adapted from Rosenbaum, R. M. A dimensional analysis of the perceived causes of success and failure. Doctoral diss. Los Angeles: University of California, 1972.

Recall our discussion of Rotter's locus-of-control concept. Rotter assumed that our expectation of future success or failure depends on whether we exhibit an internal or an external expectation. The Phares study described earlier seemed to confirm Rotter's prediction. Phares found that if we have succeeded in a skill and a chance task, we are more apt to expect future success in the skill task than the chance task. Similarly, after we have failed a skill task and a chance task, we expect future failure more in the skill task than in the chance task. However, Bernard Weiner (1980) points to a conceptual error in Rotter's theory. Skill is typically a stable factor, whereas chance reflects an unstable element. Weiner suggested that our expectation of future success or failure does not depend on whether we make an internal or external attribution but only on the stability dimension.

The Weiner, Nierenberg, and Goldstein (1976) study is one documentation of the importance of the stability attribution. They provided subjects with either 0, 1, 2, 3, 4, or 5 success experiences on a block-design task and then collected data which indicated the subjects' causal attributions for success and also their expectations of future success. Although the subjects increased their tendency to expect success as they completed successful experiences, there was a greater expectation of success for subjects who made a stable rather than an unstable attribution. This observation was true regardless of whether subjects attributed success to an internal factor or to an external one. The subjects who exhibited an internal or external stable attribution and the subjects who displayed an internal or external unstable attribution had equal expectations of success. Apparently, the stability of our attribution—not the internality or externality of attribution—determines our expectation of future success.

Causal Attributions and Behavior   Heider's theory also assumes that our attributions for past experiences determine our behavior. Meyer's (1970) study illustrates how our specific attributions influence behavior. Meyer's subjects experienced a series of five consecutive failures on a digit-symbol substitution. Failure was instituted by stopping every trial before each subject had completed the task. After each trial, Meyer assessed the subjects' causal attribution for failure and found that those subjects who had attributed their failure either to lack of ability or to a difficult task showed a decline in performance on each subsequent trial. In contrast, those subjects who believed that either lack of effort or bad luck caused their failure increased the intensity of their behavior on following trials. Meyer's results demonstrate that our causal attributions determine our subsequent behavior.

Attributions for success also affect the intensity of behavior. Although the locus-of-control dimension may not influence our expectation of future success, it does influence the strength of our behavior. We will work harder when we attribute success to an internal rather than external factor. Breit's (1969) study illustrates this effect. Breit's subjects each composed an essay and then attributed the success of completing it either to an internal or to an external factor. Breit reported that subsequent performance was greater for those subjects who had made an internal attribution rather than an external attribution for their success in completing the essay. Breit's study again shows that our causal attributions determine our future actions.

Covariation Estimates and Animal Behavior   Although no conclusive evidence documents the view that contingency judgments affect the instrumental activity of animals, a number of studies provide strong evidence suggesting that animals' instrumental behavior is affected by their view of the covariation between events. Recall our discussion of the influence of predictiveness on discrimination learning in Chapter 5. We learned that the predictive value of the S^D and S^{Δ} affects an animal's instrumental behavior. Since the predictiveness of a stimulus refers to the level of covariation between a stimulus and outcome, the importance of predictive value on discrimination learning suggests that the degree of covariance of the S^D and S^{Δ} with reward and nonreward determines an animal's performance on a discrimination task.

Covariance information is also used by animals to determine the foods they eat or avoid. Remember from Chapter 2 that the level of covariation between a specific flavor and illness is a significant determinant of whether an animal will avoid consuming a specific flavored substance. Recall the study of Klein, Davis, Cohen, and Weston (1984) in our discussion of problems with the Rescorla-Wagner model. In that study, rats experienced a nonsalient strawberry flavor and a different, more salient flavor prior to illness on each of the first four conditioning trials. This treatment resulted in a strong aversion to the strawberry flavor, which, although nonsalient, was correlated 100 percent with illness. In contrast, no aversion developed to the salient lemon flavor, which was paired with illness on the fourth conditioning trial but was correlated with illness only 25 percent of the trials. These observations provide strong evidence that animals are sensitive to covariation information and that this covariation information influences which flavor they will consume or avoid. This research also provides another example of animals using covariation information in determining their instrumental behavior.

How is covariation of stimuli, behavior, and outcomes determined? The research of Harold Kelley suggests that people use definite rules to make causal inferences. We will examine this decision process next.

Aspect 3: The Decision Process   Kelley (1967, 1973) suggests that three questions must be answered before we can formulate an accurate causal attribution. These answers tell us to which factors we attribute our successes or failures.

Distinctiveness   One question we ask following an event concerns the distinctiveness of our experiences: Is our success (or failure) unique to this setting or has it occurred in many situations? According to Kelley, we are more likely to attribute an experience to an external factor if we believe that this experience is unique than if we think that this event has happened in many settings.

Consider the following example. You enjoyed yourself at a dance. To what factor do you attribute your enjoyment? If this is the first social gathering you have enjoyed, you probably will believe that the setting (an external factor such as meeting someone to whom you are attracted) produced your enjoyment. However, if you enjoy all social gatherings, you probably attribute your enjoyment to an internal factor; you might believe that you always exert the amount of effort needed to have a good time.

Consensus We also ask about the experiences of others: Have others had a similar experience, or are we the only ones who have succeeded (or failed) at a certain task? Kelley suggests that we are more likely to attribute an experience to an external factor if we believe that others have also succeeded or failed (high consensus) at this task than if we know that we are the only ones who have encountered this experience (low consensus).

Recall our dance example. If you realize that others also enjoyed the dance, you are then apt to consider the situation, such as an exceptional band, responsible for your enjoyment, and thus you attribute your enjoyment to the excellent band. Yet, if you know that you alone had a good time, an internal factor seems the logical causal agent. Perhaps you tried harder than others to enjoy the dance.

Consistency We also ask whether we typically succeed or fail in similar settings. Consistency information allows us to determine the stability of the factor to which we attribute our experiences.

Think again about the example of enjoying a dance. If we enjoy most dances, we are likely to believe that a stable factor caused our enjoyment. We might feel that we have effective social skills (an internal, stable factor) which enable us to enjoy dances consistently. Yet, we will attribute our pleasure to an unstable factor if our enjoyment is inconsistent. Perhaps we do not always exert the effort necessary to have a good time at dances.

Empirical Support Considerable evidence validates Kelley's view of the attribution process. We will briefly examine one key study demonstrating this support (see Weiner, 1980, for a review of this literature).

McArthur (1972) tested the validity of Kelley's decision-rule system for making causal attributions. McArthur presented subjects with various situations; "John laughed at the comedian" is an example in which John's laughter could reflect his enjoyment of the situation. McArthur also gave subjects descriptions of the person's behavior (in this case, John's behavior) in order for the subjects to indicate either the degree of distinctiveness, consensus, or consistency of the person's response to the situation. Table 6.1 presents the high and low distinctiveness, consensus, and consistency items of the "John laughed at the comedian" example. After receiving these data, McArthur asked all the subjects to pick from four alternatives the perceived cause of the person's reaction to the situation (see Table 6.2). McArthur found that subjects who received the low distinctiveness, low consensus, and high consistency information chose a personal causal attribution (alternative 1). Thus, the subjects believed that an internal factor was responsible for John's enjoyment when (1) no one but John laughed at the comedian, (2) when John typically laughed at most comedians, and (3) when John almost always laughed at this comedian. Subjects who had received the high distinctiveness, high consensus,

TABLE 6.1
EXAMPLES OF CONSENSUS, DISTINCTIVENESS, AND CONSISTENCY ITEMS

Consensus information took the form:
  a. Almost everyone who hears the comedian laughs at him (high consensus).
or b. Hardly anyone who hears the comedian laughs at him (low consensus).
  Distinctiveness information took the form:
  a. John does not laugh at almost any other comedian (high distinctiveness).
or b. John also laughs at almost every other comedian (low distinctiveness).
  Consistency information took the form:
  a. In the past John has almost always laughed at the same comedian (high consistency).
or b. In the past John has almost never laughed at the same comedian (low consistency).

Source: McArthur, L. A. The how of what and why: Some determinants of consequences of causal attributions. *Journal of Personality and Social Psychology*, 1972, 22, 171–193. Copyright 1972 by the American Psychological Association. Reprinted by permission.

and high consistency information picked an external causal attribution (alternative 2). These subjects believed an environmental factor responsible for John's enjoyment when (1) everyone laughed at the comedian, (2) when John did not usually laugh at other comedians, and (3) when John almost always laughed at this comedian. Finally, subjects who received high distinctiveness and low consistency data chose an unstable attribution (alternative 3). Therefore, these subjects assumed that an external, unstable factor caused John's enjoyment when he laughed at this comedian only some of the time. Orvis, Cunningham, and Kelley (1975) found a similar influence of distinctiveness, consensus, and consistency information on the specific causal attributions that we make for our experiences.

An Animal's Covariation Decision Animals appear to use environmental information in determining the perceived level of covariation between events. Evidence of this decision making can be seen in Chapter 2 in our discussion of the influence of surprise on conditioning. Conditioned responses develop to environmental events when an animal is surprised by the occurrence of a biologically significant event, such as electric shock. This observation suggests that animals "know" when events should occur; that is, they have an idea of

TABLE 6.2
FOUR ALTERNATIVE CAUSAL ATTRIBUTIONS

a. Something about the person (John) probably caused him to make response X (laugh) to stimulus X (the comedian).
b. Something about stimulus X probably caused the person to make response X to it.
c. Something about the particular circumstances probably caused the person to make response X to stimulus X.
d. Some combination of a, b, and c above probably caused the person to make response X to stimulus X.

Source: McArthur, L. A. The how of what and why: Some determinants of consequences of causal attributions. *Journal of Personality and Social Psychology*, 1972, 22, 171–193. Copyright 1972 by the American Psychological Association. Reprinted by permission.

the covariation level between events. When this idea is challenged by an unexpected event, animals will alter their view of the contingency between events and come to expect that event under prevailing conditions.

Additional support for the view that animals have rules for determining the covariation between events can be seen in the research documenting the importance of the relative predictiveness of events. Recall the discussion of the Wagner, Logan, Haberlandt, and Price (1968) study in Chapter 5. A light S^D produced more control of responding when it was more predictive of reward availability than other discriminative stimuli than when the light cue had less predictiveness than other discriminative stimuli, even though in both instances the light cue was paired with reward on 50 percent of the trials. Thus animals are sensitive to the contingency between all stimuli paired with an event and judge the significance of a particular stimuli not only by its level of covariation with a specific outcome but also by the covariation of other stimuli with that outcome.

A similar influence of the relative predictiveness of events was noted in the Klein, Davis, Cohen, and Weston (1984) article described in Chapter 2. In that study, animals developed a strong aversion to a nonsalient strawberry flavor when that flavor was more predictive of illness than were more salient flavors. The strength of the aversion to the nonsalient strawberry flavor was not entirely determined by the number of strawberry-illness pairings, since a control group of animals receiving the same number of pairings of strawberry and illness developed only a weak aversion to the strawberry flavor. Apparently, the significance of a correlation between a stimulus and outcome depends not only on the absolute level of covariation between events but also on the relative comparison of covariation levels. People use information concerning the consistency, consensus, and distinctiveness of events in determining causal attributions; animals also appear to use environmental data in determining the perceived level of covariation of events.

Our discussion has suggested that covariation estimates are made in a rational manner; that is, an animal or person assesses the situation and makes an accurate estimate of the level of covariation between events. Unfortunately, the decision-making process is not always accurate, and bias may determine the perceived covariation level. This bias reflects the influence of experience, which causes an animal or person to come into a situation with a preconceived idea of the contingency between events and, thereby, ignore environmental circumstance.

Aspect 4: A Biased View of the World

Actor-Observer Bias   One frequently investigated bias concerns how we compare the causes of our experiences with those which we feel determine the experiences of others. Jones and Nisbett (1972) suggest that, on one hand, we are apt to attribute the causes of our experiences to the environment; on the other hand, we are likely to make personal attributions concerning others' experiences. For example, a child who has hit a peer probably attributes the behavior to the peer's actions. However, the victim's parents might attribute this behavior to the child's hostility. Our situational attribution can be self-serving, as this child's attribution was meant to maintain self-esteem.

The Nisbett, Caputo, Legant, and Maracek (1973) study demonstrates the difference between our causal attribution of our own experiences (called *actor* attributions) and those of other people (called *observer* attributions). These psychologists asked their male college students to indicate why they and their friends chose their majors and their girlfriends. Nisbett, Caputo, Legant, and Maracek discovered that for their own choices their subjects placed greater importance on external reasons than on internal causes. For example, some students believed that luck rather than their own actions was responsible for the selection of a girlfriend. But in assessing their friends' choice of girl-friends and majors, they believed their friends' personal qualities to be more important.

Jones and Nisbett (1972) suggested that attentional processes are probably responsible for different actor and observer attributions. Since we cannot see our own actions, we find it difficult to appreciate the importance which our behavior has on our experiences. In addition, since we direct our attention toward the environment, it is easy to stress the importance of situational deter-minants for our experiences. Viewing other people's experiences causes us to focus our attention on those people and thus to ignore the situation influencing them. According to this view, our attention produces causal attributions that are personal rather than situational for the experiences of other people.

Studies by McArthur and Post (1977) document the important role which attention plays in our causal attributions. Each subject in McArthur and Post's studies listened to a conversation between two men and then indicated per-ceived causes of the men's behavior during the conversation. In one study, one of the men sat under a bright light; in a second study, one of the men sat in a rocking chair. According to the attentional view, these treatments should cause each subject to focus attention on one of the men and thus to perceive his behavior as governed by internal factors to a greater extent than that of the other man (to whom the subjects would not attend). The results were as pre-dicted: the subjects felt that personality (an internal factor) played a greater part in the conversation of the man on whom their attentions had been focused.

Other Attributional Biases Although the actor-observer bias has fre-quently been reported in psychological literature, some studies (see Monson & Snyder, 1977, for a literature review) have found an opposite result: Some experiments indicate that we more frequently attribute internal causes to our experiences than to those of other people. Internal causal attributions for our experiences appear to reflect our typical attributions in achievement tasks (see Weiner, 1980). In these achievement settings, we usually attribute our suc-cesses and failures to our ability and/or effort. Perhaps our educational experi-ences lead many of us to focus on the internal determinants of success and failure, whereas most people may not have had similar interpersonal experiences. Future research will undoubtedly clarify the conditions producing a particular attributional bias.

Generalized Attributions As discussed earlier in the chapter, people often base their expectation of present success or failure on past expectations; we referred to this as a generalized expectation. An *attributional bias* is similar to a generalized expectancy in that a past attribution for success or failure is used to make a current attribution. As a result of the use of a past attribution, the individual ignores present conditions and may not attribute success or failure to the actual cause. The failure to attribute success or failure to the actual cause may result in the development of an inaccurate expectation of the future which, in turn, may cause inappropriate behavior.

We also discovered earlier in the chapter that some people generalize a single type of expectation to all situations; that is, internals always expect to be in control, while externals do not expect to have any control over their environment. Martin Seligman and his associates (see Abramson, Seligman, & Teasdale, 1978) noted a similar attributional bias. Everyone has a unique *attributional style*, or way in which he or she forms an attribution. Some people make attributions specific to the task they experience; that is, they treat each task differently and form an attribution for success or failure based on the prevailing environmental conditions. Other people generalize their attributions by assuming that the same cause determines success or failure in all situations. As we will discover shortly, the behavior pathology of depression can result from an attributional bias or style which causes the same attributions to be made in all situations.

How do some people ignore environmental circumstance and make a causal attribution based totally on preconceived beliefs? These individuals seem to ignore information discrepant from their preconceived beliefs and will, in fact, mistakenly recall the presence of situational data which provide support for their causal attribution based on their attributional style (see Metalsky & Abramson, 1981, for a discussion of the perceptual basis of biased attributions).

Two important points need mentioning here. First, several psychologists (Nisbett & Wilson, 1977) have pointed out that people do not always seem to be aware of the cognitive processes underlying their behavior. Thus, the perceived cause of behavior and actual behavior often don't correspond. For example, Nisbett and Wilson reported that consumers are unaware that the location of an item on a rack or shelf influences whether they choose the item. In one of the studies reported in Nisbett and Wilson's article, female subjects were to choose among several pairs of nylons: 80 percent of the subjects chose the pair on the right, but none of the subjects mentioned location as a factor determining their decision. Social psychologists (Worchel & Cooper, 1983) do not assume that these observations indicate that cognitive processes do not determine people's actions. Instead, they suggest that we act as if cognitions influence our behavior but are not consciously aware of the operation of the cognitive processes. Second, although cognitive processes often affect how we act, occasionally our behavior is governed by noncognitive processes. Our discussion of discrimination learning in Chapter 5 noted that some processing of information is controlled by attention, and other information is processed in an automatic or nonattentive fashion. Apparently sometimes behavior can be controlled by cognitive processes, yet at other times noncognitive processes control behavior. We will describe further evidence of this view later in the chapter during our discussion of depression and phobias.

Bias in Animal Decision Making   Animal behavior is sensitive to the contingency between stimuli, behavior, and outcomes, but preestablished covariance estimates do influence an animal's reactions to environmental events. Two lines of evidence point to a bias in an animal's perceived covariance between events. First, although the predictiveness of a stimulus does influence an animal's reaction to that stimulus, early experience with a specific stimulus' predictiveness will reduce the animal's sensitivity to changes in the level of covariation between that stimulus and the occurrence of a particular event. In support of this view, a number of studies (Benedict & Ayres, 1972; Keller, Ayres, & Mahoney, 1977; Kremer, 1971, 1974; Kremer & Kamin, 1971) have reported that experience with a CS correlated with a UCS impairs the acquisition of the estimate that the CS and UCS do not covary. The UCS-preexposure effect provides additional evidence that preconceived covariation estimates can bias an animal's response to current contingencies (see LoLordo, 1979, for a review of this literature). In these studies, preexposure to the UCS impairs the development of a CS subsequently paired with the UCS. Mikulka, Leard, and Klein (1977) suggest that the animal develops an expectation that the UCS is uncorrelated with a specific environmental event and that this preconceived belief impairs the animal from developing a covariance association between the CS and UCS. Preexposure to the CS also impairs the association of a CS and UCS. Mackintosh (1973) suggests that when an animal is exposed to a CS uncorrelated with a specific UCS, it learns that the CS is irrelevant; once an animal develops an expectation of learned irrelevance, it is very difficult for the animal to develop the idea that a CS and UCS covary.

Second, an animal's prior experience with the contingency between one stimulus and a specific outcome can affect the animal's estimate of covariance between a second stimulus and the event. The blocking literature described in Chapter 2 shows that if one stimulus is associated with a UCS, the subsequent combination of the first stimulus, a second stimulus, and the UCS results in the failure of a CS to develop to the second stimulus.

Why does blocking occur? According to Kamin (1969), animals are surprised when they experience the first cue presented with the biologically significant event. Surprise causes them to associate the first cue with the important event. In the framework of this chapter, surprise leads to the acquisition of a covariance expectancy. After conditioning, encountering the first cue causes no surprise; the animals expect the biologically significant event to follow when both the first and second cues are paired with the biologically important event. The second cue is experienced when the animal is not surprised, and, therefore, the second cue does not develop the ability to influence behavior. In terms of covariance of events, no perceived covariance between the second cue and the biologically significant event develops, since surprise does not occur when the second cue and the biologically significant event are paired in the blocking paradigm. The literature described in Chapter 2 supports the idea that blocking occurs because of an absence of surprise caused by the presence of the first cue (refer to Chapter 2 for a review of the blocking literature or to Mackintosh, 1983, for a discussion of the role of surprise in blocking). In terms of the covariance analysis, blocking occurs because a preconceived covariance estimate of the relationship between the first cue and the biologically significant event biases or prevents the development of a perceived covariance between the second cue and the biologically significant event.

We have discussed the idea that animals and people can develop estimates of the covariance of stimuli, behavior, and events as the result of experience. Animals and people can also learn that events do not covary; as we will discover in the next section, the expectation that events are unrelated can lead to the behavior pathology of depression. We will discuss depression at length: it represents an area where an extensive amount of research has shown that cognitions developed through experience affect instrumental behavior.

A LACK OF COVARIATION: A COGNITIVE VIEW OF DEPRESSION

Martin Seligman (1975) described depression as the "common cold of psychopathology." No one is immune to the sense of despair indicative of depression; each of us has become depressed following a disappointment or failure. For most, this unhappiness quickly wanes and normal activity resumes. For others, the feelings of sadness characteristic of depression last for a long time and impair the ability to interact effectively with the environment.

Why do people become depressed? According to Seligman, depression is learned and occurs when individuals assume that their failures are due to uncontrollable events and that they expect to continue to fail as long as these events are beyond their control: Depression develops because these persons believe that they are helpless to control their own destiny. Seligman's learned helplessness theory outlines the basis for his view of depression.

Learned Helplessness Theory

Imagine that none of the medical schools to which you applied admitted you. Since your dream since childhood has been to be a physician, you certainly would feel distressed for a while. If you are like most who are at first rejected, you might decide to enroll in some additional courses, study harder, and apply again. Or you could search for an alternative future occupation. However, these rejections might cause you to become severely depressed. According to Seligman, if this last alternative is your fate, self-depreciation did not cause your depression; you probably believe that you are very capable of succeeding in medical school. Seligman proposed that depression emerges when you think that failure is inevitable. Thus, you became depressed because you felt that there was nothing that you could do to erase the rejection, and you expected your reapplication to be rejected. You based your expectation of future rejection from medical school on your assumption that no matter how well you perform in school, you will be rejected. Depression, according to Seligman, is produced when individuals learn that events are independent of their behavior. Seligman labeled the expectation that events are uncontrollable *learned helplessness*. (In terms of the covariance analysis, learned helplessness represents a perceived lack of covariance between *any* behavior and a specific outcome.)

Original Animal Research　Seligman developed his learned helplessness theory of depression from his animal studies (see Maier & Seligman, 1976, for a review of this literature). The original studies (Overmier & Seligman, 1967; Seligman & Maier, 1967) used dogs as subjects. Some of these dogs were strapped in hammocks and then exposed to a series of sixty-four intense inescapable shocks. Other dogs in a second group received a series of sixty-four escapable shocks; their shock terminated when they pressed a panel with their heads. The amount of shock received by dogs in both the inescapable and escapable condition was equal: The shock ended for the dogs which received inescapable shock when the dogs in the escapable treatment successfully terminated their shock. A third group of dogs did not receive any shock during the initial stage of these studies. The experimenters placed each of the dogs in the three groups into a shuttle box twenty-four hours after the first stage. In the shuttle box, each dog received ten trials of signaled escape-avoidance training (see Chapter 2). Once the CS was presented, each dog had 10 seconds to jump over the hurdle to avoid shock. At the end of the 10-second interval, the shock was presented and the dogs could terminate (escape) the shock by jumping the hurdle. The shock remained on for 50 seconds or until the dog escaped. The experimenters reported that two-thirds of the animals which 24 hours earlier had received inescapable shocks did not learn either to escape or to avoid the intense electrical shock in the shuttle box (refer to Figure 6.5). The dogs appeared helpless: They sat in the box and endured the intense shock for the entire 50-second interval. A few of these helpless dogs occasionally jumped the hurdle and either escaped or avoided shock. However, these dogs again acted helpless on the next trial; apparently, they did not benefit from their successful experiences. In contrast, the dogs which had been given either escapable shock or no shock in the earlier phase quickly escaped shock during their initial trials in the shuttle box, and in their later trials they learned to respond to the signal and thereby avoid shock.

A wide range of animal species is susceptible to the negative impact of uncontrollable experiences. Psychologists have observed the helplessness phenomenon in cats (Seward & Humphrey, 1967; Thomas & DeWald, 1977), fish (Frumkin & Brookshire, 1969; Padilla, 1973), rats (Baker, 1976; Jackson, Alexander, & Maier, 1980; Jackson, Maier, & Rapaport, 1979; Seligman, Rosellini,

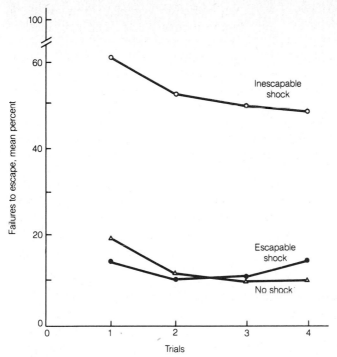

FIGURE 6.5
Percentage of trials on which dogs failed to escape shock in
the shuttle box after receiving escapable shock, inescapable
shock, or no shock in a harness. From Seligman, M. E. P., &
Maier, S. F. Failure to escape traumatic shock. *Journal of
Experimental Psychology,* 1967, *74,* 1–9. Copyright 1967 by
the American Psychological Association. Reprinted by
permission.

& Kozak, 1975), and humans (Fosco & Geer, 1971; Glass & Singer, 1972;
Hiroto, 1974; Hiroto & Seligman, 1975; Klein & Seligman, 1976; Miller &
Seligman, 1975; Rodin, 1976; Roth & Kubal, 1975). Although the human studies have demonstrated the aversive influence of uncontrollable experiences, the
effects are small when compared to those found in lower animals. These results
are not surprising; the aversive stimuli used are considerably less unpleasant in
the human than in the nonhuman studies. Exposing individuals to a treatment
sufficiently intense to induce helplessness is unethical. Thus, human experiments in this area are primarily intended to demonstrate a similar directional
influence of uncontrollable experiences in humans and lower animals.

Helplessness in Human Subjects   Hiroto's (1974) experiment with human
subjects provides a good duplication of the original helplessness studies with
dogs. Hiroto also employed the three-group design of the dog experiments.

Let's briefly examine Hiroto's study to illustrate the influence of uncontrollable experiences on human subjects. College students who volunteered to participate were assigned to one of three treatment groups. Some could terminate an unpleasant noise by pushing a button four times. Although subjects in the uncontrollable group were told that their correct response would end the noise, there was actually no response with which they could terminate the noise. Parallel to the animal studies, the noise ended (uncontrollable-condition subjects) when a comparable (controllable-condition) subject in the escapable treatment successfully terminated the noise. A third group of subjects did not receive either of these noise treatments during the first stage of the study. Following the initial part of the study, Hiroto trained all subjects to avoid or escape noise in a finger shuttle box. The noise ended when subjects moved their finger from one side of the shuttle box to the other. Hiroto reported that subjects in the uncontrollable-noise condition failed to learn either to escape or avoid the noise in the shuttle box and listened passively until the noise terminated at the end of a trial. In contrast, the group which received the controllable noise, as well as the group which was not given any initial trials, quickly learned to escape and then to avoid noise in the shuttle box. Apparently, uncontrollable experiences produce a similar negative effect on learning in both humans and lower animals.

Characteristics of Helplessness   Seligman (1975) proposed that exposure to uncontrollable events produces helplessness because of the development of an expectation that these events are independent of behavior. Once animals or humans acquire the belief that they cannot influence the occurrence of aversive events, helplessness ensues. Thus, the behavioral symptoms characteristic of helplessness are caused, according to Seligman, by the expectation of lack of control (or a perceived lack of covariation between all behavior and a specific outcome). In Seligman's view, there are three major behavior components of helplessness: (1) *motivational deficits,* (2) *cognitive deficits,* and (3) *emotional disturbance.*

Motivational Impairments   After the establishment of helplessness, animals or humans are unable to initiate voluntary behavior. The passivity of dogs or humans following uncontrollable events is thought to reflect an inability to initiate instrumental behavior. Many different behaviors appear susceptible to the influence of uncontrollable events. For example, Braud, Wepman, and Russo (1969) observed that mice exposed to uncontrollable shock later were significantly slower to escape from a water maze than were mice receiving controllable shock. Rosellini and Seligman (1975) found that rats which had previously received inescapable shock did not escape from a frustrating experience; these rats sat passively in a situation formerly associated with reward. In contrast, rats which had received either escapable shock or no shock readily learned to escape from the frustrating situation.

Hiroto and Seligman's (1975) study readily exhibits the nonspecific character of helplessness. Human subjects received uncontrollable experiences in either a cognitive task (insoluble problems) or an instrumental task (inescapable noise). Hiroto and Seligman evaluated the effect of these uncontrollable events by using either a cognitive task (unscrambling anagrams) or an instrumental task (finger–shuttle box). Results indicated that poorer performance followed uncontrollable rather than controllable events; this effect was found regardless of the nature of the uncontrollable events or the type of test situation. In addition, Hiroto and Seligman found that the uncontrollable experience and test situation did not need to be similar. For example, subjects who received uncontrollable experience in a cognitive task (insoluble problems) performed an instrumental task (anagram problems) more poorly than did subjects exposed to solvable problems.

Intellectual Impairments Cognitive deficits also characterize helplessness. The creation of the expectation that an animal has no control over environmental events renders this animal incapable of benefitting from future experiences. When animals or humans do not expect their lack of control to change, successful experiences fail to influence subsequent behavior. Overmier and Seligman (1967) and Seligman and Maier (1967) reported that their helpless dogs occasionally jumped over the hurdle and either escaped or avoided the electric shock. Despite this successful experience, these dogs did not change their behavior on subsequent trials; instead, they remained on the shock side of the shuttle box on the next trial. However, dogs in the escapable or no-shock condition learned from success: After a successful avoidance response they were more likely to respond correctly on the next trial. In addition, normal dogs changed their ineffective behavior; helpless dogs continued not to respond even though they had received punishment on each trial.

The Miller and Seligman (1975) study shows (1) a similar failure to change behavior in human subjects who were previously exposed to uncontrollable events and (2) that the reason for this failure is that the individual expects future events to be uncontrollable. The first phase of this study exposed college students to a series of escapable, inescapable, or no noise treatments. The experimenters then required all subjects to sort fifteen cards into ten categories within 15 seconds and told them that the rapidity of sorting depended on their skill. In reality, the experimenters controlled the subjects' success or failure on the sorting task; all subjects succeeded on 50 percent of the trials and failed on 50 percent of them. The experimenters determined success or failure by controlling the length of each trial so that the subjects experienced a predetermined sequence of successes and failures. They asked all subjects at the end of each trial to rate (on a scale of 0 to 10) their expectation of their success on the next trial. Miller and Seligman discovered that subjects who received the inescapable noise treatment showed little expectancy change after either success or failure; these subjects did not believe that their behavior influenced future events. In contrast, the subjects who were given either the escapable or no noise treatments displayed large expectancy changes after each trial; a successful trial increased their expectation of future success and failure on a trial decreased it. Apparently, our expectations of future events depend on our belief that we control present and past experiences. And it is the perceived ability to control events that is important, since none of Miller and Seligman's subjects in reality controlled the likelihood of success and failure.

Emotional Trauma The expectation that events are uncontrollable, according to Seligman (1975), produces emotional disturbance. Animals exposed to uncontrollable events are obviously experiencing a traumatic emotional state. For example, the dogs in the original helplessness studies sat in a corner of the shuttle box and whined until the shock ended. Human helplessness studies show a similar emotional response. For example, Roth and Kubal (1975) administered questionnaires to their human subjects following uncontrollable experiences and reported increases in feelings of helplessness, incompetence, frustration, and depression. In addition, Gatchel and Proctor (1976) found that helplessness training lowered electrodermal activity; this lowered activity is thought to be correlated with lowered motivational level (Malmo, 1965) and occurs with clinical depression (McCarron, 1973).

Similarities of Helplessness and Depression The importance of the learned helplessness phenomenon lies in its proposed relation to the clinical disorder of depression. Although a direct causal test cannot be ethically conducted, the correlational evidence supports Seligman's statement that the expectation of an inability to control events produces human depression. These comparisons show that depressed people display the cognitive characteristics of learned helplessness.

Animals and humans exposed to uncontrollable events exhibit motivational deficits. For example, college students who had previously received uncontrollable noise failed to learn to escape noise in the finger shuttle box (Hiroto, 1974). Klein and Seligman's (1976) depressed subjects similarly failed to escape noise in the shuttle box (see Figure 6.6). Their studies contained four groups of subjects: One group was classified as depressed according to the Beck Depression Inventory, and the other three groups contained nondepressed subjects. Klein and Seligman exposed one group of nondepressed subjects to uncontrollable noise—a procedure which produces helplessness. The second nondepressed group received escapable noise; the last nondepressed group and the depressed group received no noise treatment. The study's results indicated that the nondepressed subjects who were exposed to inescapable noise (the helpless group) and the depressed subjects escaped more slowly than did nondepressed subjects who received either the escapable noise or no noise treatment. Evidently, these nondepressed individuals, as a result of uncontrollable laboratory experiences, behaved as did the clinically depressed persons. We should assume not that this treatment produced clinical depression but rather that both groups did not expect to be able to control laboratory noise. Depressives have a generalized expectation of no control; their failure to escape in the study merely reflects this generalized expectancy.

Our prior discussion indicates that subjects exposed to uncontrollable events do not benefit from their experiences: These subjects do not change their expectations of future success after experiencing either success or failure. De-

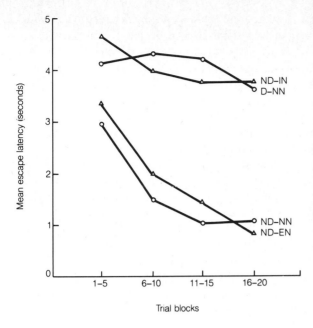

FIGURE 6.6
Escape latency to terminate noise for depressed subjects (on Beck Depression Inventory) who were not previously exposed to noise (group D-NN), for nondepressed subjects who were not previously exposed to noise (group ND-NN), for nondepressed subjects who were previously exposed to inescapable noise (group ND-IN), and for nondepressed subjects who were previously exposed to escapable noise (group ND-EN). From Klein, D. C., & Seligman, M. E. P. Reversal of performance deficits and perceptual deficits in learned helplessness and depression. *Journal of Abnormal Psychology*, 1976, *85*, 11–26. Copyright 1976 by the American Psychological Association. Reprinted by permission.

pressives show a similar failure to change their expectations after a successful experience (see Miller & Seligman, 1975). Miller and Seligman classified college students as either depressed or nondepressed and then exposed them to one of two tasks (refer to Figure 6.7). The first task, involving a test of skill, required the subjects to move a platform upward in an appropriate manner to

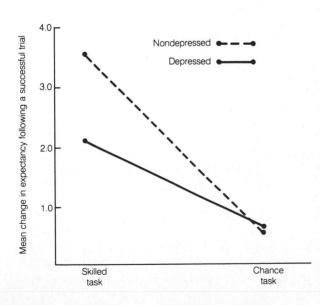

FIGURE 6.7
Average change in the expectation of future success in depressed and nondepressed subjects after success on either a skill task or a chance task. From Miller, W. R., & Seligman, M. E. P. Depression and the perception of reinforcement. *Journal of Abnormal Psychology*, 1973, *82*, 62–73. Copyright 1973 by the American Psychological Association. Reprinted by permission.

prevent a steel ball from falling. The second task, a game of chance, requested the subjects to guess which one of two slides would be presented on a given trial. Since the presentation of slides was random, success on this task was simply due to chance. All subjects estimated after each trial whether they expected to be successful on the next trial. Miller and Seligman reported that success in the skill task increased nondepressed subjects' expectation of future success, but depressed individuals showed significantly less expectancy change after having performed a successful skill task. Thus, the depressed subjects behaved as did individuals exposed to uncontrollable events: Neither changed their expectation of success very much after success. Why don't depressed and helpless subjects increase their expectation of success as much as nondepressed subjects do after a successful experience? The answer lies in the chance task behavior of both depressed and nondepressed subjects. After a successful trial on the chance task, neither depressed nor nondepressed subjects increased their expectation of future success. There was no reason to increase it, since all the subjects in this task knew that their success was due to chance and was therefore beyond their control. Depressed and helpless subjects, in Seligman's view, assumed that chance must be credited for any of their successful skill experiences, since they believed these events were uncontrollable.

Criticism of Learned Helplessness Approach   Seligman's original learned helplessness model generated interest in the role of cognitive processes involved in depression. However, his theory has encountered difficulties; it was too simplistic and did not precisely reflect the process which produces depression. Therefore, Seligman and his colleagues (Abramson, Garber, & Seligman, 1980; Abramson, Seligman, & Teasdale, 1978) revised the helplessness theory to provide a more accurate model of human depression.

Recall from the prior description of Seligman's original theory that human subjects, following exposure to uncontrollable events, did not change their future expectations in a skill task even after having success on a previous task. These results suggest that the helpless subjects believed that their success was due to chance. In contrast, the behavior of nonhelpless subjects who increased their expectation of future success after having succeeded indicates that they thought their behavior produced success. During the experiment, helpless subjects behaved as if skill tasks were chance tasks; however, when questioned after the experiment, both helpless and nonhelpless subjects described the situation as a skill task. The original helplessness model cannot explain why helpless subjects responded as if they had no control over events when they were aware that other people were able to control these same events.

A second problem with the original helplessness model is that some other studies have not observed performance deficits following uncontrollable experiences. In fact, several (Roth & Kubal, 1975; Tennen & Eller, 1977) have demonstrated improved subject performance after exposure to insoluble problems; their human subjects exposed to insoluble problems actually scored higher on subsequent tasks than did those who were exposed to solvable problems. This facilitation of subject performance after uncontrollable tasks is inconsistent with Seligman's original model of helplessness, which maintains that uncontrollable experiences should create expectations which impair—not improve—later behavior.

A third problem occurs when subjects generalize their expectation of no control to a dissimilar situation. This generalization is inappropriate because subjects have no reason to believe that all tasks are uncontrollable. Unfortunately, the original helplessness model does not explain why inappropriate generalizations appear during some circumstances but not others.

Rizley's study (1978, experiment 1) illustrates the final problem with Seligman's original helplessness theory. Rizley presented depressed and nondepressed subjects a series of fifty numbers (either 0 or 1) and then instructed the subjects to guess the next number. Although there was no pattern to the numbers, Rizley told his subjects that there were number-order trends and tendencies and that their score would be above chance if they were aware of them. The subjects were told after the presentation of fifty numbers whether they succeeded (passed the test) by scoring 26 or more or had failed by scoring 25 or less. (Since there were only two choices, a score of 25 meant chance-level performance.) The subjects then indicated the reason for their score from a list of several possibilities—luck, task difficulty, effort, or ability. Rizley's results demonstrated that depressed people attributed their success to the external factors of luck and task ease and their failure to internal factors of lack of effort and ability. In contrast, nondepressed people thought that internal factors accounted for their success, and that external factors caused their failure. Thus, depressives attribute their failure to internal processes, but they also feel helpless because they can do nothing to prevent future failures. Seligman's learned helplessness theory could not explain Rizley's observations. Fortunately, Seligman's attributional model of helplessness provides an answer to the problems inherent in the original learned helplessness theory.

An Attributional Model

Seligman (Abramson, Garber, & Seligman, 1980; Abramson, Seligman, & Teasdale, 1978) proposed that the attributions that people make for their failures determine whether they become depressed. Causal attributions of failure can be made on three dimensions: personal-universal (internal-external), global-specific, and stable-unstable. The combination of these three dimensions produces eight possible attributional outcomes. The specific attribution will determine if (1) depression occurs, (2) depression generalizes to other situations, and (3) the depression is temporary or permanent. In the examples presented in Table 6.3, if the woman attributes her rejection to an internal, stable, global factor (I'm unattractive to all men) she will become depressed. In contrast, the woman will not become depressed if she attributes rejection to an external, unstable, specific factor (he was in a rejecting mood). This attribu-

TABLE 6.3
THE ATTRIBUTIONAL MODEL OF DEPRESSION: A WOMAN REJECTED

| Dimension | Internal | | External | |
	Stable	Unstable	Stable	Unstable
Global	I'm unattractive to men.	My conversation sometimes bores men.	Men are overly competitive with intelligent women.	Men get into a rejecting mood.
Specific	I'm unattractive to him.	My conversation bores him.	He's overly competitive with women.	He was in a rejecting mood.

Note: The attribution of uncontrollability to internal causes produces personal helplessness, whereas an external causal attribution results in universal helplessness.

Source: Abramson, L. Y., Seligman, M. E. P., and Teasdale, J. D. Learned helplessness in humans: Critique and reformulation. *Journal of Abnormal Psychology*, 1978, *87*, 49–74. Copyright 1978 by the American Psychological Association. Reprinted by permission.

tional model, while certainly complex, gives us an accurate view of people's varied responses to uncontrollable experiences.

Personal versus Universal Helplessness   Consider the two following examples: (1) The economy is depressed, and the automobile industry's failure to sell enough cars forces several plants to close. An automobile worker loses her job and becomes depressed. (2) A 16-year-old who wants to play for the high school basketball team has diligently practiced summer and fall; he was not selected for the team and became depressed. In both examples, depression occurred, according to Seligman, because of each individual's perceived inability to control future events: The automobile worker could not get a job and the student could not be on the team. However, the helplessness of the automobile worker and student is quite different. The attributional model maintains two kinds of helplessness: personal and universal. The student's failure to be picked for the team is an example of *personal helplessness:* This student's inability caused failure, but other more competent students were selected for the team. *Universal helplessness* occurs when the environment is structured so that no one can control future events: The automobile worker could not control the economy; therefore, the lack of control is attributed to external forces. (In terms of the covariance analysis, personal helplessness results from depressives' perceived lack of covariance between their behavior and specific outcomes, while universal helplessness results from a perceived estimate that there is no covariance between any behavior and a specific outcome.)

Abramson (1977) ascertained from her experiments that both personal and universal helplessness produced the cognitions (expectation of future inability to control events) and motivational deficits (lack of ability to initiate voluntary behavior) which are both characteristic of depression. In addition, Abramson and Sackeim (1977) examined the attributions of depressed people and found that those who were personally depressed made internal attributions for failure, whereas those who were universally depressed made external attributions.

The nature of the helplessness determines whether loss of esteem appears. People who attribute their failure to external forces—universal helplessness—experience no loss of self-esteem, since they do not consider themselves responsible for their failure. However, the attribution of failure to internal factors—personal helplessness—produces loss of self-esteem; the incompetency of these individuals causes their failure. In support of this view, Abramson (1977) found that lowered self-esteem only occurs with personal helplessness.

Global versus Specific Causal Attributions   People who are exposed to uncontrollable events may not become depressed; their failure could be attributed to a *specific* situation, and helplessness would not occur in other circumstances. Or people could feel that their helplessness is *global,* will happen at other times, and become depressed. For instance, the automobile worker believes that a job does not exist in any other company and stops searching for a job. In contrast, the student attributing the failure to make the team to the coach could change schools and try again next year. Thus, the attribution of lack of control to global rather than to specific factors will produce helplessness which will generalize to new situations, but helplessness will be limited to a single situation if the attribution is specific.

Roth and Kubal's (1975) experiment supports the idea that global-specific attributions are important when determining whether people are helpless in new situations. First-year college students volunteered to participate in the Roth and Kubal study in two separate, very different experiments on the same day and in the same building. The first experiment was designed to fail all students. Subjects in one group (important condition) of this first experiment were told that the failed task was a "good predictor of college grades"; those in the other group (unimportant condition) were informed that they were participating in "an experiment in learning." Following the first experiment, all subjects proceeded to the second study. Since both groups experienced failure on the first experiment, the original helplessness model would predict that both groups would not perform well in the second study. However, the subjects who were told that the first experiment was a learning one did significantly better on the second experiment than did subjects who thought that the first experiment was a predictor of future success. According to the attributional model, the subjects in the important condition attributed their failure to a more global factor (absence of ability to succeed in college) than did subjects in the unimportant condition who attributed their failure to a single task. As a result, the helplessness generalized to the new situation for subjects in the important condition but not for the subjects in the unimportant treatment condition.

Stable versus Unstable Causal Attributions   Seligman proposed that a person's attribution of helplessness to a stable or unstable factor also influences the effect of uncontrollable experience on behavior. Ability is considered a stable factor; effort, an unstable one. If someone attributes failure in an uncontrollable experience to lack of effort, this attribution will increase this person's subsequent effort. However, attribution of failure to the stable factor of lack of ability will lead to helplessness, since people can change their effort but not their ability. As an example of this approach, consider what would happen if the high school student, rather than having attributed failure to lack of control, felt that not enough effort was exerted. Under this condition, failure might increase rather than decrease behavior. Thus, the facilitation which follows uncontrollable experiences in some studies probably results from the subjects' belief that increased effort leads to success. However, continued failure will eventually cause an expectation of no control over failure. A test of this view is found in Roth and Kubal's study (1975). Roth and Kubal gave their subjects one or two learned helplessness training tasks and found that those who received one task showed more motivation than control subjects but those who had two tasks exhibited helplessness. Similar results have been reported by other experimenters; see Brockner, Gardner, Bierman, Mahan, Thomas, Weiss, Winters, & Mitchell (1983) for another example.

The idea that stability or instability of the perceived cause influences helplessness also explains why depression is temporary under some situations and permanent under others. For example, with our automobile worker, the attribution to the external factor of the poor economy caused depression which will stay if the economy remains down. However, the depression will be temporary if the economy recovers (which is typical) and the worker gets a job. (If the economy improves but the worker fails to find employment, the worker may then attribute that failure to uncontrollable personal stable factors and continue to be depressed.)

Severity of Depression   Helplessness can apparently follow several different types of uncontrollable experiences. However, severe depression typically appears when individuals attribute their failure to internal, global, and stable factors. Their depression is intense because they perceive themselves as incompetent (internal attribution) in many situations (global attribution), and they believe that their incompetence is unlikely to change (stable attribution). In support of this notion, Hammen and Krantz (1976) found that depressed women attributed interpersonal failure (for example, being alone on a Friday night) to internal, global, and stable factors. In contrast, nondepressed women blamed their failure on external, specific, and unstable factors. Rizley (1978) observed a similar difference in causal attribution of failure on a cognitive task between depressed and nondepressed people.

Depressives' Attributional Style   Seligman's attributional model assumes that attributional style (perceived causes of events) influences the likelihood that a person will become depressed. To validate the attributional model, differences in attributional style between depressed and nondepressed people must be shown to be present prior to the onset of depression. Recent evidence by Seligman and his associates provides more direct support of the attributional model. Metalsky, Abramson, Seligman, Semmel, and Peterson (1982) found that knowledge of a person's attributional style enabled prediction of susceptibility to depression following failure. In their study the attributional style of college students was measured at the beginning of a semester. They discovered that those students who attributed past failures to internal, global, and stable factors were more likely to become depressed after earning a poor grade (in the student's view) on a midsemester exam than were students who had attributed their poor grade to external, specific, and unstable factors. Apparently, a person's attributional style influences the likelihood of becoming depressed when he or she fails.

Application: Cognitive Treatment of Depression   Aaron Beck (1976) developed a cognitive therapy which established rational expectations of future events in depressed people. The therapy consists of four phases: (1) *Patients become aware of their thoughts,* (2) *they learn to understand why these thoughts are inaccurate or distorted,* (3) *they replace these irrational perceptions with accurate, more objective cognitions,* and (4) *they test the validity of these cognitive beliefs.* Beck developed a twenty-hour standardized program of specific procedures for modifying depressives' cognitions. Among these procedures are distancing, decatastrophizing, and decentering. In *distancing,* patients must distinguish between a belief and a fact. Once patients recognize that their beliefs may not reflect reality, they can modify them. Patients learn to separate their experiences from those of others in *decentering.* For example, depressives must recognize that they will not lose their job because others do. *Decatastrophizing* enables patients who feel that the occurrence of certain events are catastrophic to recognize that the consequences of these events are not disastrous. In addition, in Beck's cognitive therapy, depressed people learn to substitute workable solutions for apparently insoluble problems and to identify the circumstances which produce failure. Patients are also required to test new ideas. For example, someone who has felt unable to present a speech but now feels capable is encouraged to discover the validity of the new cognition.

Beck's cognitive-restructuring therapy appears to represent a very effective treatment for depression. The Rush, Beck, Kovacs, and Hollon (1977) study demonstrates both the success of the cognitive approach when used with severely depressed individuals as well as its superiority to a tricyclic drug treatment. Their twelve-week cognitive and drug treatments revealed that although both procedures reduced depression, patients in the cognitive restructuring therapy showed greater improvement on self-ratings (the Beck Depression Inventory) and clinical ratings (the Hamilton Rating Scale). On the nonbiased blind clinical ratings, the cognitive treatment group achieved a 97 percent improvement compared with only 23 percent with the drug treatment. The cognitive treatment patients maintained their superiority to drug treatment subjects on both three-month and six-month follow-up evaluations. These results are quite impressive for several reasons. First, the cognitive treatment was compared against a recognized, effective drug treatment. The success of the drug therapy equalled previous clinical evaluations of tricyclic antidepressant therapy outcomes. Second, these therapists were not biased toward the cognitive treatment; in fact, they received their clinical training in the traditional forms of psychotherapy. Two additional results of this study need mentioning. Whereas only one of nineteen patients withdrew from the cognitive therapy, eight of twenty-two drug therapy individuals quit. The majority of these latter dropouts reported that their failure to respond to treatment was their reason for leaving therapy. These two therapies also differed in terms of how many patients required further treatment: 68 percent of the psychochemical therapy group resumed treatment for depression compared to only 16 percent of the cognitive therapy patients. McLean and Hakstein (1979) also found the cognitive therapy similarly superior.

Thus changes in the cognitive functioning are essential for a depressive's recovery. The high incidence of the return of depression following drug therapy may occur because the drug did not lead to permanent cognitive changes, and the helplessness expectations resumed control and depression returned when the drug treatment was discontinued.

Overview   Although our discussion indicates that cognitions influence the development of depressive behavior, it is important to recognize that other factors are involved in depression. Several lines of research suggest that a few factors either alone or in combination can produce depression.

Disturbances in the functioning of the brain's amine chemical transmitter systems (the catecholamines and indoleamines) are involved in people's depression. Numerous studies (see Depue & Evans, 1976) have shown that a deficiency in norepinephrine or serotonin correlates with depression, and an elevation of either reverses depression. Biochemical deficits can be caused by biological deficiencies or can be the result of experience. Jay Weiss and his associates (Weiss, Stone, & Harrell, 1970) have shown that exposing rats to uncontrollable events produced the biochemical and behavioral characteristics of depression. However, the biochemical changes are transient; that is, they are found twenty-four hours but not forty-eight hours after exposure to uncontrollable events. These changes in biochemical state are related to the occurrence of helplessness: Weiss, Stone, and Harrell found the presence of helplessness twenty-four hours after uncontrollable experiences. Furthermore, a number of studies (Sherman, Sacquitne, & Petty, 1982; Weiss, Glazer, & Pohorecky, 1976) reported that antidepressant drugs eliminated the learned helplessness effect in rats. Although these results indicate that biochemical changes are related to depression, physiological recovery does not automatically mean that feelings of helplessness will decline. The experience produced by helplessness may create psychological disturbances which will remain after an animal's or person's physiological recovery. In support of this view, Overmier and

Seligman (1967) found that their dogs, after receiving two experiences with uncontrollable events, were helpless even a month after the second experience.

Frustration appears to be involved in producing depression. Amsel's behavioral persistence model (1972) suggests that nonreward initially elicits frustration, anxiety, and hostility. These behaviors act to impair goal-oriented behavior. Continued nonreward results in the conditioning of disruptive behavior; these behaviors persist with repeated nonreward and become an animal's or human's repetitive response to frustrative nonreward. Levis (1976) proposed that behavioral persistence is responsible for the development of learned helplessness. According to Levis, animals or humans exposed to uncontrollable events experience a great deal of nonreward; this experience results in the development of persistent, disruptive, frustration-induced behaviors. When shifted to a controllable situation, the habitual disruptive activities prevent an animal or human from experiencing reward; this in turn results in nonreward continuing to be experienced. This nonreward experience acts to increase the level of arousal, thereby increasing the level of conditioning of the persistent, frustration-induced, disruptive activities. These persistent disruptive behaviors produce behavioral deficits characteristic of learned helplessness. A number of studies have reported that animals exposed to uncontrollable events develop fixed or stereotyped response patterns. This observation has been found in both rats (MacKinnon, 1968; Maier, Glazer, & Klee, 1940; Rashotte & Amsel, 1968; Ross, 1964) and humans (Deur & Parke, 1968; Linden, 1974; Marquart, 1948; Vogel-Sprott & Thurstone, 1968).

Although these studies do not provide direct evidence that behavioral persistence is involved in learned helplessness, Boyd's 1982 article provides direct support for that involvement. Some college students in Boyd's study received uncontrollable loud-noise presentations in the first phase of the study; other subjects were given either controllable loud-noise exposures or no treatment in the initial phase of the study. Half the subjects from each of these three groups received a problem-solving task in which correct responses were rewarded 100 percent of the time and other responses were never rewarded. Boyd reported the typical learned helplessness effect in these subjects: subjects given the uncontrollable problem-solving task learned more slowly than did those given controllable or no-treatment experience. The remaining half of the subjects were given a problem-solving task in which the correct response was rewarded 100 percent of the time and other responses were rewarded 50 percent of the time. If exposure to nonreward is causing the conditioning of persistent disruptive responses and leading to helplessness, the decrease in nonreward (since the disruptive responses are being rewarded 50 percent of the time) should reduce behavioral persistence and learned helplessness. However, if cognitions are mediating learned helplessness, rewarding other responses 50 percent of the time should increase the difficulty of the task and thereby increase the level of helplessness. Boyd found that this procedure (rewarding other responses 50 percent of the time) decreased the level of behavioral deficits, thus decreasing the amount of learned helplessness. Thus nonreward-induced disruptive responses play an important role in learned helplessness.

THE EXPECTATION OF ADVERSITY: A COGNITIVE VIEW OF PHOBIC BEHAVIOR

Everyone has some fears. In most cases, these fears are realistic and enable us to avoid adversity. For example, people are afraid to cross a street when cars are approaching; their fear motivates them to avoid walking in front of a car, thereby preventing them from being killed. However, some people's fears are unrealistic. These individuals have a *phobia,* a fear that was once appropriate (because an aversive event did occur) but is no longer realistic. This fear motivates avoidance behavior, which prevents learning that the phobia is unrealistic. In many situations, the original aversive event may not be readily apparent. An individual may have forgotten the unpleasant event, or the phobic response may have developed through higher-order conditioning or vicarious conditioning. The phobic response may result from stimulus generalization; for example, a child attacked by a peer generalizes this fear to all children. Research indicates that cognitive processes affect the development of phobias.

Bandura's Approach

A Phobic's Expectations   Recall our description of Marie's math phobia from the chapter's vignette. In 1977, Albert Bandura presented a cognitive theory of phobic behavior according to which two classes of expectations— outcome and efficacy—maintain Marie's phobia. Outcome expectations reflect the perceived consequences of either a behavior and/or an event. Marie expects a statistics class to be very aversive—a stimulus-outcome expectancy—and she believes that she cannot pass the course—a response-outcome expectancy. Also, Marie knows that she can prevent the aversive experience by not enrolling in the statistics course; this response-outcome expectancy motivates her phobic behavior.

Marie's phobia presents her with a dilemma typical of phobic situations. Although her phobic behavior enables her to avoid the course, her phobic actions have definite negative consequences. She realizes that she must pass this course to graduate, but her phobic behavior prevents her from obtaining her desired goal. Unfortunately, this outcome expectancy does not govern Marie's behavior, and she avoids the course even though she cannot graduate without it.

Bandura's theory suggests that a second type of expectancy is involved in motivating Marie's phobic behavior. According to Bandura's approach, Marie feels incapable of enduring the aversive experience. Bandura labeled this belief that one can or cannot execute a particular action an *efficacy expectation.* (Bandura's efficacy expectation is identical to Mischel's competency concept described earlier.) Marie's lack of self-efficacy has left her unable to register for the course.

The Importance of Our Experiences   What factors account for Marie's outcome and efficacy expectations? Marie's outcome expectation that she will fail the statistics course could have developed through direct personal experiences, through observations of the experiences of other people, or through information provided by others. Since Marie has not failed this course or any other course, her outcome expectations cannot reflect any direct personal experience. Probably Marie has observed others whom she perceived as similar to herself fail. In addition, she probably has received information from other people that the course is difficult and therefore feels that she will fail it.

Bandura (1977) suggested that we use four types of information to establish an efficacy expectation: (1) *Personal accomplishments indicate our degree of self-efficacy.* Successful experiences generally increase our mastery expectation, and failure usually decreases our sense of self-efficacy (Bandura, Jeffrey, & Gajdos, 1975). These authors discovered that the influence of success or failure on efficacy expectations depends on task difficulty, amount of effort expended, and the pattern and rate of success. We are more apt to feel competent if we usually succeed at a difficult task which requires considerable effort than if we succeed without trying. (2) *Our sense of self-efficacy is developed by observing the successes or failures of other people whom we perceive as similar to ourselves.* Seeing others successfully cope with perceived aversive events enhances our belief that we can also be effective, and observing others fail decreases our belief that we can cope with adversity. Several factors determine the effectiveness of a vicarious modeling experience. The success of the other person's behavior, or the model's behavior, must be clear; we cannot develop a sense of self-efficacy if the outcome of this other person's behavior is ambiguous (Kazdin, 1974a). Also, we acquire a stronger mastery expectation when we see several people rather than a single person cope with an aversive situation (see Bandura & Menlove, 1968; Kazdin, 1974b). Finally, Meichenbaum (1972) discovered that we develop greater self-efficacy when we see other people initially struggle with adversity and become effective slowly rather than the first time we see them succeed. (3) *We can be persuaded that we are capable of coping or unable to deal with adversity.* For example, Marie's family or her peers could attempt to convince her that she could pass the statistics course if she would try. To test the idea that verbal persuasion could alter expectancies, Lick and Bootzin (1975) suggested to their patients that they could successfully interact with a feared object. Unfortunately, they found little evidence of behavioral change with their use of verbal persuasion. Bandura (1977) proposed that the influence of verbal persuasion is short-lived unless personal experiences confirmed the altered expectancy change. (4) *Emotional arousal influences our sense of competence; we feel less able to cope with an aversive event when we are agitated or tense.* Although Bandura feels that emotional arousal plays a part in motivating phobic behavior, his view certainly differs from the drive approach outlined in Chapter 2. Bandura does not believe that fear directly causes avoidance behavior: He suggests that fear and defensive action are correlated but do not reflect a causal relationship. We are more likely to display avoidance behavior when we are afraid—but only because fear makes us feel less effective. However, since emotional arousal is only one source of information used when developing a sense of self-efficacy, other information may enable us to feel competent even though we are afraid. Under these conditions, we will interact with feared objects while we are still afraid because we perceive ourselves able to cope with adversity. Our emotional arousal extinguishes after we have interacted with an aversive event.

Bandura and Adam's (1977) study demonstrates how efficacy expectations play a role in phobic behavior. Snake-phobic patients received the systematic desensitization therapy described in Chapter 2. Bandura and Adams discovered that when patients no longer became emotionally disturbed by an imagined aversive scene, differences still existed in their ability to approach a snake. In contrast, the patients' self-efficacy expectation corresponded closely to their ability to interact with the snake: The greater the patients' perceived efficacy, the more able they were to inhibit phobic behavior and approach the snake (refer to Figure 6.8). This relation between self-efficacy and an absence of phobic behavior held true even after therapy when a new snake, different from the one used before the pretherapy and during desensitization training, was

FIGURE 6.8
Influence of desensitization therapy on the subject's level of self-efficacy and ability to approach a snake. The success of therapy on the posttest was evaluated using both the same snake used in therapy ("similar threat") and a different snake ("dissimilar threat"). From Bandura, A., & Adams, N. E. Analysis of self-efficacy theory of behavioral change. *Cognitive Therapy and Research*, 1977, *1*, 287–310.

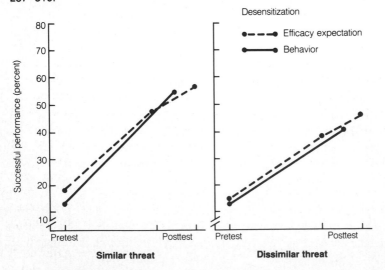

employed. These results demonstrate that if we believe ourselves competent, we will generalize our self-efficacy expectations to new situations.

Application: Modeling Treatments of Phobia

Our discussion points to the critical role of outcome and efficacy expectations in motivating phobic behavior. These expectations develop both through our experiences and through our observations of the experiences of other people. During the past twenty years, behavior therapists have employed models to interact with feared objects to treat phobic patients. The aim of this modeling treatment is to alter patients' phobic behavior by vicariously modifying their expectations.

Graduated Modeling In graduated-modeling therapy, patients see the model move closer and closer until the feared object is encountered. A study by Bandura, Grusec, and Menlove (1967) shows the effectiveness of modeling in treating phobic behavior. These psychologists allow children who feared dogs to watch a peer model interact with a dog. The children received eight 10-minute therapy sessions during a four-day period. At first, the children saw the model pat the dog while it was in a pen. During later observations, the children watched the model walk the dog around the room. In the final sessions, the model climbed into the pen and played with the dog. Other children did not see the model but saw only the dog, which occupied the pen for the first therapy session and was leashed in the last seven sessions. Bandura, Grusec, and Menlove assessed the effectiveness of modeling by determining if the phobic children could approach and play with either the dog seen in therapy sessions or a new dog. The results indicated that modeling reduced the children's phobic behavior and increased their interaction with the dog seen in the study or a new dog.

According to Bandura's approach, the success of modeling therapy must be attributed to the vicarious modifications of a patient's expectations. Support for this view is evident in a study by Bandura, Adams, and Beyer (1977). They exposed adult snake phobics to models interacting with a snake and assessed the influence of this modeling treatment on the subjects' approach response to the snake and their efficacy expectation (that is, their expectation of being able to interact fearlessly with the snake). Bandura, Adams, and Beyer found that this modeling treatment's degree of success corresponded to the increase in the phobics' self-efficacy expectation; the more the model's action altered the patient's efficacy expectation, the greater the patient's approach to the snake.

Participant Modeling In 1969, Bandura, Blanchard, and Ritter introduced a change in the modeling therapy which significantly enhanced its effectiveness. They suggested that the model (or therapist) encourage the patient to interact with the feared object in participant modeling. The model slowly moves nearer and nearer to a phobic object in a graduated modeling procedure. After each modeled behavior, the model (or therapist) asks the patient to imitate that action. During the imitation, the model (or therapist) either stands close to or is in direct physical contact with the patient. After the model (or therapist) has helped the patient interact with the feared object, the treatment's success is evaluated by having the patient encounter the feared object alone.

Bandura, Blanchard, and Ritter (1969) compared the efficacy of participant modeling with that of symbolic modeling and systematic desensitization in curing snake phobias. The symbolic-modeling-therapy patients saw a 35-minute film of children, adolescents, and adults with a snake. The desensitization treatment, identical to the procedure described in Chapter 2, employed a thirty-five-item hierarchy. Control subjects who did not receive formal therapy were assessed for their level of fear. Desensitization therapy continued until the patients could imagine the most feared item in the film without displaying any emotional response; participant-modeling therapy continued until patients could interact with their most feared item when the therapist was with them. The symbolic-modeling patients received as much modeling exposure as did patients in the participant-modeling treatment. Bandura, Blanchard, and Ritter found that while participant-modeling patients needed only 2 hours to reach the criterion, desensitization patients required 4.5 hours of therapy to imagine their most feared hierarchy item. In addition, 92 percent of the participant-modeling patients could interact alone with a snake compared to 33 percent of the symbolic-modeling patients, 25 percent of the systematic desensitization patients, and 0 percent of the control subjects. Thus symbolic-modeling and desensitization therapies are effective when compared with no treatment; both are much less effective than participant modeling. Other studies have also documented participant modeling's effectiveness in treating phobic behavior. For example, participant modeling has successfully treated phobia of heights (Ritter, 1969) and phobia of water-related activities (Hunziker, 1972).

What factors contribute to the rapid elimination of phobic behavior when participant modeling is used? Modeling provides a vicarious change in a patient's expectancies, and two processes probably account for the therapy's enhanced effectiveness when participation is also included: (1) A model (or therapist) provides patients with a sense of security. Many psychologists have realized that other people's presence can reduce the emotionality produced by aversive events (refer to Klein, 1982, for a discussion of the influence of other people on emotionality). Since Bandura's approach assumes that the emotionality level influences our efficacy expectations, the reduced arousal induced by a model's presence will increase a patient's perceived efficacy, thereby enhancing the interaction with a feared object. (2) A model's (or therapist's) encouragement places social pressure on a patient to encounter a feared object (see Klein, 1982, for a review of the social influence process). This personal experience enables patients to discover that they can interact with phobic objects without aversive consequences.

We suggested that participation alters a patient's efficacy expectations by increasing modeling therapy's effectiveness. The Bandura, Adams, and Beyer (1977) study supports this view. They discovered that the efficacy expectations of being able to fearlessly encounter a snake were higher with participant modeling than with modeling alone (refer to Figure 6.9). Furthermore, the higher the level of self-efficacy produced by participant modeling, the more able each patient was to approach the snake. Many clinical psychologists (Franks & Wilson, 1974) suggest that participant modeling represents one of the most powerful ways of altering phobic behavior. Clearly, its effectiveness lies in its ability to modify the phobics' cognitions.

An Alternative View

Not all psychologists have adopted Bandura's view of the role of anxiety in motivating avoidance behavior. Some psychologists (see Eysenck, 1978; Wolpe, 1978) have continued to advocate a drive-based view of avoidance behavior (see Chapter 4), suggesting that anxiety directly motivates avoidance

FIGURE 6.9
Influence of participant modeling, modeling, and control treatment on both the subjects' level of self-efficacy and their ability to approach a snake (Subjects' self-efficacy and avoidance behavior were measured before (pretest) and after (posttest) the treatments). Treatment effects evaluated on the posttest with the same snake used in therapy ("similar threat") and a new snake ("dissimilar threat"). From Bandura, A., Adams, N. E., & Beyer, J. Cognitive processes mediating behavioral change. *Journal of Personality and Social Psychology,* 1977, *35,* 125–129. Copyright 1977 by the American Psychological Association. Reprinted by permission.

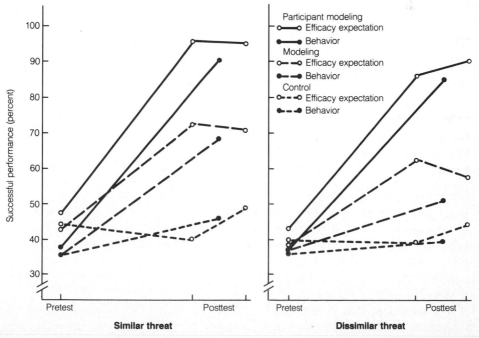

behavior. According to these psychologists, cognitions are elicited by anxiety but do not affect the occurrence of avoidance responding. Thus, Eysenck considers efficacy expectations to be merely "epiphenomenological" by-products of anxiety. Other psychologists (Borkovec, 1976, 1978; Lang, 1978) suggest that there are three types of anxiety: cognitive, physiological, and behavioral. Cognitive anxiety involves the effect of anxiety on self-efficacy, physiological anxiety affects the physiological state, and behavioral anxiety directly influences behavior. The influence of anxiety on behavior can be mediated by cognitions or physiological state, or anxiety can directly motivate behavior. According to Lang, the relative contribution of each type of anxiety differs depending on the individual's learning history and type of situation. Sometimes cognitions will mediate the effect of anxiety on behavior; under other conditions, anxiety will directly affect behavior.

Our discussion suggests that both cognitive and noncognitive processes motivate avoidance behavior. A study by Feltz (1982) supports this view. Feltz examined the variables controlling whether female college students would execute a difficult back dive. Feltz discovered that self-efficacy predicted whether the subjects executed or avoided the task on the first trial; however, the influence of self-efficacy diminished on subsequent trials, indicating an influence other than cognitive anxiety. Feltz discovered that physiological arousal also influenced whether the subjects avoided the back dive; that is, physiological measures of anxiety (i.e., heart rate) predicted behavior on trials 1 and 3. Furthermore, Feltz's research demonstrates that anxiety can directly affect behavior. On trial 2, the subjects' self-reported anxiety level was the only predictor of whether they completed the back dive or avoided it. Interestingly, self-efficacy and heart rate did correlate with self-reported anxiety prior to the first dive; however, self-reported anxiety did not correlate with either efficacy or heart rate on subsequent dives. On the basis of her research, Feltz suggested that anxiety can either directly or indirectly affect behavior by altering cognitive or physiological processes. Her study also supports the idea that both cognitive and noncognitive processes motivate avoidance behavior. Other studies have also validated this view; see Lehrer and Woolfolk (1982) for another example.

SUMMARY

During the past two decades, many psychologists have recognized the important role of cognitions in determining how we act. In contrast to the mechanistic view that we automatically respond to environmental events, a cognitive approach assumes that we have an active role in determining our responses to environmental circumstances.

Cognitive psychology began in the 1930s and 1940s with Edward Tolman's ideas. Although Tolman's cognitive approach did not receive much initial acceptance, his views represent the foundation for current cognitive theories.

Tolman proposed that our behavior is goal-oriented; we are motivated to reach specific goals and continue to search until we obtain them. Rather than representing behavior as an inflexible habit, Tolman assumed that our behavior remains flexible enough to allow us to reach our goals. Our expectations determine the specific behavior we use to obtain reward or avoid punishment. According to Tolman, we expect that behaving in a particular fashion will enable us to obtain reward or avoid adversity. In addition to understanding the means needed to reach goals, Tolman felt that environmental events guide us to our goals.

Tolman theorized that although we may know both how to obtain our goals and where these goals are located, we will not behave unless we are motivated. He proposed two classes of motives: (1) deprivation conditions and (2) incentive motivation. According to Tolman, deprivation increases our demand for goal objects, and greater reward value increases our motivation to obtain goals. Also, Tolman felt that associating environmental events with either deprivation or incentive motivation enables these environmental stimuli to develop motivational properties.

Tolman's view altered the drive theory's character (for instance, the anticipatory goal mechanism developed in response to Tolman's incentive motivation and latent-learning studies), but the drive-dominated psychology of the 1950s and 1960s all but forgot his cognitive approach. In contrast, the importance of Tolman's view is quite evident in the thinking of current psychologists investigating the influence of cognition on learning.

Contemporary research has identified three types of expectancies which motivate behavior: stimulus outcome, response outcome, and efficacy expectations. Stimulus-outcome expectancies refer to our understanding of the predictive relationships in our environment; we expect a particular stimulus to predict a biologically important event. Response-outcome expectancies represent our belief in the consequences of our actions; we expect a specific outcome when we behave in a particular way. Our efficacy expectations reflect our perceived ability to execute a particular action; we feel competent when efficacy expectations are high and inadequate when they are low. Although stimulus-outcome and efficacy expectancies direct our behavior, response-outcome expectancies determine which behavior we will exhibit to obtain desired goals.

What is an expectation? According to Alloy and Tabachnik, an expectancy is a perceived covariation between a stimulus, a behavior, and an outcome. The literature suggests that animals and people can detect the level of covariation between events. Research with humans indicates that people's covariation estimates or causal attributions can have an important impact on how they behave. We can attribute causality to personal internal factors, or we can assume that environmental external factors account for our actions and experiences. Moreover, we can believe (1) that these factors are stable and will continue to influence us or (2) that other factors may determine our future behavior and/or experiences because of the instability of the processes we assume are now governing our behavior and experiences. Some evidence indicates that the perceived level of covariance between events affects how animals act.

When developing a covariance estimate or causal attribution, we employ several rules that use the distinctiveness, consensus, and consistency of our behavior and/or experiences. Animals also appear to use environmental information in the evaluation of the level of covariance between events. However, a person's or animal's perceived covariation may not reflect actual environmental circumstances. A preconceived estimation of covariance may prevent an animal or person from accurately perceiving the covariation between stimuli, behavior, and outcomes.

In some circumstances, animals or people perceive no covariation between behavior and outcomes. The literature implicates the occurrence of this perception of covariation in the behavior pathology of depression. There appear to be two types of helplessness or depression: personal helplessness, which occurs when people consider themselves incapable of obtaining reward or avoiding punishment, and universal helplessness, which occurs when people consider the attainment of reward or the avoidance of punishment to be impossible. The duration of depression is determined by whether people make a stable attribution, which leads to long-lasting depression, or an unstable causal attribution, which results in short-lived depression. The extent of depression depends on whether a person makes a global or specific attribution; when a person makes a specific attribution helplessness is restricted to a particular circumstance, but a global attribution leads to depression in many situations. Severe depression occurs when people believe that (1) their inabilities rather than external forces cause events to be uncontrollable, (2) their inability to control events will happen in many different situations, and (3) their inability to obtain reward and avoid failure will not change with time. Psychologists have reported that therapies which change the cognitive functioning of depressed persons represent one effective method of treating depression.

Cognitions also have a powerful impact on phobias. Phobic behavior occurs when individuals expect that (1) an aversive event will occur, (2) an avoidance behavior is the only way to respond to prevent the aversive event, and (3) they cannot interact with the phobic object. Participant modeling represents an effective treatment of phobias, because it alters the cognitions which motivate the phobic's avoidance behavior.

7

COMPLEX LEARNING
TASKS

A TALKING CHIMP

Vivian had looked forward to her interview at State University for months. Attending State had been a childhood dream stemming back to Vivian's first thoughts of college, and she was certain that her life would be ruined if the university did not accept her. Vivian saw no reason to take the campus tour before her interview, but her parents insisted. Never having seen the university, they wanted to discover what the fuss was all about.

The campus tour started routinely, with the usual showing of a few dorms and a couple of classrooms. When the student guide mentioned that the next stop would be the psychology department, Vivian was not too excited. She did plan to take an introductory psychology class, since almost everyone she knew attending State had done that, but journalism was her major interest.

Vivian could not have known that touring the department's primate laboratory would alter her plans. She had seen monkeys in the zoo, of course—those cute creatures that swung from tree limbs and clowned for visitors. Although the monkeys had physically resembled humans, Vivian did not know about the other similarities. Dr. Jack Johnson, the psychologist working in the lab with the primates, introduced himself to the tour group and then gave a short lecture. He mentioned that primates and humans share many common characteristics; for example, both form close social relationships, both have developed tools for solving problems, and both can be taught to use language. Vivian was very doubtful about the last part of that statement. How could a primate learn to talk? Her skepticism vanished when Dr. Johnson introduced Joan. Joan, a 4-year-old chimpanzee, had learned to use about 150 signs of the American Sign

Language. Dr. Johnson showed Joan several objects, and she promptly gave the correct sign for each one. Vivian was even more amazed to learn that Joan could arrange groups of signs into simple sentences. Dr. Johnson instructed Joan in sign language to brush her teeth, and Joan responded in sign, "Quick, give me a toothbrush." Joan even used sign words to express new ideas. For example, Joan had learned that the sign "more" could be used to ask for more food or juice, and she continued to use this sign in other situations, such as to persuade Dr. Johnson to continue playing a game with her. Language had always intrigued Vivian, and she found it fascinating that primates could learn to use language. Vivian was so impressed by what she had learned at the primate lab that she now considered majoring in psychology so that she could study the language ability of primates. Many psychologists have reported teaching language to primates. We will look at their work later in the chapter and discuss the acquisition of language in humans and whether primates and humans use language in the same ways.

This chapter introduces the processes by which complex tasks are mastered, discussing three major complex learning tasks. First we explore how concepts are formed. A *concept* is a symbol which stands for a class or group of objects or events with common characteristics. Second, problem solving is discussed, that is, how animals and people solve problems. A *problem* exists when obstacles prevent the attaining of a desired goal. To reach the goal, the problem must be solved. Finally, the chapter describes the structure of language and how we learn to use it. *Language* is a means of communicating our thoughts and feelings. (For a more detailed discussion of complex learning tasks, readers are referred to Howard, 1983, or Wessels, 1982.)

CONCEPT LEARNING

What is an airplane? *Webster's International Dictionary* defines it as a "fixed-wing aircraft, heavier than air, which is driven by a screw propeller or by a high velocity rearward jet and supported by the dynamic reactions of the air against its wings." The word *airplane* is also a concept. Remember that a *concept* is a symbol that represents a class or group of objects or events with common properties. Thus, the concept of airplane refers to all objects that (1) have fixed wings, (2) are heavier than air, (3) are driven by a screw propeller or high-velocity rearward jet, and (4) are supported by the dynamic reactions of the air against the wings. Airplanes come in various sizes and shapes, but as long as they have the four properties listed above, they are easily identified as airplanes. We are all familiar with many concepts. *Chair, book,* and *hat* are three such concepts: they stand for groups of objects with common properties.

Concepts significantly enhance the thinking process. Instead of separately labeling and categorizing each new object or event we encounter, we simply incorporate them into existing concepts. For example, suppose a child sees a large German shepherd. Even though this child has been exposed only to smaller dogs like poodles and cocker spaniels, he or she easily identifies the barking animal with four legs and a tail as a kind of dog. Thus, concepts enable us to group objects or events that share common properties and respond in a similar manner to each example of the concept.

The Structure of a Concept

Attributes and Rules According to Wessels (1982), concepts have two main aspects: attributes and rules. An *attribute* is any feature of an object or event that varies from one instance to another. For example, height, weight, and coloring differ from person to person and therefore are attributes of each individual.

An attribute can have a fixed value; for example, the attribute of gender can only be the discrete value of either male or female. In other cases, attributes have continuous values; for instance, the shade of a certain color can vary from light to dark.

Certain properties or attributes are relevant to objects or events. For example, the attribute of four legs is relevant for cats, but the attribute of wings is not. To understand a concept, one must learn what attributes are relevant to it.

For each concept, a rule defines which objects or events are examples of that particular concept. In terms of the concept of airplane discussed earlier, the rule defining an airplane indicates that to be an airplane an object must have fixed wings, be heavier than air, be driven by a screw propeller or high-velocity rearward jet, and be supported by the dynamic reactions of the air against its wings.

Types of Rules A number of different rules may be used to define the attributes of a concept (see Table 7.1). In some instances, the rules are simple; in other cases, they are more complex. When the rule is simple, an object or event must possess only one attribute to be an example of that particular concept. Suppose that an object is green. This object belongs to the concept of green whether it is a green car, a green shirt, or a green pea.

TABLE 7.1
RULES FOR DEFINING ATTRIBUTES IN A CONCEPT

Rule	Symbolic description	Verbal description
Affirmation	L	Any large object
Negation	$\bar{L}$	Any object not large
Conjunction	$L \cap C$	Any object both large and a circle
Disjunction	$L \cup C$	Any object either large or a circle or both
Conditional	$L \Rightarrow C$	Any large object if it is a circle
Biconditional	$L \Leftrightarrow C$	Any large object if and only if it is a circle

Source: Haygood, R. C., & Bourne, L. E., Jr. Attribute and rule learning aspects of conceptual behavior. *Psychological Review,* 1965, 72, 175–195. Copyright 1965 by the American Psychological Association. Reprinted by permission.

The above example shows an affirmative rule defining a concept. An *affirmative rule* specifies that a particular attribute defines a concept. In Figure 7.1, the affirmative rule indicates that "large" is the concept. A *negative rule* states that any object or event having a certain attribute is not a member of the concept. Figure 7.1 shows that any object that is large is not an example of the concept. Another example of a concept defined by a negative rule is blindness: anyone who can see is not blind.

The rules defining other concepts may be more complex. For example, a *conjunctive rule* defines a concept based on the simultaneous presence of two or more attributes; thus, all the specified attributes must be present for an object or event to be an example of the concept (see Figure 7.1). To illustrate the conjunctive rule, consider the question, "What is poison ivy?" Poison ivy is a *vine* that has *three-leaf clusters,* each leaf is *pointed* and *tooth-edged,* and

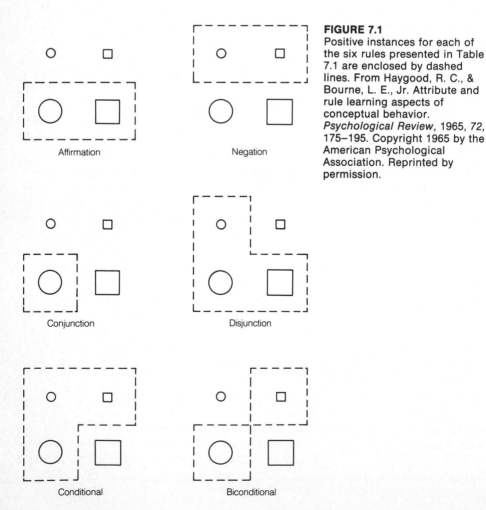

FIGURE 7.1
Positive instances for each of the six rules presented in Table 7.1 are enclosed by dashed lines. From Haygood, R. C., & Bourne, L. E., Jr. Attribute and rule learning aspects of conceptual behavior. *Psychological Review*, 1965, 72, 175–195. Copyright 1965 by the American Psychological Association. Reprinted by permission.

Affirmation

Negation

Conjunction

Disjunction

Conditional

Biconditional

each vine is *red* at the base of each branch of leaves. To be an example of the concept "poison ivy," a plant must have all the five attributes italicized above. The Virginia Creeper vine is like poison ivy but has five-leaf clusters; seedlings of the Box Elder also look like poison ivy but have straight instead of vine-like stems. Undoubtedly, many of us have mistaken other plants for poison ivy because we have not accurately learned the concept of poison ivy.

Concepts can be defined by yet another rule, the disjunctive rule. With the *disjunctive rule,* concepts are defined by the presence of one of two or both common attributes; that is, an example of the concept can possess either of the two common attributes, or it can possess both of them. In Figure 7.1, the disjunctive rule is "circle" or "large" or both. A circle is an example of the concept, as are both a large object and a large circular object. As another example of a concept defined by a disjunctive rule, consider the question, "who is schizophrenic?" A schizophrenic is an individual who persistently hallucinates and/or persistently experiences delusions. Thus, a person who has either of or both the attributes may be schizophrenic.

When a concept is defined by the *conditional rule,* the "if, then" statement can be applied. A positive instance of the concept shown in Figure 7.1 satisfies the condition: *if* an object is square, *then* it must be small. The following conditional rule might be used to define successful basketball players: If the players are small, then they must be fast; if they are tall, they must be agile.

A *biconditional rule* defines a concept using the statement "if and only if." The example shown in Figure 7.1 states that any large object is an example of the concept *if and only if* it is a circle. There are other complex rules that define concepts; interested readers are referred to Kintsch (1977) for a detailed discussion of the rules governing concept identification.

Note that how quickly a concept is learned depends on the rule defining the concept. Neisser and Weene (1962) grouped rules into three levels of complexity: Group I contains the affirmative and negative rules; group II, conjunctive and disjunctive rules; group III, conditional and biconditional rules. Neisser and Weene reported that the complexity of the rules determined how quickly a concept was learned; they found that concepts whose rules fell in Group I were learned the fastest and those with rules in group III were learned the slowest.

Similar results were observed by Bourne (1967). Bourne had different groups of subjects learn a series of concepts using either the conjunctive, disjunctive, conditional, or biconditional rule. As can be seen in Figure 7.2, the subjects learned the first concept faster when it was defined by the disjunctive rule. Concepts defined by the conjunctive rule were learned the next fastest, then those defined by the conditional rule, and finally the ones defined by the biconditional rule. Figure 7.2 also shows that the influence of rule type is only temporary. By the third concept, the rate of learning did not depend on the rule used to define the concepts. This observation indicates that the impact on how quickly a concept is learned is not an inherent characteristic of the different types of rules. Rather, the rate of learning probably reflects the subjects' greater experience with conjunctive and disjunctive rules than with conditional

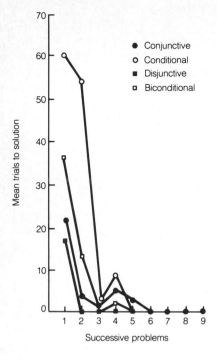

FIGURE 7.2
The number of trials to learn a problem as a function of the type of rule defining the problem. From Bourne, L. E., Jr. Learning and utilization of conceptual rules. In B. Kleinmuntz (Ed.), *Concepts and the structure of memory.* New York: Wiley, 1967.

and biconditional rules. Once people have learned concepts defined by conditional and biconditional rules, they can readily learn other concepts defined by these rules.

Our discussion suggests that for a specific object or event to be an example of a concept, it must have all the attributes characteristic of that concept. Yet, this is not always true. Consider the concept "bird." We know that birds can fly, are relatively the same size, have feathers, build nests, and head for warmer climates during the winter. However, all birds do not have all these attributes; a chicken, for example, has only one or two of these characteristics, and a robin has all. Yet, we classify both the chicken and the robin as birds. Is a robin more of a bird because it has more of the attributes?

The Prototype of a Concept   Rosch (1973, 1975, 1978) showed that all examples of a concept (or, members of a category) do not have all the attributes characteristic of that concept. Consider the concept of furniture. How exemplary of this concept is a desk, a table, or a chair? Rosch found that subjects could rank the degree to which a particular item fit a certain concept. As can be seen in Table 7.2, different pieces of furniture vary in the extent to which they are examples of the concept of furniture. "Chair" and "sofa" exemplify the concept to the greatest degree; "bureau" and "end table" to the least.

Rosch and Mervis (1978) observed not only that the extent to which objects or events exemplify a concept varies but also that objects or events which most

TABLE 7.2
RANKING OF FURNITURE AND VEGETABLES BY HOW WELL THEY
EXEMPLIFY THEIR CATEGORY

Furniture		Vegetables	
Exemplar	Goodness-of-example rank	Exemplar	Goodness-of-example rank
Chair	1.5	Peas	1
Sofa	1.5	Carrots	2
Couch	3.5	Green beans	3
Table	3.5	String beans	4
Easy chair	5	Spinach	5
Dresser	6.5	Broccoli	6
Rocking chair	6.5	Asparagus	7
Coffee table	8	Corn	8
Rocker	9	Cauliflower	9
Love seat	10	Brussels sprouts	10
Chest of drawers	11	Squash	11
Desk	12	Lettuce	12
Bed	13	Celery	13
Bureau	14	Cucumber	14
End table	15.5	Beets	15

Source: Rosch, E. Cognitive representations of semantic categories. *Journal of Experimental Psychology: General*, 1975, *104*, 192–253. Copyright 1975 by the American Psychological Association. Reprinted by permission.

closely exemplify a concept usually possess more attributes of the concept than do objects or events which exemplify the concept to a lesser degree.

Why are some objects or events better examples of a concept than are others? According to Rosch (1975), certain attributes characterize a particular concept; this commonality of attributes refers to a relation called *family resemblance*. Rosch assumes that the degree to which a member of a concept exemplifies the concept depends on the degree of family resemblance; the more attributes a specific object or event shares with other members of a concept, the more the object or event exemplifies the concept. Thus, compared with bureau and end table, sofa and chair are better examples of the concept of furniture because they share more attributes with other members of the concept. Rosch and Mervis found that the five most typical members of the concept of furniture had thirteen attributes in common, whereas the five least typical members had only two attributes in common.

When you think of the concept of vegetable, you are most likely to imagine a pea. Why? According to Rosch (1978), the *prototype* of a concept has the most attributes in common with other members of the concept and is therefore the most typical member of a category. As can be seen in Table 7.2, the pea is the prototype of the concept of vegetable because it best exemplifies a vegetable. Members of the concept which have many attributes in common with the prototype are considered typical of the concept; thus, carrots and green beans are typical of vegetable because they have many of the same attributes as the prototype. In contrast, celery, cucumbers, and beets are atypical of the concept because they share only a few attributes with the prototype.

The degree to which an object or event exemplifies a concept is important. Rosch (1978) asked subjects to indicate whether a particular object or event was a member of a specific concept. For example, subjects were asked if robins and penguins are birds. Rosch reported it took less time to say "true" when the object or event was a good example of the concept (robin) than when it was a poor example (penguin). Thus, the more an object or event differs from the prototype, the more difficult it is to identify it as an example of the concept.

Boundaries of the Concept Two objects or events may share certain attributes but not be examples of the same concept. For example, although robins and bats both have wings, the robin is a bird and the bat is a mammal. Certain rules define the boundaries of a concept. These rules indicate whether differences between the prototype of a concept and another object or event indicate either that the other object or event is less typical of the concept or that it is an example of another concept. Thus, even though robins and bats both have wings, the other differences between them mean that the bat and the robin are not members of the same concept.

Sometimes these boundaries are not clearly defined (Zazdeh, Fu, Tanak, & Shimura, 1975). For example, what is the difference between a river and a stream? Uncertainty may reflect difficulty detecting the boundary or a lack of knowledge about the rules defining the boundary. When the boundary of a concept is vague, it is difficult to know whether an object or event is a member of that concept. Rosch (1978) reported that subjects easily answered that a stone is not a bird, but they had difficulty indicating that a bat is not a bird. In fact, many subjects thought that a bat was a kind of bird. Apparently, we do not always know the boundaries defining certain concepts.

Studying Concept Learning

Before turning our attention to how concepts are acquired, let's first examine a study that investigated concept learning. Psychologists have conducted numerous experiments dealing with concept learning; an early study by Smoke (1933) is representative.

Smoke presented subjects a large number of figures that differed in terms of the shape, size, number, and location of their dots. The subjects' task was to learn the concept of DAX, which consisted of a circle with one dot inside and another dot outside (refer to Figure 7.3). The DAX concept uses the conjunctive rule; a figure which (1) is not a circle, (2) has more than two dots, or (3) has two dots inside or outside the circle is not an example of the DAX concept. Subjects saw each figure, indicated whether they thought it was an example of

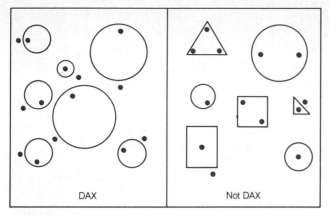

FIGURE 7.3
Samples of DAX and non-DAX figures. From Smoke, K. L.
Negative instances in concept learning. *Journal of
Experimental Psychology,* 1933, *16,* 583–588. Copyright 1933
by the American Psychological Association. Reprinted by
permission.

the concept, and received feedback about the correctness of their response.
Smoke reported that subjects readily learned the concept of DAX.

Psychologists investigating concept learning have used two methods of
training (Ellis, 1978). In the *method of reception,* each stimulus is shown separately, and subjects indicate whether they think the stimulus is an example of
the concept. After responding to each stimulus, the subjects are told whether
their response was correct. This process continues until subjects have given
each correct instance of the concept, an indication that they have fully learned
the concept. The second training procedure is the *method of selection,* a
method in which the subjects are shown all the stimuli at once and are free to
respond to them in any order. The method of selection leads to faster learning
than does the method of reception (Bourne, Ekstrand, & Dominowski, 1971).
We will see why shortly.

Concept Learning in Animals

Concept learning involves identification of the properties that characterize a
concept as well as those that do not. Can animals learn concepts? The research
of Richard Herrnstein and his associates (Herrnstein, 1979; Herrnstein & de
Villiers, 1980; Herrnstein, Loveland, & Cable, 1976) clearly shows that animals
can learn a concept.

Herrnstein, Loveland and Cable (1976) presented a series of eighty slides to
their pigeons. Half of the slides were S^D, and pecking at these slides resulted in
a food reward. The other forty slides were S^Δ, and the pigeons did not receive a
reward for pecking at them. The S^D slides contained examples of natural ob-

jects; for example, the S^D slides for some pigeons were pictures of water, for some pigeons the pictures were of trees, and for some pigeons the pictures were of a specific woman. The S^Δ slides did not contain examples of the appropriate objects. During each daily session, each of the eighty slides was briefly exposed to the pigeons. Figure 7.4 shows positive (S^D) and negative (S^Δ) instances of each concept. Herrnstein, Loveland, and Cable found that the pigeons quickly learned to respond to the S^D and not to the S^Δ.

Did these pigeons really learn a concept? Did they discover which stimuli contained examples of the concept and which stimuli did not? Or did they merely learn to respond to some stimuli but not others? Herrnstein and de Villiers (1980) evaluated whether the pigeons had actually learned a concept in two ways. First, they presented the same eighty slides to the pigeons, but this time not just the S^D slides contained examples of the concept; that is, the slides were randomly assigned to S^D and S^Δ. If the pigeons were only learning to respond to some stimuli but not to others, then the random assignment of slides should not affect how fast the pigeons learned the discrimination. Although the pigeons did learn the discrimination when the slides were randomly presented as S^D and S^Δ, Herrnstein and de Villiers reported that learning was much slower when no concept defined S^D and S^Δ. Herrnstein and de Villiers also used a positive-transfer test to show that the pigeons did learn a concept. After the pigeons had learned the discrimination in which S^D contained an example of the concept and S^Δ did not, they received two new slides of S^D and S^Δ. According to Herrnstein and de Villiers, if the pigeons had only learned to respond to certain stimuli, then learning to discriminate new slides of S^D and S^Δ should proceed at the same rate as original learning. However, if the pigeons had learned the concept, positive transfer should occur, and the pigeons should readily learn how to respond to the new slides. Herrnstein and de Villiers observed considerable positive transfer to the new slides; the pigeons responded differentially to the new examples of S^D and S^Δ almost as effectively as they had to the original slides.

Our discussion indicates that pigeons can learn which stimuli are examples of a concept and which are not. Evidently animals as well as people can organize their environment according to those events which are examples of concepts and those which are not. However, the stimuli used in the preceding studies were natural concepts; that is, the stimuli represented concrete aspects of the natural environment. Can animals also learn abstract concepts such as "same" or "different"? D'Amato and his associates (D'Amato & Salmon, 1984; D'Amato, Salmon, & Colombo, 1985) used a procedure called *matching to sample* to discover whether primates can learn abstract concepts. The matching-to-sample procedure first presented a stimulus item (e.g., a square) to monkeys and then presented two stimuli (e.g., a square and a dot). The monkeys were reinforced if they chose the appropriate stimulus on the second presentation. To evaluate whether the monkey can learn the abstract concepts of sameness or differentness, a series of sample and test stimuli was presented. If the monkey is learning the abstract concept, the level of performance should

FIGURE 7.4
Examples of stimuli used in the Herrnstein, Loveland, and Cable (1976) study. Figures A, C, and E are S^Ds. Figures B, D, and F are S^Δs. The concept of water is present in Figure A but not in Figure B. The concept of trees is present in Figure C but not in D. The particular person present in Figure E is not in Figure F. (Photographs provided by Richard Herrnstein.)

improve with each sample and presentation of test stimuli. If the monkey learned to choose on the basis of sameness (or differentness), the presentation of a new test stimulus should not affect the monkey's performance. D'Amato and his associates reported that the monkeys did perform well when presented with new stimuli; although once they have learned the initial concept, a few trials are needed before they can correctly respond to the new set of stimuli. It is evident that primates (and humans) can learn abstract concepts, but whether pigeons can also acquire abstract concepts such as sameness is unclear (see Lea, 1984, for a review of this literature).

Theories of Concept Learning

There are two main theories of concept learning. One view assumes that concept learning is an associative process; the other assumes that concept learning is a cognitive process.

Associative Theory   Clark Hull (1920) envisioned concept learning as a form of discrimination learning (see Chapter 5). In his view, concepts have both relevant and irrelevant attributes. On each trial of a concept-learning study, a subject indicates whether the object or event shown is characteristic of the concept. A subject responding correctly is reinforced by feedback (told that the response was correct). As a result of reinforcement, response strength to the attributes characteristic of the concept is increased. Failure to reinforce irrelevant attributes weakens the response to the irrelevant attributes.

Consider the Smoke study described earlier. The subjects were reinforced when they recognized DAX figures (figures of a circle with one dot on the inside of the circle and another dot on the outside). As the result of reinforcement, the stimulus (figure) and response (DAX) were associated. In contrast, subjects that identified as DAX figures that were not examples of the concept were not reinforced. The result of nonreward was a diminished response to nonexamples of the concept of DAX.

Hull's classic study (1920) seems to provide evidence for an associative view. In this study, adult subjects learned six lists of twelve paired associates. The stimuli were Chinese letters containing twelve different features. The stimuli changed from task to task, but the features did not. (Six of the features are shown in Figure 7.5.) Nonsense syllables paired with each feature served as the responses. The same feature–nonsense-syllable pairs were used in each of the lists. Hull found that the subjects learned each successive list more rapidly than they did the preceding one. In fact, on the sixth list, subjects gave the correct response 60 percent of the time on the first trial. According to Hull, the subjects learned the common feature of each stimulus in the category and were therefore able to learn later lists more quickly. Hull believed that subjects were not consciously aware of the association but instead had merely become trained to respond to a specific stimulus event.

Hull assumed that associative processes controlled concept learning. This view was advocated by most psychologists until the late 1950s, when further research revealed that cognitions also are involved in concept learning.

Cognitive Processes in Concept Learning
Testing Hypotheses   How does a person learn a concept? According to Bruner, Goodnow, and Austin (1956) a concept is learned by testing hypothe-

| Feature | List 1 | List 2 | List 3 | List 4 | List 5 | List 6 |

FIGURE 7.5
The stimuli used in Hull's concept learning study. Notice that the features shown on the left are contained in each list presented on the right. From Hull, C. L. Quantitative aspects of the evolution of concepts: An experimental study. *Psychological Monographs,* 1920, *28,* whole no. 123, Copyright 1920 by the American Psychological Association. Reprinted by permission.

ses about the correct solution. If the first hypothesis formed is correct, the individual has learned the concept. However, if the hypothesis is incorrect, another hypothesis will be generated and tested. Hypothesis testing will continue until a correct solution is discovered.

Consider the DAX concept. Suppose that on the first trial (see Figure 7.6) a figure of a circle and a dot was shown, and one subject's first hypothesis (or guess) was that this figure was an example of the concept DAX. Since DAX is a figure with a circle and two dots, the subject who responded "DAX" to the first figure was wrong. Thus, the initial hypothesis was incorrect and the subject needed to generate a new one. On trial 2, the subject hypothesized that DAX was a dot to the left of the circle. The subject learned that this hypothesis also was wrong and on trial 3 guessed that two dots represent the concept. Again the subject learned that this guess was wrong; the subject's next hypothesis was that the concept was two dots and a circle. Although trial 4 suggests that this is a possibility, trial 5 proves it to be incorrect. The subject then hypothesized that the concept of DAX must be one dot inside a circle and one dot outside. The subject tested this hypothesis on trials 6, 7, and 8 and finally concluded that it was correct. Our example suggests that, in addition to forming hypotheses to

Trial	Figure presented	Response	Feedback
1	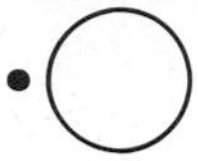	"DAX"	Wrong
2	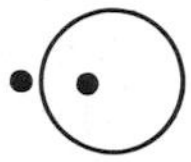	"Not DAX"	Wrong
3	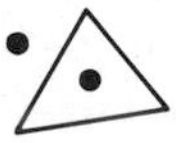	"DAX"	Wrong
4		"DAX"	Right
5	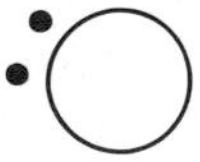	"DAX"	Wrong
6		"DAX"	Right
7		"Not DAX"	Right
8	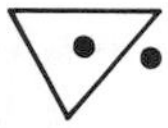	"Not DAX"	Right

FIGURE 7.6
A hypothetical series of eight trials of the DAX problem.
Successive rows show, trial by trial, the stimulus presented,
the response given, and the feedback provided by the
experimenter. From Kimble, G. A., Garmezy, N., & Zigler, E.
Psychology (6th Ed.). New York: Wiley, 1984.

learn concepts, individuals adopt a win-stay, lose-shift strategy, that is, they will stick with a hypothesis as long as it works and will generate a new one when evidence indicates that the old hypothesis is not valid. What evidence demonstrates that hypotheses are tested in concept learning? Levine's classic study (1966) provides support for a hypothesis-testing view of concept learning.

Levine (1966) developed a blank-trials procedure to evaluate the theory that people learn concepts by testing hypotheses. On each study trial, subjects were shown two letters. The letters differed in terms of color (black or white), identity (X or T), size (large or small), and position (left or right). One attribute (for example, white) was chosen by Levine to be the concept; the subjects' task was to learn which attribute had been chosen. On each study trial, the subjects chose one of the two stimuli and were told whether their response contained the correct attribute. After each study trial, subjects were given four blank trials. On each blank trial, two stimuli were presented, and the subjects again tried to choose the one that represented the concept. However, no feedback was given on these trials. The subjects' responses on the blank trials indicated whether they were testing a hypothesis about the correct attribute. If they were, a particular pattern of responses would be seen. Figure 7.7 presents the pattern of responses. Suppose that a subject hypothesized that black was the correct attribute. This subject's responses should match those depicted in the first column of Figure 7.7. In contrast, the responses of a subject who thought that large was correct should match those in the fourth column. However, a random pattern of responses would have occurred if subjects had not been testing hypotheses to learn the concept.

Levine found that subjects engaged in hypothesis testing on over 95 percent of the trials. Furthermore, he found that subjects adopted a win-stay, lose-shift strategy. When a hypothesis was confirmed on a feedback trial, subjects retained this hypothesis throughout the blank no-feedback trials and continued to use it until they found that attribute incorrect. When a hypothesis was found to be incorrect on a study trial, a new hypothesis was generated and used on the four subsequent blank no-feedback trials and then on study trials until disconfirmed.

Two additional points need to be mentioned about Levine's research. First, subjects typically do not use a specific hypothesis more than once while learning a concept. Once a hypothesis has proven to be incorrect, that hypothesis will not be evaluated again during the study. Apparently, people can remember

FIGURE 7.7
The stimuli used by Levine in his blank trials are presented in the middle of the figure. The eight possible hypothesis are shown on the left and right of the stimuli. The column below each hypothesis shows the pattern of choices which test that hypothesis. From Levine, M. Hypothesis behavior by humans during discrimination learning. *Journal of Experimental Psychology*, 1966, *71*, 311–338. Copyright 1966 by the American Psychological Association. Reprinted by permission.

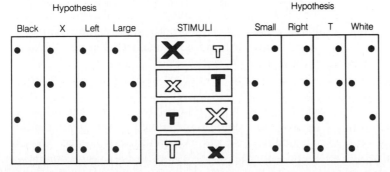

past hypotheses that have been proven invalid and will test different hypotheses until they find the correct one. Second, Levine showed that subjects can test more than one hypothesis at a time. To show this, consider the subjects' response on the first study trial. Suppose that a subject chose a large black X on the right, thinking that either black or X was the correct concept. The subject was told that the response was incorrect. This information indicates that neither black nor X is the correct attribute. Levine's results showed that in this example, subjects learned that both attributes were incorrect and, remembering that information, would not guess either black or X on blank trials. Other psychologists have also used this blank-trial technique and found that people do test hypotheses as they learn concepts; see Eimas (1969) or Ingalls and Dickerson (1969) for other examples.

The blank-trial procedure is not the only method of validating the hypothesis-testing view of concept learning. Karpf and Levine (1971) developed a procedure called *introtacts* which also shows that hypotheses are tested as a concept is learned. This procedure involves subjects stating a prediction or hypothesis about the correct attribute prior to each trial. Investigators using this method (Karpf & Levine, 1971; Kemler, 1978; Mims & Gholson, 1977; Phillips & Levine, 1975; Spiker & Cantor, 1977) have also found that subjects do systematically test hypotheses as they try to identify the correct attribute.

Do people randomly generate hypotheses, or do they use a specific strategy to learn a concept? A number of psychologists have reported that most people use strategies to learn concepts.

Strategies of Concept Learning   A *strategy* is a systematic procedure used to learn a concept. There are two major types of strategies: analytic and nonanalytic. According to Brooks (1978), *analytic strategies* represent techniques for identifying attributes, prototypes, or rules; *nonanalytic strategies* merely involve memory of particular positive instances of a concept used to determine whether new stimuli are also instances of the concept.

Analytic Strategies   Bruner, Goodnow, and Austin (1956) conducted an extensive investigation of the strategies used to learn the attributes characteristic of a concept, the prototype of a concept, or the rule defining a concept. They identified four major strategies: successive scanning, conservative focusing, simultaneous scanning, and focus gambling.

The simplest strategy identified by Bruner, Goodnow, and Austin is *successive scanning,* which involves testing only one hypothesis at a time. This is a very simple strategy, but unless an early hypothesis is correct, a good deal of time may be spent learning the concept.

A second type of strategy used to learn a concept is *conservative focusing,* which entails focusing on the first positive instance of a concept and then choosing on each subsequent trial a stimulus that differs in only one attribute from the focal stimulus. This procedure enables the subject to test the impact of that change from the focal stimulus. The subject continues to select stimuli differing in only one attribute from the focal stimulus until the concept is learned. Conservative focusing is a very efficient strategy of learning a concept; it requires only one more trial than the number of dimensions.

Consider the following example: A subject is shown stimuli differing in three dimensions: shape, size, and position (refer to Figure 7.8). The correct concept is that of a large circle. On the first trial, the subject is shown card 3, a large circle on the left side of the card. The subject learns that this is a positive instance of the concept. Using this card as the focus, the subject chooses card 1, a large square also on the left. When told that the card is negative, the subject knows that shape is relevant and that circle must be a part of the concept. To see if position is relevant, the subject chooses card 9; this stimulus differs from card 3 only in that the large circle is on the right. When told that this card is a positive instance of concept, the subject knows that position is not a relevant dimension. On the final trial, the subject selects card 4, which is the same as the focal stimulus except that the circle is small instead of large. The subject discovers that this card is not an example of the concept and now knows that size is relevant. Having systematically tested the three dimensions, the subject can identify the concept as a large circle.

Simultaneous scanning occurs when several different hypotheses are simultaneously tested on a single trial. Although this is a very efficient strategy, it involves remembering a lot of information and often leads to errors. Using the large-circle concept, the following example illustrates this second strategy. After learning on the first trial that card 3 (picture of a large circle on the left side of card) was a positive instance of the concept, subjects could hypothesize that position is relevant and that shape is irrelevant. This hypothesis could be tested by choosing card 5 (large triangle on left side of card). When told that this arrangement is not an example of the concept, the subject can deduce that shape (circle) is an attribute of the concept but that position is not.

FIGURE 7.8
Eighteen stimuli which could be used to test the large circle strategy. From *An Introduction to Cognitive Psychology* by D. R. Moates and G. M. Schumacher © 1980 by Wadsworth, Inc. Reprinted by permission of the publisher.

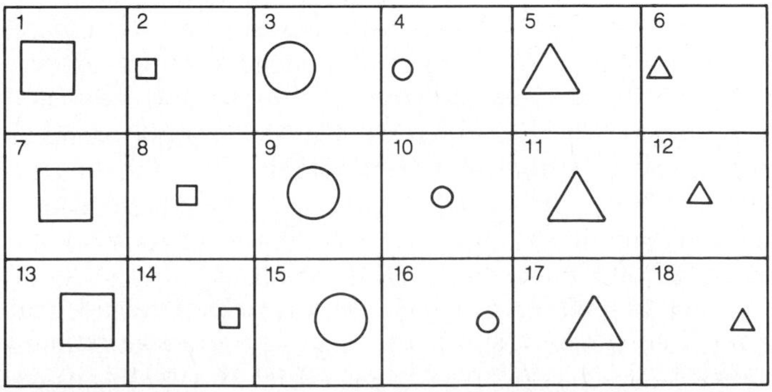

The final strategy used to learn concepts is *focus gambling*. This strategy is similar to conservative focusing in that the first positive instance becomes the focus of the concept and similar to simultaneous scanning in that more than one hypothesis is tested on each trial. This procedure can result in rapid concept learning if the guesses are accurate; however, since focus gambling tests hypotheses less systematically than conservative focusing does, more trials may be needed to identify the concept.

Nonanalytic Strategies   A person who learns a concept using a nonanalytic strategy merely remembers the positive instances of the concept and then determines whether a new stimulus is an example of the concept by comparing it with the recalled positive examples of the concept. Thus, unlike analytic strategies, which involve identifying attributes or rules, memorization is the key element in nonanalytic strategies.

Brooks (1978) provides a number of studies showing that people can learn a concept with a nonanalytic strategy. Brooks established two sets of stimuli (categories A and B). Five letters (X, V, M, R, and T) could be used to create thirty 6-letter sequences. Categories A and B had different rules governing the construction of their fifteen letter sequences. Thus, the letter sequences in category A differed from those in category B. For example, two letter sequences for category A were VVTRXR and XMVRXR, and two from category B were VVTRVV and MRMRTV.

Subjects in Brooks's study received one of three treatment conditions in the initial phase of the experiment. In the *concept-learning condition,* subjects were shown the thirty stimuli, told that two different sets of rules had been used to construct the stimuli, and asked to classify each stimulus as a member of either category A or category B. These subjects received feedback about the correctness of their responses and continued to classify stimuli until they had correctly identified all thirty. In the *memorization condition,* the subjects learned a list of thirty paired associates. The thirty letter sequences were the stimuli; the fifteen stimuli in category A were paired with names of cities as responses, and the fifteen stimuli in category B were paired with names of animals as responses. The subjects continued to receive the thirty stimuli and responses until they responded without an error. Control subjects received neither the concept learning nor the memorization treatments.

In the second phase of the study, all subjects were shown novel stimuli and asked to classify them as belonging to category A, category B, or neither. Brooks reported that subjects in the concept-learning condition correctly classified only 46 percent of the novel letter sequences. This level of performance was not much higher than that of control condition subjects, who had no knowledge of the categories. According to Brooks, the subjects in the concept-learning condition had used analytic strategies to learn the rules to classify the stimuli in the two categories, but these subjects' performance in the second phase suggests that these subjects did not learn the rules very well. In contrast, Brooks reported that memorization-condition subjects correctly classified 60 percent of the novel letter sequences. In Brooks's view, these subjects classified the novel sequences by comparing them to particular letter sequences that they had memorized to learn the paired associates. Brooks's study shows that people can learn a concept merely through exposure to positive instances of the concept; the study also supports the contention that concepts can be learned better using nonanalytic rather than analytic strategies.

You might wonder what circumstances cause people to use analytic or non-analytic strategies to learn concepts. Research indicates that a number of variables determine whether an analytic or nonanalytic strategy is employed. The following discussion briefly summarizes this research; see Brooks (1978) or Reber, Kassin, Lewis, and Cantor (1980) for a more detailed discussion.

People use analytic strategies under many circumstances. A person will use an analytic strategy to identify an attribute when stimuli characteristic of a concept have common, highly salient attributes. When the rules that define a category are salient, a person will use an analytic strategy to identify the rule. An analytic strategy is useful when the positive instances of a concept cannot be easily remembered. Finally, experience can lead people to use analytic strategies. For example, formal education requires people to classify the common attributes of events and to learn the rules for identifying common properties of these events.

In other situations, concepts can be learned best by using a nonanalytic strategy. A nonanalytic strategy is often used to learn a concept when the relevant attributes of the concept are not obvious. Experiencing only a few instances of a concept also causes people to use a nonanalytic strategy. Further, nonanalytic strategies are favored when positive instances of the concept are easily remembered and recall must be made quickly. For example, suppose that you encounter a snake and want to know whether it is poisonous—it is much more adaptive to compare this snake to other well-remembered snakes than to a prototype of a poisonous snake.

Do not assume that analytic and nonanalytic strategies are mutually exclusive. A concept can be learned using either strategy, but it is learned best when both strategies are employed. For example, Reber, Kassin, Lewis, and Cantor (1980) found that subjects acquired a concept most rapidly when they learned both the rules defining the concept and the specific instances of the concept.

Preparedness and Concept Learning

Eleanor Rosch (1973, 1975, 1978) suggested that we are more prepared to learn some concepts than we are others and that our perceptual structure enables us to learn some concepts more readily than others. Rosch refers to concepts that are quickly acquired as *natural* concepts and to those that are slowly acquired as *unnatural* concepts.

Evidence for the existence of natural concepts comes from Rosch's research with the Dani tribe of New Guinea. According to Rosch, pure colors (red, green, yellow, blue) are considered more natural and, therefore, easier to learn than less natural mixed colors. Rosch used members of the Dani tribe as subjects because they have only two color concepts in their vocabulary: *mola* for light colors and *mili* for dark colors. Unlike the people of our culture, the Dani have not learned different color concepts, thus providing Rosch with an excellent subject population to investigate the learning of color concepts.

Rosch divided the adult Dani tribe members into two groups: the natural-color condition and the unnatural-color condition. The subjects were then instructed to assign Dani family surnames to eight categories, each containing a combination of three focal and nonfocal colors. (Focal colors—red, green, blue, yellow, purple, pink, orange, and gray—are commonly recognized by members of almost every culture. Nonfocal colors are a mixture of two focal colors. For example, pure yellow is a focal color, and greenish yellow is a nonfocal color.) Rosch asked subjects in the natural-color condition to attach a family name to each of the eight categories; for this group of subjects, each category consisted of a focal color surrounded by two nonfocal colors, and all were from the same part of the color spectrum. For example, one category contained a purplish blue (nonfocal), a pure blue (focal), and a greenish-blue (nonfocal). Subjects in the unnatural-color condition were shown categories comprised of colors between the natural focal colors. For instance, these subjects were asked to name a group of colors that we might describe as reddish orange, greenish yellow, and bluish purple.

Rosch found that subjects in the natural-color condition learned to describe the various color concepts faster and made fewer errors than did the subjects in the unnatural-color condition. This suggests first that we are inherently prepared to learn that different shades of the same color represent a single color concept and second that for some reason we have difficulty learning that different parts of the color spectrum belong to the same concept. Note also that subjects in the natural-color condition found nonfocal colors more difficult to learn to name than focal colors. Apparently, focal colors are naturally highly salient and thereby provide the prototype for the color category.

Thus our perceptual abilities influence how readily we learn a concept. The inclusiveness, or the number of members, of the concept also influences how quickly a concept is learned. *Basic* concepts (concepts with a medium degree of inclusiveness) are inherently easier to learn than either *subordinate* concepts (concepts with a low degree of inclusiveness) or *superordinate* concepts (concepts with a high degree of inclusiveness). For example, the concept of vehicle contains many members and is a superordinate concept; the concept of car is a basic concept; the concept of Cadillac is a subordinate concept. Rosch found that children learn basic concepts before they learn either subordinate or superordinate concepts.

We have learned that some concepts are naturally easier to learn than are others. Yet, for various reasons, not everyone may learn all these concepts. For example, the English language has many names for colors; the Dani tribe of New Guinea has only two. We have only one word for snow; Eskimos have three. This situation of different cultures having a greater or lesser number of names for various concepts is called *linguistic relativity*.

Benjamin Whorf (1956) suggested that language determines the extent of learning; that is, we can learn only those concepts for which our language has words. Few psychologists today accept Whorf's extreme view that language determines thought. For example, people from Florida can distinguish various types of snow and can describe them with phrases. Furthermore, if these Floridans go skiing in Colorado, they are likely to add to their vocabulary new words such as *powder, corn,* and *ice* to describe the various types of snow. According to Clark and Clark (1977), different languages do not indicate different ways of thinking; instead they represent different adjustments to different environments. If you live in a land of snow, your language requires appropriate terms to distinguish between types of snow. Thus, Clark and Clark suggest that people invent language to describe important features of their environments. Linguistic relativity suggests that cultural experience influences which concepts we learn; Rosch's research shows that biological character also affects which concepts are learned. Thus, concept learning depends on both biological and experiential processes.

PROBLEM SOLVING

Examine the objects shown in Figure 7.9. How can you mount the candle on the wall so that it will not drip wax on the table or floor when lit? Although not obvious, the solution to this problem is simple (Dunker, 1945). By mounting the box on the wall with a tack, you've made a candle holder which will prevent wax from falling onto the table or floor. Every day, we are faced with many

FIGURE 7.9
The objects presented in the candle problem are shown on the left, and the solution to the problem is presented at the right. From Wingfield, A. *Human learning and memory.* New York: Harper & Row, 1979.

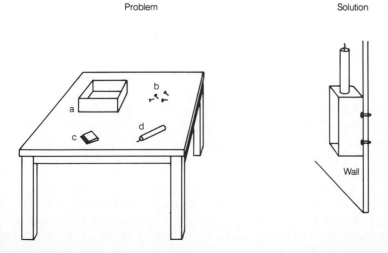

Problem   Solution

similar problems to solve. How to get an extra 10 minutes of sleep without being late to class or how to get from your car to a store without getting wet in the rain when you have no umbrella are just two examples of the type of problems we routinely confront.

The Nature of the Problem

What is a problem? A *problem* is a situation in which a person is motivated to reach a goal but attainment of the goal is blocked by some obstacle or obstacles. The person's task is to find a solution to the problem; that is, to discover a way to overcome the obstacles.

In the examples cited, sleepiness is the obstacle that needs to be overcome to get to class on time, and the rain is the obstacle that prevents you from reaching the store without getting wet. How can these obstacles be overcome?

Edward Thorndike (1898) assumed that animals and people solve problems by trial and error (see Chapter 1). For example, Thorndike did not believe that the cats in his famous puzzle box were able to figure out how to open the latch to escape from the box. Instead, the cats produced a large number of responses, and those that enabled the goal to be reached were reinforced. Wolfgang Kohler (1925) suggested a quite different view of problem solving. According to Kohler, an animal internally explores the problem before exhibiting a specific response. The animal's exploration involves considering and rejecting possible solutions and finally developing insight as to the correct solution to the problem.

Consider Kohler's classic primate studies. Kohler presented several chimpanzees with the problem of reaching a piece of fruit that was suspended over their heads in their play area. The problem was structured so that the chimps could not reach the fruit even by jumping. Kohler randomly placed several boxes and sticks throughout the play area. According to Kohler, the chimpanzees initially attempted to reach the fruit by jumping. When that failed, they stopped jumping and paced back and forth. Kohler observed that the chimps abruptly stopped pacing and, looking quite resolute, used the boxes and sticks to reach the fruit. One chimp obtained the fruit by gathering several boxes, stacking them on top of each other, and climbing up the boxes to reach the fruit. Another chimp climbed on one box and used a stick to knock down the fruit. A third chimp collected two hollow sticks and made one long stick by inserting the end of one stick into the other. Several critical observations led Kohler to suggest that insight was responsible for the chimpanzees' solutions to the problem: First, the chimps solved the problem with few or no mistakes. Second, once they had solved the problem, the chimps were able to solve quickly a similar problem in the future.

Chimpanzees are not the only animals to insightfully solve problems. Epstein (1981) observed a similar phenomenon in pigeons. In his study, Epstein initially trained pigeons to peck at a model banana to obtain food reinforcement. The pigeons were also taught to move a box across the floor of a compartment by pecking at the box. Finally, the pigeons were placed in the compartment with the movable box at one end and the model banana suspended out of reach at the other end. The pigeons' feathers had been clipped so they could not fly to reach the banana. Epstein reported that the pigeons initially looked back and forth from the box to the banana. Finally, they stopped looking, moved the box under the banana, and climbed onto the box to peck at the banana. What cognitive processes enabled Kohler's chimpanzees and Epstein's pigeons to solve the problems?

Wessels (1982) offers four steps for solving a problem: (1) define the problem, (2) devise a strategy to solve the problem, (3) execute the strategy, and (4) evaluate the effectiveness of the strategy.

Defining the Problem

Developing a definition of the problem entails identifying both the starting point, or *initial state,* of the problem and the end point, or *goal state,* of the problem. Considering the two examples again, the initial state of the first problem is that it is time to get up but you are still tired; the initial state of the second problem is that you are in your car when it is raining. The goal state of the first problem is sleeping 10 more minutes without being late for class; the goal state of the second problem is getting to the store without becoming wet.

A representation of the problem involves two additional points: (1) The operations which solve the problem need to be identified. For example, suppose that you want to receive a grade of A in this learning course. Some operations that would help you gain the knowledge needed to get an A include reading this text, attending class, and taking notes. (2) Restrictions limit what can be done to solve a problem. In our example of how to receive an A, the restrictions mean that cheating on tests and changing computer cards are not acceptable solutions to the problem.

Well-Defined versus Ill-Defined Problems   Some problems are well-defined: both the initial state and the goal state of the problem are clear. Both our examples—getting 10 more minutes of sleep and arriving at the store without becoming wet—are well-defined; that is, the starting points and goal states are obvious. However, some problems are ill-defined: they have no clear starting point or end point. Consider the problem of an instructor who wants to teach a good class. How does the instructor determine whether a class is good? Since there are no definite standards to measure the success of a course, how can the instructor know that the goal state has been reached? In this example, the end point is unclear. In some cases, the starting point is unclear. For example, a person may recognize that a car must be in good working order to run smoothly, but the individual may not be able to check the condition of the car and therefore cannot identify the starting point of the problem.

Solving Ill-Defined Problems   Reitman (1965) suggests that identifying the starting point and end point is the key to bringing an ill-defined problem closer to a well-defined one and that this objective can be accomplished by generating additional structures (subproblems). Consider the following example. Suppose that you are asked to write a term paper for a biology class. How can you best accomplish this goal? The starting point is a large body of literature that you need to analyze. The end point is a finished term paper that has a beginning, a middle, and an end, is sufficient in length and depth, and is an accurate discussion of the topic. To close the definition of the problem, you must first choose a specific topic, such as genetics. The problem can be defined further by identifying several subtopics of genetics, and these subtopics can then be broken down into even more specific groups. In Reitman's view, the subtopics establish a series of subproblems which can then be solved one at a time. Commenting on Reitman's approach, Simon (1973) suggested that creating a set of manageable subproblems provides the structure for converting an ill-defined problem into a well-defined one. Wessels (1982) believes that creating a hierarchy of clearly stated subproblems makes an ill-defined problem easier to solve. Several studies have found that the use of subproblems facilitated the solving of such ill-defined problems as designing a shop (Hayes, 1978), writing a fugue (Reitman, 1965), and building a warship (Simon, 1973).

A Strategy for Solving Problems

After the problem has been defined, the next step is to develop a plan of attack. Two major strategies can be used to solve a problem: algorithms and heuristics.

Algorithms An *algorithm* is a precise set of rules used to solve a particular type of problem. To illustrate, consider the algorithm for subtracting: One number is deducted from another to obtain the correct answer. If the algorithm is applied correctly, the solution will be accurate; in this case, following the rules of subtraction produces a correct calculation.

In some cases, a simple algorithm is all that is needed to solve the problem. The application of the subtraction algorithm, for instance, quickly leads to a correct answer. However, in many cases the set of rules that will solve the problem is not easily identified. In these situations, many alternatives must be tried before the correct solution is found. Unfortunately, this process of trial and error often uses an enormous amount of time to solve a problem, as Samuel's (1963) analysis of how this strategy could be applied to the game of checkers illustrates. Using an algorithm to develop a plan to win a checker game would involve (1) identifying all possible opening moves, (2) predicting an opponent's response to each of these moves, and (3) anticipating all the further responses of both players until all the possible outcomes of the game had been analyzed. Samuel calculated that discovering a series of moves that would guarantee a win would involve considering 10^{40} moves and take 10^{21} centuries to complete. Obviously, using an algorithm to play checkers is not very practical.

Heuristics A *heuristic*, also known as a "best guess" or "rule of thumb," is an alternative to the exhaustive search that the algorithm strategy usually entails. Heuristics increase but do not guarantee the likelihood of finding a correct solution. To illustrate this strategy, suppose that you are playing chess. Obviously, you cannot use an algorithm to discover a winning solution. You could decide to use a heuristic strategy such as maximizing the protection of the queen. However, you may not always be able to protect your queen and win (for example, when the only way to win is to sacrifice your queen), but usually this strategy will help you find a winning approach.

Consider the following real-world example of a problem solved both by an algorithm and by a heuristic. You need a special tool to fix your car, but you do not have the tool nor do you know which hardware store carries that tool. One way to solve your problem is to call every hardware store in the telephone book—using an algorithm to solve the problem. However, you might find this strategy time consuming, especially if there are hundreds of hardware stores in the telephone book. An alternative would be to call the hardware stores which have large ads in the phonebook, since these stores probably would stock the desired tool. Solving the problem this way uses a heuristic strategy.

Many heuristic strategies can be used to solve various problems (see Nisbett & Ross, 1980, for a review of this literature). Some of these heuristic strategies provide a systematic method of arriving at a solution but do not take as long to use as an algorithm. Other heuristic strategies represent cognitive shortcuts to decision making and often lead to incorrect solutions. This chapter will briefly discuss four types of heuristics. Two of them, *working backward* and *means-end analysis,* entail systematic evaluation of the problem to arrive at a reasonably accurate solution. Use of the other two heuristics, *representativeness* and *availability,* is affected by bias from past experience and therefore sometimes results in ineffective solutions.

Working Backward   How can one prove that a geometry theorem is derived from a set of geometry axioms? The starting point of the problem is the axioms; the end point, proving the theorem. One heuristic method of solving this problem is to start with the theorem and work back to the axioms. The *working-backward strategy* works well because the number of paths leading from the theorem back to the axioms is smaller than the number leading from the axioms to the theorem. Therefore, using an algorithm and searching each of these paths from the axioms will require more time to find the solution than using the working-backward heuristic and tracing the theorem back to the axioms.

The working-backward heuristic is commonly used in mathematics and other formal systems of analysis. In an elegant analysis of this type of heuristic, Newell, Shaw, and Simon (1958) found that computers programmed to use the working-backward heuristic rapidly generated proofs for mathematical theorems. In contrast, the computers programmed to work forward from the axioms required a great deal of time to prove even simple theorems.

Means-end Analysis   Another systematic heuristic used for solving problems is the *means-end analysis,* which breaks down a particular problem into a series of subproblems which are then solved. These solutions, in turn, may make it possible to solve the problem.

Newell and Simon (1972) provide a real-world example of the means-end heuristic:

> I want to take my son to nursery school. What's the difference between what I have and what I want? One of distance. What changes distance? My automobile. My automobile won't work. What is needed to make it work? A new battery. What has new batteries? An auto repair shop. I want the repair shop to put in a new battery; but the shop doesn't know I need one. What is the difficulty? One of communication. A telephone . . . and so on. (p. 416)

In this example, the starting point is an automobile that does not work; the end point is getting the child to the nursery school; the problem is how to take the child in the car to the nursery school. Solution of the problem is enhanced by creating an initial subproblem of why the automobile does not work. Recognizing that the car needs a new battery not only solves the subproblem but also increases the probability that the problem will be solved.

Note that the means-end analysis heuristic places substantial demand on the short-term store, or our memory of recent events (see Chapter 8). Each subproblem must be kept in memory until the subproblem below it is solved. To illustrate the sequence of subproblems in the short-term store, Hayes (1978) suggested the analogy of the push-down device used in some cafeterias for holding plates. As can be seen in Figure 7.10, the main problem goes in first and is pushed down as subproblems are added. Solving a subproblem causes the stack to move up to the next subproblem. Although this heuristic is demanding of the memory, it is also effective. In fact, this method can be used to solve problems which cannot be accurately solved with other heuristics.

FIGURE 7.10
Diagram shows how each subproblem is added to the push-down stack and then pops up when tested. From Hayes, J. R. *Cognitive psychology.* Homewood, Ill.: Dorsey, 1978.

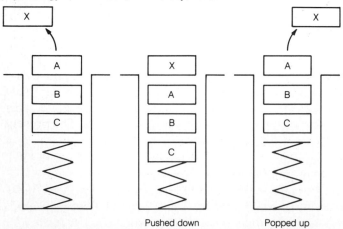

Working backward and means-end analysis both represent systematic heuristic strategies of problem solving. They seek all available information and, under most circumstances, provide accurate solutions. Other heuristics do not consider all the available information in solving problems; instead, they use only a limited amount of information. Failing to use all available information represents cognitive shortcuts, which can cause errors in judgment and lead to inaccurate solutions. Kahneman and Tversky (see Kahneman & Tversky, 1972, 1973; Tversky & Kahneman, 1973) have identified two types of heuristics—representativeness and availability—as cognitive shortcuts to solving problems.

Representativeness *Representativeness* is a heuristic that makes judgments based only on the obvious characteristics of the problem. Consider the following example: You are presented the problem, "What occupation should John pursue in college?" You are told that John is shy, helpful, good with figures, and has a passion for detail. Although you may ask for and receive further details needed to solve this problem, if you use the representativeness strategy, you will not seek additional information but will choose John's career based only on the facts initially given—facts that prompt you to decide that John should become an accountant. Although this strategy allows for faster decision making, you may be ignoring salient information (for example, John's preferences, his previous school grades, or the job opportunities in this field).

Kahneman and Tversky (1972, 1973) reported that the representativeness strategy is frequently used, even when it leads to illogical decision making. Kahneman and Tversky gave their subjects a problem similar to the last example. In addition to being given the personality sketch, subjects were told that the information was based on a psychologist's projective test given at the beginning of John's senior year of high school. Although Kahneman and Tversky's subjects expressed little faith in personality tests, they still based their decisions on information provided by John's test results. Also, the subjects overlooked the obvious point that a person's personality changes over time; certainly John's present personality could be quite different from that reported almost a year ago.

If, as suggested, use of the representative strategy may lead to error, why do people use it? There are two reasons: (1) This strategy often does work. (2) The strategy provides a quick way to make a decision. For example, suppose that you are managing a convenience store and have been robbed at gunpoint several times late at night. It is now 2 a.m.; someone enters the store alone. This person seems anxious and nervous—just like the previous robbers. The present conditions are similar to those that existed at the time of the robberies. You decide that this person is a robber and call the police. Although you may have behaved differently had you waited to gather further information, this decision is definitely the safest one. Thus, when using the representativeness strategy, we base our decisions entirely on similarities between available information and past experience.

Availability Decisions made using the *availability strategy* are based only on information that can be readily remembered. As Chapter 9 will point out, recent experiences are most easily remembered. Thus, using the availability heuristic means that decisions are usually based entirely on recent experiences. Suppose that you are trying to decide whether to drive or fly to college. If you have just read about a horrible airplane crash, your fears about the dangers of flying will be greater than if you did not have this information. Employing an availability strategy will prompt you to decide to drive, even though this choice may entail much more time and effort.

Our discussion suggests that using the heuristic strategies of representativeness or availability definitely reduces the time required to make decisions but does not always result in effective decision making. Apparently, people do not always choose the most accurate method for solving problems. Instead, their decision is often based on the effort required rather than on the accuracy of the method.

Execution of the Strategy

Once a strategy has been chosen, the next step is to decide how to execute it. For example, a person using a representativeness heuristic to decide whom to ask to the homecoming dance must then make a decision and ask that person out.

In many instances, the execution of the strategy is straightforward; that is, the strategy can readily be executed. Simple, well-defined problems can be executed in a short time. For example, if you simply want to select the most attractive date, the decision can be made quickly. However, if you want to find the perfect date, you may encounter difficulty in identifying the characteristics that define a perfect date and therefore have trouble deciding whom to ask out. This difficulty is typical of the problems encountered when trying to solve most ill-defined problems. The chosen strategy usually requires more time and effort to execute when the problem is ill-defined. Some of this difficulty may stem back to the first stage in the decision-making process, identifying the problem. Failing to make a precise identification of (1) the initial and goal states of an ill-defined problem, (2) the operations that can solve the problem, or (3) the restrictions to the solution can result in complications in executing the strategy and arriving at a solution.

The Problem Solved

The final stage of problem solving is determining the accuracy of the solution. Although we may not always know if we have solved a problem correctly, feedback often indicates whether our solution was right. This information about the accuracy of the solution is important for two reasons: (1) When we know we have chosen the right solution, we can then overcome the obstacles and reach our goals. If our solution is not accurate, this feedback lets us know that we need to find another way to solve the problem. At this point, we will start at the beginning of the problem-solving process. (2) The success or failure of our attempt to solve a problem can positively influence future problem solving by prompting us to continue using effective approaches and to abandon ineffective ones. In some cases, present problem solving can negatively affect future decisions by causing us to retain previously effective problem-solving approaches which are no longer effective as well as to overlook approaches which may have been ineffective in one situation but might be effective in another.

The Consequences of Past Experience

Functional Fixedness   After shopping at a local mall, you walk back to your car and notice that your license plate is loose. You know that it will probably fall off if you don't tighten the screws holding the plate to the frame, but how do you tighten the screws without a screwdriver? Although you might think of using a coin as a screwdriver, many other people would fail to recognize that a coin can be used in ways other than to buy things. Solving a problem often requires that we use a familiar object in a novel way. However, it is often hard to recognize these solutions. *Functional fixedness* refers to the difficulty involved in recognizing novel uses for an object. In the above example, functional fixedness would cause many people not to use a coin as a screwdriver to fix the loose license plate. Prior experience using an object to solve one problem makes it difficult to recognize that the same object can be used in a different manner to solve another problem.

The idea of functional fixedness was first discussed by Maier in 1931, and many studies have illustrated functional fixedness since (see Weisberg, DiCamillo, & Phillips, 1979, for a review of this literature). To study functional fixedness, Birch and Rabinowitz (1951) gave their subjects in the experimental groups two problems to solve. For the first problem, subjects were asked to complete an electrical circuit. Some of the subjects received a switch to use; others had a relay. Control subjects did not receive this initial problem. All subjects were then asked to solve the pendulum problem developed by Maier in 1930: Subjects are shown two strings hanging from the ceiling and told to tie the ends of the strings together. The problem was that the two strings were too far apart to hold one and reach the other. To solve this problem, subjects were given access to two heavy objects, a switch and a relay. The subjects should have then tied a heavy object to the end of one string, swung that string like a pendulum, grabbed the end of the other string, caught the first string when it swung back to them, and then tied the two strings together. Birch and Rabinowitz reported that subjects in the experimental group who had used the relay to complete the circuit in the first problem, chose the switch as the weight in the pendulum problem. In contrast, experimental-group subjects who had used the switch to solve the first problem chose the relay as the weight in the second problem. Control subjects used the relay and switch equally often. Apparently, once the experimental group subjects had established a function for the object (relay or switch) during the first problem, they did not think of using that object in a different manner to solve the second problem. Because control subjects had no prior experience with either object, the function of each object had not been fixed, and either one could have been used to solve the pendulum problem.

Functional fixedness reflects an inability to perceive objects as having more than one function. This rigidity can impair problem solving; however, there are ways to overcome functional fixedness. One way is to learn that objects can function in many ways. To illustrate this concept, Flavell, Cooper, and Loiselle (1958) asked subjects to use objects such as a switch and pliers in various ways before exposing them to the pendulum problem. Flavell, Cooper, and Loiselle reported that using one of these ordinary objects in several different ways prompted subjects to use that object again as a weight in the pendulum problem. However, if a subject had used the object in only one way, that subject did not use that object to solve the pendulum problem.

Set   Functional fixedness is not the only source of negative transfer in problem solving. People also have a tendency to attack new problems in the same way that they have solved earlier problems. The tendency to continue to use an established problem-solving method for future tasks is referred to as a *set*. It is important to note that a set is a source of negative transfer only if a new approach to solving a problem is needed. In fact, if the habitual approach will effectively solve the new problem, the set will actually be a source of positive transfer, that is, new problem solving will be enhanced as a result of the set.

Luchins's classic study (1942) showed the impact of set on problem solving. Subjects were given a series of problems that involved measuring out a given amount of water by using a water tap and three jars of specified sizes. Table 7.3 presents the sizes of the jars and the amount of water that Luchins wanted for the eleven problems. All subjects received problem 1, which could be solved by filling jar A three times and pouring the water into jar B. Subjects in the experimental group received problems 2 through 11; control-group subjects were given only problems 7 through 11. Most of the subjects in the experimental group learned that a single approach, B − A − 2C, could solve problems 2 through 6. Although problems 7 through 11 could also be solved using this approach, there was a simpler way, A + C or A − C, to solve these problems. Control subjects used the shorter solution for problems 7 through 11; in contrast, experimental subjects continued to use the longer method. Apparently, the experimental group subjects established a set, or habitual method of problem solving, as they solved problems 2 through 6, and they continued to use this approach for the remaining problems. Luchins suggested that the set created problems because it "blinded people to fresh ways of exploring problems." Other psychologists have also found that people continue to use previously successful approaches, even when other approaches would lead to faster

TABLE 7.3
LUCHINS'S WATER-MEASUREMENT PROBLEMS

Problem	Given jars of the following sizes			Obtain the amount
	A	**B**	**C**	
1.	29	3		20
2. E1	21	127	3	100
3. E2	14	163	25	99
4. E3	18	43	10	5
5. E4	9	42	6	21
6. E5	20	59	4	31
7. C1	23	49	3	20
8. C2	15	39	3	18
9.	28	76	3	25
10. C3	18	48	4	22
11. C4	14	36	8	6

Note: E = Experimental group; C = Control group
Source: Luchins, A. S. Mechanization in problem solving. *Psychological Monographs*, 1942, *54*, Whole 248. Copyright 1942 by the American Psychological Association. Reprinted by permission.

solutions; see Gardner and Runquist (1958) and Safren (1962) for other examples of the influence of set on problem solving.

Application: Becoming a Better Problem Solver

Can you improve your ability to solve problems? The answer to this question is yes. We will now examine some methods experts use to solve problems and some approaches you can use to enhance your ability to solve problems.

The Nature of Expertise People differ in terms of their ability to solve problems: some are extremely good at solving problems; others are not. Why this is true is answered by research comparing chess masters with novice players (see Chase & Simon, 1973, for a review of this literature). This research has shown that, because of repeated practice, the chess master has learned thousands of different patterns, perhaps as many as 50,000 in some cases, and can therefore automatically predict the effectiveness of all possible moves before choosing a particular one. In contrast, the novice player, before every move, must generate from scratch several possible responses to the opponent's last move and then try to anticipate the consequences of each possible reaction before deciding which move to choose. Thus an expert has more knowledge than the novice. But expertise involves more than greater knowledge; an expert also possesses more abstractions and uses more general concepts than do novices who are more concrete and employ specific bits of information. In terms of chess, experts have a general understanding of the utility of each piece and how each piece can be moved to the greatest advantage, whereas the novice has only memorized some moves that in the past have been successful.

Becoming a Better Problem Solver   Psychologists (Wicklegren, 1974) believe that problem solving in any area can be improved. Wicklegren suggests several points for improving the ability to solve problems: First, it is important to be aware of the *problem space*. The problem space is the start and end points of the problem as well as all the possible solutions to the problem. The expert chess player's knowledge of various chess positions, possible moves from each of these positions, and consequences of each move constitutes an awareness of the problem space. Second, awareness of the *various strategies for solving the problem* and knowledge of *when a particular strategy should be used* are also necessary. As discussed earlier, a number of strategies usually can be used to solve a particular problem, and the effectiveness of a certain strategy depends on the various aspects of that problem. Knowledge of different heuristic strategies (e.g., defending the queen) and of when each strategy should be employed undoubtedly contributes to the expert chess player's success. Third, the *most effective solution* must be selected. The problem solver must consider many possible solutions and then choose the one that provides the greatest likelihood of success. Finally, problem solvers must *avoid fixating on a particular strategy or a specific solution*. Changes in the nature of a problem may cause a chosen strategy to become ineffective; therefore, a problem solver must be prepared to recognize these changes and ready to try a new strategy to overcome them. Note that although knowledge of how to improve problem solving is important, only practice can significantly improve the ability to solve problems. One way to get this practice is to use Wicklegren's book, which provides examples of many problems and describes how these problems should be solved.

LANGUAGE

The Nature of Language

Language serves three very important functions in our lives: (1) *Language allows us to communicate with other people*. Just imagine how difficult life would be if we could not express our ideas to our family and friends. We could not, for example, complain to our friends about how much schoolwork we have to do this weekend or call home to ask for money. (2) *Language facilitates the thinking process*. The first two sections of this chapter discussed concept learning and problem solving. Although these two processes, like most cognitions, can occur without language, language facilitates them by providing a system of interrelated symbols and rules. (3) *Language allows us to recall information beyond the limits of our memory stores*. To study language, psychologists have developed psycholinguistics, the psychology of language. At its most elemental level, psycholinguistics describes the nature of speech sounds, called *phonemes,* and how phonemes combine to form words. A higher level of analysis, called *grammar,* discusses the rules by which words combine to form phrases and sentences. The highest level of study deals with *semantics* and *pragmatics*. Semantics is the study of the meaning of language; pragmatics concerns the everyday use of language. Psycholinguists have studied how language is learned as well as whether primates can also communicate with language.

The Structure of Language

Phonemes   A phoneme is the simplest functional speech sound. For example, consider the words *pin* and *bin*. These two words have different meanings and can be distinguished only because their initial sounds, /p/ and /b/, are two different phonemes. Note that these distinguishing sounds can occur anywhere in the word. The word pairs *but, bet* and *top, ton* illustrate that the different sounds occurring throughout words enable us to distinguish the meanings of different words.

Any language has a limited number of different sounds or phonemes. English is comprised of forty-five basic sounds, but some languages have as few as fifteen basic sounds or as many as eighty-five (Mills, 1980). Also, phonemes differ from one language to the next. For example, English contains the /l/-/r/ distinction (as in the words *late* and *rate*), but no such sound difference exists in Japanese. In fact, Miyawaki, Strange, Verbugge, Liberman, Jenkins, and Fujimura (1975) reported that the Japanese do not hear the difference between the two sounds and when learning to speak English have difficulty mastering the phoneme distinction between /l/ and /r/. Apparently we only distinguish the phonemes that exist in the languages we are familiar with. No wonder we have such difficulty learning a new language.

How do we learn to recognize phonemes? Eimas and Corbit (1973) discovered that phonemes have distinctive psychological meaning; that is, each sound has its own categorical boundaries and can be distinguished from other sounds. Consider the two syllables *ba* and *pa*. Using a speech synthesizer, Eimas and Corbit slowly changed the sound from the phoneme /b/ to the phoneme /p/, thus changing the syllable *ba* to the syllable *pa*. Although the synthesizer changed the speech sound gradually, the subjects did not respond to the subtle changes. Instead, they reported hearing an abrupt change in the syllable. Apparently, physical boundaries delineate different phonemes. Interestingly, Eimas, Siqueland, Jusczyk, and Vigorito (1971) used habituation to show that even 1-month-old babies make similar categorical distinctions between phonemes. (A habituation treatment presents a stimulus until it no longer elicits a response.) Infants from Spanish-speaking homes who had never been exposed to English (Lasky, Syrdal-Lasky, & Klein, 1975) reacted the same way as do infants from English-speaking homes. These observations suggest an innate ability to detect specific phonemes. However, experience determines which sounds gain significance and become part of our everyday vocabulary. The finding that different languages use different phonemes indicates that cultural experience governs which phonemes individuals learn to recognize. Additional support for this view can be seen in studies in which subjects are trained to make phoneme distinctions they normally do not make. For example, Streeter and Landauer (1976) reported that Spanish children could be taught to distinguish between *ba* and *pa,* a discrimination that is not part of the Spanish language.

Morphemes   A morpheme is the smallest meaningful unit of language. Whereas phonemes are single sounds that enable us to distinguish the different meanings of different words, morphemes are the simplest combinations of phonemes that can be formed and still have meaning. Some morphemes are single phonemes, such as the words *A* and *I*. Other morphemes are comprised of two or more phonemes, the words *fun, joy,* and *car,* for example. A morpheme does not have to be a word; prefixes (e.g., *un-* and *re-*) and suffixes (*-er* and *-able*) are also morphemes. Similarly, inflections that make a noun plural (leaf to leaves) or indicate that a verb is present or past (catch, caught) are also morphemes. Consider the words *pill* and *pillow.* Adding *ow* to the word *pill* creates a word with a different meaning. The word *pill* is a *free morpheme,* because it can stand alone; *-ow* is a *bound morpheme* because it must be bound to a free morpheme to have meaning.

Sentences   Words can be combined into a *phrase,* a group of two or more related words which expresses a single thought, and phrases can be connected to form a sentence. A *sentence* consists of two or more phrases and conveys an assertion, question, command, wish, or exclamation. For example, the sentence, *The couple bought the house,* consists of two major phrases: the noun phrase *the couple* and the verb phrase *bought the house.*

How is a sentence constructed? Phrases cannot be randomly combined to form a sentence. Rules govern the formation of sentences, and rules determine how phonemes are grouped to form words and how words are combined to express various ideas. These rules that govern language are called *syntax.*

Syntax: The Rules of Language

Syntax is the system of rules for combining the various units of speech. An infinite number of morphemes, phrases, and sentences can be formed by these rules. Thus, human language is generative: syntax enables us to create an infinite number of meaningful expressions. Every language has its own syntax and, therefore, its own unique way of communicating ideas.

Phonology   Languages do not use every possible phoneme combination. For example, the two phonemes /p/ and /z/ cannot be combined to begin a word in the English language. Each language restricts the way in which phonemes can be combined to produce meaningful morphemes. *Phonology* refers to the rules that dictate how phonemes can be combined into morphemes.

Grammar   *Grammar* rules establish the ways that words can be combined into meaningful phrases, clauses, and sentences. Words must be arranged to indicate mutual relations; they cannot be grouped haphazardly. Consider the following example cited by the noted psycholinguist Noam Chomsky (1957): *Colorless green ideas sleep furiously* is a meaningful, although somewhat ridiculous, sentence, whereas the same five words arranged as *Furiously sleep ideas green colorless* is not even a sentence. When words are organized according to the rules of grammar, the resulting sentence conveys some kind of meaning. However, words strung together randomly will not express a coherent thought or idea.

Linguists have studied the structure of the sentence in terms of phrases. This linguistic analysis of the constituents of a sentence is called *phrase-structure grammar*. The analysis begins by dividing a sentence into a noun phrase and a verb phrase. Figure 7.11 presents a diagram of the phrase-structure grammar for the sentence *The couple bought the house*. As the diagram illustrates, the noun and verb phrase can then be divided further. This detailed linguistic analysis identifies all the constituent structures of the sentence. The phrase-structure analysis of a simple sentence can be easy; obviously, complex sentences can be difficult to diagram. I still remember my seventh-grade English class and the considerable frustration I experienced trying to construct "grammar trees." Perhaps you have similar memories.

Note that the rules of grammar are elaborate and not always followed. However, because they are generally accepted, using these rules of grammar allows us to communicate effectively with each other.

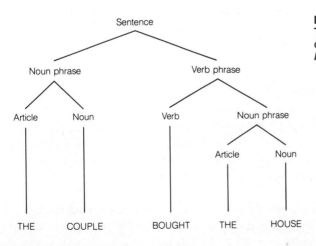

FIGURE 7.11
The phrase-structure grammar of the sentence *The couple bought the house.*

Semantics: The Meaning of Language   Consider the following two sentences: *The boy hit the ball. The ball was hit by the boy.* Shown in Figure 7.12, the grammar trees for these two sentences are quite different, but these two sentences convey the same meaning. According to Houston (1981), the fact that different sentences may have the same meaning points to one important problem of the phrase-structure grammar approach to language. Also, according to Houston, there is a second difficulty with this approach: one sentence may have two different meanings. For example, the sentence "They are growing trees" can mean either that a group of people are in the business of growing trees, or that certain trees are in the process of growing. Figure 7.13 presents the phrase-structure analyses of this ambiguous sentence.

Analyzing the grammar of a sentence is not the same as analyzing the meaning. Noam Chomsky (1965) recognized this difference. In Chomsky's view, the arrangement of the words in a sentence represents the *surface structure*. The

FIGURE 7.12
The phrase-structure grammar of the two sentences *The boy hit the ball* and *The ball was hit by the boy.*

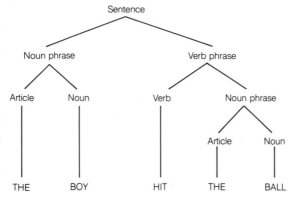

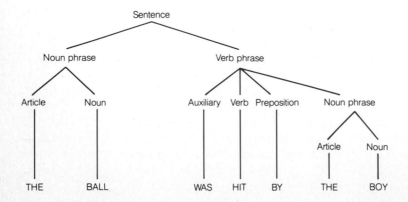

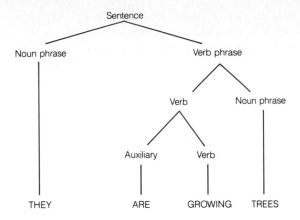

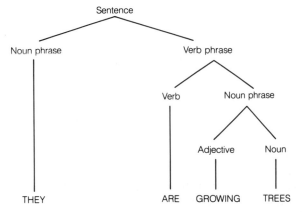

FIGURE 7.13
Two different phrase-structure grammar trees for the ambiguous sentence *They are growing trees.*

meaning or idea conveyed by the sentence is the *deep structure*. Only by determining the deep structure can the meaning of a sentence be understood.

How do we figure out the meaning of a sentence? A number of psycholinguists have described this process (Forster, 1979; Wanner & Maratsos, 1978). The first step in the comprehension of a sentence is to divide it into *clauses*. For example, the sentence, *The pitcher threw the ball, and the batter hit it,* expresses two complete thoughts or propositions; these two thoughts are clauses. Evidence of the use of this clause analysis can be found in a study by Foder, Bever, and Garrett (1974) in which subjects heard a clicking sound either in the middle of the first clause or between the two clauses. Regardless of when the click was actually presented, subjects reported hearing a click between the two clauses. Apparently, a clause is a cognitive unit which resists disruption. Thus, the click presented in the middle of the first clause "migrated" to the end of the clause, and a click presented at either point in the sentence represented a "mental comma" between the two clauses.

After a sentence has been divided into clauses, its meaning can then be determined. Let's use the sentence *The cat chased the mouse* to illustrate this process. To understand the sentence, the reader must determine who is the "doer" and who is "done-to." One approach is to use the "first-noun-phrase-did-it" strategy (Bever, 1970). Using this strategy, the sentence is assumed to be in the active voice, and the first noun clause is tentatively identified as the doer and the second noun clause as the done-to. This strategy can convey the meaning of the above sentence, and of most sentences, since the active voice is used much more frequently than the passive voice. However, it will communicate an incorrect meaning if the sentence is in the passive voice. Fortunately, some clues indicate the use of the passive voice, for example, the words *was* and *by* in the sentence *The mouse was chased by the cat*. These cue words indicate that the first-noun-phrase-did-it strategy is invalid.

Slobin (1966) suggests that an elaborate grammatical analysis is often used to determine deep structure of passive-voice sentences. To provide evidence for this view, Slobin asked his subjects to listen to a sentence, look at a picture, and then decide whether the sentence described the picture. Slobin reported that subjects took longer to react to passive-voice sentences than to active voice-sentences.

Note that shortcuts sometimes can be used to determine meaning (Slobin, 1966). For example, consider the sentence: *The flowers are watered by the girl.* Even though the sentence is in the passive voice, logically, the meaning can be quickly determined. It is plausible that girls water flowers; flowers do not water girls. However, this shortcut will not work for sentences with reversible meanings, for example, *The cat is chased by the dog.*

Not only do we receive and interpret language, we also generate it. According to Chomsky (1965) ideas can be expressed in a number of ways; that is, deep structures can be transmitted through various surface structures. Chomsky suggests that transformational rules enable the same deep structure to generate many different surface structures. Each language has its own acceptable rules of transformational grammar. Individuals in particular cultures must learn these rules so that their use of language will comply with accepted grammatical principles and thus be understood by other members of that culture.

Pragmatics: The Use of Language   The meaning of a sentence often depends on the context in which it occurs. Suppose you say, "My head is spinning." Depending on the social situation, your sentence may mean that you are dizzy from a ride on a roller coaster, that you have consumed too much alcohol, or that this class is a little too difficult. To understand the meaning of sentences, the context in which the idea being expressed was experienced must be understood.

The rules of pragmatics consider context and recognize that attitude affects the meaning of language. If your boss gives you a raise of $100 a week, you may say, "Thanks a lot." Your statement may reflect gratitude if you only expected a $10-a-week raise, or it may reflect anger if you expected a $1000-a-week raise.

Acquisition of Language

There are two major views of how the ability to use language is acquired. A learning view, first proposed by B. F. Skinner in 1957, assumes that language is acquired through the instrumental-conditioning process (see Chapter 3). According to this approach, children learn language because their parents and other people in their environment reinforce it. The psycholinguistic theory, initially described by Noam Chomsky in 1965, assumes that language acquisition is innate. In this view, humans are born with certain mechanisms that enable them to learn to communicate with only a minimal amount of linguistic experience.

A Reinforcement View   Suppose that a mother hears her young child say "mama." In all likelihood, the mother will be pleased, and she will reward the child with a hug and kiss. This affection reinforces the child's behavior and will thus increase the frequency of the child's use of language.

B. F. Skinner (1957) assumes that all responses, including language, are acquired according to the laws of instrumental conditioning (see Chapter 3). In Skinner's view, shaping is used to encourage children to learn to communicate with words. Initially, approximations of a desired verbal response are rewarded, but eventually this reinforcement stops, and adults expect a closer resemblence to the final behavior before providing reward. Consider Anne, a baby learning to talk. When Anne first makes any sound resembling a real word, such as the *m* sound for *mama,* Anne's parents are delighted and reward her with praise and affection. However, as Anne continues to make nonsense sounds, her parents gradually stop responding to them. To again receive reinforcement, Anne must learn to say something closer to the actual word "mama."

Words are not the only language units that can be acquired through the use of reinforcement. Skinner argues that phrases and sentences can also be learned by the process of shaping; initially, nongrammatical phrases and sentences may be rewarded, but eventually only correct language use will be rewarded.

Psycholinguists have been extremely critical of Skinner's reinforcement view of language acquisition (see Lennenberg, 1969, for a discussion of these criticisms). There are three major aspects of this criticism: The first problem is that Skinner's view assumes that parents will reward correct use of language and ignore or penalize incorrect use, but observations (McNeill, 1966) show that parents use rewards and punishments to influence only the content, not the grammatical correctness, of their children's language. Thus, a parent will allow a grammatically incorrect sentence to be used as long as the content is accurate. Brown, Cazden, and Bellugi's (1969) description of the language of two children, Eve and Adam, provides an excellent illustration of the influence of parental approval and disapproval on a child's use of language.

> Gross errors of word choice were sometimes corrected, as when Eve said, "What the guy idea." Once in a while an error of pronunciation was noticed and corrected. More commonly, however, the grounds on which an utterance was approved or disapproved . . . were not strictly linguistic at all. When Eve expressed the opinion that her mother was a girl by saying, "She a girl," mother answered, "That's right." The child's utterance was ungrammatical but the mother did not respond to that fact; instead she responded to the truth . . . of the proposition the child intended to express. . . . Adam's "Walt Disney comes on on Tuesday" was disapproved because Walt Disney came on on some other day. It seems then to be truth value rather than syntactic well-formedness that chiefly governs explicit verbal reinforcement by parents—which renders mildly paradoxical the fact that the usual product of such (training) is an adult whose speech is highly grammatical but not notably truthful. (pp. 70–71)

A second problem that psycholinguists have cited with a reinforcement view concerns the creative aspect of language. Children (as well as adults) frequently use an original combination of words to convey an idea. The fact that people can generate new but grammatically accurate language is difficult to explain in terms of instrumental-conditioning principles: how can children (or adults) use a combination of words that they have never said nor heard and that therefore has never been reinforced? Consider Miller's (1965) statement to illustrate this criticism of the reinforcement theory:

> By a rough, but conservative calculation there are 10^{20} sentences 20 words long, and if a child were to learn only these it would take him something on the order of 1000 times the estimated age of the earth just to learn them. . . . Any attempt to account for language acquisition that does not have a generative character will encounter this difficulty. . .
>
> Since the variety of admissible word combinations is so great, no children could learn all of them. Instead of learning specific combinations of words, he learns rules for generating admissible combinations. (pp. 176, 178)

The final and perhaps strongest evidence comes from Lennenberg's research showing that despite widely varying social conditions, most children acquire language in a relatively constant pattern. It seems reasonable to expect that children living in different cultures would show various patterns of language acquisition. Yet, Lennenberg found that nonsense sounds are always followed by one-word speech, which then develops into the use of two-word sentences, followed by telegraphic speech, and then the use of complex sentences. The observation that even children raised by deaf parents show the same pattern of language development suggests that social reinforcement is not a critical determinant of language acquisition.

Carlson (1984) argues that these criticisms of the reinforcement theory overlooked an important point. According to Carlson, language can be reinforced in ways other than direct intervention, and that, in fact, it is the effect of language, not the actual words, that is reinforced. For example, suppose that 2-year-old Billy says "milk" and is then given a glass of milk by his father. Although his father did not consider the glass of milk a reward for his son's word "milk," to Billy, the glass of milk served as a reinforcement for the verbal behavior that was instrumental in attaining it. The success of this verbal behavior will prompt Billy to use it again whenever he wants a glass of milk. Further, the effects of this reinforcement will be generative, causing Billy to realize that he can use words to get other things he wants, such as books and toys. Verbal behavior can also be used to obtain social rewards such as praise or sympathy, and receiving this kind of reinforcement will increase a child's use of language in social situations.

Increasing verbal behavior is one role of reinforcement in language acquisition. Reinforcement also affects the learning of grammar rules. According to Carlson, simple speech is sufficient to express simple ideas, and more complex language is needed for complex expressions. The future tense is one example of complex language; this tense is especially hard for children to learn because the idea expressed in a future-tense sentence is not immediately experienced and therefore not immediately reinforced. For example, the statement *We're going to the circus now* is much easier for a child to understand than the sentence *We're going to the circus next week.*

The main effect of reinforcement seems to be increased use of correct verbal behavior. However, the ability to use language appears to be innate; that is, people are born with certain mechanisms that enable them to use words to communicate. In all likelihood, this preparedness makes people very sensitive to the consequences of language use and provides an effective medium for reinforcement to increase correct language usage.

A Psycholinguistic View   Noam Chomsky (1965, 1968, 1975) was very impressed with how easily young children learned their native language. He described the universal sequence of language development from nonsense sounds to the generation of complex sentences and, on the basis of these observations, suggested that children are born with a language-generating mechanism called the *language acquisition device* (LAD). The LAD "knows" the universal aspects of language. This knowledge allows children to readily grasp the syntax relevant to their native language. In Chomsky's view, however, this biological preparedness does not result in automatic language acquisition; a child must be exposed to language to learn it. Usually, though, parents eager for their child to start talking provide more than adequate stimulation.

Chomsky's view that children are inherently prepared to learn language received a considerable amount of support from psycholinguists during the 1960s and 1970s (Dodd & White, 1980). For example, Eric Lennenberg (1967, 1969) argued that language acquisition is an innate species-specific characteristic and that its expression depends only on physical maturation and minimal exposure to language. According to Lennenberg, language is acquired in a fixed order and at a particular rate. Even when maturation is abnormally slow, as in the case of children with Down's syndrome, language is still learned in the same sequence but at a slower rate.

In recent years, however, a number of psychologists (see Bruner, 1978; Ferguson, 1977; Gleason & Weintraub, 1978; Newport, 1977; Snow, 1979) have suggested that the LAD theory expressed by Chomsky and Lennenberg may not completely explain how language is acquired. These psychologists believe that the social aspects of language, rather than simply exposure to language, govern language acquisition. Language is a method of communicating our desires to others; children are motivated to use language by various forms of reinforcement. This view does not imply that children are not prepared to learn to use language but suggests that this preparedness alone is insufficient to explain language acquisition. The idea that the ability to use language is the result of a combination of biological preparedness and reinforced experience is consistent with the material presented in Chapter 10.

Consider Moskowitz's (1978) observations to illustrate the importance of the social function of language. Moskowitz studied the language acquisition of a boy with normal hearing whose deaf parents communicated through American Sign Language. The parents had their son watch television every day in hopes that it would teach him English. Unfortunately, their idea failed; at the age of 3 their son was fluent in sign language, but he neither understood nor spoke English. Apparently, children must interact verbally with others to learn language.

Application: Teaching Chimpanzees Language

Monkeys use sounds to communicate with each other. A primate can express a variety of different emotional states in a manner that other primates understand and to which they respond. Observations of vervet monkeys in Kenya (Seyfarth, Cheney, & Marler, 1980) illustrate both the sophistication of primates' vocalizations as well as the reactions of other primates to these vocalizations. For example, the vervet monkeys made distinctive alarm calls when they spotted predators. The sight of a leopard caused them to emit a series of short, tonal calls. The sight of an eagle elicited a low pitched grunt. The reaction to a snake consisted of a series of high pitched "chutters." Each of these calls elicited a different response from vervet monkeys nearby: they ran up a tree when hearing the leopard alarm call; they looked up and ran for cover when hearing the eagle alarm call; and they looked down when hearing the snake-alarm call. Clearly, primates can communicate through vocalizations; however, these vocalizations are not language. Can primates learn to use language to communicate?

Early investigations suggested that primates could not learn language. Winthrop and Luella Kellogg (1933) raised the baby chimpanzee Gua in their home with their infant son Donald. Despite many attempts to teach Gua to speak, the chimp never uttered any English words, although she did learn to obey certain commands. Cathy and Keith Hayes (1951) were somewhat more successful in teaching the chimpanzee Vicki to speak. Vicki learned to say three words— *papa, mama,* and *cup.* Yet, these words were acquired only after a long period of training, which included manipulating the chimp's lips.

Compared with the Kelloggs and the Hayes, Beatrice and Allen Gardner (1971) were much more successful in teaching their chimp Washoe language. The Gardners believed that intellectual impairment was not responsible for earlier failures to teach chimpanzees language; instead these failures were caused by the chimpanzees' physical inability to produce the complex vocalizations necessary for speech. So instead of trying to teach Washoe to speak English, they taught her American Sign Language. Washoe lived in a trailer in the Gardner's backyard and during all her waking hours had the companionship of one or two people who talked to her only in sign language. After four years of training, Washoe had learned over 200 signs and was able to combine them into sentences, such as *Please tickle more* or *Give me sweet drink.*

Did Washoe learn to use language to communicate? The Gardners think so. Washoe's "language" certainly has many of the characteristics of human language. First, it makes sense. For example, Washoe used the sign for cat to point out a cat, and the sign for dog to identify a dog. Second, Washoe's verbalizations were in sentence form. Third, sentences created by Washoe were structured according to the rules of grammar; the sentence *Please tickle me* illustrates Washoe's mastery of syntax. Finally, Washoe responded to questions. For example, if the Gardners asked in sign language the question, "Who pretty?", Washoe answered, "Washoe."

The Gardners are not the only psychologists who have taught primates to use language. For example, Penny Patterson (1978) taught Koko, a gorilla, over 600 signs. Koko's use of language was spontaneous, and she could even generate new language. In fact, she scored only slightly below average on an intelligence test designed for humans her age.

Techniques other than sign language have been used to teach primates to communicate. Duane Rumbaugh and his colleagues (Rumbaugh & Gill, 1976; Savage-Rumbaugh, Rumbaugh, & Boysen, 1980) taught chimpanzees language with the aid of a computer. To obtain what they wanted, the chimpanzees had to press the keys that corresponded to specific words. For example, their chimpanzee Lana learned to send the following message, "Please machine make movie period." Two other chimpanzees, Austin and Sherman, even learned to communicate with each other through the computer. For example, Rumbaugh and his colleagues sometimes gave either Austin or Sherman food; the "unfed" chimpanzee had to ask the "fed" chimpanzee for food. Austin and Sherman learned to ask each other for food and for many other things. David Premack (1976) taught his chimpanzee Sarah to "read" and "write" by arranging plastic tokens into "sentences." Each plastic token represented an object, action, or attribute (see Figure 7.14). Sarah was able to construct and under-

Washoe and that this difference was responsible for Terrace's observations. The intense debate about primate ability to learn language continues, and one hopes that future research will clarify whether primates do in fact use language to communicate.

SUMMARY

A concept is a symbol that represents a class or group of objects or events that have common characteristics. Concepts enhance the thinking process by incorporating new objects and events into existing categories. A number of different rules define the characteristics, or attributes, of a particular concept. The affirmative rule states that the presence of a particular attribute defines the concept; using the negative rule, a member of the concept cannot possess a specific attribute. The presence of two or more attributes defines a concept by the conjunctive rule, whereas the disjunctive rule states that the presence of one of two or both attributes defines the concept. The if, then statement can be applied to concepts defined by the conditional rule; the statement if and only if governs concepts defined by the biconditional rule.

In some cases, not all members of a concept will have all the attributes characteristic of the concept. The prototype best exemplifies the concept because it possesses more attributes than the other members of the concept. Boundaries specify the point at which a particular object or event is not a member of a specific concept.

Concepts are learned by testing hypotheses. Various strategies can be used to systematically test hypotheses and thereby learn the concept. There are two main types of strategies: Analytic strategies represent techniques for identifying attributes, prototypes, or rules. Nonanalytic strategies involve remembering specific positive instances of a concept and using these examples to determine whether new stimuli are instances of the concept. Several analytic strategies have been identified: Successive scanning involves testing one hypothesis at a time, and conservative focusing entails focusing on the first positive instance of a concept and systematically determining which aspect of that positive instance defines the concept. Simultaneous scanning tests several hypotheses at the same time. Focus gambling is a combination of the successive-scanning and conservative-focusing strategies. Some conditions require analytic strategies to learn a concept, but in other cases nonanalytic strategies are sufficient to learn a concept.

Rosch suggested that we are inherently prepared to perceive certain concepts and that we learn concepts with a moderate degree of inclusiveness (basic concepts) more readily than either concepts with a low degree of inclusiveness (subordinate concepts) or concepts with a high degree of inclusiveness (superordinate concepts). Our culture also influences what concepts we learn; cultural differences in concept learning reflect linguistic relativity.

A problem exists when attainment of a desired goal is blocked by an obstacle or obstacles. Thorndike assumes that problems are solved by trial and error; in contrast, Kohler argued that a problem is first explored internally. Possible solutions are then tested, and finally insight into the correct solution is gained. Insight then enables the problem to be solved.

Research indicates that there are four steps to solving a problem. Defining the problem—identifying both the starting point, or initial state, of the problem and the end point, or goal state, of the problem—is the first step. In some cases, the problem is well-defined and has clear starting and end points; however, some problems are ill-defined. The key to solving an ill-defined problem is generating subproblems. The initial step in problem solving also involves identifying the operations that can be used to solve the problem as well as restrictions that cannot help to solve the problem.

The second step in problem solving is developing a strategy. There are two types of strategies: algorithms, which are precise rules, and heuristics, which are best-guess strategies. Some heuristics are systematic problem-solving methods. Using the working-backward strategy, the problem solver begins at the end point and works back to the starting point. The means-end strategy breaks the problem down into a series of subproblems. Other heuristic strategies are cognitive shortcuts which are usually effective but sometimes lead to spectacular errors. With the representative strategy, solutions are based only on the obvious characteristics of the problem; only information that can be remembered is used to solve problems with the availability strategy.

Executing the strategy is the third step and solving the problem is, obviously, the final step. Difficulties are common in solving a problem; these difficulties are sometimes caused by the influence of past experiences. In the case of functional fixedness, the difficulty found in recognizing new uses for familiar objects impairs problem solving. Another factor that creates difficulty in solving problems is the set, which attacks new problems in the same ways that earlier problems had been solved even though the old strategies are no longer effective.

Language serves three important functions: it allows us to communicate with others, it facilitates the thinking process, and it enables us to recall information beyond the limits of our memory stores. Psycholinguists have studied the nature of language. The phoneme is the simplest speech sound. Although we have an innate ability to detect many different phonemes, our culture determines how many different sounds we learn to use. Phonemes are combined to form a morpheme, the smallest meaningful unit of language. Morphemes are words (free morphemes) as well as prefixes and suffixes (bound morphemes). Words can be combined into a phrase, which expresses a single thought, and phrases can be grouped to form a sentence, which conveys an assertion, question, command, wish, or exclamation. Syntax is the system of rules governing the ways various units of speech can be combined. Phonology refers to the rules specifying how phonemes can be combined into words, whereas the rules of grammar establish how words are combined into meaningful phrases and sentences. Grammar refers to the surface structure of a sentence; the meaning conveyed by the sentence is called the deep structure. The study of the meaning of language, called semantics, has shown that the same sentence can have different meanings and different sentences can have the same meaning. According to Chomsky, transformational rules of grammar allow a specific deep structure to generate varied surface-structure sentences. The study of pragmatics has demonstrated that social context often influences the meaning of language.

Two major theories of language acquisition have been proposed. Skinner assumes that children acquire language because of reinforcement. In contrast, Chomsky assumes that humans have an innate ability to learn language and that language can be used to communicate after only a minimal amount of linguistic experience. A contemporary view suggests that both preparedness and the use of conditioning influence language; humans may be prepared to learn language, but they must also discover that language can be used to obtain nonsocial and social rewards.

Primates have been taught sign language and can use these signs in sentences. Some psycholinguists believe that these primates communicate with language and therefore argue that language is not limited to humans. However, other psycholinguists believe that primates are not actually using language but are merely imitating behavior which has been reinforced by their trainers. Whether primates can use language remains a topic for future discovery.

CHAPTER 8

MEMORY STORAGE

A FLEETING EXPERIENCE

While working at a construction site last year, Donald was hit in the head by a piece of wood. Although the accident left Donald unconscious for only several minutes, it completely altered his life. Donald could still recall events which occurred prior to the injury, but once a thought left his consciousness, it was lost.

Two events happened today which are typical of Donald's memory problem. Donald and his wife were shopping when a man whom Donald had no recollection of ever meeting approached them with a friendly greeting, "Hello, Helen and Don." After the man had walked away, Helen identified the "stranger" as a neighbor, Bill Jones, who had moved into a house down the block several months ago. Don became frustrated when Helen told him that he frequently talked with this neighbor. Helen, too, was frustrated; she often wished that Don would remember what she told him. She knew Don would ask her again about Bill Jones the next time they met.

When they arrived home, Don received a telegram from his aunt, informing him of his uncle's death. Don, immediately struck with an intense grief, cried for almost an hour over the loss of his favorite uncle. Yet, after being distracted by a phone call from a neighbor, Donald no longer remembered his uncle's death. Helen told him again, and he experienced the intense grief once more. Donald suffers from a disorder called *anterograde amnesia*. His memory problems are the direct result of his accident, which caused an injury to an area of the brain called the *dorsomedial thalamus*. The function of the dorsomedial thalamus is to store recent experiences in a permanent, or relatively permanent, way. As the result of his injury, Donald cannot store his experiences. Unfortunately, there are many people like Donald who cannot remember recent events because of brain damage.

To recall an event, two processes must take place. First, the experience must be stored as a memory. Second, the memory must be retrieved. This chapter describes the storage of experiences into memories; Chapter 9 looks at retrieval of memory. Memory losses that result from storage failure are examined in this chapter; forgetting as a result of retrieval failure will be the focus of Chapter 9. We will also discuss the physiological basis of memory storage in this chapter.

STAGES OF MEMORY STORAGE

Atkinson and Shiffrin (1971) identified three stages in the storage of information: sensory register, short-term store, and long-term store. As can be seen in Figure 8.1, external input (or external events) is initially stored in the *sensory register* for a very brief duration, usually one-half to one second. The information contained in the sensory register is an initial impression of the external environment; experiences stored in the sensory register are exact duplications of external stimuli. However, not all information in the external environment is stored in the sensory register. Also, information decays rapidly after leaving the sensory register and will be lost unless processed into the short-term store.

The *short-term store* is also a temporary storage facility. People are consciously aware of information in the short-term store; they are not aware of information in the sensory register because information is stored for a longer

FIGURE 8.1
A diagram illustrating the Atkinson-Shiffrin three-stage model of memory storage. Adapted from Atkinson, R. C., & Shiffrin, R. M. Human memory: A proposed system and its control processes. In K. W. Spence and J. T. Spence (Eds.), *The psychology of learning and motivation* (vol. E). New York: Academic, 1968.

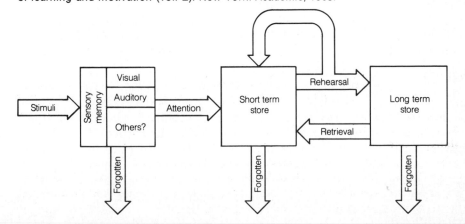

period of time in the short-term store. Memories can remain in the short-term store for 5, 10, 15 seconds, or even longer. The length of time that information remains in short-term store depends on two processes. First, experiences can be rehearsed or repeated. *Rehearsal* holds information in the short-term store. Without rehearsal, information can be lost from the short-term store before it is stored in a meaningful way. One function of rehearsal is to organize information in the short-term store. This organization makes an experience more meaningful, enhancing the likelihood that the memory will be recalled. Rehearsed information can be forgotten; rehearsal merely acts to enhance the retrievability of a memory. Furthermore, the longer information in the short-term store is rehearsed, the more likely the information will be remembered later. Also, new information entering the short-term store can result in the loss of information already held by the short-term store. Remember from Chapter 3 that concurrent interference impairs conditioning. The expulsion of information from the short-term store before it can be permanently stored may explain the impact of concurrent interference on learning.

Second, only a limited amount of information can be retained in the short-term store. When new information enters the short-term store, old information will be "bumped out" unless the short-term store has enough room for both the old and the new information. Information in the short-term store is interpreted for its meaning and then organized in a logical way. This analysis produces a more meaningful memory and thereby increases the likelihood of recall at a later time. If information lost from the short-term store is not transferred to permanent storage, it will be forgotten. Rehearsal of information in the short-term store can prevent new information from entering the short-term store; thus rehearsal prevents rehearsed information from being "bumped" from the short-term store, thereby increasing its chances of being remembered later.

Most information contained in the short-term store is transferred into the long-term store, the site of permanent memory storage. Atkinson and Shiffrin suggest that the slow decay of a memory from the long-term store can cause some information to be lost. This issue of whether information is lost from the long-term store has not been settled. Some research suggests that all information in the long-term store remains there permanently; other research indicates that decay causes some memories to be lost. However, it is clear that memories remain in the long-term store for a long time even if they are not permanently stored.

Storage of a memory in the long-term store does not guarantee the ability to recall that particular memory. Two processes help to prevent recall of information from the long-term store. First, the presence of other memories in the long-term store may prevent recollection of a particular experience; this failure to recall a specific memory because of the presence of other memories in long-term store is called *interference*. Interference is one reason that memories are not retrieved from long-term store. The other reason, according to Underwood (1983), is the absence of a specific stimulus which can retrieve the memory of a previous experience. People can use salient aspects of an event, called *memory attributes,* to remember the event. For example, a friend's visit may remind you of a past experience with this friend. Or, returning to a place you have not been for several years causes you to remember something you did there years earlier. Your friend's presence or your revisitation are the memory attributes enabling you to retrieve the earlier experiences. The absence of these environmental events can result in the failure to recall a memory from the long-term store. The identification of the salient aspects of an event for use as memory attributes occurs during the short-term-storage phase of memory storage. The failure to identify a salient aspect of an experience for use as a memory attribute can prevent later recall of an experience.

Note that the organization of experience can occur even after a memory is transferred to long-term store. The retrieval of a memory from the long-term store results in the return of the memory to the short-term store; returning the memory to the short-term store enables a person to be consciously aware of a previous experience. While the memory remains in the short-term store, it can receive additional processing. This processing may facilitate recall of that experience later. Processing can also alter the memory, which may make the memory more logical or appealing. Whether memories which have received additional processing accurately reflect the actual experience is often difficult to know.

The Metaphor of Storage and Retrieval

Our discussion suggests that after a new event, experiences are stored and later recalled. However, the memory storage and retrieval processes are not entirely similar to the storage and retrieval systems with which we are familiar. For example, we can store data on a computer disk or write data on an index card, but the brain does not store memory in a concrete location.

According to Roediger (1980), the language of memory storage and retrieval is metaphorical; that is, our description of the memory storage and retrieval process is only analogous to the way we store and retrieve information from index cards or computer disks. The metaphor of memory storage and retrieval allows us to appreciate the characteristics of how experiences are stored as memories and then later recalled from storage. Unfortunately, this language can reify the storage and retrieval processes. For example, we suggest that the short-term store acts to organize information, but the short-term store is merely a hypothetical construct, not an actual object. Although experiences are organized, we are not consciously aware of this organization nor do we understand how it is accomplished. In Chapter 1 we discussed Tolman's suggestion that we act *as if* our behavior has purpose and direction, but we are not aware of this purposefulness or direction and do not know how cognitions are translated into behaviors. Evidently, a similar process and level of knowledge exists for memory storage and retrieval. With this idea in mind, let's next examine each stage of memory storage in greater detail. The processes leading to the retrieval of information and the failure to remember experiences are discussed in the next chapter.

Sensory Register

How are memories encoded? Is an exact duplicate of the initial experience stored, or is only a partial replica of an event encoded? Several lines of evidence demonstrate that an exact copy of an experience is stored in the sensory register. However, the copy lasts for only a very short time (no more than one-half to one second). Research on the characteristics of the sensory store has investigated two sensory systems: the visual system and the auditory system. The visual copy contained in the sensory store is referred to as an *icon,* and the copy is stored in *iconic memory. Echoic memory* contains an exact replica of an auditory experience, and the *echo* is stored in the sensory store.

Iconic Memory

In Search of an Icon   The classic research of George Sperling (1960, 1963) documents the existence of the storage of visual information in the sensory register; Sperling's findings also demonstrated that (1) an icon is an exact copy of a visual experience and (2) an iconic memory lasts for only a very brief time following the event. Sperling presented to subjects an array of letters arranged in three horizontal rows of four letters each (see Figure 8.2). An apparatus called a tachistoscope is used to present the letters on a screen for 0.05 seconds. The screen was then blank for a specified retention interval of 0 to 1 second. Some of Sperling's subjects received a *partial report technique;* they were asked at the end of the interval to recall all the letters in one of the three rows. The subjects were not informed before the end of the retention interval which line they were to recall. A tone presented at the end of the retention interval indicated which line should be recalled: a high pitch indicated the first

FIGURE 8.2
Sperling's procedure for investigating the visual sensory memory. Illustration shows one trial using the partial-report technique.

Phase 1 Experimenter presents array for $1/_{20}$ second.	**Phase 2** Tone signals which row subject is to recall	**Phase 3** Suspect tries to recall correct row
X G O B T M L R V A S F	High tone means recall top row. Medium tone means recall middle row. Low tone means recall bottom row.	For example high tone signals subject to recall X G O B

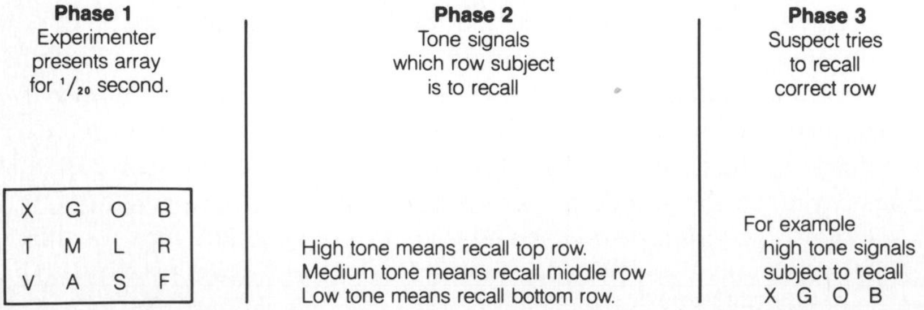

row; a medium tone, the second row; and a low tone, the third row. Presenting the tone very soon after the presentation of the array of letters enabled the subjects to remember most of the letters. However, if the retention interval was greater than 0.25 seconds, the subjects' performance declined significantly, and they could remember only about one letter per line (refer to Figure 8.3). That retention is high on an immediate but not on a delayed retention test indicates that even though subjects have access to all information contained in the sensory store, the visual copy fades quickly following entry into the sensory register.

Sperling asked some of his subjects to recall as many of the twelve letters in the array as possible. When recall occurred immediately after stimulus presentation had ended, this procedure, referred to as a *whole report technique,* resulted in subjects remembering only approximately 4.5 of the letters (see Figure 8.3). Sperling's observations with the partial report technique indicated that all twelve letters were encoded into the sensory store; why, then, could subjects receiving the whole report technique remember only about one-third

FIGURE 8.3
Performance level in Sperling's investigation of visual sensory memory. The solid line on the graph shows the number of letters recalled (left axis) and the percentage recalled (right axis) for subjects given the partial-report technique as a function of the delay between signal and recall. The bar at the right presents the number and percentage correct for the whole-report technique. From Sperling, G. The information available in brief visual presentations. *Psychological Monographs,* 1960, *74,* whole no. 498. Copyright 1960 by the American Psychological Association. Reprinted by permission.

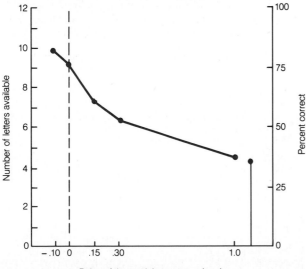

of them? Since experiences stored in the sensory register decay rapidly, the image fades before the subjects can recall more than four or five of the letters.

Note that when the retention interval was longer than 0.25 seconds, subjects were able to recall approximately 4.5 of all the letters or 1.5 of the letters in a particular row. As we learned earlier, only a limited amount (from 5–9 bits) of information can be transferred from the sensory register to short-term memory. The ability of Sperling's subjects to recall only 4.5 of all the letters or 1.5 of the letters in a particular row after a 0.5- or 1-second delay is due to the fact that only these letters were transferred from the sensory store to short-term memory, and that decay caused the rest to be lost.

Our discussion indicates that a "snapshot" of a visual experience is encoded in the sensory information store. Sperling's results provide evidence that an exact visual image of an event is stored in the sensory register. Many other studies (refer to Howard, 1983 or Wingfield & Byrnes, 1981, for a review of the literature) have shown that the sensory register contains a "mental" picture of a visual experience and that for a brief period following the event, a person can recall any of the information stored in the sensory register. These studies have also demonstrated that the icon, or visual memory, decays rapidly from the sensory register.

Eriksen and Collins (1967) presented to subjects some stimuli separated by an interval varying from 0 to 1 second. As can be seen in Figure 8.4, each separate stimulus is meaningless; however, when the stimuli overlap, the letters VOH can be seen. According to Eriksen and Collins, if an exact copy of the one stimulus had been stored in the sensory register when the next stimulus

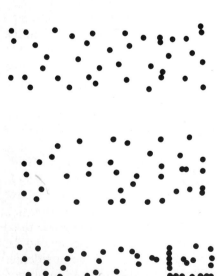

FIGURE 8.4
The stimuli used by Eriksen and Collins to study iconic memory. The top two stimuli were presented sequentially to subjects; if the two stimuli were not separated by more than 0.25 seconds, the subjects saw the nonsense syllable *VOH* which is presented in the bottom panel. From Eriksen, C. W., & Collins, J. F. Some temporal characteristics of visual pattern perception. *Journal of Experimental Psychology*, 1967, *74*, 476–484. Copyright 1967 by the American Psychological Association. Reprinted by permission.

was presented, the subjects would be able to detect the VOH letter pattern. Eriksen and Collins reported that their subjects accurately identified the letters when an interval of up to 0.25 seconds was inserted between the stimulus patterns, and they also found that the ability of the subjects to recognize the VOH letters declined to a level of no recognition when given a 1-second interval between successive stimulus presentations. Other studies have also observed that a combined image is experienced when separate stimulus events are presented close together; see Haber and Standing (1969) for another example.

Note that in the Eriksen and Collins study (1967), the subjects sometimes identified the letter pattern when a 0.5- or 0.75-second interval separated the stimuli. According to Wingfield and Byrnes (1981), some information about the first stimulus may have persisted beyond 0.25 seconds, and sometimes sufficient information about the one stimulus remained when the next stimulus was presented, which enabled the subject to identify the letter pattern. Thus, although the results of Eriksen and Collins's study demonstrate that the visual trace decays rapidly following entry into the sensory register, all information may not be lost from the sensory register 0.25 seconds after an event. Other studies (Howard, 1983) demonstrate that the length of time information is stored in the sensory register varies depending on stimulus conditions.

Duration of an Icon   Sperling's article (1960) suggests that visual images are stored in the sensory register for 0.25 seconds. However, depending on conditions, icons may persist for as much as a second or for as little as less than 0.25 seconds. The intensity of the visual events appears to affect the duration of an icon. For example, Keele and Chase (1967) and Mackworth (1963) reported that iconic memory is longer when a bright rather than dim display of letters is used. Similarly, if the preletter and postletter exposure displays are very bright, Averbach and Sperling (1961) discovered that the icon may last less than 0.25 seconds, whereas the icon may persist for more than a second when the blank displays following a visual event are very dark. Apparently, an intense stimulus experience produces a long-duration iconic memory, and a strong second visual experience can reduce the duration of the visual image of the first stimulus.

The backward-masking literature (see Breitmeyer & Ganz, 1976) shows that a visual experience can be erased from the sensory register by a new second stimulus. Thus, a second event may shorten the duration of the icon. The Averbach and Coriell study (1961) provides an excellent example of this backward-masking phenomenon. Averbach and Coriell showed their subjects an 8-by-2 array of letters for 0.05 seconds. The letters were followed by a white field for a duration ranging from 0 to 0.5 seconds. At the end of the retention interval, the subjects were instructed to recall a specific letter; the letter to be recalled was indicated by a marker. The marker was either a circle around the position the letter had occupied in the initial array or a bar over the position of the letter. Averbach and Coriell reported that with the bar marker, retention was high immediately after the array of letters terminated but declined to a recall of only four or five out of sixteen letters when the retention interval was longer than 0.25 seconds (refer to Figure 8.5). However, the use of the circle marker substantially reduced recall of the letters for intermediate intervals (0.1 to 0.2 seconds). According to Breitmeyer and Ganz (1976), no masking occurs when the circle marker either (1) comes on immediately after the letters, integrating the marker into the visual image or (2) comes on after 0.25 seconds, in which case the information has already been transferred to short-term memory. Only when the information is in the sensory register will the circle marker "mask" the to-be-called letter by taking the letter's place in the visual image. In contrast, the bar is far enough away from the letter to act as a marker indicating the letter to be recalled rather than a mask preventing recall of the letter. Other masking studies (Averbach, 1963; Sperling, 1963) report that any patterned visual event (e.g., closely meshed grid) following the letters will erase the visual image of the letters from the sensory register.

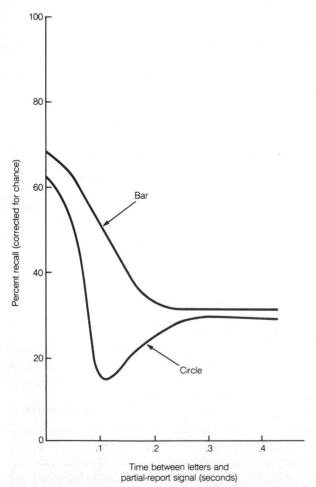

FIGURE 8.5
The percentage of recall when either a bar or a circle marker was used to indicate the letter to be recalled as a function of delay between stimuli presentation and recall test. From Averbach, E., & Coriell, A. S. Short-term memory in vision. *Bell System Technical Journal,* 1961, *40,* 309–328. Copyright 1961, The American Telephone and Telegraph Co.

Nature of Iconic Memory Our discussion indicates that for a brief time following a visual event, an exact copy of that experience is stored in the sensory register. Does visual information undergo any processing while in the sensory register? The evidence (see Howard, 1983) indicates that the analysis of visual experiences occurs *after* the sensory register stage. Furthermore, information from the sensory register can be recalled only in an unprocessed form. Subjects required to report organized visual experiences while the memory is stored in the sensory register are unable to do so. Thus, only unprocessed information is available to a subject while a memory is in the sensory register.

Coltheart, Lea, and Thompson (1974) modified Sperling's partial-report technique. They presented subjects on each trial with an array consisting of two rows of four letters each. Half the letters were red; the other half, black. Half the letters had a long *e* sound (e.g., B, C, D, G, P, and T); the other half, a short *e* sound (e.g., F, L, M, S, and X). Subjects were asked on each trial to report three kinds of information, and different tones indicated the type of information required. On some trials, subjects were asked to report the top or bottom row of letters. On other trials, they were required to report all the black letters or all the red letters. Finally, on the remaining trials, subjects were instructed to report all the letters with the long sound or all letters with the short sound. The image that subjects were shown contained two types of information: the row and the color. To obtain these two types of information, subjects did not need to process any information; they simply needed to have the information in the sensory register. Coltheart, Lea, and Thompson reported that subjects asked to report either one row of letters or all the letters of one color had high recall. The other type of information, the sound of the letter, was not contained in the visual image. To obtain this information, subjects had to have access to previously stored information about which letter had a long or short *e*. Thus, the task of reporting the sound of the letters required the subjects to process information contained in the sensory register. The authors found that recall of the sounds was low. These observations demonstrate that information stored in the sensory register is unprocessed and cannot be processed at this stage of memory storage.

Other studies (Turvey & Kravetz, 1970; Von Wright, 1968) also have reported that only unprocessed information is available from the sensory register. In these experiments, recall using a partial-report technique was high when the appropriate information was contained in the visual image, such as subjects accurately identifying items based on their shape or size. However, recall was low when the information was not contained in the visual image, such as when subjects were asked to identify items based on whether they were consonants or digits.

Thus an icon is a representation of a visual experience and is held in the sensory register for a brief time. Containing only unanalyzed information about the physical characteristics of the visual event, the icon stays in the sensory register until it either is read out into the short-term store for analysis or is lost.

Echoic Memory

In Search of an Echo   The sensory register can also contain an exact duplication of an auditory experience. Neisser (1967) called the memory of an auditory experience in the sensory register *echoic memory,* or an "echo" of a recent event. Moray, Bates, and Barnett (1965) conducted an evaluation of echoic memory comparable to Sperling's study of iconic memory. Each subject sat alone in a room containing four high-fidelity loudspeakers placed far enough apart so that subjects could discriminate the sounds coming from each speaker. At various times during the study, a list of spoken letters was emitted from each loudspeaker. The list ranged from one to four letters transmitted simultaneously from each loudspeaker. For example, at the same instant, loudspeaker 1 produced letter *e*; loudspeaker 2, letter *k*; loudspeaker 3, letter *g*, and loudspeaker 4, letter *t*.

For some trials, each subject was required to report as many letters as possible, a procedure analogous to Sperling's whole-report technique. Moray, Bates, and Barnett reported that subjects remembered only a small proportion of the letters presented from the four loudspeakers. On other trials, subjects were asked to recall the letters coming from only one of the four loudspeakers. This task was accomplished by giving a visual cue indicating from which loudspeaker the words should be reported. This procedure, analogous to Sperling's partial-report technique, resulted in subjects' recalling most of the letters when they had to report the letters emitted from only one location. These results demonstrate that an echo is an exact copy of an auditory experience and that all the information contained in an auditory experience is stored in echoic memory. Using the partial-report technique, subjects can recall any segment of the information contained in the echo; however, recall is poor using the whole-report technique.

Remember from the discussion of iconic memory the reason subjects did not recall all the visual information presented: an icon is only a brief transient copy, and subjects forgot some information stored in the icon before they had a chance to transfer it to the short-term store. An echo is also stored for only a brief time, and some of the information decays before the subjects can recall it using the whole-report technique.

Darwin, Turvey, and Crowder (1972) reported results that show that an echo lasts but a very short time. Their experiment was similar to the Moray, Bates, and Barnett study, with two exceptions: first, subjects heard simultaneous lists of letters from three rather than four locations; second, after the termination of the list, the time delay before the subjects were required to recall the letters varied. Darwin, Turvey, and Crowder used four delay intervals: 0 seconds, immediately after the letters were presented; and 1, 2, or 4 seconds later. As seen in Figure 8.6, using the partial-report technique, the level of recall declined as the interval between the auditory event and testing increased. Furthermore, using a 4-second retention interval, recall with the partial-report technique equalled recall with the whole-report technique. These results point

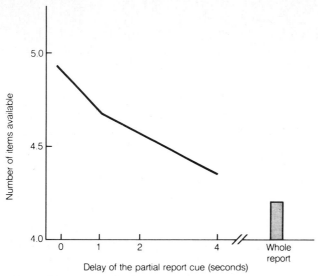

FIGURE 8.6
Performance level in Darwin, Turvey, and Crowder's study
of the auditory sensory system. The graph presents the
number of items available as a function of the delay
between signal offset and recall test. The bar at the right
shows performance with the whole-report technique.
From Darwin, C. T.; Turvey, M. T.; & Crowder, R. G. An
auditory analogue of the Sperling partial-report
procedure: Evidence for brief auditory storage. *Cognitive
Psychology*, 1972, *3*, 255–267.

out that the copy of an auditory experience stored in echoic memory is only
temporary. We learned in our discussion of iconic memory that the typical
duration of an icon is approximately 0.25 seconds. Inspection of Figure 8.7
suggests that an echo lasts several seconds. Why does the representation of an
auditory experience stored in sensory memory decay more slowly than the
trace of a visual event?

   Duration of an Echo   Although you would anticipate that an echo would
have the same duration as that of an icon, Wingfield and Byrnes (1981) suggest
that the typical duration of an echo is 2 seconds. To examine why an auditory
event is stored in the sensory register longer than a visual event, consider this
example. Suppose that you look at a chair. All the information needed to detect
that the object is a chair is contained in the visual snapshot of the chair. Thus,
salient physical characteristics of visual events can be detected by examining a
single visual image of an event from a particular moment. However, suppose
that someone says *"chair"* to you. Five separate sounds, or phonemes, are
contained in the word *chair* (see Chapter 7 for a discussion of phonemes). To
detect that the word is *chair,* you must combine the five sounds into one word.

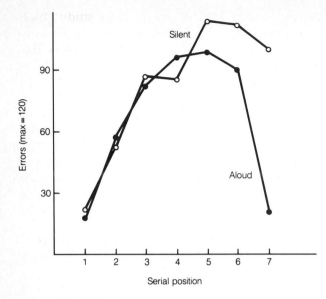

Silent

Aloud

Errors (max = 120)

Serial position

FIGURE 8.7
The number of errors as a function of the serial position of the letters for subjects who received either silent or aloud presentation of stimuli. From Crowder, R. G., & Morton, J. Precategorical acoustic storage (PAS). *Perception and Psychophysics*, 1969, 5, 365–373.

Although this combining of sounds into a word takes place in short-term memory, the detection of each of the phonemes occurs in the sensory register.

The duration of an echo must be longer than that of an icon, since the average duration of a spoken syllable is between 0.2 and 0.3 seconds. Thus, unless the memory of an auditory syllable lasts for longer than 0.3 seconds, the memory of the beginning of the syllable is lost before the speaker is able to finish the syllable. Furthermore, the recognition of a particular phoneme is "context dependent"; that is, the way an individual sound will be perceived depends on the nature of the sounds preceding or following it. Illustrating this process, Liberman, Delattre, and Cooper (1952) presented subjects with a very brief, 15-second burst of noise followed by one of several different vowel sounds. Subjects heard the burst of noise as a /p/ if it preceeded the vowel /i/ but heard the sound of /k/ if the burst occurred prior to the vowel /a/. Thus, the echo of a sound must continue for awhile after the sound ends so that sound can be detected from the next sound.

Wingfield and Byrnes (1981) suggest one additional reason that echoes last several seconds. Suppose that you are listening to a foreigner who speaks with an accent. Although you may be unable to recognize a word when initially spoken, recognition often occurs a few seconds later. According to Wingfield and Byrnes, people seem to "play it over" until they recognize a difficult sound. This suggests that we can maintain a brief, accurate sensory record of an auditory experience for several seconds to ascertain what we hear. Several studies document the duration of an echo; let's briefly examine them.

We learned earlier that when two visual stimuli are presented close together in time, the second event erases the memory of the first stimulus. Backward masking has also been observed with auditory events. Elliot's study (1967) represents one example of backward masking using auditory stimuli. Presenting a very brief 10-millisecond tone followed at various intervals by a 100-millisecond noise burst, Elliot found that if the noise burst occurred within 100 milliseconds after the tone, the subjects reported that they did not hear the tone. However, if the noise occurred 100 milliseconds, or 0.1 seconds, after the tone, the subjects did hear the tone. This observation is inconsistent with the earlier statement that the duration of the echo is 2 seconds. Yet, other studies (see Efron, 1970) have reported results similar to Elliot's. Turvey (1978) suggested an explanation for the results of these backward-masking studies. Turvey found that with a simple stimulus, such as a tone, only a very short time is needed to detect the tone. Once detected, the information is transferred to the short-term store. However, with more complex auditory events, such as the detection of phonemes, a longer echo is needed for detection. Thus, the backward-masking studies show the lower duration of an echo required for detection of a simple auditory event. Yet, echoes can and typically do last much longer than 0.1 seconds for the detection of complex auditory information. The serial-position-effect studies demonstrate that the upper limit of storage is 1 to 2 seconds for an auditory event in the sensory register. (A serial learning procedure is used to demonstrate the serial position effect. In the typical serial learning study, subjects are presented a list of items to learn. Each subject's task is to learn the items in the exact order in which they are presented. Experiments on serial learning demonstrate consistently that subjects do not learn each item on the list at the same rate. Instead, they learn items at the beginning and at the end of the list more readily than items in the middle of the list. This difference in the rate of learning of serial lists is called the *serial-position effect*. Many studies have reported the serial position effect; see Hall [1982] for a review of this literature.)

Conrad and Hull (1964) used a serial learning procedure to estimate the duration of echoic memory. Conrad and Hull presented to subjects a number of lists of random digits; each list contained seven digits presented at a rate of 100 milliseconds per digit. After finishing each list, a brief 400-millisecond delay was followed by subjects recalling as many of the seven digits as possible. Although all the digits were presented visually, some subjects were told to look at the digits and to remain silent until the time for recall. Other subjects were instructed to say the name of each digit aloud when it was presented. As can be seen in Figure 8.7, although the rate of recall did not differ for items early in the list using either the visual (silent) or auditory (aloud) presentations, the retention of the last few digits was greater with auditory than with visual presentation. The most reasonable explanation for this difference lies in the fact that iconic and echoic memory have different durations. According to Conrad and Hull, with visual presentation subjects have poor recall of the last items on the list because the visual trace of these digits has faded before the end of the 400-millisecond retention interval. In contrast, recall of the last digits is higher with the auditory presentation because the echo of the last few digits remains after the 400-millisecond delay has transpired. If it is assumed that several hundred milliseconds are required to present the last few items of the list and 400 milliseconds intervene between the last digit and recall, the duration of echoic memory is close to the 2-second estimate suggested by Darwin, Turvey, and Crowder (1972). These observations suggest that an echo can last 1 or 2 seconds if that amount of time is needed to detect the significant physical characteristics of the auditory event. We should note that mode of presentation was not important for recall of the initial four items of the list. The delay between the presentations of these items and recall was too long for either iconic or echoic memory. Recall of these first items depended entirely on whether they had been identified and transferred to the short-term store. Other studies using visual and auditory presentations also found a difference in the recall of the last few digits in a list; see Corballis (1966) or Murry (1966) for other examples.

 The Nature of Echoic Memory Recall from earlier in the chapter that an icon is an unprocessed sensory impression of a visual experience. Similarly, an echo is an exact copy of an auditory experience, and the organization and interpretation of this auditory event occurs in the short-term memory stage. Support for this view of the nature of echoic memory can even be seen in the dichotic-shadowing studies described in Chapter 5. Recall that subjects in these tasks are presented two different messages, and each message is presented to a different ear. The subject is required to repeat, or shadow, the information presented in one ear. As we discovered, nonshadowed information is detected by the sensory system; that is, the auditory experience presented over the nonattended channel is stored in the sensory register. However, unless this information is significant, it is not transferred to the short-term store and, therefore, not recalled. What types of information presented through the nonattended channel can be detected? We learned that subjects will notice a change in the pitch of the message, such as when the speaker is switched from a male to a female. This indicates that a person can detect physical changes in auditory experiences stored in sensory register. However, subjects are unable to detect a difference in meaning over the unattended channel. For example, if the language of the nonattended message is shifted from English to German (or vice versa), subjects will not notice the change. Similarly, subjects do not detect a change from technical to nontechnical material (or vice versa) when the shift occurs in the nonshadowed message. In contrast, subjects can easily detect these changes occurring in the shadow message. Our discussion shows that (1) an exact physical representation of an auditory experience is stored in the sensory register and (2) distinctions in auditory events are made only on a physical basis in echoic memory. Psychological distinctions of auditory information are made in short-term memory.

Short-Term Store

Information stored in the sensory register is transferred to short-term store where it is retained for a brief time before being permanently (or nearly permanently) stored in long-term store. The duration of a memory in the short-term store typically is 15 to 20 seconds. Although experiences do go through short-term storage to get to long-term storage, short-term storage is not merely a temporary holding facility for a memory between sensory register and the long-term storage. Instead, experiences are interpreted for their meaning and are organized in logical ways; this interpretation and logical organization require not only the physical representation of an event from the sensory register but also the use of prior information stored in long-term memory. Thus, memories can be retrieved from long-term storage and transferred into short-term storage; the retrieval of this information allows people to analyze and organize new experiences as well as to reinterpret previous events. Several psychologists (Feigenbaum, 1970; Greeno, 1974) have referred to short-term storage as the "working memory," a phrase suggesting a dynamic memory process which is the central characteristic of the short-term store. We will continue to use the conventional name for this stage of memory storage, but, clearly, people work to analyze and interpret information, and significant changes in memory can take place as the result of the attempt to find meaning in an event. We will next look at evidence indicating that information is organized in short-term storage; in the next chapter, we will examine how information is shifted from long-term memory to short-term memory.

We have identified two major characteristics of the short-term store: it has a brief storage span and it is where information is organized and analyzed. The short-term store has three additional characteristics: (1) Its storage capacity is limited—only a small amount of information can be maintained there. (2) Memories contained in the short-term store are easily disrupted by new experiences. Information already in the short-term store will be replaced if additional information overloads the storage capacity of the store. Information not sufficiently analyzed and organized prior to transfer to the long-term store may not be remembered later. (3) The short-term store has a rehearsal function; that is, the short-term store can rehearse or replay memories of prior experiences. As we will discover in a discussion of memory retrieval, the likelihood that an event will be remembered is based partly on the number of times that event has been experienced; the more times an event has been experienced, the greater the probability it will be recalled. Rehearsal has a similar impact: the more an event is rehearsed in the short-term store, the more likely that the information can be recalled later.

Why does rehearsal increase the recall of an event? One likely explanation is that rehearsal allows an experience to remain in the short-term store, and therefore the event will not be forgotten. Another explanation is that rehearsal allows for greater analysis and interpretation of experiences; the enhanced organization provided by rehearsal enables recall when the memory is transferred to the long-term store. We will next examine each of the characteristics of the short-term store.

The Span of Short-Term Memory   Say the nonsense syllable TXZ, and then start counting backward by threes, beginning with the number 632 and continuing with 629, 626, 623, 620, 617, 614, 611, 608, 605, 602, 599, 597, 594, 591, 588,

585, 582, 579, and 576. Do you remember the nonsense syllable? In all likelihood, you do not. The nonsense syllable was detected by the sensory receptors and entered into consciousness. Thus, the memory of the nonsense syllable was registered in the sensory register and entered into the short-term store. Yet, the memory of the nonsense syllable was lost as the result of the backward-counting task. Since this task required only approximately 20 seconds to complete, it appears that the memory of the nonsense syllable is rapidly forgotten after leaving the short-term store.

The preceding example was modeled after the classic Peterson and Peterson study (1959). In this study, subjects were presented a number of three-consonant trigrams, and after saying the three letters of each trigram, the subjects were given a number and required to start counting backward by threes. The numbers used were different following each trigram. The subjects were given a signal to designate when to stop counting backward and to recall the trigram; the signal was presented at different retention intervals varying from 3 to 18 seconds. Figure 8.8 represents the level of recall of a trigram as a function of

FIGURE 8.8
The percentage of correct recall of CCC trigram as a function of the interval between trigram presentation and recall test. From Peterson, L. R., & Peterson, M. J. Short-term retention of individual verbal items. *Journal of Experimental Psychology*, 1959, *58*, 193–198. Copyright 1959 by the American Psychological Association. Reprinted by permission.

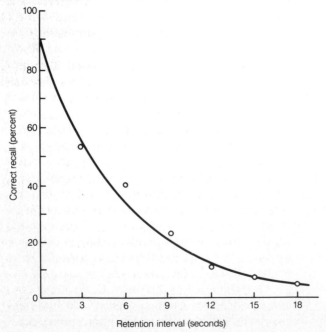

the interval between presentation of a trigram and testing. As can be seen from the figure, recall of a nonsense syllable declines rapidly: the likelihood that a subject can remember the trigram is 80 percent with a 3-second recall interval compared with only about an 18 percent recall of the trigrams with an 18-second interval. Peterson and Peterson's study illustrates the brief retention of an item after leaving the short-term store.

Why did Peterson and Peterson's subjects forget the nonsense syllable so quickly? Peterson and Peterson (1959) suggested that memories fade within a few seconds after leaving the short-term store. The decay of a short-term memory is an automatic process, and future recall of that memory occurs only if the memory has been transferred to the long-term store. Furthermore, the Petersons assumed that rehearsal postpones the onset of the decay of a short-term memory but that the memory begins to fade as soon as rehearsal stops. Melton (1963), offering another interpretation of the rapid forgetting observed in the Peterson and Peterson study, claimed that interference was responsible for the rapid forgetting of the trigrams. (Interference occurs when the memory of one event prevents the recall of another experience.) In Melton's view, subjects recalling a specific trigram encounter two sources of interference: First, the backward-counting task is a source of *retroactive interference,* occurring when the memories of recent experiences prevent the recall of earlier events. Thus, in Melton's view, the memory of the numbers interfered with recall of the trigrams. Second, the memory of trigrams experienced at the beginning of the study may have proactively interfered with the recall of trigrams presented later in the study. *Proactive interference* occurs when the memories of past events prevent the recall of recent experiences. Since Peterson and Peterson reported only the average recall of all trigrams, Melton felt that the recall of the trigrams experienced early in the study may have been greater than that reported by the Petersons.

Gleitman (1981) provides an example which should help distinguish between decay and interference. Suppose that some packages are on a loading dock, ready to be stored in a warehouse. Packages can be lost, and therefore not stored in the warehouse, if they either rot (decay) or are shoved off by other packages (interference). Which of the processes, decay or interference, causes the forgetting of short-term memories? The evidence (Wessels, 1982) indicates that in the Petersons' study, both decay and interference were responsible for a subject's inability to recall a trigram presented 18 seconds earlier.

Keppel and Underwood (1962) provided evidence that proactive interference caused most of the retention loss observed by the Petersons. Three trigrams were presented to each subject on each of three trials. Three retention intervals (3, 9, and 18 seconds) were used on each trial. Keppel and Underwood reported that on the first trial, subjects showed no decline in recall from the 3- to 18-second interval. In contrast, on the second trial, a loss of recall of the trigram occurred over the 18-second interval, and an even greater loss of retention was seen on the third trial (refer to Figure 8.9). Thus as subjects learn more trigrams, they become less able to remember them after 18 seconds.

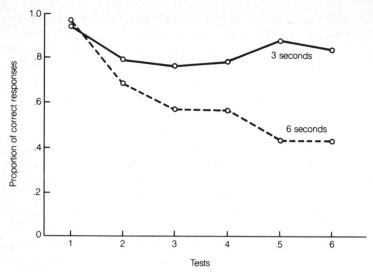

FIGURE 8.9
The proportion of correct responses as a function of the number of
previous items and length of retention interval. From Keppel, G., &
Underwood, B. J. Proactive inhibition in short-term retention of
single items. *Journal of Verbal Learning and Verbal Behavior*, 1962,
1, 153–161.

Apparently, the memories of trigrams acquired on the first trial interfered with
the recall of trigrams experienced on later trials.

Waugh and Norman (1965) evaluated the influence of retroactive interference on the recall of short-term memory. In their study, a subject received a list
of digits (for example, 1, 7, 8, 3, 4, 2, 5, 6, 3, 4, 8, 2, 9, 7*) followed by the
presentation of a tone, which is indicated (the *). The number which appeared
before the tone is the *probe digit,* and subjects were asked to recall the digit that
followed the probe digit the *first time* it was presented. Thus, in our example,
the correct digit to recall is 8. Waugh and Norman varied the number of digits
which intervened between the correct response and the probe digit. According
to Waugh and Norman, the more digits that intervened, the greater the retroactive interference and the less recall a subject should have of the correct digit.
However, more time is required when the number of intervening units is increased, and because of this time lapse between the correct digit and recall,
decay, not retroactive interference, could be responsible for the low recall. To
control for the influence of time, Waugh and Norman used two rates of presentation: four digits per second were given in the fast presentation, and only one
digit per second was provided in the slow presentation. If the number of intervening digits is critical, then recall of a twelve-item presentation, for example,
should be the same, regardless of whether those items were presented in 3
seconds or in 12 seconds. However, if short-term memories do decay, recall
should be affected by rate of presentation; that is, more forgetting should occur

when it takes 12 seconds rather than 3 to present the twelve digits. Figure 8.10 shows the results of Waugh and Norman's study: the number of intervening digits affects the level of recall; the percent correct declined from almost 100 percent with one intervening digit to that of less than 10 percent with the use of twelve intervening digits. In contrast, the rate of presentation did not affect the likelihood of subjects recalling the correct digit. These observations support the view that retroactive interference, not decay, affects the recall of short-term memory.

Some evidence suggests that decay does occur but is simply not apparent because interference is such a powerful and common cause of forgetting. There are a number of studies (Baddeley, 1976; Baddeley & Scott, 1971; Shiffrin & Cook, 1978) that indicate that the influence of decay can be observed under ideal conditions. For example, Shiffrin and Cook (1978) told their subjects that they were studying how well people forget information, not how well people can remember—a procedure which Shiffrin and Cook believed would minimize rehearsal and enhance the detection of decay. Their subjects participated in a tone-detection task in which many times during a 40-second trial, a tone was presented against a background of white noise. Also, in each 40-second trial, five consonants were presented for 2.5 seconds. The subjects were instructed to repeat the five consonants, then put them out of "mind" and continue with the tone-detection task. At the end of each trial subjects were asked to recall the letters.

Shiffrin and Cook used two kinds of tasks: on long-delay trials, the letters were presented early in the trial (32.5 seconds prior to the end of the trial and the signal to recall the letters); on short-delay trials, the letters occurred late in the trial (12.5 seconds before the trial's end and the recall signal). According to Shiffrin and Cook, if decay is a cause of forgetting, more forgetting should be

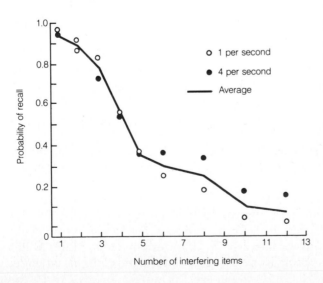

FIGURE 8.10
The probability of recall as a function of the rate of stimulus presentation and the number of intervening items. From Waugh, N. C., & Norman, D. A. Primary memory. *Psychological Review*, 1965, 72, 89–104. Copyright 1965 by the American Psychological Association. Reprinted by permission.

observed with a long-delay trial than with a short-delay trial because the longer time between presentations and recall should produce more decay. Shiffrin and Cook reported that subjects forgot 20 percent of the letters on the short-delay trials, and they forgot 30 percent on the long-delay trials; this result is consistent with the decay theory.

Increased forgetting on long-delay trials may be caused by processes other than decay. Retroactive interference from events occurring during the retention interval may explain the greater degree of forgetting observed on long-delay trials; yet, the subjects' experiences during the interval were not similar to the target letters and should thus cause a minimal amount of interference. The recall differences may have been caused by proactive interferences; however, Baddeley and Scott (1971), using a task similar to Shiffrin and Cook's, tested subjects after only one trial, a procedure designed to minimize the development of proactive interference. These experimenters also observed greater forgetting with a long-delay test than with a short delay test. Apparently, decay accounts for some forgetting of previously learned material.

The brief retention span of a short-term memory has adaptive significance—it allows us to quickly shift attention from one event to the next. As Gleitman (1981) points out, imagine how difficult a long-distance telephone operator would find remembering one telephone number while dialing another.

Limited Storage Capacity   Repeat the following list of nonsense syllables.

SYX	GXL
TRZ	QNW
BGC	RDH
KDM	HCX
NFQ	FZJ
PHY	YPC
JBD	GBX
LCN	CQT
OTS	DZP

Now repeat as many of the nonsense syllables as you can remember. If your memory is like that of most college students, you will be able to remember four or five or even six or seven of the nonsense syllables. Your inability to recall all or most of the nonsense syllables is caused by the limited storage capacity of the short-term store.

In 1956, George Miller published a classic paper entitled "The Magic Number Seven Plus or Minus Two: Some Limits on Our Capacity for Processing Information." Miller presented evidence showing that people can only hold approximately seven items at a time in their short-term store. An item may be a single letter or number; thus, the limit to the storage capacity will be 7 ± 2 letters or digits. An item can also be a word or an idea, and thus a person could have about five to nine words or ideas in the short-term memory store. Miller referred to a meaningful item as a *chunk* of information. Information is "chunked" in the short-term store; for example, three letters are chunked into a word. *Chunking,* an organizational function of the short-term store, allows the storage of more information. Thus, someone may be able to recall only seven separate letters but can remember twenty-one letters existing as seven 3-letter words.

Pollack (1952) and Garner (1953) reported that people can easily label two to four tones (or levels of loudness) but have difficulty when asked to make five or more judgments. Similarly, Kaufman, Lord, Reese, and Volkmann (1949) reported that their subjects could accurately estimate the number of dots after six or fewer dots were presented on a screen for 0.2 seconds. However, the subjects could only guess when more than six dots appeared in the pattern. Furthermore, Hayes (1952) and Pollack (1953) found that listeners recalled only six or seven items from a list of words, letters, or digits which had been read at a fast constant rate. Based on this and other information, Miller (1956) concluded that a limit exists to the amount of information which can be contained in the short-term store.

However, Watkins (1974) demonstrated that the true capacity of the short-term store is only three to four chunks. According to Watkins although the capacity of the short-term store appears to be 7 ± 2 units or chunks, some recall actually reflects information stored in the long-term store; that is, Watkins argued that information presented early in an experience has already been permanently stored. Thus, the capacity of the short-term store is actually three to four chunks. Evidence to support this view will be presented later in the chapter.

Disrupting a Short-Term Memory Consider the following series of events to illustrate how easily a memory contained in the short-term store can be disrupted: After locating a number in the telephone book, you begin dialing; then your roommate says something to you, and you stop dialing to respond. After responding, you begin to dial the number again but cannot remember it, demonstrating the susceptibility of memories contained in the short-term store to disruption by incoming information.

Evidence of the easy disruption of short-term memories can be seen in the memory-span studies discussed earlier. Recall that Peterson and Peterson (1959) found that subjects required to count backward after the presentation of a trigram were unable to recall the trigram just 18 seconds after it had been presented. Numbers had replaced the trigram in the short-term store, rendering subjects unable to recall the trigram on an 18-second recall test. Memories in the short-term store are easily disrupted because the storage capacity of this store is so limited. As the capacity is reached, new memories automatically replace older ones. And, unless stored in a meaningful way, the event will be lost forever. Thus, you forget a telephone number when someone distracts you because a telephone number contains seven units of information (seven numbers), beyond the capacity of short-term storage. The memory of the number is displaced by your roommate's words, thus creating room in the short-term store for these words. You must look up the number again because it has not been stored in a retrievable way in the long-term store.

How can the easy disruption and limited storage capacity of the short-term store be overcome? Fortunately, the short-term store has a natural organizational ability that reduces the amount of information contained in a message and thus allows the short-term store to retain more total information. Under most conditions, this organizational skill overcomes the limited storage capacity and easy disruption and allows the memory of an event to be stored in a meaningful fashion in the long-term store.

Organization in the Short-Term Store The main function of the short-term store is to organize information arriving from the sensory register. One type of organization accomplished by the short-term store is chunking. As mentioned, chunking involves combining two or more units or *bits* of information into a single unit. For example, the six letters *s, i, g, n, a, l* can be chunked into the single word *signal*. Information is also coded in the short-term store. *Coding* is the transformation of information into a new form. For example, persons using Morse code change letters into dots and dashes to transmit a message. Similarly, subjects in an experiment can code nonsense syllables into words by adding letters. The coding of the nonsense syllable ROG into the word frog illustrates this kind of coding.

The formation of associations is a third organizational process carried out by the short-term store. An *association* indicates the detection of a relation between events. Some associations are based on temporal contiguity—the occurrence of events together in time. Other associations are based on the semantic similarity of events; for example, a person can associate a dog and cat because both are animals. The temporal and semantic relations between events are identified while a memory is in the short-term store.

The organization of information by the short-term store provides some significant advantages. People can reduce the impact of the limited storage capacity of the short-term store by organizing incoming information from the sensory register. As a result of this organization, an event can become more significant or meaningful and thus more likely to be remembered. Evidence indicating that information is organized by the short-term store and that this organization increases the recall of short-term memory is examined next. Chapter 9 then discusses research demonstrating that recall of memories from the long-term store is enhanced by how the information is organized while in the short-term store.

Chunking People automatically chunk information contained in the short-term store. For example, presenting six-digit numbers to subjects to memorize, Bower and Springston (1970) found that most people chunked the six digits into groups of three digits, each separated by a pause and distinct melodic pattern. Thus, the six-digit number 427316 became 427-316. The division of a seven-digit telephone number into two separate chunks is another use of chunking. Norman (1976) describes another example of the natural use of chunking by the short-term store: Children learn the twenty-six letters of the alphabet by using rhyming and melodic rhythm to create three chunks; each chunk contains two elements, and each element has two units of one to four letters. Norman diagrammed the chunking of the alphabet: [(ab-cd) (ef-g)] [(hi-jk) (lmno-p)] [qrs-tuv) (w-xyz)].

People not only chunk letters into words but also chunk sentences into one chunk or chunks of related ideas (Johnson, 1968). Johnson assumed that people learning sentences chunk the words into higher-order units (see Chapter 7 for a discussion of language learning). For example, a noun phrase represents a chunk of the sequence *the* + adjective + noun. What evidence indicates that the words contained in a sentence are chunked into one or more units? Consider this sentence: *The tall boy saved the dying woman.* Johnson argued that the recall of one word within a unit (or chunk) is more related to the recall of other words within that unit than to the recall of words in another unit. Thus, the likelihood that a subject could recall the noun *boy* should be more influenced by the recall of the adjective *tall* than by the recall of the verb *saved*. This is true even though the noun *boy* is adjacent to both the adjective *tall* and the verb *saved*. Johnson's research shows that a subject is more likely to remember an adjacent word in the same unit than an adjacent word in a different chunk.

Does chunking increase the amount of information which can be retained in the short-term store? Simon (1974) evaluated the view that the short-term store can retain seven chunks of information, regardless of the absolute amount of information contained in each chunk. Using himself as a subject, Simon found that he could immediately recall seven 1-syllable words, about seven 2-syllable words, and about six 3-syllable words. However, Simon found that he could only remember four 2-word phrases (for example, *milky way, criminal lawyer*) and only about three longer phrases (for example, *all's fair in love and war*). Although Simon's observations indicate that chunking can increase the absolute amount of information retained in the short-term store, they also indicate that the short-term store does not contain seven chunks. Recall that Watkins (1974) suggested that the true capacity of the short-term store is three to four chunks. Watkins reported that when only a small amount of information is contained in each chunk, the capacity of the short-term store appears to be five to nine chunks; however, some of the subjects' recall actually reflects information stored in the long-term store, thus rendering the actual capacity of the short-term store back to 3 to 4 chunks. In many tasks, memories contained in both short-term and long-term stores contribute to the level of retention shown by a subject.

We have learned that more information can be retained in the short-term store as the result of chunking, but does chunking improve recall? Murdock's classic 1961 study evaluated the role of chunking in the recall of experiences. Murdock presented to his subjects a three-consonant trigram, a three-letter word, or 3 three-letter words and then required them to count backward for 0, 3, 6, 9, 12, 15, or 18 seconds. As can be seen in Figure 8.11, the retention of the three-consonant trigram was identical to that found by Peterson and Peterson

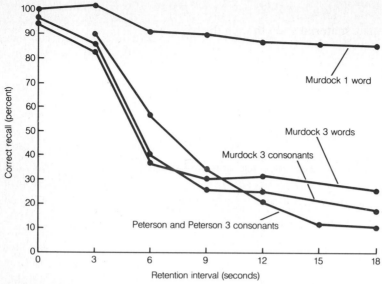

FIGURE 8.11
The percentage of correct recall as a function of the type of stimulus
material and the length of the retention interval. Adapted from Melton,
A. W. Implications of short-term memory for a general theory of memory.
Journal of Verbal Learning and Verbal Behavior, 1963, 2, 1–21.

(1959); recall of the trigram declined dramatically over the 18-second retention
interval. However, Murdock's subjects after 18 seconds exhibited a high level
of recall of the one-word unit. Furthermore, on the 18-second recall test, the
retention of the three-word unit containing nine letters equalled that of the
three-letter trigram.

Chunking does not merely improve recall; instead, the information is recalled in a specific order. Suppose that a subject is given the following list of
items:

tea	cabbage	lion	coffee
milk	seal	potato	orange
cow	spinach	lemon	elephant
apple	pear	soda	carrot

This list contains four categories of items: beverages, animals, vegetables, and
fruit. Subjects receiving the above list will recall the items in each category
together, even though the items were presented separately. The recall of material in terms of categories is called *clustering* (see Tulving & Donaldson, 1972,
for a review of this literature). The organization of material allows us to relate
similar events and contributes to a structured and meaningful world. Organization is a very important aspect of the learning process; its significance should be
apparent throughout the text.

Clustering is such an integral aspect of memory storage that subjects will attempt to organize material even though the experimenter did not provide any preorganization to the list. For example, Tulving (1966) presented subjects with an unorganized list of words. Although he varied the order of presentation of the verbal units on each trial, Tulving's subjects showed a consistency in the order in which they recalled the words from trial to trial. These observations show that people actively organize events they experience and recall the events in terms of the organization used during learning.

Coding Clearly, information is combined into smaller units of information by the short-term store. The short-term store can also code information; that is, transform an event into a totally new form. There is considerable evidence that much of our visual experiences are coded into an auditory form by the short-term store—this is acoustic coding. People can also learn other forms of coding; these coding systems will be detailed in a discussion of mnemonic techniques in Chapter 9. Although coding can enhance the storage of information, it will increase the recall of that information only if the memory can readily be decoded. Chapter 9 addresses the problem of decoding in the discussion of memory retrieval.

Conrad's study (1964) illustrates the acoustical coding of visual information. He presented visually a set of letters to his subjects and then asked them to recall all the letters. Analyzing the type of errors made by subjects on the recall test, Conrad found that errors were made based on the sound of the letters rather than on their physical appearance. For example, subjects were very likely to recall the letter *P* as the similar sounding *T*, but they were unlikely to recall the visually similar *F*. Many other studies have shown that acoustic confusions are much more common than visual confusions; see Wickelgren (1965) for another example.

People apparently learn to use *acoustical coding* for visual experiences. Conrad (1971) presented 5- and 12-year-old children with a series of pictures and then placed each picture face down. The children were then given a duplicate set of pictures and asked to match them with the pictures faced down. On half the trials, names of the duplicate pictures sounded similar to the names of the pictures faced down (e.g., *mat, bat*); on the other half of the trials, the names sounded different (e.g., *fish, house*). If the children acoustically coded the original pictures (that is, they used the names) to help them remember the pictures they had seen, they should have made more errors with items that sounded similar than with those that sounded dissimilar. In fact, Conrad did find that 12-year-old subjects made more errors with the similar than with the dissimilar list; however, the 5-year-olds made the same number of errors on both types of lists. These observations suggest that older children use acoustical coding, but younger children simply remember visual patterns.

Why does the short-term store transform visual events into an auditory representation? Why do older but not younger children use acoustical coding? According to Howard (1983), the short-term store is a working memory; it not only retains specific information but also represents a space for thinking. Since language plays a central role in thinking (see Chapter 7), it seems logical both that visual events would be acoustically coded to aid the thinking process and that acoustical coding would be more important as children mature and learn to use language in their thinking.

Association of Events   If someone asks you to respond to the word *day,* in all likelihood you will think of the word *night.* Recall from Chapter 1 that your response indicates that you have learned an association between the words *day* and *night.* One organizational function of the short-term store is to record the association of events. Two basic associations, *episodic* and *semantic,* are formed by the short-term store. Episodic associations are based on temporal contiguity. For example, if another person verbally abuses you, you will associate this person with the verbal abuse. Semantic associations are based on a similarity between the meaning of events. For example, the association of *day* and *night* reflects that both represent times of day.

Note that associations formed by the short-term store not only organize experiences; they also have a significant impact on the retrieval of an experience. Consider the following to illustrate the impact of associative learning on recall of an event: Suppose you did poorly in a course last year. Your memory of this course may contain information about many aspects of it, such as when, where, and why you did poorly.

Anderson and Bower's Human Associative Memory (HAM) model (1973) explains the associative processes involved in your recall of many details of an experience. In Anderson and Bower's view, incoming information is analyzed by a device called a *parser.* This analysis is based on the associative tree structure shown in Figure 8.12. Five types of associations are formed by the parser. The first type is the association of *fact* with *context.* Thus, a particular fact (you failed) is true in a certain context (a class last year). You also formed an association of *location* (your university) and time (last year); an association of *subject* (you) and *predicate* (failure); and an association of *relation* (failed) and *object* (the class). One more association links *concepts* to *words* (tokens) which are used to convey the memory. How do associations enhance the recall of events? We will address this issue in the next chapter.

The Rehearsal Function of the Short-Term Store   Suppose you are trying to learn the French word for *door.* To learn that the French phrase for door is *la porte,* you must form an association between the words *door* and *la porte.* In an attempt to learn the association, you repeat the two words to yourself several times. This process, called *rehearsal,* keeps the memories in the short-term store. Why do we rehearse the two words? According to Klatzky (1975), rehearsal has two functions. First, it keeps information in the short-term store so that it is not forgotten. Second, rehearsal can make information more meaningful, so that the memory will be remembered more easily when transferred to the long-term store. However, rehearsal alone does not necessarily result in greater recall: the memories must be organized in a meaningful way by the short-term store if rehearsal is to increase the future recall of that memory.

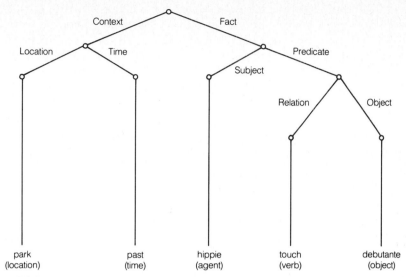

FIGURE 8.12
Diagram showing how the sentence, *In the park the hippie touched the debutante,* is stored in Anderson and Bower's Human Associative Memory System. Adapted from Anderson, J. R., and Bower, G. H. *Human associative memory.* Washington, D.C.: Winston & Sons. Copyright 1973 by Hemisphere Publishing Corporation.

Perhaps rehearsing the words *door* and *la porte* will keep the memory of the two words in the short-term store until you can form the association between them; let's next look at evidence to support this view.

Sperling (1967) found that subjects rehearsing an item presented visually say the item to themselves, hear what they say, and then store the message in long-term storage. Sperling's observation implies that rehearsal is "subvocal" or "implicit" speech. Furthermore, a person may respeak the item several times during the rehearsal process until it is finally stored in long-term storage and a new memory is allowed to enter into the short-term store.

Several types of research suggest that rehearsal is subvocal, or implicit, speech. First, recall that visual information is stored acoustically. Second, the rate of rehearsal is the same as that of vocal or overt speech (Laudauer, 1962). Laudauer asked subjects either to rehearse a series of letters ten times or to speak the letters aloud. He found that subjects could either rehearse or say about three to six letters a second. Thus, subjects appear to rehearse letters at the same rate as they would say them.

Our discussion indicates that rehearsal represents a recycling of information several times during the short-term store. Does rehearsal increase the strength of a memory in the long-term store? A series of studies by Rundus (see Rundus, 1971; Rundus & Atkinson, 1971) suggests that rehearsal does enhance the recall of an event by increasing the strength of a memory stored in the long-term store. In one of Rundus's studies, subjects were given a list of words to recall; the words were presented at a rate of one word every 5 seconds. Subjects were instructed to study the list by repeating the words during the 5-second interval between the presentation of the words. After the entire list had been presented, the subjects were required to recall as many words as possible from the list. The level of recall of a particular word was compared to the number of times it had been rehearsed during the interval between the word presentations. Rundus observed that the more times a word is rehearsed, the higher the likelihood that a subject would be able to recall the word. In other words, the more a memory is rehearsed, the greater the chances that the memory will be recalled at a later time.

You may think that rehearsal always increases the level of recall. However, evidence (Craik & Watkins, 1973; Woodward, Bjork, & Jongeward, 1973) indicates that this is not so; in fact, unless rehearsal leads to the organization of an event, rehearsal will not improve recall. Craik and Watkins (1973) presented subjects with a list of twenty-one words and instructed them to repeat the last word that began with a given letter until the next word beginning with that letter was presented. For example, suppose the given letter was *G* and the list of words was: daughter, oil, rifle, garden, grain, table, football, anchor, and giraffe. The subjects rehearsed *garden* until the word *grain* was presented, and then *grain* was rehearsed until *giraffe* was presented. Using this procedure, Craik and Watkins varied the amount of time words were rehearsed. Thus, in this list, *garden* was rehearsed for less time than *grain*. Each subject received twenty-seven lists, and the number of words between critical words varied in each list. After completing the twenty-seven lists, each subject was asked to recall as many words as possible from any of the lists. Craik and Watkins found that the amount of time a word was held in the short-term store had no impact on the level of recall, and thus the amount of rehearsal did not affect the recall of the critical word.

Why did rehearsal affect recall in the Rundus study but not in the Craik and Watkins study? The answer may lie in the difference between their studies: Subjects in the Craik and Watkins experiment rehearsed only a single word, whereas subjects in Rundus's study rehearsed several words. Thus, subjects could organize the information in the Rundus study, but no organization was possible in the Craik and Watkins study. This suggests that recitation will enhance recall only if the subject organizes the information during rehearsal.

Consider the following list of words: apple, peach, pear, orange. These words are conceptually similar; each is a type of fruit. The word fruit is associated with each word in the list and is an example of an implicit associative response (IAR) because the word *fruit* will be elicited by each word in the list. Suppose that these four words were presented within a larger list of twenty-five words. A subject would probably recall the four fruits together, even though they were not presented consecutively, and a subject able to recall the name of one of the fruits would be very likely to remember the others. Why would the fruits be remembered together? According to Underwood (1965), the IAR is responsible for the grouping. When a subject is presented with the first fruit, the IAR is elicited. Presentation of the second fruit elicits not only the IAR but also the first fruit. Thus, the IAR is the organizational basis that groups the names of the four fruits. This discussion suggests that rehearsal (remembering the first fruit as a result of the presentation of another fruit) can provide the opportunity to recall the IAR and other conceptually similar items in a list, thus tying all the items together.

Wood and Underwood's study (1967) evaluated the influence of an IAR on the recall of a list of words. They used a list of words such as *derby, coffee,* and *skunk,* words which are not ordinarily grouped together. However, adding the word *black* to the list creates an IAR for the other three words. Wood and Underwood, evaluating the influence of presenting an IAR on the recall of items conceptually related to the IAR, found that the IAR did enhance the recall of conceptually similar items. (It should be noted that the IAR must be included in the initial presentation of the list of words; the IAR has no influence if it is presented only on the recall task.) Wood and Underwood's results indicate that the IAR functions to increase the level of storage of items. Presumably, the IAR acts to increase recall by enhancing the organization of items during rehearsal.

Short-Term Memory in Animals   Recent research (Schwartz, 1984) indicates that animals have a short-term store which operates comparably to humans' short-term store. Researchers have studied animals' short-term memory process using a delayed matching-to-sample procedure. In this task, a subject is presented a specific sample stimulus. After a retention interval, the subject receives several test stimuli that match the sample stimulus. The animal is reinforced for selecting the correct test stimuli. Figure 8.13 shows a representative delayed matching-to-sample task for a pigeon. The pigeon was initially shown a red sample stimulus for 5 seconds on the middle key. After a certain interval, the pigeon was presented two-choice test stimuli: a red key on the left and a green key on the right. Pecking at the red key resulted in reinforcement, but nonreward followed a peck at the green key. Correct performance indicated that the pigeon remembered the sample stimulus presented 10 seconds earlier, whereas responding to the green key indicated that at testing the pigeon did not recall the sample stimulus.

How well does an animal remember a sample stimulus? Humans rapidly forget an event after it leaves the short-term store, and a similar finding has been observed for animals, using the delayed matching-to-sample procedure. A considerable number of studies with both pigeons (Grant, 1981) and monkeys (D'Amato, 1973) indicate that the longer the interval between termination of the sample and presentation of the test stimuli, the poorer the performance during testing.

Grant's study (1976) illustrated the rapid forgetting that occurs following the termination of the sample. Grant used pigeons as subjects and presented two test stimuli 0, 20, 40, or 60 seconds after the sample stimulus. As can be seen in

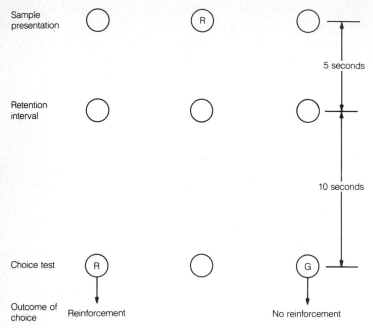

Sample
presentation

Retention
interval

5 seconds

10 seconds

Choice test

Outcome of
choice

Reinforcement

No reinforcement

FIGURE 8.13
A representative delayed matching-to-sample task in pigeons.
Reproduced from *The psychology of learning and behavior* (2d ed.)
by Barry Schwartz, by permission of W. W. Norton & Company, Inc.
Copyright 1984, 1978 by W. W. Norton & Company, Inc.

Figure 8.14, the level of performance declined with longer retention intervals. Since there were only two test stimuli, a chance level of performance was 50 percent. Evidently, a minute interval between the sample stimulus and test stimuli caused the pigeons to forget the sample stimulus.

We also discovered earlier that rehearsal decreases the amount forgotten after an event ends. A similar influence of rehearsal has been observed with animals. Increased rehearsal can be obtained in two ways. First, some studies (Grant, 1976; Roberts, 1972) varied the duration of the presentation of the sample. The results of these experiments indicate that the longer the exposure to the sample, the greater the retention of the sample. Second, other experiments (Grant & Roberts, 1976; Roberts & Grant, 1978) turned off the lights in the experimental chamber during the interval between the end of the sample and the presentation of the test stimuli. This procedure enhanced retention of the sample. Why does this second procedure lead to greater recall of the sample stimulus? According to Schwartz (1984), turning off the lights between the sample and the test stimuli eliminates distracting stimuli. The absence of distracting stimuli allows the animal to rehearse the sample stimulus, and the rehearsal increases the animal's recall of the sample at testing.

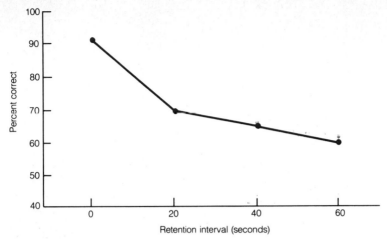

FIGURE 8.14
The accuracy of matching-to-sample as a function of the interval
between the sample stimulus and test stimuli. From Grant, D. S. Effect
of sample presentation time on long delay matching in the pigeon.
Learning and Motivation, 1976, 7, 580–590.

The technique of turning off the lights of the experimental chamber during
the retention interval may also enhance recall due to a reduction in the level of
retroactive interference. We learned earlier that interference has a significant
impact on short-term memory in humans. A number of articles (Grant, 1975;
Grant & Roberts, 1973; Jarvik, Goldfarb, & Carley, 1969) reported that interference also decreases short-term memory in animals. In these studies, another
stimulus is presented prior to the sample. The presence of the other stimulus
produces a reduced recall of the sample; proactive interference from the preceding stimulus accounts for the lower retention of the sample.

Suppose that an animal is searching for food. How can it locate food in its
environment? In addition to knowing specific instrumental activities which will
successfully obtain food, it must learn where food is located. As we discovered
in Chapter 6, Tolman suggested that animals develop cognitive maps of the
environment and use this spatial knowledge to guide them to reward. As an
animal explores its environment, it will encounter places where reward is not
located. To effectively interact with its environment, the animal must remember what places do not contain reward and avoid returning to those places. The
animal must also remember where reward is located and then return to those
places. The research of a number of psychologists (Gould, 1982; Menzel, 1978;
O'Keefe & Nadel, 1978; Olton, 1979; Shettleworth & Krebs, 1982) indicates
that animals can use their cognitive maps to remember where they previously
have or have not found reward.

Olton and his associates (Olton, 1978, 1979; Olton, Collison, & Werz, 1977;
Olton & Samuelson, 1976) constructed an eight-arm radial maze (see Figure

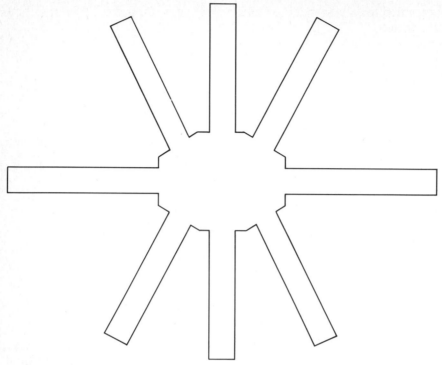

FIGURE 8.15
Figure showing the eight-arm maze used to study spatial memory. In studies of
spatial memory with this maze, Olton and his associates placed food in each arm
of the maze and required their animals to learn to visit each arm of the maze
without returning to a previously visited arm to obtain food. From Olton, D. C., &
Samuelson, R. J. Remembrance of places passed: Spatial memory in rats. *Journal
of Experimental Psychology: Animal Behavior Processes*, 1976, *2*, 96–116.
Copyright 1976 by the American Psychological Association. Reprinted by
permission.

8.15) to investigate whether an animal has a "spatial memory," or a cognitive
map, which it can use to remember where it did or did not find food. Unlike the
typical maze-learning study in which food is placed in only one arm of a maze,
Olton placed food in each of the eight arms. The rat's task is to remember
which arm it went to on the last trial and to not go to that arm again (since there
is no longer any food, return to that arm will result in no food on that trial). The
animal must use its spatial memory to go to an arm it has not already gone to in
order to receive reward on that trial. Obviously, the task becomes more difficult when only one or two arms containing food are left. Once an animal has
successfully gone to each arm, food will be again placed in each arm, and the
entire process begins again. Olton reported that his animals readily learned how
to obtain food on every trial. He found that usually by twenty trials, the rats

rarely returned to an arm that they had already visited until food was returned to all the arms.

How does the rat learn to always find food in the eight-arm maze? Olton discovered that the rats do not learn to respond to the eight arms in a specific manner; instead, the pattern of response is almost random. Also, odor cues do not seem to guide the rat to reward; Olton reported that placing strong-smelling after-shave lotion in the maze after each trial to prevent the use of odor cues did not impair the rat's performance. Apparently, the rats used the spatial cues contained in their spatial memory to guide their performance. Olton found that rotating the maze so that accurate information was no longer provided by the spatial cues caused a deterioration of the rat's performance. These observations suggest that the rat learns to get food on each trial by developing a cognitive map of the maze and uses its spatial short-term memory to keep track of where it has and has not been since the beginning of the trial. Olton's work shows not only that animals have a substantial working memory which allows them to record where they have and have not been, but also that rats are biologically prepared to efficiently forage for food (or other rewards). The efficient use of spatial memory is not limited to rats; it has been observed in other species including birds (Shettleworth, 1983; Shettleworth & Krebs, 1982) and primates (Menzel, 1978).

Long-Term Store

To review, an experience is initially encoded in the sensory register, and an exact copy of the event is transferred to the short-term store where it may be organized into a more meaningful experience. The organization of an experience increases the likelihood that the memory will be remembered at a later time. The long-term store represents the permanent (or relatively permanent) site of a memory. We will explore two aspects of the long-term storage of experiences. First, we will examine evidence that there are two types of memories: *Episodic memories* contain information about particular incidents we experience, and *semantic memories* contain our understanding of the properties of language. Second, we will discuss the physiological processes governing the long-term storage of an event as well as the psychological and physiological circumstances which can result in the failure to store an experience. Further, a memory may be encoded in the long-term store yet still not be recalled. The processes that result in the failure to recall a prior event are described in the next chapter.

Episodic versus Semantic Memory   Endel Tulving (1972, 1983) suggested that there are two different memory systems. The *episodic memory system* contains information about temporally related events, whereas the *semantic memory system* contains knowledge necessary for the use of language. Thus, an episodic memory may be of an event which you experience at a particular time and place; a semantic memory may include information about words and other symbols, their meanings and referents, relations among the words and symbols, or the rules, formulas or algorithms for the development of concepts or solutions to problems. Tulving emphasizes that the difference between episodic and semantic memory is greater than just the different types of information stored in each memory. Tulving argues that the episodic memory system is functionally distinct from the semantic memory system; he offers as evidence the fact that different operations control the storage and retrieval of episodic experiences and semantic understanding. Table 8.1 presents a list of the informational and operational differences between the episodic and semantic memory systems. Later we will discuss several studies that document the functional distinction between episodic and semantic memory. The interested reader should refer to Tulving's 1983 book *Elements of Episodic Memory* for a detailed discussion of episodic and semantic memory.

Types of Information   The types of information stored in the episodic and semantic memory systems differ. Episodic memory contains recollections of the past; semantic memory is timeless knowledge. The unit of data contained in the episodic memory is a specific event. In contrast, no single unit of information is stored in the semantic memory system. Instead, information contained in the semantic memory consists of facts, ideas, concepts, rules, propositions,

TABLE 8.1
CHARACTERISTICS OF EPISODIC AND SEMANTIC MEMORY

Diagnostic feature	Episodic	Semantic
Information		
Source	Sensation	Comprehension
Units	Events; episodes	Facts; ideas; concepts
Organization	Temporal	Conceptual
Reference	Self	Universe
Veridicality	Personal belief	Social agreement
Operations		
Registration	Experiential	Symbolic
Temporal coding	Present; direct	Absent; indirect
Affect	More important	Less important
Inferential capability	Limited	Rich
Context dependency	More pronounced	Less pronounced
Vulnerability	Great	Small
Access	Deliberate	Automatic
Retrieval queries	Time? Place?	What?
Retrieval consequences	Change system	System unchanged
Retrieval mechanisms	Synergy	Unfolding
Recollective experience	Remembered past	Actualized knowledge
Retrieval report	Remember	Know
Developmental sequence	Late	Early
Childhood amnesia	Affected	Unaffected

Source: Tulving, E. *Elements of Episodic Memory*, Clarendon Press/Oxford University Press, 1983.

schemata, and scripts which define a culture's knowledge of the world. Further, information contained in the episodic memory system is organized temporally, that is, one event precedes, occurs at the same time, or follows another event. In contrast, knowledge contained in the semantic memory system is organized conceptually. The source of episodic memory is sensory stimulation; comprehension of cultural knowledge is the source of semantic memory.

Separate Operations   The processes involved in the storage and retrieval of episodic and semantic memories also differ. According to Tulving, the episodic memory system registers immediate sensory experiences, whereas the semantic memory system records knowledge conveyed by language. The temporal order of events can be detected by the episodic memory system; problems of temporal order can be solved only by inference in the semantic memory system. Tulving reports that the episodic memory system has limited inferential capacity; that is, information stored in the episodic memory is based mainly on direct sensory impressions. In contrast, the semantic memory system has a rich inferential capacity and can therefore discover the rules of a language merely from experience with that language.

Tulving has found that the recollection of memories from the episodic system is deliberate and often requires conscious effort, whereas recall of information contained in the semantic system is automatic and can therefore be used without conscious knowledge. Although we can be aware of knowledge contained in both memory systems, we interpret episodic memories as part of our personal past and semantic memories as part of the impersonal present. Thus, we use the term *remember* when referring to episodic memories and the term *know* to describe semantic memories. According to Tulving, when information is retrieved from episodic memory, it is often changed, but memories recalled from the semantic memory system are not altered. Thus, we often reinterpret our direct experiences but not our knowledge of the use of language. Finally, the episodic memory system is much more vulnerable to interference than are memories contained in the semantic system.

Two Functionally Different Memory Systems?   Tulving (1983) detailed the results of many experiments documenting the existence of separate episodic and semantic memory systems. Let's briefly examine several studies supporting the distinction between episodic and semantic memory.

Shoben, Wescourt, and Smith (1978) compared their subjects' performances on episodic and semantic tasks. The episodic task required a subject to make recognition judgments about information contained in previously experienced sentences; the semantic task involved verifying the truth of the same sentences. The researchers also varied both the semantic relatedness of the sentences and the number of propositions about a concept contained in the sentences. Shoben, Wescourt, and Smith reported that semantic verification was influenced by semantic relatedness but not by the number of propositions. In contrast, recognition judgments were affected by the number of propositions but not by semantic relatedness. The dissociation of variables influencing performance on the episodic and semantic tasks supports the theory that the two memory systems are distinct. Other studies (Herrman & Harwood, 1980; Jacoby & Dallas, 1981; Kihlstrom, 1980; McKoon & Ratcliff, 1979) have also shown that different variables affect episodic and semantic task performance.

Warrington and Weiskrantz's study (1982) provides strong support for the distinction between episodic and semantic memory systems. Their study compared the performance of amnesic patients and nonamnesic control subjects on both a yes/no word-recognition task (an episodic task) and a word-fragment completion task (a semantic task). Warrington and Weiskrantz found no difference between amnesic and nonamnesic subjects in terms of performance on the word-fragment task. In contrast, the nonamnesic subjects' performance on the recognition task was much higher than that of the amnesic subjects, indicating that amnesics differ from nonamnesics in terms of episodic memory but not semantic memory. Other researchers have reported dissociations between performance on episodic and semantic tasks in amnesic and nonamnesic subjects; see Schacter and Tulving (1982) for a review of this literature.

Perhaps the most compelling evidence in support of separate episodic and semantic memory systems comes from a study by Wood, Taylor, Penny, and Stump (1980). These researchers compared the regional cerebral blood flow of two groups of subjects; one group was involved in a semantic memory task, the other in an episodic memory task. The authors observed differences in regional cerebral blood flow of the two groups and suggested that their results indicate "an anatomical basis for the distinction between episodic and semantic memory."

Note that a number of psychologists (Craik, 1979; Kintsch, 1980; Naus and Halasz, 1979) disagree with the idea that episodic and semantic memory systems represent two separate memory systems. Instead, they suggest that there is a single memory system and that the content of a memory in this system varies from highly context-specific episodes to abstract generalizations. Tulving (1983) asserts that the dissociation studies provide convincing evidence that there are in fact two separate memory systems. However, Tulving does recognize that the episodic and semantic memory systems are highly interdependent. Thus, an event takes on more meaning if semantic as well as episodic knowledge is involved in the storing of that experience. Yet, Tulving believes that these two memory systems can also operate independently. For example, a person can store information about a particular temporal event that is both novel and meaningless, a result which can occur only if the episodic memory system is independent of the semantic memory system.

Physiological Basis of Memory Donald Hebb (1949) proposed that the memory of an event is not immediately stored in a permanent form but instead is initially stored in a fragile form. According to Hebb, experiencing an event activates a neural circuit in the central nervous system. The activity in this neural circuit "reverberates" or lasts for a short time following the termination of the event. Hebb suggested that one function of the reverberatory activity is to act as a temporary store and retain a record of an event until it can be consolidated into a permanent representation of the event.

In Hebb's view, physiological changes in the central nervous system occur following an event and represent the permanent record of the event. Since these physiological changes occur slowly, the reverberating activity must be maintained until the memory is permanently stored. If reverberatory activity is disrupted, the consolidation process stops, and no further physiological changes take place. Thus, a second function of reverberating activity, in Hebb's view, is the transfer of the storage of a memory from a temporary to a more permanent form.

The strength of a memory depends on how long the memory had to consolidate. Disruption of reverberating activity early in the consolidation process leads to a weak or nonexistent permanent memory of an event, resulting in an inability to recall the event. However, disruption late in the consolidation process usually has little impact: the permanent physiological changes have almost been completed, the permanent memory is strong, and recall of the event is probable. Next we discuss evidence evaluating whether reverberatory neural activity (1) follows an event, (2) is essential for the storage of a memory into permanent form, and (3) is followed by permanent physiological changes representing the permanent record of an event. We can only briefly examine the physiological basis of memory; for a more detailed discussion of this topic, see Rozenzweig and Bennett (1976) or Thompson, Hicks, and Shvyrok (1980).

Do Reverberatory Circuits Exist? Considerable evidence supports Hebb's idea (1949) that following an event, activity reverberates in a neural circuit. This neural activity continues sequentially through the circuit, and the activity is sustained for a short time following the event. Attempting to document the existence of a reverberating circuit, Burns (1958) first isolated a section of cortical tissue by undercutting a section of the cortex so that the section was no longer neurally connected to other parts of the brain. (Burns was careful not to disturb any of the blood supply running along the top of the cortex.) Next, he electrically stimulated part of the neural tissue and observed bursts of activity. This electrical activity continued following termination of the stimulation. Depending on the intensity of the electrical stimulation, the continued neural activity lasted up to 30 minutes. Although reverberation seems the most reasonable explanation for the sustained neural activity following an event, Burns provided more direct evidence of reverberation. He reasoned that if all the neurons in the circuit were stimulated simultaneously, then the sustained activity would stop when all the neurons were in the refractory period. To demonstrate this possibility, Burns applied a single intense shock to the middle of the cortical tissue. He noted an initial activity in the entire neural tissue followed by a cessation of neural activity. Apparently, for the continued neural activity to continue after an event, it must only reverberate through a specific neural circuit.

Other studies (Verzeano & Negishi, 1960; Verzeano, Laufer, Spear, & McDonald, 1970) also show reverberatory activity in neural tissue. In these studies, electrodes were implanted close together (30–200 μm apart) and arranged in a row to record electrical activity in adjacent neurons. Results show that brain stimulation produced a wave of neural activity which began with the stimulated neurons and continued sequentially in adjacent neurons. Further-more, the activity occurred in recurrent waves of excitation from one neuron to another. These observations suggest that recirculating or reverberating activity is initiated by stimulation. Verzeano and his associates also observed that the pattern of neural activity varied as a function of the stimulus presented, imply-ing that different reverberatory circuits are activated by different events. It seems reasonable to assume that the activation of different neural circuits by various events accounts for the differentiation of memories.

Is Reverberatory Activity Essential for Memory Storage?   Hebb's theory (1949) is not only that activity reverberates in a neural circuit after an event but also that consolidation requires this reverberation. If the encoding of an event in the long-term store requires reverberatory activity, disruption of activity in the neural circuit early in the consolidation of a memory should prevent encod-ing of the event as a memory. Duncan's study (1949) provided evidence sup-porting the critical role of reverberating activity in memory consolidation.

Duncan (1949) trained rats to avoid electric shock in the shuttle box. A light serving as the conditioned stimulus was presented 10 seconds prior to the shock. Each animal received one trial per day for eighteen days. After each training trial, the rats in eight experimental groups received an electroconvul-sive shock (ECS). The time lapse between the end of the training trial and the ECS varied from 20 seconds to 14 hours. A control group of rats did not receive the ECS. Since electroconvulsive shock produces intense activity in many neurons, Duncan assumed that synchronized reverberating activity would be disrupted, and that this in turn would lead to an end of memory consolidation. It would then follow that the shorter the interval between the training trial and the ECS, the less of the memory that is stored and the lower the recall of the experience. As predicted from a consolidation viewpoint, Duncan reported that the longer the interval between training trial and ECS, the higher the level of avoidance performance (see Figure 8.16). The reduced memory following ECS treatment is *retrograde amnesia,* and it is assumed to result from the disruption of memory consolidation caused by the ECS-induced termination of reverber-ating activity. Note that Duncan's study showed that consolidation occurred slowly. Avoidance performance was impaired even when several hours passed between training and ECS.

Following Duncan's initial observations, a number of studies (Leukel, 1957; Ransmeier, 1953; Thompson & Dean, 1955) reported that ECS produced deficits in the retention of a response. The studies also showed that when ECS immediately follows an event, a retention test shows no recall of that event. Furthermore, the effects of ECS on retention were shown in a variety of tasks: Leukel (1957) and Ransmeier (1953) used a maze learning situation, and Thompson and Dean (1955) employed a visual discrimination task. Retrograde amnesia with ECS has also been reported in human subjects (Cronholm & Molander, 1958; Flesher, 1941; Williams, 1950; Zubin & Barrera, 1941).

However, these early studies contain a methodological problem. Subjects were exposed to a series of ECSs, and since electroconvulsive shocks are an

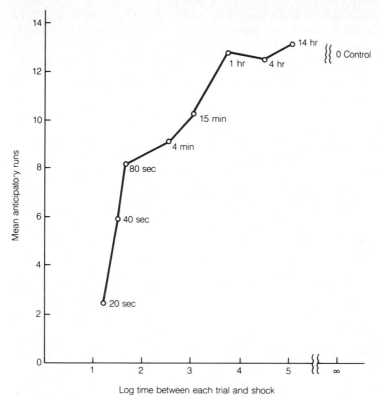

FIGURE 8.16
Active-avoidance performance as a function of the interval between
avoidance training and presentation of ECS. Anticipatory runs are
trials in which shock is avoided. From Duncan, C. P. The retroactive
effect of electroshock on learning. *Journal of Comparative and
Physiological Psychology*, 1949, *42*, 32–44. Copyright 1949 by the
American Psychological Association. Reprinted by permission.

aversive event, using multiple ECS presentations would lead to the association
of the aversive properties of ECS to the environment in which ECS was presented. The aversive qualities of this environment would lead to longer latencies, and the longer latencies would be attributed to poor recall when, in fact,
they were caused by avoidance of the situation in which ECS was received.
The temporal gradient showing greater performance as the interval between
learning trial and ECS increased would be attributed to more consolidation
when, in fact, it resulted from lower aversive conditioning caused by the delay
between the end of the training trial and ECS.

Support for the argument that the poor performance of subjects in these ECS
studies resulted from aversive conditioning rather than interrupted consolidation is found in Miller and Coons's study (1955), which shows that ECS does
have aversive properties and that multiple ECSs can lead to increased avoid-

ance latency. Miller and Coons first trained rats to run down an alley to obtain food and then shocked them while they ate. Electroconvulsive shocks were delivered at various intervals after the electrical shock was presented. If ECS does indeed disrupt consolidation of the shock experience, the rats should forget being shocked and run quickly to food. However, if ECS has aversive properties, avoidance latency would increase. Miller and Coons reported that rats given ECS after being shocked showed greater avoidance latency than did rats that received shocks but not ECS. Furthermore, the longer the interval between the shock and the ECS, the faster the latency to run for food. A similar development of anxiety as the result of ECS has been observed in humans (Gallinek, 1956).

Since multiple ECSs produce fear and lead to poorer active-avoidance performance, studies employing ECS after the 1950s have used a single ECS. This procedure minimizes the aversive conditioning by the ECS. Experimenters have also employed passive-avoidance tasks (see Chapter 4). In the passive-avoidance task, the aversive qualities of ECS would lead to greater avoidance performance. If ECS does affect memory, it could be detected: if ECS induces memory deficits, then the use of ECS would result in decreased avoidance performance; but if ECS causes aversive conditioning, then the result would be greater avoidance performance. Articles using single-trial passive-avoidance tasks have reported that ECS will induce memory deficits only when administered very shortly after passive-avoidance training (Lewis, 1969).

Chorover and Schiller (1965) used a step-down apparatus to train rats to avoid electric shock passively. This step-down apparatus consists of a chamber with a grid floor and a small wooden platform in the middle of the chamber (see Figure 8.17). Rats stepping off the platform were shocked. After being shocked, rats in the experimental groups received ECS. Chorover and Schiller varied the interval between the end of training and ECS from 3 to 30 seconds. Control-group rats either did not receive ECS after being shocked or were given neither training nor ECS. Chorover and Schiller reported that when tested the next day, control-group rats that had not received ECS after training showed evidence of remembering they were shocked in the apparatus by refusing to step off the platform; however, the control animals which had not re-

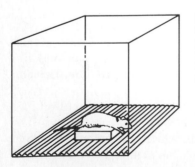

FIGURE 8.17
Step-down apparatus used for training passive-avoidance response. When animal steps off the platform, it receives electrical footshock. Reluctance to step off platform on test indicates level of conditioning of passive-avoidance response.

ceived either shock or ECS the previous day readily stepped off the platform. The presentation of ECS after training did disrupt passive-avoidance performance; the occurrence of ECS after passive-avoidance training caused the animals to step off the platform quickly on the retention test. Chorover and Schiller also established the temporal gradient of retrograde amnesia; that is, they measured what time was required before the ECS no longer affected the performance of a learned response. Unlike the results of Duncan (1949) and other studies using multiple training trials and ECS, Chorover and Schiller found ECS to be ineffective when presented more than 30 seconds after training (refer to Figure 8.18). These observations point out that memory consolidation occurs quickly, within a matter of seconds, and that the behavioral deficits following ECS gradients observed in other studies were caused by processes other than the failure to consolidate. Other experiments have also found that ECS is effective for only a short time following training; see Quartermain, Paolino, and Miller (1965) for another example.

Our discussion suggests that a memory consolidates quickly, and that consolidation is susceptible to disruption for only a few seconds after an event. A number of articles (Lewis, 1979; Miller & Springer, 1973) suggest that memories are consolidated in a fraction of a second. Furthermore, these articles argue that one function of the short-term store is to organize or elaborate on the stored memory; this organization or elaboration enhances an animal or person's ability to retrieve the memory. This theory assumes that ECS affects not

FIGURE 8.18
Percentage of subjects avoiding stepping off platform for at least 20 seconds as a function of training-ECS interval. From Chorover, S. L., & Schiller, P. H. Short-term retrograde amnesia in rats. *Journal of Comparative and Physiological Psychology*, 1965, 59, 73–78. Copyright 1965 by the American Psychological Association. Reprinted by permission.

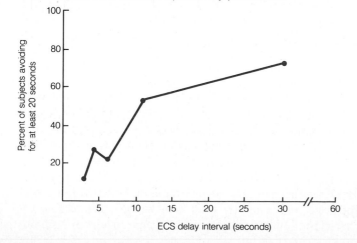

the consolidation of a memory but rather the retrieval of that memory. Thus, ECS is thought to interfere with the retrieval rather than storage of an experience.

Misanin, Miller, and Lewis (1968) provide evidence that ECS interferes with the retrieval of a memory. They trained their rats to passively avoid electric shock in a one-trial passive-avoidance step-down situation. Twenty-four hours after training, some subjects received the light CS followed by an ECS. The authors reported that ECS produced retrograde amnesia twenty-four hours after original training. Since consolidation of the memory of passive-avoidance training was undoubtedly completed after twenty-four hours, the retrograde amnesia could not have resulted from disruption of memory consolidation. Instead, Misanin, Miller, and Lewis suggested that there are two kinds of memory systems: active and passive. Their active memory system corresponds to the short-term store; the passive memory system, to the long-term store. In their view, retrograde amnesia can be produced only when a memory is active; that is, ECS can interfere with retrieval only when the memory of an event is being actively recalled. Why did ECS, presented twenty-four hours after training, produce retrograde amnesia? In Misanin, Miller, and Lewis's view, the CS reactivated the memory of original training, and the recall of the passive-avoidance response enabled ECS to be an effective amnesic agent.

Further evidence that ECS inhibits only the retrieval of a memory and not consolidation can be seen in the Lewis, Miller, and Misanin study (1969). In this study, one group of animals received a foot shock after stepping down from the platform; another group was given a foot shock followed by an ECS; a third group received only an ECS; and a fourth group did not receive any treatment. On a retention test the next day, Lewis, Miller, and Misanin found that animals receiving the foot shock alone showed a high level of fear, indicating that they remembered the foot shock from the previous day. When an ECS had followed the foot shock, the animals showed no fear when tested. A similar lack of fear was observed in animals that had received either ECS or no treatment. A fifth group of animals was given a "reminder shock" in a different environment four hours after receiving a foot shock and ECS. On a retention test twenty-four hours later, Lewis, Miller, and Misanin found that the reminder shock had eliminated the retrograde amnesia induced by ECS; that is, animals given the foot shock followed by ECS and then a reminder shock four hours later remembered the foot shock they had received the day before and showed fear in the step-down apparatus. Note that the reminder shock alone is not sufficient to produce fear of the step-down; Lewis, Miller, and Misanin still found no fear in animals receiving only the reminder shock on the first day. The authors suggested that the second foot shock reminded the rats of the first foot shock and the ECS. This reminder treatment caused the animals to overcome the retrieval failure produced by the ECS and thereby enabled them to avoid being shocked. These results also show that the memory of passive-avoidance training had been consolidated; otherwise, the reminder treatment would have had no effect. Other studies have reported that the reminder treatment produces a significant amount of memory return; see Geller and Jarvik (1968) or Koppenaal, Jogoda, and Cruce (1967) for other examples.

We have learned that a memory consolidates very rapidly. Electroconvulsive shock produces forgetting only when the memory of a past experience is active. The forgetting produced by ECS results from interference and can be reduced by a reminder treatment. Chapter 9 discusses how the reminder treatment eliminates ECS-induced forgetting.

In Search of the Engram What physical changes provide the basis for the permanent record of an event? Many scientists (Agranoff, 1980; Dunn, 1980) have suggested that a change in nucleic acids (RNA and DNA) produces the storage site of memories. This view, called *nucleotide-rearrangement theory,* assumes that a permanent change in RNA and DNA occurs as the result of learning. The modified RNA and DNA contains information about the experience. For several reasons, scientists have found the nucleotide-rearrangement theory attractive. First, considerable evidence implies that hereditary information is stored in the DNA molecule. Since innate information can be stored, it seems reasonable to assume that acquired information could also be stored in DNA. Second, an enormous amount of information is accumulated in a lifetime. DNA possesses sufficient complexity to store this vast amount of information. A considerable number of studies evaluating the nucleotide-rearrangement theory have provided evidence which seems to support this view; however, some scientists (see Briggs & Kitto, 1962) argue that the DNA structure cannot be changed by neural activity. E. Roy John's view (1967) suggests a mechanism whereby DNA action can be altered by experience without changing DNA structure. We will examine John's idea following a discussion of evidence indicating an involvement of nucleic acids in the storage of information.

Three approaches have been employed to validate the nucleotide-rearrangement view of memory storage. Some studies have measured biochemical changes associated with learning. Other experiments have attempted to inhibit changes in nucleotides. Still other studies have removed the nucleotides from experienced animals and injected them into untrained animals, reasoning that if changes in the nucleotides do underlie memory storage, this transfer should facilitate learning in unexperienced animals.

Chemical Changes Associated with Learning Many studies have evaluated whether learning produces quantitative or qualitative changes in RNA. (Since the lifespan of RNA is limited and its manufacture is controlled by DNA, changes in RNA are assumed to reflect DNA changes.) Some of these articles have measured RNA changes after learning. While not all these experiments have reported positive results, many have found RNA changes following learning (see Rose, Hambley, & Haywood, 1976, for a view of this literature). For example, Hyden and Egyhazi (1964) found that rats forced to reach for food with their nonpreferred paw showed a significant increase in cortical RNA in the hemisphere contralateral to the nonpreferred paw, compared with control rats allowed to reach with their preferred paw. Qualitative changes in RNA were also observed by Hyden and Egyhazi. They found changes in the ratios of nucleotide bases, the building blocks of RNA and DNA, for experimental animals, but they reported no changes in control subjects.

Other studies have attempted to discover a specific protein change following learning. (Since protein synthesis is controlled by RNA, altered protein synthesis is assumed to reflect nucleotide alteration.) George Ungar and his associates (Ungar, Galvan, & Clark, 1968) successfully identified a protein specific to fear. To identify this protein, rats were shocked when they entered a dimly lit chamber. Analysis of the brains of these animals revealed a protein not present in untrained animals. Ungar, Galvan, and Clark named the protein *scotophobin* after the Greek word for "fear of the dark."

Still other experiments have indirectly measured nucleotide changes. In these studies, a radioactive nucleotide or one of its precursors was injected prior to learning, and then the level of the radioactive substance was measured after learning. Increased radioactivity is thought to reflect increased RNA synthesis as the result of learning. One study using this technique is Horn, Rose, and Bateson's study of imprinting (1973). In their study, newly hatched chicks were exposed to either a flashing or continuous light for various amounts of time. Control chicks were kept in the dark. Horn, Rose, and Bateson found that chicks imprinted on the flashing light but did not react to the continuous light. Furthermore, they reported that RNA synthesis was increased more by exposure to the flashing light than by exposure to the continuous light. These observations show a relationship between learning and changes in RNA synthesis; that is, greater changes occur in RNA when an animal imprints than when imprinting does not occur. Horn, Rose, and Bateson also found that the longer the exposure to the flashing light, the greater the change in RNA synthesis (see Figure 8.19). Apparently, the more an animal learns about an event, the greater the change in RNA.

Inhibition of RNA Synthesis   Another way to assess the nucleotide-rearrangement theory is to administer drugs which temporarily impair or prevent RNA synthesis. The effect of these drugs should block memory storage as the result of the temporary reduction or elimination of RNA synthesis. Many studies have reported that inhibition of RNA synthesis results in memory impairment (see Quarterman, 1976, for a review of this literature).

In an early study in this area, Flexner, Flexner, and Stellar (1963) intracerebrally injected puromycin, a drug which interferes with protein synthesis, following the acquisition of an avoidance response. They found that puromycin prevented the recall of the avoidance response. Other experiments have also shown that puromycin impairs retention; however, research by Cohen, Ervin, and Barondes (1966) observed that puromycin also produces abnormal activity in the hippocampus, an effect comparable to delivering electroconvulsive shock. Thus, it is not clear whether puromycin's effects on memory are caused by its effect on protein synthesis or by the electrical activity it produces.

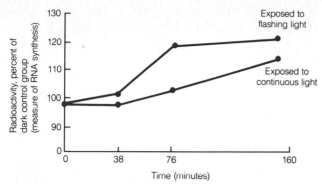

FIGURE 8.19
Alterations in RNA synthesis in the tectum area of chick's
brain after exposure to a flashing or steady light. From Horn,
G.; Rose, S. D. R.; & Bateson, P. P. G. Experience and
plasticity in the central nervous system. *Science*, 1973, *181*,
506–514. Copyright 1973 by the American Association for
the Advancement of Science.

Researchers in this area have used other drugs which impair RNA synthesis.
For example, Barondes and Cohen (1967) used cycloheximide, which inhibits
protein synthesis, and Agranoff, Davis, Casola, and Lim (1967) administered
8-azaquanine, which inhibits RNA action. However, these studies suffer from
two major methodological problems. First, since toxic doses of these drugs are
necessary to produce amnesia, animals show signs of illness during the studies,
and some die. Thus, perhaps illness rather than suppression of RNA and protein synthesis accounts for the effects of these drugs on memory. Second, the
drugs are only effective following weak training; extended training could overcome the drug's effect on memory and lead to retention of the response. As an
example of this finding, Barondes and Cohen reported that when mice were
trained to avoid to a criterion of three correct responses in four successive
trials, cycloheximide eliminated the memory of the response. However, the
drug had no effect, even though it inhibited protein synthesis by about 90
percent, when training was to a criterion of nine correct responses out of ten
trials. The significance of level of training questioned the role of the nucleotides
in memory storage.

The use of a new protein inhibitor, anisomycin, solved these two problems.
Flood, Bennett, Rozenzweig, and Orme (1973) found anisomycin to be an
effective amnesic drug at low doses; the lethal dose is 25 times the effective
amnesic dose. Furthermore, since low doses are safe, the drug can be given in
repeated doses. Flood, Bennett, Rozenzweig, and Orme reported that repeated
injections produce amnesia, even after extended training. Figure 8.20 shows
the results of their study in which mice were trained to avoid electric shock
passively. The level of training was manipulated by varying shock intensity; the
greater the intensity of shock, the higher the training strength. The mice re-

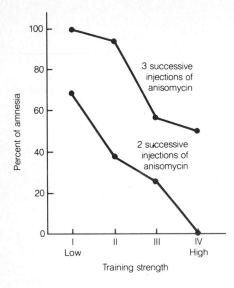

FIGURE 8.20
The percentage of mice showing amnesia as a function of the level of training and the number of injections of anisomycin, a protein inhibitor. From Flood, J. F.; Bennett, E. L.; Rosenzweig, M. R.; & Orme, A. E. The influence of duration of protein synthesis inhibition on memory. *Physiology and Behavior*, 1973, *10*, 555–562. Copyright 1973, Pergamon Press, Ltd.

ceived one, two, or three successive injections of anisomycin. The first injection was given 15 minutes before training; the subsequent injections were given at 2-hour intervals after training. As can be seen in Figure 8.20, the higher the number of injections, the greater the amnesia of prior avoidance training. Furthermore, at a high level of training three injections were needed to produce amnesia, indicating that with stronger training, protein synthesis must be inhibited longer to produce forgetting. Flood, Bennett, Orme, and Rosenzweig (1975) observed a similar influence of training strength and length of inhibition on the level of amnesia of an active-avoidance response.

Memory Transfer Studies   Some scientists have attempted to validate the nucleotide-rearrangement theory by training animals on a specific behavior and then injecting nucleic acids from the trained animals into untrained animals. If this transfer results in improved learning compared with control animals receiving nucleic acids from untrained animals, chemical changes in the nucleic acids can be assumed to cause the storage of a memory. Some of these studies have injected entire brain extracts into untrained animals; others have administered only the nucleic acids of the donor animals. These transfer studies have involved a variety of different animals and a large number of different training situations. Many studies have reported results indicating that memories can be transferred from one animal to another. Table 8.2 presents a list of studies in which animals were trained to perform various tasks and then the memory of their training was reportedly transferred to other animals.

Note that many researchers have been unable to replicate the early memory-transfer studies (Gaito, 1974). Chapouthier (1983) in a review of the literature suggests that methodological differences are responsible for the negative results of these later studies. For example, the time interval between injecting and testing of the receipt animals is critical; studies using a short interval

TABLE 8.2

SOME STUDIES REPORTING MEMORY TRANSFER FROM TRAINED TO
UNTRAINED ANIMALS

Task	Study
Acquired avoidance of saccharin	Revusky & DeVenuto, 1967; Moos, Levan, Mason, Mason, & Hebron, 1969
Alimentary conditioned reflexes	Reinis, 1965, 1968
Black-white discrimination	Dyal & Golub, 1967
Conditioned approach	Jacobson, Babich, Bubash, & Jacobson, 1965; McConnell, Shigehisha, & Salive, 1968
Conditioned avoidance of drinking	Weiss, 1970
Dark avoidance	Gay & Raphelson, 1967; Ungar, Galvan, & Clark, 1968; Fjerdingstad, 1969; Golub, Epstein, & McConnell, 1969; Wolthuis, 1969
Escape in a water maze	Essman & Lehrer, 1966
Habituation to sound	Ungar & Oceguera-Navarro, 1965
Instrumental learning in an operant chamber	Rosenblatt & Miller, 1966; Rosenblatt, Farrow, & Rhine, 1966; Byrne & Samuel, 1966; Byrne & Hughes, 1967; Dyal, Golub, & Marrone, 1967; Dyal & Golub, 1968; Golub & McConnell, 1968; McConnell, Shigehisha, & Salive, 1968
Left-right discrimination	Rosenblatt & Miller, 1966; Essman & Lehrer, 1967; Ungar, 1967a,b; Ungar & Irwin, 1967; Krylov, Kalyuzhnaya, & Tongur, 1969
Wire climbing	Gibby & Crough, 1967

obtained mostly negative results, but studies using a sufficient interval between the injection and testing have consistently obtained positive results. However, Chapouthier asserts that in many cases the positive results of the early studies can be attributed to nonspecific action of the injected substance rather than to the transfer of any specific information.

Recall that Ungar and his associates detected the presence of the protein scotophobin in animals trained to avoid dark places, but they did not detect it in animals that had not received the avoidance training. Ungar, Galvan, and Clark (1968) went a step further and injected scotophobin into untrained mice. They observed that these mice, which naturally prefer dark places, avoided a dark chamber. Apparently, fear-related information can be transferred from one animal to another. Furthermore, Ungar, Desiderio, and Parr (1972) synthesized scotophobin from inorganic chemicals and injected it into untrained animals. These animals also avoided dark places. However, a number of researchers (DeWied, Sarantakis, & Weinstein, 1973; Miller, Small, & Berk, 1975; Misslin, Ropartz, Ungerer, & Mandel, 1978) suggest that the effects of scotophobin are nonspecific; that is, the scotophobin acts to decrease emotionality, and decreased emotionality accounts for the greater time spent in a lighted environment rather than a specific fear of darkness.

Let's use Misslin, Ropartz, Ungerer, and Mandel's study to document this nonspecific effect of scotophobin. The researchers placed scotophobin-treated and control animals in an open field and noted that the animals given scotopho-bin were significantly more active and, therefore, less emotional in the open field than were control animals not given scotophobin. Since more emotional animals spend more time in dark places, Misslin, Ropartz, Ungerer, and Mandel assumed that the reduced emotionality caused by scotophobin explains the reduced time spent in the black chamber by scotophobin-treated animals.

Our discussion suggests that nucleic acids may be involved in the storage of information; however, this idea remains unproved, and many researchers are still skeptical. Other psychologists (John, 1967; Rosenblatt, 1967; Ungar, 1976) assert that the nucleic acids represent a logical basis of memory storage. How might memories be stored in nucleic acid? In an elegant discussion, John (1967) details a mechanism through which experience can lead to a change in nucleo-tide action. We can only briefly describe John's theory view, but interested readers are referred to John's *Mechanisms of Memory* for a complete discus-sion of his theory and evidence supporting it.

John's Theory of Memory Storage   John (1967) suggests that every event produces a unique and distinctive spacial-temporal pattern of neural activity. The representation of this experience is then permanently stored in the central nervous system. According to John, the storage of a memory occurs in three phases. In the first phase, an experience is registered in the nervous system. This stage corresponds to the sensory register and is almost instantaneous; the reminder studies described earlier support this aspect of John's view.

John's second phase, containing two parts, corresponds to the short-term store. One part of this phase provides the temporary retention characteristic of the short-term store; the second aspect serves as the template for long-term information storage. In John's view, short-term recall results from prolonged cellular responsiveness, which appears to be caused by ionic hyperpolariza-tion. Considerable evidence supports John's theory that increased neural re-sponsivity is responsible for short-term recall. For example, Haycock, van Buskirk, and McGaugh (1977) observed that recall is enhanced by injections of catecholamines, which increase neural reactivity when the drug is administered immediately following training. Similarly, Stein, Belluzzi, and Wise (1975) and Jensen, Martinez, Messing, Spiehler, Vasquez, Soumireu-Mourat, Liang, and McGaugh (1978) found that when injected shortly after learning, drugs which lower catecholamine levels and thereby decrease neuron responsivity impair short-term recall.

The short-term store also serves as the template for long-term information storage. John (1967) suggests that, instead of an experience permanently chang-ing DNA, DNA action is modified as a result of an event. According to John, neural responsivity is governed by DNA action. The activity of small segments of DNA is in turn controlled by regressor genes, and modification of repressor-gene activity would also modify DNA action, thereby changing responsivity of a neuron or neurons.

How does an event modify repressor-gene function? In John's view, a newly synthesized RNA molecule, produced by an event, alters repressor-gene function. This new RNA molecule has a limited lifespan and serves as the holding mechanism only until the memory is permanently stored. John presents a number of studies supporting his view. For example, Barondes and Cohen (1966) found that actinomycin D_1, a compound which inhibits RNA synthesis, interferes with the acquisition (storage) of a response but not with its retention (retrieval).

Information, in John's view, is permanently stored in the last phase of memory processing. According to John, the modified DNA action produces new RNA and protein. The new RNA and protein have two effects: (1) to reproduce the spacial-temporal neural activity associated with the recall of an event and (2) to maintain the altered DNA action through the continued influence on repressor-gene function. John presents evidence to support this aspect of his theory. For example, he suggests that the drug puromycin interferes with long-term retention by inhibiting the use of newly formed RNA and protein.

The storage of information can also be influenced by the action of several key CNS structures. Damage to these structures can lead to anterograde, or posttraumatic, amnesia. *Anterograde amnesia* is an inability to recall events which occur after some disturbance to the brain, such as a head injury or certain degenerative brain diseases. The case described in the opening vignette of the chapter is one example of the inability to permanently store information as the result of an injury to the brain.

Anatomical Basis of Memory Formation   In 1889, the Russian neurologist Korsakoff described a serious and dramatic memory deficit. His patients failed to recall past events; if an event recurred, these individuals showed no evidence of remembering the event. This disorder, called *Korsakoff's syndrome,* is typically seen in chronic alcoholics and occurs when certain brain structures malfunction.

Research on Korsakoff's syndrome has focused on two important issues, the first being the extent of the memory impairment in patients suffering from this disease. According to Carlson (1981), recent evidence indicates that these patients suffer from an inability to code information efficiently in the short-term store. This inefficient coding impairs the ability to store an event in a meaningful fashion, which in turn results in an inability to remember the event at a later date. Early research with these patients suggested an inability to store any information; however, more recent studies show that Korsakoff patients can remember certain types of information or events which do not require coding. For example, Sidman, Stoddard, and Mohr (1968) trained a patient with Korsakoff's syndrome to press a square containing the image of a circle, giving a penny as a reward for each correct response. The patient quickly learned to press the circle, and could select a circle from a display containing one circle and seven ellipses of various shapes. Even after several minutes of working on other tasks, the patient could select the appropriate stimulus. These observations indicate that this particular patient could remember the correct response.

However, although he responded appropriately physically, he soon forgot the words for what he had learned. When asked during the first task what he was doing, he replied that he was choosing the circle. However, after several minutes, he could no longer verbally describe his actions. Apparently, the patient retained knowledge of the contingency between behavior and reinforcement but forgot exactly what he was doing. In a similar study with additional patients, El-Wakil (1975) observed that patients with Korsakoff's syndrome could remember previously acquired contingencies but did not recall the logic behind their actions. These observations indicate that the memory deficit of Korsakoff patients represents a failure to code and store information.

The second aspect of the Korsakoff syndrome involves identifying nonfunctioning structures which cause the memory deficit seen in these patients. In 1954, Scoville demonstrated that bilateral removal of the medial temporal lobe in humans resulted in memory impairment identical to that seen in Korsakoff syndrome patients. These operations, conducted on thirty psychotic patients in an attempt to reduce their behavioral problems, resulted in anterograde amnesia.

Other studies (Penfield & Milner, 1958; Penfield & Mathieson, 1974) have implicated the hippocampus, a structure in the limbic system, not in the temporal lobe, as responsible for the consolidation of memories. These experiments pointed out that removing the temporal lobe alone does not lead to memory impairments; but removal of the hippocampus, which often is also removed with the temporal lobe, does result in severe anterograde amnesia.

For many years the hippocampus has been considered responsible for the consolidation of memories, but recent evidence collected by Horel and his associates (see Horel, 1978; Horel & Misantone, 1974, 1976) indicates that the destruction of the dorsomedial thalamic nucleus causes the memory impairments characteristic of Korsakoff's syndrome. Horel (1978), examining published studies concerning memory loss in humans suffering from Korsakoff's syndrome, reported that the memory impairments seen with this disease correlate with damage to the dorsomedial thalamus but not with damage to the hippocampus. Furthermore, Horel and Misantone (1974, 1976) observed that the destruction of the dorsomedial thalamus but not the hippocampus affected primates' ability to distinguish new from familiar objects. In contrast, dorsomedial thalamic lesions had no influence on the monkeys' retention of a visual discrimination. These results suggest that the memory deficits observed in patients with Korsakoff's syndrome can be reproduced in primates by destroying the dorsomedial thalamus but not the hippocampus. Apparently, the coding of an event and then the storage of the event in the long-term store are functions of the dorsomedial thalamus area of the brain. Chapter 9 will discuss how the hippocampus functions to retrieve the memory of prior events.

Levels of Memory Processing

Craik and Lockhart (1972) suggested that the multiple-store memory model proposed by Atkinson and Shiffrin does not accurately describe the memory process. They did not believe that memory reflected a transfer from one stage (e.g., short-term store) to another (e.g., long-term store); instead their *levels-of-processing* approach argues that memories differ in the extent to which they have been processed. According to Craik and Lockhart, a memory can be processed at many different levels. An event can receive only shallow superficial analysis, or it can be interpreted at a deeper level. Consider the various levels at which the word *car* can be processed. The initial processing involves analysis of the physical characteristics of the word, such as determining the lines and angles of those individual letters. A deeper level of processing involves identification of the three letters. A still deeper level of processing leads to identification of the word, and determination of the word's meaning represents an even higher level of memory processing.

The level of processing that an event receives is a very important aspect of Craik and Lockhart's view. They propose that all experiences result in a permanent memory trace but that the strength of the trace depends on the level of processing that memory has received. Craik and Lockhart assume that the more an event is processed, the more durable its memory trace will be and the greater the likelihood that it will be recalled.

Experiences are definitely processed at various levels. The discussion of language in Chapter 7 showed that determination of the deep structure allows us to understand the meaning of words and ideas. Chapter 9 will examine the observation that the recall of information is affected by the extent to which experiences are analyzed. However, Craik and Lockhart's level-of-processing theory does not necessarily describe accurately the storage and retrieval of information. Considerable evidence indicates that the Atkinson-Shiffrin multistage memory model is a valid explanation of the memory process; that is, most psychologists support the theory that experiences can be retained in stores of differing permanence. Next we will examine evidence which validates the Atkinson-Shiffrin multistage memory model (see Howard, 1983, for a detailed discussion of this literature). Other research shows that although experiences that receive extensive processing are more likely to be recalled than are events that receive less processing, on some occasions experiences that receive only superficial processing can be more readily recalled than can deeply processed information. Our discussion of memory storage ends with a brief description of this research (refer to Bransford, Franks, Morris, & Stein, 1979, for presentation of this experimentation).

Support for Multistage Memory Model   Two lines of evidence provide convincing proof that more than one memory system exists. First, individuals with Korsakoff's syndrome can retain new experiences for only a short time but are able to recall information experienced prior to the onset of the disease. This pattern of memory loss is thought to be caused by damage to the dorsomedial thalamus and to reflect a failure to permanently store experiences. In contrast, Chapter 9 will show that damage to the hippocampus results in an individual who can remember recent information but is unable to recall previously stored experiences. The different pattern of memory deficits provides strong support for distinct short-term stores and long-term stores.

The second line of research validating the theory of distinct memory stores is provided by research on the serial-position effect. Recall that people learn the items at the beginning and end of the list more readily than items in the middle of the list. The serial-position effect is also observed during recall (see Figure 8.21). One interpretation of the serial-position effect (Howard, 1983) argues that the recency aspect of the serial-position effect—the better recall of the last items—results from continued rehearsal of these items during testing and, therefore, reflects the operation of the short-term store. In contrast, the primacy aspect of the serial-position effect—the higher recall of initial items— is thought to occur because subjects can spend more time processing the initial items and storing them in the long-term store. This interpretation suggests that two distinct memory-storage systems are involved in the serial-position effect—the short-term store causes the recency effect, and the long-term store accounts for the primacy effect.

Is this dual-storage theory of the serial-position effect valid? A considerable amount of research (Howard, 1983) indicates that different variables influence the primacy and recency effects; these observations are consistent with the idea that different memory systems are responsible for the primacy and recency effects. For example, Murdock (1962) and Postman and Phillips (1965) presented some of their subjects with a list of thirty words and then asked them to count backward by threes for 2 minutes; other subjects were tested immediately. A multistage memory model predicts that this procedure should influence the recency but not the primacy effect, since counting backward affects short-term but not long-term memory. In support of this prediction, the researchers found that although the counting-backward technique did not influence recall of the items presented at the beginning of the list, recall was significantly poorer

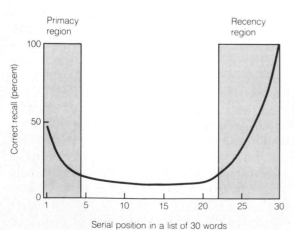

FIGURE 8.21
Figure shows the serial-position effect in terms of percentage of correct recall. The shaded areas indicate that recall is better for items at the beginning (primacy portion) and the end (recency portion) of the list than for items in the middle of the list. From Howard, D. V. *Cognitive psychology.* New York: Macmillan, 1983.

for end-of-the-list items when testing was delayed rather than immediate. Murdock (1962) and Postman and Phillips (1965) also varied the rate at which the words were presented. It is assumed that the presentation rate should not influence short-term memory and, therefore, the recency effect. In contrast, a slower rate of presentation should allow for more long-term storage of information and thus increase the primacy effect and lead to greater recall of items early in the list. Consistent with this view, the authors reported that increasing the rate of presentation affected the primary but not the recency effect.

Shallowly Processed Information Can Be Recalled Craik and Lockhart (1972) proposed that we have only one memory system and that the ability to remember a past experience depends on how deeply we process that event. In their view, information that is deeply processed will be remembered better than will experiences that are only shallowly processed. However, a number of researchers (Morris, Bransford, & Franks, 1977; Stein, 1978) have reported that in some instances an event that receives a shallower processing is retained better than another experience which receives a deeper level of processing. These results indicate that the depth of information processing does not completely control the recall of previous experiences. Let's look at the Morris, Bransford, and Franks (1977) study to illustrate that retention of a shallowly processed event is not necessarily less than that of a more deeply processed experience.

Morris, Bransford, and Franks (1977) presented their subjects two types of problems intended to produce two kinds of information processing, phonemic or semantic. Phonemic (or sound) processing was induced with problems such as "_____ rhymes with legal?" A problem like "The _____ had a silver engine" is assumed to stimulate semantic processing. Since semantic problems require a greater level of processing than do phonemic tasks, the Craik and Lockhart levels-of-processing view suggests that subjects will always recall semantically processed information better.

Morris, Bransford, and Franks's study does not support this prediction; these researchers showed that shallowly processed information can sometimes be recalled better than deeply processed information. In their study, subjects were given one of two types of retention tests. One test was a standard recognition test consisting of an equal number of target (previously experienced) and of nontarget words. The subjects' task on this test was to indicate which words they had already heard. The other subjects received a rhyming recognition test which was comprised of words that either rhymed or did not rhyme with the target words; the subjects' task was to indicate which words rhymed with the target words. Morris, Bransford, and Franks reported that although semantic processing leads to better retention on the standard test, retention was superior for phonemically processed words on the rhyming tests. These results not only are inconsistent with the Craik and Lockhart model, they also indicate that the type of test used to measure recall is important. According to Morris, Bransford, and Franks, semantic processing will only aid retention when certain kinds of retention tests are used. On the rhyming test, semantic processing is less effective than phonemic processing and, therefore, leads to poorer recall.

Other studies show that in certain situations shallowly processed information can be recalled well. For example, Kolers (1979) found that people can remember for long periods the type of print that they read. Other experiments indicate that reexperiencing an event can lead to improved recall even though the level of processing does not increase. Nelson's (1979) study illustrates this observation. He found that asking a question like "Does the word *train* have an *n* sound?" twice leads to better recall of the question. According to Nelson, the second presentation of the question does not lead to any deeper processing of information, yet it does result in better retention.

Our discussion indicates that memory storage does not depend on the depth of information processing. Cermack and Craik (1979) suggested that retention depends less on the level of processing than on the elaborativeness of processing. Elaboration is one function of the short-term store; in the next chapter we will examine evidence that it also has an important influence on the recall of past experiences.

SUMMARY

There are three stages in the storage of an experience. The first stage is the sensory register, which stores an exact copy of the external stimuli. The visual copy contained in the sensory store is referred to as an icon and is stored in the iconic memory. Echoic memory contains an exact replica of an auditory experience, and the echo is stored in the sensory store. Data are stored in the sensory register for only a very short time; icons usually last about 0.25 seconds, the echoes approximately 2 seconds. Echoes last longer than icons because a visual experience provides all the information needed to detect the salient characteristics, whereas the recognition of an auditory event requires sounds to be retained in the sensory store until detection of the event is achieved and a record of the event is formed. All the information about an experience is not contained in the sensory store; in fact, only a small amount of external information is retained there. Also, information decays rapidly after leaving the sensory register and is lost unless transferred into the short-term store.

The short-term store serves as a temporary storage facility, and people are consciously aware of information stored there. Information remains in the short-term store for approximately fifteen to twenty seconds, and during this time experiences are interpreted for their meaning and then organized in logical ways. This interpretation and organization produces a more meaningful experience, which in turn increases the likelihood of recall occurring at a later time. The short-term store also has limited storage capacity; only three or four units of information can be retained at one time. One effect of the interpretation and organization is overcoming this limited storage capacity. Memories contained in the short-term store are easily disrupted and replaced by new information.

The short-term store can rehearse or replay prior experiences, and this rehearsal functions to retain information in the short-term store for a longer period. This increased rehearsal enhances interpretation and organization of the memory, improving the likelihood that the memory will later be available for recall.

Most information in the short-term store is transferred into the long-term store, the site of permanent memory. Although a memory contained in the long-term store may not be remembered at a later time, memories can be lost as the result of decay, or fail to be recalled because of interference or the absence of memory attributes.

There are two types of long-term memories. The episodic memory system contains information about temporally dated events; the semantic memory system contains knowledge of words or other symbols or about the rules, formulas or algorithms for developing concepts or solutions to problems. The type of information contained is not the only difference between the two systems. The episodic and semantic memory systems are also functionally distinct, controlled by different operations for the storage and retrieval of past experiences.

Activity reverberates in a neural circuit following the experiencing of an event. This reverberatory activity represents the interpretive and organizational function of the short-term store. Disruption of this neural activity prior to the elaboration of an experience can produce a memory that cannot be retrieved from the long-term store.

According to John, modification of repressor-gene action occurs following an experience; the change in repressor-gene function alters the action of DNA. The modified DNA acts to change neural responsivity and also represents the site of permanent memory storage. Changes in RNA have been observed following an event; these findings provide support for John's theory of memory storage.

The dorsomedial thalamus functions to code and store an event in the long-term store. Individuals suffering from Korsakoff's syndrome are unable to store information permanently. Evidence suggests that Korsakoff's syndrome is caused by the failure of the dorsomedial thalamus to function properly.

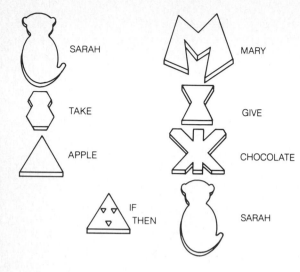

SARAH

TAKE

APPLE

MARY

GIVE

CHOCOLATE

IF
THEN

SARAH

FIGURE 7.14
A few of Sarah's "words" which
she arranged to form complex
sentences. From Premack, A. J.,
& Premack, D. Teaching
language to an ape. *Scientific
American,* 1972, 227, 92–99.

stand a number of different sentences. For example, she learned the agent-action-object word order and created new sentences such as *Debby cut banana.*

Despite the fact that primates appear to use language to communicate, Herbert Terrace (1979) does not believe that primates are capable of learning language. Teaching American Sign Language to a chimpanzee named Nim Chimpsky, Terrace noted some important differences between Nim's vocalizations and human language: an intense, directed effort was required to teach Nim even very simple signs, whereas children do not need to be taught language; they learn to talk simply by being in an environment where language is used. Terrace found no evidence that Nim could create unique grammatically correct sentences. According to Terrace, the chimpanzee did not learn the creative aspect of language; that is, she did not know how to use rules to create an infinite number of new experiences and complex sentences. Instead, Terrace argued that the chimpanzee's multiword sentences merely imitated the order used by the trainer. Why did the chimpanzee even bother to use the signs at all? According to Terrace, reinforcement of imitative behavior motivated the primate's behavior. Also, by reviewing the transcripts of communications of Washoe and several other chimpanzees, Terrace concluded that these animals were unable to generate syntactically correct novel combinations of signs. Terrace also noted that few of Nim's statements were spontaneous; most of them were in response to a human's statement. This lack of spontaneous speech is quite different from the spontaneity characteristic of human speech.

Although a number of psychologists (Marx, 1980; Thompson & Church, 1980) have supported Terrace's view, others (Bindra, 1981; Gardner, 1981; Pate & Rumbaugh, 1983; Patterson, 1981) have disagreed with him. For example, Beatrice Gardner (1981) argued that Nim was raised quite differently from

CHAPTER 9

MEMORY RETRIEVAL

A MEMORABLE EXPERIENCE

Reading the morning newspaper, Rene was drawn to an ad for a workshop that offered techniques in memory improvement to be given at the local college. "Techniques are available to enable you to remember better. Let us teach you these techniques in only one day." Rene has a terrible memory. She forgets the names of people to whom she has just been introduced. She often forgets her errands and even forgets to attend meetings, both of which are detrimental to her career as a real estate agent. Although skeptical about the prospects for improvement of her memory, Rene decided to attend the workshop anyway.

Jim Brewer, the instructor for the workshop, is somewhat of a celebrity. Rene had seen him on several television shows where he demonstrated a remarkable memory, recalling all the names of people in the audience or pages of telephone numbers from the local directory. Rene thought that Jim Brewer's extraordinary memory capacity must have been inherited; however, if Rene could learn just a few techniques to improve her feeble memory, she certainly would be grateful.

The large number of people attending the workshop surprised Rene. Jim Brewer began the session by saying that everyone has the capacity for a good memory but that the ability to remember previous experiences must be developed. He explained that a number of techniques called *mnemonics* have been developed to improve memory and that the aim of the workshop would be to learn these techniques. Brewer continued by emphasizing that these mnemonic techniques are easily learned and can readily enhance the ability to remember. To illustrate this point, he asked members of the workshop to perform a mnemonic exercise to learn the name of the person sitting in front of them. Rene, surprised by the effectiveness of the technique, still remembers the name. However, Brewer also emphasized that the techniques must be practiced to have a meaningful impact. Like most skills, the more they are used, the better the results they produce.

The workshop lasted only one day, but Rene learned many techniques to help her remember things like names, appointments, and phone numbers. She even learned how to use her memory to improve her bridge game. Rene was very pleased with the workshop and vowed to practice the techniques she had learned.

ATTRIBUTES OF MEMORY

Benton Underwood (1969, 1983) suggested that memory can be thought of as a collection of different types of information. Each type of information is called a *memory attribute*. For example, the memory of an event contains information regarding where the event occurred. This aspect is referred to as the *spatial* attribute of that memory. A memory also contains information about the temporal characteristics of an event; Underwood calls this information the *temporal* attribute. According to Underwood, there are ten major memory attributes: acoustic, orthographic, frequency, spatial, temporal, modality, context, affective, verbal associative, and transformational.

The Function of an Attribute

Before discussing each type of memory attribute, let us first look at the two basic functions of attributes as described by Underwood. First, *the establishment of a specific aspect of an experience as a memory attribute can act to decrease forgetting*. Interference, a major cause of forgetting, often occurs as a result of the failure to differentiate between memories. Information contained in a memory attribute provides a basis for distinguishing memories and thus can prevent forgetting. Second, *the presence of the stimulus contained in the memory attribute can act to retrieve a memory*. When we encounter or reexperience the stimulus which characterizes a salient aspect of a past event, the presence of that stimulus will act to recall the memory of the event. We will discuss the development of memory attributes and their role in the recall of past experiences in more detail later.

Note that although there are ten major attributes of memory, information about each attribute may not be contained in every memory. Thus, even though a stimulus characterizes a particular aspect of a past experience, if it is not a memory attribute of that experience, its presence will not lead to the recall of the event. For example, you have a traffic accident on a particular day. If the day is not an attribute of the memory of the accident, the anniversary of the accident will not remind you of your misfortune. Furthermore, one or two aspects of an experience may be more salient for a particular experience; these aspects will become memory attributes of the event, and retrieval will be based solely on the presence of the stimuli which represent these attributes.

Types of Attributes

Acoustic Attribute   Recall from Chapter 8 that experiences are acoustically coded by the short-term store. Underwood suggested that one attribute of a memory provides information about the acoustical properties of an event. Since speech communication would be impossible if people could not discriminate between verbal signals, an event's acoustical properties are clearly important.

Long and Allen's (1973) study illustrates the important influence of the acoustic attribute on the recall of an experience. Long and Allen presented to their subjects a list of eighteen words organized in one of two ways: six groups of three rhyming words (e.g., Ted, red, head; Jack, black, back) or six groups of three conceptually related words (e.g., Ted, Jack, Jean; red, black, green). After the list was presented, the subjects were asked to recall as many words from it as they could. Remember subjects organize a list of words during their presentation and cluster them in terms of the way they were organized. Long and Allen, interested in whether their subjects would cluster the words based on the acoustic attribute or on the conceptual attribute, found the words were clustered according to the way they rhymed rather than their conceptual similarity. These observations indicate that the acoustic attribute had a dominant influence on the recall of the words.

Underwood (1969) suggested that the *acoustic attribute* does not always play the dominant role in memory. Sometimes acoustical features may not be the most salient aspect of the experience. In these circumstances, other types of information are used to recall prior experiences. Clearly, other characteristics of an event also can become an attribute of a memory, and these attributes can lead to the retrieval of a memory.

Orthographic Attribute   Events differ in their structural characteristics. For example, different letters have different shapes. Different words have different structures: words differ in length, in number of syllables, in number of repeated letters, and in terms of unusual or infrequently appearing sequences. Underwood referred to the feature characteristics of events as their *orthographic attribute*.

To differentiate items, for example to distinguish an *A* from a *K,* a person must recognize feature characteristics of each item. Evidence indicates that people can detect these orthographic characters of an event. For example, Zechmeister (1969) reported that subjects rated words based on their orthographic distinctiveness.

Furthermore, people can use the orthographic attribute to recall a particular event. To illustrate the influence of orthographic attribute on the retrieval of a memory, Hintzman, Block, and Inskeep (1972) presented to subjects eight successive eighteen-word lists. Half the words on each list were presented in upper-case block letters; the other half, in lower-case script letters. Hintzman, Block, and Inskeep found that, on a free recall task (a task in which subjects can recall items in any order), subjects reported words in the script type in one group and words in the block type in another group, indicating that the orthographic attribute of type style was used to retrieve the words on the list. We should note that other attributes were also used to recall the words, since all the subjects did not cluster the words based on type style. The use of the orthographic attribute to recall material has been reported by other researchers; for example, Kolers (1976) had subjects read some material upside down and found that subjects could recall items a year later based on whether they had been read upside down.

Frequency Attribute   According to Underwood, a counting mechanism which registers every experience provides a record of the number of times a specific event is experienced. In Underwood's view, the frequency of an event's occurrence, or the *frequency attribute,* that can be used to recall the memory of that event.

Ekstrand, Wallace, and Underwood (1966) presented to subjects a list of 8 four-letter words and asked them to guess how frequently each of the words appeared in everyday print such as books and newspapers. The results showed that these estimates corresponded well to the actual frequency that the words did appear (Figure 9.1). Thus people do have information about how frequently certain events occur.

Can this information about frequency be used to recall a specific memory? Ekstrand, Wallace, and Underwood (1966) also evaluated this aspect of attribute theory. Subjects in this study received a list of 75 words, 40 of which were presented only once; 20 were presented twice; 10, three times; and 5, four times. After the list had been presented, the subjects were shown pairs of the words from the list and asked to indicate which of the two words had occurred more frequently. If frequency is an attribute of memory, then the subjects should be able to recognize the word in the pair that had occurred more frequently. Ekstrand, Wallace, and Underwood reported that their subjects did use the frequency information and identified the correct word. Note that identification was not perfect but that the greater the difference in how frequently the two words appeared, the more accurate the recall. For example, subjects were better able to identify the correct word if 1 word had been presented one time and the other word presented four times than if the words had been presented two and three times.

Spatial Attribute   Students will occasionally tell me that they can remember the number of the page where a particular study is described in a textbook. These people have information about the spatial location of a certain item. This knowledge represents the *spatial attribute* of a memory.

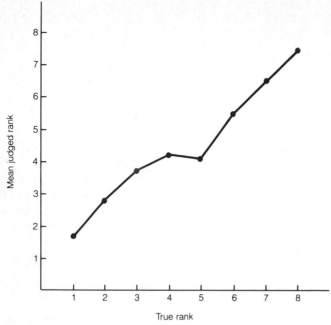

FIGURE 9.1
The subjects' mean judgments of the frequency with which
words occur in printed discourse as a function of the actual
frequency of occurrence. From *Attributes of memory* by B. J.
Underwood. Copyright 1983 by Scott, Foresman and Company.
Reprinted by permission.

According to Underwood (1969, 1983) material can occupy different positions, and spatial information automatically becomes part of a person's memory of an event. A study by Weeks (1975) shows that the stimulus contained in the spatial attribute can retrieve a memory. In Weeks's study, subjects received five successive lists of trigrams presented through either a single speaker or two speakers placed 120 degrees apart. When all five lists were presented through the same speaker, proactive interference developed, and subjects had difficulty remembering words from later lists. However, if the first four lists were presented through one speaker and the fifth through a second speaker, the subjects could readily remember the words presented in the last list. Apparently, the spatial location of the speaker became an attribute for remembering the last list and was responsible for subjects' ability to recall the words on it.

Let's use one further example to show the influence of the spatial attribute. When trying to remember the details of a particular story, you recall the specific newspaper or magazine in which the story appeared. You can then use this spatial information to remember the story.

Temporal Attribute When it is September 15th, I know that it's my birthday. Obviously, one attribute of my birthday is the date on which my birth occurred. The knowledge of my birth date is the *temporal attribute* of that event. Everyone knows the date of his or her birthday as well as the dates of other significant events. These observations clearly indicate that time can be a very important part of a memory. Even so, research shows that only *significant* temporal information is used to recall an experience.

Underwood (1977) presented to college students a list of eight events; the events occurred approximately a year apart, and Underwood made certain that the subjects knew about them. The students were asked to rank the events in the order that they had taken place. Underwood reported that of 108 students, only 2 did so correctly. Apparently, the temporal attribute does not always contain sufficient information for retrieval; a person may know that an event occurred but may not know exactly when. For example, you may have received an excellent grade on a particular date last year, but that date this year does not remind you of the event. It seems reasonable to assume that only when the date becomes associated with the event will the temporal attribute contain the date of the occurrence and therefore lead to the retrieval of the memory of the event.

Modality Attribute Underwood (1969, 1983) asserts that memories may also contain information regarding the sensory modality which experienced the event. Thus, one attribute of a memory is knowledge of whether the event being recalled was seen or heard or touched. What is the function of this *modality attribute* of a memory? In Underwood's view, the modality attribute serves the same purpose as any other attribute: it is used to differentiate between memories, and the presence of specific sensory information can retrieve a particular memory. Hintzman, Block, and Inskeep's 1972 study provides support for this view.

Hintzman, Block, and Inskeep (1972) presented several lists of words visually and other lists of words orally. Subjects were then asked to identify which words had been spoken and which had been shown. The authors reported that their subjects identified the words correctly 74 percent of the time, indicating that the memory of each word contained information regarding the sensory modality which had registered the word. Hintzman, Block, and Inskeep also asked subjects to recall as many words as possible and found that subjects had clustered the words based on the input modality, indicating that subjects used the modality attribute to remember the words.

Underwood notes that although the input modality is an attribute of a memory, there is a high level of interchange between memories established via different modalities. To understand information often requires other information received by other modalities. Underwood presents the following example to illustrate this cross-modality interchange. Suppose you use your index finger to write letters of the alphabet on the back of another person. Can this person tell which letters you have drawn? Evidence indicates the answer is yes. According to Underwood, the correct detection occurs because the tactile stimulation was translated into a memory system having access to visual information about the letters. This visual information is used to identify the letters that were printed tactilely.

Context Attribute   An event's background can become an attribute of memory, and reexposure to that background context can produce the retrieval of the memory of that event. For example, in the beginning of the classic movie *Casablanca,* Ingrid Bergman did not recognize Humphrey Bogart, even though they had had a love affair many years earlier. However, the song "As Time Goes By" reminded her of past experiences with the male character. The song was part of the context in which their love affair had taken place, and thus the song was a memory attribute of the affair. Hearing the song reminded the woman of the events surrounding her affair. The experience of Ingrid Bergman's character is not unique. You have undoubtedly been reminded of a past event by reexperiencing one aspect of the event.

Underwood's view suggests that context is a memory attribute. A considerable amount of research has been conducted to investigate the *context attribute.* Some of this research has involved human subjects (Smith, Glenberg, & Bjork, 1978; Underwood, 1983); other studies have used animals as subjects (Gordon, 1983; Spear, 1973, 1978). Both types of research show that context is an important memory attribute.

Bilodeau and Schlosberg (1951) placed two groups of human subjects in the "drum room," a dingy storeroom filled with old equipment, and asked them to learn a list of ten paired associates. (In a paired-associates learning task, subjects are presented a list of stimuli and responses. The list usually consists of ten to fifteen pairs, and subjects are required to learn the correct response to each stimulus.) The subjects had to learn the paired associates while looking at the nonsense syllables that were printed on a memory drum. One group of subjects then learned a second list of paired associates in this same room, but the other group received the interpolated list in another room. This other room, called the "card room," was described by Bilodeau and Schlosberg as being as different from the drum room as possible. The card room was a large basement classroom where nonsense syllables were presented on a card-flipping device similar to a desk calendar. Seated in front of this apparatus, the subjects learned the paired associates as the experimenter flipped the cards every 2 seconds. Following the interpolated paired-associate learning, all subjects relearned the original material in the drum room. Bilodeau and Schlosberg reported that subjects who learned the interpolated material in a different environment recalled the original material significantly better than did the subjects who learned both lists in the same room. These results indicate that the environment in which an event is experienced becomes a part of the memory of the event. The use of different contexts allowed the second group of subjects to differentiate the memories and thereby recall the memory of the desired list. In contrast, the subjects who learned both lists in the same room could not distinguish between the memories of the two lists and showed a substantial amount of retroactive interference. Apparently, the use of different contexts led to greater recall of verbal information. Greenspoon and Ranyard in 1957 observed findings similar to Bilodeau and Schlosberg's. In a more recent study, Smith, Glenberg, and Bjork (1978) discovered that subjects' recall of a list of words was significantly higher when testing occurred in the original context than when subjects were tested in a novel environment.

The influence of context in memory retrieval in animals can be seen in a study by Gordon, McCracken, Dess-Beech, and Mowrer (1981). Animals in this study were trained in a distinctive environment to actively respond to avoid shock in a shuttle box. Forty-eight hours later, the rats were placed either in the shuttle box in the original training room or in an identical shuttle box located in another room that differed from the training room in terms of size, lighting, odor, ambient noise level, and holding cage. Gordon, McCracken, Dess-Beech, and Mowrer reported high retention when the rats were tested in the training context and significantly poorer performance when testing occurred in a novel context (refer to Figure 9.2). Apparently, the context in which the active-avoidance response is learned influences an animal's ability to recall the avoidance response. If an animal is in the learning context, it will remember the past experience; if it is in a different context, the avoidance will not be recalled.

Note that not all studies have shown that a change in context leads to forgetting (Underwood, 1983). Although context is one attribute of memory, a memory also contains information about other characteristics of an event. Undoubtedly, the significance and availability of other attributes influence whether a memory is recalled in another context. If the context is the unique or significant aspect of a memory, retrieval will depend on the presence of the context; however, if other attributes are important and available, retrieval will occur even in a new context.

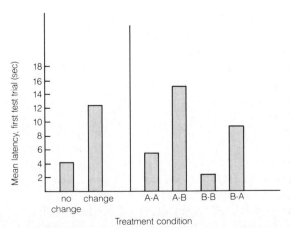

FIGURE 9.2
The mean latencies to cross to the black chamber on retention test for groups A-A and B-B (trained and tested in the same environment) and groups A-B and B-A (trained in one environment and tested in another environment). From Gordon, W. C.; McCraken, K. M.; Dess-Buch, N.; & Mowrer, R. R. Mechanisms for the cueing phenomenon: The addition of the cueing context to the training memory. *Learning and Motivation*, *1981, 12*, 196–211.

The reminder-treatment studies (Gordon, 1983) demonstrate that retrieval can occur in a new context when other attributes are able to produce recall. The reminder treatment consists of presenting subjects during testing with a subset of the stimuli that were present in training. Although this reminder treatment is insufficient to produce learning, it can induce retrieval of a past experience, even in a novel context. The Gordon, McCracken, Dess-Beech, and Mowrer (1981) study shows this influence of the reminder treatment. Recall that in this study, changing the context caused animals to forget their prior active-avoidance responses. Another group of animals in the study received reminder treatment 4 minutes before they were placed in the novel environment. The reminder treatment involved placing animals for 15 seconds in a cueing chamber—a white, translucent box identical to the white chamber of the avoidance apparatus where shock had occurred during training. Following the reminder treatment, animals were placed in a holding cage for 3.5 minutes and then transferred to the shuttle box in the novel context. Gordon, McCracken, Dess-Beech, and Mowrer found that animals receiving the reminder treatment performed as well as the animals that had been in the training context. Apparently, exposure to the cueing chamber prevented the forgetting that normally occurs in a novel context. These observations indicate that the presence of stimuli which are contained in other memory attributes can also reduce the impact of a change in context cues.

Smith (1979, 1982) discovered that a reminder treatment could be used in human subjects to reduce forgetting that occurs when context is changed from training to testing. In Smith's studies, some subjects received training and testing in the same environment; other subjects were given a list of thirty-two words to learn in one context and then asked to recall the list in a new context. A third group of subjects was exposed to a context-recall technique prior to testing in a new environment. The context-recall technique involved instructing subjects to think of the original training context and ignore the new context when trying to recall the list of words. Smith reported that subjects in the context-recall technique group remembered as many words in a new room as did subjects tested in their original learning room. In contrast, subjects who were tested in a new context but did not receive the reminder treatment remembered only two-thirds as many words. Apparently, a reminder treatment can prevent forgetting that would normally be seen in both animals and humans as a result of a context change.

Affective Attribute   Underwood (1969, 1983) asserted that the emotional responses produced by different events are effective attributes of memories. Some events are pleasant; others, unpleasant. The memory of an event contains much information regarding the emotional character of that event. This *affective attribute* enables a person to distinguish between memories of pleasant and unpleasant events, as well as to retrieve the memory of a particular event.

The Wickens and Clark study (1968) provides evidence of an affective attribute of memory. Wickens and Clark gave subjects a list of words that had been rated pleasant to learn. After the subjects had learned the first list of words, they were given a second list. If the second list also contained pleasant words, the memory of the first list interfered with the recall of the second list. However, if the second list of words was unpleasant, no proactive interference was observed. These observations indicate that the subjects' memory of the lists contained knowledge of the affect of the words, and this information facilitated recall of the second list of words and interfered with recall of the first list.

Underwood theorized that the affective attribute could be viewed as an internal contextual attribute; that is, it contained information about the internal consequences of an event. Events not only produce internal changes, they also occur during a particular internal state. Suppose you are intoxicated at a party. The next day a friend asks you if you had an enjoyable time, but you do not remember. This situation is an example of *state-dependent learning* (Overton, 1964, 1971). In a state-dependent learning study, an experience encountered during one internal state will not be recalled when the internal state is changed. According to our memory attribute framework, internal state is an attribute of memory; that is, knowledge of the internal state is contained in our memory of an event. A change in internal state removes the presence of an attribute of memory, which can lead to a failure to recall the event.

State-Dependent Learning   Overton (1964) trained rats to obtain food in a T maze. Half the animals were trained after receiving a pentobarbital injection (a depressant); the remaining half were trained after receiving a saline injection. The two groups of animals were subdivided again during testing: half of each group was tested after receiving a pentobarbital injection; the other half, after a saline injection. As can be seen in Table 9.1, half the animals were tested when they were in the same internal state as they had been during training; the other half were tested during a state different from that experienced during training. Overton found a high recall of the prior instrumental appetitive response if rats had received pentobarbital or saline prior to both training and testing. In contrast, retention was impaired if animals had been given either pentobarbital

TABLE 9.1
RETENTION OF RESPONSE AS A FUNCTION
OF TRAINING AND TESTING CONDITIONS

Training	Testing	
	Drug	**No drug**
Drug	Good retention	Poor retention
No drug	Poor retention	Good retention

Note: The good-retention areas had conditions the same during both training and testing.

before training and saline prior to testing, or saline before training and pentobarbital prior to testing. Thus, forgetting of a previously learned response can occur when the internal state is altered between training and testing. State-dependent learning has been reported for a variety of behaviors, including approach in the T maze (Overton, 1964), escape and avoidance responding in the shuttle box (Holmgren, 1964), and bar pressing in an operant chamber (Kubena & Barry, 1969). State-dependent learning has also been observed in rats, monkeys, cats, dogs, goldfish, and humans. The human studies used alcohol (Goodwin, Powell, Bremer, Hoine, & Stein, 1969; Modill, 1967), amphetamine (Swanson & Kinsbourne, 1979), or marijuana (Eich, Weingartner, Stillman, & Gillin, 1975).

Events can also be experienced during a particular internal emotional state, and a change in this emotional state can lead to forgetting. Using hypnosis, Bower (1981) manipulated mood state (either happy or sad) before training and again prior to testing. Some subjects experienced the same mood prior to both training and testing, and other subjects had one mood state present before training and the other present before testing. Bower found significantly better recall when the emotional state induced before testing matched the state present during training than when the training and testing states were not the same. Apparently, a change in mood state, as well as drug state, can lead to forgetting.

Kamin Effect   Naturally occurring changes in internal state can also lead to forgetting because of the absence of the internal attributes of a memory. In 1957, Kamin reported that rats were unable to perform a previously learned active-avoidance response on an intermediate retention test (one to three hours after original training), whereas avoidance performance was excellent both immediately and twenty-four hours after the initial aversive experience (see Figure 9.3). This U-shaped retention function, the *Kamin effect,* has been consistently replicated (Brush, 1971), and the poor performance on the intermediate retention interval has been attributed to retrieval failure. A number of studies (Baum, 1968; Bintz, 1970; Klein, 1972; Klein & Spear, 1969, 1970a, 1970b; Spear, Klein, & Riley, 1971) support a retrieval-failure explanation of the Kamin effect. When the memory of original training is available (both immediately and twenty-four hours after training), subjects respond according to prior training in the same situation (Klein & Spear, 1969, 1970b), acquire a new response more readily than do untrained animals in a positive transfer situation (Baum, 1968), and show an acquisition deficit comparable to that of untrained animals in a negative transfer situation (Klein & Spear, 1970a, 1970b). However, when the memory of prior avoidance responding is unavailable (on an intermediate retention test), subjects do not respond according to prior training in the original situation; they act like untrained rats in a new situation.

Why are animals unable to recall the memory of prior response on an intermediate retention test? The answer lies in the difference in internal state which exists between an immediate or twenty-four-hour test and the intermediate

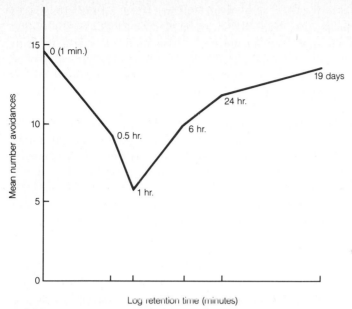

FIGURE 9.3
The mean number of active-avoidance responses as a function of
the time between training and testing. From Kamin, L. J.
Retention of an incompletely learned avoidance response.
Journal of Comparative and Physiological Psychology, 1957, *50,*
457–460. Copyright 1957 by the American Psychological
Association. Reprinted by permission.

retention test. Since avoidance training is aversive, a number of physiological
changes take place during the acquisition of the avoidance response. One physiological response that occurs during avoidance training is the release of adre-
nocorticotrophic hormone (ACTH) from the pituitary gland. An important
physiological effect of ACTH is the excitement of neural systems, and this
excitement produces motivational and emotional arousal (Grossman, 1967).
Approximately one hour after a stressful experience, a central inhibition of the
ACTH release is caused by the presence of adrenal corticotrophic hormones
released by the adrenal cortex. This inhibition of ACTH release lasts several
hours and results in a lowered responsivity to stressful experiences. The
corticoid inhibition is no longer present on the twenty-four-hour test, and,
therefore, the internal responsivity has returned to the normal state. Our discussion suggests that the internal state that exists during an intermediate retention test is different than that which occurs on an immediate or twenty-four-
hour retention test. Two lines of evidence support a state-dependent-learning
explanation of the Kamin effect. First, Spear, Klein, and Riley (1971) found
that avoidance learning acquired during the intermediate interval state has been
forgotten when animals are tested under the conditions present on a twenty-

four-hour test. Second, Klein (1972) observed that direct implantation of ACTH into the lateral anterior hypothalamus or electrical stimulation of the lateral anterior hypothalamus enabled animals to respond according to prior avoidance training at the intermediate retention interval (see Figure 9.4). These treatments are assumed to produce retrieval at the intermediate interval because of the reinstatement of the internal state that had been present during prior avoidance training.

Relative Contributions of Internal versus External Memory Attributes   The internal state experienced during training is one attribute of memory. Although a change in internal state can lead to retrieval failure, in some circumstances forgetting does not occur despite a change in internal state. For example, although intoxicated people do forget some events, they can clearly remember others. The attribute model of memory suggests that the presence of other memory attributes can lead to retrieval, despite the change in internal state.

Eich, Weingartner, Stillman, and Gillin (1975) examined the state-dependent effects of the drug marijuana. With the permission of appropriate government agencies, subjects smoked either a marijuana cigarette (drug condition) or a cigarette with the active ingredient THC removed (nondrug condition). Some subjects smoked the marijuana 20 minutes before learning a list of words and again before testing which occurred 4 hours after training. Other subjects were given the marijuana prior to training and the nondrug before testing; still other

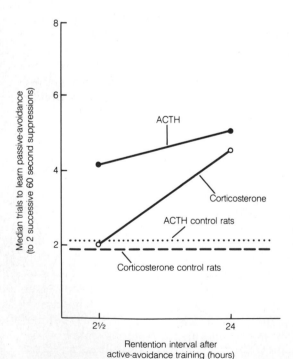

FIGURE 9.4
The median trials to learn a passive-avoidance response for groups receiving either ACTH or corticosterone prior to a 2.5-hour or 24-hour retention test. Control animals had not received prior active-avoidance training. A high score indicates good retention of active-avoidance response. From Klein, S. B. Adrenal-pituitary influence in reactivation of avoidance-learning memory in the rat after intermediate intervals. *Journal of Comparative and Physiological Psychology,* 1972, 79, 341–359. Copyright 1972 by the American Psychological Association. Reprinted by permission.

subjects received the nondrug before training and the marijuana before testing. A final group of subjects smoked the nondrug before both training and testing. Eich, Weingartner, Stillman, and Gillin evaluated the influence of marijuana by measuring heart rate (marijuana increases heart rate) and the subjective experience of being "high." They found that compared with the nondrug condition, marijuana produced a strong physiological and psychological effect. Half the subjects were tested using a free-recall task; the other half, using category names of the words given in training as retrieval cues. In the free-recall testing, state-dependent learning had occurred: the subjects remembered more words when the same state was present during both training and testing than when the states differed during testing and training (see Table 9.2). The lower recall of words on the free-recall test was true whether the subjects were in a drug state during training and a nondrug state in testing or a nondrug state during training and a drug state during testing. In contrast to the state-dependent effects with the free-recall test, subjects receiving the cued-recall test had no state-dependent effects. When the subjects received the category words at testing, they showed a high level of recall in all four treatment conditions.

Why did a change in internal state not lead to forgetting in the cued-recall testing procedure? Eich (1980) suggested that people typically rely on external cues. If these cues are unavailable, they will use subtle cues associated with their physiological or mental state to retrieve memories. The cued-recall procedure provided external retrieval cues which eliminated the reliance on internal retrieval cues to recall the training. What memory attributes did the cued-recall procedure give to the subjects? In Underwood's view (1983), the cued recall provided subjects with stimuli contained in the verbal associative attributes.

Verbal Associative Attributes   According to Underwood (1983), when a person hears or sees a word, the word may produce a variety of verbal associates. For example, the word *cat* may elicit the associative response of *animal*.

TABLE 9.2
TREATMENT CONDITIONS AND RESULTS OF A
STATE-DEPENDENT-LEARNING STUDY

Condition		Average number of words recalled	
Study	Test	Free recall	Cued recall
Nondrug	Nondrug	11.5	24.0
Nondrug	Drug	9.9	23.7
Drug	Nondrug	6.7	22.6
Drug	Drug	10.5	22.3

Source: Eich, J. E., Weingartner, H., Stillman, R. C., & Gillin, J. C. State dependent accessibility of retrieval cues in the retention of a categorized list. *Journal of Verbal Learning and Verbal Behavior,* 1975, *14,* 408–417.

The category word *animal* is a memory attribute of the memory of *cat,* and its presence may act to retrieve the word *cat* on a retention test. In our discussion of the short-term store, we learned that associations are formed by the short-term store. One consequence of this associative learning is the establishment of *verbal associative attributes.* These verbal associative attributes undoubtedly are responsible for the enhanced recall which occurs as the result of associative learning. Underwood suggested that there are two types of verbal associative attributes: parallel associates and class associates.

Parallel Associates   Underwood (1983) proposed three major types of parallel associates: antonyms, synonyms, and functional associates. Functional associates are formed because of functional contiguity and include pairs such as cup-saucer, table-chair, and key-lock. The presence of a parallel associate during testing can result in the retrieval of a memory which would not have been recalled if the associate had not been present.

The influence of parallel associates on retrieval can be seen in the study by Jenkins, Mink, and Russell (1958). They constructed four lists of words, and each list consisted of twelve pairs of words. Thus, the four lists combined contained forty-eight pairs, all of which differed in terms of the strength of the individual associates. Some had high associative strength (e.g., man-woman); others had low associative strength (e.g., comfort-chair). Four different associative strengths were used—76, 43, 32, and 12; the strengths varied according to the number of subjects producing the same associative responses. Each list contained three pairs of each associative strength. As seen in Figure 9.5, the higher the associative strength of a pair, the higher the recall of the words, indicating that the presence of a parallel associate in the list increases the retrieval of the associated word.

Class Attribute   Underwood (1983) proposed that when a word elicits the category name that includes that word, the category name is a class attribute of the word. The presence of the category name can act to retrieve the word during testing. For example, the category name *animal* can act as a memory attribute of the word *cat.*

Recall the implicit associative response study conducted by Wood and Underwood (1967) described in Chapter 8. The presence of the word *black* on a list of words enhanced the retrieval of three apparently unrelated words: *derby, coffee,* and *skunk. Black* was a class associate of each word; that is, it has conceptual similarity to each of the other three words. Thus, *black* was a memory attribute of each word: If subjects remembered the word *black,* they would also remember the three other words. The observation that the inclusion of the word *black* facilitated the recall of its class associates but not the other words on the list supports Underwood's view.

Underwood points out an important idea to remember when considering the influence of class attributes on the retrieval of words. The class attribute must be elicited during conditioning and also during testing. If the class attribute is not present during both training and testing, retrieval will not be enhanced. For example, Wood and Underwood (1967) found that if the word *black* was

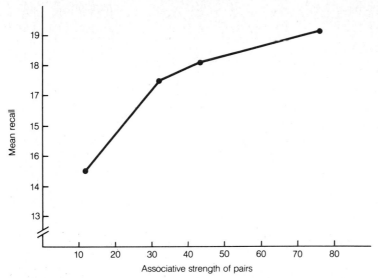

FIGURE 9.5
The mean recall of twelve pairs of words in a twenty-four-word list as
a function of the associative strength of word pairs. Adapted from
Jenkins, J. J.; Mink, W. P.; & Russell, W. A. Associative clustering as a
function of verbal association strength. *Psychological Reports*, 1958, *4*,
127–136, Figure 2.

present only during training or only during testing, the recall of its three class
associates was no better than if the word *black* had not been presented at all.
Apparently, class attributes can function to retrieve a memory if an association
is formed between the class attribute and the word and if the class attribute is
present during testing.

Transformational Attributes   The final class of memory attributes is referred to by Underwood (1983) as the *transformational attribute*. Recall from
our discussion of the short-term store that information can be transformed
there. For example, the nonsense syllable *tfx* can be coded or transformed by
the short-term store into the word *tax*. During testing, the word *tax* must be
decoded into the nonsense syllable *tfx*. According to Underwood, a part of the
memory of the nonsense syllable must consist of the information for decoding.
This decoding information constitutes the transformational attribute. This section discusses three major types of transformational attributes: images, natural
language mediators, and order transformations.

Images   Many words or ideas can be transformed into images. For example, the word *car* can be transformed into the image of a car. According to
Underwood (1983), the image is a transformational attribute of the word or
idea. Remembering the image will enable a person to recall the word or idea.
Suppose you are trying to remember your friend's name, "Betty." To learn
the friend's name, you must associate her with the name. This is a difficult

association to learn; that many people have problems remembering names attests to the difficulty of forming the association of a person with a name. You could form an image of your friend sitting in a bed. Seeing your friend will elicit the image of a bed, which you can decode into the name "Betty." We will address the use of this mnemonic technique again later.

Research by Allan Paivio (1969, 1978) showed that the use of imagery enhances the recall of experiences. In one study, Paivio, Yuille, and Madigan (1968) asked people to rate on a scale of 1 to 7 a large number of nouns based on how easily they could form images of the words. In general, concrete nouns such as *blood* or *hyena* were rated high, and abstract nouns such as *democracy* or *truth* were rated low. Paivio reported that his subjects remembered high-imagery words much more readily than low-imagery words.

Why does the amount of imagery elicited by a word affect the amount of recall? According to Paivio, both high- and low-imagery words activate verbal codes (or attributes). However, only high-imagery words also elicit imaginal codes (or attributes). In Paivio's view, the fact that high-imagery words activate two codes (or attributes), whereas low-imagery words activate only one code, accounts for the greater recall of high-imagery words.

Natural Language Mediators   Consider the following example. In a paired-associate learning task, a subject is learning the associate "dog-car." If a subject injects the word *chase* between *dog* and *car,* the natural language mediator is *dog-chase-car*. According to Underwood (1983), the mediator produces a meaningful link between the stimulus and the response. Underwood reports that subjects attempting to learn verbal material use language mediators. For example, subjects learning a serial list of words often will add a word or two to the list to create a story.

Does the use of natural language mediators enhance the recall of verbal information? Many studies (Spear, 1971) have reported that retrieval of verbal material is increased by the use of natural language mediators. Montague, Adams, and Kiess (1966) gave to subjects a single presentation of a list of twenty-five pairs of nonsense syllables and then asked the subjects to report whether they used natural language mediators to learn each pair. Twenty-four hours later the subjects returned to the laboratory to recall the pairs of nonsense syllables. Montague, Adams, and Kiess observed greater recall of pairs learned with a mediator than those learned without one.

Although natural language mediators can enhance the retrieval of verbal material, this is not always true. Underwood (1983) observed that subjects attempting to recall a particular verbal unit often make errors. In Underwood's view, in order for a subject to accurately recall a previously learned response that had been coded by a natural language mediator, the subject's memory of the verbal unit must contain decoding information (or knowledge of words to be deleted). Errors occur because subjects lack a systematic decoding procedure. In our discussion of mnemonics, we will discover that some very effective mnemonic techniques use natural language mediators and contain specific decoding procedures.

Order Transformations Underwood (1983) suggests that relatively meaningless nonsense syllables can be recoded to create more meaningful verbal units. For example, the nonsense syllable *rac* can become the word *car*. As was true of the use of natural language mediators, order transformations can increase the recall of verbal units. A number of studies (Spear, 1971) have shown that order transformation can enhance recall. However, this is true only if subjects have available to them during testing a simple rule for rearranging the verbal units into the original form.

Underwood and Keppel (1963) presented college students with a list of ten trigrams to learn. Each trigram could be arranged into words by changing two letters. Some subjects were instructed to rearrange the trigrams into words during training; other subjects were not. Underwood and Keppel reported that rearranging the trigrams into words during training facilitated recall of the trigrams only if the subjects were free to recall the words in any order. If the subject had to recall the trigrams in the correct order, recall was actually poorer than for subjects who had not rearranged the trigrams.

The poor recall of subjects instructed to rearrange the trigrams and then remember them in the original order was due to the absence of simple coding and decoding instructions. To show the importance of coding and decoding rules, Underwood and Erlebacher (1965) provided some of their subjects with specific rules for arranging (coding) and rearranging (decoding) the twelve trigrams they were to learn. Some subjects could code and decode each trigram with the same rule. For example, each trigram in the list could be coded into a word and decoded back into the correct trigram with the 1-3-2 rule (switching second and third letters). Other subjects had two or four coding and decoding rules to use, and a final group had no rules. Underwood and Erlebacher found that order transformation during training improved recall for subjects having only a single rule to learn compared with subjects who did not code the words during training. In contrast, when subjects needed two or four rules to code and decode the trigrams, recall was impaired. One of the advantages of the mnemonic techniques to be discussed shortly is that they provide a simple rule for coding experiences and then decoding them during testing.

FORGETTING

Having examined the process which enables us to recall previous experiences, let's now look at the reasons why people forget past events. Three theories have been used to explain the forgetting of previous experiences. First, some psychologists (McGeoch, 1932) have suggested that memories decay, a view which assumes that memory is lost through disuse; that is, that memories that are not used will not survive. Second, interference between memories has been proposed as a cause of forgetting (McGeoch, 1932; Underwood, 1957). Interference reflects a person's inability to recall a specific event as the result of having experienced another event. The third theory is that the absence of a specific stimulus can lead to forgetting (Underwood, 1969, 1983). This view holds that a memory contains a collection of different types of information, and each type of information is an attribute of the memory. The retrieval of a memory depends on the presence of the stimulus contained in the memory attribute.

Decay of a Memory

It is generally assumed that specific physiological changes take place that relate to the event being learned (see Chapter 8). The *engram,* or physical representation of an event, enables a person to recall an experience at a later time. A few psychologists (see McGeoch, 1932) have proposed that the engram fades with disuse; that is, that the physiological changes that took place during learning and that represent the record of the experience will diminish unless the memory is retrieved from time to time. Retrieval may prevent decay or strengthen a decaying memory.

In a classic study, Jenkins and Dallenbach (1924) evaluated the decay view of forgetting by teaching subjects a list of nonsense syllables to a criterion of one trial without errors. The retention of the nonsense syllables was evaluated one, two, four, or eight hours later. Half the subjects spent their retention interval awake; the other half of the subjects slept during the interval. If the decay view is accurate and the time between learning and recall determines the level of forgetting, an equal amount of forgetting should be found regardless of whether the subjects were asleep or awake during the retention interval. As can be seen in Figure 9.6, more forgetting was seen in the subjects who were awake than in those asleep during the retention interval, suggesting that activities that occurred while the subjects were awake contributed greatly to the amount of

FIGURE 9.6
The number of syllables recalled as a function of time between training and testing in subjects who were either asleep or awake during the retention interval. From Jenkins, J. G., & Dallenbach, K. M. Oblivescence during sleep and waking. *American Journal of Psychology,* 1924, *35,* 605–612.

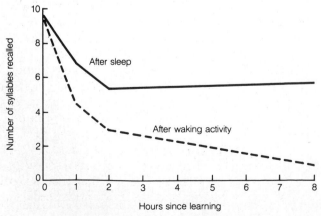

forgetting. We will discover that the activities of the subjects who were awake during the retention interval produced interference, which accounted for some of the difference in the level of forgetting between the subjects in the awake and those in the asleep conditions.

Note that subjects who slept during the interval forgot a considerable amount during that time. Is this forgetting a result of decay? According to Underwood (1957), the methods employed by Jenkins and Dallenbach (1924) were inadequate by contemporary standards. In addition, Jenkins and Dallenbach's subjects had been in other studies; this previous participation could have produced high levels of proactive interference, which in turn caused the forgetting seen in the asleep condition. Conducting a tightly controlled investigation of the effects of sleep on retention, Ekstrand (1967) used subjects who had not experienced prior paired-associate tasks. One group of subjects slept the eight-hour retention interval after learning a list of paired associates; the other group was awake during the retention interval. Ekstrand observed that the subjects in the awake condition forgot 23 percent of the paired associates, whereas subjects in the sleep condition forgot only 11 percent. These observations indicate that proactive interference due to prior experience with paired associates caused much of the forgetting seen by Jenkins and Dallenbach in the asleep condition subjects. However, subjects in the asleep condition did forget some material. Decay of memory may have been responsible for this forgetting. It is also feasible that extraexperimental sources of interference (interference from verbal material learned outside the laboratory) contributed to the forgetting seen in the asleep condition. We will next examine some research supporting a decay view; extraexperimental sources of interference as a cause of forgetting will be discussed later in the chapter.

Rozin and Gleitman (cited in Gleitman, 1971) used fish as their subjects and trained them to avoid shock in a shuttle box. The fish spent either a four-week or an eight-week retention interval in either the training temperature (25–26°C) or in a hot tank (33°C). Rozin and Gleitman reasoned that since fish are cold-blooded, heating the fish tank would accelerate their metabolic processes, thereby increasing the rate of decay of the memory of the avoidance training. Rozin and Gleitman reported that the fish kept in the hot tank forgot more during the retention interval than did the fish in the training tank. Other investigators have attempted to slow down metabolic rate to decrease the decay of memory and thereby reduce the amount of forgetting. Rensch and Dücker (1966) observed that goldfish treated with chloropromazine during the retention interval exhibited greater retention of a visual discrimination than did goldfish not given chloropromazine during the retention interval. A similar decrease in forgetting was observed by Dücker and Rensch (1968) in goldfish kept in the dark during the retention interval and by Alloway (1969) in grain beetles kept in a cold environment after learning an avoidance response in the T maze.

Gleitman (1981) points to one problem in concluding that decay is a source of forgetting. Studies evaluating the decay view have inferred that treatments such as heat or sleep affect forgetting by altering the metabolic processes that prevent or increase erosion of the memory trace. Unfortunately, no study has proved that this relation exists; thus decay remains only a possible source of forgetting. In contrast, considerable evidence indicates that interference is a major cause of forgetting.

Interference

There are two types of interference: proactive and retroactive. *Proactive interference* (PI) involves an inability to recall recent experiences because of the memory of an earlier experience. For example, a group of subjects learns one list of paired associates (A-B list) and then learns a second list of paired associates (A-C). At some later time, the subjects are asked to recall the associates from the second list but are unable to because the memory of the first list interferes. How do we know that these subjects would not have forgotten the response to the second list even if they had not learned the first list? To show that it is the memory of the first list which caused the forgetting of the second list, a control group of subjects learned only the second list (see Table 9.3 for a diagram of the treatments given to experimental and control subjects). Any poorer recall of the second list by the experimental subjects than by the control subjects is assumed to be due to proactive interference.

Retroactive interference (RI) occurs when people cannot remember distant events because the memory of more recent events intervenes. Retroactive interference can be observed in the following procedure: Experimental subjects learn two lists of paired associates (A-B, A-C) and then take a retention test that asks them to recall the responses from the first list. The retention of the first list of responses for experimental subjects is compared with the retention for a control group required to learn only the first list (refer to Table 9.4 for a diagram of the treatment given the experimental and control subjects). If the recall of the first list is poorer for experimental subjects than for the control-group subjects, retroactive interference is assumed to be the cause of the difference.

Why does interference occur? In 1940, Melton and Irwin offered a two-factor view of interference. Although many observations support their view,

TABLE 9.3
DESIGN OF A PROACTIVE INTERFERENCE STUDY

	Stage of experiment		
Group	**I**	**II**	**III**
Experimental	Learn first materials	Learn materials to be remembered	Test for recall
Control	Unrelated activity	Learn materials to be remembered	Test for recall

TABLE 9.4
DESIGN OF A RETROACTIVE INTERFERENCE STUDY

Group	Stage of experiment		
	I	II	III
Experimental	Learn materials to be remembered	Learn new materials	Test for recall
Control	Learn materials to be remembered	Unrelated activity	Test for recall

others do not. Several psychologists (Keppel, 1968; Postman, Stark, & Fraser, 1968; Underwood, 1969; Underwood & Postman, 1960) commenting on these observations have suggested new ideas for why interference occurs between memories. Let's first look at Melton and Irwin's two-factor theory.

Melton and Irwin's Two-Factor Theory of Interference According to Melton and Irwin (1940), competition between memories is a source of both proactive and retroactive interference. Consider the A-B, A-C paradigm, in which the same stimulus (A) has been associated with two responses (B and C). Since the task required subjects to recall only one response, the task will elicit the response with the strongest association to the stimulus. Thus, a subject may forget response C owing to competition from response B with a stronger association to the stimulus A. Or, if the stimulus response A-C is stronger than that of A-B, the subject will be unable to recall the responses from task A-B.

Melton and Irwin proposed that although competition is the only cause of proactive interference, a second factor, unlearning, can also produce retroactive interference. According to Melton and Irwin, for subjects to learn the second list (A-C), they must unlearn or extinguish the first list (A-B). They do not view unlearning as an erasure of A-B associations. Instead, they suggest that A-B associations are suppressed so that subjects can learn the second task. Unlearning of first-task responses causes subjects to forget these first-list responses when they take a retention test given immediately after second-list acquisition.

Melton and Irwin suggested that the suppression of first-list responses is only temporary and that the association will spontaneously recover during the interval after second-list learning. The recovery of the strength of first-task associations may lead to a recall of the first-list responses. As the memory of first-list responses becomes available, response competition becomes the sole determinant of which memory the subject will recall.

Evidence Supporting Melton and Irwin Several lines of evidence support the Melton and Irwin two-factor theory of interference. First we will discuss research suggesting that competition influences the level of PI and RI, and then we'll describe some evidence that implies that unlearning is a source of RI.

The competition theory suggests that the degree of first- and second-task associative learning should affect the level of PI and RI. If the level of first-task learning is greater than that of second-task acquisition, associative strength to the first-task responses should be greater than to second-task responses. According to the competition approach, the stronger first-task associations should lead to high levels of PI. A number of studies (Atwater, 1953; Postman & Riley, 1959; Underwood, 1945) have evaluated how the degree of original task learning relates to the amount of PI. These experiments show that as the level of original-list learning increases, PI also increases.

The competition view also assumes that increased degree of second-list, or interpolated, learning should cause greater levels of RI. We assume that the increased RI is caused by the greater associative strength of the second-list responses that results from increased levels of interpolated list learning. The research (Lewis, Smith, & McAllister, 1952; Postman & Riley, 1959; Thune & Underwood, 1943) evaluating the role of the degree of interpolated task learning on the amount of RI has demonstrated that as interpolated lists are learned to greater degrees, the level of RI increases (see Hall, 1966, for a review of how the degree of original-list and interpolated list learning affects the amount of PI and RI).

To review, the greater the degree of original (or interpolated) task learning, the higher the PI (or RI). We assume that the influence of the degree of learning on the level of interference is caused by the effect of degree of learning on the associative strength of stimulus-response pairs; a greater degree of learning increases the associative strength, and a stronger association enables the memory of a particular stimulus-response association to compete with the memory of another stimulus-response association, thereby increasing the likelihood of interference. These observations support Melton and Irwin's view that competition is a source of interference.

Melton and Irwin (1940) conducted a study assessing the influence of unlearning as a source of RI. They provided subjects with a list of eighteen nonsense syllables to learn in serial order. After original training, subjects were given an interpolated eighteen-item list of nonsense syllables for five, ten, twenty, or forty trials, followed by the relearning of the original list. Examining the total amount of RI, Melton and Irwin found that the greater the number of interpolated list trials was, the higher the RI. Melton and Irwin also measured the interpolated list intrusions which occurred during the relearning of the original list. If competition is responsible for RI, interpolated list intrusions should be related to the level of RI; that is, as RI increases, so should the number of interpolated list intrusions. Melton and Irwin found no perfect relation between the number of interpolated list intrusions and the total amount of retroactive interference. As can be seen in Figure 9.7, the amount of RI attributed to interpolated list intrusion (competition) increases a maximum point between five and ten trials of interpolated list learning and then declines. Note that even when interpolated list intrusions are greatest, they do not completely account for all RI. Thus, Melton and Irwin assumed that a factor other than

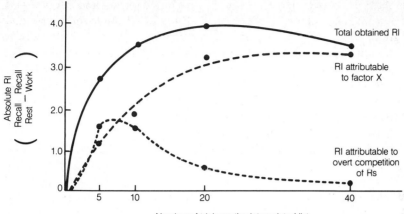

FIGURE 9.7
The amount of retroactive interference as a function of the degree of
interpolated list training. From Melton, A. W., & Irwin, J. M. The influence of
degree of interpolated learning on retroactive inhibition and the overt transfer
of specific responses. *American Journal of Psychology,* 1940, *53,* 173–203.

competition must be responsible for the occurrence of RI. They called this
factor X, but they suggested that it represented unlearning as a source of RI.
Similar results were obtained by Thune and Underwood (1943) with two lists of
paired associates.

Although these observations indicate that a second factor contributes to the
level of RI, they do not indicate that unlearning is that second cause. However,
a number of studies (see Hall, 1966) support Melton and Irwin's view that
factor X is, indeed, unlearning.

Barnes and Underwood's (1959) experiments suggest that unlearning is a
source of RI. Their subjects learned two lists (A-B, A-C) of paired associates;
the two lists had the same stimuli but different responses. After 1, 5, 10, or 20
trials of interpolated list learning, the subjects were given a piece of paper and
asked to write down the two responses for each stimulus. If unlearning is a
cause of RI, then subjects learning the second list would not be able to recall
the responses of the first list. In contrast, if competition is the sole cause of RI,
subjects given sufficient time should be able to provide both responses. Barnes
and Underwood reported that their subjects' ability to report responses in the
first list declined as they learned the responses of the second list (see Figure
9.8). These observations point out that first list responses become increasingly
unavailable as subjects learn the second list, an idea consistent with the view
that unlearning is a source of RI.

Melton and Irwin (1940) conceptualized the unlearning of original task
sponses as analogous to the extinction of a conditioned response. Recall from
Chapter 2 that conditioned responses will spontaneously recover several hours
after extinction. If unlearning is a cause of RI, the spontaneous recovery of the

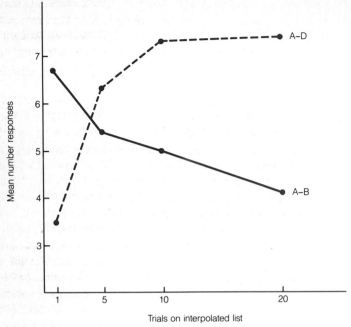

FIGURE 9.8
The frequency of recall of the first list (A-B) and the second list
(A-D) as a function of the number of second-list trials when the
subject is asked to recall the responses from both lists. From
Barnes, J. M., & Underwood, B. J. "Fate" of first-list associations
in transfer theory. *Journal of Experimental Psychology*, 1959, *58,*
97–105. Copyright 1959 by the American Psychological
Association. Reprinted by permission.

first-task response should result in reduced RI and increased PI. A number of
studies (see Hall, 1966) have measured the changes in PI and RI following
interpolated list learning. Experimentation demonstrates that immediately following the learning of the second task, subjects can remember only the second
task. Thus, RI is maximal, and no PI occurs when testing takes place immediately after acquisition of the second list. As the time lapse after learning of the
second task increases, the subjects' ability to remember the second list decreases while their ability to recall the first list increases. Therefore, with an
increased retention interval, the level of RI diminishes and PI increases. We
assume that the changes in interference with time reflect the spontaneous recovery of original-list responses.

   We have learned that Melton and Irwin (1940) suggested that competition is
the cause of PI and that competition and unlearning are sources of RI. The past
twenty-five years have seen several changes in the interference theory of forgetting. Our discussion of interference will conclude by examining these devel-
opments.

Extraexperimental Sources of Interference   Underwood and Postman (1960) addressed two important issues about forgetting. The first issue concerns the forgetting which occurs after a subject learns a single task. For example, the classic Ebbinghaus (1885) study showed a rapid forgetting following acquisition of a list of nonsense syllables. Ebbinghaus learned a list of ten to twelve nonsense syllables and then relearned the list after various retention intervals. As can be seen in Figure 9.9, Ebbinghaus forgot almost half the prior list after twenty-four hours, and six days later only one-fourth of prior learning was recalled. (In Ebbinghaus's study, savings in relearning the lists was used to indicate how much of the list was retained; the greater the savings, the higher the recall.) Why did Ebbinghaus forget so much of the single list of nonsense syllables? In an admirable piece of detective work, Underwood (1951) examined fourteen studies which reported the recall of a list of nonsense syllables on a twenty-four-hour retention test and found considerable differences among the studies. Some articles reported only a little forgetting after twenty-four hours;

FIGURE 9.9
Percentage retained as a function of the interval between training and testing. Adapted from Ebbinghaus, H. *Memory: A contribution to experimental psychology*. H. A. Ruger & C. E. Bussenins (Trans.). New York: Dover, 1885.

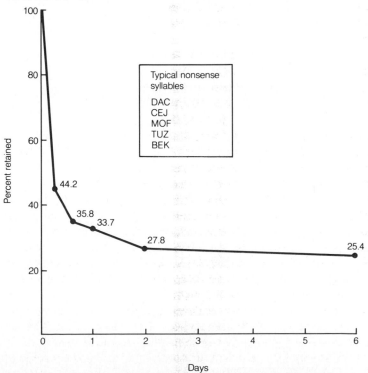

others showed substantial forgetting. Figure 9.10 shows the results of Underwood's investigation. He reported that as the number of prior lists increased, so did the amount of forgetting. Note that in a number of studies subjects had no experience in learning lists of nonsense syllables, but these studies still showed 15 to 25 percent forgetting after twenty-four hours.

The second question addressed by Underwood and Postman (1960) was why untrained subjects still forgot some of their prior learning on a twenty-four-hour retention test. According to Underwood and Postman, language habits acquired before entering the laboratory were responsible for the forgetting seen after presenting a single list of nonsense syllables to untrained subjects. Underwood and Postman referred to the natural language habits which produce forgetting of laboratory material as *extraexperimental sources of interference*. Furthermore, two types of extraexperimental sources of interference interfere proactively with the recall of material learned in the laboratory. First, *letter sequences* used in the laboratory conflict with grammatically correct letter sequences. For example, if the nonsense syllable to be learned is QTX, the QT letter sequence conflicts with the previously learned QU letter sequence. To learn the QT sequence, the subject must unlearn the QU sequence; the spontaneous recovery of the QU letter sequence occurring after laboratory experience will cause the subject to forget the QT sequence. *Unit-sequence* interference is the second kind of extraexperimental source of interference. Suppose that a subject must learn the paired associate *ice-dog* in the laboratory. This unit sequence conflicts with the previously learned sequence *ice-cold*. Again,

FIGURE 9.10
The amount of proactive interference as a function of the number of previously learned lists on the recall of a list of nonsense syllables on a 24-hour retention test. Adapted from Underwood, B. J. Interference and forgetting. *Psychological Review*, 1957, *64*, 49–60. Copyright 1957 by the American Psychological Association. Reprinted by permission.

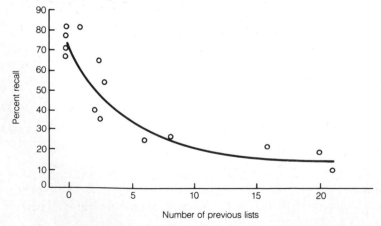

the response *cold* must be unlearned as a subject learns the response *dog,* and the spontaneous recovery of the response *cold* will interfere with the recall of the response *dog.*

Underwood and Postman (1960) evaluated whether letter- and unit-sequence interference was responsible for the forgetting of a single list of nonsense syllables. Comparing the level at which task material conflicted with language letter- and unit-sequences and with the amount of forgetting, Underwood and Postman found that extraexperimental sources proactively interfere with the recall of material learned in the laboratory. Keppel (1968) suggested that linguistic activity occurring during the retention interval is also a source of retroactive interference. A number of studies (see Keppel, Henschel, & Zavortink, 1969) have reported that the similarity between linguistic activities learned in the task and those occurring during the retention interval influences the level of the recall of task material.

The Influence of Distributed Practice   Underwood and Postman (1960) assumed that language habits acquired outside of the laboratory interfere with the recall of material learned in the laboratory, but the level of forgetting seen after a single task is only modest. Why do language habits fail to produce greater interference with laboratory material? The answer lies in the way in which language habits are typically learned in the real world. Although subjects usually learn material in the laboratory in a short time (under what psychologists call *massed practice*), language habits acquired in the real world are usually learned slowly (under *distributed practice*). According to Underwood and Postman, less interference is found with distributed than with massed practice. A considerable amount of evidence (see Keppel, 1964; Underwood & Ekstrand, 1966) supports this view.

In Underwood and Ekstrand's study (1966), one group of subjects learned the initial list over a four-day period (distributed practice); other subjects acquired the first list in a single session (massed practice). All subjects learned the second list under massed practice. Underwood and Ekstrand then evaluated the level of interference, finding greater interference with massed practice than with distributed practice. These observations show that materials acquired with distributed practice are less susceptible to the effects of interference. Our discussion has suggested why people do not forget massive amounts of linguistic activities. Because much of our verbal material is acquired under distributed practice, verbal memories are less likely to be interfered with and less likely to be a source of interference.

Why does distributed practice have such a dramatic influence on the level of forgetting? Underwood's list-differentiation view of interference provides an answer.

Underwood's List Differentiation View   Underwood (1969, 1983) suggested that interference is due not to response competition, but instead to a failure of task differentiation. According to Underwood, subjects do remember responses from both tasks but are unable to remember which task a particu-lar response was associated. Thus, subjects asked to recall the response learned from the first task can remember the response from both tasks but will appear to forget them because they cannot remember which response came from the first list. A considerable amount of research indicates that the failure of list differentiation—not competition—is a source of forgetting. Let's briefly look at the evidence.

We learned earlier that interference is not seen in subjects who learned one task in one environment and another task in a different environment. Accord-ing to Underwood, the use of different environments enables a subject to differ-entiate between memories, and thereby no interference is seen. Although these responses from the tasks are still in associative competition, interference will not occur because the subjects are able to differentiate between the two tasks. In Underwood's view, interference occurs when a subject cannot differentiate between memories.

According to Underwood, any treatment which increases the distinctiveness of memories will reduce the level of interference. We know that interference is reduced when the distribution of practice on the first list differs from that present on the second list. Furthermore, Underwood and Freund (1968) ob-served less interference when original-list and interpolated-list learning were separated by three days, even when the two lists were acquired with the same distribution of practice. Each of these treatments (different distribution of prac-tice, different times, different environments) increased the distinctiveness of both memories, and this increased list differentiation was responsible for the observed reduced interference in Underwood's view.

Postman's Generalized Competition View   We know that the level of PI increases following interpolated list learning, whereas the amount of RI de-clines. We assume that the changes in interference were caused by the sponta-neous recovery of the original-list responses. However, this statement is an inference; the use of the recall procedure introduced by Barnes and Under-wood (1959) made it possible to determine whether changes in interference were, in fact, caused by spontaneous recovery of the first-list responses. Some studies have observed spontaneous recovery, but others have not (see Keppel, 1968; Postman, Stark, & Fraser, 1968). On the basis of these studies, Postman, Stark, and Fraser (1968) suggested that "it is clear that long-term spontaneous recovery is not a dependable phenomenon."

These observations suggest that spontaneous recovery cannot be responsi-ble for the predictable changes in interference which follow interpolated list learning. They also imply that unlearning is not responsible for the unavailabil-ity of original-list responses during interpolated list acquisition. Postman and his associates (Postman, 1967; Postman, Stark, & Fraser, 1968) suggest that generalized competition rather than unlearning is responsible for a subject's inability to recall first-list responses as the second list is acquired. Further-more, reduced generalized competition—not spontaneous recovery of original list responses—causes the changes in interference seen after interpolated list learning, in Postman's view.

According to Postman, generalized competition is a "set" to continue to respond in the manner learned most recently. A selector mechanism excludes from subjects' response repertoire all responses except those being learned. Thus, it is this selector mechanism, not unlearning, which prevents a subject from being able to remember original list responses. Postman suggests that following interpolated list acquisition, generalized competition decreases; this decline in the selector mechanism is responsible for the increased PI and decreased RI. Throughout the text we have seen that recency plays an important role in determining a person's behavior. Postman's generalized competition merely assumes that a mechanism exists which ensures that recency will have a significant impact on behavior.

What evidence indicates that generalized competition exists? Melton and Irwin (1940) assumed that the relative strength of corresponding responses from each list determines the level of interference. Yet, it is the relative degree of learning on each list, not individual response strength, which governs the amount of interference (see Runquist, 1957). The influence of the entire task, rather than the memory of individual responses, supports the view that a selector mechanism exists which limits responses to the most recent task for a short time following learning.

In summary, we have discovered two types of interference: proactive interference and retroactive interference. This interference appears to be due to generalized competition and failure of list differentiation.

The Importance of Elaboration

In Chapter 8 we discovered that our experiences are organized by the short-term store and that rehearsal enables our experiences to be interpreted, analyzed, and stored in the long-term store. We learned in this chapter that interpretation and analysis have a critical impact on whether we can recall a past experience. The identification of salient aspects of an experience provides resistance to interference from similar memories and enhances recall. Also, the presence of environmental circumstances that represent the key aspects or attributes of a memory are necessary for the retrieval of an experience.

It is important to recognize the link between the discussion of the organization and rehearsal of experiences in Chapter 8 and the description of memory attributes and interference in this chapter. We have been discussing two aspects of the same process: experiences are interpreted and analyzed by the short-term store prior to permanent storage in the long-term store, and the ability to retrieve the experience from the long-term store depends on whether salient aspects of the experience were identified when the experience was organized in the short-term store. Thus, organization occurs in the short-term store but is critical to the retrieval of that experience from the long-term store. Craik and Tulving (1975) discuss how elaboration of experiences influences the recall of those events. According to Craik and Tulving, the elaborateness of memory encoding refers to what extent events are related to or organized with other events. For example, suppose that you learn a list containing the words *grief, love, forgotten,* and *spinster*. The word spinster could be encoded in an elaborate fashion by relating it to the other words in the list. A less elaborate encoding would be to analyze the meaning of the word without attempting to relate the word spinster to the other list words.

According to Craik and Tulving, there are also differences in the extent to which an event is analyzed independent of its relation to other events. An experience can be interpreted phonetically in terms of its physical characteristics and semantically in terms of its meaning. Thus, you could analyze the physical attributes of the word *spinster* as well as identify the numerous semantic features of the word. Craik and Tulving assume that although both the physical and semantic features of an event are analyzed, events differ in terms of the levels of phonetic and semantic elaboration. Some events may receive little semantic or physical elaboration, and other experiences undergo substantial physical or semantic elaboration. Consider the following two examples to illustrate how semantic and phonetic elaboration vary. In the first case, you are reading about the predatory behavior of lions. While reading, you concentrate on the meaning of the words rather than the physical attributes of the words. In the second case, you are attempting to evaluate the rhythm of a poem. In this case, you need to analyze the physical features of the words more than the semantic aspects.

We have discovered that experiences undergo varying degrees of elaboration prior to storage. According to Craik and Tulving (1975), the level of elaboration determines the amount of recall of previously experienced events. They presented to subjects several words and asked them whether each word made sense in various sentences. For example, one word was *watch,* and two sentences that different subjects received for the word *watch* were *He dropped the _____* and *The old man hobbled across the room and picked up the valuable _____ from the mahogany table*. According to Craik and Tulving, semantic analysis is required to determine whether the insertion of the word *watch* makes sense in each question, but subjects given the latter sequence had to use greater elaboration than did subjects receiving the first sentence. An unannounced memory test showed that the level of recall was affected by the degree of elaboration: the greater the elaboration, the higher the level of retention of the words. Other studies have also showed that the level of recall of previously experienced events depends on the elaborateness of processing; see Cermack and Craik (1979) for a review of this literature.

AN IMPERFECT RECORD

How accurate is a person's recollection of an experience? Elizabeth Loftus (1980) argued that a memory of an experience is often inaccurate. Sometimes details of an event are forgotten, creating an imperfect memory. To create a logical and realistic experience, people may add information to the memory during recall. Or an experience may not make sense to an individual, and some information will be deleted or new information added to establish a memory consistent with the individual's view of the world. The alteration of a memory to correspond to the individual's expectations is called *memory reconstruction*. This memory reconstruction process was studied by Frederic Bartlett years ago.

Reconstruction Studies

Bartlett (1932) examined the alteration of a memory during recall. He gave subjects stories from folklore of other cultures and then asked them to recall the stories. Bartlett noted that the subjects' memory of the stories often differed from the original story. He found that some aspects of the stories were deleted, some overemphasized, and in other cases, new information was added. According to Bartlett, the content and structure of the folklore was quite different from actual events that the subjects had experienced. Because of their unfamiliarity with the folklore, the subjects reconstructed their memory of the folklore to be more consistent with their own cultural expectations.

To demonstrate how extensively a memory can be altered by reconstruction, Bartlett presented a figure to a subject, and the subject was then told to reproduce it for a second subject. In some cases, the transmission of information continued through ten subjects. Bartlett noted that not only did the final drawing differ from the original, but the changes were quite extensive. Also, the figure changed from subject to subject. Figure 9.11 shows the change in each subject's recollection of the figure presented.

The Accuracy of Eyewitness Testimony

Loftus (1980) pointed out the significant relation between the memory reconstruction process and the accuracy of eyewitness testimony. According to Loftus, trial witnesses recall what they think they saw or heard. The literature on memory reconstruction suggests that their recollections may not always be accurate. In all likelihood, the incident they are recalling occurred months or years earlier, and the witnesses may have forgotten some aspects of the event. To create a logical and realistic account, the witnesses will fill in information consistent with the aspects actually remembered.

Loftus (1980) contends that a memory can be altered by information received from others. Because of this information, the memory of the past event is inaccurate, and the memory is subsequently changed to conform to the information received from other people. Consider Loftus's 1975 study to illustrate this process. In her study, subjects first were shown a film of a car accident. During the first discussion of the accident, experimental subjects were asked the question, "Did you see the children getting into the school bus?" Control subjects did not receive this question. A week later, all subjects

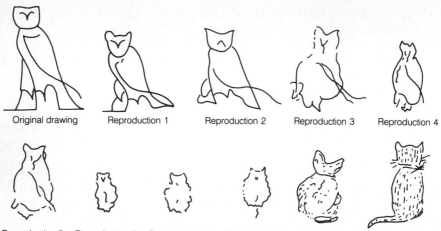

| Original drawing | Reproduction 1 | Reproduction 2 | Reproduction 3 | Reproduction 4 |

| Reproduction 5 | Reproduction 6 | Reproduction 7 | Reproduction 8 | Reproduction 9 | Reproduction 10 |

FIGURE 9.11
Subject 1 was shown original drawing and asked to reproduce it after half an hour. The reproduction of the original drawing was shown to subject 2 whose reproduction was presented to subject 3, and so on through subject 10. This figure presents the original drawing and the ten reproductions. From Barlett, F. C. *Remembering: A study in experimental and social psychology*. Cambridge: Cambridge University, 1932.

were asked to recall the accident. Loftus found that although there was no school bus, experimental subjects were three to four times more likely to say they saw a school bus than were control subjects. Did the question about the school bus during the initial interview cause many of the experimental subjects to think that the school bus was present in the film? According to Loftus, the wording of the question implied that the school bus was present during the accident, and thus the experimental subjects altered their memory of the accident to include a school bus. These results show that a memory can be altered by information received during recall. They also demonstrate that a clever attorney may be able to change a witness's memory of a crime by asking leading questions, thereby altering the outcome of the trial. Other psychologists have also found that suggestion can alter the content of memory; see Dodd and Bradshaw (1980) for another example.

Changing a witness's memory can be accomplished by very subtle wording of a question: Loftus and Zanni (1975) asked subjects one of two questions about a car accident. Some subjects were asked, "Did you see the broken headlight?" Other subjects were questioned, "Did you see a broken headlight?" Subjects who heard the word *the* were much more likely to say that they did see a broken headlight than were those who heard the word *a*. According to Loftus and Zanni, the use of the word *the* led subjects to believe that there had been a broken headlight in the film. These observations suggest that a good lawyer can reconstruct a witness's memory and lead the witness to believe that the event happened in the manner suggested by the attorney. On the basis of the Loftus and Zanni study, as well as similar studies, it is no wonder that many psychologists and legal scholars question the accuracy of eyewitness testimony.

Altering the Memories of Animals

Can memories also be reconstructed in animal subjects? The research of William Gordon and his associates (Gordon, 1983; Mowrer & Gordon, 1983; Wittrup & Gordon, 1982) indicates that an animal's memory of an event can be changed by information experienced during recall. Mowrer and Gordon's 1983 study illustrated this reconstruction process. In their study, rats were first trained to avoid shock in a shuttle box. Some rats received avoidance training and testing in the same context; other rats were trained and tested in different contexts. Mowrer and Gordon reported that retention of the avoidance response was impaired when the context was changed from training to testing. As we learned earlier in the chapter, the absence of the environmental stimuli contained in the contextual memory attribute is responsible for forgetting observed in animals trained and tested in different environments. Mowrer and Gordon treated a third group of animals differently; these animals were trained in one context, were given a cueing treatment in a second context, and then were retested in the original training context. They reported that this third group performed worse on the avoidance task during testing than did animals that had not received the cueing treatment in the second context. According to Mowrer and Gordon, the cueing treatment caused the animals to remember their previous avoidance training in the new context. This treatment altered the memory of avoidance learning by adding the second context as a memory attribute. The addition of the new context to the animal's memory caused that context to function as if it had been the training context. And since forgetting occurred when the animal was returned to the original training context, Mowrer and Gordon concluded that the training context was no longer a part of the animal's memory of the initial avoidance training. Apparently, an animal's memory of past experiences can also be reconstructed by the presence of new information during recall.

ANATOMICAL BASIS OF MEMORY RETRIEVAL

In Chapter 8, we learned that the coding and storing function of the short-term store is carried out by the dorsomedial thalamus. Damage to this area can lead to Korsakoff's syndrome, an inability to organize and store complex material. Also recall from Chapter 8 that hippocampal damage had been implicated in the Korsakoff syndrome. However, a number of scientists (Huppert & Piercy, 1979; Poon, 1980; Signoret & Lhermitte, 1976; Warrington & Weiskrantz, 1968, 1970; Weiskrantz & Warrington, 1975) have suggested that the amnesia resulting from hippocampal damage differs from that seen in a Korsakoff patient with a damaged dorsomedial thalamus. Patients with Korsakoff syndrome have difficulty coding and storing information, but individuals with hippocampal damage encounter problems with the retrieval of information. In Chapter 8 we examined evidence indicating that dorsomedial thalamus malfunction causes the coding and storage memory deficits characteristic of Korsakoff's syndrome. Several studies showing that hippocampal damage can lead to retrieval difficulty are examined next.

Warrington and Weiskrantz (Warrington & Weiskrantz, 1968, 1970; Weiskrantz & Warrington, 1975) conducted a number of studies comparing the memory of amnesics with the memory of individuals who were able to recall prior events. One study (refer to Warrington & Weiskrantz, 1968) provided subjects a list of words to remember. The amnesics seemed unable to remember these simple lists of words even after several repetitions; however, Warrington and Weiskrantz noted that as the amnesics were given list after list, they began to give responses from earlier lists. In contrast, fewer prior-list intrusions were observed in nonamnesic subjects. Apparently, the amnesics had stored the responses from earlier lists but were unable to retrieve the appropriate response. This observation suggests that amnesics are more susceptible to interference than are nonamnesics and that the greater interference led to more retrieval failure in amnesics than in nonamnesic patients.

Further evidence of a retrieval problem in amnesic patients can be seen in Warrington and Weiskrantz's 1970 study. They used three testing procedures: recall, recognition, and fragmented words. In the recall procedure, subjects were asked to recall as many words as they could from a previously learned list; in the recognition procedure, subjects were asked to identify the words they had previously learned from an equal number of alternative words; in the fragmented words procedure, subjects were presented five-letter words in a partial form by omitting two or three of the letters. As can be seen in Figure 9.12, the percentage of correct responses for both amnesic and nonamnesic subjects was greater for the recognition than for the recall procedure. Further, the level of recall was equal for the amnesic and nonamnesic subjects in the fragmented words procedure. These results point out that the amnesic subjects had stored the words but were unable to retrieve them on the recall test. According to Warrington and Weiskrantz, the fragmented word treatment provided the subjects with the cues necessary for retrieval and, therefore, enabled amnesic subjects to remember the training words as well as nonamnesic subjects. Other studies by Weiskrantz and Warrington (1975) showed that giving cues to amnesics at the time of recall significantly increased the retention of amnesic patients on a recall test.

Thus retrieval failure caused the memory deficits seen in the amnesic patients in Warrington and Weiskrantz's studies. Let's examine evidence showing that this retrieval failure results from hippocampal malfunctions.

Mishkin (1978) evaluated the effect of damage to the hippocampus on the acquisition and retention of a discrimination task in monkeys. He found that although the hippocampus does not seem to be essential for the acquisition of the correct response, animals with hippocampal lesions required significantly

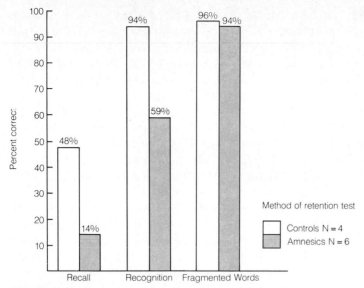

FIGURE 9.12
The percentage of correct responses for amnesic and control
subjects on either a free-recall, a recognition test, or a
fragmented-word test. From Warrington, E. L., & Weiskrantz, L.
Amnesic syndrome: Consolidation or retrieval. *Nature,* 1970, *228,*
628–630. Reprinted by permission from *Nature,* Vol. 228, p.p.
628–630. Copyright © 1970—Macmillan Journals Limited.

more trials to relearn the task than did nonlesioned primates. In fact, hippo-
campal-lesioned animals required almost as many trials to relearn the task as
they did during original training. These observations show that the hippocampus is not involved in the formation of a memory; instead, it functions to
retrieve a memory.

We have learned that some amnesics have difficulty coding and storing
information as the result of a malfunction in the dorsomedial thalamus; hippocampal deficits cause other patients to have problems in the retrieval of memories. Huppert and Piercy (1978, 1979) found that Korsakoff patients have difficulty coding and storing information. If these patients were given longer
periods of exposure to stimuli and, therefore, more time to store an event,
Huppert and Piercy observed that later recognition of the event was equivalent
in Korsakoff patients and normal subjects. In contrast, Huppert and Piercy
found that other amnesics learned a task as rapidly as normal subjects but
forgot the task more readily. Furthermore, Zola-Morgan, Squire, and Mishkin
(1981) found that destruction of the dorsomedial thalamus impaired learning but
not recall of a visual discrimination in monkeys, whereas hippocampal lesions
did not affect learning but did disrupt recall of a response. Apparently, brain
structures that play a part in the storage of memories differ from those involved
in the retrieval of memories.

APPLICATION: MNEMONICS

My youngest son recently asked me to give him some questions for his science test. One question required him to list five items. As he recalled the list to me, it was evident that he had a system for remembering the list. He had memorized the first letter of each item and was using these letters to recall each item on the list. Although he was unaware of it, he was using a *mnemonic technique* to recall the list of items. People often unknowingly use mnemonic techniques to increase recall. For example, medical students trying to remember the bones in a person's hand often use a mnemonic device; they take the first letter of each bone, construct a word from the letters, and use the word to recall the bones on a test. Perhaps you have used a similar mnemonic technique to recall some information.

You may have noted that the two cases just described are examples of the coding process detailed in our discussion of the short-term store. Your observation is accurate. There is nothing mystical about mnemonics. Mnemonic techniques merely use the short-term store efficiently. You have undoubtedly seen memory experts on television. Although they seem to possess an extraordinary memory, their high ability to recall information stems from their use of mnemonic techniques. There are a number of these techniques, each having in common the ability to take unorganized material and store it in a meaningful way.

The remainder of this chapter discusses several mnemonic techniques. Students in my courses using these mnemonic techniques have found them to be effective ways of enhancing recall. Since this chapter gives only a brief discussion of mnemonics, interested readers should refer to *The Memory Book* by Lorayne and Lucas (1974) to master the use of mnemonics.

Method of Loci

Suppose you need to give a memorized speech in one of your classes. Trying to remember the words by rote memorization would be a time-consuming process and could cause you to make many mistakes. The method of loci is one mnemonic technique you might use to recall the speech. This method, developed by the Greeks to memorize speeches, first involves establishing an ordered series of known locations. For example, the person can take "a mental walk" through his or her home, such as entering the house through the living room, proceeding into the dining room, and so on. The individual would then separate the speech into several key thoughts. The key thoughts are then associated in the order corresponding to the walk through the house. Perhaps your speech will be on Pavlov's research on the classical conditioning process. The first key thought may be to remember that Pavlov used dogs to investigate conditioning. You need to associate this thought with your living room. To do this, you might form a mental image of Pavlov and a dog in your living room. When you give the speech you need only to image going into the living room and seeing Pavlov and his dog there. This mental image will enable you to tell your class that Pavlov investigated conditioning processes using dogs. Perhaps you can see from our discussion that the method of loci represents a structured technique for using the associative and organizational capacities of the short-term store to remember a speech. The use of imagery increases the meaningfulness of the material and thus acts to enhance the recall of the speech.

The method of loci can be used to remember any list, either in a specific order or in a random one. For example, you need to buy five items at the grocery store. You could write the items on a piece of paper or use the method of loci to remember them. Perhaps one item you need is milk. You could associate a large carton of milk with your living room. Using this method to recall lists of items will show you that your memory can be improved and will document the power of the mnemonic techniques.

Peg Word System

Another popular mnemonic technique used to enhance recall of a list is the *peg word* system. An example of a popular peg word system is:

One is a bun.
Two is a shoe.
Three is a tree.
Four is a door.
Five is a hive.
Six is sticks.
Seven is heaven.
Eight is a gate.
Nine is wine.
Ten is a hen.

Let's see how this peg word mnemonic system works. Suppose you wanted to learn the following list of words: table, candle, firewood, glass, cigar, picture, book, ashtray, car, and lamp. To use the peg word system to remember the list, first associate the word *table* with the first peg word, *bun*. To do this, perhaps imagine a bun sitting on a table. Next, associate the word *candle* with the second peg word, *shoe*. To do this, imagine a candle burning a hole in the shoe. Associate each word in the list with the appropriate peg word. The peg word system works like the method of loci: both efficiently use the associative and organizational capacity of the short-term store. This system is also effective because a person can recall any item without having to start at the beginning of the list.

Lorayne and Lucas (1974) offer a different peg word system in *The Memory Book*. Although more difficult to learn, it provides more useful applications than the systems described above. For example, Lorayne and Lucas's peg word system can be used to remember a variety of things, including phone numbers, playing cards, weekly appointments, and anniversaries. The system begins by matching a letter to each of the numbers from 0 to 9. The pegs are:

1 = t or d
2 = N
3 = M
4 = r
5 = l
6 = sh, j, ch, soft g
7 = k, L and C, hard g
8 = f, v, ph
9 = p or b
0 = z, s, soft c

There is a rationale for each of the pegs. For example, four is *r* because the word *four* ends in the letter *r*. The system so far is a code for transforming numbers to letters. To create the peg words, vowels and consonants not used for other pegs are added. For example, the peg for five is *law*. Peg words above 9 can be easily created; the peg word for 55 is *lily*. In fact, an infinite number of peg words can be created (refer to Table 9.5). Let's look at one example of the use of this peg word system to remember a telephone number. Suppose your doctor's number is 940-8212. To learn this number, Lorayne and Lucas suggest that you associate doctor (perhaps by using a stethoscope) to *brass fountain*. The italic letters refer to the letters that correspond to the numbers in the peg word system. To form this association, visualize a stethoscope around a brass fountain.

A word of caution. Much practice is needed to use this mnemonic system efficiently. You need to (1) learn the peg, (2) use the peg to code information, and (3) decode the peg to recall information correctly. In our example, you need to know how to transform the peg word *brass fountain* into the correct phone number. The efficient use of this peg word system, like any skill, requires time and effort. Do not expect rapid results. However, if you work at it you will in all likelihood be pleased with the outcome. One problem experienced by many people is difficulty remembering names. The last example of a mnemonic technique is a description of its use in recalling names.

Remembering Names

Why do many people have such a hard time remembering other people's names? To recall a name, an individual must associate the person with his or her name, store this association, and then be able to retrieve the person's name. The main problem with remembering a person's name lies in the storage process: the association of a person's name with that individual is a difficult one to form. As is true with many recall problems, the association will eventually be formed with repeated repetition and, therefore, eventually will be recalled. Mnemonics offer a technique for enhancing the association between a name

TABLE 9.5
ONE HUNDRED PEG WORDS

1. tie	26. notch	51. lot	76. cage
2. Noah	27. neck	52. lion	77. coke
3. Ma	28. knife	53. loom	78. cave
4. rye	29. knob	54. lure	79. cob
5. law	30. mouse	55. lily	80. fuzz
6. shoe	31. mat	56. leech	81. fit
7. cow	32. moon	57. log	82. phone
8. ivy	33. mummy	58. lava	83. foam
9. bee	34. mower	59. lip	84. fur
10. toes	35. mule	60. cheese	85. file
11. tot	36. match	61. sheet	86. fish
12. tin	37. mug	62. chain	87. fog
13. tomb	38. movie	63. chum	88. fife
14. tire	39. mop	64. cherry	89. fob
15. towel	40. rose	65. jail	90. bus
16. dish	41. rod	66. choo choo	91. bat
17. tack	42. rain	67. chalk	92. bone
18. dove	43. ram	68. chef	93. bum
19. tub	44. rower	69. ship	94. bear
20. nose	45. roll	70. case	95. bell
21. net	46. roach	71. cot	96. beach
22. nun	47. rock	72. coin	97. book
23. name	48. roof	73. comb	98. puff
24. Nero	49. rope	74. car	99. pipe
25. nail	50. lace	75. coal	100. disease

Source: Lorayne, H., & Lucas, J. *The Memory Book.* New York: Stein & Day, 1974.

and a person; the enhanced storage of this association enables a person to recall a name after a single experience.

Lorayne and Lucas (1974) provide many examples of the use of mnemonics to recall people's names. Let's examine several of them. Suppose that you meet a person named Bill Gordon. Perhaps Bill Gordon has very bushy eyebrows. Lorayne and Lucas suggest that when you first meet him, you might visualize his eyebrows as being a *garden* with dollar *bills* growing there. The mental image formed when you first meet someone and then elicited when you see this person again will provide you with the information needed to recall the person's name.

What if you meet a woman named Ms. Pukczyva? How can you possibly use the mnemonic technique to recall her name? Perhaps she has a tall hairdo; you could see *shivering* hockey *pucks* flying out of her hair. After you have formed this association, the next time you meet Ms. Pukczyva you will remember her name.

This mnemonic technique can create a mental image which contains not only a person's name but also other bits of information about the individual. For example, suppose that Mr. Gordon works for U.S. Steel. You can put this information into your mental image by seeing an American flag (*U.S.*) made of *steel* growing out of the garden. Note that, as with the other mnemonic techniques discussed in this chapter, practice is required before you will be able to rapidly form a mental image of a person's name and then remember the name. The more you practice, the more efficient you will become at remembering names.

Do mnemonics work? The empirical evidence indicates that they are effective (see Norman, 1976, for a review of this literature). Bugelski's study (1968) provides one example of the effectiveness of mnemonic techniques. Bugelski had an experimental group learn a list of words using the "one is a bun" peg word system, and control subjects learn the list without the aid of the mnemonic technique. Bugelski then asked subjects to recall specific words; for example, he asked them, "What is the seventh word?" Bugelski reported that experimental subjects recalled significantly more words than did control subjects.

SUMMARY

According to Underwood, a memory is a collection of different types of information, called memory attributes. A memory attribute can decrease interference by providing a basis for distinguishing memories. Also, reexperiencing one aspect of an experience prompts the attribute of that event to act to recall the entire memory.

There are ten major memory attributes. The acoustic attribute stores information about the auditory properties of an event, and the physical characteristics of an event are contained in the orthographic attribute. In the frequency attribute, a record of the number of times an event is experienced is stored; the time that an event occurred is recorded in the temporal attribute, and the place where it occurred is contained in the spatial attribute of the memory. The modality attribute provides information about the sensory modality which experienced that event; the background in which an event took place is stored in the context attribute.

The affective attribute of a memory provides information about the emotional condition surrounding an event. The affective attribute can be viewed as an internal contextual attribute: it registers internal changes which may be natural reactions to the event or may be drug-induced. The associates of verbal items are also attributes of a memory. There are two types of verbal associative attributes: parallel attributes (antonyms, synonyms, and functional associates of the verbal item) and class attributes (the category name of the verbal item). The transformational attribute contains information about how to decode items that were coded during learning. The three types of transformational attributes are: images, natural language mediators, and order transformations.

The failure to remember an experience can result from one of three processes. The absence of an environmental stimulus representative of the memory attributes is one; another is decay. Memories decay when the physiological changes that took place during memory formation and that represent the record of the past event diminish with time. Interference is the third cause of forgetting; interference occurs when the memory of one experience prevents the retrieval of the memory of another event. There are two types of interference: Proactive interference is the inability to recall recent events because of the memory of a past experience; retroactive interference is the inability to remember distant events because of the memory of recent events.

Melton and Irwin's two-factor theory assumes that interference is caused by competition and unlearning. Competition among memories produces both proactive and retroactive interference, whereas unlearning, which is the temporary suppression of distant memories during current learning, causes only retroactive interference. As the effect of unlearning diminishes, competition alone determines which type of interference occurs. A more contemporary view of forgetting states that list differentiation and generalized competition, rather than competition and unlearning, are responsible for interference. According to Underwood, the failure to distinguish memories is one cause of interference. Postman suggests that generalized competition, a "set" that continues to respond in the manner most recently learned, is another source of interference.

The level of elaboration that an experience receives during processing influences the recall of that event; the more elaborately an event is encoded, the more likely that the memory will be retrievable later. Elaboration affects retrieval presumably by enhancing the identification of the important aspects of an experience. This enhanced identification can provide memory attributes which allow retrieval during testing as well as enable the memory to be distinguished from other experiences, thereby reducing interference as a source of forgetting.

The memory of an experience is not always accurate. Sometimes details of an event are forgotten, creating an imperfect memory. To produce a logical and realistic memory of an event, information will be added to the memory during recall. If an experience does not make sense, some information may be deleted, new information may be added, or both, to establish a memory of an event that is consistent with the animal's or person's perception of the world. Environmental input received during retrieval can also lead to a change in the memory of a past experience. The alteration of a memory after initial storage is called memory reconstruction. Research in the area of memory reconstruction has special significance because it relates to the accuracy of much or all eyewitness testimony.

The hippocampus area of the central nervous system appears to be responsible for the retrieval of memories. Hippocampal damage leads to amnesia due to the failure to retrieve stored memories.

Memory can be improved by the use of techniques called mnemonics. There are a number of mnemonic techniques, and the effectiveness of each mnemonic results from enhanced organization of information during the storage process, and this increased organization leads to improved ability to remember information.

CHAPTER 10

BIOLOGICAL INFLUENCE ON LEARNING

A NAUSEATING EXPERIENCE

For weeks, Sean has looked forward to spending the spring semester break in Florida with his roommate John and John's parents. Never having visited Florida, Sean was certain that his anticipation would make the long eighteen-hour car ride tolerable. When they arrived Sean felt genuinely welcome; John's parents had even planned many sightseeing tours for all of them during the week's stay. Sean was glad that he had come.

John had often mentioned that his mother was a gourmet cook. Sean was certainly relishing the thoughts of her meals, especially since his last enjoyable food had been his own mother's cooking. Sean was also quite tired of the many fast food restaurants at which they had stopped during their drive. When John's mother called them to dinner, Sean felt very hungry. However, the sight of lasagna on the dining table almost immediately turned Sean's hunger to nausea. As he sat down at the table, the smell of the lasagna intensified his nausea. Sean began to panic; he did not want to offend his hosts, but he hated lasagna. Although he had stopped John's mother after she had served only a small portion, Sean did not know if he could eat even one bite. When he put the lasagna to his mouth, he began to gag and the nausea became unbearable. He quickly asked to be excused, bolting to the bathroom, where he proceeded to vomit everything he had eaten that day.

Embarrassed, Sean apologetically explained his aversion to lasagna. Although he liked most Italian food, he had become intensely ill several hours after eating lasagna, and now he cannot stand even the sight or smell of lasagna.

John's mother said that she understood: she herself had a similar aversion to seafood. She offered to make Sean a sandwich, and he readily accepted.

This chapter explains the biological process which caused Sean to develop his aversion to lasagna but not to other foods. Biological processes also affect other types of learning: in some instances, biological processes ensure that animals learn adaptive behavior; in other cases, they prevent the learning of effective behaviors.

GENERALITY OF THE LAWS OF LEARNING

Why do psychologists train rats or monkeys to press a bar for food or present a buzzer prior to food presentation for cats or dogs, since these situations bear little resemblance to those of the real world? (In natural settings, rats and monkeys do not have to bar-press for food, just as cats or dogs do not hear a buzzer before they eat.) The answer to this question lies in the belief that there are some general laws of learning. These laws will be revealed by studying any behavior, even behaviors not exhibited in natural settings.

Psychologists investigating instrumental conditioning use the bar-press response because it is a behavior easily acquired in many different species. But the same rules governing the acquisition or extinction of an instrumental response could be demonstrated by using a maze or alley to study the instrumental conditioning process. Furthermore, the unnaturalness of bar pressing is desirable because the animal comes into the conditioning situation without any past experience which may affect its behavior. The following statement by Skinner illustrates the belief that the study of any behavior shows that there are specific laws governing the instrumental conditioning process: "The general topography of operant behavior is not important, because most if not all specific operants are conditioned. I suggest that the dynamic properties of operant behavior may be studied with a single reflex" (1938, pp. 45–46).

Although Skinner studied operant conditioning using the bar-press response, the observations reported in Chapter 3 show that the rules detailed by Skinner governing the acquisition and extinction of the pressing response control the instrumental conditioning process with many different behaviors and in many species. Also, much research demonstrates that many varied reinforcers can be employed to increase the rate of bar pressing and that the rules described by Skinner have been found to operate in both laboratory and real-world settings. It is not surprising that psychologists felt confident in training rats and primates to bar-press for food to reveal the general laws of instrumental conditioning.

Similarly, psychologists who present a buzzer prior to food assume that any rules uncovered governing the acquisition or extinction of a conditioned salivation response will represent general laws of classical conditioning. Further, the choice of a buzzer and food is arbitrary: cats or dogs could be conditioned to salivate as readily to a wide variety of visual, auditory, or tactile stimuli. The following statement by Pavlov illustrates the view that all stimuli are capable of becoming conditioned stimuli: "Any natural phenomenon chosen at will may be converted into a conditioned stimulus . . . any visual stimulus, any desired sound, any odor, and the stimulation of any part of the skin'' (1928, p. 86). Also, the specific UCS used is arbitrary: any event that can elicit an unconditioned response can become associated with the environmental events which precede it. Thus, Pavlov's buzzer could have as easily been conditioned to elicit fear through pairing it with shock as it was conditioned to elicit salivation through being presented prior to food. The equivalent associability of events is described in the following statement by Pavlov: "It is obvious that the reflex activity of any effector organ can be chosen for the purpose of investigation, since signalling stimuli can get linked up with any of the inborn reflexes'' (1927, p. 17). Pavlov found that many different stimuli can become associated with the UCS of food. Other psychologists documented the conditioning of varied stimuli with a multitude of UCSs. Also, the literature points out that different CSs and UCSs can become associated in both laboratory and natural situations. The idea that any environmental stimulus can become associated with any unconditioned stimulus seemed a reasonable conclusion based on the research conducted in classical conditioning.

THE IDEA OF PREPAREDNESS

Martin Seligman (1970) suggested that the biological equipment of a particular species determines what an animal can or cannot learn. In some situations, the biological character of a species facilitates learning; in other circumstances, the biological structure of the species thwarts learning. In still other conditions, the biological character neither facilitates nor prevents learning. Seligman assumes that a species is *prepared* to learn when its biological structure facilitates learning, *contraprepared* to learn when its biological character prevents learning, and *unprepared* when its biological character neither facilitates nor prevents learning.

Seligman assumes that there is a continuum of preparedness and that the "relative preparedness of an animal for learning about a situation is defined by the amount of input (e.g., number of trials, pairings, bits of information, etc.) which must occur before that output (responses, acts, repertoire, etc.), which is construed as evidence of acquisition, reliably occurs" (1970, p. 408). If an animal responds appropriately after the presentation of just one reward or after the pairing of the CS with the UCS, the animal is prepared to learn, according to Seligman. In this situation, the animal is at the extreme of the prepared end of the dimension, and instinctive processes produce rapid learning. When only a few pairings of the CS and UCS are needed for conditioning or when effective responding occurs after a few reinforcer presentations, the animal is somewhat prepared to learn. An animal is unprepared to learn if the conditioned response develops only after many CS and UCS pairings or if many reinforcements are necessary for an instrumental response to be acquired. If an animal learns only after *very* many pairings of the CS and UCS, or after *very* many presentations of reinforcement following a specific behavior, or if no learning occurs at all, the animal is contraprepared to learn a particular CS-UCS association or a specific instrumental response.

Why is an animal prepared to learn some associations or responses but contraprepared or unprepared to learn others? According to Seligman, an animal comes into an experiment with certain biological equipment and predispositions. The biological structure contains specialized sensory and receptor apparatus, and the predispositions reflect its associative apparatus. The biological character and predispositions have developed through a long and specialized evolutionary history, and this history reflects the development of biological equipment and predispositions which have enabled that species to survive in its natural habitat. If an experiment is structured in a certain way, an animal's evolutionary history may have prepared it to associate a specific CS and UCS or specific response and outcome. However, the animal's evolutionary heritage may have produced a biological structure or predisposition that causes it to be either unprepared or contraprepared to learn. Seligman points out that learning theorists have experimented using situations in which animals are unprepared to learn. This research has created the impression that some general laws of learning are characteristic of all species. However, ethologists for many years have investigated circumstances in which an animal's evolutionary history prepared it to learn. Unfortunately, these observations were ignored by the general learning camp until recently. The research of several psychologists during the 1960s forced general learning theorists to recognize the significant influence that an animal's biological heritage plays in learning. During the 1970s and 1980s, a considerable body of literature emerged indicating the role of preparedness and contrapreparedness in learning.

Research on biological processes in learning demonstrates that species differ in their ability to associate a specific CS with a particular UCS. The biological predispositions of each species determine what will or will not become associated in classical conditioning situations as well as the rapidity of associations that can be acquired. Furthermore, biological processes govern which behavior can be acquired for an animal to obtain reward in an instrumental conditioning setting; biological systems also govern whether a specific event can serve as a reinforcer in instrumental learning. An animal's biological inheritance may cause it to exhibit unreinforced behaviors in an instrumental conditioning situation: The use of reward can evoke both unrewarded and rewarded behaviors in some species. Finally, developmental factors can influence whether learning occurs. For example, responses acquired during one developmental stage may not be learned at another stage of a species's development. In this chapter, we will discover that an animal's biological heritage influences what it can or cannot learn as well as when it can learn in classical and instrumental conditioning situations. We now turn our attention to research documenting Seligman's view that animals are prepared to develop some associations, unprepared to learn others, and contraprepared to acquire other associations.

Animal Misbehavior

Several summers ago my family visited Busch Gardens. We observed some unusual behavior in birds during our visit; they walked on a wire, pedaled a bicycle, pecked certain keys on a piano, and so on. The birds had been trained to exhibit these behaviors using the operant conditioning techniques detailed in Chapter 3. Keller Breland and Marian Breland (see Breland & Breland, 1961) initiated the use of operant procedures to teach exotic behaviors to animals. They conducted their research at Animal Behavior Enterprises, Hot Springs, Arkansas, to see if the techniques described by Skinner could be used in the real world. The Brelands, finding Skinner's operant procedures to be very effective, trained thirty-eight species, including reindeer, cockatoos, raccoons, porpoises, and whales. In fact, they have trained over six thousand animals to emit a wide range of behaviors, including hens playing a 5-note tune on a piano and performing a "tap dance," pigs turning on a radio and eating breakfast at a table, chicks running up an inclined platform and sliding off, a calf answering questions in a quiz show by lighting either a yes or no sign, and two turkeys playing hockey. Established by the Brelands and many other individuals, these exotic behaviors have been shown at many municipal zoos and museums of natural history, in department store displays, at fair and trade convention exhibits, tourist attractions, and on television shows. These demonstrations have not only provided entertainment for millions of people but have also documented the power and generality of the operant conditioning procedures detailed by Skinner.

Although Breland and Breland (1961, 1966) were able to condition a wide variety of exotic behaviors using operant conditioning, they noted that the efficiency of some operant responses, although initially performed effectively, deteriorated with continued training despite repeated food reinforcements. According to Breland and Breland, elicitation by food of instinctive food-foraging and food-handling behaviors caused the decline in the effectiveness of an operant response reinforced by food. These instinctive behaviors, strengthened by food reward, eventually dominate the operant behavior. Breland and Breland called the deterioration of an operant behavior with continued reinforcement *instinctive drift,* and the instinctive behavior which prevented the continued effectiveness of the operant response is an example of *animal misbehavior*.

Breland and Breland attempted to condition pigs to pick up a large wooden coin and deposit it in a piggy bank several feet away. Each pig was required to deposit four or five coins to receive one reinforcement. According to Breland and Breland, "pigs condition very rapidly, they have no trouble taking ratios, they have ravenous appetites (naturally), and in many ways are the most trainable animals we have worked with." However, each pig they conditioned exhibited an interesting pattern of behavior following conditioning. At first, the pigs picked up a coin, carried it rapidly to the bank, deposited it, and readily returned for another coin. However, over a period of weeks, the pigs' operant behavior became slower and slower. Each pig still rapidly approached the coin, but rather than carry it until depositing it in the bank, the pigs "would repeat-edly drop it, root it, drop it again, root it along the way, pick it up, toss it up in the air, drop it, root it some more, and so on." Why did the pigs' operant behavior deteriorate after conditioning? According to Breland and Breland, the pigs merely exhibited instinctive behaviors associated with eating. The presen-tation of food during conditioning not only reinforces the operant response but also elicits instinctive food-related behaviors. The reinforcement of these in-stinctive food-gathering and food-handling behaviors strengthens these instinc-tive food-related behaviors, which results in the deterioration of the pigs' operant responses (depositing the coin in the bank). The more dominant the instinctive food-related behaviors become, the longer it takes for the operant response to occur. The slow deterioration of the operant depositing response provides support for Breland and Breland's instinctive drift view of animal misbehavior.

Breland and Breland (1961) observed a similar misbehavior problem in rac-coons. Their raccoons, required to deposit two coins in a bank to obtain food reward, were easily conditioned to pick up the coin. However, they had diffi-culty learning to drop it in the bank: they rubbed it up against the inside of the bank, pulled it back out, and held onto it for several seconds before dropping it in the bank. When the raccoons were required to drop two coins in the bank, the raccoons' coin-dropping behavior deteriorated further. The animals spent minutes rubbing them together and dipping them in and out of the bank before depositing them. As was the case with the pigs, the behavior became progres-sively worse with continued reinforcement.

Another example of animal misbehavior is that of a chicken learning to play baseball. In this situation, the chicken is placed in a cage approximately 4-feet long, with a miniature baseball field alongside the cage. At one end of the cage is a food dispenser; at the other end, an opening through which the chicken can reach and pull a loop on a bat. If the chicken pulls the loop with sufficient force, the bat will swing, hitting a small baseball into the playing field. The chicken will be reinforced with food if the ball passes the miniature toy baseball players on the field and hits the back fence; however, no reward occurs if the ball does not reach the field. Although the chickens are reinforced only on a variable-ratio schedule, Breland and Breland noted that their chickens quickly learned to hit the ball hard enough to be reinforced. The misbehavior occurred when the cage was removed, allowing the chickens access to the playing field. The chickens, very excited when they hit the ball, jumped onto the playing field, and chased the ball all over it. Occasionally, they knocked the ball off the field and onto the floor, where they pecked and chased it. The chickens' behavior was so persistent and disruptive that they no longer received reinforcement. Breland and Breland had to replace the cage to reinstate the original high level of performance. Why did the chickens chase the ball? According to Breland and Breland, chickens instinctively chase and peck at insects for food; the presentation of food caused the elicitation of instinctive food-related behaviors, which thereby disrupted the chickens' instrumental behavior.

Breland and Breland have reported many other instances of animal misbehavior. For example, they found hamsters that stopped responding in a glass case, porpoises and whales that swallowed balls or inner tubes instead of responding to them to receive reinforcement, cats that refused to leave the area around the food dispenser, and rabbits that refused to approach their feeder. Breland and Breland also reported extreme difficulty in conditioning many bird species to vocalize to obtain food reward. In each case of animal misbehavior, Breland and Breland suggested that the instinctive food-seeking behavior prevented the continued high level of performance of an instrumental response required to receive reinforcement. Apparently, the effectiveness of food reinforcement used to establish instrumental behavior is limited. This research, although contrary to the behaviorist orientation outlined in Chapters 1 through 3, is definitely consistent with the idea that there are biological influences on learning.

The Brelands observed misbehaviors in a wide variety of animal species. In a recent article, Boakes, Poli, Lockwood, and Goodall (1978) established a procedure for producing animal misbehavior in the laboratory. Boakes, Poli, Lockwood, and Goodall trained rats to press a flap to obtain a ball bearing to be deposited in a chute to obtain food reinforcement. They reported that although all the rats initially released the ball bearing readily, the majority of the animals became reluctant to let go of the ball bearing after several training sessions. These rats repeatedly mouthed, pawed, and retrieved the ball bearing before finally depositing it in the chute.

Breland and Breland (1961, 1966) suggested that elicitation of instinctive food-related behaviors (food-seeking and ingestive behaviors) by reward and the strengthening of these instinctive responses during operant conditioning is responsible for animal misbehavior. Boakes, Poli, Lockwood, and Goodall (1978) proposed another explanation. In their view, animal misbehavior is produced by Pavlovian conditioning rather than by operant conditioning. The association of environmental events with food during conditioning causes these environmental events to elicit species-typical foraging and food-handling behaviors; the elicitation of these behaviors competes with the occurrence of efficient operant behavior. Consider the misbehavior of the pig detailed earlier. According to Breland and Breland, the pigs rooted the tokens because the reward presented during operant conditioning produced rooting behavior and reward strengthened the intensity of the instinctive food-related behavior; in contrast, Boakes, Poli, Lockwood, and Goodall suggested that the association of the token with food caused the token to elicit the rooting behavior.

Timberlake, Wahl, and King (1982) conducted a series of studies to evaluate the validity of Breland and Breland's operant conditioning instinctive drift hypothesis and Boakes, Poli, Lockwood, and Goodall's Pavlovian conditioning view of animal misbehavior. The results of the experiments conducted by Timberlake, Wahl, and King show that both operant and Pavlovian conditioning contribute to producing animal misbehavior. In their appetitive structure view, misbehavior represents species-typical foraging and food-handling behaviors which are elicited by pairing food with the natural cues controlling food-gathering activities. Thus, misbehavior will occur only if the stimuli present during operant conditioning resemble the natural cues in terms of similarity and temporal proximity to food. According to Timberlake, Wahl, and King, the pigs rooted tokens because of the physical similarity of tokens to the cues eliciting and controlling rooting in natural settings as well as because of the temporal relation of these cues to food. In addition, the instinctive food-gathering behaviors must be reinforced if the misbehavior is to dominate the operant behavior. Furthermore, animal misbehavior does not occur in most operant conditioning situations because (1) the cues present during conditioning do not resemble the natural cues eliciting instinctive foraging and food-handling behaviors and (2) these instinctive behaviors are not reinforced. Let's examine how Timberlake, Wahl, and King validated their appetitive structure view of animal misbehavior.

Timberlake, Wahl, and King used the ball bearing procedure developed by Boakes, Poli, Lockwood, and Goodall to investigate animal misbehavior. Recall that rats in this situation repeatedly mouth, paw, and retrieve the ball bearing before releasing it down the chute to obtain food reinforcement. Timberlake, Wahl, and King (experiment 1) assessed the contribution of Pavlovian conditioning to animal misbehavior by pairing the ball bearing with food in experimental subjects. Experimental treatment animals received food after the ball bearing had rolled out of the chamber. Also, this study used two control conditions to evaluate the importance of ball bearing–food presentations: animals in one control condition were given random pairings of the ball bearing and food (random group); subjects in the second control condition received only the ball bearing (CS-only group). Timberlake, Wahl, and King reported that animals in the experimental group exhibited a significant amount of misbehavior toward the ball bearing: they touched it, carried it about the cage, placed it in their mouth, and bit it while holding it in their forepaws. In contrast, infrequent misbehavior occurred in animals in the two control groups. These observations indicate that the ball bearing and food must be presented together for a high level of misbehavior to occur.

According to Timberlake, Wahl, and King, the pairings of the ball bearing with food are necessary but not sufficient for the development of misbehavior. Timberlake, Wahl, and King also assert that the misbehavior must be reinforced by food presentation for misbehavior to dominate instrumental responding. Timberlake, Wahl, and King's experiments 3 and 4 evaluated the importance of operant conditioning to the establishment of animal misbehavior. In experiment 3, contact with the ball bearing caused food to be omitted. Timberlake, Wahl, and King assumed that if reinforcement of contact with the ball bearing is necessary for the dominance of animal misbehavior, the contingency that contact with the ball bearing would prevent reinforcement would lead to an absence of animal misbehavior. The results of experiment 3 show that if contact with the ball bearing prevents reward, then the animals exhibit no contact with the ball bearing. Timberlake, Wahl, and King then reinforced contact with the ball bearing in experiment 4. If the animal did not touch the ball bearing, it

received no food on that trial. Timberlake, Wahl, and King reported that reinforcement of contact with the ball bearing produced a rapid increase in the level
of animal misbehavior. It is interesting that the effect of reward caused by
increasing contact with the ball bearing inhibited the animals' instrumental
response toward the food source and thereby prolonged the eating time. Timberlake, Wahl, and King also discovered that removal of the contingency between contact with the ball bearing and food presentation (extinction) caused
a decrease in the amount of misbehavior. Apparently, for misbehavior to
develop, stimuli (e.g., ball bearings) resembling the natural cues controlling
food-gathering activities must be consistently paired with food (Pavlovian conditioning), and the presentation of food must reinforce the occurrence of
species-typical foraging and food-handling behaviors elicited by the natural
cues (operant conditioning).

Does misbehavior occur in humans? Research needs to be conducted to
answer this question. However, a few years ago during the banquet of my
youngest son's football team, a young girl seated across from me exhibited a
pattern of eating behavior definitely resembling the misbehavior described by
Breland and Breland. The girl spent several minutes playing with her eating
utensils before putting a bite of food in her mouth. At the end of the 1½-hour
banquet, she had not even half finished her food. Her parents indicated that this
was not atypical behavior for their daughter; it was not unusual for her to spend
several hours eating, and she had, in fact, spent her entire last birthday party
eating rather than playing with her friends. Furthermore, they said that her
older brother also took a long time to eat but not nearly as long as his sister.
Surely other children also show excessively long periods of eating behavior;
undoubtedly, it may be the association of the utensils with food as well as the
reinforcement of the misbehavior which contributes to their pattern of eating
behavior.

Schedule-Induced Behavior

B. F. Skinner (1948) described an interesting pattern of behavior exhibited by
pigeons reinforced for key pecking on a fixed-interval schedule. When food
reinforcement was delivered to the pigeons on a fixed-interval 15-second schedule, they developed a "ritualistic" stereotyped pattern of behavior during the
interval. The pattern of behavior differed from bird to bird: some walked in
circles between food presentations; others scratched on the floor; still others
moved their heads back and forth. Once a particular pattern of behavior
emerged, the pigeons repeatedly exhibited it, with the frequency of the behavior increasing as the birds received more reinforcement. Skinner referred to the
behavior of his pigeons on the interval schedule as an example of *superstitious
behavior*.

Why do animals exhibit superstitious behavior? One reasonable explanation
suggests that animals have associated superstitious behavior with reinforcement and that this association causes the animals to exhibit high levels of

superstitious behavior. However, Staddon and Simmelhag's (1971) analysis of superstitious behavior indicates that it is not an example of the instrumental behavior detailed in Chapter 3. They identified two types of behavior produced when reward (for example food) is programmed to occur on a regular basis: (1) *Terminal behavior* occurs during the last few seconds of the interval between reward presentations, and it is reward oriented. Staddon and Simmelhag's pigeons pecking on or near the food hopper which delivered food is an example of terminal behavior. (2) *Interim behavior,* in contrast, is not reward oriented. Although contiguity influences the development of terminal behavior, interim behavior does not occur contiguously with reinforcement. Terminal behavior falls between interim behavior and reward but does not interfere with the exhibition of interim behavior. According to Staddon and Simmelhag, terminal behavior occurs in stimulus situations which are highly predictive of the occurrence of reinforcement; that is, terminal behavior is typically emitted just prior to reward availability on a fixed-interval schedule. In contrast, interim behavior occurs during stimulus conditions which have a low probability of the occurrence of reinforcement; that is, interim behavior is observed most frequently in the period *following* reinforcement. The strange superstitious behavior described initially by Skinner is only one example of interim behavior. Animals exhibit a wide variety of other behaviors (i.e., drinking, running, grooming, nest building, aggression) when reward occurs regularly. The elicitation of high levels of interim behavior by fixed-interval schedules of reinforcement is referred to as *adjunctive behavior.* Let's now examine evidence of the occurrence of adjunctive behaviors on fixed-interval reinforcement schedules.

Schedule-Induced Polydipsia   The most extensively studied form of adjunctive behavior is the excessive intake of water (polydipsia) when animals are reinforced with food on a fixed-interval schedule. John Falk (1961) was the first investigator to observe *schedule-induced polydipsia.* Falk deprived rats of food until their bodyweight was approximately 70 to 80 percent of their initial bodyweight and then trained them to bar-press for food reinforcement. When water was available in an operant chamber, Falk found that the rats consumed excessive amounts of water. Even though Falk's rats were not water deprived, they drank large amounts of water; in fact, under certain conditions animals provided food reinforcement on an interval schedule will consume as much as one-half their weight in water in a few hours. Note that this level of excessive drinking cannot be produced with water deprivation or heat stress or by providing a similar amount of food in one meal. Apparently, some important aspects of providing food on an interval schedule can elicit excessive drinking.

Is schedule-induced polydipsia an example of interim behavior? Recall Staddon and Simmelhag's definition—interim behavior occurs in stimulus situations which have a low probability of reward occurrence. Schedule-induced drinking does fit their definition: animals rewarded on an interval schedule typically drink in the period *following* food consumption. In contrast, drinking usually does not occur in the period which *precedes* the availability of food reward. Evidently, schedule-induced polydipsia is an example of interim behavior.

Schedule-induced polydipsia has been consistently observed in rats given food reward on an interval schedule; see Falk (1971) or Staddon (1977) for a review of this literature. A variety of different interval schedules of reinforcement have been found to produce polydipsia. For example, Falk (1966a) observed polydipsia in rats on a fixed-interval schedule and also reported (1967) the occurrence of schedule-induced polydipsia in rats receiving a variable-interval schedule. Also with rats, Segal and Holloway (1963) found polydipsia using a differential rate of low reinforcement (DRL) schedule, and Jacquet (1972) and Rosenblith (1970) observed polydipsia on a variety of multiple schedules of reinforcement.

Schedule-induced polydipsia has been found in species other than rats. For example, Shanab and Peterson (1969) reported this behavior in pigeons on an interval schedule of food reward, and Schuster and Woods (1966) observed it in primates.

Level of Schedule-Induced Polydipsia Four factors have been identified as contributing to the amount of polydipsia. First, the intensity of food deprivation affects the level of polydipsia observed. Falk (1969) initially established polydipsia in animals of 70 to 80 percent normal body weight and then decreased the level of deprivation to 95 to 100 percent of their initial body weight. Falk discovered that the amount drunk declined as body weight increased. These results indicate that the level of polydipsia is influenced by motivation level: as the motivation level declines, the amount of polydipsia declines.

Second, Falk (1964, 1966a) reported that the palatability of the available fluid affects the amount of schedule-induced polydipsia. Falk observed that level of intake declined substantially when animals were given an NaCl solution instead of water. In a similar study, Gilbert (1974) discovered that rats drank significantly less ethanol solution than water. Furthermore, as the concentration of ethanol was increased, the amount of polydipsia declined. Apparently, schedule-induced polydipsia can be inhibited by the presence of an unattractive liquid.

Third, the amount of reward also influences the degree of polydipsia produced in animals on an interval schedule of reward. Hawkins, Schrot, Githens, and Everett (1972) reported an increase in the level of polydipsia with an increase in the magnitude of reward. Bond (1973) and Couch (1974) also observed that polydipsia increased as a function of the level of reward magnitude.

Finally, the level of polydipsia is affected by the length of time between reinforcements. A number of studies (Falk, 1966a, 1967; Flory, 1971) show that an inverted-U–shaped relation exists between the time interval between reinforcements and the level of polydipsia: the amount of polydipsia increases as the interval length increases up to 180 seconds, and then it declines with increased interval length. Falk's 1966a study illustrates this effect. He varied the fixed-interval (FI) length from 20 seconds to 300 seconds. As can be seen in Figure 10.1, the level of polydipsia increased as the FI was increased to 180

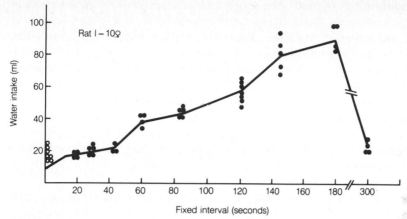

FIGURE 10.1
The amount of water intake as a function of the length of fixed-interval
schedule of food reinforcement. Adapted from Falk, J. L. Schedule-induced
polydipsia as a function of fixed-interval length. *Journal of the Experimental
Analysis of Behavior,* 1966, *9,* 37–39. Copyright 1966 by the Society for the
Experimental Analysis of Behavior. Reprinted by permission.

seconds and then dropped sharply with a 300-second interval. Flory (1971)
observed a gradual drop in the level of polydipsia from an FI of 240 seconds to
an FI of 480 seconds.

Nature of Schedule-Induced Polydipsia   Two classes of theories have been
offered to explain polydipsia. Some explanations suggest that factors *specific* to
thirst cause polydipsia; others imply that a *general* process causes all schedule-
induced behavior and that the specific behavior depends only on the animal's
capability of exhibiting that behavior. These general process theorists propose
that if water is unavailable, an animal on an interval schedule would exhibit an
instinctive behavior other than polydipsia. The evidence clearly shows that the
specific factor of thirst is not responsible for polydipsia; instead a general
process causes all schedule-induced behavior.

Several psychologists (Stein, 1964; Teitelbaum, 1966) have suggested that
the ingestion of food produces a dry mouth, and this in turn motivates drinking
behavior. A substantial amount of research indicates that a dry mouth is not
responsible for polydipsia. For example, Falk (1969) and Stricker and Adair
(1966) used reinforcers that were one-third water by weight. Although this
reinforcement should not produce a dry mouth, substantial levels of polydipsia
were still observed. Also, Falk (1967) reported polydipsia when liquid reinforcers were used. Furthermore, polydipsia has been observed with the use
of a secondary reinforcer rather than a primary reinforcement (see Corfield-
Sumner, Blackman, & Stainer, 1977; Rosenblith, 1970). Apparently, an
animal's dry mouth is not responsible for polydipsia occurring on an interval
schedule.

Teitelbaum (1966) suggested that polydipsia was the result of thirst produced by cellular dehydration; this dehydration is caused by food pulling water out of the tissues and into the stomach. However, Falk's 1969 study shows that dehydration is not responsible for schedule-induced polydipsia. In Falk's study, the animals prior to training were preloaded with water through a rubber catheter which had been passed down the esophagus into the stomach. Falk found that preloading, which would eliminate cellular dehydration, did not influence the level of polydipsia. Our discussion indicates that the physiological condition of thirst is not responsible for schedule-induced polydipsia. We now turn our attention to other instinctive behaviors which occur on interval schedules of reinforcement.

Schedule-Induced Wheel Running   A number of psychologists (King, 1974; Levitsky & Collier, 1968; Skinner & Morse, 1958; Staddon & Ayres, 1975) have reported that interval schedules of reward produce high levels of wheel running. *Schedule-induced wheel running* has been observed using both food and water reward. Furthermore, variables affecting schedule-induced polydipsia also influence schedule-induced wheel running. For example, Levitsky and Collier (1968) reported the intensity of wheel-running to be greater on an interval schedule than on a ratio schedule. Also, Levitsky and Collier found that the highest rate of wheel running occurs in the time immediately following reward and then decreases as the time for the next reward nears. Moreover, Staddon and Ayres (1975) reported an inverted-U–shaped relationship between the rate of wheel-running and the interval length between rewards: as the interreward interval increases, the intensity of wheel running initially increases and then declines.

Schedule-Induced Aggression   Animals receiving reward on an interval schedule will attack an appropriate target of aggressive behavior. For example, Azrin, Hutchinson, and Hake (1966), Cohen and Looney (1973), and Flory and Ellis (1973) reported that pigeons will attack another bird or a stuffed model of a bird which is present during key pecking for reward on an interval schedule. Similar *schedule-induced aggression* has been observed in squirrel monkeys (Hutchinson, Azrin, & Hunt, 1968) and rats (Gentry & Schaeffer, 1969; Knutson & Kleinknecht, 1970; Thompson & Bloom, 1966). Schedule-induced aggression has been found using a variety of interval schedules, including fixed-interval (Richards & Rilling, 1972), differential reinforcement of low rate (Knutson & Kleinknecht, 1970), and response-independent fixed-time schedules (Flory, 1969).

Schedule-induced aggression, like schedule-induced wheel running, is affected by those variables influencing the level of schedule-induced polydipsia. For example, Azrin, Hutchinson, and Hake (1966) found that the deprivation level affected the duration of attack. In their study, the greater the deprivation level, the shorter the duration of schedule-induced aggression. In addition, Azrin, Hutchinson, and Hake (1966) and Knutson and Kleinknecht (1970) re-

ported that the greatest intensity of aggressive behavior occurred in the immediate postreinforcement period. Finally, an excessive level of aggressive behavior is produced on interval schedules of reinforcement. Azrin, Hutchinson,
and Hake (1966) observed that pigeons on an interval schedule of reinforcement often badly injure live target birds, and Flory (1969) found that pigeons on
this schedule will rapidly destroy realistic model birds.

Other Schedule-Induced Behaviors   Several other instinctive behaviors are
observed in animals on interval schedules. For example, Mendelson and Chillag (1970) found that rats provided access to a continuous air stream from a
drinking tube will lick from the tube in the postreinforcement period. The
intensity of *schedule-induced air licking* is also affected by deprivation. Chillag
and Mendelson (1971) reported that the level of schedule-induced air licking
increases as the animal's deprivation level is increased. Furthermore, Mendelson and Chillag (1970) observed that the greatest intensity of air licking
occurs in the period immediately following reward.

Villareal (1967) reported that rhesus monkeys will ingest wood shavings
covering the floor of the experimental chamber during the postreinforcement
period of an interval schedule. The ingestion of wood shavings in animals on an
interval schedule is called *schedule-induced pica*. Villareal observed that monkeys will only ingest the wood shavings on an interval schedule; food-deprived
animals will not ingest freely available wood shavings in the absence of an
interval reinforcement schedule.

The Nature of Schedule-Induced Behavior   Three major general theories
have been proposed to explain schedule-induced behavior (see Davey, 1981,
for a review of this literature). One view (Clark, 1962; Segal, 1965) suggests that
adventitious reinforcement causes schedule-induced behavior; that is, the oc-
casional occurrence of behaviors such as drinking, attacking, or running prior
to reinforcement causes these behaviors to be increased in intensity like any
other reinforced behavior. Numerous research argues against an adventitious
reinforcement explanation of schedule-induced or adjunctive behavior. The
most persuasive evidence against an adventitious reinforcement explanation
lies in the temporal locus of adjunctive behavior. If adventitious reinforcement
causes schedule-induced behavior, the highest level of responding should take
place just prior to reward. Yet, the literature clearly shows that the greatest
intensity of schedule-induced behavior can be produced, even with long delays
between rewards (Schuster & Woods, 1966; Stein, 1964). As we learned in
Chapter 3, instrumental behavior is weak, with long delays of reward; however, schedule-induced behavior is *excessive,* despite the occurrence of a long-
delay between the adjunctive behavior and reward. One final observation is the
strongest against an adventitious reinforcement explanation of adjunctive behavior. Several investigators (Cherek, Thompson, & Heistad, 1973; Falk, 1964;
Flory, 1969) have added an additional contingency to their interval schedule.
This contingency specifies that the occurrence of the adjunctive behavior in the

15-second period prior to reward causes the animal not to receive reinforcement. Although this procedure successfully suppresses the adjunctive behavior during the 15-second period prior to reward, therefore preventing any possible adventitious reward, the level of adjunctive behavior *after* reward is not affected by the additional contingency. Apparently, reward of adjunctive behavior is not responsible for schedule-induced behavior.

A second explanation of schedule-induced behavior (see Lotter, Woods, & Vasselli, 1973; Stein, 1964) proposed that adjunctive behavior is an unconditioned response elicited by reinforcement. Several aspects of schedule-induced behavior seem to support this view: the greatest intensity of adjunctive behavior does occur in the period following reinforcement, and the reliability and excessive character of adjunctive behavior is also found in unconditioned responses. However, other aspects of schedule-induced behavior indicate that adjunctive behavior is not an unconditioned response to reward. First, unlike unconditioned responses, adjunctive behavior requires several training sessions to develop (Falk, 1971). Also, the greater the training, the higher the level of schedule-induced behavior. Second, several studies (Flory & O'Boyle, 1972; Gilbert, 1974; Knutson & Kleinknecht, 1970; Segal & Holloway, 1963) prevented the occurrence of adjunctive behavior in the immediate postreward period but allowed it to occur later in the interval between rewards. If reward was, indeed, eliciting the adjunctive behavior, this technique should have eliminated schedule-induced behavior. However, excessive levels of behavior were still observed, despite the prevention of the occurrence in the immediate postreward period.

Bolles (1972, 1979) offered a third and apparently accurate explanation of schedule-induced behavior. According to Bolles, after an animal receives reward on an interval schedule, it does not expect another reward for a while. This expectation of no reward is aversive, activating frustration-induced behavior. Thus, frustration elicits the excessive level of instinctive appetitive behavior seen during interval schedules. Several types of evidence support this frustration view of schedule-induced behavior. First, stimuli which have been present during extinction and thereby signal nonreward have been observed to elicit excessive levels of instinctive appetitive behavior. For example, Azrin, Hutchinson, and Hake (1966) observed that pigeons attacked a restrained target pigeon during the extinction period of a multiple schedule (see Chapter 3). Also, Hutchinson, Azrin, and Hunt (1968) reported that signaled extinction periods elicited aggressive behavior in squirrel monkeys. Furthermore, Panksepp, Toates, and Oatley (1972) found that excessive drinking occurred in rats during the presentation of the stimulus which signaled extinction or during multiple schedules of reinforcement. Second, the level of frustration influences the magnitude of schedule-induced behavior. Thomka and Rosellini (1975) decreased the reward magnitude, which thereby intensified frustration and increased the level of schedule-induced polydipsia.

Why does frustration produced by the expectation of nonreward cause schedule-induced behavior? Recall from Chapter 4 that aggression in a frustrated animal is pleasurable. All instinctive consummatory behavior (eating, drinking, sex, etc.) is pleasurable, and these behaviors induce pleasure by activating a specific neural system. Furthermore, stimulation of this pleasure system also acts to inhibit activity in another neural system which, if aroused, causes pain. In all likelihood, excessive levels of instinctive appetitive behaviors occur on interval schedules because these behaviors arouse pleasure and inhibit the aversive frustration produced by the expectation that reward will be unavailable for some time.

Does Schedule-Induced Behavior Occur in Humans?   In many situations in our society, reinforcement is programmed to occur on an interval schedule. Furthermore, excessive levels of instinctive appetitive behaviors do often occur in humans. A likely cause of people's excessive eating, drinking, and aggressive behavior is the frustration produced by the expectation of nonreward for some time. Gilbert (1974) suggested that interval schedules could be responsible for the excessive drinking (or alcoholism) of many people. Gilbert's demonstration that excessive levels of ethanol were consumed by rats on an interval schedule supports his view. Note that animals do not normally drink any ethanol and that the use of an interval schedule of reward is one of the few ways of producing drinking of alcohol in animals. A recent study by Granger, Porter, and Christoph (1983) reported that water intake was increased when reward (M&Ms) was presented on an interval schedule; the heightened water intake occurred after reward presentation and, therefore, was a demonstration of adjunctive behavior in humans. Furthermore, several researchers (Cantor & Wilson, 1984; Cherek, 1982; Wallace, Singer, Wayner, & Cook, 1975) have observed excessive levels of activities such as eating, smoking, or nailbiting in the interval following reward in real-world settings. While additional research is necessary to document that people's excessive behavior reflects an example of schedule-induced behavior, animal research on adjunctive behavior suggests techniques to eliminate excessive appetitive behavior in humans.

We have seen that instinctive behavior elicited by reward can interfere with the development of the instrumental response producing reward (animal misbehavior) and that the expectation that reward will not occur for some time will elicit instinctive responses which reduce frustration (schedule-induced behavior). We next examine the biological processes affecting flavor-aversion learning.

Flavor-Aversion Learning

I have a friend who refuses to walk down an aisle in a supermarket where tomato sauce is displayed; he says that even the sight of cans of tomatoes makes him ill. My oldest son once got sick after eating string beans, and now he refuses to touch them. I once was very nauseated several hours after eating at a local restaurant, and I have not returned since. Almost all of us have some food that we will not eat or a restaurant that we avoid. Often the reason for this behavior is that at some time we experienced illness after eating a particular food or in a particular place, and associated the event with the illness through classical conditioning. Such an experience engenders a *conditioned aversion* to the taste of the food or the place itself. Subsequently, we avoid it.

Our discussion of flavor-aversion learning begins with the classic research of John Garcia and his associates (see Garcia, Kimeldorf, & Koelling, 1955; Garcia, Kimeldorf, & Hunt, 1957). Although rats have a strong preference for saccharin, consuming large quantities even when nondeprived, Garcia and his colleagues discovered that these animals will not subsequently drink saccharin if illness followed its consumption. In their studies, rats after consuming saccharin were made ill by agents such as *x-ray irradiation* or *lithium chloride;* they subsequently avoided that taste.

Long-Delay Learning   You probably do not find the observation that animals avoid the taste cues preceding illness surprising: we described many examples of the acquisition of emotional responses (CRs) when a novel stimulus (CS) precedes a biologically important event (UCS) in our discussion of classical conditioning in Chapter 2. Although flavor aversion does reflect the operation of the Pavlovian conditioning process, it differs from all other examples of classical conditioning in one important way. Recall from Chapter 2 that contiguity plays a critical role in the acquisition of a conditioned response: little conditioning occurs if the CS precedes the UCS by several seconds or minutes. However, animals will develop aversions to taste cues even when the taste stimulus preceded illness by *several hours*. This observation indicates that unlike other conditioned responses, contiguity is not essential for the establishment of a flavor aversion. The association of a flavor with illness is often referred to as *long-delay learning;* the use of this term suggests a difference between flavor-aversion learning and other examples of classical conditioning.

The research of Garcia and his associates attracted the attention of many psychologists during the late 1960s and early 1970s. As a result, hundreds of experiments were conducted investigating flavor-aversion learning. A number of important characteristics of long-delay learning have been uncovered in the past fifteen years (see Logue, 1979, for a review of this literature). Let's examine what psychologists have discovered about flavor-aversion learning.

Delay Gradient   Like other conditioned responses, there is a delay gradient whereby the closer the occurrence of the CS and UCS, the faster the conditioning of the CR as well as the greater the final level of conditioning. In the case of flavor-aversion learning, the delay gradient lasts several hours rather than seconds or minutes (see Chapter 2 for characteristics of delay gradients for other conditioned responses). Garcia, Clark, and Hankins's (1973) results provide a delay gradient representative of flavor-aversion learning. In their study, rats consumed saccharin and were then injected with apormorphine 30, 45, 75, 120, or 180 minutes later. As can be seen in Figure 10.2, strong aversions to saccharin were observed with delays up to 75 minutes. In contrast, delay intervals of 2 or 3 hours between taste and illness produced no aversion: animals in these

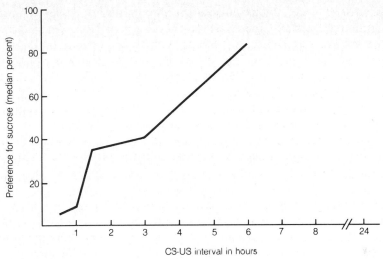

FIGURE 10.2
Median percentage preference for sucrose solution as a function of the
interval between flavor and illness. From Kalat, J. W., & Rozin, P. Role of
interference in taste-aversion learning. *Journal of Comparative and
Physiological Psychology*, 1971, *77*, 53–58. Copyright 1971 by the
American Psychological Association. Reprinted by permission.

delay treatments drank as much saccharin as did control animals injected with
saline rather than apormorphine. A number of other studies have also investigated the relation between the delay between flavor and illness and the strength
of the aversion. Most of these studies have found results similar but not identical to those of Garcia, Clark, and Hankins. For example, Kalat and Rozin
(1971) found a strong aversion to saccharin with delay intervals up to 60 minutes, a weak aversion to saccharin with 1.5- or 3-hour delay intervals, and no
aversion with 6- or 24-hour delay intervals. However, a few studies (for example, Andrews & Braveman, 1975; Etscorn & Stephens, 1973) reported some
aversion to saccharin, even with a 24-hour interval between the flavor and
illness. It is thought that only under optimal conditions can an aversion be
established with a 24-hour delay; under less than ideal circumstances, weak
aversions are established at 1.5 to 3 hours, and no aversions occur with longer
intervals. One condition (salience) which affects the strength of a flavor aversion is described next. Other variables (predictiveness, CS intensity, UCS
intensity) also influence flavor-aversion learning: the effects of these factors
were discussed in Chapter 2.

   The Salience of the CS   Recall from Chapter 2 that stimuli differ in salience;
that is, some stimuli are more likely to become associated with a particular
UCS than other stimuli are. Garcia and Koelling's classic study (1966) shows
that a taste is more salient when preceding illness than when preceding shock,

whereas a light or tone is more salient when presented prior to shock than is illness. In Garcia and Koelling's study, rats were exposed to either a saccharin taste cue or a light and tone compound stimulus. Following exposure to one of these cues, animals received either an electric shock or irradiation-induced illness. Figure 10.3 presents the results of the study. The animals exhibited an aversion to saccharin when it was paired with illness but not when it was paired with shock. In addition, they developed a fear of the light and tone stimulus when it was paired with shock but not when it was paired with illness.

On the basis of the Garcia and Koelling study, Seligman (1970) proposed that rats have an evolutionary preparedness to associate tastes with illness. Further support for this view is the observation that an intense aversion to a flavor is acquired in adult rats after a single taste-illness pairing. Young animals also acquire a strong aversion after one taste-illness pairing (see Galef & Sherry, 1973; Klein, Domato, Hallstead, Stephens, & Mikulka, 1975; Rudy & Cheatle, 1977). Apparently, taste cues are very salient in terms of their associability with illness.

Seligman also suggested that rats are contraprepared to become afraid of a light or tone paired with illness. However, other research (for example, Best, Best, & Mickley, 1973; Klein, Freda, & Mikulka, 1985; Morrison & Collyer, 1974; Revusky & Parker, 1976) indicates that rats can associate an environmental cue with illness. Best, Best, and Mickley (1973) and Klein, Freda, and Mikulka (1985) found that rats avoided a distinctive black compartment previously paired with an illness-inducing apormorphine or lithium chloride injection. Morrison and Collyer (1974) reported that rats developed an aversion to a light cue preceded by illness, and Revusky and Parker (1976) observed that rats did not eat out of a container which had been paired with illness induced by lithium chloride. Note that although animals can acquire environmental aversions, more trials and careful training procedures are necessary to establish an

FIGURE 10.3
Effects of pairing a gustatory cue or an auditory cue with either external pain or internal illness. Adapted from Garcia, J.; Clark, J. C.; & Hankins, W. G. Natural responses to scheduled rewards. In P. P. G. Bateson & P. H. Klopfer (Eds.), *Perspectives in ethology* [vol. 1]. New York: Plenum, 1973.

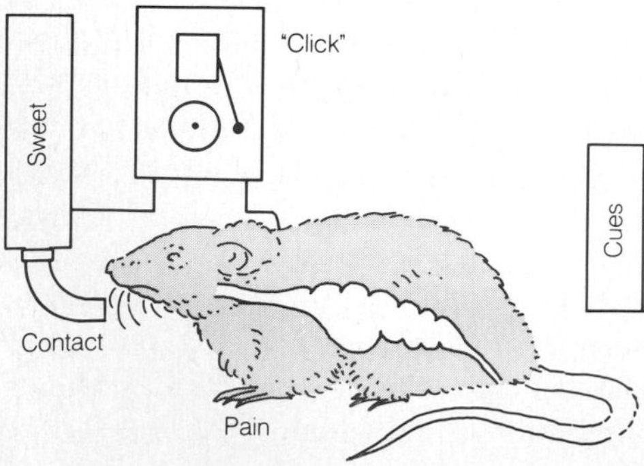

		Consequences	
		Nausea	Pain
Cues	Sweet	Acquires aversion	Does not
	"Click"	Does not	Learns defense

environmental aversion than a flavor aversion (for example, Klein, Freda, & Mikulka, 1985; Riccio & Haroutunian, 1977). Also, extinction is more rapid, and the delay interval during which an aversion can be acquired is shorter with an environmental aversion than with a flavor aversion (Best, Best, & Henggeler, 1977).

The literature also shows that taste cues are more salient when paired with illness than with an odor. For example, Garcia and Koelling (1967) and Garcia, McGowan, Ervin, and Koelling (1968) reported that a taste cue, when compared with an odor cue, was more readily associated with illness. Similar results were found by Kalat and Rozin (1970) and Klein, Davis, Cohen, and Weston (1984). Thus a rat is prepared to associate a taste with illness, but it is *unprepared* to learn an environmental or odor aversion.

Although rats form flavor aversions more readily than they do environmental aversions, other species do not show this pattern of stimulus salience. Unlike rats, birds acquire visual aversions more rapidly than taste aversions. For example, Wilcoxin, Dragoin, and Kral (1971) poisoned quail that had consumed sour blue water, reporting that an aversion was formed to the blue color but not to the sour taste. In the same vein, Capretta (1961) found greater salience of visual cues than taste cues in chickens.

Why are visual cues more salient than taste stimuli in birds? According to Garcia, Hankins, and Rusiniak (1974), this salience hierarchy is adaptive. Since birds' seeds are covered by a hard flavorless shell, they must use visual cues to assess whether food is poisoned, and thus, these visual cues enable birds to avoid consuming poisonous seeds. Although this view seems reasonable, it does not appear to be completely accurate. According to Braveman (1974, 1975), the feeding time characteristic of a particular species determines the relative salience of stimuli becoming associated with illness. Rats, which are nocturnal animals, locate their food at night and therefore rely less on visual information than on gustatory information to identify poisoned food. In contrast, birds search for their food during the day, and thus visual information plays an important role in controlling their food intake. Braveman evaluated this view by examining the salience hierarchy of guinea pigs, which, like birds, seek their food during the day. Braveman found visual cues to be more salient than taste stimuli for guinea pigs.

Flavor-Aversion Learning in Humans   Does a person's dislike for a particular food reflect the establishment of a flavor aversion? It seems reasonable that people's aversion to a specific food often develops after they eat it and become ill. Informally questioning the students in my learning class last year, I found that many of them indeed had an experience in which illness followed eating a certain food and that these students no longer could eat that food. If you have had a similar experience, perhaps you too can identify the cause of your aversion to some food. In a more formal investigation, Garb and Stunkard (1974) questioned 696 subjects about their food aversions, reporting that 38 percent of the subjects had at least one strong food aversion. Garb and Stunkard found that 89 percent of the people reporting a strong food aversion could identify a specific instance in which they became ill after eating the food, refusing to consume it thereafter. Even though most often the illness did not begin until several hours after consumption of the food, their subjects still avoided the food in the future. Also, Garb and Stunkard's survey indicated that the subjects were more likely to develop aversions between the ages of 6 and 12 years old than at any other time of life.

Experimentation has documented the establishment of food aversion in people (see Logue, 1985, for a review of this literature). In one study, Bernstein (1978) found that children in the early stages of cancer acquired an aversion to a distinctively flavored Mapletoff ice cream (maple and black walnut flavor) consumed before toxic chemotherapy in the gastrointestinal (GI) tract. Instead of eating Mapletoff ice cream, these children now preferred either to play with a toy or to eat another flavor ice cream. In contrast, both children who had previously received the toxic therapy to the GI tract without the Mapletoff ice cream and children who had been given the Mapletoff ice cream before toxic chemotherapy not involving the GI tract continued to eat the Mapletoff ice cream. Bernstein and Webster (1980) reported similar results in adults. Cancer patients receiving radiation therapy typically show a loss of appetite and weight (Morrison, 1976); the association of hospital food with illness could be reduced by presenting radiation therapy prior to meals, a procedure which would lead to greater eating and a better chance of recovery.

Nature of Flavor-Aversion Learning   Why do animals and people develop aversions to a specific food consumed prior to illness, despite a delay of several hours between consumption of the food and illness? Two very different explanations of long-delayed flavor-aversion learning have been proposed: (1) Kalat and Rozin's (1971) learned-safety theory and (2) Revusky's (1977) concurrent interference theory. Research evaluating both views suggests that each process contributes to flavor-aversion learning. Let's now briefly examine both views, as well as the evidence that the process detailed by each view enables an animal or person to learn to avoid a poisoned food.

Learned-Safety View   Kalat and Rozin's (1971) learned-safety view suggests that a unique process is responsible for flavor-aversion learning. The contiguity process detailed in Chapter 2 has obvious adaptive significance for most classical conditioning situations. For example, a child touches a flame and experiences pain. The association of the flame with pain produces the conditioned response of fear; fear elicited on subsequent exposure to the flame motivates this child to avoid pain. However, since the consumption of poisoned food rarely produces immediate illness, the contiguity process characteristic of other classical conditioning situations will not enable an animal to associate food and illness. In Kalat and Rozin's view, a mechanism unique to learning a flavor aversion evolved to allow animals to avoid potentially lethal foods. Kalat and Rozin called this process used by animals to avoid poisoned food *learned safety*.

An animal exposed to a new food consumes only a small portion of it. This low consumption of a novel food, *neophobia*, has obvious adaptive significance: it prevents animals from consuming a large quantity of a potentially poisoned food so that if the food is poisonous, the animals will become sick but not die. According to Kalat and Rozin, if an animal becomes sick within several hours after food consumption, it will associate the food with illness and develop an aversion to that food. However, if illness does not occur, the animal can assume that the food is not poisonous and that it can safely be consumed again. Thus, learned safety overcomes an animal's reluctance (neophobia) to consume new foods, enabling it to eat foods which enhance its survival.

Kalat and Rozin (1973), providing support for their learned-safety view, gave animals one of three treatments: One group of rats received a novel flavor four hours before being poisoned (4-P treatment). A second group was poisoned half an hour after receiving the novel food (½-P treatment). A third group was given access to the novel flavor and was again exposed to it three and a half hours later; illness followed half an hour later (3½-½-P treatment). A contiguity view of classical conditioning predicts equal strength of the flavor aversion in the second and third groups, since a half-hour interval separated the flavor and illness in both groups, and a weaker aversion should be found in the first group because a four-hour interval separated the flavor and illness. In contrast, the learned-safety view assumes a strong aversion in the second group and a weak aversion in the first and third groups, since the rats in both groups 1 and 3 had four hours after consumption of the novel flavor to learn it was safe. As can be seen in Figure 10.4, the results of Kalat and Rozin's study support a learned-safety view of flavor-aversion learning.

Some psychologists (Best, 1975; Revusky, 1977) have criticized Kalat and

FIGURE 10.4
Mean casein hydrolysate consumption for ½-P, 3½-½-P and 4-P treatment conditions. From Kalat, J. W., & Rozin, P. "Learned safety" as a mechanism in long-delay taste-aversion learning in rats. *Journal of Comparative and Physiological Psychology*, 1973, *83*, 198–207. Copyright 1973 by the American Psychological Association. Reprinted by permission.

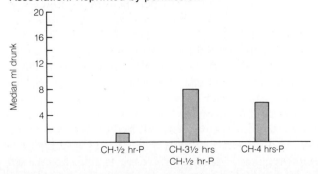

Rozin's learned-safety explanation of flavor-aversion learning. There are two main aspects of this criticism. First, Kalat and Rozin's view assumes that it takes only a single experience for an animal to learn that a food is safe. However, the degree of difficulty in establishing an aversion depends on the amount of prior experience to the food: the more experiences the subject has had with a food without illness, the longer it takes to establish an aversion. This observation does not necessarily mean that safe consumption is not being learned when a food is consumed without illness. Instead, like any other association, the strength of learned safety may vary with experience, and the degree of certainty with which a food can be safely consumed may increase with greater exposure to it without illness. Second, Best (1975) and Taukulis and Revusky (1975) reported that the presence of a familiar food will not cause animals to consume a different food previously paired with illness. Best suggested that exposure to a food without illness results in animals learning that the food is meaningless rather than safe. However, Kalat and Rozin's learning-safety view does not imply that animals can be nonselective in choosing their food, only that they can safely consume a particular food.

It should be noted that animals can learn that even a dangerous food can be consumed under some conditions. This knowledge, requiring the use of conditioned inhibition training (see Chapter 2), is illustrated by Taukulis and Revusky's (1975) study. In Taukulis and Revusky's study, rats drinking saccharin alone became ill; however, they did not become ill after drinking saccharin smelling of amyl acetate. Apparently, the amyl acetate odor inhibited the rats' aversion, allowing them to drink saccharin. A person learning that a specific food can be eaten safely in one restaurant but not another represents a real-world example of the operation of conditioned inhibition in flavor-aversion situations.

Concurrent Interference View   Revusky (1971) assumes that the associative processes influencing other forms of classical conditioning also affect flavor aversion learning. In all cases, classical conditioning reflects the association of a CS with a UCS. However, since animals often experience several stimuli prior to the UCS, which stimulus becomes associated with the UCS? According to Revusky, proximity is a critical factor in conditioning; the stimulus occurring closest to the UCS will become able to elicit the CR. In this view, a CS may be unable to elicit a CR if other stimuli occur between the CS and UCS. The failure of conditioning to occur when a stimulus is experienced between the CS and the UCS is called *concurrent interference* by Revusky. Revusky asserts that contiguity is essential in classical conditioning because a delay between the CS and UCS probably will produce concurrent interference. However, after eating a food, an animal is unlikely to consume another food for several hours. Thus, long-delay learning occurs in flavor-aversion learning as a result of the absence of concurrent interference.

Two areas of research support Revusky's concurrent interference view. First, instrumental responses can be learned with relatively long delays between the response and reinforcement when interference is minimized (see Chapter 3 for a discussion of this literature). Second, Revusky (1971) conducted a number of studies showing that the presence of other taste cues can interfere with the establishment of a flavor aversion. In a typical study, rats received initial exposure to saccharin (CS) followed by illness 75 minutes later. A second flavor was introduced 15 minutes after the CS and 1 hour before the UCS. For some subjects, tap water was the second solution; for others, it was vinegar. Revusky reported a weaker aversion to saccharin when vinegar rather than water was used as the second solution, indicating that the presentation of vinegar interfered with the establishment of the saccharin aversion. Furthermore, the amount of concurrent interference was related to the intensity of the vinegar: the stronger the vinegar, the weaker the aversion to saccharin. Revusky found maximum concurrent interference if the second flavor had previously been paired with illness and minimal concurrent interference if the second flavor had previously been experienced without illness.

Thus, when animals or people eat a new food and become ill, they form an association between the food and illness. This association causes them to subsequently avoid consuming that food; however, if no illness results, they learn that the food is safe and will consume it again in the future. An aversion may not develop if other foods are experienced between the initial food and illness.

Conditioned Medicine Effect

Suppose that your diet did not contain an essential nutrient. Research conducted during the 1930s indicates that you would stop eating the deficient diet and try new diets until you located one containing the required nutrient. After identifying the diet containing the needed nutrient, you would eat only this diet. How do you locate the diet with the required nutrient? According to Richter (1936), animals possess specialized receptors capable of detecting the presence of a dietary deficiency. For example, we know that animals whose adrenal glands are removed have an increased need for salt. Richter found that *adrenalectomized* rats show an increased preference for salt, consuming levels that normal rats avoid. Animals show an increased consumption of a large number of substances (for example, calcium, phosphorus, vitamins, and proteins) when their diets are deficient in these substances, or when a biological malfunction creates an additional need for them.

Recent evidence indicates that an animal's increased intake of the needed substance does not reflect an innate biological sensory system which can detect the presence of the nutrient; rather, the intake reflects a learned preference for a diet containing the deficient substance (Rozin & Kalat, 1971). According to Rozin and Kalat, an animal becomes ill because of a deficiency and develops an aversion to the deficient diet. The animal's taste aversion to its familiar diet causes it to search for and consume a new diet. If the new diet contains the needed nutrient, enabling the animal to recover, the animal then associates the new diet with recovery from illness and develops a strong preference for it.

In Rodgers and Rozin's study (1966), rats deprived of *thiamine* (vitamin B_{12}) rejected their diet, dug the food out of their dishes without eating it, and chewed on other objects in their cages. This behavior is identical to that of animals given unpalatable quinine. The old, deficient diet had apparently become aversive. When rats were given a new diet containing thiamine, they consumed large quantities of the new food. When offered a choice between the new diet containing the deficient nutrient and a second new diet, they showed a preference for the diet containing the needed nutrient. Similar results were reported by Rozin and Kalat (1971).

The preference for the new diet developed because the new diet was associated with recovery from illness. Garcia, Ervin, Yorke, and Koelling (1967) also placed animals on a thiamine-deficient diet. After several days of the deficient diet, they paired saccharin with an injection of thiamine. The thiamine injection produced a rapid recovery from the deficiency, and these animals consumed more saccharin than control animals that were not deficient when they received the saccharin-thiamine pairing. Also, Garcia, Hankins, and Rusiniak (1974) found that any taste presented during a rat's recovery from illness induced by lithium chloride will become a preferred taste. Animals are apparently capable of learning which foods produced a recovery from illness, as well as which foods induce illness (see Figure 10.5). One might speculate that many of our homemade remedies for illness (for example, chicken soup) may have coincidentally been paired with our natural recovery from illness. The treatment we think will make us well may merely reflect a "conditioned medicine effect."

Sign Tracking

Konrad Lorenz (1969) suggested that the instinctive systems of lower animals and people are programmed to change in response to both successful and failed experiences. These experiences, referred to as *conditioning,* provide additional

FIGURE 10.5
Temporal sequence of events which lead to a conditioned medicine effect.
Adapted from Garcia, J.; Hankins, W. G.; & Rusiniak, K. W. Behavioral regulation of the milieu interne in man and rat. *Science,* 1974, *185,* 824–831. Copyright 1974 by the American Association for the Advancement of Science. Reprinted by permission.

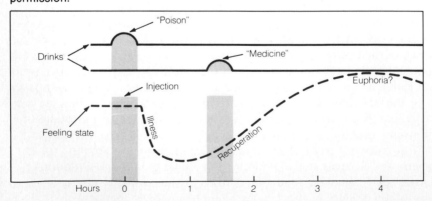

knowledge about the environment, which, in turn, enhances adaptability. According to Lorenz, conditioning can alter instinctive behavior, the stimuli which release instinctive behavior, or both. Only the *consummatory response* at the end of the behavior chain, according to Lorenz, is resistant to modification. Depending on the nature of the conditioning experience, this change can be either increased or decreased sensitivity. In addition, new behaviors or releasing stimuli can be developed through conditioning. All these modifications increase an animal's or person's ability to adapt to the environment.

Howard Liddell's experiment (reported by Lorenz, 1969) illustrates Lorenz's view. Working in Pavlov's laboratory, Liddell observed that Pavlov's dogs, conditioned to salivate when a metronome was presented, ran to the machine when they were released from their harness. The dogs then wagged their tails, barked, and jumped on the machine. What caused this behavior? According to Lorenz, these dogs behaved as they would if begging another dog for food. Apparently as the result of conditioning, the machine developed the capacity to release in dogs the same instinctive actions as those which might have been produced by their seeking another dog with food. When hungry, my family dog behaves in a manner similar to Pavlov's dogs. She approaches the bag containing her food and paws it until she is fed.

Studying Sign Tracking   Psychologists have not always appreciated the importance of Liddell's and Lorenz's observations. Traditionally, Pavlovian conditioning has been viewed from a narrow perspective. Through Pavlovian conditioning, environmental events become able to elicit instinctive visceral and skeletal responses. Conditioned responses can motivate instrumental behavior, which enables an animal to obtain reward or avoid punishment. However, the significance of conditioned stimuli to animals in natural settings has not been apparent until recently. During the late 1960s and 1970s, research conducted (Hearst, 1975; Jenkins, 1977) on *sign tracking* or *autoshaping* points to a valuable contribution of conditioned stimuli in the elicitation of instinctive behavior which enables animals to obtain reward, a view consistent with the observations of Liddell and Lorenz.

Animals need to locate reward (e.g., food, water) in their natural environment. How do they find these rewards? Environmental events, or stimuli, signaling the availability of reward are approached and contacted by animals seeking reward. By tracking these environmental stimuli an animal is able to obtain reward. Consider a predator tracking its prey: Certain sights, movements, odors, or noises are characteristic of the prey. The predator can catch the prey only by approaching and then contacting these stimuli. Research indicates that experience increases a predatory animal's ability to aim its instinctive biting response toward the desired part of the prey (Eibl-Eibesfeldt, 1970) and to attack motionless prey (Fox, 1969; Eibl-Eibesfeldt, 1961). Instrumental conditioning is not responsible for the establishment of effective predatory behavior, since a young predator's attack response improves even when its predatory behavior is unsuccessful. Furthermore, although nonpredatory animals can learn to kill other animals for food, they do not exhibit the instinctive species-specific response characteristic of predatory behavior. Pavlovian conditioning undoubtedly contributes to the enhancement of the predatory attack by causing the animal to approach and contact the stimuli characteristic of the prey.

Brown and Jenkins (1968) conducted the first sign tracking, or autoshaping, experiment. They placed pigeons in an operant chamber (see Figure 3.1); the environmental chamber contained a small circular key, which could be illuminated, and a food dispenser. Hungry pigeons were fed at 15-second intervals, and the key was illuminated for 8 seconds prior to each food presentation. The pigeons did not have to do anything to obtain food. Brown and Jenkins reported that the pigeons, instead of approaching the food dish when the food was presented, started to peck at the key. The animals' response toward the key resembles the manner in which they peck at grain. Remember that the pigeons did not have to peck at the key to obtain food, but the presentation of the illuminated key prior to food sufficiently established a key-pecking response. In fact, Williams and Williams (1969) reported that the pigeons pecked at the key even when pecking decreased the amount of food obtained. Many experiments on autoshaping have been conducted since Brown and Jenkins's initial observations. These studies (see Jenkins, 1977), indicating that Pavlovian conditioning is responsible for the pigeons' pecking at the illuminated key, use the illuminated key as the conditioned stimulus and food as the unconditioned stimulus. As the result of conditioning, the conditioned stimulus can elicit the instinctive pecking response identical to that naturally elicited by food. In natural settings, animals' response toward stimuli associated with food brings them in contact with food, thereby enabling them to obtain food.

Jenkins (1977) described several characteristics of the autoshaping process which point to an involvement of Pavlovian conditioning. First, pigeons' initial pecking at the illuminated key is not accidental: the pairing of the signal and food is necessary to produce pecking. Second, the predictiveness of the stimulus is a crucial element in the establishment of autoshaping. If the illuminated key does not reliably predict the occurrence of food, pigeons will not continue to peck at the key. Gamzu and Williams's (1971) study shows the influence of predictiveness on autoshaping. In their study, food was presented only when the key was illuminated for contingency subjects. Noncontingency subjects were given half their food when the key was illuminated and half when it was not. The results showed that when no contingency existed between the signal and food, autoshaping did not occur. Furthermore, Gamzu and Williams found that if the contingency was removed after the development of the key pecking, the pigeons stopped pecking at the key.

Perhaps you think that the pigeons' key pecking is an instrumental response reinforced by food rather than a conditioned response elicited by the illuminated key. If the key pecking is, indeed, an instrumental response, its characteristics would not differ with the use of various rewards. However, if the illuminated key is producing an instinctive response identical to that previously elicited by reward, the animals' response will differ with various rewards. The research on autoshaping with rewards other than that of food reveals that the key-pecking response observed by Brown and Jenkins is a conditioned response rather than an instrumental behavior.

Jenkins and Moore (1973) used either food or water as the reward in their autoshaping study. Observations of the pigeons' key-pecking responses demonstrated distinct differences between pigeons receiving the reward of food and those receiving water. Pigeons autoshaped with food key-pecked sharply and vigorously; their behavior resembled their response toward food. Animals autoshaped with water exhibited a slower, more sustained contact with the key. Furthermore, these pigeons frequently made swallowing movements; their behavior toward the key resembled their response to water. Jenkins and Moore also autoshaped pigeons using two keys: one with food reward, the other with water reward. They reported that these pigeons responded with intense short pecks to the key associated with food and with slow sustained contact to the key paired with water. Supporting Jenkins and Moore's observations, other studies also show that the response toward the key with the use of food reward differs from that used with water reward; see Wolin (1968) for another example.

In an interesting study of autoshaping, Rackham (1971) reported conditioned fetish behavior in pigeons. Rackham used four mated pairs of birds, housing the male and female of each pair in adjacent compartments of a large chamber with a sliding door separating the two birds. The stimulus, a light, was turned on daily just prior to the removal of the sliding door (moving the door allowed the male to initiate courtship with the female). Rackham initially observed that the pigeons' first reaction to the light was to approach it, nodding and bowing. The pigeons then began cooing, strutting, and pirouetting. Finally, midway through the study Rackham observed the pigeons emitting nest calls. The pigeons' response to the light stimulus was similar to that exhibited to the female. Also, the conditioned courtship response, like the autoshaped eating and drinking responses observed by Jenkins and Moore (1973), was directed toward the conditioned stimulus.

We have learned that animals approach and contact stimuli associated with reward. Further, the autoshaping process enables animals to track distant reward. The Hearst and Jenkins (1974) study illustrates the sign-tracking function of autoshaping. Hearst and Jenkins placed pigeons in a 6-ft alley with a food dish in the middle (see Figure 10.6); at each end of the alley a circular disk could be illuminated. One key was illuminated prior to food presentation; illumination of the other key was uncorrelated with food. Note that the pigeons had only 4 seconds to get food after the presentation; failure to walk to the food dish within 4 seconds resulted in no food on that trial.

Hearst and Jenkins reported that the pigeons, following several illuminated key-food pairings, ran to the end of the alley having the illuminated key associated with food, pecked at the key, and then ran to the center of the alley for food. The pigeons did not respond to the key unassociated with food presenta-

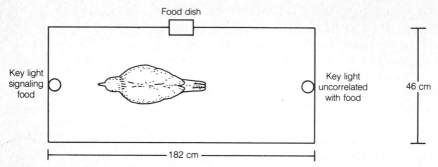

FIGURE 10.6
Illustration of top view of the apparatus used by Hearst and Jenkins to study sign tracking. From *The principles of learning and behavior* by M. Domjan and B. Burkhard. Copyright © 1982 by Wadsworth Inc. Reprinted by permission of Brooks/Cole Publishing Company, Monterey, Calif., 93940.

tion. Since the alley was long, the pigeons did not always reach the food dish before removal of the food, but they continued to respond to the illuminated key prior to going to the food, demonstrating the strong attraction of animals to stimuli associated with reward: the pigeons in the Hearst and Jenkins study did not have to peck to obtain food; they simply had to sit in the middle of the alley and wait for it. The birds' responding to the light associated with food indicates the power of a classically conditioned signal of reward.

Sign Tracking in Humans   Does the autoshaping process influence human behavior? Do we respond instinctively to signals for reward? Consider our response to a refrigerator to answer these questions. Certainly your refrigerator is associated with food. Traditionally, going to it to obtain food is considered to be an instrumental response; that is, a response which a person learns to get food. However, this may not be the case! Your response to the refrigerator is similar to your response to food: you approach, contact, open the refrigerator, and check out the many foods in it. The automatic reflexive character of going to the refrigerator is consistent with the idea that it is an instinctive response conditioned to a signal rather than an acquired instrumental response. People also show approach and contact behavior to signals associated with other rewards (e.g., water and sex). Research is necessary to show conclusively an involvement of Pavlovian conditioned instinctive behavior in the attainment of reward; the reflexive character of goal-seeking behavior in humans points to an influence of the autoshaping process in our responses to reach our goals.

Imprinting

Infant Love   You have undoubtedly seen young ducks swimming behind their mother in a lake. What process is responsible for the young birds' attachment to their mother? Konrad Lorenz (1952) investigated this social attachment process, calling it *imprinting*. Lorenz found that a newly hatched bird approaches, follows, and forms a social attachment to the first moving object it encounters. Although typically the first object that the young bird sees is its mother, birds have imprinted to many different and sometimes peculiar objects. In a classic demonstration of imprinting, newly hatched goslings imprinted on Konrad Lorenz and thereafter followed him everywhere. Birds have imprinted to colored boxes and other inanimate objects as well as to animals of different species. After imprinting, the young bird prefers the imprinted object to its real mother; this shows the strength of imprinting. Animal behaviorists (or ethologists) have conducted many studies investigating the imprinting process, and their research indicates that a number of factors affect an animal's social attachment.

Nature of Imprinting Object   Although animals have imprinted to a wide variety of objects, certain characteristics of the object affect the likelihood of imprinting. For example, Klopfer (1971) found that ducklings imprinted more readily to a moving object than to a stationary object. Also, ducks are more likely to imprint to an object that (1) makes "lifelike" rather than "gliding" movements (Fabricius, 1951); (2) vocalizes rather than remains silent (Collias & Collias, 1956); (3) emits short rhythmic sounds rather than long high-pitched sounds (Weidman, 1956); and (4) measures about 10 cm in diameter (Schulman, Hale, & Graves, 1970). Bateson (1966) and Kovach (1971) reported that chicks responded more to lights at the red rather than the green end of a visual spectrum. Harry Harlow (1971) observed that primates readily became attached to a soft terry cloth surrogate mother but developed no attachment to a wire mother. Harlow and Suomi (1970) found that infant monkeys preferred a terry cloth mother over a rayon, vinyl, or sandpaper surrogate; liked clinging to a rocking mother rather than to a stationary mother; and chose a warm (temperature) mother over a cold one. Mary Ainsworth and her associates (see Blehar, Lieberman, & Ainsworth, 1977), reporting a similar importance of a warm, responsive mother in the social attachment of human infants, found a strong attachment to mothers who were responsive and sensitive to their children's needs. In contrast, infants showed little attachment to anxious or indifferent mothers.

Sensitive Period   Age plays an important role in the imprinting process. Not only does imprinting occur readily in certain sensitive periods, but also imprinting is less likely to occur following this sensitive period. Illustrating the importance of age in imprinting, Jaynes's (1956) study exposed newly hatched New Hampshire chicks to cardboard cubes at different times. Jaynes reported that five-sixths of the chicks imprinted within one to six hours after hatching. However, only five-sevenths of the chicks met the criterion for imprinting when exposed to the cardboard cube six to twelve hours after hatching. The percentage declined to three-fifths at twenty-four to thirty hours, two-fifths at thirty to thirty-six hours, and only one-fifth at forty-eight to fifty-four hours.

However, the sensitive period merely reflects a greater difficulty of forming an attachment; when sufficient experience is given, imprinting will occur after the sensitive period has lapsed. For example, Boyd and Fabricius (1965) reported that ducklings not exposed to the imprinting object until ten days after hatching still formed an attachment. Brown (1975) trained ducklings ranging in age from 20 to 120 hours to follow an object to an equivalent degree. Brown found that although the older the duck, the longer the time required for the duckling to follow the imprinting object, all the ducklings with sufficient training showed an equal degree of attachment to the imprinted object.

The sensitive period for social attachment differs between species; in sheep and goats, it is two to three hours after birth (see Klopfer, Adams, & Klopfer, 1964); in primates, three to six months; and in humans, six to twelve months (Harlow, 1971).

Law of Effort   According to Hess (1973), the greater the effort expended by an animal during initial exposure to follow the imprinted object, the more likely imprinting is to occur. Consider a study by MacDonald and Solandt (1966) to illustrate the *law of effort*. They exposed 12- to 20-hour-old White Rock cornish chicks to a flickering light and a metronome sound. Some of the chicks were injected with the drug Flaxedril before experiencing the light and sound; Flaxedril blocks overt motor movements, thereby limiting the amount of effort expended by the chicks to interact with the imprinting object. Other chicks did not receive this drug, and thus could freely follow the light and sound. MacDonald and Solandt reported that nondrugged chicks showed a significantly stronger attachment to the imprinted object than did the drugged chicks. Other animal behaviorists have found an important influence of the amount of effort on the strength of imprinting (see Gottlieb, 1965, for another example).

A young animal's or person's attachment to "mother" is not the only form of imprinting. Imprinting is also responsible for the establishment of sexual, food, and location preferences. In addition, song learning in birds also appears to reflect the imprinting process.

Sexual Preference   Konrad Lorenz (1952) reported an interesting behavior in one of his male jackdaws. The bird attempted courtship feeding with him: it finely minced worms mixed with saliva and attempted to place the worms in Lorenz's mouth. When Lorenz did not open his mouth, he got an earful of worm pulp. Lorenz suggested that the male jackdaw had sexually imprinted to him. The sexual preference of many birds is established during a sensitive period (Eibl-Eibesfeldt, 1970; Lorenz, 1970). Also, the birds' sexual preference does not have to be for their own species; although in the absence of the preferred, imprinted species, sexual behavior will occur with their own species. Since sexual preference develops in immature birds when copulation is impossible, the establishment of the birds' sexual preference does not depend on sexual reinforcement. Furthermore, the imprinted birds' sexual fixation is not modified, even after sexual experience with another bird species. Perhaps this sexual imprinting is a cause of the development and persistence of human sexual preferences.

Food Preference   According to Hess (1962, 1964), animals' experience with food during a sensitive period of development results in the establishment of a food preference. This preference can develop to a nonpreferred food and, once established, is permanent. Consider Hess's (1973) study to illustrate the imprinting of a food preference. Chicks innately prefer to peck at a white circle on a blue background rather than a white triangle on a green background. Hess gave different groups of chicks of various ages experience with the less-preferred stimulus. As can be seen in Figure 10.7, the chicks developed a strong preference for the green-triangle stimulus experienced during days 3 to 4 after the chicks had hatched. Preference did not change if the experience occurred on day 1 or 2 or day 7 or 9 after hatching. These observations indicate that the sensitive period for the establishment of food preference in chicks is 3 to 4 days following hatching. Hess suggests that this time period for the establishment of a food preference is critical because 3-day-old chicks (1) no longer use the yolk sac for nutrients, and (2) can peck with maximum accuracy.

Humans differ considerably in their food preferences (Rozin, 1977). These preferences may to some degree reflect experience with a specific food during the sensitive period of development. People typically seem to prefer familiar foods, which suggests an imprinting influence in food preference. Food aversions in humans may also be sensitive to a developmental stage; Garb and Stunkard's (1974) observation that people are most apt to develop food aversions between the ages of 6 and 12 years old provides additional evidence that imprinting affects the establishment of food preferences and aversions.

Locality Imprinting   Evidence suggests that animals learn to prefer their initial environment. For example, Hess (1972) observed environmental imprinting in mallard ducklings. In Hess's study, one group of ducks hatched in a simulated-open-group nest; a second group hatched in a simulated-nest box.

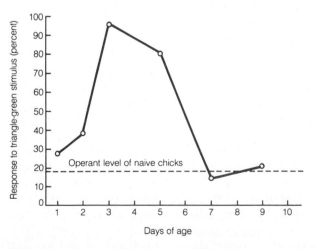

FIGURE 10.7
Percentage of responses to triangle-green stimulus as a function of age of initial exposure to stimulus. Adapted from Hess, E. H. Imprinting in birds. *Science,* 1964, *113,* 1132–1139. Copyright 1973 by the American Association for the Advancement of Science.

Some of the ducklings were kept in the nest for one day; others stayed there for two days. Hess reported that when these ducks later bred and nested in the wild, the ducks hatched in the simulated-open-ground nest used natural ground nests; in contrast, ducks kept in a simulated-nest box used elevated nest boxes in the wild. Note that this locality preference was seen only in ducks that stayed in the simulated nests for two days, not in ducks experiencing only one day of the simulated nest. Thus the time from one to two days is apparently the sensitive period for the establishment of locality preference in ducks. Other animal behaviorists have found locality preferences developing as the result of early experience; see Thorpe (1944, 1945) and Loehol (1959) for other examples.

Song Learning in Birds Experience plays an important role in the development of song in many bird species. These birds acquire song by imitating the song of experienced members of their species. Thorpe (1961) proposed that the song learning of these bird species exemplified imprinting. Several observations support this view (see Nottebohm, 1980, for a review of the song learning literature). First, there is a sensitive period for the establishment of song learning in these bird species: exposure to a conspecific after the sensitive period results in a lower likelihood of song learning. Second, even a short exposure to song during the sensitive period leads to permanent song learning. For example, Thielcke-Poltz and Thielcke (1960) observed song learning in blackbirds with 1-minute exposure to song during the sensitive period.

Nature of Imprinting What process accounts for animals' developing a social attachment (or food preference, sexual preference, locality preference, or song) during a specific developmental period? Two different views of imprinting have been offered: one suggests that associative learning is responsible for imprinting, and the other proposes that genetic programming produces imprinting. The evidence indicates that both instinctive and associative processes contribute to imprinting.

Associative Learning View Moltz (1960, 1963) proposed that classical and instrumental conditioning are responsible for social imprinting. Consider the imprinting of a chick to its mother to illustrate the associative learning view. When the chick is old enough to move around in its environment, large objects (for example, mother) in the environment attract the chick's attention, and it orients toward the object. The chick at this developmental age has little fear of new objects in its environment; therefore, only a low level of arousal will be conditioned to these objects. When the chick's fear system does emerge, new environmental objects will elicit high levels of arousal. Since familiar objects produce only low levels of arousal, their presence elicits relief. This relief reduces the chick's fear and reinforces its approach response, which enables it to reach the familiar object. Thus, the chick develops an attachment to mother (or any other object) because her presence elicits relief and, thereby, reduces the young chick's fear. A considerable amount of literature indicates that the imprinted object does have fear-reducing properties. For example, Bateson (1969) and Hoffman (1968) noted that the imprinting object's presence reduced distress vocalizations in birds. Harry Harlow's (1971) classic research with primates clearly shows the fear-reducing properties of "mama."

Harlow (1971) observed that young primates up to 3 months old do not exhibit any fear of new events; after 3 months, a novel object elicits intense fear. Young primates experience a rapid reduction in fear when clinging to their mother. For example, 3-month-old primates are extremely frightened when introduced to a mechanical monster or plastic toy and will run to their mother; clinging to her apparently causes the young primates' fear to dissipate. Human children show a similar development of fear at approximately 6 months of age (Schaffer & Emerson, 1964). Before this time, they exhibit no fear of new objects. After children are 6 months old, an unfamiliar object elicits fear, and children react by running to mother and clinging to her, which causes fear to subside.

Is this fear reduction responsible for the young primate's or human's attachment to "mother"? Harlow developed two inanimate surrogate mothers to investigate the factors influencing the attachment to the mother (see Figure 10.8). Each mother had a bare body of welded wire; one mother retained only the wire body, and the other was covered with soft terry cloth. In typical studies, primates were raised with both a wire and a cloth-covered surrogate mother. Frightened young primates experienced fear reduction when clinging to the cloth mother but showed no loss of distress when with their wire mother. When aroused, the infants were extremely motivated to reach their cloth

FIGURE 10.8
Cloth and wire surrogate mothers. (Courtesy of Harlow Primate Laboratory, University of Wisconsin.)

mother, even jumping over a high plexiglass barrier to get to it. In contrast, the frightened young primates showed no desire to approach the wire mother. Also, the young primate preferred to remain with the cloth mother in the presence of a dangerous object than to run away alone; however, if the wire mother was present, the frightened primate ran away.

Blehar, Lieberman, and Ainsworth (1977) reported a similar importance of security in human infants. They initially observed the maternal behavior of white middle-class Americans feeding their infants from birth to 54 weeks of age. They identified two categories of maternal care: one group of mothers showed responsivity and sensitivity to their children during feeding; the other mothers were indifferent to their infants' needs. During the second stage of their study, Blehar, Lieberman, and Ainsworth examined the behavior in a strange environment of these same infants at age 1 year. In the unfamiliar place, the interested mothers' children occasionally sought their mothers' attention; when left alone in a strange situation, these children were highly motivated to remain with the mother when reunited. In addition, once these children felt secure in the new place, they explored and played with toys. The researchers called this type of mother-infant bond a *secure relationship*. The behavior of these secure children strikingly resembles the response of Harlow's rhesus monkeys to the cloth mother. In contrast to this secure relationship, children of indifferent mothers frequently cried and were apparently distressed. Their alarm was not reduced by the presence of the mother. Also, Blehar, Lieberman, and Ainsworth reported that these children avoided contact with their mothers, either because the mothers were uninterested or because the mothers actually rejected them. The researchers labeled this mother-infant interaction an *anxious relationship*. The failure of the mothers of these anxious children to induce security certainly parallels the infant primates' response to the wire surrogate mother.

Our discussion indicates that the association of the mother with security determines the formation of social attachment of the infant to its mother. This observation supports the view that associative learning is involved in the imprinting process. However, other observations are inconsistent with a purely associative learning explanation of imprinting. Moltz's associative learning view suggests that initial conditioning of low arousal to the imprinting objects develops because the object is attention-provoking, orienting the animal toward the imprinting object. But we learned earlier that chicks imprint more readily to objects moving away than to objects moving toward them. One would assume that advancing objects would be more attention-provoking than retreating objects. Chicks' greater imprinting to objects moving away argues against an explanation of imprinting based only on simple associative learning. This observation points to another problem with an associative learning view. Some objects are more likely than others to become imprinting objects. For example, animals imprint more readily to objects having characteristics of adult members of their species. A simple associative explanation of imprinting would not assume that the characteristics of the imprinting object are important: any object attracting the animal's attention prior to the development of fear should become able to provide security and, therefore, a strong attachment should ensue. The importance of the specific attributes of the object in the formation of a social attachment argues against a purely associative explanation of imprinting. Further, observations concerning the other forms of imprinting argue against a purely associative view. Sexual preference develops in many bird species prior to the development of sexual maturity; the reinforcement mechanism for the establishment of sexual preference remains unclear. Song learning also appears to develop in the absence of any reward or punishment, and birds learn some songs more readily than others.

Thus associative learning cannot completely explain the imprinting process. Since the characteristics of imprinting objects are important, instinctive processes also affect imprinting.

Instinctive View of Imprinting   Konrad Lorenz (1935) suggested that imprinting is a genetically programmed form of learning. Imprinting is adaptive because it ensures that environmental events elicit instinctive reactions that enhance the animal's survival. Sensitivity to the imprinting object for only a brief period in an animal's life is also adaptive because it enhances the likelihood of survival. Hess (1973) also proposed that inheritance governs the imprinting process. The following quotation by Hess (1973) eloquently describes his view of the role of instinct in the social attachment of the young mallard to its mother:

> We must consider that young ducks innately possess a schema of the natural imprinting object, so that the more a social object fits this schema, the stronger the imprinting that occurs to the object. This innate disposition with regard to the type of object learned indicates that social imprinting is not just simply an extremely powerful effect of the environment upon the behavior of an animal. Rather, there has been an evolutionary pressure for the young bird to learn the right thing—the natural parent—at the right time—the first day of life—the time of the sensitive period that has been genetically provided for." (p. 380)

Several observations indicate that imprinting differs from other forms of associative learning (Graham, 1981). First, unlike other associative learning, imprinting is most likely to occur during a brief specified period of an animal's life. Second, the animal's response to the imprinting object is less susceptible to change than is an animal's reaction to events acquired through conventional associative learning. For example, conditioned stimuli which elicit saliva quickly extinguish when food is discontinued. Similarly, the absence of shock produces a rapid extinction of fear. In contrast, the elimination of reward does not typically lead to a loss of reaction to an imprinting object. Hess (1962, 1964) observed that once a 3- to 4-day-old chick developed a food preference to a less preferred object, this preference remained, despite the discontinuance of food reinforcement when the chick pecked at this object. In addition, punishment quickly alters an animal's response to conditioned stimuli associated with reward. Yet, animals seem insensitive to punishment from an imprinting object.

Kovach and Hess (1963) found that chicks approached the imprinting object despite its administration of electric shock. Harlow's (1971) classic research shows how powerful the social attachment of the infant primate is to its surrogate mother. Harlow constructed four very abusive "monster mothers." One rocked violently from time to time; a second projected an air blast in the infant's face. Primate infants clung to these mothers even while being abused. The other two monster mothers were even more abusive: one of them tossed the infant off her, and the other shot brass spikes as the infant approached. Although the infants were unable to cling to these mothers continuously, they resumed clinging as soon as possible when the abuse stopped. Harlow's observations indicate why abused children typically desire to return to their abusive parent (or parents). Apparently, a child's love for the parent makes possible the forgiveness of even the strongest abuse.

Our discussion indicates that instinct affects the imprinting process. Recall the evidence demonstrating that experience also influences an animal's or person's response to an imprinting object. Apparently, both associative and instinctive processes contribute to imprinting.

The Avoidance of Adversity

Species-Specific Defense Reactions   We discovered earlier in the chapter that animals possess instinctive responses enabling them to obtain reward (i.e., food, water, mate). Robert Bolles (1970, 1978) suggested that animals also have a *species-specific defense reaction* (*SSDR*), which allows them to avoid dangerous events. According to Bolles, animals have little opportunity to learn to avoid danger: they either possess instinctive means of keeping out of trouble or they perish. For example, a deer does not have time to learn to avoid its predator. If the deer does not possess instinctive means of avoiding the predator, it probably will wind up as the predator's meal.

The instinctive responses which enable animals to avoid adversity differ. An animal's evolutionary history determines which behaviors will become SSDRs: responses which enable animals to avoid adversity will remain in their genetic programming, whereas nonadaptive responses will not be passed on to future generations. According to Bolles, animals experiencing danger narrow their response repertoire to those behaviors which they expect will eliminate the danger. Since evolution has proved the species-specific defense reactions to be effective and other behaviors likely to produce failure, behaviors other than the species-specific defense reactions probably would be nonadaptive. Thus, animals limit their reactions to SSDRs as they attempt to avoid danger.

Rats employ three different species-specific defense reactions: running, freezing, and fighting. Rats attempt to run from a distant danger; a close danger motivates freezing. When these two responses fail, rats use aggressive behavior to avoid adversity. Other animals employ different instinctive responses to avoid danger: the mouse, as Bolles suggests in a quote from Robert Burns' ("To a Mouse"), is "a wee timorous beastie" when experiencing danger because this is the only way this small and relatively defenseless animal can avoid danger. In contrast, the bird just flies away to avoid adversity.

A study by Bolles and Collier (1976) demonstrates that the cues which predict danger not only motivate defensive behavior but also determine which response rats will exhibit when they expect danger. Bolles and Collier's rats received shock in a square or a rectangular box. After they had shocked the rats, the rats either remained in the dangerous environment or were placed in the other box where no shocks were given. They found that defensive behavior occurred only when the rats remained in the previously shocked compartment. These results indicate that physiological state does not control avoidance behavior, since all the rats were aroused; rather, it is the expectation of danger which motivates responding. Also, Bolles and Collier found that a dangerous square compartment produced a freezing response, while a running behavior occurred in the rectangular box. Apparently, the particular SSDR produced depends on the nature of the dangerous environment.

Psychologists have found that animals easily learn to avoid an aversive event when they can use an SSDR. For example, rats readily learn to run to avoid being shocked. Similarly, pigeons easily learn to avoid shock by flying from perch to perch. In contrast, animals have difficulty learning to avoid an aversive event when they must emit a behavior other than an SSDR to avoid adversity. D'Amato and Schiff's (1964) study provides an example of this difficulty. Trying to train rats to bar-press to avoid electric shock, D'Amato and Schiff reported that over half of their rats, even after having participated in more than 7000 trials over a 4-month period, failed to learn an avoidance response. Bolles (1969) reported that rats quickly learned to run in an activity wheel to avoid electric shock but found no evidence of learning when his rats were required to stand on their hind legs to avoid shock (see Figure 10.9). Although Bolles's rats stood on their hind legs in an attempt to escape from the compartment where they were being shocked, these rats did not learn the same behavior to avoid shock. According to Bolles, failure of the rats to stand on their hind legs is another example of animal misbehavior; their natural response in a small compartment was to freeze, and this innate SSDR prevented their learning a non-species-specific defensive reaction as the avoidance behavior.

Bedford and Anger (1968) observed the significant impact of instinct on the acquisition of an avoidance response. Although their pigeons had little difficulty learning to fly from one perch to another to avoid electric shock, Bedford and Anger reported that it was almost impossible to train the pigeons to peck at a key to avoid shock. Other psychologists have also found that pigeons experience great difficulty learning to key-peck to avoid shock; see Smith and Keller (1970) for another example.

A few rats eventually learn to bar-press to avoid electric shock. How do these rats learn an avoidance response which is not an SSDR? Bolles (1970) suggested that an animal learns a new avoidance response only by adapting an SSDR to the situation. In Bolles's view, if a rat is touching the bar when shock begins, this rat will freeze. The freezing then activates the bar and terminates

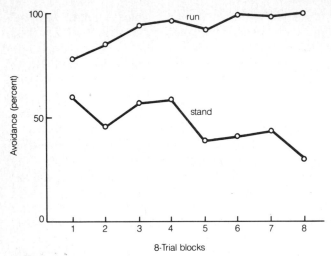

FIGURE 10.9
Percentage of avoidance responses during training in
animals that could avoid shock by running or standing on
their hind legs. From Bolles, R. C. Avoidance and escape
learning. *Journal of Comparative and Physiological
Psychology*, 1969, *68*, 355–358. Copyright 1969 by the
American Psychological Association. Reprinted by
permission.

the shock. Those animals which do not freeze on the bar will never learn to bar-press.

The Nature of Avoidance Learning   We saw earlier in the chapter that environmental events associated with reward will acquire the ability to elicit instinctive food-gathering behaviors as a conditioned response. This conditioned response causes animals to approach and contact reward, thereby enabling them to obtain reinforcement. This process is called sign tracking or autoshaping. Bolles (1978) suggested that *autoshaping* is also responsible for the development of avoidance learning. In Bolles's view, aversive events elicit instinctive species-specific defensive responses. The environment present during adversity becomes able to produce these instinctive defensive reactions as a conditioned response. Whereas instinctive CRs to cues associated with reward elicit approach and contact behavior which enables an animal to obtain reward, stimuli associated with adversity produce instinctive defensive responses which allow the animal to avoid adversive events. To illustrate the autoshaping approach to avoidance learning, consider Foree and LoLordo's (1970) study in which pigeons were trained to depress an 8-in triangle mounted 1.2 inches above the floor to avoid electric shock. Foree and LoLordo reported that their pigeons readily learned to depress the lever to avoid being shocked. According to Foree and LoLordo, jumping and wing flapping are instinctive uncondi-

tioned responses elicited by shock. These instinctive responses, when produced by cues associated with shock, enable pigeons to avoid shock effectively.

Bolles's approach assumes that Pavlovian conditioning rather than instrumental conditioning is responsible for avoidance learning. This theory considers avoidance behavior a conditioned rather than an instrumental behavior.
Also, the association of environmental stimuli with adversity rather than reinforcement is responsible for the development of avoidance behavior.

Bolles and Riley's (1973) study shows that reinforcement is not responsible
for the rapid acquisition of avoidance behavior. In their study, some animals
could avoid being shocked by freezing. Bolles and Riley reported that after only
a few minutes of training, their animals were freezing most of the time. Two
additional groups were included in their study: one group punished for freezing
could avoid shock by not freezing; the other group was shocked regardless of
their behavior. Bolles and Riley observed that the rats punished for freezing
still froze much of the time. Furthermore, rats punished for freezing froze as
much as rats shocked regardless of their behavior. According to Bolles, when
an animal is in a small confined area and anticipates adversity, it freezes. The
animals punished for freezing would still have frozen all the time, in Bolles's
view, had frequent shocks not disrupted their freezing. Yet, as soon as the
shock ended, the anticipation elicited the instinctive freezing response. Thus,
with the exception of shock-induced disruption of freezing in the animals punished for freezing, animals either rewarded or punished for freezing showed
equivalent levels of freezing. Apparently, the contingency between responding
and adversity did not affect the animals' behavior in Bolles and Riley's study.

Animals quickly learn to avoid adversity when a species-specific defensive
reaction enables them to avoid the aversive event, but they either cannot learn
or learn only with great difficulty to avoid adversity when a nonspecies-specific
defensive reaction is necessary for avoiding danger. What process is responsible for how quickly animals learn to avoid adversity? According to Bolles,
animals are prepared to learn the environmental events signaling danger. Once
animals anticipate danger, they possess an instinctive expectation that their
instinctive species-specific defensive reaction will enable them to avoid danger.
Thus, the environmental cues which signal danger also elicit a species-specific
defensive reaction to avoid that danger. In contrast, animals are contraprepared to learn that a new behavior will enable them to avoid adversity. This
contrapreparedness is based on the necessity to limit an animal's response to
danger since any animal which does not readily learn to avoid danger will
perish.

One additional topic deserves our attention. An animal or person's ability to
experience the pleasure of reward or the adversity of danger depends upon the
effective functioning of two central nervous system (CNS) structures. These
two CNS structures are involved in an animal's learning to obtain reward or
avoid adversity. We end our discussion by examining the biological basis of
reward and punishment.

THE BIOLOGY OF REWARD AND PUNISHMENT

Responses to reward and punishment differ considerably. Some of us are intensely motivated to obtain reward; others show a lack of interest in reinforcement. Similarly, punishment can readily modify some people's behavior; others seem totally oblivious to punishment. Although psychological factors clearly can affect our sensitivity to reward and punishment, physiological research during the past thirty years demonstrates that several brain systems are significantly involved in our responses to both reinforcers and adversity. Effective functioning of these systems allows us to obtain socially acceptable reward and avoid potential punishment. Malfunctions in these systems lead to pathological behavior.

Electrical Stimulation of the Brain

James Olds and Peter Milner's research (Olds & Milner, 1954) is a significant contribution to psychology. Olds and Milner found that stimulating some areas of the brain is reinforcing and that stimulating other areas is aversive. It is interesting that they made their classic observations accidentally when trying to determine the effects of activating the reticular formation. Their electrode placement mistakenly swung forward into the hypothalamus. When this area was aroused, their rats behaved as if stimulation was reinforcing. For example, the rats strongly preferred the place on the long table where they received the stimulation.

To evaluate their findings further, Olds and Milner made the electrical stimulation contingent on pressing a bar in an operant chamber (see Figure 10.10). They found that the rats pressed a bar to receive brain stimulation. The animals' behavior to obtain brain stimulation is called either *electrical stimulation of the brain* (ESB) or *intracranial self-stimulation* (ICSS). Many species, including pigeons (Goodman & Brown, 1966), rats (Olds & Milner, 1954), cats and dogs (Stark & Boyd, 1963), primates (Brady, 1961), and humans (Heath, 1955) have demonstrated that brain stimulation can be reinforcing.

Although Olds and Milner found that stimulating many brain areas provided reinforcement, activation of other brain areas was aversive. Animals receiving this aversive stimulation learned a new behavior to terminate or avoid it. For example, Delgado, Roberts, and Miller (1954) discovered that cats learned to turn a paddlewheel to terminate brain stimulation, just as they would have done to escape an electrical shock to the feet.

Anatomical Location of Reward and Punishment

Larry Stein and his associates (Stein, 1969) presented evidence indicating that a group of nerve fibers, the *medial forebrain bundle* (MFB) located in the limbic system, is the brain's reward center. Stimulation of the MFB motivates us to approach reward. In addition, another limbic system fiber tract, the *periventric-*

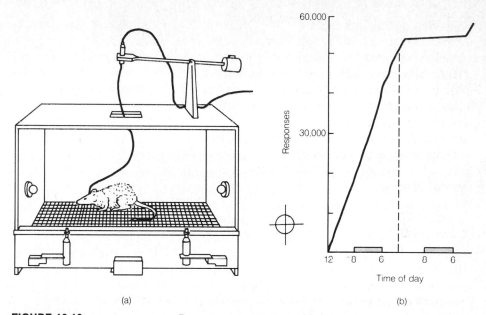

FIGURE 10.10
(a) Rat pressing a bar for electrical brain stimulation (ESB). (b) Sample cumulative record.
Note the extremely high rate of responding (over 2000 bar presses per hour) which
occurred for more than 24 hours and was followed by a period of sleep. Adapted from
Olds, J. Self-stimulation experiments and differentiated rewards. In H. H. Jasper, L. D.
Proctor, R. S. Knighton, W. C. Noshav, & R. T. Costello (Eds.), *Reticular formation of the
brain.* Boston: Little, Brown, 1958. Copyright 1958 by Little, Brown, and Company.

ular tract (PVT), represents the brain's punishment center. Activation of the
PVT motivates us to avoid punishment.

Stein also described how the reward (MFB) and punishment (PVT) systems
exert control over instrumental behavior. Activity in the PVT inhibits our
tendency to approach events. Stimulation of the MFB—by either internal activation or the presence of a reinforcing event—inhibits the amygdala. The
amygdala excites the PVT through the medial thalamus and hypothalamus;
inhibiting the amygdala lessens this excitation and thereby suppresses the effectiveness of the PVT punishment system. Stein's theory portrays animals and
humans as normally cautious when encountering new events. The MFB reward
system inhibits our hesitancy and motivates approach behavior.

MFB Reward System

Is This the Site of Reward?   Not only are most of the brain sites for reward
located in the MFB, but MFB stimulation causes more intense reinforcing
effects than stimulation of other brain areas does. For example, Olds, Travis,
and Schwing (1960) found that rats press a bar up to 10,000 times per hour for

MFB stimulation and only 500 times per hour for septum and amygdala stimulation.

Lesion studies also demonstrate the importance of the MFB in motivating reward-seeking behavior. These experiments (Morgane, 1961; Teitelbaum & Epstein, 1962) showed that destruction of the MFB impairs reward-seeking behavior. Apparently, the MFB must be intact if we are to be motivated by reward.

MFB Influence   Chapter 2 described Rescorla and Solomon's concept of the central appetitive motivational state. In this section we will see that the MFB is the site of the central appetitive motivational system.

The appetitive motivational state and stimulation of the MFB share four characteristics: (1) Activation of the central appetitive motivational state elicits appetitive behavior. Psychologists have discovered that MFB arousal motivates approach behavior too. (2) Stimulation of the MFB is highly reinforcing; animals will exert considerable effort to activate this system. We exert considerable effort to obtain stimuli (secondary reinforcers) which stimulate the central appetitive motivational state, indicating that arousal of this state is also reinforcing. (3) Reward and stimuli associated with reward activate the central appetitive motivational state, and evidence collected by numerous psychologists shows that reward enhances MFB functioning. (4) Deprivation increases the intensity of the approach behavior activated by the central appetitive motivational state. A similar influence of drive is found in MFB effectiveness.

The MFB's reinforcing and motivational abilities should not be surprising because conventional reinforcers (for example, money) also possess motivational properties. For example, the extreme measures taken by many children to obtain ice cream indicates that ice cream reinforces them, but the presence of ice cream often motivates them to consume large servings of it. Evidence which indicates that MFB stimulation is both reinforcing and motivating follows in the next sections.

Reinforcing Power of Stimulation of the MFB   Stimulation of the MFB is extremely reinforcing. Valenstein and Beer's study (1964) illustrating the impact of brain stimulation on rats found that for weeks, rats pressed a bar continuously up to thirty times per minute, stopping for only a short time to eat and groom. These rats responded until exhausted, fell asleep for several hours, and awoke to resume bar pressing. In addition, electrical stimulation of the brain (ESB) is more powerful than conventional reinforcers such as food, water, or sex. To illustrate that ESB has greater reinforcing value than other rewards, Routtenberg and Lindy (1965) constructed a situation in which pressing one lever caused brain stimulation and pressing another lever produced food. The experimental animals (rats) were placed in this situation for only one hour a day and had no other food source. All the rats spent the entire hour pressing for brain stimulation and eventually starved to death.

The pleasurable aspect of brain stimulation has also been demonstrated in humans. For example, Ervin, Mark, and Stevens (1969) reported that MFB stimulation not only eliminated pain in cancer patients but also produced a euphoric feeling (approximately equivalent to the effect of two martinis) lasting for several hours. Sem-Jacobson (1968) found brain stimulation to be pleasurable to patients suffering intense depression, fear, or physical pain; patients who felt well experienced only mild pleasure.

Motivational Influence of MFB Stimulation   The research of Elliot Valenstein and his associates (Valenstein, Cox, & Kakolewski, 1969) demonstrated that activation of the reward system also motivates behavior. The specific response motivated by brain stimulation depends on the prevailing environmental conditions. Thus, brain stimulation will motivate eating if food is available or drinking when water is present. This phenomenon is named *stimulus-bound behavior* to indicate that the stimulus environment determines which action is motivated by brain stimulation.

Electrical brain stimulation motivates behavior even when no internal deprivation exists. Why would brain stimulation cause an animal to eat food when not hungry or drink when not thirsty? Mendelson's study (1966) suggests that MFB activity makes environmental events more reinforcing and thereby motivates us to obtain these events. Mendelson placed his rats in a T maze (see Chapter 3); movement to one side of the maze produced ESB; movement to the other side produced both ESB and food. What did Mendelson's rats do in this situation? The previous discussion pointed out that animals will learn a new behavior to obtain ESB. Thus, we might predict that Mendelson's rats would favor both sides equally since they are not hungry. However, Mendelson reported that his subjects learned to go to the side producing both ESB and food.

Mendelson's rats first received the brain stimulation and then ate their food. Apparently, they experienced pleasurable brain stimulation which made their eating more enjoyable. This observation implies that the influence of reinforcement increases the reinforcing ability of other events.

Influence of Reward   Many people report that sexual intercourse is more pleasurable after watching an erotic film (Klein, 1982). According to our view of MFB functioning, the movie activates the MFB reward center, which then increases the reinforcing quality of sex. A number of studies have demonstrated that the presence of reward or stimuli associated with reward increases the reinforcing value of MFB activity.

Mendelson's study (1967) illustrates the influence of water on the reward value of ESB. Mendelson compared how often his rats pressed a bar to obtain brain stimulation when water was available with how often they pressed it in the absence of water. His results showed that rats pressed significantly more often when water was present. Coons and Cruce (1968) found that the presence of food increased the effort expended to obtain brain stimulation, and Hoebel (1969) discovered that a peppermint odor or a few drops of sucrose in the mouth produced a heightened self-stimulation response. These results indicate that the presence of reward makes brain stimulation more reinforcing.

Influence of Drive   Drinking ice water is very satisfying on a hot day, yet on a cold day ice water has little reinforcing quality. This example illustrates one characteristic of deprivation: drive increases the value of rewards. In this example, the presence of thirst on a hot day enhances the reward value of ice water. Increasing the activity of the brain's reward system probably is one mechanism that accounts for this drive effect. Studies which show that drive increases the value of brain stimulation definitely support that view. Let's look at several of these demonstrations.

Using rats, Brady (1961) showed that the rate of self-stimulation depends on the level of hunger; the longer his rats were deprived of food, the more intense was their rate of brain stimulation. Using water deprivation, Olds (1962) found that the value of brain stimulation is enhanced in rats deprived of water. The male sex hormone testosterone and the female sex hormone estrogen increase sexual motivation (Klein, 1982). Caggiula and Szechtman (1972) discovered that injecting rats with testosterone increased ESB; Prescott (1966) reported that the rate of brain stimulation increased in rats when estrogen levels increased during the estrus cycle and decreased when estrogen levels declined.

We know that MFB activity is pleasurable and that environmental reinforcers and internal drives activate the MFB system. Stimulating this reward system will motivate approach behavior to obtain reward. However, we also avoid aversive events.

PVT Punishment System　Chapter 2 detailed Rescorla and Solomon's central aversive motivational state, which is activated by aversive events and the anticipation of adversity. This stimulation results in terminating approach to reward and avoiding aversive and potentially aversive events. Much research indicates that the periventricular tract (PVT) is the site of Rescorla and Solomon's punishment system. Let's examine some of this evidence.

Stimulation of the PVT produces three effects identical to those induced by aversive events such as electrical shock (see Olds, 1962). First, PVT stimulation elicits jumping, biting, and vocalizations, all behaviors which electrical shock and other painful agents can produce. Second, both PVT stimulation and conventional punishers suppress reward-seeking behavior. Third, animals are motivated to terminate PVT stimulation as well as to acquire behaviors which prevent activation of the PVT. Shock and other aversive events also motivate escape and avoidance behaviors.

Destruction of the PVT produces animals insensitive to aversive events. For example, Margules and Stein (1969) noted that rats with PVT lesions showed large deficits in their ability to avoid electrical shock. Apparently, effective avoidance and escape from aversive events depend on the effective functioning of the PVT. In the next section we will see that malfunctions in the MFB and PVT can lead to behavioral disturbances in humans.

Reward and Punishment Systems in Behavior Pathology

Many prominent psychologists (Snyder, 1974; Stein & Wise, 1971, 1973; Valenstein, 1973) have suggested that behavioral disturbances can result from failure of the reward and punishment systems to operate effectively. Two major categories of abnormal behavior—depression and phobias—have been linked to malfunctions in the reward and punishment systems. Contemporary evidence implicates a reward system that functions at low levels in depressives' failure to obtain satisfaction from reward. Phobics' extreme fear is thought to be caused by intense arousal of the punishment system.

Chemistry of Reward and Punishment

MFB Reward System   Many studies support the idea that two catecholamine substances, *norepinephrine* and *dopamine*, are the chemical transmitter substances in the MFB reward system (Stein, 1969; Stein & Wise, 1969). Several of these studies are briefly described.

Margules (1969) found that an injection of amphetamine, a drug which stimulates the release of both norepinephrine and dopamine, enhances the reinforcing value of ESB. Olds (1970) and Stein and Wise (1974) made similar observations. Other experiments (Olds, 1975; Stein & Wise, 1973) have discovered that direct administration of the catecholamines into the MFB reward system also increases the rate of brain stimulation.

Drugs which inhibit the MFB reward system decrease the reinforcing effect of self-stimulation. Stein and Wise (1969) reported that administration of a-methyl-paratyrosine (AMPT), a drug which prevents the synthesis of both norepinephrine and dopamine, decreases the rate of brain stimulation. Also, administration of chlorpromazine, a drug which blocks both norepinephrine and dopamine neural transmission, attenuates the reinforcing value of ESB. Other experiments (Cooper, Cott, & Breese, 1974; Liebman & Butcher, 1974; Wauguier & Niemegeers, 1975) have also concluded that drugs which antagonize noradrenergic and dopaminergic neurons (those neurons for which dopamine is the transmitter substance) either reduce or eliminate responding aimed at brain stimulation.

The PVT Punishment System   The chemical transmitter substance *acetylcholine* has been implicated in the motivation of escape and avoidance behavior (Carlton, 1969; Stein, 1969). Injections of drugs which activate cholinergic neurons (those neurons for which acetylcholine is the transmitter substance) increase the influence of punishing agents. In contrast, drugs which block cholinergic activity reduce the effectiveness of punishment.

The experiments by Margules and Stein (1967) provide direct evidence of cholinergic transmission in the PVT punishment system. They injected directly into the punishment area drugs which either increase cholinergic activity (for example, carbachol) or decrease it (for example, atropine). Before being injected, their rats had been trained to press a bar for a reward (milk) and had experienced a tone paired with electrical shocks. Margules and Stein administered the injections while presenting this tone. They reported that drugs which aroused cholinergic neurons increased the effectiveness of the tone in suppressing bar pressing. Drugs which inhibit cholinergic neurons decreased the suppressive ability of the tone.

The Pharmacology of Behavioral Disturbance   We have seen that adrenergic and dopaminergic neurons in the MFB reward system are activated when we seek reward. Moreover, cholinergic neurons in the PVT punishment system are aroused when we avoid adversity. Under ideal conditions, the effective functioning of these two systems enables us to obtain reward and avoid punishment. Evidence suggests that malfunctions in either the reward or the punishment system are involved in depression and phobic behavior.

Depression   A central characteristic of depression is a lack of interest in reward (Klein, 1982). Considerable evidence indicates that lowered responsivity of the catecholamine neurons in the MFB reward system contributes to the development of depression in humans (see Chapter 6).

Studies evaluating amine levels have demonstrated a deficiency in depressed individuals (Depue & Evans, 1976). For example, Ashcroft, Crawford, and Eccleston (1966) measured the level of a serotonin metabolite (5-hydroxyindole acetic acid or 5HIAA) in the cerebrospinal fluid of depressed and nondepressed persons and found lower levels of 5HIAA in the depressives. Similarly, several other studies (for example, Maas, Dekirmenjian, & Fawcett, 1971) point to a low level of the cerebrospinal metabolite (3-methoxy-4-hydroxyphenylethylene glycol or MHPG) of norepinephrine in depressives.

Drugs which decrease brain amine levels induce depressive behavior. Lemieux, Davignon, and Genest (1956) reported that reserpine, a drug which reduces levels of serotonin and norepinephrine, produced depression. In contrast, drugs which elevate brain amine levels are able to decrease depressive symptoms. For example, the tricyclic compounds increase brain norepinephrine by interfering with its reuptake after the neuron fires. Davis, Klerman, and Schildkraut (1967) found tricyclic drugs effective in the treatment of many depressives.

The research of Thomas and Balter (1975) provides support for the role of the MFB in depression. The septum area of the limbic system inhibits the MFB. The chemical transmitter within the septum is acetylcholine. Thomas and Balter found that chemical stimulation of the septum produced the behavioral passivity characteristic of depression. In another study, Thomas and Balter noted that if rats which had received uncontrollable shock were injected with atropine, their behavioral passivity was reduced. Since atropine blocks acetylcholine activity, the lowered depression produced by atropine supports the idea that the central reward system is involved in depression. Janowsky, El-Yousef, Davis, Hubbard, and Sekerke (1972) noticed a similar influence of cholinergic drugs in humans. Injecting nondepressives with physotigmine—a drug which increases acetylcholine level by blocking its breakdown during neural transmission—produced feelings of helplessness and suicidal wishes. Atropine reduced their feelings of depression. Thus the normal functioning of the catecholamine neurons in the MFB reward system is necessary for us to appreciate reinforcing events.

Phobic Behavior   Phobics are intensely motivated to avoid adversity. Although psychological processes undoubtedly contribute to phobic behavior, some evidence indicates that an overresponsive PVT punishment system contributes to a phobic's preoccupation with avoiding a specific aversive event.

Suppose that you feel extremely anxious about your forthcoming examinations and do not know whether you can take them. Your doctor might prescribe a tranquilizer as treatment for this excessive fear. Two frequently prescribed tranquilizers used to treat anxiety are chlordiazepoxide (Librium) and diazepam (Valium). Other common antianxiety drugs are the barbiturates (for example, pentobarbital) and alcohol.

Animal research clearly demonstrates the capacity of the antianxiety drugs to reduce fear (see Gray, 1971). Conger (1951) trained rats to run down an alley to obtain food and then shocked them before they entered the goal box. This procedure established an approach-avoidance conflict (see Chapter 2). Conger discovered that an alcohol injection reduced the suppressive effects of the electrical shock: the animals that received alcohol ran into the goal box. In contrast, animals given a control injection of water would not approach the goal box. It is possible that the effect of alcohol was not to reduce fear but to increase hunger. Conger used Brown's concept of strength of approach-avoidance tendencies to test this assertion. He measured his rats' approach to reward or avoidance of punishment. Testing either mildly drunk or sober rats, he found that alcohol reduced the aversiveness of punishment but had no effect on the attractiveness of reward. These results demonstrate that alcohol directly antagonizes the suppressive effects of punishment. Bailey and Miller (1952) discovered that the barbiturate sodium amytal also reduced the influence of electric shock in an approach-avoidance situation.

The observation that the antianxiety drugs antagonize fear suggests that these drugs affect the PVT punishment system. Margules and Stein (1967) provided additional direct evidence by finding that the barbiturate oxazempam not only reduced the suppressive effects of conventional aversive events (for example, electric shock or bitter quinine) but also antagonized the punishing effects of brain stimulation.

SUMMARY

Psychologists have generally assumed that some laws govern the learning of all behaviors. This view has enabled psychologists in the laboratory to study behaviors not exhibited in natural settings. However, psychologists have recently discovered that the biological character of a species determines what an animal can or cannot learn. A species's biological structure sometimes prepares it to learn some behavior rapidly; at other times, its biological equipment causes it to be contraprepared to learn—to learn slowly or not at all. An animal is unprepared to learn when its biological character neither facilitates nor prevents learning.

Breland and Breland trained many exotic behaviors in a wide variety of animal species; however, they found that some operant responses, although initially performed effectively, deteriorated with continued training despite repeated food reinforcements. The deterioration of the operant behavior is called instinctive drift, and the instinctive behavior which prevents continued effectiveness of the operant response is an example of animal misbehavior. Recent research indicates that animal misbehavior occurs when (1) the stimuli present during operant conditioning resemble the natural cues controlling food-gathering activities, (2) these stimuli are paired with food reinforcement, and (3) the instinctive food-gathering behaviors elicited by the stimuli present during conditioning are reinforced.

Animals receiving reinforcement on an interval schedule of reinforcement exhibit a wide variety of instinctive behaviors (e.g., drinking, running, grooming, nest building, aggression). Although there is no contingency between these behaviors and reward, excessive levels of these schedule-induced behaviors occur; the highest level, called adjunctive behavior, is observed in the time period following reward. Several factors increase the intensity of adjunctive behavior: (1) higher levels of deprivation, (2) greater reward value, and (3) shorter interval length. Schedule-induced behavior occurs because an animal expects reward to be unavailable for a specified period of time after reinforcement. This expectation elicits the emotion of frustration, with the instinctive appetitive behavior producing pleasure and, thereby, reducing the negative emotional frustration state.

When an animal or person experiences illness after eating a particular food, an association between the food and illness develops. Subsequently, this association causes the animal or person to avoid that food. A flavor aversion can be formed even when illness occurs several hours after experience with the food: the association of the flavor with delayed illness is often referred to as long-delayed learning. Like other conditioned responses, there is a delay gradient whereby the closer the occurrence of the flavor and illness, the faster the conditioning of the flavor aversion. However, in the case of flavor-aversion learning, the delay gradient lasts several hours rather than seconds or minutes. Salience affects the strength of flavor-aversion learning: some stimuli are more likely to become associated with illness than others are. Nocturnal animals, like rats, associate flavor more readily with illness than with environmental events. In contrast, visual stimuli are more salient than flavor cues in diurnal animals like birds or guinea pigs.

Two views have been offered to explain flavor-aversion learning: Kalat and Rozin's learned-safety view and Revusky's concurrent interference theory. When an animal eats a food and no illness results, it learns that the food can be safely consumed in the future; however, if the animal becomes ill after eating, an association between the food and illness is formed, and the animal will subsequently avoid that food. An aversion may not develop if other foods are experienced between the initial food and illness.

Animals not only develop an aversion to foods associated with illness, they also learn to prefer foods paired with the recovery from illness. This preference, called a conditioned medicine effect, develops even if the food does not produce the recovery. There are occasions when an animal's diet is deficient. In these cases, the animal becomes ill and develops an aversion to the deficient diet. The animal's flavor aversion to its familiar diet causes it to search for and consume a new diet. If the new diet contains the needed nutrient, the animal will recover, associate the new diet with recovery from illness, and develop a strong preference for it.

Animals need to locate reward in their environment. Environmental events signaling the availability of reward are approached and contacted by animals seeking reward. The animal's response to these events enables it to obtain desired rewards. The ability of these events to elicit approach and contact behavior is acquired through classical conditioning. As the result of conditioning, the conditioned stimulus becomes able to elicit instinctive responses identical to those naturally elicited by reward. The process of an animal learning to reach a desired reward by using conditioned instinctive behaviors is called sign tracking or autoshaping.

Young animals through the imprinting process develop strong attachments to their mother; this attachment has considerable adaptive significance during the young animal's years of dependency. Animals are more likely to imprint during a specified period of development called a sensitive period. Although animals can imprint to any object experienced during the sensitive period, they are more likely to imprint to objects having characteristics of their species. Also, during initial exposure to an object, the more effort an animal expends to follow this object, the more likely that imprinting will occur. The animal's attachment to the imprinted object reflects both associative and instinctive processes. Animals during sensitive periods of development also show other forms of imprinting: they develop sexual preferences, food preferences, and locality preferences, and they learn to sing.

Animals possess instinctive responses called species-specific defense reactions which allow them to avoid dangerous events. These instinctive means of keeping out of trouble are programmed into animals' genetic structure, since they have little opportunity to learn to avoid danger in the real world. Bolles suggested that animals are prepared to learn the environmental events signaling danger. Once animals anticipate danger, they will readily learn to avoid it if a species-specific defense reaction is effective. However, if a non-species-specific defense reaction is required to avoid an aversive event, animals will learn with extreme difficulty or will not learn at all.

Specialized neural systems control our responses to reinforcers and punishers. Arousal of the medial forebrain bundle (MFB), the brain's reward system, causes pleasure. Research indicates that the presence of reward activates the MFB; arousal of the MFB motivates us to seek the reward. Drive also increases MFB activity, thereby increasing the value of reinforcers. In contrast, activity in the periventricular tract (PVT), the brain's punishment center, is unpleasant. Punishers activate this system, motivating escape and avoidance behavior. Behavioral disturbances can result when reward and punishment systems operate ineffectively. Contemporary evidence implicates a low-level functioning of the reward system in depressives' failure to obtain satisfaction from reward, and phobics' extreme fear is thought to be caused by intense arousal of the punishment system.

REFERENCES

Abramson, L. Y. Universal versus personal helplessness: An experimental test of the reformulated theory of learned helplessness and depression. Doctoral dissertation, University of Pennsylvania, 1977.

———; Garber, J.; & Seligman, M. E. P. Learned helplessness in humans: An attributional analysis. In J. Garber and M. E. P. Seligman (Eds.), *Human helplessness: Theory and applications*. New York: Academic, 1980.

———, & Sackeim, H. A. A paradox in depression: Uncontrollability and self-blame. *Psychological Bulletin,* 1977, *84,* 838–851.

———; Seligman, M. E. P.; & Teasdale, J. D. Learned helplessness in humans: Critique and reformulation. *Journal of Abnormal Psychology,* 1978, *87,* 49–74.

Adelman, H. M., & Maatsch, J. L. Learning and extinction based upon frustration, food reward and exploratory tendency. *Journal of Experimental Psychology,* 1956, *52,* 311–315.

Agranoff, B. W. Biochemical events mediating the formation of short-term and long-term memory. In Y. Tsukada and B. W. Agranoff (Eds.), *Neurobiological basis of learning and memory*. New York: Wiley, 1980.

———; Davis, R. E.; Casola, L.; & Lim, R. Actinomycin D blocks formation of memory of shock avoidance in goldfish. *Science,* 1967, *158,* 1600–1601.

Alford, G. S., & Turner, S. M. Stimulus interference and conditioned inhibition of auditory hallucinations. *Journal of Behavior Therapy and Experimental Psychiatry,* 1976, *7,* 155–160.

Alloway, T. M. Effects of low temperature upon acquisition and retention in the grain beetle (*Tenebrio molitor*). *Journal of Comparative and Physiological Psychology,* 1969, *69,* 1–8.

Alloy, L. B., & Abramson, L. Y. Judgment of contingency in depressed or nondepressed students: Sadder but wiser? *Journal of Experimental Psychology: General,* 1979, *108,* 441–485.

———, & Tabachnik, N. Assessment of covariation by humans and animals: The joint influence of prior expectations and current situational information. *Psychological Review*, 1984, *91*, 112–149.

Amsel, A. The combination of a primary appetitional need with primary and secondary emotionally derived needs. *Journal of Experimental Psychology*, 1950, *40*, 1–14.

―――. The role of frustrative nonreward in noncontinuous reward situations. *Psychological Bulletin*, 1958, *55*, 102–119.

―――. Behavior habituation, counterconditioning, and a general theory of persistence. In A. H. Black and W. F. Prokasy (Eds.), *Classical conditioning II: Current research and theory*. New York: Appleton-Century-Crofts, 1972.

―――, & Roussel, J. Motivational properties of frustration. I. Effect on a running response of the addition of frustration to the motivational complex. *Journal of Experimental Psychology*, 1952, *43*, 363–368.

Anderson, J. R., & Bower, G. H. *Human associative memory*. Washington, D.C.: Winston, 1973.

Anderson, N. H. Comparison of different populations: Resistance to extinction and transfer. *Psychological Review*, 1963, *70*, 162–179.

Andrews, E. A., & Braveman, N. S. The combined effects of dosage level and interstimulus interval on the formation of one-trial poison-based aversions in rats. *Animal Learning and Behavior*, 1975, *3*, 287–289.

Annau, Z., & Kamin, L. J. The conditioned emotional response as a function of intensity of the US. *Journal of Comparative and Physiological Psychology*, 1961, *54*, 428–432.

Appel, J. B. Punishment and shock intensity. *Science*, 1963, *14*, 528–529.

Armus, H. L. Effect of magnitude of reinforcement on acquisition and extinction of a running response. *Journal of Experimental Psychology*, 1959, *58*, 61–63.

Aronfreed, J., & Leff, R. The effects of intensity of punishment and complexity of discrimination upon the generalization of an internalized inhibition. Manuscript, University of Pennsylvania, 1963.

Ashcroft, G.; Crawford, T.; & Eccleston, E. 5-Hydroxyindole compounds in the cerebrospinal fluid of patients with psychiatric or neurological disease. *Lancet*, 1966, *2*, 1049–1052.

Atkinson, J. W. *Motives in fantasy, action and society*. Princeton, N.J.: Van Nostrand, 1958.

―――. *An introduction to motivation*. Princeton, N.J.: Van Nostrand, 1964.

Atkinson, R. C., & Shiffrin, R. M. The control of short-term memory. *Scientific American*, 1971, *225*, 82–90.

Atwater, S. K. Proactive inhibition and associative facilitation as affected by degree of prior learning. *Journal of Experimental Psychology*, 1953, *46*, 400–404.

Averbach, E. The span of apprehension as a function of exposure duration. *Journal of Verbal Learning and Verbal Behavior*, 1963, *2*, 60–64.

―――, & Coriell, A. S. Short-term memory in vision. *Bell System Technical Journal*, 1961, *40*, 309–328.

―――, & Sperling, G. Short-term storage of information in vision. In C. Cherry (Ed.), *Fourth London Symposium on Information Theory*. London and Washington, D.C.: Butterworth, 1961.

Ayllon, T., & Azrin, N. H. The measurement and reinforcement of behavior of psychotics. *Journal of the Experimental Analysis of Behavior*, 1965, *8*, 357–383.

―――, & ―――. *The token economy: A motivation system for therapy and rehabilitation*. New York: Appleton-Century-Crofts, 1968.

————; Layman, D.; & Kandel, H. J. A behavioral-educational alternative to drug control of hyperactive children. *Journal of Applied Behavior Analysis,* 1975, *8,* 137–146.

Azrin, N. H. Some effects of two intermittent schedules of immediate and nonimmediate punishment. *Journal of Psychology,* 1956, *42,* 3–21.

————. Sequential effects of punishment. *Science,* 1960, *13,* 605–606.

————. Aggression. Paper presented at the American Psychological Association Meeting, Los Angeles, September 1964.

————; Hake, D. F.; Holz, W. C.; & Hutchinson, R. R. Motivational aspects of escape from punishment. *Journal of the Experimental Analysis of Behavior,* 1965, *8,* 31–44.

————, & Holz, W. C. Punishment. In W. K. Honig (Ed.), *Operant behavior: Areas of research and application.* New York: Appleton-Century-Crofts, 1966.

————; Holz, W. C.; & Hake, D. F. Fixed-ratio punishment. *Journal of the Experimental Analysis of Behavior,* 1963, *6,* 141–148.

————; Hutchinson, R. R.; & Hake, D. F. Extinction-induced aggression. *Journal of the Experimental Analysis of Behavior,* 1966, *9,* 191–204.

————; ————; & McLaughlin, R. The opportunity for aggression as an operant reinforcer during aversive stimulation. *Journal of the Experimental Analysis of Behavior,* 1965, *8,* 171–180.

————; ————; & Sallery, R. D. Pain aggression toward inanimate objects. *Journal of the Experimental Analysis of Behavior,* 1964, *7,* 223–228.

————; Sneed, T. J.; & Foxx, R. M. Drybed. A rapid method of eliminating bedwetting (enuresis) of the retarded. *Behavior Research and Therapy,* 1973, *11,* 427–434.

Bacon, W. E. Partial-reinforcement extinction following different amounts of training. *Journal of Comparative and Physiological Psychology,* 1962, *55,* 998–1003.

Baddeley, A. D. *The psychology of memory.* New York: Basic Books, 1976.

————, & Scott, D. Short-term forgetting in the absence of proactive inhibition. *Quarterly Journal of Experimental Psychology,* 1971, *23,* 275–283.

Baer, D. M. Laboratory control of thumbsucking by withdrawal and representation of reinforcement. *Journal of the Experimental Analysis of Behavior,* 1962, *5,* 525–528.

Bailey, C. J., & Miller, N. E. The effect of sodium amytal on an approach-avoidance conflict in cats. *Journal of Comparative and Physiological Psychology,* 1952, *45,* 205–208.

Bailey, J. S.; Wolf, M. M.; & Phillips, E. L. Home-based reinforcement and the modification of pre-delinquents' classroom behavior. *Journal of Applied Behavior Analysis,* 1970, *3,* 223–233.

Baker, A. G. Learned irrelevance and learned helplessness: Rats learn that stimuli, reinforcers and responses are uncorrelated. *Journal of Experimental Psychology: Animal Behavior Processes,* 1976, *2,* 130–141.

————, & Mackintosh, N. J. Excitatory and inhibitory conditioning following uncorrelated presentations of CS and US. *Animal Learning and Behavior,* 1977, *5,* 315–319.

————, & ————. Pre-exposure to the CS alone, US alone or CS and US uncorrelated: Latent inhibition, blocking by context, or learned irrelevance? *Learning and Motivation,* 1979, *10,* 278–294.

————; Mercier, P.; Gabel, J.; & Baker, P. A. Contextual conditioning and the US preexposure effect in conditioned fear. *Journal of Experimental Psychology: Animal Behavior Processes,* 1981, *7,* 109–128.

Balsam, P. D., & Schwartz, A. L. Rapid contextual conditioning in autoshaping. *Journal of Experimental Psychology: Animal Behavior Processes,* 1981, *7,* 382–393.

Bandura, A. *Social learning theory*. Morristown, N.J.: General Learning, 1971.

———. Self-efficacy: Toward a unifying theory of behavior change. *Psychological Review*, 1977, *84*, 191–215.

———, & Adams, N. E. Analysis of self-efficacy theory of behavioral change. *Journal of Personality and Social Psychology*, 1977, *1*, 287–310.

———; ———; & Beyer, J. Cognitive processes mediating behavioral change. *Journal of Personality and Social Psychology*, 1977, *35*, 125–129.

———; Blanchard, E. B.; & Ritter, R. The relative efficacy of desensitization and modeling approaches for inducing behavioral, affective, and attitudinal changes. *Journal of Personality and Social Psychology*, 1969, *13*, 173–199.

———; Grusec, J. E.; & Menlove, F. L. Vicarious extinction of avoidance behavior. *Journal of Personality and Social Psychology*, 1967, *5*, 16–23.

———; Jeffrey, R. W.; & Gajdos, F. Generalizing change through participant modeling with self-directed mastery. *Behavior Research and Therapy*, 1975, *13*, 141–152.

———, & Menlove, F. L. Factors determining vicarious extinction of avoidance behavior through symbolic modeling. *Journal of Personality and Social Psychology*, 1968, *8*, 99–108.

———, & Perloff, B. Relative efficacy of self-monitored and externally imposed reinforcement systems. *Journal of Personality and Social Psychology*, 1967, *7*, 111–116.

———, & Rosenthal, T. L. Vicarious classical conditioning as a function of arousal level. *Journal of Personality and Social Psychology*, 1966, *3*, 54–62.

———; Ross, D.; & Ross, D. A. Imitation of film-mediated aggressive models. *Journal of Abnormal and Social Psychology*, 1963, *66*, 3–11.

———, & Walters, R. H. *Adolescent aggression*. New York: Ronald, 1959.

Banks, R. K., & Vogel-Sprott, M. Effect of delayed punishment on an immediately rewarded response in humans. *Journal of Experimental Psychology*, 1965, *70*, 357–359.

Barlow, D. H.; Agras, W. S.; Leitenberg, H.; & Wincze, J. P. An experimental analysis of the effectiveness of "shaping" in reducing maladaptive avoidance behavior: An analogue study. *Behaviour Research and Therapy*, 1970, *8*, 165–173.

Barnes, G. W. Conditioned stimulus intensity and temporal factors in spaced-trial classical conditioning. *Journal of Experimental Psychology*, 1956, *51*, 192–198.

Barnes, J. M., & Underwood, B. J. "Fate" of first-list associations in transfer theory. *Journal of Experimental Psychology*, 1959, *58*, 97–105.

Baron, A. Delayed punishment of a runway response. *Journal of Comparative and Physiological Psychology*, 1965, *60*, 131–134.

Barondes, S. H., & Cohen, H. D. Puromycin effect on successive phases of memory storage. *Science*, 1966, *151*, 594–595.

———, & ———. Comparative effects of cycloheximide and puromycin on cerebral protein synthesis and consolidation of memory in mice. *Brain Research*, 1967, *4*, 44–51.

Barry, H., III. Effects of strength of drive on learning and on extinction. *Journal of Experimental Psychology*, 1958, *55*, 473–481.

Bartlett, F. C. *Remembering: A study in experimental and social psychology*. London: Cambridge University Press, 1932.

Barton, E. S.; Guess, D.; Garcia, E.; & Baer, D. M. Improvement of retardates' mealtime behaviors by time-out procedures using multiple baseline techniques. *Journal of Applied Behavior Analysis*, 1970, *3*, 77–84.

Bass, M. J., & Hull, C. L. The irradiation of a tactile conditioned reflex in man. *Journal of Comparative Psychology,* 1934, *17,* 47–65.

Bateson, P. P. G. The characteristics and contexts of imprinting. *Biological Reviews of the Cambridge Philosophical Society,* 1966, *41,* 177–220.

———. Imprinting and the development of preferences. In A. Ambrose (Ed.), *Stimulation in early infancy.* New York: Academic, 1969.

Batten, D. E., & Shoemaker, H. A. The effect of incentive palatability on a conditioned operant response. *Journal of Comparative and Physiological Psychology,* 1961, *54,* 577–579.

Bauer, R. H. The effects of CS and US intensity on shuttle box avoidance. *Psychonomic Science,* 1972, *27,* 266–268.

Baum, M. Reversal learning of an avoidance response and the Kamin effect. *Journal of Comparative and Physiological Psychology,* 1968, *66,* 495–497.

Baumrind, D. *Early socialization and the discipline controversy.* Morristown, N.J.: General Learning, 1975.

Bechterev, V. M. *La psychologie objective.* Paris: Alcan, 1913.

Beck, A. T. Thinking and depression. I. Idiosyncratic content and cognitive distortions. *Archives of General Psychiatry,* 1963, *9,* 324–333.

———. *Cognitive therapy and the emotional disorders.* New York: International Universities Press, 1976.

Becker, H. C., & Flaherty, C. F. Influence of ethanol on contrast in consummatory behavior. *Psychopharmacology,* 1982, *77,* 253–258.

———, & ———. Chlordiazepoxide and ethanol additively reduce gustatory negative contrast. *Psychopharmacology,* 1983, *80,* 35–37.

Bedford, J., & Anger, D. Flight as an avoidance response in pigeons. Paper presented to the Psychonomic Society, St. Louis, November 1968.

Benedict, J. O., & Ayres, J. J. B. Factors affecting conditioning in the truly random control procedure in the rat. *Journal of Comparative and Physiological Psychology,* 1972, *78,* 323–330.

Beneke, W. N., & Harris, M. B. Teaching self-control of study behavior. *Behaviour Research and Therapy,* 1972, *10,* 35–41.

Berger, S. M. Conditioning through vicarious instigation. *Psychological Review,* 1962, *69,* 450–466.

Berkowitz, L. *Aggression: A social psychological analysis.* New York: McGraw-Hill, 1962.

———. *Roots of aggression.* New York: Atherton, 1969.

———. The contagion of violence: An S-R mediational analysis of some effects of observed aggression. In M. Page (Ed.), *Nebraska Symposium on Motivation, 1970.* Lincoln: University of Nebraska Press, 1971.

———. Do we have to believe we are angry with someone in order to display "angry" aggression toward that person? In L. Berkowitz (Ed.), *Cognitive theories in social psychology: Papers reprinted from the Advances in Experimental Social Psychology.* New York: Academic, 1978.

———. *A survey of social psychology* (2d ed.). New York: Holt, Rinehart & Winston, 1980.

———, & Le Page, A. Weapons as aggression-eliciting stimuli. *Journal of Personality and Social Psychology,* 1967, *7,* 202–207.

Berman, J., & Katzev, R. Factors involved in the rapid elimination of avoidance behavior. *Behaviour Research and Therapy,* 1972, *10,* 247–256.

Bernard, L. L. *Instinct: A study in social psychology*. New York: Henry Holt, 1924.

Bernstein, I. L. Learned taste aversions in children receiving chemotherapy. *Science,* 1978, *200,* 1302–1303.

———, & Webster, M. M. Learned taste aversions in humans. *Physiology and Behavior,* 1980, *25,* 363–366.

Berscheid, E., & Walster, E. U. *Interpersonal attraction*. Reading, Mass.: Addison-Wesley, 1978.

Bersh, P. J. The influence of two variables upon the establishment of a secondary reinforcer for operant responses. *Journal of Experimental Psychology,* 1951, *41,* 62–73.

Best, M. R. Conditioned and latent inhibition in taste-aversion learning: Clarifying the role of learned safety. *Journal of Experimental Psychology: Animal Behavior Processes,* 1975, *1,* 97–113.

———, & Domjan, M. Characteristics of the lithium-mediated proximal US-preexposure effect in flavor-aversion conditioning. *Animal Learning and Behavior,* 1979, *7,* 433–440.

———, & Gemberling, G. A. Role of short-term processes in the conditioned stimulus preexposure effect and the delay of reinforcement gradient in long-delay taste-aversion learning. *Journal of Experimental Psychology: Animal Behavior Processes,* 1977, *3,* 253–263.

Best, P. J.; Best, M. R.; & Henggeler, S. The contribution of environmental non-ingestive cues in conditioning with aversive internal consequences. In L. M. Barker, M. R. Best, and M. Domjan (Eds.), *Learning mechanisms in food selection*. Waco, Tex.: Baylor University Press, 1977.

———; ———; & Mickley, G. A. Conditioned aversion to distinct environmental stimuli resulting from gastrointestinal distress. *Journal of Comparative and Physiological Psychology,* 1973, *85,* 250–257.

Bever, T. G. The cognitive basis for linguistic structures. In J. R. Hayes (Ed.), *Cognition and development of language*. New York: Wiley, 1970.

Biederman, G. B.; D'Amato, M. R.; & Keller, D. M. Facilitation of discriminated avoidance learning by dissociation of CS and manipulandum. *Psychonomic Science,* 1964, *1,* 229–230.

Bilodeau, I. M., & Schlosberg, H. Similarity in stimulating conditions as a variable in retroactive inhibition. *Journal of Experimental Psychology,* 1951, *41,* 199–204.

Bindra, D. Ape language. *Science,* 1981, *211,* 86.

Bintz, J. Time-dependent memory deficits of aversively motivated behavior. *Learning and Motivation,* 1970, *1,* 405–406.

Birch, H. G., & Rabinowitz, H. S. The negative effect of previous experience on productive thinking. *Journal of Experimental Psychology,* 1951, *41,* 121–125.

Black, A. H. The effect of CS-US interval on avoidance conditioning in the rat. *Canadian Journal of Psychology,* 1963, *17,* 174–182.

Black, R. W. Shifts in magnitude of reward and contrast effects in instrumental selective learning: A reinterpretation. *Psychological Review,* 1968, *75,* 114–126.

Blakemore, C. B.; Thorpe, J. G.; Barker, J. C.; Conway, C. G.; & Lavin, N. I. The application of faradic aversion conditioning in a case of transvestism. *Behaviour Research and Therapy,* 1963, *1,* 29–34.

Blehar, M. C.; Lieberman, A. F.; & Ainsworth, M. D. S. Early face-to-face interaction and its relation to later infant-mother attachment. *Child Development,* 1977, *48,* 182–194.

Blodgett, H. C., & McCutchan, K. Place versus response-learning in a simple T-maze. *Journal of Experimental Psychology,* 1947, *37,* 412–422.

——, & ——. The relative strength of place and response learning in the T-maze. *Journal of Comparative and Physiological Psychology,* 1948, *41,* 17–24.

Bloomfield, T. M. Behavioral contrast and relative reinforcement frequency in two multiple schedules. *Journal of the Experimental Analysis of Behavior,* 1967, *10,* 151–158.

——. Contrast and inhibition in discrimination learning by the pigeon: Analysis through drug effects. *Learning and Motivation,* 1972, *3,* 162–178.

Blough, D., & Blough, P. Animal psychophysics. In W. K. Harris and J. E. R. Staddon (Eds.), *Handbook of operant behavior.* Englewood Cliffs, N.J.: Prentice-Hall, 1977.

Boakes, R. A.; Poli, M.; Lockwood, M. J.; & Goodall, G. A study of misbehavior: Token reinforcement in the rat. *Journal of the Experimental Analysis of Behavior,* 1978, *29,* 115–134.

Boe, E. E., & Church, R. M. Permanent effects of punishment during extinction. *Journal of Comparative and Physiological Psychology,* 1967, *63,* 486–492.

Bolles, R. C. Avoidance and escape learning: Simultaneous acquisition of different responses. *Journal of Comparative and Physiological Psychology,* 1969, *68,* 355–358.

——. Species-specific defense reactions and avoidance learning. *Psychological Review,* 1970, *77,* 32–48.

——. Reinforcement, expectancy and learning. *Psychological Review,* 1972, *79,* 394–409.

——. *Theory of motivation* (2d ed.). New York: Harper & Row, 1975.

——. The role of stimulus learning in defensive behavior. In S. H. Hulse, H. Fowler, and W. K. Honig (Eds.), *Cognitive processes in animal behavior.* Hillsdale, N.J.: Erlbaum, 1978.

——. *Learning theory* (2d ed.). New York: Holt, Rinehart & Winston, 1979.

——, & Collier, A. C. The effect of predictive cues on freezing in rats. *Animal Learning and Behavior,* 1976, *4,* 6–8.

——; ——; Bouton, M. E.; & Marlin, N. A. Some tracks for ameliorating the trace-conditioning deficit. *Bulletin of the Psychonomic Society,* 1978, *11,* 403–406.

——; Grossen, N. E.; Hargrave, G. E.; & Duncan, P. M. Effects of conditioned appetitive stimuli on the acquisition and extinction of a runway response. *Journal of Experimental Psychology,* 1970, *85,* 138–140.

——, & Riley, A. Freezing as an avoidance response: Another look at the operant-respondent distinction. *Learning and Motivation,* 1973, *4,* 268–275.

——, & Seelbach, S. Punishing and reinforcing effects of noise onset and termination for different responses. *Journal of Comparative and Physiological Psychology,* 1964, *58,* 127–132.

——, & Tuttle, A. V. A failure to reinforce instrumental behavior by terminating a stimulus that had been paired with shock. *Psychonomic Science,* 1967, *9,* 255–256.

——; Uhl, C. N.; Wolfe, M.; & Chase, P. B. Stimulus learning versus response learning in a discriminated punishment situation. *Learning and Motivation,* 1975, *6,* 439–447.

Bond, N. Schedule-induced polydipsia as a function of the consummatory rate. *The Psychological Record,* 1973, *23,* 377–382.

Borkovec, T. D. Physiological and cognitive processes in the regulation of fear. In G. E.

Schwartz and D. Shapiro (Eds.), *Consciousness and self-regulation: Advances in research.* New York: Plenum, 1976.

———. Self-efficacy: Cause or reflection of behavioral change? In S. Rachman (Ed.), *Advances in behaviour research and therapy* (vol. 1). Oxford: Pergamon, 1978.

Boroczi, G.; Storms, L. H.; & Broen, W. E. Response suppression and recovery of responding at different deprivation levels as functions of intensity and duration of punishment. *Journal of Comparative and Physiological Psychology,* 1964, *58,* 456–459.

Bourne, L. E., Jr. Learning and utilization of conceptual rules. In B. Kleinmuntz (Ed.), *Concepts and the structure of memory.* New York: Wiley, 1967.

———; Ekstrand, D. R.; & Dominowski, R. L. *The psychology of thinking.* Englewood Cliffs, N.J.: Prentice-Hall, 1971.

Bower, G. H. Mood and memory. *American Psychologist,* 1981, *36,* 129–148.

———; Fowler, H.; & Trapold, M. A. Escape learning as a function of amount of shock reduction. *Journal of Experimental Psychology,* 1959, *48,* 482–484.

———, & Hilgard, E. R. *Theories of learning* (5th ed.). Englewood Cliffs, N.J.: Prentice-Hall, 1981.

———, & Springston, F. Pauses as recoding points in letter series. *Journal of Experimental Psychology,* 1970, *83,* 421–430.

———; Starr, R.; & Lazarovitz, L. Amount of response-produced change in the CS and avoidance learning. *Journal of Comparative and Physiological Psychology,* 1965, *59,* 13–17.

Boyd, H., & Fabricius, E. Observations on the incidence of following of visual and auditory stimuli in naive mallard ducklings (*Anas platyrhynchos*). *Behaviour,* 1965, *25,* 1–15.

Boyd, T. L. Learned helplessness in humans: A frustration-produced response pattern. *Journal of Personality and Social Psychology,* 1982, *42,* 738–752.

Brady, J. V. Motivational-emotional factors and intracranial self-stimulation. In D. E. Sheer (Ed.), *Electrical stimulation of the brain.* Austin: University of Texas Press, 1961.

Bramel, D.; Taub, B.; & Blum, B. An observer's reaction to the suffering of his enemy. *Journal of Personality and Social Psychology,* 1968, *8,* 384–392.

Bransford, J. D.; Franks, J. J.; Morris, C. D.; & Stein, B. S. Some general constraints on learning and memory research. In L. S. Cermak and F. I. M. Craik (Eds.), *Levels of processing in human memory.* Hillsdale, N.J.: Erlbaum, 1979.

Braud, W.; Wepman, B.; & Russo, D. Task and species generality of the "helplessness" phenomenon. *Psychonomic Science,* 1969, *16,* 154–155.

Braveman, N. S. Poison-based avoidance learning with flavored or colored water in guinea pigs. *Learning and Motivation,* 1974, *5,* 182–194.

———. Formation of taste aversions in rats following prior exposure to sickness. *Learning and Motivation,* 1975, *6,* 512–534.

Breit, S. Arousal of achievement motivation with causal attributions. *Psychological Reports,* 1969, *25,* 539–542.

Breitmeyer, B. B., & Ganz, L. Implications of sustained and transient channels for theories of visual pattern masking, saccadic suppression, and information processing. *Psychological Review,* 1976, *83,* 1–36.

Breland, K., & Breland, M. The misbehavior of organisms. *American Psychologist,* 1961, *61,* 681–684.

————, & ————. *Animal behavior*. New York: Macmillan, 1966.

Briggs, M. H., & Kitto, G. B. The molecular basis of memory. *Psychological Review*, 1962, *69*, 537–541.

Bristol, M. M., & Sloane, H. N., Jr. Effects of contingency contracting on study rate and test performance. *Journal of Applied Behavior Analysis*, 1974, *7*, 271–285.

Broadbent, D. E. *Perception and communication*. New York: Pergamon, 1958.

Brockner, J.; Gardner, M.; Bierman, J.; Mahan, T.; Thomas, B.; Weiss, W.; Wintend, L.; & Mitchell, A. The roles of self-esteem and self-consciousness in the Wortman-Brehm model of reactance and learned helplessness. *Journal of Personality and Social Psychology*, 1983, *45*, 199–209.

Brogden, W. J. Sensory pre-conditioning. *Journal of Experimental Psychology*, 1939, *25*, 323–332.

Brooks, C. I. Effect of prior nonreward on subsequent incentive growth during brief acquisition. *Animal Learning and Behavior*, 1980, *8*, 143–151.

Brooks, L. R. Nonanalytic concept formation and memory for instances. In E. Rosch and B. B. Lloyd (Eds.), *Cognition and categorization*. Hillsdale, N.J.: Erlbaum, 1978.

Brown, J. L. *The evolution of behavior*. New York: Norton, 1975.

Brown, J. S. Factors determining conflict reactions in different discriminations. *Journal of Experimental Psychology*, 1942, *31*, 272–292.

————. Gradients of approach and avoidance responses and their relation to level of motivation. *Journal of Comparative and Physiological Psychology*, 1948, *41*, 450–465.

————, & Jacobs, A. The role of fear in the motivation and acquisition of responses. *Journal of Experimental Psychology*, 1949, *39*, 747–759.

Brown, P. L., & Jenkins, H. M. Autoshaping of the pigeon's key peck. *Journal of the Experimental Analysis of Behavior*, 1968, *11*, 1–8.

Brown, R.; Cazden, C.; & Bellugi, U. The child's grammar from I to III. In J. P. Hill (Ed.), *Minnesota Symposium on Child Psychology* (vol. 2). Minneapolis: University of Minnesota Press, 1969.

Brucke, E. *Lectures on physiology*. Vienna: University of Vienna, 1874.

Bruner, J. S. Learning the mother tongue. *Human Nature*, 1978, *1*, 42–49.

————; Goodnow, J. J.; & Austin, G. A. *A study of thinking*. New York: Wiley, 1956.

Brush, F. R. (Ed.). *Aversive conditioning and learning*. New York: Academic, 1970.

————. Retention of aversively motivated behavior. In F. R. Brush (Ed.), *Aversive conditioning and learning*. New York: Academic, 1971.

Buchanan, G. U. The effects of various punishment-escape events upon subsequent choice behavior of rats. *Journal of Comparative and Physiological Psychology*, 1958, *51*, 1958, *51*, 355–362.

Bucher, B., & Fabricatore, J. Use of patient-administered shock to suppress hallucinations. *Behavior Therapy*, 1970, *1*, 382–385.

Bugelski, B. R. Images as mediators in one-trial paired-associate learning. II: Self-timing in successive lists. *Journal of Experimental Psychology*, 1968, *77*, 328–334.

Burchard, J. D. Systematic socialization: A programmed environment for the habilitation of antisocial retardates. *Psychological Record*, 1967, *17*, 461–476.

Burgess, E. P. The modification of depressive behaviors. In R. D. Rubin and C. M. Franks (Eds.), *Advances in behavior therapy*. New York: Academic, 1968.

Burns, B. D. *The mammalian cerebral cortex*. London: Arnold, 1958.

Burns, R. A. Effects of sequences of sucrose reward magnitudes with short ITIs in rats. *Animal Learning and Behavior,* 1976, *4,* 473–479.

Butler, R. A., & Harlow, H. F. Persistence of visual exploration in monkeys. *Journal of Comparative and Physiological Psychology,* 1954, *47,* 257–263.

Butter, C. M., & Thomas, D. R. Secondary reinforcement as a function of the amount of primary reinforcement. *Journal of the Experimental Analysis of Behavior,* 1958, *51,* 346–348.

Byrne, W. L., & Hughes, A. Behavioral modification by injection of brain extract from trained donors. *Federation Proceedings,* 1967, *26,* 676.

————, & Samuel, D. Behavioral modification by injection of brain extract prepared from a trained donor. *Science,* 1966, *154,* 418.

Caggiula, A. R., & Szechtman, H. Hypothalamic stimulation: A biphasic influence on the copulation of the male rate. *Behavioral Biology,* 1972, *7,* 591–598.

Cain, N. W., & Baenninger, R. Effects of prior experience with the US on the formation of learned taste aversions in rats. *Animal Learning and Behavior,* 1977, *5,* 359–364.

Caldwell, W. E., & Jones, H. B. Some positive results on a modified Tolman and Honzik insight maze. *Journal of Comparative and Physiological Psychology,* 1954, *47,* 416–418.

Camp, D. S.; Raymond, G. A.; & Church, R. M. Response suppression as a function of the schedule of punishment. *Psychonomic Science,* 1966, *5,* 23–24.

————; ————; & ————. Temporal relationship between response and punishment. *Journal of Experimental Psychology,* 1967, *74,* 114–123.

Campbell, B. A., & Church, P. M. *Punishment and aversive behavior.* New York: Appleton-Century-Crofts, 1969.

————, & Kraeling, D. Response strength as a function of drive level and amount of drive reduction. *Journal of Experimental Psychology,* 1953, *45,* 97–101.

Campbell, P. E.; Knouse, D. B.; & Wroten, J. D. Resistance to extinction in the rat following regular and irregular schedules of partial reinforcement. *Journal of Comparative and Physiological Psychology,* 1970, *72,* 210–215.

Campbell, S. L. Resistance to extinction as a function of number of shock-termination reinforcements. *Journal of Comparative and Physiological Psychology,* 1959, *52,* 754–758.

Cannon, D.; Berman, R.; Baker, T.; & Atkinson, C. Effect of preconditioning unconditioned stimulus experience on learned taste aversions. *Journal of Experimental Psychology: Animal Behavior Processes,* 1975, *104,* 270–284.

Cantor, M. B., & Wilson, J. F. Feeding the face: New directions in adjunctive behavior research. In F. R. Brush and J. B. Overmier (Eds.), *Affect, conditioning, and cognition.* Hillsdale, N.J.: Erlbaum, 1984.

Capaldi, E. D., & Hovancik, J. R. Effects of previous body weight level on rats' straight-alley performance. *Journal of Experimental Psychology,* 1973, *97,* 93–97.

Capaldi, E. J. Effect of N-length, number of different N-lengths and number of reinforcements on resistance to extinction. *Journal of Experimental Psychology,* 1964, *68,* 230–239.

————. Partial reinforcement: A hypothesis of sequential effects. *Psychological Review,* 1966, *73,* 459–479.

————. A sequential hypothesis of instrumental learning. In K. W. Spence & J. T. Spence (Eds.), *The psychology of learning and motivation* (vol. 1). New York: Academic, 1967.

————. Memory and learning: A sequential viewpoint. In W. K. Honig and P. H. R. James (Eds.), *Animal memory*. New York: Academic, 1971.

————; Hart, D.; & Stanley, L. R. Effect of intertrial reinforcement on the aftereffect of nonreinforcement and resistance to extinction. *Journal of Experimental Psychology,* 1963, *65,* 70–74.

————, & Spivey, J. E. Stimulus consequences of reinforcement and nonreinforcement: Stimulus traces or memory. *Psychonomic Science,* 1964, *1,* 403–404.

————, & Stanley, L. R. Percentage of reward vs. N-length in the runway. *Psychonomic Science,* 1965, *3,* 263–264.

Capretta, P. J. An experimental modification of food preference in chickens. *Journal of Comparative and Physiological Psychology,* 1961, *54,* 238–242.

Carlson, N. R. *Physiology of behavior* (2d ed.). Boston: Allyn & Bacon, 1981.

————. *Psychology: The science of behavior.* Boston: Allyn & Bacon, 1984.

Carlton, P. L. The interacting effects of deprivation and reinforcement schedule. *Journal of the Experimental Analysis of Behavior,* 1961, *4,* 379–381.

————. Brain-acetylcholine and inhibition. In J. T. Tapp (Ed.), *Reinforcement and behavior.* New York: Academic, 1969.

Carter, L. F. Intensity of conditioned stimulus and rate of conditioning. *Journal of Experimental Psychology,* 1941, *28,* 481–490.

Catania, A. C. *Learning.* Englewood Cliffs, N.J.: Prentice-Hall, 1979.

————, & Reynolds, G. S. A quantitative analysis of the responding maintained by interval schedules of reinforcement. *Journal of the Experimental Analysis of Behavior,* 1968, *11,* 327–383.

Catell, R. B.; Kawash, G. F.; & De Young, G. E. Validation of objective measures of ergic tension: Response of the sex urge to visual stimulation. *Journal of Experimental Research in Personality,* 1972, *6,* 76–83.

Cautela, J. R. The use of covert conditioning in modifying pain behavior. *Journal of Behavior Therapy and Experimental Psychiatry,* 1977, *8,* 45–52.

Cermak, L. S., & Craik, F. I. M. *Levels of processing in human memory.* Hillsdale, N.J.: Erlbaum, 1979.

Chadwick, B. A., & Day, R. C. Systematic reinforcement: Academic performance of underachieving students. *Journal of Applied Behavior Analysis,* 1971, *4,* 311–319.

Channell, S., & Hall, G. Facilitation and retardation of discrimination learning after exposure to the stimuli. *Journal of the Experimental Analysis of Behavior,* 1981, *7,* 437–446.

Chapouthier, G. Molecular basis of memory. In J. A. Deutsch (Ed.), *The physiological basis of memory.* New York: Academic, 1983.

Chase, W. G., & Simon, H. A. The mind's eye in chess. In W. G. Chase (Ed.), *Visual information processing.* New York: Academic, 1973.

Cherek, D. R. Schedule-induced cigarette self-administration. *Pharmacology, Biochemistry, and Behavior,* 1982, *17,* 523–527.

————; Thompson, T.; & Heistad, G. T. Responding maintained by the opportunity to attack during an interval food reinforcement schedule. *Journal of the Experimental Analysis of Behavior,* 1973, *19,* 113–123.

Cherry, E. C. Some experiments on the recognition of speech, with one and with two ears. *Journal of the Acoustical Society of America,* 1953, *25,* 975–979.

Cheyne, J. A.; Goyeche, J. R.; & Walters, R. H. Attention, anxiety, and rules in resistance-to-deviation in children. *Journal of Experimental Child Psychology,* 1969, *8,* 127–139.

Chillag, D., & Mendelson, J. Schedule-induced airlicking as a function of body-weight deficit in rats. *Physiology and Behavior,* 1971, *6,* 603–605.

Chomsky, N. *Syntactic structures.* The Hague: Mouton, 1957.

———. *Aspects of the theory of syntax.* Cambridge, Mass.: M.I.T. Press, 1965.

———. *Language and mind.* New York: Harcourt Brace Jovanovich, 1968.

———. *Reflections on language.* New York: Pantheon, 1975.

Chorover, S. L., & Schiller, P. H. Short-term retrograde amnesia in rats. *Journal of Comparative and Physiological Psychology,* 1965, *59,* 73–78.

Christensen, F. E., & Sprague, R. L. Reduction of hyperactive behavior by conditioning procedures alone and combined with methylphenitate. *Behaviour Research and Therapy,* 1973, *11,* 331–334.

Church, R. M. Response suppression. In B. A. Campbell and R. M. Church (Eds.), *Punishment and aversive behavior.* New York: Appleton-Century-Crofts, 1969.

———, & Black, A. H. Latency of the conditioned heart rate as a function of the CS-US interval. *Journal of Comparative and Physiological Psychology,* 1958, *51,* 478–482.

———; Brush, F. R.; & Solomon, R. L. Traumatic avoidance learning: The effects of CS-UCS interval with a delayed conditioning procedure in a free-responding situation. *Journal of Comparative and Physiological Psychology,* 1956, *49,* 301–308.

———; Raymond, G. A.; & Beauchamp, R. D. Response suppression as a function of intensity and duration of a punishment. *Journal of Comparative and Physiological Psychology,* 1967, *63,* 30–44.

Cicala, G. A., & Kremer, E. The effects of shock intensity and d-amphetamine on avoidance learning. *Psychonomic Science,* 1969, *14,* 41–42.

Clark, F. C. Some observations on the adventitious reinforcement of drinking under food reinforcement. *Journal of the Experimental Analysis of Behavior,* 1962, *5,* 61–63.

Clark, H. H., & Clark, E. V. *Psychology and language.* New York: Harcourt Brace Jovanovich, 1977.

Clayton, K. N. T-maze choice learning as a joint function of the reward magnitudes for the alternatives. *Journal of Comparative and Physiological Psychology,* 1964, *58,* 333–338.

Cohen, D. H. Effect of conditioned stimulus intensity on visually conditioned heart rate change in the pigeon: A sensitization mechanism. *Journal of Comparative and Physiological Psychology,* 1974, *87,* 495–499.

Cohen, H. D.; Ervin, F.; & Barondes, S. H. Puromycin and cycloheximide: Different effects on hippocampal electrical activity. *Science,* 1966, *154,* 1552–1558.

Cohen, P. S., & Looney, T. A. Schedule-induced mirror responding in the pigeon. *Journal of the Experimental Analysis of Behavior,* 1973, *19,* 395–408.

Collerian, I. J. Frustration odor of rats receiving small numbers of prior rewarded running trials. *Journal of Experimental Psychology: Animal Behavior Processes,* 1978, *4,* 120–130.

———, & Ludvigson, H. W. Hurdle-jump responding in the rat as a function of conspecific odor of reward and nonreward. *Animal Learning and Behavior,* 1977, *5,* 177–183.

Collias, N. E., & Collias, E. C. Some mechanisms of family integration in ducks. *Auk,* 1956, *73,* 378–400.

Collier, G.; Hirsch, E.; & Hamlin, P. H. The ecological determinants of reinforcement in the rat. *Physiology & Behavior,* 1972, *9,* 705–716.

Coltheart, M.; Lea, C. D.; & Thompson, K. In defense of iconic memory. *Quarterly Journal of Experimental Psychology*, 1974, *26*, 633–641.

Conger, J. J. Effect of alcohol on conflict behavior in the albino rat. *Quarterly Journal of Studies of Alcohol*, 1951, *12*, 1–29.

Conrad, D. G., & Sidman, M. Sucrose concentration as reinforcement for lever pressing by monkeys. *Psychological Reports*, 1956, *2*, 381–384.

Conrad, R. Acoustic confusions in immediate memory. *British Journal of Psychology*, 1964, *55*, 75–84.

————. The chronology of the development of covert speech in children. *Developmental Psychology*, 1971, *5*, 398–405.

————, & Hull, A. J. Information, acoustic confusion, and memory span. *British Journal of Psychology*, 1964, *55*, 429–432.

Coons, E. E., & Cruce, J. A. F. Lateral hypothalamus: Food and current intensity in maintaining self-stimulation of hunger. *Science*, 1968, *159*, 1117–1119.

Cooper, D. R.; Cott, J. A.; & Breese, G. R. Effects of acetylamine-depleting drugs and amphetamine on self-stimulation of the brain following various 6-hydroxydopamine treatments. *Psychopharmacologia*, 1974, *37*, 235–248.

Corballis, M. C. Rehearsal and decay in immediate recall of visually and aurally presented items. *Canadian Journal of Psychology*, 1966, *20*, 43–51.

Corey, J. R., & Shamov, J. The effects of fading on the acquisition and retention of oral reading. *Journal of Applied Behavior Analysis*, 1972, *5*, 311–315.

Corfield-Sumner, P. K.; Blackman, D. E.; & Stainer, G. Polydipsia induced in rats by second-order schedules of reinforcement. *Journal of the Experimental Analysis of Behavior*, 1977, *27*, 265–273.

Couch, J. V. Reinforcement magnitude and schedule-induced polydipsia: A reexamination. *The Psychological Record*, 1974, *24*, 559–562.

Cowles, J. T., & Nissen, H. W. Reward expectancy in delayed responses of chimpanzees. *Journal of Comparative Psychology*, 1937, *24*, 345–358.

Craig, K. D., & Weinstein, M. S. Conditioning vicarious affective arousal. *Psychological Reports*, 1965, *17*, 955–963.

Craik, F. I. M. Human memory. *Annual Review of Psychology*, 1979, *30*, 63–102.

————, & Lockhart, R. S. Levels of processing: A framework for memory research. *Journal of Verbal Learning and Verbal Behavior*, 1972, *11*, 671–684.

————, & Tulving, E. Depth of processing and the retention of words in episodic memory. *Journal of Experimental Psychology: General*, 1975, *104*, 268–294.

————, & Watkins, M. J. The role of rehearsal in short-term memory. *Journal of Verbal Learning and Verbal Behavior*, 1973, *12*, 599–607.

Creer, T. L.; Chai, H.; & Hoffman, A. A single application of an aversive stimulus to eliminate chronic cough. *Journal of Behavior Research and Experimental Psychiatry*, 1977, *8*, 107–109.

Crespi, L. P. Quantitative variation of incentive and performance in the white rat. *American Journal of Psychology*, 1942, *55*, 467–517.

————. Amount of reinforcement and level of performance. *Psychological Review*, 1944, *51*, 341–357.

Crider, S.; Schwartz, G. E.; & Shapiro, D. Operant suppression of electrodermal response rate. *Journal of Experimental Psychology*, 1970, *83*, 333–334.

Cronholm, B., & Molander, L. Influence of an interpolated ECS on retention of memory material. *University of Stockholm Psychological Laboratory Reports*, 1958, *61*.

Crooks, J. L. Observational learning of fear in monkeys. Manuscript, University of Pennsylvania, 1967.

Crowell, C. R.; Hinson, R. E.; & Siegel, S. The role of conditional drug responses in tolerance to the hypothermic effects of ethanol. *Psychopharmacology,* 1981, *73,* 51–54.

Cruser, L., & Klein, S. B. The role of schedule-induced polydipsia on temporal discrimination learning. *Psychological Reports,* 1984, *58,* 443–452.

Cunningham, C. E., & Linscheid, T. R. Elimination of chronic infant ruminating by electric shock. *Behavior Therapy,* 1976, *1,* 231–234.

Daly, H. B. Reinforcing properties of escape from frustration aroused in various learning situations. In G. H. Bower (Ed.), *The psychology of learning and motivation* (vol. 8). New York: Academic, 1974.

D'Amato, M. R. Secondary reinforcement and magnitude of primary reinforcement. *Journal of Comparative and Physiological Psychology,* 1955, *48,* 378–380.

———. *Experimental psychology: Methodology, psychophysics, and learning.* New York: McGraw-Hill, 1970.

———. Delayed matching and short-term memory in monkeys. In G. H. Bower (Ed.), *The psychology of learning and motivation* (vol. 7). New York: Academic, 1973.

———, & Fazzaro, J. Discriminated lever press avoidance learning as a function of type and intensity of shock. *Journal of Comparative and Physiological Psychology,* 1966, *61,* 313–315.

———; ———; & Etkin, M. Anticipatory responding and avoidance discrimination as factors in avoidance conditioning. *Journal of Experimental Psychology,* 1968, *77,* 41–47.

———; Keller, D.; & DiCara, L. V. Facilitation of discriminated avoidance learning by discontinuous shock. *Journal of Comparative and Physiological Psychology,* 1964, *58,* 344–349.

———, & Salmon, D. P. Cognitive processes in cebus monkeys. In H. L. Roitblat, R. G. Bever, and H. S. Terrace (Eds.), *Animal cognition.* Hillsdale, N.J.: Erlbaum, 1984.

———; ———; & Colombo, M. Extent and limits of the matching concept in monkeys (*Cebus apella*). *Journal of Experimental Psychology: Animal Behavior Processes,* in press.

———; Safarjan, W. R.; & Salmon, D. P. Long-delay conditioning and instrumental learning: Some new findings. In N. E. Spear and R. R. Miller (Eds.), *Information processing in animals: Memory mechanisms.* Hillsdale, N.J.: Erlbaum, 1981.

———, & Schiff, E. Further studies of overlearning and position reversal learning. *Psychological Reports,* 1964, *14,* 380–382.

Darwin, C. *Origin of species* (1936 ed.). New York: Modern Library, 1859.

Darwin, C. J.; Turvey, M. T.; & Crowder, R. G. An auditory analogue of the Sperling partial report procedure: Evidence for brief auditory storage. *Cognitive Psychology,* 1972, *3,* 255–267.

Davey, G. C. *Animal learning and conditioning.* University Park: Pennsylvania State University Press, 1981.

Davidson, R. S. *Aversive modification of alcoholic behavior: Punishment of an alcohol-reinforced operant.* Manuscript, U.S. Veterans Administration Hospital, Miami, Florida, 1972.

Davis, J. M.; Klerman, G.; & Schildkraut, J. Drugs used in the treatment of depression.

In L. Efron, J. O. Cole, D. Levine, and J. R. Wittenborn (Eds.), *Psychopharmacology, A review of progress*. Washington, D.C.: U.S. Clearinghouse of Mental Health Information, 1967.

Davison, G. C. Systematic desensitization as a counterconditioning process. *Journal of Abnormal Psychology,* 1968, *73,* 91–99.

Davitz, J. R.; Mason, D. J.; Mowrer, O. H.; & Vick, P. Conditioning of fear: A function of the delay of reinforcement. *American Journal of Psychology,* 1957, *70,* 69–74.

Delgado, J. M. R.; Roberts, W. W.; & Miller, N. E. Learning motivated by electric stimulation of the brain. *American Journal of Physiology,* 1954, *179,* 587–593.

Denny, M. R. Relaxation theory and experiments. In F. R. Brush (Ed.), *Aversive conditioning and learning*. New York: Academic, 1971.

———, & King, G. R. Differential response learning on the basis of differential size of reward. *Journal of Genetic Psychology,* 1955, *87,* 317–320.

———, & Weisman, R. G. Avoidance behavior as a function of the length of nonshock confinement. *Journal of Comparative and Physiological Psychology,* 1964, *58,* 252–257.

Depue, R. A., & Evans, R. *The psychobiology of the depressive disorders: Implications for the effects of stress*. New York: Academic, 1976.

Deur, J. L., & Parke, R. D. Resistance to extinction and continuous punishment in humans as a function of partial reward and partial punishment. *Psychonomic Science,* 1968, *13,* 91–92.

Dews, P. B. The effect of multiple S^Δ periods on responding on a fixed-interval schedule. *Journal of the Experimental Analysis of Behavior,* 1962, *5,* 369–374.

Dewey, J. *Psychology*. New York: Harper & Row, 1886.

De Wied, D.; Sarantakis, D.; & Weinstein, B. Behavioral evaluation of peptides related to scotophobin. *Neuropharmacology,* 1973, *12,* 1109–1115.

Dickinson, A. Appetitive-aversive interactions: Facilitation of aversive conditioning by prior appetitive training in the rat. *Animal Learning and Behavior,* 1976, *4,* 416–420.

———. *Contemporary animal learning theory*. Cambridge: Cambridge University Press, 1980.

———; Colwill, R. M.; & Pearce, J. M. Post-trial stimulation and the acquisition of conditioned suppression in the rat. *Quarterly Journal of Experimental Psychology,* 1980, *32,* 149–158.

———; Hall, G.; & Mackintosh, N. J. Surprise and the attenuation of blocking. *Journal of Experimental Psychology: Animal Behavior Processes,* 1976, *2,* 313–322.

Dodd, D. H., & Bradshaw, J. M. Leading questions and memory: Pragmatic constraints. *Journal of Verbal Learning and Verbal Behavior,* 1980, *19,* 695–704.

———, & White, R. M. *Cognition: Mental structures and processes*. Boston: Allyn & Bacon, 1980.

Domjan, M., & Gemberling, G. A. Effects of expected vs. unexpected proximal US preexposure on taste-aversion learning. *Animal Learning and Behavior,* 1980, *8,* 204–210.

Dorry, G. W., & Zeaman, D. The use of a fading technique in paired-associate teaching of a reading vocabulary with retardates. *Mental Retardation,* 1973, *11,* 3–6.

———, & ———. Teaching a simple reading vocabulary to retarded: Effectiveness of fading and nonfading procedures. *American Journal of Mental Deficiency,* 1975, *79,* 711–716.

Drabman, R., & Spitalnik, R. Social isolation as a punishment procedure: A controlled study. *Journal of Experimental Child Psychology,* 1973, *16,* 236–249.

Dryer, P. L., & Church, R. M. Reinforcement of shock-induced fighting. *Psychonomic Science*, 1970, *18*, 147–148.

Ducker, G., & Rensch, B. Verzogerung des Vergessens erlernter visuellen Aufgaben bei Fischen durch Dunkelhaltung. *Pfluegers Archiv für die Gesamte Physiologie des Menschen und der Tiere*, 1968, *301*, 1–6.

Du Nann, D. G., & Weber, S. J. Short- and long-term effects of contingency managed instruction on low, medium, and high GPA students. *Journal of Applied Behavior Analysis*, 1976, *9*, 375–376.

Duncan, C. P. The retroactive effect of electroshock on learning. *Journal of Comparative and Physiological Psychology*, 1949, *42*, 32–44.

Dunker, K. On problem solving. *Psychological Monographs*, 1945, *58*, Whole no. 270.

Dunn, A. J. Neurochemistry of learning and memory: An evaluation of recent data. *Annual Review of Psychology*, 1980, *31*, 343–390.

Dunstone, J. J.; Cannon, J. T.; Chickson, J. T.; & Burns, W. K. Persistence and vigor of shock-induced aggression in gerbils (*Meriones unguiculatus*). *Psychonomic Science*, 1972, *28*, 272–274.

Dyal, J. A., & Golub, A. M. An attempt to obtain shifts in brightness preference as a function of injection of brain homogenates. *Journal of Biological Psychology*, 1967, *9*, 29–33.

——, & ——. Further positive transfer effects obtained by intraperitoneal injections of brain homogenates. *Psychonomic Science*, 1968, *11*, 13–14.

——; ——; & Marrone, R. L. Transfer effects of intraperitoneal injection of brain homogenates. *Nature*, 1967, *214*, 720–721.

Ebbinghaus, H. *Memory: A contribution to experimental psychology*, H. A. Ruger & C. E. Bussenius (Trans.). New York: Dover, 1885.

Efron, R. The relationship between the duration of a stimulus and the duration of a perception. *Neuropsychologia*, 1970, *8*, 37–55.

Eibl-Eibesfeldt, I. The fighting behavior of animals. *Scientific American*, 1961, *205*, 112–122.

——. *Ethology: The biology of behavior*. New York: Holt, 1970.

Eich, J. E. The cue-dependent nature of state-dependent retrieval. *Memory and Cognition*, 1980, *8*, 157–173.

——; Weingartner, H.; Stillman, R. C.; & Gillin, J. C. State-dependent accessibility of retrieval cues in the retention of a categorized list. *Journal of Verbal Learning and Verbal Behavior*, 1975, *14*, 408–417.

Eimas, P. D. A developmental study of hypothesis behavior and focusing. *Journal of Experimental Child Psychology*, 1969, *8*, 160–172.

——, & Corbit, J. D. Selective adaptation of linguistic feature detectors. *Cognitive Psychology*, 1973, *4*, 99–109.

——; Siqueland, E. R.; Jusczyk, P.; & Vigorito, J. Speech perception in infants. *Science*, 1971, *171*, 303–306.

Eisenberger, R.; Myers, A. K.; & Kaplan, R. M. Persistent deprivation-shift effect opposite in direction to incentive contrast. *Journal of Experimental Psychology*, 1973, *99*, 400–404.

Ekstrand, B. R. Effect of sleep on memory. *Journal of Experimental Psychology*, 1967, *75*, 64–72.

——; Wallace, W. P.; & Underwood, B. J. A frequency theory of verbal-discrimination learning. *Psychological Review*, 1966, *73*, 566–578.

Elkins, R. L. Attenuation of drug-induced bait shyness to a palatable solution as an increasing function of its availability prior to conditioning. *Behavioral Biology,* 1973, *9,* 221–226.

Elliot, L. L. Development of auditory narrow-band frequency contours. *Journal of the Acoustical Society of America,* 1967, *42,* 143–153.

Ellis, H. C. *Fundamentals of human learning, memory and cognition* (2d ed.). Dubuque, Iowa: Wm. C. Brown, 1978.

Ellison, G. D. Differential salivary conditioning to traces. *Journal of Comparative and Physiological Psychology,* 1964, *57,* 373–380.

El-Wakil, F. W. Master's thesis, University of Massachusetts—Amherst, 1975.

Emshoff, J. G.; Redd, W. H.; & Davidson, W. S. Generalization training and the transfer of prosocial behavior in delinquent adolescents. *Journal of Behavior Therapy and Experimental Psychiatry,* 1976, *7,* 141–144.

Engberg, L. A.; Hansen, G.; Welker, R. L.; & Thomas, D. R. Acquisition of keypecking via autoshaping as a function of prior experience: "Learned laziness?" *Science,* 1973, *178,* 1002–1004.

Epstein, R. On pigeons and people: A preliminary look at the Columban Simulation Project. *The Behavior Analyst,* 1981, *4,* 43–55.

Eriksen, C. W., & Collins, J. F. Some temporal characteristics of visual pattern perception. *Journal of Experimental Psychology,* 1967, *74,* 476–484.

————, & ————. Sensory traces versus the psychological moment in the temporal organization of form. *Journal of Experimental Psychology,* 1968, *77,* 376–382.

Ervin, F. R.; Mark, V. H.; & Stevens, J. R. Behavioral and affective responses to brain stimulation in man. In J. Zubin and C. Shagass (Eds.), *Neurological aspects of psychopathology.* New York: Grune & Stratton, 1969.

Essman, W. B., & Lehrer, G. M. Is there a chemical transfer of learning? *Federation Proceedings,* 1966, *25,* 208.

————, & ————. Facilitation of maze performance by "RNA extracts" from mazetrained mice. *Federation Proceedings,* 1967, *26,* 263.

Estes, W. K. An experimental study of punishment. *Psychological Monographs,* 1944, *57,* Whole no. 263.

————. Outline of a theory of punishment. In B. A. Campbell and R. M. Church (Eds.), *Punishment and aversive behavior.* New York: Appleton-Century-Crofts, 1969.

————, & Skinner, B. F. Some quantitive properties of anxiety. *Journal of Experimental Psychology,* 1941, *29,* 390–400.

Etscorn, F., & Stephens, R. Establishment of conditioned taste aversions with a 24-hour CS-US interval. *Physiological Psychology,* 1973, *73,* 252–253.

Eysenck, M. W. Levels of processing: A critique. *British Journal of Psychology,* 1978, *68,* 157–169.

Fabricius, E. Zur Ethologie Junger Anatiden. *Acta Zoologica Fennica,* 1951, *68,* 1–175.

Fairweather, G. W.; Sanders, D. H.; Maynard, H.; & Cressler, D. C. *Community life for the mortally ill: An alternative to institutional care.* Chicago: Aldine, 1969.

Falk, J. L. Production of polydipsia in normal rats by an intermittent food schedule. *Science,* 1961, *133,* 195–196.

————. Studies on schedule-induced polydipsia. In M. J. Wayner (Ed.), *Thirst.* Oxford: Pergamon, 1964.

————. The motivational properties of schedule-induced polydipsia. *Journal of the Experimental Analysis of Behavior,* 1966a, *9,* 19–25.

————. Schedule-induced polydipsia as a function of fixed interval length. *Journal of the Experimental Analysis of Behavior,* 1966b, *9,* 37–39.

————. Control of schedule-induced polydipsia: Type, size, and spacing of meals. *Journal of the Experimental Analysis of Behavior,* 1967, *10,* 199–206.

————. Conditions producing psychogenic polydipsia in animals. *Annals of the New York Academy of Sciences,* 1969, *157,* 569–593.

————. The nature and determinants of adjunctive behavior. *Physiology and Behavior,* 1971, *6,* 577–588.

Fazzaro, J., & D'Amato, M. R. Resistance to extinction after varying amounts of nondiscriminative or cue-correlated escape training. *Journal of Comparative and Physiological Psychology,* 1969, *68,* 373–376.

Feather, B. W. Human salivary conditioning: A methodological study. In G. A. Kimble (Ed.), *Foundations of conditioning and learning.* New York: Appleton-Century-Crofts, 1967.

Feigenbaum, E. A. Information processing and memory. In D. A. Norman (Ed.), *Models of human memory.* New York: Academic, 1970.

Feldman, M. D., & MacCulloch, M. J. *Homosexual behavior: Therapy and assessment.* Oxford: Pergamon, 1971.

Felton, M., & Lyon, D. O. The post-reinforcement pause. *Journal of the Experimental Analysis of Behavior,* 1966, *9,* 131–134.

Feltz, D. L. The analysis of the causal elements in Bandura's theory of self-efficacy and an anxiety-based model of avoidance behavior. *Journal of Personality and Social Psychology,* 1982, *42,* 764–781.

Fenwick, S.; Mikulka, P. J.; & Klein, S. B. The effect of different levels of preexposure to sucrose on acquisition and extinction of conditioned aversion. *Behavioral Biology,* 1975, *14,* 231–235.

Ferguson, C. A. Baby talk as a simplified register. In C. E. Snow and C. A. Ferguson (Eds.), *Talking to children: Language input and acquisition.* New York: Cambridge University Press, 1977.

Ferraro, D. P. Response suppression and recovery under some temporally defined schedules of intermittent punishment. *Journal of Comparative and Physiological Psychology,* 1967, *64,* 133–139.

Ferster, C. B., & Skinner, B. F. *Schedules of reinforcement.* New York: Appleton-Century-Crofts, 1957.

Fjerdingstad, E. J. Chemical transfer of learned preference. *Nature,* 1969, *222,* 1079–1080.

Flaherty, C. F. *Animal learning and cognition.* New York: Knopf, 1985.

————, & Davenport, J. W. Successive brightness discrimination in rats following regular versus random intermittent reinforcement. *Journal of Experimental Psychology,* 1972, *96,* 1–9.

————, & Driscoll, C. Amobarbital sodium reduces successive gustatory contrast. *Psychopharmacology,* 1980, *69,* 161–162.

————; Hamilton, L. W.; Gandelman, R. J.; & Spear, N. E. *Learning and memory.* Chicago: Rand-McNally, 1977.

————; Uzwiak, A. J.; Levine, J.; Smith, M.; Hall, P.; & Schuler, R. Apparent hyperglycemic and hypoglycemic conditioned responses with exogenous insulin as the unconditioned stimulus. *Animal Learning and Behavior,* 1980, *8,* 382–386.

Flakus, W. J., & Steinbrecher, B. C. Avoidance conditioning in the rabbit. *Psychological Reports,* 1964, *14,* 140.

Flavell, J. H.; Cooper, A.; & Loiselle, R. H. Effect of the number of pre-utilization functions on functional fixedness in problem solving. *Psychological Reports*, 1958, *4*, 343–350.

Flesher, D. L'amnesia refrograda dropo l'eltroshiek: Contributo allo studio della patogenesi della amnesia in genere. *Schweiz Archives Neurologia Psychiatry*, 1941, *48*, 1–28.

Flexner, J. B.; Flexner, L. B.; & Stellar, E. Memory in mice as affected by intracerebral puromycin. *Science*, 1963, *141*, 57–59.

Flood, J. F.; Bennett, E. L.; Orme, A. E.; & Rosenzweig, M. R. Relation of memory formation to controlled amounts of brain protein synthesis. *Physiology and Behavior*, 1975, *15*, 97–102.

——; ——; Rosenzweig, M. R.; & Orme, A. E. The influence of duration of protein synthesis inhibition on memory. *Physiology and Behavior*, 1973, *15*, 97–102.

Flory, R. K. Attack behavior as a function of minimum inter-food interval. *Journal of the Experimental Analysis of Behavior*, 1969, *12*, 825–828.

——. The control of schedule-induced polydipsia: Frequency and magnitude of reinforcement. *Learning and Motivation*, 1971, *2*, 215–227.

——, & Ellis, B. B. Schedule-induced aggression against a slide-image target. *Bulletin of the Psychonomic Society*, 1973, *2*, 287–290.

——, & O'Boyle, M. D. The effect of limited water availability on schedule-induced polydipsia. *Physiology and Behavior*, 1972, *8*, 147–149.

Fodor, J. A.; Bever, T. G.; & Garrett, M. F. *The psychology of language: An introduction to psycholinguistics and generative grammar*. New York: McGraw-Hill, 1974.

Foree, D. D., & LoLordo, V. M. Attention in the pigeon: The differential effects of food-getting vs. shock avoidance procedures. *Journal of Comparative and Physiological Psychology*, 1973, *85*, 551–558.

Forster, K. I. Levels of processing and the structure of the language processor. In W. E. Cooper and T. Walker (Eds.), *Sentence processing*. Hillsdale, N.J.: Erlbaum, 1979.

Fosco, F., & Geer, J. H. Effects of gaining control over aversive stimuli after differing amounts of no control. *Psychological Reports*, 1971, *29*, 1153–1154.

Fowler, H., & Miller, N. E. Facilitation and inhibition of runway performance by hind- and forepaw shock of various intensities. *Journal of Comparative and Physiological Psychology*, 1963, *56*, 801–805.

——, & Trapold, M. A. Escape performance as a function of delay of reinforcement. *Journal of Experimental Psychology*, 1962, *63*, 464–467.

Fox, M. W. Ontogeny of prey-killing behavior in canidae. *Behaviour*, 1969, *35*, 259–272.

Franks, C. M., & Wilson, G. T. *Annual review of behavior therapy: Theory and practice* (vol. 2). New York: Brunner/Mazel, 1974.

Freedman, P. E.; Hennessy, J. W.; & Groner, D. Effects of varying active/passive shock levels in shuttle box avoidance in rats. *Journal of Comparative and Physiological Psychology*, 1974, *86*, 79–84.

Frey, P. W. Within- and between-session CS intensity performance effects in rabbit eyelid conditioning. *Psychonomic Science*, 1969, *17*, 1–2.

——, & Butler, C. S. Rabbit eyelid conditioning as a function of unconditioned stimulus duration. *Journal of Comparative and Physiological Psychology*, 1973, *85*, 289–294.

——, & Ross, L. E. Classical conditioning of the rabbit eyelid response as a function of interstimulus interval. *Journal of Comparative and Physiological Psychology,* 1968, *65,* 246–250.

Frumkin, K., & Brookshire, K. H. Conditioned fear training and later avoidance learning in goldfish. *Psychonomic Science,* 1969, *16,* 159–160.

Fuchs, C. Z., & Rehm, L. P. Self-control depression program. *Journal of Consulting and Clinical Psychology,* 1977, *45,* 206–215.

Gaito, J. A biochemical approach to learning and memory: Fourteen years later. *Advances in Psychobiology,* 1974, *2,* 225–239.

Galbraith, D. A.; Byrick, R. J.; & Rutledge, J. T. An aversive conditioning approach to the inhibition of chronic vomiting. *Canadian Psychiatric Association Journal,* 1970, *15,* 311–313.

Galef, B. G. Aggression and timidity: Responses to novelty in feral Norway rats. *Journal of Comparative and Physiological Psychology,* 1970a, *70,* 370–381.

———. Target novelty elicits and directs shock-associated aggression in wild rats. *Journal of Comparative and Physiological Psychology,* 1970b, *71,* 87–91.

———, & Sherry, D. F. Mother's milk: A medium for the transmission of cues reflecting the flavor of mother's diet. *Journal of Comparative and Physiological Psychology,* 1973, *83,* 374–378.

Gamzu, E., & Williams, D. R. Classical conditioning of a complex skeletal act. *Science,* 1971, *171,* 923–925.

Gantt, W. H. Experimental basis for neurotic behavior. In H. D. Kimmel (Ed.), *Experimental psychopathology: Recent research and theory.* New York: Academic, 1971.

Ganz, L. An analysis of generalization behavior in the stimulus deprived organism. In G. Newton and S. Levine (Eds.), *Early experience and behavior.* Springfield, Ill.: Charles C. Thomas, 1968.

———, & Riesen, A. H. Stimulus generalization to hue in the dark-reared macaque. *Journal of Comparative and Physiological Psychology,* 1962, *55,* 92–99.

Garb, J. J., & Stunkard, A. J. Taste aversions in man. *American Journal of Psychiatry,* 1974, *131,* 1204–1207.

Garcia, J.; Clark, J. C.; & Hankins, W. G. Natural responses to scheduled rewards. In P. P. G. Bateson and P. H. Klopfer (Eds.), *Perspectives in ethology.* New York: Plenum, 1973.

———; Ervin, F. R.; Yorke, C. H.; & Koelling, R. A. Conditioning with delayed vitamin injections. *Science,* 1967, *155,* 716–718.

———; Hankins, W. G.; & Rusiniak, K. W. Behavioral regulation of the milieu interne in man and rat. *Science,* 1974, *185,* 824–831.

———; Kimeldorf, D. J.; & Hunt, E. L. Spatial avoidance in the rat as a result of exposure to ionizing radiation. *British Journal of Radiology,* 1957, *30,* 318–322.

———; ———; & Koelling, R. A. Conditioned aversion to saccharin resulting from exposure to gamma radiation. *Science,* 1955, *122,* 157–158.

———, & Koelling, R. A. Relation of cue to consequence in avoidance learning. *Psychonomic Science,* 1966, *4,* 123–124.

———, & ———. A comparison of aversions induced by x-rays, toxins, and drugs in the rat. *Radiation Research Supplement,* 1967, *7,* 439–450.

———; McGowan, B. K.; Ervin, F. R.; & Koelling, R. A. Cues: Their relative effectiveness as a function of the reinforcer. *Science,* 1968, *160,* 794–795.

———, & Rusiniak, K. W. What the nose learns from the mouth. In D. Muller-Schwarze and R. M. Silverskin (Eds.), *Chemical senses.* New York: Plenum, 1980.

Gardner, B. J., & Gardner, R. A. Two-way communication with an infant chimpanzee. In A. M. Schrier and F. Stolnitz (Eds.), *Behavior of nonhuman primates: Modern research trends*. New York: Academic, 1971.

Gardner, R. A., & Runquist, W. N. Acquisition and extinction of problem-solving set. *Journal of Experimental Psychology*, 1958, *55*, 274–277.

Garner, W. R. An information analysis of absolute judgements of loudness. *Journal of Experimental Psychology*, 1953, *46*, 373–380.

Gatchel, R. J., & Proctor, J. D. Physiological correlates of learned helplessness in man. *Journal of Abnormal Psychology*, 1976, *85*, 27–34.

Gay, R., & Raphelson, A. "Transfer of learning" by injection of brain RNA: A replication. *Psychonomic Science*, 1967, *8*, 369–370.

Gelfand, D. M.; Hartmann, D. P.; Lamb, A. K.; Smith, C. L.; Mahan, M. A.; & Paul, S. C. The effects of adult models and described alternatives on children's choice of behavior management techniques. *Child Development*, 1974, *45*, 585–593.

Geller, A., & Jarvik, M. E. The time relations of ECS-induced amnesia. *Psychonomic Science*, 1968, *12*, 169–170.

Gentry, G. D.; Weiss, B.; & Laties, V. G. The microanalysis of fixed-interval responding. *Journal of the Experimental Analysis of Behavior*, 1983, *39*, 327–343.

Gentry, W. D., & Schaeffer, R. W. The effect of FR response requirement on aggressive behavior in rats. *Psychonomic Science*, 1969, *14*, 236–238.

Gibby, R. G., & Crough, D. G. RNA-induced enhancement of wire climbing in the rat. *Psychonomic Science*, 1967, *9*, 413–414.

Gibson, E. J. *Perceptual learning and development*. New York: Appleton, 1969.

———, & Walk, R. D. The effect of prolonged exposure to visually presented patterns on learning to discriminate them. *Journal of Comparative and Physiological Psychology*, 1956, *49*, 239–242.

———; ———; & Tighe, R. J. Enhancement and deprivation of visual stimulation during rearing as factors in visual discrimination learning. *Journal of Comparative and Physiological Psychology*, 1959, *52*, 74–81.

Gilbert, R. M. Ubiquity of schedule-induced polydipsia. *Journal of the Experimental Analysis of Behavior*, 1974, *21*, 277–284.

Giles, D. K., & Wolf, M. M. Toilet training in institutionalized, severe retardates: An application of operant behavior modification techniques. *American Journal of Mental Deficiency*, 1966, *70*, 766–780.

Glass, D. C., & Singer, J. E. *Urban stress: Experiments on noise and social stressors*. New York: Academic, 1972.

Gleason, J. B., & Weintraub, S. Input language and the acquisition of communicative competence. In K. E. Nelson (Ed.), *Children's language* (vol. 1). New York: Gardner, 1978.

Gleitman, H. Forgetting of long-term memories in animals. In W. K. Honig and P. H. R. James (Eds.), *Animal memory*. New York: Academic, 1971.

———. *Psychology*. New York: Norton, 1981.

Glueck, S., & Glueck, E. *Unraveling juvenile delinquency*. Cambridge, Mass.: Harvard University Press, 1950.

Gollin, E. S. Solution of conditional discrimination problems by young children. *Journal of Comparative and Physiological Psychology*, 1966, *62*, 454–456.

———, & Savoy, P. Fading procedures and conditional discrimination in children. *Journal of the Experimental Analysis of Behavior*, 1968, *48*, 371–388.

Golub, A. M.; Epstein, L.; & McConnell, J. V. The effect of peptides, RNA extracts, and whole brain homogenates on avoidance behavior in rats. *Journal of Biological Psychology,* 1969, *11,* 44–49.

———, & McConnell, J. V. Transfer of a response bias by injection of brain homogenates: A replication. *Psychonomic Science,* 1968, *11,* 1–2.

Goodman, I. J., & Brown, J. L. Stimulation of positively and negatively reinforcing sites in the avian brain. *Life Sciences,* 1966, *5,* 693–704.

Goodwin, D. W.; Powell, B.; Bremer, D.; Hoine, H.; & Stein, J. Alcohol and recall: State-dependent effects in man. *Science,* 1969, *163,* 1358–1360.

Gordon, W. C. Malleability of memory in animals. In R. L. Mellgren (Ed.), *Animal cognition and behavior.* New York: North Holland, 1983.

———; McCracken, K. M.; Dess-Beech, N.; & Mowrer, R. R. Mechanisms for the cueing phenomenon: The addition of the cueing context to the training memory. *Learning and Motivation,* 1981, *12,* 196–211.

Gormezano, I. Investigations of defense and reward conditioning in the rabbit. In A. H. Black and W. F. Prokasy (Eds.), *Classical conditioning II: Current theory and research.* New York: Academic, 1972.

Gottlieb, G. Imprinting in relation to parental and species identification by avian neonates. *Journal of Comparative and Physiological Psychology,* 1965, *59,* 354–356.

Gould, J. L. *Ethology: The mechanisms and evolution of behavior.* New York: Norton, 1982.

Granger, R. G.; Porter, J. H.; & Christoph, N. L. Adjunctive behavior in children as a function of interreinforcement interval length. Paper presented at Southeastern Psychological Association Convention, Atlanta, Georgia, March 1983.

Grant, D. A., & Schipper, L. M. The acquisition and extinction of conditioned eyelid responses as a function of the percentage of fixed ratio random reinforcement. *Journal of Experimental Psychology,* 1952, *43,* 313–320.

———, & Schneider, D. E. Intensity of the conditioned stimulus and strength of conditioning: I. The conditioned eyelid response to light. *Journal of Experimental Psychology,* 1948, *38,* 690–696.

———, & ———. Intensity of the conditioned stimulus and strength of conditioning: II. The conditioned galvanic skin response to an auditory stimulus. *Journal of Experimental Psychology,* 1949, *39,* 35–40.

Grant, D. S. Proactive interference in pigeon short-term memory. *Journal of Experimental Psychology: Animal Behavior Processes,* 1975, *1,* 207–220.

———. Effect of sample presentation time on long delay matching in the pigeon. *Learning and Motivation,* 1976, *7,* 580–590.

———. Short-term memory in the pigeon. In N. E. Spear and R. R. Miller (Eds.), *Information processing in animals: Memory mechanisms.* Hillsdale, N.J.: Erlbaum, 1981.

———, & Roberts, W. A. Trace interaction in pigeon short-term memory. *Journal of Experimental Psychology,* 1973, *101,* 21–29.

———, & ———. Sources of retroactive inhibition in pigeon short-term memory. *Journal of Experimental Psychology: Animal Behavior Processes,* 1976, *2,* 1–16.

Gray, J. A. *The psychology of fear and stress.* New York: McGraw-Hill, 1971.

Gray, T., & Appignanesi, A. A. Compound conditioning: Elimination of the blocking effect. *Learning and Motivation,* 1973, *4,* 374–380.

Green, K. F., & Churchill, P. A. An effect of flavors on strength of conditioned aversions. *Psychonomic Science,* 1970, *21,* 19–20.

Green, L. Temporal and stimulus factors in self-monitoring by obese persons. *Behavior Therapy*, 1978, *9*, 328–341.

Greene, J. E. Magnitude of reward and acquisition of a black-white discrimination habit. *Journal of Experimental Psychology*, 1953, *46*, 113–119.

Greeno, J. G. Hobbits and orcs: Acquisition of a sequential concept. *Cognitive Psychology*, 1974, *6*, 270–292.

Greenspoon, J., & Ranyard, R. Stimulus conditions and retroactive inhibition. *Journal of Experimental Psychology*, 1957, *53*, 55–59.

Greiner, J. M., & Karoly, P. Effects of self-control training on study activity and academic performance: An analysis of self-monitoring, self-reward, and systematic planning components. *Journal of Counseling Psychology*, 1976, *23*, 495–502.

Grice, G. R. The relation of secondary reinforcement to delayed reward in visual discrimination learning. *Journal of Experimental Psychology*, 1948, *38*, 1–16.

——. Stimulus intensity and response evocation. *Psychological Review*, 1968, *75*, 359–373.

——. Conditioning and a decision theory of response evocation. In G. H. Bower (Ed.), *The psychology of learning and motivation*. New York: Academic, 1972.

——, & Hunter, J. J. Stimulus intensity effects depend upon the type of experimental design. *Psychological Review*, 1964, *71*, 247–256.

Griffin, J. C.; Locke, B. J.; & Landers, W. F. Manipulation of potential punishment parameters in the treatment of self-injury. *Journal of Applied Behavior Analysis*, 1975, *8*, 458.

Grossen, N. E.; Kostensek, D. J.; & Bolles, R. C. Effects of appetitive discriminative stimuli on avoidance behavior. *Journal of Experimental Psychology*, 1969, *81*, 340–343.

Grosslight, J. H.; Hall, J. F.; & Murnin, J. Patterning effect in partial reinforcement. *Journal of Experimental Psychology*, 1953, *46*, 103–106.

Grossman, S. P. *A textbook of physiological psychology*. New York: Wiley, 1967.

Grusec, J. E. Demand characteristics of the modeling experiment: Altruism as a function of age and aggression. *Journal of Personality and Social Psychology*, 1972, *22*, 139–148.

Guthrie, E. R. Reward and punishment. *Psychological Review*, 1934, *41*, 450–460.

——. *The psychology of learning*. New York: Harper, 1935.

Gutman, A.; Sutterer, J. R.; & Brush, R. Positive and negative behavioral contrast in the rat. *Journal of the Experimental Analysis of Behavior*, 1975, *23*, 377–384.

Guttman, N. Operant conditioning, extinction, and periodic reinforcement in relation to concentration of sucrose used as reinforcing agent. *Journal of Experimental Psychology*, 1953, *46*, 213–224.

——, & Kalish, H. I. Discriminability and stimulus generalization. *Journal of Experimental Psychology*, 1956, *51*, 79–88.

Guyer, M. J., & Rapoport, A. 2 × 2 games played once. *Journal of Conflict Resolution*, 1972, *16*, 409–431.

Haber, A., & Kalish, H. I. Prediction of discrimination from generalization after variations in schedule of reinforcement. *Science*, 1963, *142*, 412–413.

Haber, R. N., & Standing, L. G. Direct measures of short-term visual storage. *Quarterly Journal of Experimental Psychology*, 1969, *21*, 43–45.

Habley, P.; Gipson, M.; & Hause, J. Acquisition and extinction in the runway as a joint function of constant reward magnitude and constant reward delay. *Psychonomic Science*, 1972, *29*, 133–136.

Hake, D. F.; Azrin, N. H.; & Oxford, R. The effects of punishment intensity on squirrel monkeys. *Journal of the Experimental Analysis of Behavior,* 1967, *10,* 95–107.

Halgren, C. R. Latent inhibition in rats: Associative or nonassociative? *Journal of Comparative and Physiological Psychology,* 1974, *86,* 74–78.

Hall, G. Exposure learning in young and adult laboratory rats. *Animal Behavior,* 1979, *27,* 586–591.

Hall, J. F. Studies in secondary reinforcement: I. Secondary reinforcement as a function of the frequency of primary reinforcement. *Journal of Comparative and Physiological Psychology,* 1951a, *44,* 246–251.

———. Studies in secondary reinforcement: II. Secondary reinforcement as a function of the strength of drive during primary reinforcement. *Journal of Comparative and Physiological Psychology,* 1951b, *44,* 462–466.

———. *The psychology of learning.* Philadelphia: Lippincott, 1966.

———. *Classical conditioning and instrumental learning: A contemporary approach.* Philadelphia: Lippincott, 1976.

———. *An invitation to learning and memory.* Boston: Allyn & Bacon, 1982.

Hammen, C. L., & Krantz, S. Effect of success and failure on depressive cognitions. *Journal of Abnormal Psychology,* 1976, *85,* 577–586.

Hammond, L. J. Increased responding to CS- in differential CER. *Psychonomic Science,* 1966, *5,* 337–338.

Hanratty, M. A.; Liebert, R. M.; Morris, L. W.; & Fernandez, L. E. Imitation of film-mediated aggression against live and inanimate victims. In American Psychological Association, *Proceedings of the 77th annual convention of the American Psychological Association.* Washington, D.C., 1969, 457–458.

Hanson, H. M. Effects of discrimination training on stimulus generalization. *Journal of Experimental Psychology,* 1959, *58,* 321–334.

Harlow, H. F. *Learning to love.* San Francisco: Albion, 1971.

———, & Suomi, S. J. Nature of love—Simplified. *American Psychologist,* 1970, *25,* 161–168.

Harris, M. B. Self-directed program for weight control: A pilot study. *Journal of Abnormal Psychology,* 1969, *74,* 264–270.

Harris, V. W., & Sherman, J. A. Use and analysis of the "Good Behavior Game" to reduce disruptive classroom behavior. *Journal of Applied Behavior Analysis,* 1973, *6,* 405–417.

Hartman, T. F., & Grant, D. A. Effect of intermittent reinforcement on acquisition, extinction, and spontaneous recovery of the conditioned eyelid response. *Journal of Experimental Psychology,* 1960, *60,* 89–96.

Hawkins, R. D.; Schrot, J. F.; Githens, S. H.; & Everett, P. B. Schedule-induced polydipsia: Analysis of water and alcohol ingestion. In R. M. Gilbert and J. D. Kechn (Eds.), *Schedule effects: Drugs, drinking, and aggression.* Toronto: Toronto University Press, 1972.

Haycock, J. W.; van Buskirk, R.; & McGaugh, J. L. Effects of catecholaminergic drugs upon memory storage processes in mice. *Behavioral Biology,* 1977, *20,* 281–310.

Hayes, J. R. *Cognitive Psychology.* Homewood, Ill.: Dorsey, 1978.

Hayes, J. R. M. Memory span for several vocabularies as a function of vocabulary size. In *Quarterly progress report.* Cambridge, Mass.: Acoustics Laboratory, Massachusetts Institute of Technology, 1952.

Hayes, K. J., & Hayes, C. The intellectual development of a home-raised chimpanzee. *Proceedings of the American Philosophical Society,* 1951, *95,* 105–109.

Hayes, S. C., & Cone, J. D. Reducing residential electrical energy use: Payments, information, and feedback. *Journal of Applied Behavior Analysis,* 1977, *10,* 425–435.

Hearst, E. The classical-instrumental distinction: Reflexes, voluntary behavior, and categories of associative learning. In W. K. Estes (Ed.), *Handbook of learning and cognitive processes,* vol. 2: *Conditioning and behavior theory.* Hillsdale, N.J.: Erlbaum, 1975.

———; Besley, S.; & Farthing, G. W. Inhibition and the stimulus control of operant behavior. *Journal of the Experimental Analysis of Behavior,* 1970, *14,* 373–409.

———, & Jenkins, H. M. *Sign tracking: The stimulus-reinforcer relation and direct action.* Austin, Tex.: Monograph of the Psychonomic Society, 1974.

———, & Koresko, M. B. Stimulus generalization and amount of prior training on variable interval reinforcement. *Journal of Comparative and Physiological Psychology,* 1968, *66,* 133–138.

———, & Sidman, M. Some behavioral effects of a concurrently positive and negative stimulus. *Journal of the Experimental Analysis of Behavior,* 1961, *4,* 251–256.

Heath, R. G. Correlations between levels of psychological awareness and physiological activity in the central nervous system. *Psychosomatic Medicine,* 1955, *17,* 383–395.

Hebb, D. O. *The organization of behavior.* New York: Wiley, 1949.

Heider, F. *The psychology of interpersonal relations.* New York: Wiley, 1958.

Heinemann, E. G., & Rudolph, R. L. The effect of discriminative training on the gradient of stimulus-generalization. *American Journal of Psychology,* 1963, *76,* 653–658.

Herrmann, D. J., & Harwood, J. R. More evidence for the existence of separate semantic and episodic stores in long-term memory. *Journal of Experimental Psychology: Human Learning and Memory,* 1980, *6,* 467–478.

Herrnstein, R. J. Acquisition, generalization and discrimination reversal of a natural concept. *Journal of Experimental Psychology: Animal Behavior Processes,* 1979, *5,* 116–129.

———, & de Villiers, P. A. Fish as a natural category for people and pigeons. In G. H. Bower (Ed.), *Psychology of learning and motivation* (vol. 14). New York: Academic, 1980.

———; Loveland, D. H.; & Cable, C. Natural concepts in pigeons. *Journal of Experimental Psychology: Animal Behavior Processes,* 1976, *2,* 285–302.

Hess, E. H. Space perception in the chick. *Scientific American,* 1956, *195,* 71–80.

———. Ethology: An approach toward the complete analysis of behavior. In R. Brown, E. Galanter, E. H. Hess, and G. Mandler (Eds.), *New directions in psychology.* New York: Holt, 1962.

———. Imprinting in birds. *Science,* 1964, *146,* 1128–1139.

———. *Imprinting.* Princeton, N.J.: Van Nostrand-Reinhold, 1973.

Hilgard, E. R., & Marquis, D. G. *Conditioning and learning.* New York: Appleton-Century-Crofts, 1940.

Hill, W. F., & Spear, N. E. Extinction in a runway as a function of acquisition level and reinforcement percentage. *Journal of Experimental Psychology,* 1963, *65,* 495–500.

———, & Wallace, W. P. Effects of magnitude and percentage of reward on subsequent patterns of runway speed. *Journal of Experimental Psychology,* 1967, *73,* 544–548.

Hines, B., & Paolino, R. M. Retrograde amnesia: Production of skeletal but not cardiac response gradient by electroconvulsive shock. *Science,* 1970, *169,* 1224–1226.

Hintzman, D. L.; Block, R. A.; & Inskeep, N. R. Memory for mode of input. *Journal of Verbal Learning and Verbal Behavior,* 1972, *11,* 741–749.

Hirayoshi, I., & Warren, J. M. Overtraining and reversal learning by experimentally naive kittens. *Journal of Comparative and Physiological Psychology,* 1967, *64,* 507–509.

Hiroto, D. S. Locus of control and learned helplessness. *Journal of Experimental Psychology,* 1974, *102,* 187–193.

————, & Seligman, M. E. P. Generality of learned helplessness in man. *Journal of Personality and Social Psychology,* 1975, *31,* 311–327.

Hobbs, T. R., & Holt, M. M. The effects of token reinforcement on the behavior of delinquents in cottage settings. *Journal of Applied Behavior Analysis,* 1976, *9,* 189–198.

Hockman, C. H., & Lipsitt, L. P. Delay-of-reward gradients in discrimination learning with children for two levels of difficulty. *Journal of Comparative and Physiological Psychology,* 1961, *54,* 24–27.

Hoebel, B. G. Feeding and self-stimulation: Neural regulation of food and water intake. *Annals of the New York Academy of Sciences,* 1969, *157,* 758–778.

Hoffman, H. S. The control of stress vocalization by an imprinting stimulus. *Behaviour,* 1968, *30,* 175–191.

————. Stimulus factors in conditioned suppression. In B. A. Campbell and R. M. Church (Eds.), *Punishment and aversive behavior.* New York: Appleton-Century-Crofts, 1969.

Hokanson, J. E. Psychophysiological evaluation of the catharsis hypothesis. In E. I. Megargee and J. E. Hokanson (Eds.), *The dynamics of aggression.* New York: Harper & Row, 1970.

————, & Burgess, M. The effects of three types of aggression on vascular processes. *Journal of Abnormal and Social Psychology,* 1962a, *64,* 446–449.

————, & ————. The effects of status, type of frustration, and aggression on vascular processes. *Journal of Abnormal and Social Psychology,* 1962b, *65,* 232–237.

————; ————; & Cohen, M. F. Effects of displaced aggression on systolic blood pressure. *Journal of Abnormal and Social Psychology,* 1963, *67,* 214–218.

————, & Shelter, S. The effect of overt aggression on level of physiological arousal. *Journal of Abnormal and Social Psychology,* 1961, *63,* 446–448.

Holland, P. C., & Rescorla, R. A. The effects of two ways of devaluing the unconditioned stimulus after first- and second-order appetitive conditioning. *Journal of Experimental Psychology: Animal Behavior Processes,* 1975, *1,* 355–363.

Hollis, K. Pavlovian conditioning of signal-centered action patterns and autonomic behavior: A biological analysis of function. In J. S. Rosenblatt, R. A. Hinde, C. Beer, and M. Busnel (Eds.), *Advances in the study of behavior* (vol. 12). New York: Academic, 1982.

Holmgren, B. Nivel de vigilia y relfecjos condicionados. *Boletin del Instituto de Investigaciones de la Actividad Nerviosa Superior (Havana),* 1964, *1,* 33–50.

Homme, L. W.; deBaca, P. C.; Devine, J. V.; Steinhorst, R.; & Rickert, E. J. Use of the Premack principle in controlling the behavior of nursery school children. *Journal of the Experimental Analysis of Behavior,* 1963, *6,* 544.

Horel, J. A. The neuroanatomy of amnesia: A critique of the hippocampal memory hypothesis. *Brain,* 1978, *101,* 403–445.

————, & Misantone, L. G. The Kluver-Bucy syndrome produced by partial isolation of the temporal lobe. *Experimental Neurology,* 1974, *42,* 101–112.

————, & ————. Visual discrimination impaired by cutting temporal lobe connections. *Science,* 1976, *193,* 336–338.

Horn, G.; Rose, S. P. R.; & Bateson, P. P. G. Experience and plasticity in the central nervous system. Is the nervous system modified by experience? Are such modifications involved in learning? *Science,* 1973, *181,* 506–514.

Horner, R. D., & Keilitz, I. Training mentally retarded adolescents to brush their teeth. *Journal of Applied Behavior Analysis,* 1975, *8,* 301–310.

Houston, J. P. Stimulus selection as influenced by degrees of learning, attention, prior associations, and experience with the stimulus components. *Journal of Experimental Psychology,* 1967, *73,* 509–516.

––––––. *Fundamentals of learning and memory.* New York: Academic, 1981.

Hoveland, C. I. The generalization of conditioned responses: IV. The effects of varying amounts of reinforcement upon the degree of generalization of conditioned responses. *Journal of Experimental Psychology,* 1937, *21,* 261–276.

Howard, D. V. *Cognitive psychology: Memory, language, and thought.* New York: Macmillan, 1983.

Hull, C. L. Quantitative aspects of the evolution of concepts: An experimental study. *Psychological Monographs,* 1920, *28,* Whole no. 123.

––––––. Goal attraction and directing ideas conceived as habit phenomena. *Psychological Review,* 1931, *38,* 487–506.

––––––. *Principles of behavior.* New York: Appleton, 1943.

––––––. *A behavior system.* New Haven: Yale University Press, 1952.

Hulse, S. H., Jr. Amount and percentage of reinforcement and duration of goal confinement in conditioning and extinction. *Journal of Experimental Psychology,* 1958, *56,* 48–57.

––––––; Fowler, H.; & Honig, W. K. (Eds.), *Cognitive processes in animal behavior.* Hillsdale, N.J.: Erlbaum, 1978.

Hume, D. *A treatise of human nature: Being an attempt to introduce the experimental method of reasoning into moral subjects.* London: J. Noon, 1739.

Humphreys, L. G. Acquisition and extinction of verbal expectations in a situation analogous to conditioning. *Journal of Experimental Psychology,* 1939, *25,* 294–301.

Hunziker, J. C. The use of participant modeling in the treatment of water phobias. Master's thesis, Arizona State University, 1972.

Huppert, F. A., & Piercy, M. Dissociation between learning and remembering in organic amnesia. *Nature,* 1978, *275,* 317–318.

––––––, & ––––––. Normal and abnormal forgetting in organic amnesia: Effect of locus of lesion. *Cortex,* 1979, *15,* 385–390.

Hurwitz, H. M. B. Method for discriminative avoidance training. *Science,* 1964, *145,* 1070–1071.

Hutchinson, R. R.; Azrin, N. H.; & Hunt, G. M. Attack produced by intermittent reinforcement of a concurrent operant response. *Journal of the Experimental Analysis of Behavior,* 1968, *11,* 498–495.

Hyden, H., & Egyhazi, E. Changes in RNA content and base composition in cortical neurons of rats in a learning experiment involving transfer of handedness. *Proceedings of the National Academy of Sciences,* 1964, *52,* 1030–1035.

Ingalls, R. P., & Dickerson, D. J. Development of hypothesis behavior in human concept identification. *Developmental Psychology,* 1969, *1,* 707–716.

Innis, N. K. Stimulus control of behavior during postreinforcement pause of FI schedules. *Animal Learning and Behavior,* 1979, *7,* 203–210.

Ison, J. R., & Cook, P. E. Extinction performance as a function of incentive magnitude and number of acquisition trials. *Psychonomic Science,* 1964, *7,* 203–210.

Iwata, B. A., & Bailey, J. S. Reward versus cost token systems: An analysis of the effects on students and teacher. *Journal of Applied Behavior Analysis,* 1974, *7*, 567–576.

Jackson, R. L.; Alexander, J. H.; & Maier, S. F. Learned helplessness, inactivity, and associative deficits. Effects of inescapable shock on response choice escape learning. *Journal of Experimental Psychology: Animal Behavior Processes,* 1980, *6*, 1–20.

————, Maier, S. F.; & Rapaport, P. M. Exposure in inescapable shock produces both activity and associative deficits in the rat. *Learning and Motivation,* 1979, *9*, 69–98.

Jacobson, A. L.; Babich, F. R.; Bubash, S.; & Jacobson, A. Differential approach tendencies produced by injection of RNA from trained rats. *Science,* 1965, *150*, 636–637.

Jacoby, L. L., & Dallas, M. On the relationship between autobiographical memory and perceptual learning. *Journal of Experimental Psychology: General,* 1981, *110*, 306–340.

Jacquet, Y. F. Schedule-induced licking during multiple schedules. *Journal of the Experimental Analysis of Behavior,* 1972, *17*, 413–423.

James, C. T., & Greeno, J. G. Stimulus selection at different stages of paired-associate learning. *Journal of Experimental Psychology,* 1967, *74*, 75–83.

James, J. P.; Ossenkop, P.; & Mostoway, W. W. Avoidance learning as a function of amount and direction of change in CS intensity without a constant background intensity. *Bulletin of the Psychonomic Society,* 1973, *2*, 18–20.

James, W. A. *The principles of psychology* (vols. I and II). New York: Holt, 1890.

Janowsky, D. S.; El-Yousef, M. K.; Davis, J. M.; Hubbard, B.; & Sekerke, H. J. Cholinergic reversal of manic symptoms. *Lancet,* 1972, *1*, 1236–1237.

Jarvik, M. E.; Goldfarb, R.; & Corley, J. L. Influence of interference on delayed matching in monkeys. *Journal of Experimental Psychology,* 1969, *81*, 1–6.

Jaynes, J. Imprinting: The interaction of learned and innate behavior: I. Development and generalization. *Journal of Comparative and Physiological Psychology,* 1956, *49*, 201–206.

Jenkins, H. M. Sensitivity of different response systems to stimulus-reinforcer and response-reinforcer relations. In H. Davis and H. M. B. Hurwitz (Eds.), *Operant-Pavlovian interactions.* Hillsdale, N.J.: Lawrence Erlbaum Associates, 1977.

————, & Harrison, R. H. Generalization gradients of inhibition following auditory discrimination learning. *Journal of the Experimental Analysis of Behavior,* 1962, *5*, 435–441.

————, & Moore, B. R. The form of the autoshaped response with food or water reinforcers. *Journal of the Experimental Analysis of Behavior,* 1973, *20*, 163–181.

Jenkins, J. G., & Dallenbach, K. M. Oblivescence during sleep and waking. *American Journal of Psychology,* 1924, *35*, 605–612.

Jenkins, J. J.; Mink, W. D.; & Russell, W. A. Associative clustering as a function of verbal association strength. *Psychological Reports,* 1958, *4*, 127–136.

Jenkins, W. O. A temporal gradient of derived reinforcement. *American Journal of Psychology,* 1950, *63*, 237–243.

————; McFann, H.; & Clayton, F. L. A methodological study of extinction following aperiodic and continuous reinforcement. *Journal of Comparative and Physiological Psychology,* 1950, *43*, 155–167.

Jennings, H. S. *Contributions to the study of the behavior of lower organisms.* New York: Columbia University Press, 1904.

Jensen, G. D. Learning and performance as functions of ration size, hours of deprivation, and effort requirement. *Journal of Experimental Psychology,* 1960, *59,* 261–268.

Jensen, R. A.; Martinez, J. L.; Messing, R. B.; Spiehler, V. R.; Vasquez, B. J.; Soumireu-Mourat, B.; Liang, K. C.; & McGaugh, J. L. Morphine and naloxone alter memory in rats. *Society for Neuroscience Abstracts,* 1978, *4,* 260.

John, E. R. *Mechanisms of memory.* New York: Academic, 1967.

Johnson, D. F., & Cumming, W. W. Some determiners of attention. *Journal of the Experimental Analysis of Behavior,* 1968, *11,* 157–166.

Johnson, E. E. The role of motivational strength in latent learning. *Journal of Comparative and Physiological Psychology,* 1952, *45,* 526–530.

Johnson, J. L., & Church, R. M. Effects of shock intensity on non-discriminative avoidance learning of rats in a shuttlebox. *Psychonomic Science,* 1965, *3,* 497–498.

Johnson, N. F. Sequential verbal behavior. In T. R. Dixon and D. L. Horton (Eds.), *Verbal behavior and general behavior theory.* Englewood Cliffs, N.J.: Prentice-Hall, 1968.

Jones, E. E., & Nisbett, R. E. The actor and the observer: Divergent perceptions of the causes of behavior. In E. E. Jones, D. E. Kanouse, H. H. Kelley, R. E. Nisbett, S. Valins, and B. Weiner (Eds.), *Attribution: Perceiving the causes of behavior.* Morristown, N.J.: General Learning, 1972.

Jones, M. C. The elimination of children's fears. *Journal of Experimental Psychology,* 1924, *7,* 383–390.

Kahneman, D., & Tversky, A. Subjective probability: A judgment of representativeness. *Cognitive Psychology,* 1972, *3,* 430–454.

———, & ———. On the psychology of prediction. *Psychological Review,* 1973, *80,* 237–251.

Kalat, J. W. Taste salience depends on novelty, not concentration, in taste-aversion learning in the rat. *Journal of Comparative and Physiological Psychology,* 1974, *86,* 47–50.

———, & Rozin, P. "Salience": A factor which can override temporal contiguity in taste-aversion learning. *Journal of Comparative and Physiological Psychology,* 1970, *71,* 192–197.

———, & ———. Role of interference in taste-aversion learning. *Journal of Comparative and Physiological Psychology,* 1971, *77,* 53–58.

———, & ———. "Learned safety" as a mechanism in long-delay learning in rats. *Journal of Comparative and Physiological Psychology,* 1973, *83,* 198–207.

Kalish, H. I. Stimulus generalization. In M. H. Mary (Ed.), *Learning: Processes.* London: Macmillan, 1969.

———. *From behavioral science to behavior modification.* New York: McGraw-Hill, 1981.

Kallman, W. M.; Hersen, M.; & O'Toole, D. H. The use of social reinforcement in a case of conversion reaction. *Behavior Therapy,* 1975, *6,* 411–413.

Kamin, L. J. Traumatic avoidance learning: The effects of CS-UCS interval with a trace-conditioning procedure. *Journal of Comparative and Physiological Psychology,* 1954, *47,* 65–72.

———. The effects of termination of the CS and avoidance of the US on avoidance learning. *Journal of Comparative and Physiological Psychology,* 1956, *49,* 420–424.

———. The retention of an incompletely learned avoidance response. *Journal of Comparative and Physiological Psychology,* 1957, *50,* 457–460.

————. The delay-of-punishment gradient. *Journal of Comparative and Physiological Psychology,* 1959, *52,* 434–437.

————. "Attention-like" processes in classical conditioning. In M. R. Jones (Ed.), *Miami symposium on the prediction of behavior: Aversive stimulation.* Miami: University of Miami Press, 1968.

————. Predictability, surprise, attention, and conditioning. In B. A. Campbell and R. M. Church (Eds.), *Punishment and aversive behavior.* New York: Appleton-Century-Crofts, 1969.

————; Brimer, C. J.; & Black, A. H. Conditioned suppression as a monitor of fear of the CS in the course of avoidance training. *Journal of Comparative and Physiological Psychology,* 1963, *56,* 497–501.

————, & Schaub, R. E. Effects of conditioned stimulus intensity on the conditioned emotional response. *Journal of Comparative and Physiological Psychology,* 1963, *56,* 502–507.

Kanarek, R. B. *The energetics of meal patterns.* Doctoral dissertation, Rutgers—The State University, 1974.

Kaplan, M.; Jackson, B.; & Sparer, R. Escape behavior under continuous reinforcement as a function of aversive light intensity. *Journal of the Experimental Analysis of Behavior,* 1965, *8,* 321–323.

Kaplan, P. S. The importance of relative temporal parameters in trace autoshaping: From excitation to inhibition. *Journal of Experimental Psychology: Animal Behavior Processes,* 1984, *10,* 113–126.

————, & Hearst, E. Bridging temporal gaps between CS and US in autoshaping: Insertion of other stimuli before, during, and after CS. *Journal of Experimental Psychology: Animal Behavior Processes,* 1982, *8,* 187–203.

Karli, P. The Norway rat's killing response to the white mouse. *Behavior,* 1956, *10,* 81–103.

Karpf, D., & Levine, M. Blank-trial probes and introtacts in human discrimination learning. *Journal of Experimental Psychology,* 1971, *90,* 51–55.

Karsh, E. B. Effects of number of rewarded trials and intensity of punishment on running speed. *Journal of Comparative and Physiological Psychology,* 1962, *55,* 44–51.

Kauffman, J. M., & Hallahan, D. P. Control of rough physical behavior using novel contingencies and directive teaching. *Perceptual and Motor Skills,* 1973, *36,* 1225–1226.

Kaufman, E. L.; Lord, M. W.; Reese, T. W.; & Volkmann, J. The discrimination of visual number. *American Journal of Psychology,* 1949, *62,* 498–525.

Kaufman, K. F., & O'Leary, K. D. Reward, cost, and self-evaluation procedures for disruptive adolescents in a psychiatric hospital school. *Journal of Applied Behavior Analysis,* 1972, *5,* 293–309.

Kazdin, A. E. Response cost: The removal of conditioned reinforcers for therapeutic change. *Behavior Therapy,* 1972, *3,* 533–546.

————. Covert modeling, modeling similarity, and reduction of avoidance behavior. *Behavior Therapy,* 1974a, *5,* 325–340.

————. Effects of covert modeling and modeling reinforcement on assertive behavior. *Journal of Abnormal Psychology,* 1976, *83,* 240–252.

Keele, S. W., & Chase, W. G. Short-term visual storage. *Perception and Psychophysics,* 1967, *2,* 383–385.

Kehoe, E. J.; Gibbs, C. M.; Garcia, A.; & Gormezano, I. Associative transfer and stimulus selection in classical conditioning of the rabbit's nictitating membrane response to serial compound CS. *Journal of Experimental Psychology: Animal Behavior Processes,* 1979, *5,* 1–19.

Keith-Lucas, T., & Guttman, N. Robust-single-trial delayed backward conditioning. *Journal of Comparative and Physiological Psychology,* 1975, *88,* 468–476.

Kelleher, R. T., & Morse, W. H. Schedules using noxious stimuli: III. Responding maintained with response-produced electric shocks. *Journal of the Experimental Analysis of Behavior,* 1968, *11,* 819–838.

Keller, F. S., & Hull, L. M. Another "insight" experiment. *Journal of Genetic Psychology,* 1936, *48,* 484–489.

Keller, R. J.; Ayres, J. J.; & Mahoney, W. J. Brief versus extended exposure to truly random control procedures. *Journal of Experimental Psychology: Animal Behavior Processes,* 1977, *3,* 53–65.

Kelley, H. H. Attribution theory in social psychology. In D. Levine (Ed.), *Nebraska symposium on motivation.* Lincoln: University of Nebraska Press, 1967.

————. The process of causal attribution. *American Psychologist,* 1973, *28,* 107–128.

Kellogg, W. N., & Kellogg, L. A. *The ape and the child.* New York: McGraw-Hill, 1933.

Kemler, D. G. Patterns of hypothesis testing in children's discriminative learning: A study of the development of problem solving strategies. *Developmental Psychology,* 1978, *14,* 653–673.

Kendler, H. H. Learning. In *Annual review of psychology.* Stanford, Calif.: Annual Reviews, 1959.

————, & Gasser, W. P. Variables in spatial learning: I. Number of reinforcements during training. *Journal of Comparative and Physiological Psychology,* 1948, *41,* 178–187.

Kenny, F. T.; Solyom, L.; & Solyom, C. Faradic disruption of obsessive ideation in the treatment of obsessive neurosis. *Behavior Therapy,* 1973, *4,* 448–457.

Keppel, G. Facilitation in short- and long-term retention of paired associates following distributed practice in learning. *Journal of Verbal Learning and Verbal Behavior,* 1964, *3,* 91–111.

————. Retroactive and proactive inhibition. In T. R. Dixon and D. L. Horton (Eds.), *Verbal behavior and general behavior theory.* Englewood Cliffs, N.J.: Prentice-Hall, 1968.

————; Henschel, D. M.; & Zavortink, B. Influence of nonspecific interference on response recall. *Journal of Experimental Psychology,* 1969, *81,* 246–255.

————, & Underwood, B. J. Proactive inhibition in short-term retention of single items. *Journal of Verbal Learning and Verbal Behavior,* 1962, *1,* 153–161.

Kihlstrom, J. F. Posthypnotic amnesia for recently learned material: Interactions with "Episodic" and "Semantic" memory. *Cognitive Psychology,* 1980, *12,* 227–251.

Kimble, G. A., & Reynolds, B. Eyelid conditioning as a function of the interval between conditioned and unconditioned stimuli. In G. A. Kimble (Ed.), *Foundations of conditioning and learning.* New York: Appleton-Century-Crofts, 1967.

Kimble, G. H. *Hilgard and Marquis' conditioning and learning* (2d ed.). New York: Appleton-Century, 1961.

Kimmel, H. D. Instrumental inhibitory factors in classical conditioning. In W. F. Prokasy (Ed.), *Classical conditioning: A symposium.* New York: Appleton-Century-Crofts, 1965.

King, G. D. Wheel running in the rat induced by a fixed-time presentation of water. *Animal Learning and Behavior*, 1974, *2*, 325–328.

Kintsch, W. On comprehending stories. In M. A. Just and P. A. Carpenter (Eds.), *Cognitive processes in comprehension*. Hillsdale, N.J.: Erlbaum, 1977.

———. Semantic memory: A tutorial. In T. D. Nickerson (Ed.), *Attention and performance VIII*. Hillsdale, N.J.: Lawrence Erlbaum Associates, 1980.

Klatzky, R. L. *Human memory*. San Francisco: Freeman, 1975.

Klein, D. C., & Seligman, M. E. P. Reversal of performance deficits and perceptual deficits in learned helplessness and depression. *Journal of Abnormal Psychology*, 1976, *85*, 11–26.

Klein, S. B. Adrenal-pituitary influence in reaction of avoidance-learning memory in the rat after intermediate intervals. *Journal of Comparative and Physiological Psychology*, 1972, *79*, 341–359.

———. *Motivation: Biosocial approaches*. New York: McGraw-Hill, 1982.

———; Davis, T.; Cohen, L.; & Weston, D. Relative influence of cue predictiveness and salience on flavor aversion learning. *Learning and Motivation*, 1984, *15*, 188–202.

———; Domato, G. C.; Hallstead, C.; Stephens, I.; & Mikulka, P. J. Acquisition of a conditioned aversion as a function of age and measurement technique. *Physiological Psychology*, 1975, *3*, 379–384.

———; Freda, J. S.; & Mikulka, P. J. The influence of a taste cue on an environmental aversion: Potentiation or overshadowing. *Psychological Record*, 1985, *35*, 101–112.

———, & Spear, N. E. Influence of age on short-term retention of active-avoidance learning in rats. *Journal of Comparative and Physiological Psychology*, 1969, *69*, 583–589.

———, & ———. Forgetting by the rat after intermediate intervals ("Kamin effect") as retrieval failure. *Journal of Comparative and Physiological Psychology*, 1970a, *71*, 165–170.

———, & ———. Reactivation of avoidance learning memory in the rats after intermediate retention intervals. *Journal of Comparative and Physiological Psychology*, 1970b, *72*, 498–504.

Klopfer, P. H. Imprinting: Determining its perceptual basis in ducklings. *Journal of Comparative and Physiological Psychology*, 1971, *75*, 378–385.

———; Adams, D. K.; & Klopfer, M. S. Maternal "imprinting" in goats. *National Academy of Science Proceedings*, 1964, *52*, 911–914.

Knecht vs. *Gillman*, 488 F. 2d 1136 (8th Cir. 1973).

Knutson, J. F., & Kleinknecht, R. A. Attack during differential reinforcement of low rate of responding. *Psychonomic Science*, 1970, *19*, 289–290.

Koegel, R. L.; Firestone, P. B.; Kramme, K. W.; & Dunlap, G. Increasing spontaneous play by suppressing self-stimulation in autistic children. *Journal of Applied Behavior Analysis*, 1974, *7*, 521–528.

Kohlenberg, R. J. The punishment of persistent vomiting: A case study. *Journal of Applied Behavior Analysis*, 1970, *3*, 241–245.

Kohler, W. *The mentality of apes*. London: Routledge & Kegan Paul, 1925.

———. Simple structural functions in the chimpanzee and the chicken. In W. D. Ellis (Ed.), *A source book of gestalt psychology*. New York: Harcourt Brace, 1939.

Kolers, P. A. Pattern-analyzing memory. *Science*, 1976, *191*, 1280–1281.

———. A pattern-analyzing basis of recognition. In L. S. Cermak and F. I. M. Craik (Eds.), *Levels of processing human memory*. Hillsdale, N.J.: Erlbaum, 1979.

Koppenaal, R. J.; Jogoda, E.; & Cruce, J. A. Recovery from ECS-produced amnesia following a reminder. *Psychonomic Science,* 1967, *9,* 293–294.

Kovach, J. K. Interaction of innate and acquired: Color preferences and early exposure learning in chicks. *Journal of Comparative and Physiological Psychology,* 1971, *75,* 386–398.

———, & Hess, E. H. Imprinting: Effects of painful stimulation upon the following response. *Journal of Comparative and Physiological Psychology,* 1963, *56,* 461–464.

Krapft, J. E. Differential ordering of stimulus presentation and semiautomated versus live treatment in the systematic desensitization of snake phobia. Doctoral dissertation, University of Missouri, 1967.

Krechevsky, I. "Hypotheses" in rats. *Psychological Review,* 1932, *39,* 516–532.

Kremer, E. F. Truly random and traditional control procedures in CER conditioning in the rat. *Journal of Comparative and Physiological Psychology,* 1971, *76,* 441–448.

———. The truly random control procedure: Conditioning to the static cues. *Journal of Comparative and Physiological Psychology,* 1974, *86,* 700–707.

———, & Kamin, L. J. The truly random control procedure: Associative or nonassociative effects in rats. *Journal of Comparative and Physiological Psychology,* 1971, *74,* 203–210.

———; Specht, T.; & Allen, R. Attenuation of blocking with the omission of a delayed US. *Animal Learning and Behavior,* 1980, *8,* 609–616.

Kubena, R. K., & Barry, H. Generalization by rats of alcohol and atropine stimulus characteristics to other drugs. *Psychopharmalogia,* 1969, *15,* 196–206.

Kurtz, K. H., & Pearl, J. The effects of prior fear experiences on acquired-drive learning. *Journal of Comparative and Physiological Psychology,* 1960, *53,* 201–206.

Kushner, M. The operant control of intractible sneezing. In C. D. Spielberger, R. Fox, and D. Masterton (Eds.), *Contributions to general psychology.* New York: Ronald, 1968.

———, & Sandler, J. Aversion therapy and the concept of punishment. *Behaviour Research and Therapy,* 1966, *4,* 179–186.

Lachman, R. The influence of thirst and schedules of reinforcement-nonreinforcement ratios upon brightness discrimination. *Journal of Experimental Psychology,* 1961, *62,* 80–87.

Landauer, T. K. Rate of implicit speech. *Perceptual and Motor Skills,* 1962, *15,* 646.

Lang, P. J. Self-efficacy theory: Thoughts on cognition and unification. In S. Rachman (Ed.), *Advances in behaviour research and therapy* (vol. 1). Oxford: Pergamon, 1978.

———, & Melamed, B. G. Avoidance conditioning of an infant with chronic ruminative vomiting. *Journal of Abnormal Psychology,* 1969, *74,* 1–8.

Lashley, K. S. *Brain mechanisms and intelligence.* Chicago: University of Chicago Press, 1929.

———, & Wade, M. The Pavlovian theory of generalization. *Psychological Review,* 1946, *53,* 72–87.

Lasky, R. E.; Syrdal-Lasky, A.; & Klein, R. E. VOT discrimination by four- to six-and-a-half-month-old infants from Spanish environments. *Journal of Experimental Child Psychology,* 1975, *20,* 215–225.

Lawrence, D. H. The transfer of a discrimination along a continuum. *Journal of Comparative and Physiological Psychology,* 1952, *45,* 511–516.

———, & DeRivera, J. Evidence for relational transposition. *Journal of Comparative and Physiological Psychology,* 1954, *47,* 475–471.

Lawson, E. A. Decisions concerning the rejected channel. *Quarterly Journal of Experimental Psychology*, 1966, *18*, 260–265.

Lawson, R. Brightness discrimination performance and secondary reward strength as a function of primary reward amount. *Journal of Comparative and Physiological Psychology*, 1957, *50*, 35–39.

Lazarus, A. A. *Behavior therapy and beyond*. New York: McGraw-Hill, 1971.

Le, A. D.; Poulos, C. X.; & Cappell, H. Conditioned tolerance to the hypothermic effect of ethyl alcohol. *Science*, 1979, *206*, 1109–1110.

Le Boeuf, A. Aversion treatment of headbanging in a normal adult. *Journal of Behavior Therapy and Experimental Psychiatry*, 1974, *5*, 197–199.

Lea, S. E. A. In what sense do pigeons learn concepts? In H. L. Roitblat, T. G. Bever, and H. S. Terrace (Eds.), *Animal cognition*. Hillsdale, N.J.: Erlbaum, 1984.

Leary, R. W. Homogeneous and heterogeneous reward of monkeys. *Journal of Comparative and Physiological Psychology*, 1958, *51*, 706–710.

Leff, R. Effects of punishment intensity and consistency on the internalization of behavioral suppression in children. *Developmental Psychology*, 1969, *1*, 345–356.

Lefkowitz, M. M.; Walder, L. O.; & Eron, L. D. Punishment, identification, and aggression. *Merrill-Palmer Quarterly*, 1963, *9*, 159–174.

Lehrer, P. M., & Woolfolk, R. L. Self-report assessment of anxiety: Physiological, cognitive, and behavioral modalities. *Behavioral Assessment*, 1982, *4*, 167–177.

Lemieux, G.; Davignon, A.; & Genest, J. Depressive states during rauwolfia therapy for arterial hypertension. *Canadian Medical Association Journal*, 1956, *74*, 522–526.

Lenneberg, E. H. *Biological foundations of language*. New York: Wiley, 1967.

———. On explaining language. *Science*, 1969, *164*, 635–643.

Lett, B. T. Delayed reward learning: Disproof of the traditional theory. *Learning and Motivation*, 1973, *4*, 237–246.

———. Long delay learning in the T-maze. *Learning and Motivation*, 1975, *6*, 80–90.

———. Taste potentiation in poison-avoidance learning. In R. Herrnstein (Ed.), *Harvard symposium on quantitative analysis of behavior* (vol. 4). Hillsdale, N.J.: Erlbaum, 1982.

Leukel, F. A. A comparison of the effects of ECS and anesthesia on acquisition of the maze habit. *Journal of Comparative and Physiological Psychology*, 1957, *50*, 300–306.

Levine, M. Hypothesis behavior by humans during discrimination learning. *Journal of Experimental Psychology*, 1966, *71*, 331–338.

Levine, S. UCS intensity and avoidance learning. *Journal of Experimental Psychology*, 1966, *71*, 163–164.

Levis, D. J. Learned helplessness: A reply and an alternative S-R interpretation. *Journal of Experimental Psychology: General*, 1976, *105*, 47–65.

Levitsky, D., & Collier, G. Schedule-induced wheel running. *Physiology and Behavior*, 1968, *3*, 571–573.

Lewis, D. J. Partial reinforcement in the gambling situation. *Journal of Experimental Psychology*, 1952, *43*, 447–450.

———. Partial reinforcement: A selective review of the literature since 1950. *Psychological Bulletin*, 1960, *57*, 1–28.

———. Sources of experimental amnesia. *Psychological Review*, 1969, *76*, 461–472.

———. Psychobiology of active and inactive memory. *Psychological Bulletin*, 1979, *86*, 1054–1083.

————, & Cotton, J. W. Effect of runway size and drive strength on acquisition and extinction. *Journal of Experimental Psychology, 1960, 59*, 402–408.

————, & Duncan, C. P. Effect of different percentages of money reward on extinction of a lever-pulling response. *Journal of Experimental Psychology, 1956, 52*, 23–27.

————, & ————. Expectation and resistance to extinction of a lever-pulling response as functions of percentage of reinforcement and amount of reward. *Journal of Experimental Psychology, 1957, 54*, 115–120.

————, & ————. Expectation and resistance to extinction of a lever-pulling response as a function of percentage of reinforcement and number of acquisition trials. *Journal of Experimental Psychology, 1958, 55*, 121–128.

————, & Maher, B. A. Neural consolidation and electroconvulsive shock. *Psychological Review, 1965, 72*, 225–239.

————; Miller, R. R.; & Misanin, J. R. Selective amnesia in rats produced by electroconvulsive shock. *Journal of Comparative and Physiological Psychology, 1969, 69*, 136–140.

————; Smith, P. N.; & McAllister, D. E. Retroactive facilitation and interference in performance on the modified two-hand coordinator. *Journal of Experimental Psychology, 1952, 44*, 44–50.

Liberman, A. M.; Delattre, P.; & Cooper, F. S. The role of selected stimulus-variables in the perception of the unvoiced stop consonants. *American Journal of Psychology, 1952, 65*, 497–516.

Liberman, R. P., & Raskin, D. E. Depression: A behavioral formulation. *Archives of General Psychiatry, 1971, 24*, 515–523.

Lick, J., & Bootzin, R. Expectancy factors in the treatment of fear: Methodological and theoretical issues. *Psychological Bulletin, 1975, 82*, 917–931.

Liebman, J. M., & Butcher, L. I. Comparative involvement of dopamine and noradrenaline in rate-free self-stimulation in the substantia nigra, lateral hypothalamus and mesencephalic central gray. *Naunyn-Schmiedeberg's Archives of Pharmacology, 1974, 284*, 167–194.

Linden, D. R. The effect of intensity of intermittent punishment in acquisition on resistance to extinction of an approach response. *Animal Learning and Behavior, 1974, 2*, 9–12.

Lindsey, G., & Best, P. Overshadowing of the less salient of two novel fluids in a taste-aversion paradigm. *Physiological Psychology, 1973, 1*, 13–15.

Lipsitt, L. P., & Castaneda, A. Effects of delayed reward on choice behavior and response speeds in children. *Journal of Comparative and Physiological Psychology, 1958, 51*, 65–67.

Lockhart, R. A., & Steinbrecher, C. D. Temporal avoidance conditioning in the rabbit. *Psychonomic Science, 1965, 3*, 121–122.

Loeb, J. *Einleitung in die vergleichende Gehirnphysiologie und vergleichende Psychologie.* Leipzig: Barth, 1899.

Loehol, H. Zur Frage des Zeitpunktes einer Praqung auf die Heimatregion beim Halsbandschnapper (*Ficedulla albiocollis*). *Journal für Ornithologie, 1959, 100*, 132–140.

Loftus, E. F. Leading questions and the eyewitness report. *Cognitive Psychology, 1975, 7*, 560–572.

————. *Memory.* Reading, Mass.: Addison, Wesley, 1980.

————, & Zanni, G. Eyewitness testimony: The influence of the wording of a question. *Bulletin of the Psychonomic Society, 1975, 5*, 86–88.

Logan, F. A. The role of delay of reinforcement in determining reaction potential. *Journal of Experimental Psychology,* 1952, *43,* 393–399.

———. *Incentive.* New Haven: Yale University Press, 1960.

Logue, A. W. Taste aversion and the generality of the laws of learning. *Psychological Bulletin,* 1979, *86,* 276–296.

———. Conditioned food aversion learning in humans. *Annals of the New York Academy of Sciences,* 1985.

LoLordo, V. M. Selective associations. In A. Dickinson and R. A. Boakes (Eds.), *Mechanisms of learning and motivation.* Hillsdale, N.J.: Erlbaum, 1979.

Lombardi, B. R., & Flaherty, C. F. Apparent disinhibition of successive but not of simultaneous negative contrast. *Animal Learning and Behavior,* 1978, *6,* 30–42.

Long, D., & Allen, G. A. Relative effects of acoustic and semantic relatedness on clustering free recall. *Bulletin of the Psychonomic Society,* 1973, *1,* 316–318.

Longenecker, E. G.; Krauskopf, J.; & Bitterman, M. E. Extinction following alternating and random reinforcement. *American Journal of Psychology,* 1952, *65,* 580–587.

Lorayne, H., & Lucas, J. *The memory book.* New York: Ballantine, 1974.

Lorenz, K. Der Kumpan in der Umwelt des Vogels. *Journal of Ornithology,* 1935, *83,* 137–213, 289–413.

———. The past twelve years in the comparative study of behavior. In C. H. Schiller (Ed.), *Instinctive behavior.* New York: International Universities Press, 1952.

———. *On aggression.* New York: Harcourt Brace Jovanovich, 1966.

———. Innate bases of learning. In K. H. Pibram (Ed.), *On the biology of learning.* New York: Harcourt, Brace, & World, 1969.

———. Companions as factors in the bird's environment. In R. Martin (Trans.), *Studies in animal and human behaviour* (vol. 1). Cambridge, Mass.: Harvard University Press, 1970.

Lotter, E. C.; Woods, S. C.; & Vasselli, J. R. Schedule-induced polydipsia: An artifact. *Journal of Comparative and Physiological Psychology,* 1973, *83,* 478–484.

Lovaas, O. I.; Koegel, R.; Simmons, J. Q.; & Long, J. S. Some generalization and follow-up measures on autistic children in behavior therapy. *Journal of Applied Behavior Analysis,* 1973, *6,* 131–166.

———, & Simmons, J. Q. Manipulation of self-destruction in three retarded children. *Journal of Applied Behavior Analysis,* 1969, *2,* 143–157.

Lovibond, S. H., & Caddy, G. Discriminated aversive control in the moderation of alcoholics' drinking behavior. *Behavior Therapy,* 1970, *1,* 437–444.

Lovitt, T. C.; Guppy, T. E.; & Blattner, J. E. The use of free-time contingency with fourth graders to increase spelling accuracy. *Behaviour Research and Therapy,* 1969, *7,* 151–156.

Lowell, E. L. The effect of need for achievement on learning and speed of performance. *Journal of Psychology,* 1952, *33,* 31–40.

Lubow, R. E., & Moore, A. U. Latent inhibition: The effect of nonreinforced preexposure to the conditioned stimulus. *Journal of Comparative and Physiological Psychology,* 1959, *52,* 415–419.

———; Rifkin, B.; & Alek, M. The context effect: The relationship between stimulus preexposure and environmental preexposure determines subsequent learning. *Journal of Experimental Psychology: Animal Behavior Processes,* 1976, *2,* 38–47.

Luchin, A. S. Mechanization in problem solving. *Psychological Monographs,* 1942, *54,* Whole no. 248.

Ludvigson, H. W.; McNeese, R. R.; & Collerain, I. Long-term reaction of the rat to conspecific (frustration) odor. *Animal Learning and Behavior,* 1979, *7,* 251–258.

Maas, J. W.; Dekirmenjian, H.; & Fawett, J. Catecholamine metabolism, depression and stress. *Nature,* 1971, *230,* 330–331.

MacCorquodale, K., & Meehl, P. E. Edward C. Tolman. In W. K. Estes et al. (Eds.), *Modern learning theory.* New York: Appleton, 1954.

MacCrimmon, K., & Messick, D. Framework of social motives. *Behavioral Science,* 1976, *21,* 86–100.

MacDonald, G. E., & Solandt, A. Imprinting: Effects of drug induced immobilization. *Psychonomic Science,* 1966, *5,* 95–96.

MacDuff, M. M. The effect of retention of varying degrees of motivation during learning in rats. *Journal of Comparative and Physiological Psychology,* 1946, *39,* 207–240.

MacFarlane, D. A. The role of kinesthesis in maze learning. *University of California Publications in Psychology,* 1930, *4,* 277–305.

MacKinnon, J. R. Competing responses in a differential magnitude of reward discrimination. *Psychonomic Science,* 1968, *12,* 333–334.

Mackintosh, N. J. Selective attention in animal discrimination learning. *Psychological Bulletin,* 1965, *64,* 124–150.

————. Stimulus selection: Learning to ignore stimuli that predict no change in reinforcement. In R. A. Hinde and J. Stevenson-Hinde (Eds.), *Constraints on learning.* London: Academic, 1973.

————. *The psychology of animal learning.* London: Academic, 1974.

————. A theory of attention: Variations in the associability of stimuli with reinforcement. *Psychological Review,* 1975, *82,* 276–298.

————. Overshadowing and stimulus intensity. *Animal Learning and Behavior,* 1976, *4,* 186–192.

————. Cognitive or associative theories of conditioning: Implications of an analysis of blocking. In S. H. Hulse, H. Fowler, and W. K. Honig (Eds.), *Cognitive processes in animal behavior.* Hillsdale, N.J.: Erlbaum, 1978.

————. *Conditioning and associative learning.* Oxford: Oxford University Press, 1983.

————; Bygrave, D. J.; & Picton, D. M. B. Locus of the effect of a surprising reinforcer in the attenuation of blocking. *Quarterly Journal of Experimental Psychology,* 1977, *29,* 327–336.

————; Dickinson, A.; & Cotton, M. M. Surprise and blocking: Effects of the number of compound trials. *Animal Learning and Behavior,* 1980, *8,* 387–391.

Mackworth, J. F. The duration of the visual image. *Canadian Journal of Psychology,* 1963, *17,* 62–81.

MacPherson, E. M.; Candee, B. L.; & Hohman, R. J. A comparison of three methods for eliminating disruptive lunchroom behavior. *Journal of Applied Behavior Analysis,* 1974, *7,* 287–297.

Madigan, R. J. Reinforcement context effects on fixed-interval responding. *Animal Learning and Behavior,* 1978, *6,* 193–197.

Madsen, C. H.; Madsen, C. K.; Saudargas, R. A.; Hammond, W. R.; & Edgar, D. E. Classroom RAID (Rules, Approval, Ignore, Disapproval): A cooperative approach for professionals and volunteers. *Journal of School Psychology,* 1970, *8,* 180.

Mahoney, M. J. Self-reward and self-monitoring techniques for weight control. *Behavior Therapy,* 1974, *5,* 48–57.

Maier, N. R. F. Reasoning in humans: I. On direction. *Journal of Comparative Psychology,* 1930, *10,* 115–143.

————. Reasoning in humans: II. The solution of a problem and its appearance in consciousness. *Journal of Comparative and Physiological Psychology*, 1931, *12*, 181–194.

————. *Frustration: The study of behavior without a goal*. New York: McGraw-Hill, 1949.

————; Glazer, N. M.; & Klee, J. B. Studies of abnormal behavior in the rat: III. The development of behavior fixations through frustration. *Journal of Experimental Psychology*, 1940, *26*, 521–546.

————, & Klee, J. B. Studies of abnormal behavior in the rat: XVII. Guidance versus trial and error in the alteration of habits and fixations. *Journal of Psychology*, 1945, *19*, 133–163.

Maier, S. F., & Seligman, M. E. P. Learned helplessness: Theory and evidence. *Journal of Experimental Psychology: General*, 1976, *105*, 3–46.

Maleske, R. T., & Frey, P. W. Blocking of eyelid conditioning: Effect of changing the CS-US interval and introducing an intertrial stimulus. *Animal Learning and Behavior*, 1979, *7*, 452–456.

Malmo, R. B. Finger sweat prints in differentiation of low and high incentive. *Psychophysiology*, 1965, *1*, 231–240.

Maloney, D. M.; Harper, T. M.; Braukmann, C. M.; Fixsen, D. L.; Phillips, E. L.; & Wolf, M. M. Teaching conversation-related skills to predelinquent girls. *Journal of Applied Behavior Analysis*, 1976, *9*, 371.

Mann, J.; Berkowitz, L.; Sidman, J.; Starr, S.; & West, S. Satiation of the transient stimulating effect of erotic films. *Journal of Personality and Social Psychology*, 1974, *30*, 729–735.

Mansfield, J. G., & Cunningham, C. L. Conditioning and extinction of tolerance to the hypothermic effect of ethanol in rats. *Journal of Comparative and Physiological Psychology*, 1980, *94*, 962–969.

Margules, D. L. Noradrenergic rather than serotonergic basis of reward in dorsal tegmentum. *Journal of Comparative and Physiological Psychology*, 1969, *67*, 25–32.

————, & Stein, L. Neuroleptics versus tranquilizers: Evidence from animal behavior studies of mode and site of action. In H. Brill et al. (Eds.), *Neuropsychopharmacology*. Amsterdam: Elsevier, 1967.

————, & ————. Cholinergic synapses of a periventricular punishment system in the medial hypothalamus. *American Journal of Physiology*, 1969, *217*, 475–480.

Marquart, D. I. The pattern of punishment and its relation to abnormal fixation in adult human subjects. *Journal of General Psychology*, 1948, *39*, 107–144.

Marsh, G. An evaluation of three explanations for the transfer of discrimination effect. *Journal of Comparative and Physiological Psychology*, 1969, *68*, 268–275.

Marshall, W. L.; Boutilier, J.; & Minnes, P. The modification of phobic behavior by covert reinforcement. *Behavior Therapy*, 1974, *5*, 469–480.

Martin, L. K., & Riess, D. Effects of US intensity during previous discrete delay conditioning on conditioned acceleration during avoidance extinction. *Journal of Comparative and Physiological Psychology*, 1969, *69*, 196–200.

Marx, J. L. Ape-language controversy flares up. *Science*, 1980, *207*, 1330–1333.

Masserman, J. H. *Behavior and neurosis*. Chicago: University of Chicago Press, 1943.

Masterson, F. A. Escape from noise. *Psychological Reports*, 1969, *24*, 484–486.

Mattson, M., & Moore, J. W. Intertrial responding and CS intensity in classical eyelid conditioning. *Journal of Experimental Psychology*, 1964, *68*, 396–401.

Mayer, J. Genetic, traumatic, and environmental factors in the etiology of obesity. *Psychological Review*, 1953, *33*, 472–508.

McAllister, W. R.; McAllister, D. E.; & Douglass, W. K. The inverse relationship between shock intensity and shuttle-box avoidance learning in rats. *Journal of Comparative and Physiological Psychology*, 1971, *74*, 426–433.

McArthur, L. A. The how of what and why: Some determinants and consequences of causal attributions. *Journal of Personality and Social Psychology*, 1972, *22*, 171–193.

———, & Post, D. L. Figural emphasis and perception. *Journal of Experimental Social Psychology*, 1977, *13*, 520–535.

McCalden, M., & Davis, C. *Report on priority lane experiment on the San Francisco-Oakland Bay Bridge*. Sacramento, Calif.: Department of Public Works, 1972.

McCarron, L. R. Psychophysiological discriminants of reactive depression. *Psychophysiology*, 1973, *10*, 223–230.

McClintock, C. G., & McNeel, S. P. Reward level and game playing behavior. *Journal of Conflict Resolution*, 1966, *10*, 98–102.

McConnell, J. V.; Shigehisha, T.; & Salive, H. Attempts to transfer approach and avoidance responses by RNA injections in rats. *Journal of Biological Psychology*, 1968, *10*, 32–50.

McCord, W.; McCord, J.; & Zola, I. K. *Origins of crime: A new evaluation of the Cambridge-Somerville Youth Study*. New York: Columbia University Press, 1959.

McGaugh, J. L., & Landfield, P. W. Delayed development of amnesia following electroconvulsive shock. *Physiology and Behavior*, 1970, *5*, 1109–1113.

McGeoch, J. A. Forgetting and the law of disuse. *Psychological Review*, 1932, *39*, 352–370.

McGuigan, F. J. Covert oral behavior and auditory hallucinations. *Psychophysiology*, 1966, *3*, 73–80.

McGuire, R. J., & Vallance, M. Aversion therapy by electric shock, a simple technique. *British Medical Journal*, 1964, *1*, 151–152.

McKoon, G., & Ratcliff, R. Priming in episodic and semantic memory. *Journal of Verbal Learning and Verbal Behavior*, 1979, *18*, 463–480.

McLaughlin, T. F., & Malaby, J. Intrinsic reinforcers in a classroom token economy. *Journal of Applied Behavior Analysis*, 1972, *5*, 263–270.

McLean, D. D., & Hakstian, A. R. *Clinical depression: Comparative efficacy of outpatient treatments*. Manuscript, University of British Columbia, Vancouver, Canada, 1979.

McNamara, H. J.; Long, J. B.; & Wike, E. L. Learning without response under two conditions of external cues. *Journal of Comparative and Physiological Psychology*, 1956, *49*, 477–480.

McNeill, D. Developmental psycholinguistics. In F. Smith and G. A. Miller (Eds.), *The genesis of language*. Cambridge, Mass.: M.I.T. Press, 1966.

Meichenbaum, D. H. Examination of model characteristics in reducing avoidance behavior. *Journal of Behavior Therapy and Experimental Psychiatry*, 1972, *3*, 225–227.

Mellgren, R. L. Positive and negative contrast effects using delayed reinforcement. *Learning and Motivation*, 1972, *3*, 185–193.

———, & Ost, J. W. P. Transfer of Pavlovian differential conditioning to an operant discrimination. *Journal of Comparative and Physiological Psychology*, 1969, *67*, 390–394.

Melton, A. W. Implications of short-term memory for a general theory of memory. *Journal of Verbal Learning and Verbal Behavior*, 1963, *2*, 1–21.

————, & Irwin, J. M. The influence of degree of interpolated learning on retroactive inhibition and the overt transfer of specific responses. *American Journal of Psychology,* 1940, *53,* 173–203.

Mendelson, J. The role of hunger in T-maze learning for food by rats. *Journal of Comparative and Physiological Psychology,* 1966, *62,* 341–353.

————. Lateral hypothalamic stimulation in satiated rats: The rewarding effects of self-induced drinking. *Science,* 1967, *157,* 1077–1979.

————, & Chillag, D. Schedule-induced air licking in rats. *Physiology and Behavior,* 1970, *5,* 535–537.

————, & Chorover, S. L. Lateral hypothalamic stimulation in satiated rats: T-maze learning for food. *Science,* 1965, *149,* 559–561.

Menzel, E. W. Cognitive mapping in chimpanzees. In S. H. Hulse, H. Fowler, and W. K. Honig (Eds.), *Cognitive processes in animal behavior.* Hillsdale, N.J.: Erlbaum, 1978.

Metalsky, G. I., & Abramson, L. Y. Attributional styles: Toward a framework for conceptualization and assessment. In P. C. Kendall and S. D. Hollon (Eds.), *Assessment strategies for cognitive-behavioral interventions.* New York: Academic, 1981.

————; ————; Seligman, M. E. P.; Semmel, A.; & Peterson, C. Attributional styles and life events in the classroom: Vulnerability and invulnerability to depressive mood reactions. *Journal of Personality and Social Psychology,* 1982, *43,* 612–617.

Meyer, W. U. Selbstverantwortlichkeit and Leitungs motivation. Doctoral dissertation. Ruhr University, Bochum, Germany, 1970.

Mikulka, P. J.; Leard, B.; & Klein, S. B. The effect of illness (US) exposure as a source of interference with the acquisition and retention of a taste aversion. *Journal of Experimental Psychology: Animal Behavior Processes,* 1977, *3,* 189–201.

Milby, J. B. Delay of shock-escape with and without stimulus change. *Psychological Reports,* 1971, *29,* 315–318.

Miles, R. C. The relative effectiveness of secondary reinforcers throughout deprivation and habit-strength parameters. *Journal of Comparative and Physiological Psychology,* 1956, *49,* 126–130.

Miller, G. A. The magical number seven, plus or minus two: Some limits on our capacity for processing information. *Psychological Review,* 1956, *63,* 81–97.

————. Some preliminaries to psycholinguistics. *American Psychologist,* 1965, *20,* 15–20.

Miller, H. R., & Nawas, M. M. Control of aversive stimulus termination in systematic desensitization. *Behaviour Research and Therapy,* 1970, *8,* 57–61.

Miller, N. E. The frustration-aggression hypothesis. *Psychological Review,* 1941, *48,* 337–342.

————. Studies of fear as an acquirable drive: I. Fear as motivation and fear-reduction as reinforcement in learning of new responses. *Journal of Experimental Psychology,* 1948, *38,* 89–101.

————. Comments on multiple-process conceptions of learning. *Psychological Review,* 1951, *58,* 375–381.

————, & Coons, E. E. Conflict versus consolidation of memory to explain "retrograde amnesia" produced by ECS. *American Psychologist,* 1955, *10,* 394.

————, & Dollard, J. *Social learning and imitation.* New Haven: Yale University Press, 1941.

Miller, R. R.; Small, D.; & Berk, A. M. Information content of rat scotophobin. *Behavioral Biology,* 1975, *15,* 463–472.

————, & Springer, A. D. Amnesia, consolidation and retrieval. *Psychological Review*, 1973, *80*, 69–79.

Miller, W. R., & Seligman, M. E. P. Depression and learned helplessness in man. *Journal of Abnormal Psychology*, 1975, *84*, 228–238.

Mills, C. B. Effects of context on reaction time to phonemes. *Journal of Verbal Learning and Verbal Behavior*, 1980, *19*, 75–83.

Mims, R. M., & Gholson, B. Effects of type and amount of feedback upon hypothesis sampling systems among seven- and eight-year-old children. *Journal of Experimental Child Psychology*, 1977, *24*, 358–371.

Minnesota Department of Public Welfare, Program and Health Services Division. Aversion and deprivation guidelines. August 8, 1977.

Mis, F. W., & Moore, J. W. Effects of pre-acquisition UCS exposure on classical conditioning of the rabbit's nictitating membrane response. *Learning and Motivation*, 1973, *4*, 108–114.

Misanin, J. R.; Miller, R. R.; & Lewis, D. J. Retrograde amnesia produced by electroconvulsive shock after reactivation of a consolidated memory trace. *Science*, 1968, *160*, 554–555.

Mischel, W. Toward a cognitive social learning reconceptualization of personality. *Psychological Review*, 1973, *80*, 252–283.

————, & Grusec, J. E. Determinants of the rehearsal and transmission of neutral and aversive behaviors. *Journal of Personality and Social Psychology*, 1966, *3*, 197–205.

Mishkin, M. Memory in monkeys severely impaired by combined but not by separate removal of amygdala and hippocampus. *Nature*, 1978, *273*, 297–298.

Misslin, R.; Ropartz, P.; Ungerer, A.; & Mandel, P. Nonreproducibility of the behavioral effects induced by scotophobin. *Behavioral Processes*, 1978, *3*, 45–56.

Miyawaki, K.; Strange, W.; Verbugge, R. R.; Liberman, A. M.; Jenkins, J. J.; & Fujimura, O. An effect of linguistic experience: The discrimination of [r] and [l] by native speakers of Japanese and English. *Perception and Psychophysics*, 1975, *18*, 331–340.

Moltz, H. Imprinting: Empirical basis and theoretical significance. *Psychological Bulletin*, 1960, *57*, 291–314.

————. Imprinting: An epigenetic approach. *Psychological Review*, 1963, *70*, 123–138.

Monson, T. C., & Snyder, M. Actors, observers, and the attribution process: Toward a reconceptualization. *Journal of Experimental Social Psychology*, 1977, *13*, 89–111.

Montague, W. E.; Adams, J. A.; & Kiess, H. O. Forgetting and natural language mediation. *Journal of Experimental Psychology*, 1966, *72*, 829–833.

Monti, P. M., & Smith, N. F. Residual fear of the conditioned stimulus as a function of response prevention after avoidance or classical defensive conditioning in the rat. *Journal of Experimental Psychology: General*, 1976, *105*, 148–162.

Moore, J. W. Stimulus control: Studies of auditory generalization in rabbits. In A. H. Black and W. F. Prokasy (Eds.), *Classical conditioning II*. New York: Appleton-Century-Crofts, 1972.

————, & Gormezano, I. Effects of omitted versus delayed UCS on classical eyelid conditioning under partial reinforcement. *Journal of Experimental Psychology*, 1963, *65*, 248–257.

Moore, R., & Goldiamond, I. Errorless establishment of visual discrimination using fading procedures. *Journal of the Experimental Analysis of Behavior*, 1964, *7*, 269–272.

Moos, W. S.; Levan, H.; Mason, B. T.; Mason, H. C.; & Hebron, D. L. Radiation induced avoidance behavior transfer by brain extracts of mice. *Experientia*, 1969, *25*, 1215–1219.

Moray, N. Attention in dichotic listening: Affective cues and the influence of instructions. *Quarterly Journal of Experimental Psychology*, 1959, *11*, 56–60.

———; Bates, A.; & Barnett, R. Experiments on the four-eared man. *Journal of the Acoustical Society of America*, 1965, *38*, 196–201.

Morgane, J. P. Alterations in feeding and drinking of rats with lesions in the globi pallidi. *American Journal of Physiology*, 1961, *201*, 420–428.

Morris, C. C.; Bransford, J. D.; & Franks, J. J. Levels of processing versus transfer appropriate processing. *Journal of Verbal Learning and Verbal Behavior*, 1977, *16*, 519–533.

Morrison, G. R., & Collyer, R. Taste-mediated conditioned aversion to an exteroceptive stimulus following LiCl poisoning. *Journal of Comparative and Physiological Psychology*, 1974, *86*, 51–55.

Morrison, S. D. Control of food intake in cancer cachexia: A challenge and a tool. *Physiology and Behavior*, 1976, *17*, 705–714.

Morse, W. H.; Mead, R. N.; & Kelleher, R. T. Modulation of elicited behavior by a fixed-interval schedule of electric shock presentation. *Science*, 1967, *157*, 215–217.

Moscovitch, A., & LoLordo, V. M. Role of safety in the Pavlovian backward fear conditioning procedure. *Journal of Comparative and Physiological Psychology*, 1968, *66*, 673–678.

Moskowitz, B. A. The acquisition of language. *Scientific American*, 1978, *239*, 92–108.

Mostofsky, D. I. *Stimulus generalization*. Stanford, Calif.: Stanford University Press, 1965.

Mowrer, O. H. Preparatory set (Expectancy): A determinant in motivation and learning. *Psychological Review*, 1938, *45*, 62–91.

———. A stimulus-response analysis and its role as a reinforcing agent. *Psychological Review*, 1939, *46*, 553–565.

———. On the dual nature of learning—A reinterpretation of "conditioning" and "problem solving." *Harvard Educational Review*, 1947, *17*, 102–148.

———. Two-factor learning theory reconsidered, with special reference to secondary reinforcement and the concept of habit. *Psychological Review*, 1956, *63*, 114–128.

———. *Learning theory and behavior*. New York: Wiley, 1960.

———, & Jones, H. M. Habit strength as a function of the pattern of reinforcement. *Journal of Experimental Psychology*, 1945, *35*, 293–311.

———, & Lamoreaux, R. R. Avoidance conditioning and signal duration: A study of secondary motivation and reward. *Psychological Monographs*, 1942, *54*, Whole no. 247.

Mowrer, R. R., & Gordon, W. C. Cueing in an "irrelevant" context. *Animal Learning and Behavior*, 1983, *11*, 401–406.

Moyer, K. E. *The psychobiology of aggression*. New York: Harper & Row, 1976.

———, & Korn, J. H. Effect of UCS intensity on the acquisition and extinction of an avoidance response. *Journal of Experimental Psychology*, 1964, *67*, 352–359.

———, & Korn, J. H. Effect of UCS intensity on the acquisition and extinction of a one-way avoidance response. *Psychonomic Science*, 1966, *4*, 121–122.

Murdock, B. B., Jr. The retention of individual items. *Journal of Experimental Psychology*, 1961, *62*, 618–625.

———. The serial position effect of free recall. *Journal of Experimental Psychology*, 1962, *64*, 482–488.

————. Auditory and visual stores in short-term memory. *Acta Psychologica,* 1967, *27,* 316–324.

Murry, R. G., & Hobbs, S. A. The use of a self-imposed timeout procedure in the modification of excessive alcohol consumption. *Journal of Behavior Therapy and Experimental Psychiatry,* 1977, *8,* 377–380.

Musante, G. J. The dietary rehabilitation clinic: Evaluative report of a behavioral and dietary treatment of obesity. *Behavior Therapy,* 1976, *7,* 198–204.

Myer, J. S., & Riccio, D. Delay of punishment gradients for the goldfish. *Journal of Comparative and Physiological Psychology,* 1968, *66,* 417–421.

Naus, M. J., & Halasz, F. G. Developmental perspectives on cognitive processing and semantic memory. In L. S. Cermak and F. I. M. Craik (Eds.), *Levels of processing in human memory.* New York: Erlbaum, 1979.

Nation, J. R.; Wrather, D. M.; & Mellgren, R. L. Contrast effects in escape conditioning of rats. *Journal of Comparative and Physiological Psychology,* 1974, *86,* 69–73.

Neely, J. H., & Wagner, A. R. Attenuation of blocking with shifts in reward: The involvement of schedule-generated contextual cues. *Journal of Experimental Psychology,* 1974, *102,* 751–763.

Neisser, U. *Cognitive psychology,* New York: Appleton-Century-Crofts, 1967.

————, & Weene, P. Hierarchies in concept formation. *Journal of Experimental Psychology,* 1962, *64,* 644–645.

Nelson, D. L. Remembering pictures and words: Appearance, significance, and name. In C. S. Cermak and F. I. M. Craik (Eds.), *Levels of processing in human memory.* New York: Erlbaum, 1979.

Nelson vs. *Heyne,* 491 F. 2d 352 (1974).

Nevin, J. A. The maintenance of behavior. In J. A. Nevin (Ed.), *The study of behavior: Learning, motivation, emotion, and instinct.* Glenview, Ill.: Scott, Foresman, 1973.

————, & Shettleworth, S. J. An analysis of contrast effects in multiple schedules. *Journal of the Experimental Analysis of Behavior,* 1966, *9,* 305–315.

Newell, A., & Simon, H. *Human problem solving.* Englewood-Cliffs, N.J.: Prentice-Hall, 1972.

————; Shaw, J. C.; & Simon, H. A. Elements of a theory of human problem solving. *Psychological Review,* 1958, *65,* 151–166.

Newport, E. L. Motherese: The speech of mothers to young children. In N. Castellan, D. P. Pisoni, and G. Potts (Eds.), *Cognitive theory* (vol. 2). Hillsdale, N.J.: Erlbaum, 1977.

Nisbett, R. E.; Caputo, C.; Legant, P.; & Maracek, J. Behavior as seen by the actor and by the observer. *Journal of Personality and Social Psychology,* 1973, *27,* 154–164.

————, & Ross, L. *Human inference: Strategies and shortcomings of social judgment.* Englewood Cliffs, N.J.: Prentice-Hall, 1980.

————, & Wilson, T. D. Telling more than we can know: Verbal reports on mental processes. *Psychological Review,* 1977, *84,* 231–259.

Nissen, H. W. Analysis of a complex conditional reaction in chimpanzee. *Journal of Comparative and Physiological Psychology,* 1951, *44,* 9–16.

Noble, C. E. S-O-R and the psychology of human learning. *Psychological Reports,* 1966, *18,* 923–943.

Noble, M., & Harding, G. E. Conditioning of rhesus monkeys as a function of the interval between CS and US. *Journal of Comparative and Physiological Psychology,* 1963, *56,* 220–224.

Norman, D. A. *Memory and attention* (2d ed.). New York: Wiley, 1976.

Nottebohm, F. Brain pathways for vocal learning in birds: A review of the first 10 years. In J. M. Sprague and A. N. Epstein (Eds.), *Progress in psychology and physiological psychology* (vol. 9). New York: Academic, 1980.

Ohio Rev. Code Ann., sec. 5122.271(E) (1977).

O'Keefe, J., & Nadel, L. *The hippocampus as a cognitive map*. Oxford: Oxford University Press, 1978.

Olds, J. Hypothalamic substrates of reward. *Psychological Review*, 1962, *42*, 554–604.

———, & Milner, P. Positive reinforcement produced by electrical stimulation of septal area and other regions of rat brain. *Journal of Comparative and Physiological Psychology*, 1954, *47*, 419–427.

———; Travis, R. D.; & Schwing, R. C. Topographic organization of hypothalamic self-stimulation functions. *Journal of Comparative and Physiological Psychology*, 1960, *53*, 23–32.

Olds, M. E. Comparative effects of amphetamine, scopolamine, chloriazepoxide and diphenylhydantoin on operant and extinction behavior with brain stimulation and food reward. *Neuropharmacology*, 1970, *9*, 519–532.

———. Effects of intraventricular 6-hydroxydopamine and replacement therapy with norepinephrine, dopamine and serotonin on self-stimulation in the diencephalic and mesencephalic regions in the rat brain. *Brain Research*, 1975, *98*, 327–342.

Olton, D. S. Characteristics of spatial memory. In S. H. Hulse, H. Fowler, and W. K. Honig (Eds.), *Cognitive processes in animal behavior*. Hillsdale, N.J.: Erlbaum, 1978.

———. Mazes, maps and memory. *American Psychologist*, 1979, *34*, 583–596.

———; Collison, C.; & Werz, M. A. Spatial memory and radial arm maze performance of rats. *Learning and Motivation*, 1977, *8*, 289–314.

———, & Samuelson, R. J. Remembrance of places passed: Spatial memory in rats. *Journal of Experimental Psychology: Animal Behavior Processes*, 1976, *2*, 97–116.

Orvis, B. R.; Cunningham, J. D.; & Kelley, H. H. A closer examination of causal inference: The role of consensus, distinctiveness, and consistency information. *Journal of Personality and Social Psychology*, 1975, *32*, 605–616.

Osborne, S. R. A quantitative analysis of the effects of amount of reinforcement on two response classes. *Journal of Experimental Psychology: Animal Behavior Processes*, 1978, *4*, 297–317.

Overmier, J. B., & Seligman, M. E. P. Effects of inescapable shock upon subsequent escape and avoidance learning. *Journal of Comparative and Physiological Psychology*, 1967, *63*, 28–33.

Overton, D. A. State dependent or "dissociated" learning produced with pentobarbital. *Journal of Comparative and Physiological Psychology*, 1964, *57*, 3–12.

———. Discriminative control of behavior by drug states. In T. Thompson and R. Pickens (Eds.), *Stimulus properties of drugs*. New York: Appleton-Century-Crofts, 1971.

Padilla, A. M. Effects of prior and interpolated shock exposures on subsequent avoidance learning by goldfish. *Psychological Reports*, 1973, *32*, 451–456.

Paivio, A. Mental imagery in associative learning and memory. *Psychological Review*, 1969, *76*, 241–263.

———. The relationship between verbal and perceptual codes. In E. C. Carterette and M. P. Friedman (Eds.), *Handbook of perception* (vol. VIII). New York: Academic, 1978.

———; Yuille, J. C.; & Madigan, S. A. Concreteness, imagery, and meaningfulness values for 925 nouns. *Journal of Experimental Psychology Monograph Supplement,* 1968, *76,* 1, (pt. 2).

Palmerino, C. C.; Rusiniak, D. W.; & Garcia, J. Flavor-illness aversions: The peculiar roles of odor and taste in memory for poison. *Science,* 1980, *208,* 753–755.

Panksepp, J.; Toates, F. M.; & Oatley, K. Extinction induced drinking in hungry rats. *Animal Behavior,* 1972, *20,* 461–462.

Parke, R. D., & Deur, J. L. Schedule of punishment and inhibition of aggression in children. *Developmental Psychology,* 1972, *7,* 266–269.

————, & Walters R. H. Some factors determining the efficacy of punishment for inducing response inhibition. *Monograph of the Society for Research in Child Development,* 1967, *32,* Whole no. 109.

Pate, J. L., & Rumbaugh, D. M. The language-like behavior of Lana chimpanzee: Is it merely discrimination learning and paired-associate learning? *Animal Learning and Behavior,* 1983, *11,* 134–138.

Patterson, F. G. Conversations with a gorilla. *National Geographic,* 1978, *154,* 438–465.

————. Ape language. *Science,* 1981, *211,* 86–87.

Paul, G. L. Behavior modification research: Design and tactics. In C. M. Franks (Ed.), *Behavior therapy: Appraisal and status.* New York: McGraw-Hill, 1969.

Paul, G. P., & Lentz, R. J. *Psychosocial treatment of chronic mental patients: (Milieu vs. social learning programs).* Cambridge, Mass.: Harvard University Press, 1977.

Paulson, K.; Rimm, D. C.; Woodburn, L. T.; & Rimm, S. A. A self-control approach to inefficient spending. *Journal of Consulting and Clinical Psychology,* 1977, *45,* 433–435.

Pavlov, I. The scientific investigation of the psychical faculties or processes in the higher animals. *Science,* 1906, *24,* 613–619.

————. *Conditioned reflexes.* Oxford: Oxford University Press, 1927.

————. *Lectures on conditioned reflexes: The higher nervous activity of animals* (vol. 1), H. Gantt (Trans.). London: Lawrence and Wishart, 1928.

Pearce, J. M., & Hall, G. A model for Pavlovian learning. *Psychological Review,* 1980, *87,* 532–552.

————; Nicholas, D. J.; & Dickinson, A. The potentiation effect during serial conditioning. *Quarterly Journal of Experimental Psychology,* 1981, *33,* 159–179.

Penfield, W. W., & Mathieson, G. Memory: Autopsy findings and comments on the role of hippocampus in experiential recall. *Archives of Neurology (Chicago),* 1974, *31,* 145–154.

————, & Milner, B. Memory deficit produced by bilateral lesions in the hippocampal zone. *AMA Archives of Neurology and Psychiatry,* 1958, *79,* 475–497.

Penney, R. K. The effects of non-reinforcement on response strengths as a function of number of previous reinforcements. *Canadian Journal of Psychology,* 1960, *14,* 206–215.

————. Children's escape performance as a function of schedules of delay of reinforcement. *Journal of Experimental Psychology,* 1967, *73,* 109–112.

————, & Coskery, J. Instrumental avoidance conditioning of anxious and nonanxious children. *Journal of Comparative and Physiological Psychology,* 1962, *55,* 847–849.

————, & Kirwin, P. M. Differential adaptation of anxious and nonanxious children in instrumental escape conditioning. *Journal of Experimental Psychology,* 1965, *70,* 539–549.

Perin, C. T. Behavior potentiality as a joint function of the amount of training and the degree of hunger at the time of extinction. *Journal of Experimental Psychology,* 1942, *30,* 93–113.

———. A quantitative investigation of the delay-of-reinforcement gradient. *Journal of Experimental Psychology,* 1943, *32,* 37–51.

Peterson, L. R., & Peterson, M. J. Short-term retention of individual verbal items. *Journal of Experimental Psychology,* 1959, *58,* 193–198.

Peterson, N. Effect of monochromatic rearing on the control of responding by wave-length. *Science,* 1962, *136,* 774–775.

Peterson, R. F., & Peterson, L. R. The use of positive reinforcement in the control of self-destructive behavior in a retarded boy. *Journal of Experimental Child Psychology,* 1968, *6,* 351–360.

Phares, E. J. Expectancy changes in skill and chance situations. *Journal of Abnormal and Social Psychology,* 1957, *54,* 339–342.

Phillips, E. L. Achievement place: Token reinforcement procedures in a home-style rehabilitation setting for "predelinquent" boys. *Journal of Applied Behavior Analysis,* 1968, *1,* 213–223.

———; Phillips, E. A.; Fixen, D. L.; & Wolf, M. M. Achievement place: Modification of the behaviors of predelinquent boys within a token economy. *Journal of Applied Behavior Analysis,* 1971, *4,* 45–59.

Phillips, S., & Levine, M. Probing for hypotheses with adults and children. Blank trials and introtacts. *Journal of Experimental Psychology: General,* 1975, *104,* 327–354.

Piliavin, I. M.; Piliavin, J. A.; & Rodin, J. Costs, diffusion, and the stigmatized victim. *Journal of Personality and Social Psychology,* 1975, *32,* 429–438.

Piliavin, J. A.; Dovidio, J. F.; Gaertner, S. L.; & Clark, R. D., III. Responsive by-standers: The process of intervention. In J. Grzelak and V. Derlega (Eds.), *Living with other people: Theory and research on cooperation and helping.* New York: Academic, 1981.

Plotnick, R.; Mir, D.; & Delgado, J. M. R. Aggression, noxiousness and brain stimulation in unrestrained rhesus monkeys. In B. E. Eleftheriou and J. P. Scott (Eds.), *The physiology of aggression and defeat.* New York: Plenum, 1971.

Plummer, S.; Baer, D. M.; & LeBlanc, J. M. Functional considerations in the use of procedural time out and an effective alternative. *Journal of Applied Behavior Analysis,* 1977, *10,* 689–706.

Pollack, I. The information in elementary auditory displays. *Journal of the Acoustical Society of America,* 1952, *24,* 745–749.

———. The information of elementary auditory displays II. *Journal of the Acoustical Society of America,* 1953, *25,* 765–769.

Poon, L. W. A system approach for the assessment and treatment of memory problems. In J. W. Ferguson and C. B. Taylor (Eds.), *The comprehensive handbook of behavioral medicine,* vol. 1: *Systems intervention.* New York: SP Medican and Scientific Books, 1980.

Porterfield, J. K.; Herbert-Jackson, E.; & Risley, T. R. Contingent observation: An effective and acceptable procedure for reducing disruptive behavior of young children in group setting. *Journal of Applied Behavior Analysis,* 1976, *9,* 55–64.

Posner, M. E. Cumulative development of attentional theory. *American Psychologist,* 1982, *37,* 168–179.

Postman, L. Mechanisms of interference in forgetting. Vice-presidential address given at the annual meeting of the American Association for Advancement of Science. New York, 1967.

————, & Phillips, L. Short-term temporal changes in free recall. *Quarterly Journal of Experimental Psychology*, 1965, *17*, 132–138.

————, & Riley, D. A. Degree of learning and interserial interference in retention: A review of the literature and an experimental analysis. *University of California Publications in Psychology*, 1959, *8*, 271–396.

————; Stark, K.; & Fraser, J. Temporal changes in interference. *Journal of Verbal Learning and Verbal Behavior*, 1968, *7*, 672–694.

Powell, D. R., Jr., & Perkins, C. C., Jr. Strength of secondary reinforcement as a determiner of the effects of duration of goal response on learning. *Journal of Experimental Psychology*, 1957, *53*, 106–112.

Powell, J., & Azrin, N. The effects of shock as a punisher for cigarette smoking. *Journal of Applied Behavior Analysis*, 1968, *1*, 63–71.

Powley, R. L. The ventromedial hypothalamic syndrome, satiety, and a cephalic phase hypothesis. *Psychological Review*, 1977, *84*, 89–126.

Premack, A. J., & Premack, D. Teaching language to an ape. *Scientific American*, 1972, *227*, 92–99.

Premack, D. Toward empirical behavior laws: I. Positive reinforcement. *Psychological Review*, 1959, *66*, 219–233.

————. Reinforcement theory. In D. Levine, (Ed.), *Nebraska symposium on motivation*. Lincoln: University of Nebraska, 1965.

————. *Intelligence in ape and man*. Hillsdale, N.J.: Erlbaum, 1976.

————; Schaeffer, R. W.; & Hundt, A. Reinforcement of drinking by running: Effect of fixed ratio and reinforcement time. *Journal of the Experimental Analysis of Behavior*, 1964, *7*, 91–96.

Prescott, R. G. W. Estrous cycle in the rat: Effects on self-stimulation behavior. *Science*, 1966, *152*, 796–797.

Prewitt, E. P. Number of preconditioning trials in sensory preconditioning using CER training. *Journal of Comparative and Physiological Psychology*, 1967, *64*, 360–362.

Prochaska, J.; Smith, N.; Marzilli, R.; Colby, J.; & Donovan, W. Remote-control aversive stimulation in the treatment of head-banging in a retarded child. *Journal of Behavior Therapy and Experimental Psychiatry*, 1974, *5*, 285–289.

Prokasy, W. F., Jr.; Grant, D. A.; & Myers, N. A. Eyelid conditioning as a function of unconditioned stimulus intensity and intertrial interval. *Journal of Experimental Psychology*, 1958, *55*, 242–246.

————, & Hall, J. F. Primary stimulus generalization. *Psychological Review*, 1963, *70*, 310–322.

Pubols, B. H., Jr. Incentive magnitude, learning and performance in animals. *Psychological Bulletin*, 1960, *51*, 89–115.

Quartermain, D. The influence of drugs on learning and memory. In M. R. Rosenzweig and E. L. Bennett (Eds.), *Neural mechanisms of learning and memory*. Cambridge, Mass.: M.I.T. Press, 1976.

————; Paolino, R. M.; & Miller, N. E. A brief temporal gradient of retrograde amnesia independent of situational change. *Science*, 1965, *149*, 1116–1118.

Rackham, D. Conditioning of the pigeon's courtship and aggressive behavior. Master's thesis, Dalhousie University, 1971. Cited in E. Hearst and H. M. Jenkins, *Sign-tracking: The stimulus-reinforcer relation and directed action*. Austin, Tex.: The Psychonomic Society, 1974.

Randich, A., & LoLordo, V. M. Preconditioning exposure to the unconditioned stimulus affects the acquisition of a conditioned emotional response. *Learning and Motivation,* 1979, *10,* 245–275.

————, & Ross, R. T. Contextual stimuli mediate the effects of pre-and postexposure to the unconditioned stimulus on conditioned suppression. In P. D. Balsam and A. Tomie (Eds.), *Context and learning.* Hillsdale, N.J.: Erlbaum, 1985.

Ransmeier, R. E. The effects of convulsion, hypoxia, hypothermia, and anesthesia on retention in the master. Ph.D. thesis, University of Chicago, 1953.

Rapport, M. D., & Bostow, D. E. The effects of access to special activities on the performance in four categories of academic tasks with third-grade students. *Journal of Applied Behavior Analysis,* 1976, *9,* 372.

Rashotte, M. E., & Amsel, A. Transfer of slow-response rituals to extinction of a continuously rewarded response. *Journal of Comparative and Physiological Psychology,* 1968, *66,* 432–433.

Razran, G. H. S. Stimulus generalization of conditioned responses. *Psychological Bulletin,* 1949, *46,* 337–365.

Reber, A. S.; Kassin, S. M.; Lewis, S.; & Cantor, B. On the relationship between implicit and explicit modes in the learning of a complex rule structure. *Journal of Experimental Psychology: Human Learning and Memory,* 1980, 6, 492–502.

Redd, W. H.; Morris, E. K.; & Martin, J. A. Effects of positive and negative adult-child interactions on children's social preference. *Journal of Experimental Child Psychology,* 1975, *19,* 153–164.

Rehm, L. P. A self-control model of depression. *Behavior Therapy,* 1977, *8,* 787–804.

Reichle, J.; Brubakken, D.; & Tetrault, G. Eliminating perserverative speech by positive reinforcement and time-out in a psychotic child. *Journal of Behavior Therapy and Experimental Psychiatry,* 1976, *1,* 179–183.

Reinis, S. The formation of conditioned reflexes in rats after the parenteral administration of brain homogenate. *Activitas Nervosa Superior,* 1965, *7,* 167–168.

————. Block of "memory transfer" by actinomycin D. *Nature,* 1968, *200,* 177–178.

Reisinger, J. J. The treatment of "anxiety-depression" via positive reinforcement and response cost. *Journal of Applied Behavior Analysis,* 1972, *5,* 125–130.

Reiss, M. L.; Piotrowski, W. D.; & Bailey, J. S. Behavioral community psychology: Encouraging low-income parents to seek dental care for their children. *Journal of Applied Behavior Analysis,* 1976, *9,* 387–397.

Reitman, W. R. *Cognition and thought: An information processing approach.* New York: Wiley, 1965.

Renner, K. E. Delay of reinforcement and resistance to extinction: A supplementary report. *Psychological Reports,* 1965, *16,* 197–198.

————. Temporal integration: Relative value of rewards and punishments as a function of their temporal distance from the response. *Journal of Experimental Psychology,* 1966, *71,* 902–907.

Rensch, B., & Ducker, G. Verzogerung des Vergessens erlernter visuellen Aufgaben bei Tieren durch Chlorpromazin. *Pfluegers Archiv für die Gesamte Physiologie des Menschen und der Tiere,* 1966, *289,* 200–214.

Rescorla, R. A. Probability of shock in presence and absence of CS in fear conditioning. *Journal of Comparative and Physiological Psychology,* 1968, *66,* 1–5.

————. Pavlovian conditioned inhibition. *Psychological Bulletin,* 1969, *72,* 77–94.

————. Summation and retardation tests of latent inhibition. *Journal of Comparative and Physiological Psychology,* 1971, *75,* 77–81.

————. Effects of US habituation following conditioning. *Journal of Comparative and Physiological Psychology,* 1973, *82,* 137–143.

————. Effect of inflation of the unconditioned stimulus value following conditioning. *Journal of Comparative and Physiological Psychology,* 1974, *86,* 101–106.

————. Pavlovian excitatory and inhibitory conditioning. In W. K. Estes (Ed.), *Handbook of learning and cognitive processes: Conditioning and behavior theory* (vol. 2). Hillsdale, N.J.: Erlbaum, 1975.

————. Some implications of a cognitive perspective on Pavlovian conditioning. In S. H. Hulse, H. Fowler, and W. K. Honig (Eds.), *Cognitive processes in animal behavior.* Hillsdale, N.J.: Erlbaum, 1978.

————. Simultaneous associations. In P. Harzum and M. D. Zeiler (Eds.), *Predictability, correlation and contiguity.* New York: Wiley, 1981.

————. Effect of a stimulus intervening between CS and US in autoshaping. *Journal of Experimental Psychology: Animal Behavior Processes,* 1982, *8,* 131–141.

————; Durlach, P. J.; & Grau, J. W. Contextual learning in Pavlovian conditioning. In P. D. Balsam and A. Tomie (Eds.), *Context and learning.* Hillsdale, N.J.: Erlbaum, 1985.

————, & Holland, P. C. Behavioral studies of associative learning in animals. *Annual Review of Psychology,* 1982, *33,* 265–308.

————, & LoLordo, V. M. Inhibition of avoidance behavior. *Journal of Comparative and Physiological Psychology,* 1965, *59,* 406–412.

————, & Skucy, J. C. Effect of response-independent reinforcers during extinction. *Journal of Comparative and Physiological Psychology,* 1969, *67,* 381–389.

————, & Solomon, R. L. Two-process learning theory: Relations between Pavlovian conditioning and instrumental learning. *Psychological Review,* 1967, *74,* 151–182.

————, & Wagner, A. R. A theory of Pavlovian conditioning: Variations in the effectiveness of reinforcement and non-reinforcement. In A. H. Black and W. F. Prokasy (Eds.), *Classical conditioning II.* New York: Appleton-Century-Crofts, 1972.

Revusky, S. The role of interference in association over a delay. In W. K. Honig and P. H. R. James (Eds.), *Animal memory.* New York: Academic, 1971.

————. The concurrent interference approach to delay learning. In L. M. Barker, M. R. Best, and M. Domjan (Eds.), *Learning mechanisms in food selection.* Waco, Tex.: Baylor University Press, 1977.

————, & Bedarf, E. W. Association of illness with prior ingestion of novel foods. *Science,* 1967, *155,* 219–220.

————, & Devenuto, F. Attempt to transfer aversion to saccharine solution by injection of RNA from trained to naïve rats. *Journal of Biological Psychology,* 1967, *9,* 18–22.

————, & Parker, L. A. Aversions to drinking out of a cup and to unflavored water produced by delayed sickness. *Journal of Experimental Psychology: Animal Behavior Processes,* 1976, *2,* 342–353.

Reynolds, G. S. Behavioral contrast. *Journal of the Experimental Analysis of Behavior,* 1961a, *4,* 57–71.

————. Attention in the pigeon. *Journal of the Experimental Analysis of Behavior,* 1961b, *4,* 203–208.

————. An analysis of interactions in a multiple schedule. *Journal of the Experimental Analysis of Behavior,* 1961c, *4,* 107–117.

————. *A primer of operant conditioning.* Glenview, Ill.: Scott, Foresman, 1968.

Reynolds, W. F., & Pavlik, W. B. Running speed as a function of deprivation period and reward magnitude. *Journal of Comparative and Physiological Psychology*, 1960, *53*, 615–618.

Riccio, D. C., & Haroutunian, V. Failure to learn in a taste aversion paradigm: Associative or performance deficit? *Bulletin of the Psychonomic Society*, 1977, *10*, 219–222.

Richards, R. W., & Rilling, M. Aversive aspects of a fixed-interval schedule of food reinforcement. *Journal of the Experimental Analysis of Behavior*, 1972, *71*, 405–411.

Richter, C. P. Increased salt appetite in adrenalectomized rats. *American Journal of Psychology*, 1936, *115*, 155–161.

Ridgers, A., & Gray, J. A. Influence of amylobarbitone on operant depression and elation effects in the rat. *Psychopharmacologia*, 1973, *32*, 265–270.

Rimm, D. C., & Mahoney, M. J. The application of reinforcement and participant modeling procedures in the treatment of snake-phobic behavior. *Behaviour Research and Therapy*, 1969, *7*, 369–376.

———, & Masters, J. C. *Behavior therapy*. New York: Academic, 1979.

Risley, T. R. The effects and side effects of punishing the autistic behaviors of a deviant child. *Journal of Applied Behavior Analysis*, 1968, *1*, 21–34.

Ritter, B. The use of contact desensitization, demonstration-plus-participation, and demonstration alone in the treatment of acrophobia. *Behavior Research and Therapy*, 1969, *7*, 157–164.

Rizley, R. C. Depression and distortion in the attribution of causality. *Journal of Abnormal Psychology*, 1978, *87*, 32–48.

———, & Rescorla, R. A. Associations in higher order conditioning and sensory preconditioning. *Journal of Comparative and Physiological Psychology*, 1972, *81*, 1–11.

Robbins, D. Partial reinforcement: A selective review of the alleyway literature since 1960. *Psychological Bulletin*, 1971, *76*, 415–431.

Roberts, W. A. Free recall of word lists varying in length and rate of presentation: A test of the total-time hypotheses. *Journal of Experimental Psychology*, 1972, *92*, 365–372.

———, & Grant, D. S. An analysis of light-induced retroactive inhibition of pigeon short-term memory. *Journal of Experimental Psychology: Animal Behavior Processes*, 1978, *4*, 219–236.

Robinson, N. M., & Robinson, H. B. A method for the study of instrumental avoidance conditioning with children. *Journal of Comparative and Physiological Psychology*, 1961, *54*, 20–23.

Rodgers, W., & Rozin, P. Novel food preferences in thiamine-deficient rats. *Journal of Comparative and Physiological Psychology*, 1966, *61*, 1–4.

Rodin, J. The relationship between external responsiveness and the development and maintenance of obesity. In D. Novin, W. Wyrwicka, and G. A. Bray (Eds.), *Hunger: Basic mechanisms and clinical implications*. New York: Raven, 1976.

Roediger, H. L., III. Memory metaphors in cognitive psychology. *Memory and cognition*, 1980, *8*, 231–246.

Roitblat, H. L.; Bever, T. C.; & Terrace, H. S. (Eds.), *Animal cognition*. Hillsdale, N.J.: Erlbaum, 1984.

Rosch, E. On the internal structure of perceptual and semantic categories. In T. E. Moore (Ed.), *Cognitive development and the acquisition of language*. New York: Academic, 1973.

———. Cognitive representations of semantic categories. *Journal of Experimental Psychology: General*, 1975, *104*, 192–253.

————. Principles of categorization. In E. Rosch and B. Lloyd (Eds.), *Cognition and categorization*. Hillsdale, N.J.: Erlbaum, 1978.

————, & Mervis, C. B. Family resemblances: Studies in the internal structure of categories. *Cognitive Psychology, 1978, 7,* 573–605.

Rose, S. P. R.; Hambley, J.; & Haywood, J. Neurochemical approaches to developmental plasticity and learning. In M. R. Rosenzweig and E. L. Bennett (Eds.), *Neural mechanisms of learning and memory*. Cambridge, Mass.: M.I.T. Press, 1976.

Rosellini, R., & Seligman, M. E. P. Learned helplessness and escape from frustration. *Journal of Experimental Psychology: Animal Behavior Processes, 1975, 1,* 149–158.

Rosenbaum, R. M. *A dimensional analysis of the perceived causes of success and failure*. Doctoral dissertation, University of California, Los Angeles, 1972.

Rosenblatt, F. Recent work on theoretical models of biological memory. In J. Tou (Ed.), *Computer and information sciences* (vol. 2). New York: Academic, 1967.

————; Farrow, J. T.; & Rhine, S. The transfer of learned behavior from trained to untrained rats by means of brain extracts, I and II. *Proceedings of the National Academy of Sciences USA, 1966, 55,* 548–555, 787–792.

————, & Miller, R. G. Behavioral assay procedures for transfer of learned behavior by brain extracts, I and II. *Proceedings of the National Academy of Sciences USA, 1966, 56,* 1423–1430, 1683–1688.

Rosenblith, J. Z. Polydipsia induced in the rat by a second order schedule. *Journal of the Experimental Analysis of Behavior, 1970, 14,* 139–144.

Rosenzweig, M. R., & Bennett, E. L. (Eds.), *Neural mechanisms of learning and memory*. Cambridge, Mass.: M.I.T. Press, 1976.

Ross, R. R. Positive and negative partial reinforcement effects carried through continuous reinforcement, changed motivation, and changed response. *Journal of Experimental Psychology, 1964, 68,* 492–592.

Roth, S., & Kubal, L. The effects of noncontingent reinforcement on tasks of differing importance: Facilitation and learned helplessness effects. *Journal of Personality and Social Psychology, 1975, 32,* 680–691.

Rotter, J. B. *Social learning and clinical psychology*. Englewood Cliffs, N.J.: Prentice-Hall, 1954.

————. Generalized expectancies for internal versus external control of reinforcement. *Psychological Monographs, 1966, 80,* Whole no. 609.

Routtenberg, A., & Lindy, J. Effects of the availability of rewarding septal and hypothalamic stimulation on bar-pressing for food under conditions of deprivation. *Journal of Comparative and Physiological Psychology, 1965, 60,* 158–161.

Rovee-Collier, C. K., & Capatides, J. B. Positive behavioral contrast in 3-month-old infants on multiple conjugate reinforcement schedules. *Journal of the Experimental Analysis of Behavior, 1979, 32,* 15–27.

Rozin, P. The significance of learning mechanisms in food selection: Some biology, psychology, and sociology of science. In L. M. Barker, M. R. Best, and M. Domjan (Eds.), *Learning mechanisms in food selection*. Waco, Tex.: Baylor University Press, 1977.

————, & Kalat, J. W. Specific hungers and poison avoidance as adaptive specializations of learning. *Psychological Review, 1971, 78,* 459–486.

Rudy, J. W., & Cheatle, M. D. Odor-aversion learning in neonatal rats. *Science, 1977, 198,* 845–846.

Rumbaugh, D. M., & Gill, R. V. The mastery of language-type skills by the chimpanzee (Pan). *Annals of the New York Academy of Sciences, 1976, 280,* 562–578.

Rundus, D. Analysis of rehearsal processes in free recall. *Journal of Experimental Psychology,* 1971, *89,* 63–77.

———, & Atkinson, R. C. Rehearsal processes in free recall: A procedure for direct observation. *Journal of Verbal Learning and Verbal Behavior,* 1970, *9,* 99–105.

Runquist, W. N. Retention of verbal associates as function of strength. *Journal of Experimental Psychology,* 1957, *54,* 369–375.

Rush, A. J.; Beck, A. T.; Kovacs, M.; & Hollon, S. Comparative efficacy of cognitive therapy and pharmacotherapy in the treatment of depressed outpatients. *Cognitive Therapy and Research,* 1977, *1,* 17–37.

Rusiniak, K. W.; Palmerino, C. C.; & Garcia, J. Potentiation of odor by taste in rats: Tests of some nonassociative factors. *Journal of Comparative and Physiological Psychology,* 1982, *96,* 775–780.

Russell, R. K., & Sipich, J. F. Cue-controlled relaxation in the treatment of test anxiety. *Journal of Behavior Therapy and Experimental Psychiatry,* 1973, *4,* 47–49.

Safren, M. A. Associations, set, and solution of word problems. *Journal of Experimental Psychology,* 1962, *64,* 40–45.

Sajwaj, T.; Libet, J.; & Agras, S. Lemon-juice therapy: The control of life-threatening rumination in a six-month-old infant. *Journal of Applied Behavior Analysis,* 1974, *7,* 557–563.

Samuel, A. L. Some studies in machine learning using the game of checkers. In E. A. Feigenbaum and J. Feldman (Eds.), *Computers and thought.* New York: McGraw-Hill, 1963.

Sand, L. I., & Biglan, A. Operant treatment of a case of recurrent abdominal pain in a 10-year-old boy. *Behavior Therapy,* 1974, *5,* 677–681.

Savage-Rumbaugh, E. S.; Rumbaugh, D. M.; & Boysen, S. Do apes use language? *American Scientist,* 1980, *68,* 49–61.

Schacter, D. L., & Tulving, E. Memory, amnesia, and the episodic/semantic distinction. In R. L. Isaacson and N. E. Spear (Eds.), *Expression of knowledge.* New York: Plenum, 1982.

Schachter, S. Some extraordinary facts about obese humans and rats. *American Psychologist,* 1971a, *26,* 129–144.

———. *Emotion, obesity, and crime.* New York: Academic, 1971b.

Schaefer, H. H., & Martin, P. L. *Behavioral therapy.* New York: McGraw-Hill, 1969.

Schaffer, H. R., & Emerson, P. E. The development of social attachments in infancy. *Monographs Social Research in Child Development,* 1964, *29,* 1–77.

Schlosberg, H., & Solomon, R. L. Latency of response in a choice discrimination. *Journal of the Experimental Psychology,* 1943, *33,* 22–39.

Schneider, B. A. A two-state analysis of fixed-interval responding in the pigeon. *Journal of the Experimental Analysis of Behavior,* 1969, *12,* 677–687.

Schneider, W., & Shiffrin, R. M. Controlled and automatic human information processing: I. Detection, search, and attention. *Psychological Review,* 1977, *84,* 1–66.

Scholander, T. Case reports and technique innovations treatment of an unusual case of compulsive behavior by aversive stimulation. *Behavior Therapy,* 1972, *3,* 290–293.

Schoonard, J., & Lawrence, D. H. Resistance to extinction as a function of the number of delay of reward trials. *Psychological Reports,* 1962, *11,* 275–278.

Schreibman, L., & Koegel, R. T. Autism: A defeatable honor. *Psychology Today,* 1975, *8,* 60–67.

Schrier, A. M., & Harlow, H. F. Effect of amount of incentive on discrimination learning by monkeys. *Journal of Comparative and Physiological Psychology*, 1956, *49*, 117–125.

Schubot, E. D. The influence of hypnotic and muscular relaxation in systematic desensitization. Doctoral dissertation, Stanford University, California, 1966.

Schulman, A. H.; Hale, E. B.; & Graves, H. B. Visual stimulus characteristics for initial approach response in chicks (*Gallus domesticus*). *Animal Behaviour*, 1970, *18*, 461–466.

Schuster, C. R., & Woods, J. H. Schedule-induced polydipsia in the rhesus monkey. *Psychological Reports*, 1966, *19*, 823–828.

Schuster, R., & Rachlin, H. Indifference between punishment and free shock: Evidence for the negative law of effect. *Journal of the Experimental Analysis of Behavior*, 1968, *11*, 777–786.

Schusterman, R. J. Serial discrimination-reversal learning with and without errors by the California sea lion. *Journal of the Experimental Analysis of Behavior*, 1966, *9*, 593–600.

Schwartz, B. *Psychology of learning and behavior* (2d ed.). New York: Norton, 1984.

Schwitzgebel, R. L., & Schwitzgebel, R. K. *Law and psychological practice*. New York: Wiley, 1980.

Scoville, W. B. The limbic lobe in man. *Journal of Neurosurgery*, 1954, *11*, 64–66.

Sears, R. R.; Maccoby, E. E.; & Levin, H. *Patterns of child rearing*. Evanston, Ill.: Row Peterson, 1957.

Seaver, W. B., & Patterson, A. H. Decreasing fuel-oil consumption through feedback and social commendation. *Journal of Applied Behavior Analysis*, 1976, *9*, 147–152.

Segal, E. F. The development of water drinking on a dry-food free-reinforcement schedule. *Psychonomic Science*, 1965, *2*, 29–30.

———, & Holloway, S. M. Timing behavior in rats with water drinking as a mediator. *Science*, 1963, *140*, 888–889.

Seligman, M. E. P. On the generality of laws of learning. *Psychological Review*, 1970, *77*, 406–418.

———. *Helplessness: On depression, development, and death*. San Francisco: Freeman, 1975.

———, & Campbell, B. A. Effects of intensity and duration of punishment on extinction of an avoidance response. *Journal of Comparative and Physiological Psychology*, 1965, *59*, 295–297.

———, & Maier, S. F. Failure to escape traumatic shock. *Journal of Experimental Psychology*, 1967, *74*, 1–9.

———; Rosellini, R. A.; & Kozak, M. Learned helplessness in the rat: Reversibility, time course, and immunization. *Journal of Comparative and Physiological Psychology*, 1975, *88*, 542–547.

Sem-Jacobson, C. W. *Depth-electrographic stimulation of the human brain and behavior: From fourteen years of studies and treatment of Parkinson's disease and mental disorders with implanted electrodes*. Springfield, Ill.: Thomas, 1968.

Senkowski, P. C. Variables affecting the overtraining extinction effect in discrete-trial lever pressing. *Journal of Experimental Psychology: Animal Behavior Processes*, 1978, *4*, 131–143.

Seward, J. P., & Humphrey, G. L. Avoidance learning as a function of pretraining in the cat. *Journal of Comparative and Physiological Psychology*, 1967, *63*, 338–341.

Seybert, J. A.; Baer, L. P.; Harvey, R. J.; Ludwig, D.; & Gerard, I. C. Resistance to extinction as a function of percentage of reward: A reinforcement-level interpretation. *Animal Learning and Behavior,* 1979, *7,* 233–238.

——; Mellgren, R. L.; & Jobe, J. B. Sequential effects on resistance to extinction as widely spaced trials. *Journal of Experimental Psychology,* 1973, *101,* 151–154.

Seyfarth, R. M.; Cheney, D. L.; & Marler, P. Monkey responses to three different alarm calls: Evidence of predator classification and semantic communication. *Science,* 1980, *210,* 801–803.

Sgro, J. A.; Dyal, J. A.; & Anastasio, E. J. Effects of constant delay of reinforcement on acquisition asymptote and resistance to extinction. *Journal of Experimental Psychology,* 1967, *73,* 634–636.

Shafto, F., & Sulzbacher, S. Comparing treatment tactics with a hyperactive preschool child: Stimulant medication and programmed teacher intervention. *Journal of Applied Behavior Analysis,* 1977, *10,* 13–20.

Shanab, M. E., & Birnbaum, D. W. Durability of the partial reinforcement and partial delay of reinforcement extinction effects after minimal acquisition training. *Animal Learning and Behavior,* 1974, *2,* 81–85.

——; Sanders, R.; & Premack, D. Positive contrast in the runway obtained with delay of reward. *Science,* 1969, *164,* 724–725.

——, & Peterson, J. L. Polydipsia in the pigeon. *Psychonomic Science,* 1969, *15,* 51–52.

Sheffield, F. D. Relation between classical conditioning and instrumental learning. In W. F. Prokasy (Ed.), *Classical conditioning.* New York: Appleton-Century-Crofts, 1965.

——. New evidence on the drive-induction theory of reinforcement. In R. N. Haber (Ed.), *Current research in motivation.* New York: Holt, 1966.

——, & Roby, T. B. Reward value of a non-nutritive sweet taste. *Journal of Comparative and Physiological Psychology,* 1950, *43,* 471–481.

Sherman, A. D.; Sacquitne, J. L.; & Petty, F. Specificity of the learned helplessness model of depression. *Pharmacology, Biochemistry, and Behavior,* 1982, *16,* 449–454.

Sherman, J. E. US inflation with trace and simultaneous fear conditioning. *Animal Learning and Behavior,* 1978, *6,* 463–468.

Sherrington, C. S. *Integrative action of the nervous system.* New Haven: Yale University Press, 1906.

Shettleworth, S. J. Memory in food hoarding birds. *Scientific American,* 1983, *248,* 102–110.

——, & Krebs, J. R. How marsh tits find their hoards: The roles of site preference and spatial memory. *Journal of Experimental Psychology: Animal Behavior Processes,* 1982, *8,* 342–353.

Shiffrin, R. M., & Cook, J. R. Short-term forgetting of item and order information. *Journal of Verbal Learning and Verbal Behavior,* 1978, *17,* 189–218.

——, & Schneider, W. Controlled and automatic human information processing: II. Perceptual learning, automatic attending, and a general theory. *Psychological Review,* 1977, *84,* 127–196.

Shimoff, E.; Catania, A. C.; & Matthews, B. A. Uninstructed human responding: Sensitivity of low-rate performance to schedule contingencies. *Journal of the Experimental Analysis of Behavior,* 1981, *36,* 207–220.

Shipley, R. H. Extinction of conditioned fear in rats as a function of several parameters of CS exposure. *Journal of Comparative and Physiological Psychology*, 1974, *87*, 699–707.

Shipley, R. H.; Mock, L. A.; & Levis, D. J. Effects of several response prevention procedures on activity, avoidance responding, and conditioned fear in rats. *Journal of Comparative and Physiological Psychology*, 1971, *77*, 256–270.

Shoben, E. J.; Wescourt, K. T.; & Smith, E. E. Sentence verification, sentence recognition and the semantic-episodic distinction. *Journal of Experimental Psychology: Human Learning and Memory*, 1978, *4*, 304–317.

Sidman, M., & Stebbins, W. C. Satiation effects under fixed-ratio schedules of reinforcement. *Journal of Comparative and Physiological Psychology*, 1954, *47*, 114–116.

——, & Stoddard, L. T. The effectiveness of fading in programming and simultaneous form discrimination for retarded children. *Journal of the Experimental Analysis of Behavior*, 1967, *10*, 3–15.

——; ——; & Mohr, J. P. Some additional quantitative observations of immediate memory in a patient with bilateral hippocampal lesions. *Neuropsychologia*, 1968, *6*, 245–254.

Siegel, S. Effect of CS habituation on eyelid conditioning. *Journal of Comparative and Physiological Psychology*, 1967, *64*, 471–477.

——. Effect of CS habituation on eyelid conditioning. *Journal of Comparative and Physiological Psychology*, 1969, *69*, 157–159.

——. Evidence from rats that morphine tolerance is learned response. *Journal of Comparative and Physiological Psychology*, 1975, *89*, 498–506.

——. Morphine analgesic tolerance: Its situation specificity supports a Pavlovian conditioning model. *Science*, 1976, *193*, 323–325.

——. Morphine tolerance acquisition as an associative process. *Journal of Experimental Psychology: Animal Behavior Processes*, 1977, *3*, 1–13.

——. A Pavlovian conditioning analysis of morphine tolerance. In N. A. Krasnegor (Ed.), *Behavioral tolerance: Research and treatment implications*. NIDA Research Monograph no. 18. Washington, D.C.: U.S. Government Printing Office, 1978.

——. The role of conditioning in drug tolerance and addiction. In J. D. Keehn (Ed.), *Psychopathology in animals: Research and clinical implications*. New York: Academic, 1979.

——, & Andrews, J. M. Magnitude of reinforcement and choice behavior in children. *Journal of Experimental Psychology*, 1962, *63*, 337–341.

——, & Domjan, M. Backward conditioning as an inhibitory procedure. *Learning and Motivation*, 1971, *2*, 1–11.

——; Hinson, R. E.; & Krank, M. D. The role of predrug signals in morphine analgesic tolerance: Support for a Pavlovian conditioning model of tolerance. *Journal of Experimental Psychology: Animal Behavior Processes*, 1978, *4*, 188–196.

——; Hinson, R. E.; Krank, M. D.; & McCully, J. Heroin "overdose" death: Contribution of drug-associated environmental cues. *Science*, 1982, *216*, 436–437.

——; Sherman, J. E.; & Mitchell, D. Extinction of morphine analgesic tolerance. *Learning and Motivation*, 1980, *11*, 289–301.

Signoret, J. L., & Lhermitte, F. The amnesic syndromes and the encoding process. In M. R. Rosenzweig and E. L. Bennett (Eds.), *Neural mechanisms of learning and memory*. Cambridge, Mass.: M.I.T. Press, 1976.

Simon, H. A. The structure of ill-structured problems. *Artificial Intelligence*, 1973, *4*, 181–202.

——. How big is a chunk? *Science,* 1974, *183,* 482–488.

——. *Models of thought.* New Haven: Yale University Press, 1979.

Skinner, B. F. *The behavior of organisms. An experimental analysis.* New York: Appleton-Century-Crofts, 1938.

——. Superstition in the pigeon. *Journal of Experimental Psychology,* 1948, *38,* 168–172.

——. *Science and human behavior.* New York: Macmillan, 1953.

——. *Verbal behavior.* New York: Appleton, 1957a.

——. The experimental analysis of behavior. *American Scientist,* 1957b, *45,* 343–371.

——, & Morse, W. H. Concurrent activity under fixed-interval reinforcement. *Journal of Comparative and Physiological Psychology,* 1957, *50,* 279–281.

Slobin, D. I. Grammatical transformations and sentence comprehension in childhood and adulthood. *Journal of Verbal Learning and Verbal Behavior,* 1966, *5,* 219–227.

Smith, J. C., & Roll, D. L. Trace conditioning with X-rays as an aversive stimulus. *Psychonomic Science,* 1967, *9,* 11–12.

Smith, M. C.; Coleman, S. R.; & Gormezano, I. Classical conditioning of the rabbit's nictitating membrane response at backward, simultaneous and forward CS-US intervals. *Journal of Comparative and Physiological Psychology,* 1969, *69,* 226–231.

Smith, M. P. The stimulus trace gradient in visual discrimination learning. *Journal of Comparative and Physiological Psychology,* 1951, *44,* 154–161.

Smith, R. F., & Keller, F. R. Free-operant avoidance in the pigeon using a treadle response. *Journal of the Experimental Analysis of Behavior,* 1970, *13,* 211–214.

Smith, S. M. Remembering in and out of context. *Journal of Experimental Psychology: Human Learning and Memory,* 1979, *5,* 460–471.

——. Enhancement of recall using multiple environmental contexts during learning. *Memory & Cognition,* 1982, *19,* 405–412.

——; Glenberg, A.; & Bjork, R. A. Environmental context and human memory. *Memory & Cognition* 1978, *6,* 342–353.

Smoke, K. L. Negative instances in concept learning. *Journal of Experimental Psychology,* 1933, *16,* 583–588.

Snow, C. E. Mother's speech research: From input to interaction. In C. E. Snow and C. A. Ferguson (Eds.), *Talking to children: Language input and acquisition.* Cambridge: Cambridge University Press, 1979.

Snyder, S. H. Catecholamines as mediators of drug effects in schizophrenia. In F. D. Schmitt and F. G. Worden (Eds.), *The neurosciences: Third study program.* Cambridge, Mass.: M.I.T. Press, 1974.

Solnick, J. V.; Rincover, A.; & Peterson, C. R. Some determinants of the reinforcing and punishing effects of time-out. *Journal of Applied Behavior Analysis,* 1977, *10,* 415–424.

Solomon, R. L. The opponent-process theory of acquired motivation: The costs of pleasure and the benefits of pain. *American Psychologist,* 1980, *35,* 691–712.

——, & Wynne, L. C. Traumatic avoidance learning: Acquisition in normal dogs. *Psychological Monographs,* 1953, *67,* Whole no. 354.

——, & ——. Traumatic avoidance learning: The principles of anxiety conservation and partial irreversibility. *Psychological Review,* 1954, *61,* 353–385.

Spear, N. E. Forgetting as retrieval failure. In W. K. Honig and H. P. R. James (Eds.), *Animal memory.* New York: Academic, 1971.

——. Retrieval of memory in animals. *Psychological Review,* 1973, *80,* 163–194.

————. *The processing of memories: Forgetting and retention.* Hillsdale, N.J.: Erlbaum, 1978.

————; Klein, S. B.; & Riley, E. P. The Kamin effect as "state-dependent learning": Memory-retrieval failure in the rat. *Journal of Comparative and Physiological Psychology,* 1971, *74,* 416–425.

Spence, K. W. The nature of discrimination learning in animals. *Psychological Review,* 1936, *43,* 427–449.

————. *Behavior theory and conditioning.* New Haven: Yale University, 1956.

Sperling, G. The information available in brief visual presentations. *Psychological Monographs* 1960, *74,* Whole no. 498.

————. A model for visual memory task. *Human Factors,* 1963, *5,* 19–31.

————. Successive approximations to a model for short-term money. *Acta Psychologia,* 1967, *27,* 285–292.

Spiker, C. C., & Cantor, J. H. Introtacts as predictors of discrimination performance in kindergarten children. *Journal of Experimental Child Psychology,* 1977, *23,* 520–538.

Spinetta, J. J., & Rigler, D. The child-abusing parent: A psychological review. *Psychological Bulletin,* 1972, *77,* 296–304.

Spivey, J. E. Resistance to extinction as a function of number of N-R transitions and percentage of reinforcement. *Journal of Experimental Psychology,* 1967, *75,* 43–48.

Staats, C. K., & Staats, A. W. Meaning established by classical conditioning. *Journal of Experimental Psychology,* 1957, *54,* 74–80.

Staddon, J. E. R. Schedule induced behaviors. In W. K. Honig and J. E. R. Staddon (Eds.), *Handbook of operant behavior.* Englewood Cliffs, N.J.: Prentice-Hall, 1977.

————, & Ayres, S. L. Sequential and temporal properties of behavior induced by a schedule of periodic food delivery. *Behavior,* 1975, *54,* 26–49.

————, & Simmelhag, V. L. The "superstition" experiment; A reexamination of its implications for the principles of adaptive behavior. *Psychological Review,* 1971, *78,* 3–43.

Stapleton, J. V. Legal issues confronting behavior modification. *Behavioral Engineering,* 1975, *2,* 35.

Stark, P., & Boyd, E. S. Effects of cholinergic drugs on hypothalamic self-stimulation response rates of dogs. *American Journal of Physiology,* 1963, *205,* 745–748.

Stein, B. S. Depth of processing reexamined: The effects of the precision of encoding and test appropriateness. *Journal of Verbal Learning and Verbal Behavior,* 1978, *17,* 165–174.

Stein, L. Excessive drinking in the rat: Superstition or thirst? *Journal of Comparative and Physiological Psychology,* 1964, *58,* 237–242.

————. Chemistry of purposive behavior. In J. T. Tapp (Ed.), *Reinforcement and behavior.* New York: Academic, 1969.

————; Belluzzi, J. D.; & Wise, C. D. Memory enhanced by central administration of norepinephrine. *Brain Research,* 1975, *84,* 329–335.

————, & Wise, C. D. Release of norepinephrine from the hypothalamus and amygdala by rewarding medial forebrain bundle stimulation and amphetamine. *Journal of Comparative and Physiological Psychology,* 1969, *67,* 189–198.

————, & ————. Possible etiology of schizophrenia: Progressive damage to the noradrenergic reward system of 6-hydroxydopamine. *Science,* 1971, 1032–1036.

————, & ————. Amphetamine and noradrenergic reward pathways. In E. Usdin and S. H. Snyder (Eds.), *Frontiers in catecholamine research.* New York: Pergamon, 1973.

————, & ————. Serotonin and behavioral inhibition. In E. Costa and P. Greengard (Eds.), *Advances in biochemical psychopharmacology.* New York: Raven, 1974.

Steinbrecher, C. D., & Lockhart, R. A. Temporal avoidance conditioning in the cat. *Psychonomic Science.* 1966, *5,* 441–442.

Stephens, C. E.; Pear, J. J.; Wray, L. D.; & Jackson, G. C. Some effects of reinforcement schedules in teaching picture names to retarded children. *Journal of Applied Behavior Analysis,* 1975, *8,* 435–447.

Steuer, F. B.; Applefield, J. M.; & Smith, R. Televised aggression and the interpersonal aggression of preschool children. *Journal of Experimental Child Psychology,* 1971, *11,* 442–447.

Storms, L. H.; Boroczi, G.; & Broen, W. E., Jr. Punishment inhibits an instrumental response in hooded rats. *Science,* 1962, *135,* 1133–1134.

————; ————; & ————. Effects of punishment as a function of strain of rat and duration of shock. *Journal of Comparative and Physiological Psychology,* 1963, *56,* 1022–1026.

Streeter, L. A., & Landauer, J. K. Effects of learning English as a second language on the acquisition of new phonetic contrast. *Journal of the Acoustical Society of America,* 1976, *59,* 448–451.

Stricker, E. M., & Adair, E. R. Body fluid balance, taste, and post-prandial factors in schedule-induced polydipsia. *Journal of Comparative and Physiological Psychology,* 1966, *62,* 449–454.

Stuart, R. B. Behavioral control of eating. *Behavior Research and Therapy,* 1967, *5,* 357–365.

————. A three-dimensional program for the treatment of obesity. *Behavior Research and Therapy,* 1971, *9,* 177–186.

Suboski, M. P. UCS intensity and the latency of the classically conditioned eyelid response. *Journal of Experimental Psychology,* 1967, *74,* 31–35.

Sutherland, N. S., & Holgate, V. Two-cue discrimination learning in rats. *Journal of Comparative and Physiological Psychology,* 1966, *61,* 198–207.

————, & Mackintosh, N. J. *Mechanisms of animal discrimination learning.* New York: Academic, 1971.

Swanson, J. M., & Kinsbourne, M. State-dependent learning and retrieval: Methodological cautions against theoretical considerations. In J. F. Kihlstrom and F. J. Evans (Eds.), *Functional disorders of memory.* Hillsdale, N.J.: Erlbaum, 1979.

Tait, R. W.; Marquis, H. A.; Williams, R.; Weinstein, L.; & Suboski, M. S. Extinction of sensory preconditioning using CER training. *Journal of Comparative and Physiological Psychology,* 1969, *69,* 170–172.

Tanner, B. A., & Zeiler, M. Punishment of self-injurious behavior using aromatic ammonia as the aversive stimulus. *Journal of Applied Behavior Analysis,* 1975, *8,* 53–57.

Tarpy, R. M. Reinforcement difference limen (RDL) for delay in shock escape. *Journal of Experimental Psychology,* 1969, *79,* 116–121.

————. *Basic principles of learning.* Glenview, Ill.: Scott, Foresman, 1975.

————, & Koster, E. D. Stimulus facilitation of delayed-reward learning in the rat. *Journal of Comparative and Physiological Psychology,* 1970, *71,* 147–151.

————, & Mayer, R. E. *Foundations of learning and memory.* Glenview, Ill.: Scott, Foresman, 1978.

————, & Sawabini, F. L. Reinforcement delay: A selective review of the last decade. *Psychological Bulletin,* 1974, *81,* 984–987.

Taukulis, H. K., & Revusky, S. Odor as a conditioned inhibitor: Applicability of the Rescorla-Wagner model to feeding behavior. *Learning and Motivation*, 1975, *6*, 11–27.

Teitelbaum, P. The use of operant methods in the assessment and control of motivational states. In W. K. Honig (Ed.), *Operant behavior: Areas of research and application*. New York: Appleton-Century-Crofts, 1966.

————, & Epstein, A. N. The lateral hypothalamic syndrome: Recovery of feeding and drinking after lateral hypothalamic lesions. *Psychological Review*, 1962, *69*, 74–90.

Tennen, H., & Eller, S. J. Attributional components of learned helplessness and facilitation. *Journal of Personality and Social Psychology*, 1977, *35*, 265–271.

Terrace, H. S. Discrimination learning with and without "errors." *Journal of the Experimental Analysis of Behavior*, 1963a, *6*, 1–27.

————. Errorless transfer of a discrimination across two continua. *Journal of the Experimental Analysis of Behavior*, 1963b, *6*, 223–232.

————. Errorless discrimination learning in the pigeon: Effects of chlorpromazine and imipramine. *Science*, 1963c, 140, 318–319.

————. Wavelength generalization after discrimination learning with and without errors. *Science*, 1964, *144*, 78–80.

————. Stimulus control. In W. K. Honig (Ed.), *Operant behavior: Areas of research and application*. New York: Appleton-Century-Crofts, 1966a.

————. Behavioral contrast and the peak shift. Effects of extended discrimination training. *Journal of the Experimental Analysis of Behavior*, 1966b, *9*, 613–617.

————. *Nim*. New York: Knopf, 1979.

Terrell, G., & Ware, R. Role of delay of reward in speed of size and form discrimination learning in childhood. *Child Development*, 1961, *32*, 409–415.

Tharp, R. G., & Wetzel, R. J. *Behavior modification in the natural environment*. New York: Academic, 1969.

Theios, J.; Lynch, A. D.; & Lowe, W. F., Jr. Differential effects of shock intensity on one-way and shuttle avoidance conditioning. *Journal of Experimental Psychology*, 1966, *72*, 294–299.

Thielke-Poltz, H., & Thielke, G. Akustiches Lernen verschieden alter schallisolierter Amseln (Turdus merula L.) und die Entwicklung erlernter Motive ohne und mit kunstlichen Einfluss von Testosteron. *Zeitschrift für Tierpsychologie*, 1960, *17*, 211–244.

Thomas, D. R., & Switalski, R. W. Comparison of stimulus generalization following variable-ratio and variable-interval training. *Journal of Experimental Psychology*, 1966, *76*, 365–376.

Thomas, E., & Balter, A. L. Learned helplessness: Amelioration of symptoms by cholinergic blockage of the septum. Cited in M. E. P. Seligman, *Helplessness*. San Francisco: Freeman, 1975.

————, & Dewald, L. Experimental neurosis: Neuropsychological analysis. In J. D. Master and M. E. P. Seligman (Eds.), *Psychopathology: Experimental models*. San Francisco: Freeman, 1977.

Thomka, M. L., & Rosellini, R. A. Frustration and the production of schedule-induced polydipsia. *Animal Learning and Behavior*, 1975, *3*, 380–384.

Thompson, C. R., & Church, R. M. An explanation of the language of a chimpanzee. *Science*, 1980, *208*, 313–314.

Thompson, R., & Dean, W. A. A further study on the retroactive effects of ECS. *Journal of Comparative and Physiological Psychology*, 1955, *48*, 488–491.

Thompson, R. F.; Hicks, L. H.; & Shvyrok, V. B. *Neural mechanisms of goal-directed behavior and learning.* New York: Academic, 1980.

Thompson, T., & Bloom, W. Aggressive behavior and extinction-induced response rate increase. *Psychonomic Science,* 1966, *5,* 335–336.

Thorndike, E. L. Animal intelligence: An experimental study of the associative processes in animals. *Psychological Review Monograph Supplement,* 1898, *2,* 1–109.

———. *Educational psychology,* vol. II: *The psychology of learning.* New York: Teachers College, Columbia University, 1913.

———. *Fundamentals of learning.* New York: Teachers College, Columbia University, 1932.

Thorpe, W. H. Type of learning in insects and other anthropods, Part III. *British Journal of Psychology,* 1944, *34,* 66–76.

———. The evolutionary significance of habitat selection. *Journal of Animal Ecology,* 1945, *14,* 67–70.

———. *Bird song: The biology of vocal communication and expression in birds.* Cambridge: Cambridge University Press, 1961.

Thune, L. E., & Underwood, B. J. Retroactive inhibition as a function of degree of interpolated learning. *Journal of Experimental Psychology,* 1943, *32,* 185–200.

Tiffany, S. T., & Baker, T. B. Morphine tolerance in rats: Congruence with a Pavlovian paradigm. *Journal of Comparative and Physiological Psychology,* 1981, *95,* 747–762.

Timberlake, W., & Allison, J. Response deprivation: An empirical approach to instrumental performance. *Psychological Review,* 1974, *81,* 146–164.

———; Wahl, G.; & King, D. Stimulus and response contingencies in the misbehavior of rats. *Journal of Experimental Psychology: Animal Behavior Processes,* 1982, *8,* 62–85.

Tinklepaugh, O. L. An experimental study of representative factors in monkeys. *Journal of Comparative Psychology,* 1928, *8,* 197–236.

Todd, G. E., & Cogan, D. C. Selected schedules of reinforcement in the black-tailed prairie dog (*Cynomys ludovicianus*). *Animal Learning and Behavior,* 1978, *6,* 429–434.

Toister, R. P.; Condron, C. J.; Worley, L.; & Arthur, D. Faradic therapy of chronic vomiting in infancy: A case study. *Journal of Behavior Therapy and Experimental Psychiatry,* 1975, *6,* 55–59.

Tolman, E. C. *Purposive behavior in animals and men.* New York: Century, 1932.

———. Cognitive maps in rats and men. *Psychological Review,* 1948, *55,* 189–208.

———. Principles of purposive behavior. In S. Koch (Ed.), *Psychology: A study of a science* (vol. 2). New York: McGraw-Hill, 1959.

———, & Honzik, C. H. "Insight" in rats. *University of California Publications in Psychology,* 1930a, *4,* 215–232.

———, & ———. Degrees of hunger; reward and nonreward; and maze learning in rats. *University of California Publications in Psychology,* 1930b, *4,* 241–256.

———; Ritchie, B. F.; & Kalish, D. Studies of spatial learning: II. Place learning versus response learning. *Journal of Experimental Psychology,* 1946, *36,* 221–229.

Tombaugh, T. N. Resistance to extinction as a function of the interaction between training and extinction delays. *Psychological Reports,* 1966, *19,* 791–798.

Tomie, A.; Murphy, A. L.; & Fath, S. Retardation of autoshaping following unpredictable food: Effects of changing the context between pretraining and testing. *Learning and Motivation,* 1980, *11,* 117–134.

Touchette, P. E. Tilted lines as complex stimuli. *Journal of the Experimental Analysis of Behavior,* 1969, *12,* 211–214.

Trabasso, T. R., & Bower, G. H. *Attention in learning: Theory and research.* New York: Wiley, 1968.

Tracy, W. K. Wavelength generalization and preference in monochromatically reared ducklings. *Journal of the Experimental Analysis of Behavior,* 1970, *13,* 163–178.

Trapold, M. A., & Fowler, H. Instrumental escape performance as a function of the intensity of noxious stimulation. *Journal of Experimental Psychology,* 1960, *60,* 323–326.

————, & Winokur, S. Transfer from classical conditioning and extinction to acquisition, extinction, and stimulus generalization of a positively reinforced instrumental response. *Journal of Experimental Psychology,* 1967, *73,* 517–525.

Traupmann, K. L. Drive, reward, and training parameters and the overlearning-extinction effect (OEE). *Learning and Motivation,* 1972, *3,* 359–368.

Treisman, A. M. Contextual cues in selective listening. *Quarterly Journal of Experimental Psychology,* 1960, *12,* 242–248.

————, & Geffen, G. Selective attention: Perception or response? *Quarterly Journal of Experimental Psychology,* 1967, *19,* 1–17.

Trenholme, I. A., & Baron, A. Intermediate and delayed punishment of human behavior by loss of reinforcement. *Learning and Motivation,* 1975, *6,* 62–79.

Troland, L. T. *The fundamentals of human motivation.* New York: Van Nostrand, 1928.

Tulving, E. Subjective organization and effects of repetition in multi-trial free recall learning. *Journal of Verbal Learning and Verbal Behavior,* 1966, *5,* 193–197.

————. Episodic and semantic memory. In E. Tulving and W. Donaldson (Eds.), *Organization of memory.* New York: Academic, 1972.

————. *Elements of episodic memory.* Oxford: Clarendon Press/Oxford University Press, 1983.

————, & Donaldson, W. *Organization of memory.* New York: Academic, 1972.

Turner, L. H., & Solomon, R. L. Human traumatic avoidance learning: Theory and experiments on the operant-respondent distinction and failures to learn. *Psychological Monographs,* 1962, *76,* Whole no. 559.

Turvey, M. T. Visual processing and short-term memory. In W. K. Estes (Ed.), *Handbook of learning and cognitive processes* (vol. 5). Hillsdale, N.J.: Erlbaum, 1978.

————, & Kravetz, S. Retrieval from iconic memory with shape as the selection criterion. *Perception and Psychophysics,* 1970, *8,* 171–172.

Tversky, A., & Kahneman, A. Availability: A heuristic for judging frequency and probabililty. *Cognitive Psychology,* 1973, *5,* 207–232.

Tyszka, T., & Grzelak, J. L. Criteria and mechanisms of choice behavior in n-person games. *Journal of Conflict Resolution,* 1976, *20,* 352–376.

Ullmann, L. P., & Krasner, L. *Case studies in behavior modification.* New York: Holt, Rinehart & Winston, 1965.

Ulrich, R. E. Pain as a cause of aggression. *American Zoologist,* 1966, *6,* 643–662.

————; Wolff, P. C.; & Azrin, N. H. Shock as an elicitor of intra- and inter-species fighting behavior. *Animal Behavior,* 1964, *12,* 14–15.

Underwood, B. J. The effect of successive interpolations on retroactive and proactive inhibition. *Psychological Monographs,* 1945, *59,* Whole no. 273.

————. Associative transfer in verbal learning as a function of response similarity and degree of first-list learning. *Journal of Experimental Psychology,* 1951, *42,* 44–53.

————. Interference and forgetting. *Psychological Review,* 1957, *64,* 48–60.

————. False recognition produced by implicit verbal response. *Journal of Experimental Psychology*, 1965, *70*, 122–129.

————. Attributes of memory. *Psychological Review*, 1969, *76*, 559–573.

————. *Temporal codes for memories: Issues and problems*. Hillsdale, N.J.: Erlbaum, 1977.

————. *Attributes of memory*. Glenview, Ill.: Scott, Foresman, 1983.

————, & Ekstrand, B. R. An analysis of some shortcomings in the interference theory of forgetting. *Psychological Review*, 1966, *73*, 540–549.

————, & Erlebacher, A. H. Studies of coding in verbal learning. *Psychological Monographs*, 1965, *79*, Whole no. 606.

————, & Freund, J. S. Effect of temporal separation of two tasks on proactive inhibition. *Journal of Experimental Psychology*, 1968, *78*, 50–54.

————; Ham, M.; & Ekstrand, B. R. Cue selection in paired-associate learning. *Journal of Experimental Psychology*, 1962, *64*, 405–409.

————, & Keppel, G. Coding processes in verbal learning. *Journal of Verbal Learning and Verbal Behavior*, 1963, *1*, 250–257.

————, & Postman, L. Extraexperimental sources of interference in forgetting. *Psychological Review*, 1960, *67*, 73–95.

Ungar, G. Transfer of learned behavior by brain extracts. *Journal of Biological Psychology*, 1967a, *9*, 12–27.

————. Chemical transfer of acquired information. *Proceedings of the Vth International Congress of the Collegium Internationale Neuropsychopharmacologicum*. Amsterdam: Excerpta Media, 1967b, 169–175.

————. Biochemistry of intelligence. *Research Communications in Psychology, Psychiatry and Behavior*, 1976, *1*, 597–606.

————; Desiderio, D. M.; & Parr, W. Isolation. Identification and synthesis of a specific-behavior-inducing brain peptide. *Nature (London)*, 1972, *238*, 198–202.

————; Galvan, L.; & Clark, R. H. Chemical transfer of learned fear. *Nature*, 1968, *217*, 1259–1261.

————, & Irwin, L. N. Transfer of acquired information by brain extracts. *Nature*, 1967, *214*, 453–455.

————, & Oceguera-Navarro, C. Transfer of habituation by material extracted from brain. *Nature*, 1965, *207*, 301–302.

Valenstein, E. S. *Brain control*. New York: Wiley, 1973.

————, & Beer, B. Continuous opportunities for reinforcing brain stimulation. *Journal of Experimental Analysis of Behavior*, 1964, *7*, 183–184.

————; Cox, V. C.; & Kakolewski, J. W. The hypothalamus and motivated behavior. In J. T. Tapp (Ed.), *Reinforcement and behavior*. New York: Academic, 1969.

Vasta, R. Coverant control of self-evaluations through temporal cueing. *Journal of Behavior Therapy and Experimental Psychiatry*, 1975, *7*, 35–37.

Verzeano, J.; Laufer, M.; Spear, S.; & McDonald, S. The activity of neuronal networks in the thalamus of the monkey. In K. H. Pribram and D. E. Broadbent (Eds.), *Biology of memory*. New York: Academic, 1970.

Verzeano, M., & Negishi, K. Neuronal activity in cortical and thalamic networks. *Journal of General Physiology*, 1960, *43*, Suppl., 177.

Villareal, J. Schedule-induced pica. Paper presented at the meeting of the Eastern Psychological Association, Boston, November 1967.

Voeks, V. W. Acquisition of S-R connections: A test of Hull's and Guthrie's theories. *Journal of Experimental Psychology*, 1954, *47*, 137–147.

Vogel-Sprott, M., & Thurstone, E. Resistance to punishment and subsequent extinction of a response as a function of its reward history. *Psychological Reports*, 1968, *22*, 631–637.

Vogler, R. E.; Lunde, S. E.; Johnson, G. R.; & Martin, P. L. Electrical aversion conditioning with chronic alcoholics. *Journal of Consulting and Clinical Psychology*, 1970, *34*, 302–307.

——; ——; & Martin, P. L. Electrical aversion conditioning with chronic alcoholics: Follow-up and suggestions for research. *Journal of Consulting and Clinical Psychology*, 1971, *36*, 450.

Von Wright, J. M. Selection in visual immediate memory. *Quarterly Journal of Experimental Psychology*, 1968, *20*, 62–68.

Wagner, A. R. Conditioned frustration as a learned drive. *Journal of Experimental Psychology*, 1963, *66*, 142–148.

——. Stimulus selection and a "modified continuity theory." In G. H. Bower and J. T. Spence (Eds.), *The psychology of learning and motivation* (vol. 3). New York: Academic, 1969.

——; Logan, F. A.; Haberlandt, K.; & Price, T. Stimulus selection in animal discrimination learning. *Journal of Experimental Psychology*, 1968, *76*, 171–180.

——; Rudy, J. W.; & Whitlow, J. W. Rehearsal in animal conditioning. *Journal of Experimental Psychology Monograph*, 1973, *97*, 407–426.

Wahler, R. G.; Winkel, G. H.; Peterson, R. F.; & Morrison, D. C. Mothers as behavior therapists for their own children. *Behaviour Research and Therapy*, 1965, *3*, 113–124.

Walk, R. D.; Gibson, E. J.; Pick, H. L., Jr.; & Tighe, T. J. The effectiveness of prolonged exposure to cutouts vs. painted patterns for facilitation of discrimination. *Journal of Comparative and Physiological Psychology*, 1959, 52, 519–521.

——, & Walters, C. P. Effect of visual deprivation on depth discrimination of hooded rats. *Journal of Comparative and Physiological Psychology*, 1973, *85*, 559–563.

Wall, A. M.; Walters, G. C.; & England, R. S. The lickometer: A simple device for the analysis of licking as an operant. *Behavior Research Methods and Instrumentation*, 1972, *4*, 320–322.

Wallace, M.; Singer, G.; Wayner, M. J.; & Cook, P. Adjunctive behavior in humans during game playing. *Physiology and Behavior*, 1975, *14*, 651–654.

Waller, R. G. Effect of consistency of reward during runway training on subsequent discrimination performance in rats. *Journal of Comparative and Physiological Psychology*, 1973, *83*, 120–123.

Walters, G. C., & Glazer, R. D. Punishment of instinctive behavior in the Mongolian gerbil. *Journal of Comparative and Physiological Psychology*, 1971, *75*, 331–340.

——, & Grusec, J. F. *Punishment*. San Francisco: Freeman, 1977.

Walters, R. H. Delay of reinforcement gradients in children's learning. *Psychonomic Science*, 1964, *1*, 307–308.

Wanner, E., & Maratsos, M. An ATN approach to comprehension. In M. Halle, J. Bresnan, and G. A. Miller (Eds.), *Linguistic theory and psychological reality*. Cambridge, Mass.: M.I.T., Press, 1978.

Warren, J. M., & McGonigle, B. Attention theory and discrimination learning. In R. M. Gilbert and N. S. Sutherland (Eds.), *Animal discrimination learning*. New York: Academic, 1969.

Warrington, E. K., & Weiskrantz, L. A study of learning and retention in amnesic patients. *Neuropsychologia*, 1968, *6*, 283–291.

——, & ——. Amnesic syndrome: Consolidation or retrieval? *Nature*, 1970, *228*, 628–630.

————, & ————. Amnesia: A disconnection syndrome? *Neuropsychologia*, 1982, *20*, 233–318.

Watkins, M. J. When is recall spectacularly higher than recognition? *Journal of Experimental Psychology*, 1974, *102*, 161–163.

Watson, J. B. The place of the conditioned reflex in psychology. *Psychological Review*, 1916, *23*, 89–116.

————. *Behaviorism*. New York: Norton, 1925.

————, & Morgan, J. J. B. Emotional reactions and psychological experimentation. *American Journal of Psychology*, 1917, *28*, 163–174.

————, & Raynor, R. Conditional emotional reactions. *Journal of Experimental Psychology*, 1920, *3*, 1–14.

Waugh, N. C., & Norman, D. A. Primary memory. *Psychological Review*, 1965, *72*, 89–104.

Wauguier, A., & Niemegeers, C. J. E. The effects of dexetimide on pimozide-halopendol- and pipamperone-induced inhibition of brain stimulation in rats. *Archives Internationales de Pharmacodynamie et de Therapie*, 1975, *217*, 280–292.

Weeks, R. A. Auditory location as an encoding dimension. *Journal of Experimental Psychology: Human Learning and Memory*, 1975, *104*, 316–318.

Weidman, U. Some experiments on the following and the flocking reaction of mallard ducklings. *British Journal of Animal Behavior*. 1956, *4*, 78–79.

Weiner, B. *Human motivation*. New York: Holt, 1980.

————; Nierenberg, R.; & Goldstein, M. Social learning (locus of control) versus attributional (causal stability) interpretations of expectancy of success. *Journal of Personality*, 1976, *44*, 52–68.

Weinstock, S. Acquisition and extinction of a partially reinforced running response at a 24-hour intertrial interval. *Journal of Experimental Psychology*, 1958, *56*, 151–158.

Weisberg, R.; DiCamillo, M.; & Phillips, D. Transferring old associations to new situations: A nonautomatic process. *Journal of Verbal Learning and Verbal Behavior*, 1979, *17*, 219–228.

Weiskrantz, L., & Warrington, E. K. The problem of the amnesic syndrome in man and animals. In R. L. Isaacson and K. H. Pribram (Eds.), *The hippocampus*. New York: Plenum, 1975.

Weisman, R. G., & Palmer, J. A. Factors influencing inhibitory stimulus control: Discrimination training and prior nondifferential reinforcement. *Journal of the Experimental Analysis of Behavior*, 1969, *12*, 229–237.

Weiss, J. M.; Glazer, H. I.; & Pohorecky, L. A. Coping behavior and neurochemical changes: An alternative explanation for the original "learned helplessness" experiments. In G. Serban and A. King (Eds.), *Animal models in human psychobiology*. New York: Plenum, 1976.

————; Stone, E. A.; & Harrell, N. Coping behavior and brain norepinephrine in rats. *Journal of Comparative and Physiological Psychology*, 1970, *72*, 153–160.

Weiss, K. P. Measurement of the effects of brain extract on interorganism information transfer. In W. L. Byrne (Ed.), *Molecular approaches to learning and memory*. New York: Academic, 1970.

Wells, M. J. *Brain and behavior in cephalopods*. London: Heinemann, 1962.

Wells, U. C.; Forehand, R.; Hickey, K.; & Green, K. D. Effects of a procedure derived from the overcorrection principle on manipulated and nonmanipulated behavior. *Journal of Applied Behavior Analysis*, 1977, *10*, 679–688.

Wessels, M. G. *Cognitive psychology*. New York: Harper & Row, 1982.

White, M. A. Natural rates of teacher approval and disapproval in the classroom. *Journal of Applied Behavior Analysis,* 1975, *8,* 367–372.

Whorf, B. L. Science and linguistics. In J. B. Carrol (Ed.), *Language, thought and reality: Selected writings of Benjamin Lee Whorf.* New York: Wiley, 1956.

Wickelgren, W. A. Acoustic similarity and retroactive interference in short-term memory. *Journal of Verbal Learning and Verbal Behavior,* 1965, *4,* 53–61.

———. *How to solve problems.* San Francisco: Freeman, 1974.

Wickens, D. D., & Clark, S. Osgood dimensions as an encoding class in short-term memory. *Journal of Experimental Psychology,* 1968, *78,* 580–584.

———, & Harding, G. B. Effect of UCS strength on GSR conditioning: A within-subject design. *Journal of Experimental Psychology,* 1965, *70,* 152–153.

Wilcott, R. C. A search for subthreshold conditioning at four different auditory frequencies. *Journal of Experimental Psychology,* 1953, *46,* 271–277.

Wilcoxin, H. C.; Dragoin, W. B.; & Kral, P. A. Illness-induced aversions in rat and quail: Relative salience of visual and gustatory cues. *Science,* 1971, *7,* 489–493.

Williams, D. C. The elimination of tantrum behavior by extinction procedures. *Journal of Abnormal and Social Psychology,* 1959, *59,* 269.

Williams, D. R., & Williams, H. Auto-maintenance in the pigeon: Sustained pecking despite contingent non-reinforcement. *Journal of the Experimental Analysis of Behavior,* 1969, *12,* 511–520.

Williams, M. The effects of experimentally induced needs upon retention. *Journal of Experimental Psychology,* 1950, *40,* 139–151.

Williams, S. B. Resistance to extinction as a function of the number of reinforcements. *Journal of Experimental Psychology,* 1938, *23,* 506–522.

Wilson, G. T., & Tracey, D. A. An experimental analysis of aversive imagery vs. electrical aversive conditioning in the treatment of chronic alcoholics. *Behaviour Research and Therapy,* 1976, *14,* 41–51.

Wingfield, A., & Byrnes, D. L. *The psychology of human memory.* New York: Academic, 1981.

Winston, H.; Lindzey, G.; & Connor, J. Albinism and avoidance learning in mice. *Journal of Comparative and Physiological Psychology,* 1967, *63,* 77–81.

Wittrup, M., & Gordon, W. C. The alteration of a training memory through cueing. *American Journal of Psychology,* 1982, *95,* 495–507.

Wolf, M. M.; Hanley, E. L.; King, L. A.; Lachowicz, J.; & Giles, D. K. The timer-game: A variable interval contingency for the management of out-of-seat behavior. *Exceptional Children,* 1970, *37,* 113–117.

———; Risley, T.; & Mees, H. L. Application of operant conditioning procedures to the behavior problems of an autistic child. *Behaviour Research and Therapy,* 1964, *1,* 305–312.

Wolin, B. R. Difference in manner of pecking a key between pigeons reinforced with food and water. In A. C. Catania (Ed.), *Contemporary research in operant behavior.* Glenview, Ill.: Scott, Foresman, 1968.

Wolpe, J. *Psychotherapy by reciprocal inhibition.* Stanford, Calif.: Stanford University Press, 1958.

———. *Theme and variations: A behavior therapy casebook.* Elmsford, N.Y.: Pergamon, 1976.

———. Self-efficacy theory and psychotherapeutic change: A square peg for a round hole. In S. Rachman (Ed.), *Advances in behavior research and therapy* (vol. 1). Oxford: Pergamon, 1978.

Wolthuis, O. L. Inter-animal information transfer by brain extracts. *Archives Internationales de Pharmacodynamie,* 1969, *182,* 439–442.

Wood, F.; Taylor, B.; Penny, R.; & Stump, D. Regional cerebral blood flow response to recognition memory versus semantic classification tasks. *Brain and Language,* 1980, *9,* 113–122.

Wood, G., & Underwood, B. J. Implicit responses and conceptual similarity. *Journal of Verbal Learning and Verbal Behavior,* 1967, *6,* 1–10.

Woodard, W. T. Classical respiratory conditioning in the fish: CS intensity. *American Journal of Psychology,* 1971, *84,* 549–554.

Woodruff, G. Behavioral contrast and type of reward: Role of elicited response topography. *Animal Learning and Behavior,* 1979, *7,* 339–346.

Woods, P. J.; Davidson, E. H.; & Peters, R. J. Instrumental escape conditioning in a water tank: Effects of variations in drive stimulus intensity and reinforcement magnitude. *Journal of Comparative and Physiological Psychology,* 1964, *57,* 466–470.

———, & Holland, C. H. Instrumental escape conditioning in a water tank: Effects of constant reinforcement at different levels of drive stimulus intensity. *Journal of Comparative and Physiological Psychology,* 1966, *62,* 403–408.

Woodward, A. E., Jr.; Bjork, R. A.; & Jongeward, R. H., Jr. Recall and recognition as a function of primary rehearsal. *Journal of Verbal Learning and Verbal Behavior,* 1973, *12,* 608–617.

Woodworth, R. S. *Dynamic psychology.* New York: Columbia University Press, 1918.

Worchel, S., & Cooper, J. *Understanding social psychology.* Homewood, Ill.: Dorsey, 1983.

Wright v. *McMann,* 460 F. 2d 126 (2d Cir., 1972).

Wulbert, M., & Dries, R. The relative efficacy of methylphenidate (ritalin) and behavior-modification techniques in the treatment of a hyperactive child. *Journal of Applied Behavior Analysis,* 1977, *10,* 21–31.

Zazdeh, L. A.; Fu, K. S.; Tanak, K.; & Shimura, M. (Eds.), *Fuzzy sets and their applications to cognitive and decision processes.* New York: Academic, 1975.

Zeaman, D. Response latency as a function of the amount of reinforcement. *Journal of Experimental Psychology,* 1949, *39,* 466–483.

Zechmeister, E. B. Orthographic distinctiveness. *Journal of Verbal Learning and Verbal Behavior,* 1969, *8,* 754–761.

Zola-Morgan, S.; Squire, L. R.; & Mishkin, M. The anatomy of amnesia: Amygdalahippocampus vs. temporal stem. *Society for Neuroscience Abstracts,* 1981, *7,* 236.

Zubin, J., & Barrera, S. E. Effect of electric convulsive therapy on memory. *Proceedings for the Society of Experimental Biology,* 1941, *48,* 596–597.

INDEXES

INDEXES

NAME INDEX

SUBJECT INDEX